W9-AVK-890

SOUTHWEST FRANCE

DORDOGNE
LOT & BORDEAUX

Cadogan Books plc
London House, Parkgate Road, London SW11 4NQ

The Globe Pequot Press
6 Business Park Road, PO Box 833, Old Saybrook,
Connecticut 06475–0833

Copyright © Dana Facaros and Michael Pauls 1994
Illustrations © Mary Kuper 1994

Book and cover design by Animage
Cover illustrations by Horatio Monteverde
Maps © Cadogan Guides, drawn by Thames Cartographic Ltd

Editing: Dominique Shead
Series Editors: Rachel Fielding and Vicki Ingle

Copyediting: Eric Smith
Proofreading: Anne Greenshields
Indexing: James Pargiter
Production: Rupert Wheeler Book Production Services
Mac Help: Jacqueline Lewin

A catalogue record for this book is available from the British Library
ISBN 0–947754–709

US Library of Congress Cataloging-in-Publication-Data:
Facaros, Dana
     Southwest France / Dana Facaros and Michael Pauls.
            p. cm.--(Cadogan guides)
     Includes bibliographical references and index.
     ISBN 1–56440–487–6
     1. France, Southwest--Guidebooks.   I. Pauls, Michael   II. Title   III. Series
DC609.3.F33   1994
914.4'704839--dc20   94-3018
                        CIP

Printed and bound in Great Britain by The Lavenham Press, Lavenham, Suffolk
on Jordan Opaque supplied by McNaughton Publishing Papers Ltd.

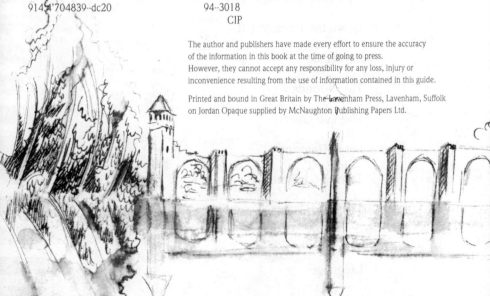

About the Authors

Michael and Dana, their two kids, three cats and a fierce bad rabbit live in a leaky old Quercy farmhouse in the middle of nowhere. They have written 14 guides for Cadogan.

Acknowledgements

Our thanks go out to all the local tourist offices and scores of helpful autochtones who offered us stacks of facts and words of wisdom. Also, great big *bisous* to Pauline, Carole, Trebor, Victor, Kate and Penny for a thousand kindnesses, car rides, restaurant discoveries and inspiration *en vrac*. A big thank you to Dominique for being such a sweetie and for all her hard work. And last but not least, to George, Joanne, Carolyn, Chris, Robin, Judy, Mike and Marge who crossed the Atlantic to keep us and the *dolmens* company.

The publishers would like to thank Animage for their design, Thames Cartographic Services for the maps, Eric Smith for copyediting, Anne Greenshields for proofreading and James Pargiter for indexing.

Please help us to keep this guide up to date

We have done our best to ensure that the information in this guide is correct at the time of going to press. But places and facilities are constantly changing, and standards and prices in hotels and restaurants fluctuate. We would be delighted to receive any comments concerning existing entries or omissions. All contributors will be acknowledged in the next edition, and will receive a copy of the Cadogan Guide of their choice.

Contents

Travel   1–8

Practical A–Z   9–28

History   29–40

List of Maps

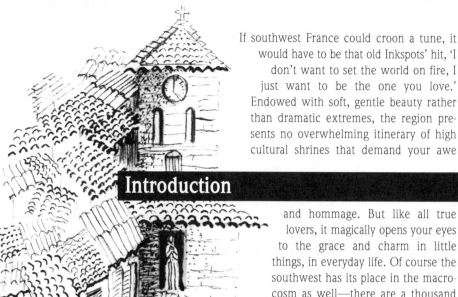

If southwest France could croon a tune, it would have to be that old Inkspots' hit, 'I don't want to set the world on fire, I just want to be the one you love.' Endowed with soft, gentle beauty rather than dramatic extremes, the region presents no overwhelming itinerary of high cultural shrines that demand your awe

Introduction

and hommage. But like all true lovers, it magically opens your eyes to the grace and charm in little things, in everyday life. Of course the southwest has its place in the macro-cosm as well—there are a thousand proud châteaux and as many medieval villages, the world's foremost wine region and its very first art. These long-secret paintings and carvings that pre-date the dawn of history have an uncanny beauty and power all of their own.

Apart from Bordeaux and Toulouse, the two great cities that form the limits of this book, nothing much has happened here since the Hundred Years' War. Out of history, out of mind, this region has since the last war been slowly rediscovered as a land that retains something that most of the industrialized world has lost in its mad rush towards modernity. If you talk to an old farmer, he may mention *eime*, the Occitan word for soul similar to the Catalan *seny*—the intangible spirit of the nation, its good sense, its spirit of measure and modera-tion. The southwest may be the land of mystical troubadours, but it is also the land of France's most reasonable thinkers, of Montaigne, Fénelon, La Boétie and Montesquieu.

For if nothing else, southwest France is a fine place to hear yourself think. The great wine helps, of course, and the delicious regional cuisine puts your digestion in harmony with the universe. The pace of life is slow, and there's time to contemplate that old stone farm on the next hill, blending into the environment naturally and effortlessly. The wall by your chair is covered with eglantine and honeysuckle; fragrance, warm sun and the blackbird trilling and jamming away in the poplar overhead make you delightfully drowsy and once again all plans and outings are postponed. You can't put it off forever, of course—we have a full schedule of sights and surprises for you in this book—but the true purpose of this land is helping us to pause for a moment and regain some perspective. Or, as in the words of Montaigne:

> The value of life lies, not in the length of days, but in the use we make of them; a man may live long, yet live very little. Satisfaction in life depends not on the number of your years, but on your will.

A Guide to the Guide

This book covers the Aquitaine Basin, a great bay in the ocean millions of years ago and now divided into the *départements* of the Dordogne, Gironde, Lot, Lot-et-Garonne and Tarn-et-Garonne. This is river country par excellence—once the Dordogne, Lot, Tarn and Garonne plunge from their sources in the Pyrenees and Massif Central and carve out their steep gorges, we pick them up where they put on their watery brakes to weave gracefully down to the broad estuary of the Gironde and the Atlantic.

If you're driving down from Britain, chances are you'll pass through the verdant valleys and woodlands of the northern *département* of the Dordogne or **Périgord**, a lush land dotted with fairytale castles and domed Romanesque churches, culminating in the astonishing St-Front in the handsome town of Périgueux. The next chapter, still within the boundaries of the Dordogne, delves into the misty past along the enchanting **Vézère Valley**, whose caves and shelters hold the densest concentration of prehistoric art on this planet, including the sublime Grotte de Lascaux.

Next come two chapters following the valley of the **Dordogne** river, first descending from Argentat to Domme, passing by way of some of the busiest tourist attractions in the southwest—the immense chasm and underground river at Padirac, the medieval pilgrimage town of Rocamadour, and the beautiful Renaissance town of Sarlat. The next chapter, **Down the Dordogne II**, follows the river past the first vineyards, from Bergerac (also home to the national tobacco museum) to lovely Saint-Emilion, Montaigne's château and ending up at the mighty citadel of Blaye.

Bordeaux with all its 18th-century frippery and fine museums gets a chapter all to itself, followed by its *département*, the **Gironde**. This is not only home to France's most celebrated vineyards and its rarefied wine châteaux (Mouton, Lafite, Yquem, Margaux) but to long beaches of silver sand, deep pine forests, the busy bird sanctuary at La Teich and the grand old seaside resort and oyster haven of Arcachon.

Next we backtrack east, to head down the wild limestone plateaux and the river **Lot**, wiggling dramatically under cliffs, castles, picturesque old villages such as St-Cirq-Lapopie and the medieval city of Cahors, with its landmark triple-towered Pont Valentré. The Lot flows next into the *département* and chapter of **Lot-et-Garonne**, a rolling land of orchards dotted with charming medieval new towns, or bastides, as well as French prune capitals Villeneuve and Agen, and more picture postcard castles at Bonaguil, Duras and Nérac.

From here we head south into rural **Tarn-et-Garonne**, a *département* decorated with hundreds of dovecotes and the delightful brick city of Montauban, not to mention the great abbey of Moissac, one of Romanesque Europe's greatest masterpieces. Last of all comes **Toulouse**, the dynamic, cosmopolitan 'Ville Rose' of the southwest, boasting a clutch of medieval masterpieces, worthy museums, charming brick streets and squares and the best shopping and nightlife in this book.

Unravelling the Names

Perhaps the biggest source of confusion for newcomers to southwest France is that underneath the tidy departmental names bestowed by the French Revolution, older regional names have survived—like peeling circus posters, one atop the other. 'Aquitaine' sufficed for the whole region from Roman times until the Middle Ages, when things began to get confusing and new names appeared: Gascony, for the lands west of the Garonne, and Languedoc, for those to the east, while everything owned by the English crown after the marriage of Eleanor of Aquitaine and Henry II became known as Guyenne, from the English inability to pronounce Aquitaine properly. Guyenne's borders fluctuated greatly until the end of the Hundred Years' War, and the name survives to this day whenever anyone feels like using it.

Within Guyenne, what is now the *département* of the Dordogne was the county of Périgord until the Revolution, and the name is still synonymous with the Dordogne *département.* The Lot, and most of the Tarn-et-Garonne were known (and still are) as Quercy. The Lot-et-Garonne and the Gironde were always the heartland of Aquitaine/Guyenne, although their southern reaches belong to Gascony; Toulouse was the medieval capital of the Languedoc, but in the new division of French regions (since 1981) the name Languedoc migrated to the Mediterranean, leaving Toulouse the capital of an artificial region called the Midi-Pyrénées, which encompasses the Lot and Tarn-et-Garonne, among others, while the region of Aquitaine includes the Dordogne, Gironde and Lot-et-Garonne with Bordeaux as the capital. Get it?

Restaurants: L'Aubergade, Puymirol; St-James, Bouliac; Le Centenaire, Les Eyzies.

Hotels: Moulin de l'Abbaye, Brantôme; Le Vieux Logis, Trémolat.

Prehistoric Art: Lascaux; Les Eyzies; Rouffignac; Pech-Merle.

Natural Wonders: Dune du Pilat; Gouffre de Padirac.

Most Beautiful Villages: Domme; Rocamadour; St-Cirq-Lapopie; Saint-Emilion; Le Mas d'Agenais; Martel.

Most Beautiful Towns: Sarlat-la-Canéda; Périgueux; Cahors.

Seaside resorts: Arcachon.

Castles: Bonaguil; Biron; Beynac-et-Cazenac; Jumilhac.

Art and Architecture: Moissac Abbey; church of Saint-Sernin, Toulouse; church of Les Jacobins, Toulouse; museums in Toulouse, Bordeaux and Agen; church of Sainte-Marie, Souillac.

Travel

A little preparation will help you get much more out of your holiday in southwest France. Check the list of events (see p.11) to help you decide where you want to be and when, and book accommodation early: if you plan to base yourself in one area, write ahead to the local tourist offices listed in the text for complete lists of self-catering accommodation, hotels, and camp sites in their areas, or else contact one of the many agencies in the UK or USA (see p.26). For more general information, get in touch with a French Government Tourist Office:

UK: 178 Picadilly, London, W1V OAL, ℂ (071) 491 7622, fax (071) 493 6594.

Ireland: 35 Lower Abbey St, Dublin 1, ℂ (1) 77 18 71, fax (1) 74 73 24.

Australia: BWP House, 12 Castlereigh St, Sydney NSW 2000, ℂ (612) 213 5244.

USA: 610 Fifth Ave, New York, NY, 10020, ℂ (212) 757 1125, fax (212) 247 6468; 645 N. Michigan Ave, Chicago, IL 60611; 9454 Wiltshire Blvd, No. 303, Beverly Hills, CA 90212. Nationwide information ℂ (900) 420 2003.

Canada: 1981 Av. McGill College, No. 490, Montreal, Quebec H3A 2W9, ℂ (514) 288 4264, fax (514) 845 4868; 1 Dundas St W., No. 2405 Box 8, Toronto, Ontario M5G 1Z3, ℂ (416) 593 4723, fax (416) 979 7587.

Getting There

By Air

The international airports in the region are at Bordeaux and Toulouse, both of which have direct connections with London on Air France or British Airways (in France BA has a toll-free information and reservation number, ℂ 05 12 51 25). Neither Bordeaux nor Toulouse get enough holiday volume to offer special fares or charter flights; at the time of writing return fares on BA are £230. You can usually save money by purchasing your ticket in advance; check with your travel agent for details, or your major Sunday newspaper for any bargains or packages. If you're flying from any place but London, it's often cheaper to pick up a flight to Paris and catch a cheap Air Inter flight to Bordeaux or Toulouse. Air Inter offers a number of discounts: *Super Loisirs* on return flights that include a Saturday night and Sunday, and a *Super Loisirs Jeunes* for everyone under 25, or students under 27. Other discounts are possible (up to 46%) if you fly in a low-occupancy 'Blue period' with a *Carte Evasion*, valid for one year. In Paris, contact Air Inter at ℂ 45 46 90 10; in the UK, Nouvelles Frontières, 11 Blenheim St, London W1, ℂ (071) 629 7772.

Another domestic airline, Air Littoral, has flights from Paris (ℂ 47 35 70 71) to Agen and Périgueux. Another possibility, from June to mid September only, are TAT's Saturday non-stop flights from London to Brive in the upper Dordogne (in Brive ℂ 55 86 88 36). TAT also has flights from Paris (ℂ 42 79 05 05) to Bordeaux, with discounts for anyone under 27 and anyone of the female sex (on certain flights).

Students equipped with relevant ID cards are eligible for considerable reductions, not only on flights, but on trains and admission fees to museums, concerts, and more. Agencies specializing in student and youth travel can help in applying for the cards, as well as filling you in on the best deals. Try STA, ℂ (071) 937 9921, and Campus Travel, ℂ (071) 730 3402, in London or branches throughout the UK; STA, ℂ (03) 347 6911, in Australia; Council Travel, ℂ (800) 223 7402, and STA, ℂ (800) 777 0112, in the US; ℂ (416) 979 2406 in Canada.

By Train

Air prices and airport hassles make France's high-speed TGVs (*train à grande vitesse*) an attractive alternative. TGVs shoot along at an average of 170mph when they're not breaking world records: the journey from Paris' Gare de Montparnasse on the TGV Atlantique to Bordeaux takes 2 hours 58 min, and continues on to Toulouse by way of Agen in slightly under 5 hours. Costs are only minimally higher on a TGV. Some weekday departures require a supplement (30–40F) and seat reservations (20F), which you can make when you buy your ticket or at the station before departure. Another pleasant way of getting there is by overnight sleeper (slower trains for the southwest all depart from the Gare d'Austerlitz in Paris). People under 26 are eligible for a 30 per cent discount on fares (*see* the travel agencies listed above) and there are other discounts if you're over 65, available from major travel agents.

If you plan on making several long train journeys, look into the variety of rail passes: France's national railroad, the SNCF, offers a *France Railpass* that gives you either four days (they don't have to be consecutive) of unlimited travel in a 15-day period, or nine days of travel within 30 days. It includes extras like a day's free travel in Paris (from the airport, the métro, etc), TGV supplements (except the seat reservation), and discounts on car rentals and Channel crossings. Get it before you leave from travel agents or the SNCF office at 'The Rail Shop', 179 Piccadilly, London W1, ℂ (071) 495 4933 for bookings. For simple information the SNCF has created a new number that charges you for the pleasure of asking, at 48p a minute peak time, ℂ (0891) 515 477. In the US contact 610 Fifth Ave, New York, NY 10020, ℂ (212) 582 2816 (or ℂ (800) 848 7245). Other alternatives include the well-known InterRail pass for European residents under age 26, which offers a month's unlimited travel in Europe and 50 per cent reductions on Channel ferries, and various Eurail passes for non-Europeans, valid from 15 days to three months.

By Coach

The cheapest way to get from London to southwest France is by National Express Eurolines coach, ℂ (071) 730 0202; tickets available from any National Express office. There are at least three journeys a week to Cahors, Périgueux and Bordeaux and all take about a day and aren't much fun, although the coach saves you the hassle of crossing Paris to change trains.

By Car

A car entering France must have its registration and insurance papers. If you're coming from the UK or Ireland, the dip of the headlights must be adjusted to the right. Carrying a warning triangle is mandatory, and should be placed 50m behind the car if you have a breakdown. Drivers with a valid licence from an EU country, Canada, the USA or Australia don't need an international licence. If you plan to hire a car, look into air and holiday package deals to save money, or consider leasing a car if you mean to stay three weeks or more. Prices vary widely from firm to firm, and beware the small print about service charges and taxes: a couple of firms to try in the US are France Auto Vacances, ℭ (800) 234 1426 and Europe by Car Inc, ℭ (800) 223 1516 or Renault, ℭ (800) 221 1052.

If you're driving down from the UK you may face going through or around Paris on the abominable *périphérique*, a task best tackled on either side of rush hour. To avoid it, seasoned travellers favour the Portsmouth–Caen ferry (Brittany Ferries), offering a direct and not-too-frenetic drive via Le Mans, Tours and Poitiers. From Caen (360 miles to Périgueux) or Le Havre (390 miles to Périgueux) take the N 158/N 138 to Le Mans and Tours, and continue on the N 10 to Poitiers, from which you can branch off for either Bordeaux, via Angoulême, or Cahors, via Limoges. Another Bordeaux alternative is the autoroute A 10 from Tours. You may also consider taking a ferry to Le Havre or Cherbourg from Portsmouth, Poole or Southampton (P&O Ferries or Brittany Ferries). If you're visiting the west end of the region, you could sail to St-Malo (from Portsmouth with Brittany Ferries) and take in Rennes, Nantes, La Rochelle and Saintes, picking up the A 10 there towards Bordeaux. If you want to put your car on a train, the only option in the area is from Calais to Brive.

Entry Formalities

Passports and Visas

Holders of EU, US, or Canadian passports do not need a visa to enter France for stays up to three months, but everyone else still does. Apply at your nearest French Consulate: the most convenient visa is the *visa de circulation*, allowing for multiple stays of three months over a three-year period. If you intend on **staying longer**, the law says you need a *carte de séjour*, a requirement EU citizens can easily get around as passports are rarely stamped. On the other hand, non-EU citizens had best apply for an extended visa at home, a complicated procedure requiring proof of income, etc. You can't get a *carte de séjour* without this visa, in itself a trial run for the *ennuis* you'll undergo in applying for a *carte de séjour* at your local *mairie*.

Health and Travel Insurance

Citizens of the EU who bring along their E-111 forms are entitled to the same health services as French citizens. This means paying up front for medical care and presciptions, of which costs 75–80 per cent are reimbursed later—a complex procedure for the non-French. As an alternative, consider a travel insurance policy, covering theft and losses and offering 100 per cent medical refund; check to see if it covers extra expenses if you get bogged down in airport or train strikes. Beware that accidents resulting from sports are rarely covered by ordinary insurance. Canadians are usually covered in France by their provincial health coverage; Americans and others should check their individual policies.

By Train

The southwest has a decent network of trains, although many of the smaller lines have only two or three connections a day, making it rather difficult to see much of the country by rail; in places SNCF buses have taken over former train routes. Prices, if not a bargain, are still reasonable, and discounts are available especially if you travel off-peak in a *période bleue* with a return ticket and go at least 1000km (25 per cent discounts). Married (or not—they don't really check) couples are eligible for a free *Carte Couple* (bring a pair of photos) which entitles one to pay half fare when travelling together on blue days. People over 65 can purchase a *Carte Vermeille*, valid for a year of half-price blue period travel; under 26-year-olds can buy a *Carte Jeune* for half-price blue day travel from June to September. The more children you have, the more economical an expensive *Carte Kiwi* becomes: the card is in the name of one child, and family members each purchase complementary cards. The child then pays full fare, and everyone else half. As you can see, the SNCF delights in complexity; their super-intelligent new computerized reservation system, called 'Socrates', has become a chaotic nightmare, enraging both riders and employees. Watch out; they haven't got it fixed yet.

Tickets must be **stamped** in the little orange machines by the door to the tracks that say *Compostez votre billet* (this puts the date on the ticket, to keep you from using the same one over and over again). Any time you interrupt a journey until another day, you have to re-compost your ticket. Long-distance *Trains Corails* can be utterly delightful when not too crowded. They have snack trolleys and bar/cafeteria cars (the food isn't bad), and some offer play areas for small children. Nearly every station has banks of mechanical lockers (*consignes automatiques*) that spit out a slip with the lock combination when you use them; they take about half an hour to puzzle out the first time you use them, so plan accordingly.

By Bus

Do not count on seeing any part of rural France by public transport. The bus network is barely adequate between major cities and towns (places often already well-served by rail) and rotten in rural areas, where the one bus a day fits the school schedule, leaving at the crack of dawn and returning in the afternoon; more remote villages are linked to civilization only once a week or not at all. Buses are run either by the SNCF (replacing discontinued rail routes) or private firms. Rail passes are valid on SNCF buses and they generally coincide with trains. Private bus firms, especially when they have a monopoly, tend to be a bit more expensive than trains; some towns have a *gare routière* (coach station), usually near the train station, while in others the buses stop at bars or any other place that catches their fancy. Stops are hardly ever marked, while on the other hand in some areas there are conspicuous bus stops everywhere, where in fact no service exists. The posted schedules are not always to be trusted. The tourist office or shopkeepers near the bus stop may have a more accurate instinct for when a bus is likely to appear.

Unless you plan to stick to the major towns, cycle, or walk, a car is regrettably the only way to see the southwest. This too has its drawbacks: high rental car rates and Europe's costliest petrol, and an accident rate double that of the UK (and much higher than the US). The vaunted French logic and clarity breaks down completely on the asphalt. Go slow and be careful; never expect any French driver to be aware of the possibility of a collision.

Roads are generally excellently maintained, but anything of less status than a departmental route (D-road) may be uncomfortably narrow. Petrol stations are rare in rural areas and closed on Sunday afternoons, so consider your fuel supply while planning any forays into the back country—especially if you're on unleaded. The scoundrels will expect a tip for oil, windscreen-cleaning or air. The French have one admirably civilized custom of the road; if oncoming drivers unaccountably flash their headlights at you, it means the *gendarmes* are lurking just up the way.

Always give **priority to the right** at any intersection—anywhere, unless you're on a motorway or on a road with a yellow diamond 'priority route' sign. This French anachronism is a major cause of accidents; most people only follow the rule when they're feeling generous. If you are new to France, think of every intersection as a new and perilous experience. Watch out for Byzantine street parking rules (which would take pages to explain: do as the natives do, and especially be careful about village centres on market days).

Unless sweetened in an air or holiday package deal, car hire in France is an expensive proposition (350–400F a day, without mileage for the cheapest cars). Petrol (*essence*) is at the time of writing about 5F 90 a litre for super. Speed limits are 130km/80mph on the *autoroutes* (toll motorways); 110km/69mph on dual carriageways (divided highways); 90km/55mph on other roads; 50km/30mph in an 'urbanized area': as soon as you pass a white sign with a town's name on it and until you pass another sign with town's name barred. Fines for speeding, payable on the spot, begin at 1300F and can be astronomical if you flunk the breathalyser. If you wind up in an accident, the procedure is to fill out and sign a *constat aimable*. If your French isn't sufficient to deal with this, hold off until you find someone to translate for you so you don't accidently incriminate yourself. If you have a breakdown and are a member of a motoring club affliated with the Touring Club de France, ring the latter; if not, ring the police.

A plethora of tiny rural roads and lack of strenuous mountains make the Dordogne and Lot valleys ideal for a cycling holiday, and there are a number of companies (*see* list below) ready to make them even easier by arranging all the hotels along your route and carrying your suitcase for you. French drivers, not always courteous to fellow motorists, usually give cyclists a wide berth; and yet on any given summer day, half the patients in a French hospital are there from accidents on two wheeled transport. Consider a helmet. Maps and info are available from the Fédération Française de Cyclotourisme, 8 Rue Jean-Marie Jégo, 75013 Paris, ℂ 45 80 30 21; in Britain information on cycle touring in France is available from the Cyclists Touring Club, Cotterell House, 69 Meadrow, Godalming, Surrey GU7 3HS, ℭ (0483) 68 7217.

Getting your own bike to France is fairly easy: Air France and British Airways carry them free from Britain. From the US or Australia most airlines will carry them as long as they're boxed and included in your total baggage weight. In all cases, telephone ahead. Certain French trains (with a bicycle symbol in the timetable) carry bikes free; otherwise you have to send it as registered luggage and pay a 40F fee, with delivery guaranteed within 5 days.

You can hire bikes of varying quality (most of them 10-speed) at most SNCF stations and in major towns. The advantage of hiring from a station means that you can drop it off at another, as long as you specify where when you hire it. Rates run around 50F a day, with a deposit of 300–400F or credit card number. Private firms hire mountain bikes and better-quality touring bikes by the week.

By Foot

A network of long distance paths, the *Grandes Randonnées*, or GRs for short (marked by distinctive red and white signs) take in some of the most beautiful scenery in southwest France. Each GR is described in a *Topoguide*, with maps and details about camping sites, *refuges*, and so on, available in area bookshops or from the Comité National des Sentiers de Grande Randonnée, 8 Ave Marceau, 75008 Paris, ℭ 47 23 62 32; the most popular have been translated by Robertson-McCarta, 122 Kings Cross Road, London WC1X 9DS, ℭ (071) 278 8276. Among the most scenic walking paths are the GR36, following the Lot valley from St-Cirq-Lapopie to Bonaguil, where it veers north through Biron, Belvès and the Vézère Valley; GR6 and GR46 run through central Périgord, from Figeac to Les Eyzies passing Rocamadour, Bergerac, and Sarlat; GR8 follows the Atlantic coast from Pointe de Grave to the Lac de Cazaux.

Special Interest Holidays

There are a number of ways to combine a holiday with study or a special interest. For more information, contact the French Centre, ℭ (071) 221 8134, or the Cultural Department of the French Embassy, 23 Cromwell Road, London SW7, ℭ (071) 581 5292, or at 972 Fifth Av, New York, NY 10021, ℭ (212) 439 1400.

Alternative Travel, 69–71 Banbury Road, Oxford, OX2 6PE, ℭ (0865) 310399, fax (0865) 310299: walking and cycling in the Dordogne and wine tours in the Bordeaux region.

Arblaster & Clarke, 104 Church Road, Steep, Petersfield GU32 2DD, ℭ (0730) 266883: wine tours of Bordeaux.

Belle France, Bayham Abbey, Lamberhurst TN3 8BG, ℭ (0892) 890 885, fax (0892) 890180): walking and cycling tours in the Dordogne.

Blakes Holidays, Wroxham, Norwich, NR12 8DH ℭ (0603) 784 131: sailing boat charters in the Bassin d'Arcachon.

Erna Low Consultants, 9 Reece Mews, London SW7 3HE, © (071) 584 2841, fax (071) 589 9531, brochure line (071) 584 7820: golfing holidays.

Explore Worldwide, 1 Frederick St, Aldershot, GU11 1LQ, © (0252) 333031, fax (0252) 343170: 15-day rafting tours down the Dordogne.

GEM: Neo-Medicis Workshop, Patrick Nicolas, Bourgade, 47150 Monflanquin, France, © 53 01 79 04: learn to paint in the Renaissance *technique mixte* of Jan Van Eyck in 5-month sessions.

Headwater Holidays, 146 London Road, Northwich CW9 5HH, © (0606) 42220, fax (0606 48761): cycling and walking tours along the Lot and Célé valleys.

Inntravel, Hovingham, York YO6 4JZ, © 0439 7111, © (0653) 628811, fax (0653) 628741: city breaks to Toulouse, cycling tours and riding in the Dordogne.

La France des Villages, Model Farm, Rattlesden, Bury St Edmunds IP30 0SY, © (0449) 737664, fax (0449) 737850: canoeing, riding and painting holidays; gypsy caravans in the Lot.

LSG Theme Holidays, 201 Main Street, Thornton LE67 1AH, © (0509) 231713: a French-operated company offering cycling and walking day trips, two-week language courses, painting and drawing and cookery courses from local chefs in the Dordogne.

Luigi and Gail Mustafic, 12 John Street, Penarth, S. Glamorgan, CF64 1DN, © (0222) 707955: small operator offering wine holidays in the Dordogne, with introductions to local vineyard owners.

Susi Madron's Cycling for Softies, 2/4 Birch Polygon, Rufholme, Manchester M14 5HX, © (061)248 8282, fax (061) 248 5140: easy cycling in the Dordogne.

Voyages Jules Verne, 21 Dorset Square, London NW1 6QG, © (071) 723 6556, fax (071) 723 8629: painting holidays in Ribérac, in the Dordogne.

Disabled Travellers

When it comes to providing access for all, France is not exactly in the vanguard of nations; many Americans who come over are appalled. But things are beginning to change, especially in newer buildings. Access and facilities in 90 towns in France are covered in *Touristes quand même! Promenades en France pour les voyageurs handicapés*, a booklet usually available in the tourist offices of large cities, or write ahead to the Comité National Français de Liaison pour la Réadaptation des Handicapés, 30–32 Quai de la Loire, 75019 Paris. Hotels with handicapped facilities are listed in Michelin's *Red Guide to France*.

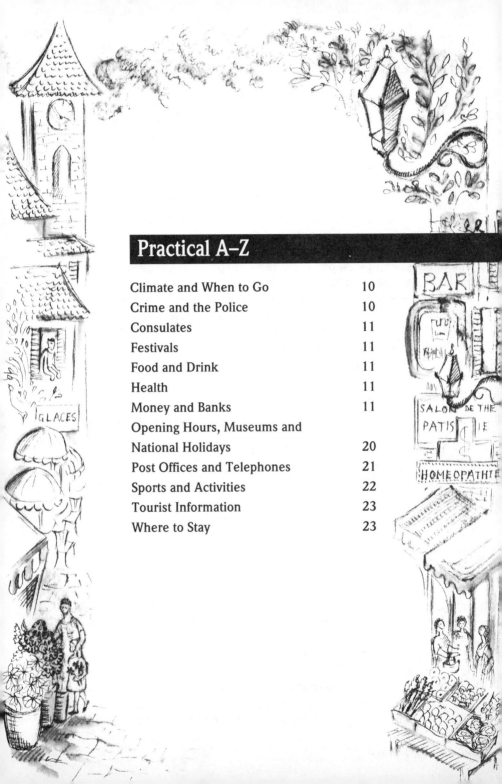

Practical A–Z

The Aquitaine Basin, shielded from intemperate Continental influences by the Massif Central, has a fairly balmy, humid Atlantic climate, with long hot summers broken by heavy thunderstorms; early spring and late autumn usually get the most rainfall—and it can rain for weeks or even months at a time. Winters are fairly mild, with only 20–40 days of frost a year, although every 30 years (on average) killer frosts descend—the last one happened in 1985, the year of the great mimosa massacre. Of late the weather has been capricious and strange; after five years of drought that produced some of the greatest wine of this century, the autumns of 1992 and '93 saw endless rain and floods, followed by spring-like Januarys and Februarys, and soggy wet Mays and Junes.

Unless you're coming to learn about the intricacies of preparing foie gras, winter is the bleakest time to visit; hotels, restaurants and sights simply close down, and the skies are often cloudy all day. The first crocuses often show up in January, but no matter how lovely the weather is nothing really opens up until the first tourist rush of the year—Palm Sunday and Easter week. May and June, usually warm and not too crowded, are among the best times to visit. Hot July, August and early September are French school holidays; the southwest is invaded by Parisians and other French as well as thousands of Dutch, German and British holiday-makers. Towns and attractions are crowded, more expensive than usual and there are scores of village *fêtes*, fairs, concerts, and races. The region often looks its best in October, when the tourists have gone and everyone is concentrating on the *vendange*; November and December can be dismal, but wild mushrooms, truffles, walnuts, and game dishes offer some consolation.

average maximum temperatures in °C /°F

	Jan	Feb	Mar	Apr	May	June	July	Aug	Sept	Oct	Nov	Dec
Cahors	11/52	13/55	15/59	17/63	20/68	22/73	26/79	26/79	24/75	20/68	14/57	11/52
Périgueux	10/50	12/54	14/57	17/63	19/66	23/75	25/77	26/79	22/73	18/65	15/59	12/54
Agen	9/48	11/52	15/59	17/63	19/66	23/75	25/77	26/79	21/70	18/64	15/59	10/50

Crime and the Police

Southwest France isn't exactly a high crime area. Isolated holiday homes get burgled, as anywhere else; cars are occasionally broken into or stolen. Generally the police are more annoying than the crooks, especially the customs officers; these can turn up anywhere in the interior, and they have nothing better to do than arbitrarily stop cars from outside their *département* and give them the once over. Report thefts to the nearest *gendarmerie*, not a pleasant task but the reward is the bit of paper you need for an insurance claim. If your passport is stolen, contact the police and your nearest consulate for emergency travel documents. By law, the police in France can stop anyone anywhere and demand ID; in practice, they only tend to do it to harass minorities, the homeless, and scruffy hippy types. If they really don't like the look of you they can salt you away for a long time without any reason.

The drug situation is the same in France as anywhere in the West: soft and hard drugs are widely available, and the police only make an issue of victimless crime when it suits them (your being a foreigner just may rouse them to action). Smuggling any amount of marijuana into the country can mean a prison term, and there's not much your consulate can or will do about it.

Consulates

US: 22 Cours Maréchal Foch, Bordeaux, © 56 52 65 95

UK: 15 Cours de Verdun, Bordeaux © 56 52 28 35

Festivals

Every single village or town in this book puts on a party at least once a year, usually in honour of its patron saint. These events happen all through the summer, and can be good corny fun. Up go the Christmas lights and flags, the big tables and folding chairs for the feast, and a platform for the band or bands in the main *place*—larger towns can afford both a *bal musette* (accordian waltzes and tangos and French songs for the oldsters) and a local rock band of dubious merit for the teenagers. There is invariably plenty of *animation* (everything from a local merchant chattering away on a portable microphone, jumping motorcycles, or dogs pulling sleds on wheels to international folklore events). In larger villages, a travelling funfair and/or circus pulls into town for the small fry; there may even be fireworks if the *mairie* has some money to blow.

calendar of events

March

Thurs before Mardi Gras	Promenade des Boeufs, **Bazas**
Last Sunday	Mascarade de Soufflets, **Nontron**

May

1	Traditional rural fair near **St-Aulaye** in the Forêt de la Double
Early month	Flower and strawberry festival, **Marmande**
Last week	Polo, *dressage*, jumping, racing etc. in the *Mai du cheval*, even-numbered years only, in **Bordeaux** and nearby châteaux

June

22	St John's day, with bonfires, **La Teste**
23	St John's day bonfires, homage to the bull and a week of events, **Bazas**

July

All month	International folklore festival, **Montignac**; jazz festivals, **Souillac**
Beginning	Jazz Festival, **Montauban**
1st Sun	*La Félibrée*, Occitan folk festivities, costumes, floats, music and theatre, in a different town in Périgord each year (run by Lo Bornat dau Périgord, 11 Rue Ernest-Guiller, Périgueux). Huge Antiques fair in **Belvès**
Mid-month	Jazz Festivals, **Andernos**; Blues Festival, **Cahors**
13-14	Big Bastille day celebrations at **Arcachon**
14	Regattas on the Dordogne, **Bergerac**
3rd weekend	Fête de la Madeleine, lively festival, wine and fun fair at **Duras**
3rd Sat	Entre-Deux-Mers wine festival, **Sauveterre-de-Guyenne**
End July–early Aug	Theatre festival, **Sarlat**; Goose fair, **Rouffignac** in odd-numbered years; music festival, **St-Céré**

August

All month	Pantomine festival, **Périgueux**
1–15	Music festival at **Bonaguil**
1st week	Oyster fair, **Gujan-Mestras** and **Claouey**; harvest festival, **Gourdon**
2nd week	Medieval festival, **Monflanquin**
Sun preceeding 15	*Fête du Chabrol*, folklore, crafts and food, **Varaignes**
15	Music festival, four days of music, **Uzeste**; huge flea market (*brocante*) in **Duras**; sea festival, **Arcachon**; grand laser light up of **Rocamadour**
Mid-month	Demonstration of high-wire artistry, **Castillonnès**
End of month	Festival of the Unusual, **La Tour-Blanche**

September

8	Pilgrimage at **Rocamadour**
3rd Sun	Fête du chasselas, **Moissac**; Proclamation of the beginning of the *vendanges* by the Jurade, **St-Emilion**
Mid-month	Prune fairs, **Agen** and **Nerac**
29	St Michael's fair and horse races, **Langon**

November

All month	SIGMA—theatre, dance and music, **Bordeaux**
1	Traditional week-long All Saints' fair, **La Réole**
11	16th-century Turkey Fair, **Varaignes**
25	St Catherine fête in **Quinsac**, with wine flowing from the public fountain

December

| Throughout month | *Marchés de gras*—foie gras, fattened ducks and geese markets—are held in most towns |

Food and Drink

When the French talk about abandoning the charms of *nouvelle cuisine* for good old country cooking, or *cuisine de terroir*, southwest France is often the first *terroir* that springs to mind. Intensely rural, sprinkled with small traditional family farms and overflowing with the good things of the earth, it serves a hearty cuisine of fresh ingredients, and so delicious that eating and drinking are two of the most compelling reasons to visit. Indeed, everyone is so pleased with it that it's hard to find a restaurant in the southwest that serves anything else.

The cuisine of Périgord and Quercy

Yet for all the talk of tradition, the dishes that bring hungry Parisians down *en masse* only date as popular fare from the 19th century; before then, the barons who ruled the land were so rapacious that the peasants' diet was based on red cabbage, chestnuts, turnips, fruit, and fish if they lived near the river, with little meat; hunting was a privilege of the nobility. These days, perhaps to make up for the past, meat is liable to appear in every course except dessert, to the dismay of France's minuscule vegetarian minority. The otherwise diet-conscious can take courage from recent studies showing that the basic southwest diet, with all of its duck and goose fat and red wine is actually good for you and your heart; heart disease is half the rate it is in the United States and many natives live well into their nineties. The region eagerly awaits an entrepreneur to set up a duck fat and wine spa to take advantage of a potential fad.

The best place to tuck into a traditional meal is the *ferme-auberge*, or farm restaurant, one of the delights awaiting diners in southwest France, where most of what you eat has been raised on the spot. A typical meal in a *ferme-auberge* or a good traditional restaurant may start with an *apéritif*, a *kir* (maybe with vin de Cahors instead of white wine) or a *fenelon*, a delightful cocktail of walnut liqueur, cassis, and red wine. Then comes the *tourain* (or *tourin*), an onion and garlic soup cooked in a broth with duck or goose fat and lard, ladelled over slices of country bread and cheese. The proper way to finish up the dregs is to *faire chabrot*, pour in a dash of red wine, swish it around, and drink it directly from the bowl.

The next dish is generally a pâté, often duck or goose, or *rillons* (the meat left over after preparation of foie gras and *confits*, mixed with a bit of fat to make a smooth paste) or foie gras, the enlarged liver of either a goose or duck (*see* 'Topics', p.50), often served with a bit of truffle it doesn't really need but jacks the price up even further. Foie gras comes raw (*nature*) or half-cooked (*mi-cuit*) in a frying pan, with a bit of lemon or *verjus* (the tart juice of underripe grapes), salt and pepper, white grapes, and served with slices of toasted *pain de campagne* and ideally with a glass of Sauternes, Loupiac, or Monbazillac. Goose is finer and more delicate, duck is tastier (and cheaper). Other popular starters include a salad of *gésiers*, or gizzards, cooked and sliced, or a plate of *charcuterie*. In the spring, asparagus often makes an appearance, and sometimes in Périgord you'll see *boutons de scorsonères*—flowers of black salsify—cooked in omelettes. For a real autumn delicacy, try an omelette with *cèpes* (boletus mushrooms) or truffles.

Main courses often star duck and goose as well, in the form of *confits* (the southwest's traditional way of keeping meat: thighs, legs, or wings are cooked and then put up in their own fat, and reheated in the oven). *Magrets* (also spelled *maigrets*) are filets of duck or goose breast, best simply grilled and served with a very light cream sauce with parsley and garlic, or in the autumn, with fresh *cèpes*. *Cou d'oie*, goose neck stuffed with a truffled minced pork and foie gras, and *demoiselles*, carcasses of fattened ducks grilled on a wood fire, are traditional peasant favourites that occasionally make it onto pricey restaurant menus. The duck or goose fat from *confits* is used for the accompanying *pommes de terre sarladaise*—sliced potatoes sautéed in goose fat or lard, with garlic and parsley, and *cèpes* in the autumn, a combination that lifts the humble spud to culinary heaven (they used to have truffles in them too, back when truffles were still affordable). Another main destination for *confits* is *cassoulet*—white beans, a dish that reaches its epiphany in Toulouse (*see* p.364).

Poultry—free-range Gascon chickens with black feet, or guinea fowl, capon, pheasant and pigeon—is always delicious, occasionally served in a fricasée, in a *ballotine* (a roll of poultry and stuffing in galantine) or *alicuit*, a traditional Gascon ragoût of poultry giblets, (even testicles) wings, potatoes, carrots and onions. Occasionally on the menus of *ferme-auberges* you'll see a *mique*, a dumpling cooked in bouillon that was long a staple in old Quercy and Périgord.

Game dishes are few, although there are places that specialize in boar and *marcassin* (young boar, served in a *civet* or red wine stew). Beef dishes are fairly rare, outside of *tournedos* in Périgord—filet of beef with foie gras and truffles. Lamb, especially *agneau de causse*, is very popular and prepared in a number of ways (most simply as a *gigot* or leg, roasted with garlic) and served too rare for many Anglo-Saxon tastes; *ris d'agneau* are lamb's sweetbreads). Pork appears in sausages—the omnipresent fat *saucisse de Toulouse*, or thinner *chipolatas* and spicey *merguez*—a contribution of the southwest's Spanish immigrants. *Andouillettes* are chitterling sausages; much rarer are pinkish *anguettes*, made with turkey's blood, unappetizing to look at but much appreciated fried in goose fat, with a spoonful of vinegar, garlic, and nutmeg. In the Lot-et-Garonne, pork is often cooked with prunes and wine, in a delicious sweet and savoury combination. Trout, pike (*brochet*, often prepared as *quenelles*, or cakes), and *écrevisse* (crayfish), *sandre* (pike-perch), *alose* (shad) and salmon are the principal fish on the menu, although sometimes you'll even see sturgeon and caviare (*see* p.81).

The classic salad is made of dandelion leaves (*pissenlits*) and walnuts, and seasoned vinegar and walnut oil, the perfect accompaniment to the most famous cheese of the region, AOC *cabecou* goat cheese rounds from Rocamadour, wrapped in vine leaves, or coated with pepper, ashes, or ground pistachios. Another popular cheese from the region is *bleu des Causses*, similar to Roquefort.

The locals are very sweet toothed and in some restaurants the desserts are the stars of the show. Traditional specialities often involve walnuts (*tarte aux noix,* walnut tart, *gâteaux aux noix,* walnut cake, sometimes coated wtih bitter chocolate) or prunes (in a *tourtière,* marinated in Armagnac and orange blossom water and topped with layers of paper thin pastry called *pastis*, of one part butter to four parts flour); sometimes apples replace the prunes and it's called a *croustade*. A *flognarde* is a *clafoutis* (flan) with pieces of apples, pears or plums; light crispy *échaudés* are flavoured with aniseed liqueurs, *vieille prune* (old prune) or *eau de noix* (made with green walnuts). A *toureau* is a Sunday or holiday bread-like cake in a ring served as a dessert, flavoured with orange blossom water, lemon, orange rum, vanilla and Grand Marnier, with homemade jam (leftovers are good toasted). Fresh strawberries in season go into a wide variety of desserts; melons, *pêches de vigne* (peaches grown between vines, now rare), apricots or cherries in Armagnac round off a meal in style.

The cuisine of the Bordelais

Cross over into the Bordelais and menus take on a whole new cast of ingredients, beginning with the oysters of Arcachon, among the finest in France, served raw with little grilled sausages called *crépinettes*. Mussels, *coques* (cockles) and *praires* (clams) are other tasty local shellfish; from the Gironde estuary come *pibales* or tiny baby elvers fried in oil, shrimp, shad (especially as *alose à l'oseille* stuffed with sorrel and grilled over vine cuttings, which helps dissolve its many fine bones), eels, salmon, salmon trout and for daring diners, lamprey, a dish so prized that the canons of Saint Seurin in Bordeaux gave up all their rights to property in the city in 1170, in exchange for 12 good fat lampreys a year (*see* p.183).

If garlic is the totem elsewhere in the Midi, shallots are just as essential to the Bordelais: *à la bordelaise* means topped with a *hachis* of parsley and shallots (but, confusingly, it can also mean accompanied with *cèpes*, or red wine sauce). Chopped shallots attain a kind of epiphany on grilled steaks—the famous *entrecôte à la bordelaise*. A good deal of passion is reserved for *cèpes*, and hunting them in the autumn, especially on someone else's property, leads to huge rows, slit tyres, dog bites and gunshots. There are two kinds: the true *cèpe bordelais* (*cèpe de chêne*) and less tasty *cèpe de pins*. Asparagus, both green and white, is one of the joys of spring in the region, served especially as a starter.

A speciality revived since 1985 is milk-fed lamb, or *agneau de Pauillac*, which holds pride of place among meat dishes along with the beef from Bazas and capons from Grignols; in the autumn, wood pigeon is a favourite dish, although few would countenance the way they are caught—netted a flock at a time in migrating season. Amongst the sweets, look for *compote de vigneron*, apples melted in red Bordeaux; in the big city itself, try a *canelé*, a delicious pastry made according to a recipe invented by the nuns of the Annonciade in the 16th century.

restaurant basics

Restaurants generally serve between 12 and 2 and in the evening from 7 to 9pm, with later summer hours. In the southwest people tend to arrive early, to have a better choice of dishes, and to get a crack at the specials, or *plats du jour*—turn up at 1 for lunch or 8 for dinner and your choice may be very limited. All post menus outside the door so you'll know what to expect; if prices aren't listed, you can bet it's not because they're a bargain. If you have the appetite to eat the biggest meal of the day at noon, you'll spend a lot less money. Almost all restaurants have a choice of set-price menus. Many expensive places offer a cheaper lunch special—the best way to experience some of the finer gourmet temples. Eating à la carte will always be much more expensive, in many cases twice as much; in most average spots no one ever does it.

Menus sometimes include the house wine (*vin compris*); if you choose a better wine anywhere, expect a scandalous mark-up. Don't be dismayed, it's a long-established custom (as in many other lands); the French wouldn't dream of a meal without wine, and the arrangement is a simple device to make food prices seem lower. If service is included it will say *service compris* or *s.c.*, if not *service non compris* or *s.n.c.*. Some restaurants offer a set-price gourmet *menu dégustation*—a selection of chef's specialities, which can be a great treat. On the other end of the scale, in the bars and brasseries, is the *plat du jour* (daily special) and the no-choice *formule*, which is more often than not steak and *frites*.

A full French meal may begin with an *apéritif*, hors d'oeuvres, a starter or two, followed by the entrée, cheese, dessert, coffee and chocolates, and perhaps a *digestif* to finish things off. If you order a salad it may come before or after but never with your main course. In everyday eating, most people condense this feast to a starter, main course, and cheese or dessert. Vegetarians will have a hard time in the southwest, but most establishments will try to accommodate them somehow.

When looking for a restaurant, homing in on the one place crowded with locals is as sound a policy in France as anywhere. Don't overlook hotel restaurants, some of which are absolutely top notch even if a certain red book refuses on some obscure principles to give them three stars. To avoid disappointment, call ahead in the morning to reserve a table, especially at the smarter restaurants, and especially in the summer. One thing you'll notice in the cities is an growing choice of ethnic restaurants, mostly North African (a favourite for their economical *couscous*—spicy meat and vegetables on a bed of steamed semolina, served with *harisa*, a hot red pepper sauce); Asian (usually Vietnamese, sometimes Chinese, Cambodian, or Thai); and Italian, the latter sometimes combined with a pizzeria (the pizza will be all right if there's a proper pizza oven, but with anything else Italian you're taking your chances).

markets, picnic food and snacks

In most villages, market day is the event of the week, and rightfully so. The food markets of the southwest are celebrated for their fresh farm produce. They are fun to visit on their own, and become even more interesting if you're cooking for yourself or are just gathering the ingredients for a picnic. In the larger cities they take place every day, while smaller towns and villages have markets just one day a week, and double as social occasions for the locals. Most markets finish up around noon.

Other good sources for picnic food are the *charcuteries* or *traiteurs*, both of which sell prepared dishes sold by weight in cartons or tubs. You can also find counters at larger supermarkets. Cities are snack-food wonderlands, with outdoor counters selling pastries, crêpes, pizza slices, *frites*, *croque monsieurs* (toasted ham and cheese sandwiches) and a wide variety of sandwiches made from *baguettes* (long thin loaves of bread).

drinks

Cafés are also a home away from home, places to read the papers, play cards, meet friends, and just unwind, sit back and watch the world go by. You can sit for hours over one coffee and no one will try to hurry you along. Prices are listed on the *Tarif des Consommations*: note they go up depending whether you're served at the bar (*comptoir*), at a table (*la salle*) or outside (*la terrasse*).

French coffee is strong and black, but lacklustre next to the aromatic brews of Italy or Spain. If you order *un café* you'll get a small black *express*; if you want milk, order *un crème*. If you want more than a few drops of caffeine, ask them to make it *grand*. For decaffinated, the word is *déca*; in the summer try a *frappé* (iced coffee). The French only order *café au lait* (a small coffee topped off with lots of hot milk) when they stop in for breakfast, and if what your hotel offers is expensive or boring, consider joining them. There are baskets of *croissants* and pastries, and some bars will make you a *baguette* with butter, jam or honey. If you want to go native, try the Frenchman's Breakfast of Champions: a *pastis* or two, and five non-filter *Gauloises*. *Chocolat chaud* (hot chocolate) is usually good; if you order *thé* (tea), you'll get an ordinary bag. An *infusion* is an herbal tea—*camomile*, *menthe* (mint), *tilleul* (lime or linden blossom), or *verveine* (verbena). These are kind to the all-precious *foie*, or liver, after you've over-indulged at the table.

Mineral water (*eau minérale*) can be addictive, and comes either sparkling (*gazeuse* or *pétillante*) or still (*non-gazeuse* or *plate*). If you feel run down, Badoit has lots of peppy magnesium in it—it's the current trendy favourite. The usual international corporate soft drinks are available, and all kinds of bottled fruit juices (*jus de fruits*). Some bars also do fresh lemon and oranges juices (*citron* or *orange pressé*). The French are also fond of fruit syrups—red *grenadine* and ghastly green *diabolo menthe*.

Beer (*bière*) in most bars and cafés is run-of-the-mill big brands from Alsace, Germany, and Belgium. Draft (*à la pression*) is cheaper than bottled beer. Nearly all resorts have bars or pubs offering wider selections of drafts, lagers, and bottles.

The strong spirit of the Midi comes in a liquid form called *pastis*, first made popular in Marseilles as a plague remedy; its name comes from the Latin *passe-sitis*, or thirst quencher. A pale yellow 90°-nectar flavoured with aniseed, vanilla, and cinnamon, *pastis* is drunk as an *apéritif* before lunch and in rounds after work. The three major brands, Ricard, Pernod and Pastis 51, all taste slightly different; most people drink their '*pastaga*' with lots of water and ice (*glaçons*), which help make it more tolerable.

wine

One of the pleasures of travelling in France is drinking great wines for a fraction of what you pay at home, and discovering new varieties that you've never seen in your local shop. Unless someone else is paying, smart restaurants are the last place to make your discoveries, with their prices marked up to triple or quadruple the retail. If you love wine but have to watch expenses (and who doesn't these days?) buy it direct from the producers, the *vignerons*. In the text we've included a few addresses for each wine to get you started.

The wines of the southwest are divided into two general groups, Bordeaux and the Haut Pays. The wines of Bordeaux, all in the *département* of the Gironde, the largest wine region in the world, cover 102,000 hectares and produce 500 million litres a year, enough to launch a battleship. Three quarters of this wine is AOC (*appellation d'origine contrôlée*), divided into 40 different *appellations*, including some of the most prestigious in France—Pomerol, Sauternes, Saint-Emilion, Pauillac, Margaux—and encompass 3500 red and white *crus*, or growths; a Premier Cru, or First Growth is the top of the top, a Château Lafite, Latour, d'Yquem or Ausone that you have to own several oil wells to afford. But even wines not designated as *crus* are now made better than ever, thanks to the introduction of new techniques and care.

Similar improvements have been made in the AOC wines of the Haut Pays—Côtes de Duras, Buzet, Cahors, Bergerac and the sweet white wine of Monbazillac. Many were famous in the Middle Ages, and even preferred to Bordeaux wines, but because they were upriver they were denied access to northern markets for centuries—by the Bordelais, of course. If you like to visit wineries or *chais* (a Gascon word meaning the building where the wine is stored in oak barrels, before being bottled and laid in the *cave* or cellar), these tend to be friendly and easy to get into without reservations for a look around and a taste, often with the proprietor.

Don't neglect the wines with less exalted labels, especially those labelled VDQS (*Vin de Qualité Supérieure*) or *Vin de Pays* (guaranteed to originate in a certain region—Côtes de Quercy and Vin du Tsar are worth a try), with *Vin Ordinaire* (or *Vin de Table*) at the bottom, which may not send you to seventh heaven but is usually drinkable and cheap. In a restaurant if you order a *rouge* or *blanc* or *rosé*, this is what you'll get, either by the glass (*un verre*), by the quarter-litre (*un pichet*) or bottle (*une bouteille*). *Brut* is very dry, *sec* dry, *demi-sec* and *moelleux* are sweetish, *doux* and *liquéroux* sweet, and *méthode champenoise*, sparkling.

A Guide to Bordeaux Red Vintages

The red wines of Bordeaux have an inherent sophistication which, with age, makes them inimitable. All but the leading *crus bourgeois* and *crus classés* wines can certainly be drunk with pleasure after about five years, especially under modern methods of vinification, but the wines of the top properties come into their own with age when all their nuances of bouquet and flavour make them as appealing to the intellect as they are to the palate.

1989: This was the hottest of a whole decade of superb summers and the vintage was the earliest since 1893. The wines are opulent and generous, with deep colour and 'fleshy' flavour—a flamboyant vintage. The *petits châteaux* are drinking now, the *crus classés* will continue to improve for many years.

1988: Not a large crop but a first-rate vintage nevertheless. Initially it was thought that the St-Emilions and Pomerols were more successful than the Médocs, but with subsequent re-tasting it has become increasingly apparent how very good the wines of the other communes of Bordeaux are.

1986: Coming between the opulent 1985 and early-maturing 1987 vintages, 1986 is a year that shows the rewards and advantages of giving fine claret time to develop. The *crus classés* and best *crus bourgeois* need more time, while some of the others are starting to open up and already show great character. A real claret-drinker's vintage.

1985: The rich concentration of fruit and smoothness of style enabled many of the wines from this vintage to show well earlier than is perhaps traditional for claret. The top *crus classés* are already proving accessible but further patience will be greatly rewarded. The vintage is living up to its excellent reputation.

1984: This was an irregular vintage which saw the Cabernets perform best. These '84s will never be classics, but make very good-value drinking.

1983: A delightful vintage, the wines of which are now beginning to open up fully. In comparison to the 1982s which were, if anthing, overpraised, the 1983s were initially rather overlooked. This is certainly changing now, as the wines show their breeding.

1982: 1982 continues to hold the highest reputation, even among all the excellent vintages of the 1980s. The top *crus classés* will celebrate the beginning of the next millennium.

1978: One of the very best vintages of the 1970s; the top wines are now approaching their optimum period for drinking having emerged from a restrained early life.

1976: The heatwave of 1976 and the resulting fully ripe grapes have produced fine, elegant wines with a good structure, which are now showing at their best.

Reproduced courtesy of Berry Bros. & Rudd Ltd, 3 St James's St, London SW1, © 071–396 9600.

If you're buying direct from the producer (or a wine co-operative, or *syndicat*, a group of producers), you'll be offered glasses to taste, each wine older than the previous one until you are feeling quite jolly and ready to buy the oldest (and most expensive) vintage. On the other hand, many producers (especially in the Haut Pays) sell loose wine à la petrol pump, or *en vrac*; many *chais* even sell the little plastic barrels to put it in.

Health

Local hospitals are the place to go in an emergency (*urgence*). If you need an ambulance (SAMU) dial 15; police and ambulance, © 17; fire, © 18. Doctors take turns going on duty at night and on holidays even in rural areas: pharmacies will know who to contact, or else telephone the local *SOS Médecins*—if you don't have access to a phone book or Minitel, dial directory assistance © 12. To be on the safe side, always carry a phone card (*see* Telephones, below). If it's not an emergency, pharmacies have addresses of local doctors (including those who speak English), or outpatient clinic (*centre hospitalier*). Pharmacists themselves are trained to administer first aid, and dispense free advice for minor problems. In cities pharmacies themselves open at night on a rotating basis; addresses are posted in their windows or in the local newspaper. In most rural pharmacies you can ring the doorbell after hours and roust the pharmacist on duty.

Money and Banks

The franc is divided into 100 centimes. Banknotes come in denominations of 500, 200, 100, 50 and 20F; coins in 20, 10, 5, 2, 1 and ½F, and 20, 10, and 5 centimes. You can bring in as much currency as you like, but by law are only allowed to take out 5000F in cash. Traveller's cheques or Eurocheques are the safest way of carrying money; the most widely recognized credit card is *Visa* (*Carte Bleu* in French) which is accepted almost everywhere and will give you cash out of the automatic tellers. If you plan to spend a lot of time in rural areas, where banks are few and far between, you may want to opt for International Giro Cheques, exchangeable at any post office.

Banks are generally open from 8.30–12.30 and 1.30–4; they close on Sundays, and most close either on Saturdays or Mondays as well. Exchange rates vary, and nearly all take a commission of varying proportions. Places that do nothing but exchange money (and hotels and train stations) usually have the worst rates or take out the heftiest commissions, so be careful. It's always a good bet to purchase some francs before you ago, especially if you arrive during the weekend.

Opening Hours, Museums, and National Holidays

Most shops close down on Sunday afternoons and Mondays, though some grocers and *supermarchés* open on Monday afternoons. In many towns Sunday morning is a big shopping period. Markets (daily in the cities, weekly in villages) are usually open mornings only, although clothes, flea and antique makets run into the afternoon.

Museums, with a few exceptions, close for lunch as well, and often on Mondays or

Tuesdays, and sometimes for all of November or the entire winter. Hours change with the season: longer summer hours begin in May or June and last through September—usually. Some change their hours every month. We've done our best to include them in the text, but don't be surprised if they're not exactly right. Most close on national holidays and give discounts if you have a student ID card, or are an EU citizen under 18 or over 65 years old; most charge admission ranging from 10–30F. Churches are usually open all day, or closed all day and only open for mass. Sometimes notes on the door direct you to the *mairie* or priest (*presbytère*) where you can pick up the key. If not, ask at the nearest house—they may well have it. There are often admission fees for cloisters, crypts, and special chapels.

On French **national holidays**, banks, shops and businesses close; some museums do, but most restaurants stay open. They are: January 1, Easter Sunday, Easter Monday, May 1, May 8 (VE Day), Ascension Day, Pentecost and the following Monday, July 14 (Bastille Day), August 15 (Assumption of the BVM), November 1 (All Saints'), November 11 (World War I Armistice), and Christmas Day.

Post Offices and Telephones

Known as the *PTT* or *Bureau de Poste*, marked by a kind of blue bird on a yellow background, French post offices are open in the cities Monday to Friday 8am–7pm, and Saturdays 8am until 12. In villages offices may not open until 9am, close for lunch, and close at 4.30 or 5. You can receive mail *poste restante* at any of them; the postal codes in this book should help your mail get there in a timely fashion. To collect it, bring some ID. You can purchase stamps in tobacconists as well as post offices.

Post offices offer free use of a Minitel electronic directory; they've done away with most printed directories, and using these slow, cumbersome and complicated technological marvels can be a major nuisance. Offices usually have at least one telephone booth with a meter—the easiest way to phone overseas. Almost all other public telephones have switched over from coins to *télécartes*, which you can purchase at newspaper kiosks, tobacco shops and the post office for 40F for 50 *unités* or 96F for 120 *unités*.

The French have eliminated area codes, giving everyone an eight-digit telephone number, which is all you have to dial within France, except when phoning Paris, where the prefix is 16 1 before the eight-digit number. For international calls, first dial 19, wait for the change in the dial tone, then dial the country code (UK 44; US and Canada 1; Ireland 353; Australia 61; New Zealand 64), and then the local code (minus the 0 for UK numbers) and number. The easiest way to call collect is to spend a few francs ringing the number you want to call and giving them your number in France, which is always posted in the box; alternatively ring your national operator and ask him or her that you want to call reverse charges (for the UK dial 19 00 44; for the US 19 00 11). France's international dialling code is 33. For directory assistance, dial 12; international directory assistance is 19 33 12 followed by the country code, but note that you'll have to wait around for them to ring you back with your requested number.

bicycling

See 'Travel', p.6.

canoeing and kayaking

The Dordogne, the Vézère, the Lot and Célé are among the prettiest rivers in France for a week-long canoe or kayak trip. You can organize excursions through UK operators or in France. Among the larger firms are Canoës Loisirs, 407 Le Colombier, Sarlat-la-Canéda, 24200, © 53 28 23 43 or Canoë Raid (which also has trips down the Vézère), Siorac-en-Périgord, Campeyral 24170, © 53 31 64 11, and Safaraid, Albas 46140 Luzech, © 65 36 23 54, offer canoe trips down the Lot, Dordogne and Célé from June–September.

caves

Speleology, potholing, spelunking—whatever you want to call it, it's very popular, especially in the pocked limestone hills and mountains of the *causse de Gramat* in the Lot. For information and keys contact the Comité Départemental de Spéléologie, M. Jean-Robert Broqua, 46230 Bach, © 65 31 70 81.

fishing

You can fish in the sea without a permit as long as your catch is for local consumption. Fresh water fishing (extremely popular in this region of rivers and lakes) requires an easily-obtained permit from a local club; tourist offices can tell you where to find them. Often the only outdoor vending machine in a town sells worms and other bait. Ocean-fishing excursions (for tuna and other denizens of the deep) are organized by the day and half day, arranged in advance (in Arcachon, © 56 54 60 32).

gambling

The only casinos in this book are in Arcachon and Soulac-sur-Mer or you can do as the locals do and play for a side of beef, a lamb, or VCR in a **Loto**, in a local café or municipal *salle de fête*. Loto is just like bingo, although some of the numbers have names: 11 is *las cambas de ma grand* (my grandmother's legs) and 75, the number of the *département* of Paris, is *los envaïssurs* (the invaders). Everybody plays the horses at the local bar with the *PMU* (off-track betting) outlet.

golf

You'll find courses at Périgueux, Bergerac, Belvès, Le Bugue, and Sarlat (all in the Dordogne); Arcachon, St Loubes, Lacanau-Océan, and Bordeaux (three courses), in the Gironde; Agen, Villeneuve-sur-Lot, and Barbaste in Lot-et-Garonne; and at Martel, in the Lot.

horse-riding

Each tourist office has a list of *centres hippiques* or *centres equestres* that hire out horses.

Most offer group excursions, although if you prove yourself an experienced rider you can usually head down the trails on your own.

parachuting

Lessons for beginners (minimum age 15), jumps and gear are available from the Centre Ecole de Parachutisme du Bassin d'Arcachon, Aérodrome de Villemarie, La Teste 33260, © 56 54 73 11.

pétanque

Like *pastis* and olive oil, *pétanque* is one of the essential ingredients of the whole south of France, and even the smallest village has a rough, hard court under the plane trees for its practitioners—nearly all male, although women are welcome to join in. Similar to *boules*, the object is to get your metal ball closest to the marker (*bouchon* or *cochonnet*). Tournaments are frequent and well attended.

rugby

Since 1900 rugby, perfectly adapted to the Gascon temperament and physique, has been the national sport of the southwest, and the cradle of most of the players on the national team (although movements to change one of the Five Nations from France to Occitania have so far fallen flat). Agen and Bordeaux are among the top teams in France; in some places, especially towards Toulouse, they play heretical 'Cathar rugby'—13 to a side instead of 15. There's a women's version without tackling called *barette*.

walking

See 'Getting Around', p.7.

Tourist Information

Every city and town and most villages have a tourist information office, either called a *Syndicat d'Initiative* or an *Office du Tourisme*. In smaller villages this service is provided by the town hall (*mairie*). They distribute free maps and town plans, hotel, camping, and self-catering accommodation lists for their area, and can inform you on sporting events, leisure activities, wine estates open for visits and festivals. Addresses and telephones are listed in the text, and if you write to them they'll post you their booklets to help you plan your holiday before you leave.

Where to Stay

hotels

Like most countries in Europe, the tourist authorities grade hotels by their facilities (not by charm or location) with stars from four (or four with a L for luxury—a bit confusing, so in the text luxury places are given five stars) to one, and there are even some cheap but adequate places undignified by any stars at all.

We would have liked to put the exact prices in the text, but in France this is not possible. Almost every establishment has a wide range of rooms and prices—a very useful and logical way of doing things, once you're used to it. In some hotels, every single room has its own personality and the difference in quality and price can be enormous: a large room with antique furniture, a television or a balcony over the sea and a complete bathroom can cost much more than a pokey back room in the same hotel, with a window overlooking a parking lot, no antiques, and the WC down the corridor. Some proprietors will drag out a sort of menu for you to choose what sort of price and facilities you would like. Most two-star hotel rooms have their own showers and WCs; most one stars offer rooms with or without. The following guide will give you an idea of what prices to expect. The first number gives the range you'll encounter in 90% of the hotels (there are always exceptions); the second, in parenthesis, the average.

Note: all prices listed here and elsewhere in this book are for a double room.

★★★★Luxe	1400–2800F (1800F)
★★★★	550–1400F (900F)
★★★	250–600F (350F)
★★	140–350F (230F)
★	90–220F (150F)

Hotels with **no stars** are not necessarily dives; their owners probably never bothered filling out a form for the tourist authorities. Their prices are usually the same as one-star hotels.

Although it's impossible to be more precise, we can add a few more generalizations. **Single rooms** are relatively rare, and usually two thirds the price of a double, and rarely will a hotelier give you a discount if only doubles are available (again, because each room has its own price); on the other hand, if there are three or four of you, **triples** or **quads** or adding extra beds to a double room is usually cheaper than staying in two rooms. Prices are posted at the reception desk and in the rooms to keep the management honest. **Flowered wallpaper**, usually beige, comes in all rooms with no extra charge—it's an essential part of the French experience. **Breakfast** (usually coffee, a croissant, bread and jam for 20F or 30F) is nearly always optional: you'll do as well for less in a bar. As usual rates rise in the holidays and summer, when many hotels with restaurants will require that you take **half-board** (*demi-pension*—breakfast and a set lunch or dinner). Many hotel restaurants are superb and described in the text; non-guests are welcome. At worst the food will be boring, and it can be monotonous eating in the same place every night when there are so many tempting restaurants around. Don't be put off by obligatory dining. It's traditional; French hoteliers think of themselves as innkeepers, in the old-fashioned way. In the off-season board requirements vanish into thin air.

Your holiday will be much sweeter if you **book ahead**, especially from May to October. July and August are the only really impossible months; otherwise it usually isn't too difficult to find something. Phoning a day or two ahead is always a good policy, although beware that hotels will usually only confirm a room with the receipt of a cheque covering the first night (not a credit card number). Tourist offices have complete lists of accommodation in their given areas or even *départements*, which come in handy during the peak season; many will even call around and book a room for you on the spot for free or a nominal fee.

Chain hotels (Climat, Formula One, etc) are in most cities, but always dreary and geared to the business traveller more than the tourist, so you won't find them in this book. Don't confuse chains with the various **umbrella organizations** like *Logis et Auberges de France*, *Relais de Silence*, or the prestigious *Relais et Châteaux* which promote and guarantee the quality of independently-owned hotels and their restaurants. Many are recommended in the text. Larger tourist offices usually stock their booklets, or you can pick them up before you leave from the French National Tourist Office. If you plan to do a lot of driving, you may want to pick the English translation of the French truckers' bible, *Les Routiers*, an annual guide with maps listing reasonably priced lodgings and food along the highways and byways of France (£8.99, Routiers Limited, 25 Vanston Place, London SW6 1AZ).

Bed and breakfast: In rural areas, there are plenty of opportunities for a stay in a private home or farm. *Chambres d'hôtes*, in the tourist office brochures, are listed separately from hotels with the various *gîtes* (*see below*). Some are connected to *ferme-auberge* restaurants, others to wine estates or a château; prices tend to be moderate to inexpensive. Local tourist offices can provide you with a list.

youth hostels, gîtes d'étape, and refuges

Most cities have youth hostels (*Auberges de Jeunesse*) which offer simple dormitory accommodation and breakfast to people of any age for around 40–70F a night. Most offer kitchen facilities as well, or inexpensive meals. They are the best deal going for people travelling on their own; for people travelling together a one-star hotel can be just as cheap. Another down side is that most are in the most ungodly locations—in the suburbs where the last bus goes by at 7pm, or miles from any transport at all in the country. In the summer the only way to be sure of a room is to arrive early in the day. Most require a Youth Hostels Association membership card, which you can usually purchase on the spot, although regulations say you should buy them in your home country (the UK from YHA, 14 Southampton Street, London WC2; the USA from AYH, P.O. Box 37613, Washington DC 20013; Canada from CHA, 1600 James Maysmyth Dr, 6th floor, Gloucester Ottawa, Ontario K1B 5N4; Australia from AYHA, 60 Mary St, Surry Hills, Sydney, New South Wales 2010). Another option in cities is the single sex dormitories for young workers, *Foyers de Jeunes Travaillers et de Jeunes Travailleuses*, which will rent out individual rooms if any are available for slightly more than a youth hostel.

A *gîte d'étape* is a simple shelter with bunk beds and a rudimentary kitchen set up by a village along GR walking paths or scenic bike route. Again, lists are available for each *département*; the detailed maps listed under 'Walking' above mark them as well. In the mountains similar rough shelters along the GR paths are called *refuges*, most of them open summer only. Both charge around 40 or 50F a night.

Camping is a very popular way to travel, especially among the French themselves, and there's at least one camp site in every town, often an inexpensive, no frills site run by the town itself (*camping municipal*). Other camp sites are graded with stars like hotels from four to one: at the top of the line you can expect lots of trees and grass, hot showers, a pool or beach, sports facilities, and a grocer, bar and/or restaurant, and prices rather similar to one-star hotels (although these, of course, never have all the extras). Camping on a farm is especially big in the southwest, and is usually less expensive than organized sites. If you want to camp wild, it's imperative to ask the permission of the landowner first, or risk a furious farmer, his dog and perhaps even the police.

Tourist offices have lists of camp sites in their regions, or if you plan to move around a lot the *Guide Officiel Camping/Caravaning* is available in most French book shops. A number of UK holiday firms book camping holidays and offer discounts on Channel ferries: Canvas Holidays, © (0992) 553535; Eurocamp Travel, © (0565) 55399; Keycamp Holidays, © (081) 661 1836. The French National Tourist Office has complete lists.

Gîtes de France and other self-catering accommodation

Southwest France offers a vast range of self-catering accommodation from inexpensive farm cottages to history-laden châteaux and fancy villas, or even on board canal boats. The *Fédération Nationale des Gîtes de France* is a French government service offering inexpensive accommodation by the week in rural areas. Lists with photos for each *département* are available from the French National Tourist office, from most local tourist offices, or in the UK from the official rep: **Gîtes de France**, 178 Picadilly, London W1V 9DB, © (071) 493 3480. Prices range from 1000 to 3000F a week, depending very much on the time of year as well as facilities; nearly always you'll be expected to begin your stay on a Saturday. Many *départements* also have a second (and usually less expensive) listing of *gîtes* in a guide called *Cléconfort*.

The Sunday papers are full of options, or contact one of the firms listed below. The accommodation they offer will nearly always be more comfortable and costly than a *gîte*, but the discounts holiday firms offer on the ferries, plane tickets, or car rentals can make up for the price difference.

In the UK

Allez France, 27 West Street, Storrington, West Sussex RH20 4DZ, © (0903) 742345, fax (0903) 745044: wide variety of accommodation from cottages to châteaux.

Angel Travel, 34 High Street, Borough Green, Sevenoaks TN15 8BJ, © (0732) 884109: villas, gîtes and flats in Aquitaine.

Aquitaine Holidays, Hill Place, London Road, Southborough, Tunbridge Wells, TN4 0PX, © (0892) 516500: villas, cottages and farmhouses.

Beach Villas, 8 Market Passage, Cambridge CB2 3QR, ✆ (0223) 311113: villas and gîtes in the Dordogne.

Bonnes Vacances, 10 Hill Street, Richmond, TW9 1TN, ✆ (081) 9483467: villlas, cottages, flats.

Bowhills, Mayhill Farm, Mayhill Lane, Swanmore, Southampton SO3 2QW, ✆ (0489) 877627: farmhouses, watermills, châteaux and cottages in the Dordogne.

Bridgewater Travel, 217 Monton Road, Monton, Manchester M30 9PN, ✆ (061) 707 8547: villas and appartments.

Brittany Ferries, The Brittany Centre, Wharf Road, Portsmouth, PO2 8RU, ✆ (0705) 827701: gîtes and appartments by the sea.

Crystal Holidays, Crystal House, Arlington Road, Surbiton KT6 6BW, ✆ (081) 390 3335: villas in the Dordogne.

Dominique's Villas, 13 Park House, 140 Battersea Park Road, London SW11 4NB, ✆ (071) 738 8772, fax (071) 498 6014: large villas and châteaux with pools etc in the whole region.

La France des Villages, Model Farm, Rattlesden, Bury St Edmunds, IP30 0SY, ✆ (0449) 737678: cottages, manors, farmhouses and mills in the Dordogne, Lot and Lot-et-Garonne.

Francophile Holidays, Bishop Crewe House, North Street, Daventry, NN11 5PN, ✆ (0327) 300565: villas, cottages with pools.

French Affair, 5/7 Humbolt Road, London W6 8QH, ✆ (071) 381 8519: cottages.

French Character Cottages, 8 Market Passage, Cambridge, CB2 8QR, ✆ (0223) 350777: villas, cottages, farmhouses.

French Life Holidays, 26 Church Street, Horsforth, Leeds LS18 5LG, ✆ (0532) 390077: self-catering in the Dordogne.

French Villas, 175 Selsdon Park Road, Croydon CR2 8JJ, ✆ (081) 651 1231: gîtes, villages de vacances, and villas in the Dordogne.

International Chapters, 126 St Johns Wood Terrace, London NW8 7ST, ✆ (071) 586 9451: farmhouses, châteaux and villas in the Dordogne.

Unicorn Holidays, 2 Place Farm, Wheathampstead, Hertfordshire, AL4 8SB, ✆ (0582) 834400: châteaux holidays.

Vacances en Campagne, Bignor, Pulborough, West Sussex RH20 1QD, ✆ (0798) 7433: farmhouses, villas and gîtes in the Lot, Dordogne, and Lot-et-Garonne.

VFB, Normandy House, High Street, Cheltenham, GL50 3HW, ✆ (0242) 526338: gîtes, cottages and flats.

Vintage France, 75 Rampton Road, Willingham, Cambridge, CB4 5JQ, ✆ (0954) 261431: farmhouses with pools.

In the USA

Villas International, 71 W. 23 St, New York, NY 10010, ✆ (800) 221 2260.

At Home Abroad, 405 East 56th St, New York, NY 10022, ✆ (212) 421 9165.

Four Star Living, 964 Third Avenue, New York, NY 10022, ✆ (212) 891 8199.

Hideaways International, P.O. Box 1464, Littleton, MA 01460, ✆ (617) 486 8955.

Homeowners International, 1133 Broadway, NY 10010, ✆ (212) 769 1170 or (800) 367 4668.

Overseas Connections, 70 West 71 St, Suite 1C, New York, NY 10023, ✆ (212) 769 1170.

Resort Villas International, 30 Spring St, Stamford CT 06901, ✆ (203) 965 0161.

RAVE (Rent-a-Vacation-Elsewhere), 328 East Main St, Suite 526, Rochester, NY 14604, ✆ (716) 454 6440.

History

400,000–600 BC: the southwest gets off to an extremely precocious start, and humanity comes to the Dordogne for its first summer art course

Europeans tend to think of 'early man' as some low-browed troglodyte living in Africa or the Middle East. But the roots of humanity are as deep in Europe as anywhere—going back perhaps a million years in some places. Even more startling to contemplate is the fact that destiny chose this particular corner of France to be the scene of some of the earliest and most significant developments in culture and art. A mere 400,000 years ago, somebody was poking around Périgord and other parts of the southwest, laboriously making flint tools and somehow managing to get a fire lit. The crossing from the Lower to the Middle Palaeolithic occurred in this area about 75,000 years ago; the newcomer was Neanderthal man (presumably accompanied by Neanderthal woman). These come across as thick-skulled brutes in most accounts, but were really rather clever, inventing better tools and techniques, and developing the first rituals and burials: the elements of the 'Mousterian culture' in the southwest. The Neanderthals get pushed off the stage at about 40–35,000 years by Cro-Magnon Man, or *Homo sapiens sapiens*—us, more or less; books on Cro-Magnon man usually mention with a touch of whimsy that if one of them got on the bus today in a business suit, nobody would notice.

The creations of the Cro-Magnon (named after the hamlet in Périgord where their bones were first discovered) are many and varied enough for scholars to define various distinct Upper Paleolithic cultures: notably, the Perigordian and Aurignacian (35–20,000 BC), who left us jewellery, finely-crafted spear points, and—best of all—the world's first painting and sculpture (*see* 'Topics', p.49). In the Solutrean culture (20–15,000 BC), art was less of a passion, but people brought their stone tools—axes, spear points, arrowheads, knives, even sewing needles—to a point of perfection. The Upper Paleolithic reached its height with the Magdalenian culture (15–9000 BC), with the beautiful paintings in the caves at Lascaux and elsewhere. This period was the slow end of an ice age, and it is possible that the people who made Magdalenian art gradually migrated northwards, following the herds of reindeer and other animals they hunted. The Mesolithic cultures that followed them (9000–4000 BC) did not paint, nor do much of anything else that was interesting.

Neolithic culture reached the area about 4000 BC, either by migrations or simply by transmission of ideas—a lot of ideas: better tools, the first pottery, sedentary agricultural life, the domestication of animals, and a complex religion. The Neolithic peoples made Europe's first great civilization, and they were its first builders. Their dolmens, menhirs, stone circles and tumuli are common all along the Continent's coasts, but the Lot and the Dordogne have the greatest inland concentration of them anywhere. The Neolithic age was a peaceful one, and probably matriarchal; they lived in unfortified villages, and evidences of warfare are singularly lacking. Lost so far back in time, hard facts are few, and Neolithic culture leaves us with a tangle of fascinating riddles: the purposes of their megalithic monuments and their siting of them, their considerable achievements in astronomy, and above all the vision of an extremely sophisticated culture, living in close harmony with nature and living well, without metals or technology.

This world lasted for over three millennia in many areas. But the unity of Neolithic civilization was broken c. 2000 BC, with the arrival of new peoples like the metalworking Artenac civilization, around Bordeaux. Over the next millennia and a half the picture grows increasingly confused, as ever more peoples and cultures pass through. The first to have a name, courtesy of later Roman writers, are the Aquitanii; they arrived in the 7th century BC (or much earlier, according to some opinions), and they may have been related to the various tribes of Celts who followed them.

600 BC–507 AD: in which the Celts and the Romans first bash swords, and later clink glasses

In the 6th–4th centuries BC, new waves of Celtic peoples slowly spread over what came to be called Gaul. The Romans, when they arrived, found the area inhabited by a number of Gaulish tribes and wrote down their names: the Petrocorii north of the *Duranus*, or Dordogne, and south of it the Eleuteti and the fierce Cadurcii, who gave their name to Divona Cadurcorum (Cahors) on the *Oltis*, or Lot. In what is now the lower Lot-et-Garonne lived the Nitiobroges; while the plains around Toulouse were home to the Tolosates and Volcae Tectosages. The region around Bordeaux was occupied by the Biturges Vibiscii, who called themselves the 'Kings of the World'. A culturally complex people who nevertheless preferred pretty jewellery to the less mobile trappings of civilization—like temples and cities—the Celts, or Gauls, did settle a number of small towns, or *oppida*, which often served as trading stations. Even in this remote age, the 'Gallic isthmus' between the Atlantic and Mediterranean was a busy trade route; tin from Cornwall went one way, and back the other came imports from the Greek world including wine, of which the Gauls were especially fond.

Rome's conquest of Gaul was hardly an overnight affair. Julius Caesar, who arrived on his historic campaign in 59 BC, gets credit for the job, but Roman influence in the south at least was already strong—a Roman garrison was installed at Tolosa (Toulouse) around the middle of the 2nd century BC. Caesar's invasion came in response to revolts among Gauls who already found Roman control a little too heavy for their tastes. Burdigala (Bordeaux) was captured in 56 BC by Caesar's political partner Crassus, a wealthy magnate who, like Caesar, had bought a command because conquest was not only the path to power but also the only business more profitable to a Roman than city land speculation. The last great effort of the Gaulish nation and its leader, Vercingetorix, ended in total defeat at Gergovia in the Auvergne. The last Gaulish redoubt to fall, Uxellodunum, was somewhere in the Lot or perhaps Périgord (as with Gergovia, scholars are still arguing today over just where Uxellodunum was). The southwest, from the Loire to the Pyrenees, was organized into the Roman province of Aquitania.

Under direct Roman rule, southern Gaul became completely integrated into the Mediterranean economy. The new rulers apportioned out much of the land to Roman investors and veterans of the legions. Among the many new crops they introduced to the area was the grape, and soon the new Gallo-Roman Aquitania was not only meeting its own considerable demand for wine, but actually exporting it to Italy. Some of the *oppida* grew into towns—Tolosa, Burdigala and Divona Cadurcorum among many others; others naturally declined and died, and their ruins can be seen at such places as Mursens and Luzech, in the Lot. Mines and quarries were exploited, and many towns made a good living on manufactures, especially ceramics. By the 1st century AD, the larger towns were looking quite opulent, with forums, temples, public baths and amphitheatres imitating the cities of Italy.

Despite all this, life in Aquitania would not have looked so rosy to the average man. As else-where in the western Empire, Roman Gaul was a profoundly sick society, a pyramid with a few fantastically wealthy landowning families at the top, their estates tilled by vast armies of slaves. In the last centuries of the Empire, things got progressively worse. The small middle class in the towns was ground into poverty, as taxes rose and trade declined. Like the equally small class of free farmers, the middle class found itself gradually pushed into serfdom by debt. Not surprisingly, at the end of the Empire large areas of the country were controlled or at least threatened by the *bagaudae*—guerrilla bands out to destroy the system, and especially strong in Aquitania.

The Germanic raids of the mid 3rd century were an omen of troubles to come. In 256, the Franks and the Alemanni broke through the Rhine frontier. For two decades, they roamed over Gaul almost at will. Though the legions eventually recovered and drove them out, things would never be the same. The towns suffered most—such as Tolosa and Vesunna (Périgueux), which contracted after the invasions to a fraction of their former size, hud-dling inside circuits of hastily built walls. By this time the elite had already given up on urban life, and in the 4th century their sumptuous villas grew into cities in themselves; well-defended and self-supporting, these were the centres of what economic life remained in the last days. The fatal invasions came after 407; both Vandals and Visigoths passed through the region, and after 420 it found itself part of the new Visigothic kingdom, with its capital at Tolosa. Barbarian Franks replaced the barbarian Goths in 507, after the Battle of Vouillé, but this meant little to a part of Gaul that had effectively dropped out of history altogether.

507–1000: in which Aquitania is Frankly demoralized

Christianity had come to the region in the 4th century, the age when it was being estab-lished everywhere as the state religion of the Empire. The first recorded bishops are at Burdigala, in 314. Under the newly Christianized Franks, the Church in the 6th century strengthened its power everywhere. While the Frankish Merovingian kings held only a ten-uous control over most of Gaul, and only brought their army down to meet a foreign invasion, or when tribute was slow in coming, the real day-to-day government was usually in the hands of the landowners and their younger brothers in the Church. One bright light in the Dark Ages was Cahors. Controlled by a long line of powerful bishops beginning with the legendary Didier, the city survived and somehow prospered through the troubles; Cahors's aqueduct and baths were even restored in the grim 7th century.

Under the Merovingians, Frankish and Roman landowners gradually fused through inter-marriage into a new ruling class much like the old one. Over generations their villas began to metamorphose into castles, while the landowners themselves gradually made their logical transformation into feudal barons. The Merovingians created the duchy of Aquitaine in the 7th century; for seven centuries the largely independent dukes would be in control of all the western coast from Poitou to the Pyrenees. In this poor backwater, they weren't always up to the task. The Arabs roared through from Spain in the early 700s, seizing Bordeaux and dominating the area until Charles Martel beat them at Poitiers in 732. Soon afterwards, the Frankish kingdom under its new Carolingian dynasty—headed by Charles's son Pepin the Short—tried to seize the duchy, while the duke, Waiofer, sheltered refugeee lords who had been disposessed by the Carolingians and led the southern resistance to the ambitious new power descending from the north. The result was a bloody war of three decades; Aquitaine was not completely brought under control until 774.

Pepin's son Charlemagne found a compromise solution—raising the duchy of Aquitaine into a kingdom—the first 'king' of which was his son Louis; this title lasted only until 877. The height of Frankish power under the Carolingians was a peaceful time for most of France, though it was short-lived. Charlemagne was still warm in the grave when his empire started to disintegrate, and the western shores suffered the visits of the worst barbarians ever: the Normans, or Vikings. In 848 they sacked Bordeaux, and all through the century their regular raids brought terror and destruction to all the river valleys as far as Toulouse. The bits and shards of Roman civilization that had survived this long now finally faded out. Many people in the 9th century, looking forward to the millennium, were convinced that the end of the world was at hand, when in fact the ground was only being swept clean for something new and better.

1000–1271: the southwest creates a civilization, and the French and English come down to make nuisances of themselves

If the 9th century was the low point for the southwest and many other parts of Europe, the sudden strong impulse of cultural achievement and economic power that followed—the dawning of the Middle Ages—is all the more surprising. The Vikings settling down in Normandy marked an end to foreign invasions, and in a period of relative tranquillity (marked by constant but not-too-serious feudal warfare) the feudal system in the southwest reached its perfection. The crazy quilt of *comtés*, *vicomtés*, *sénéchaussées* and *duchés*, interspersed with huge areas where local barons were free to do what they liked within the limits of their feudal oaths, made for a finely balanced anarchy that somehow managed to permit a rapid rebirth of towns, trade, wealth and culture.

In the brilliant 12th century, great abbey complexes appeared under the patronage of local rulers, and new stone churches in the Romanesque style were under way in every town and village—the biggest one in Europe, St-Sernin, went up under the wealthy and enlightened counts of Toulouse, strongest lords of the southwest, who tended to all be named Raymond. Along the coast lived their near-equals, the dukes of Aquitaine; all of these were Guillaumes, and the list included Guillaume IX (1086–1127), who besides his capable political leadership was one of the first of the troubadours, heralding the rebirth of poetry in

Europe. That poetry was written in Occitan, the *langue d'oc*, and it was the pride of an Occitan nation, stretching from the Atlantic to the Alps, that was just beginning to become aware of itself when it was overwhelmed by invaders from the north.

Guillaume had a granddaughter, a beautiful and wilful woman whose life would be the stuff of romances, and whose career would change history: Eleanor of Aquitaine. She was sole heir to the rich duchy, and when she married Louis VII in 1137, the French crowed for having plucked the biggest feudal plum imaginable. Eleanor did her best with the cold, pious Louis, and even accompanied him on a crusade. Her manifest discontent led inevitably to a divorce, in 1152, and two years later she found a more convivial marriage with Louis's mortal enemy: Henry Plantagenet, Duke of Anjou, soon to be Henry II, King of England. Along with Eleanor came the land, and for the next three centuries Aquitaine would be a possession of the English crown. The Plantagenets, in constant need of cash, introduced an intelligent and well-organized administration; if the tax burden was high, the resources were there to pay it. The English proved good rulers, usually sympathetic to local concerns, and they gained a high degree of loyalty from the people of Aquitaine. (One sour note at the beginning came with the depredations of Henry and Eleanor's sons—worst of all Richard the Lion-Heart, a fellow who gets off all too easily in history and legend. Richard battled and pillaged across the region more to line his pockets than to solidify English rule, and in Aquitaine, as elsewhere, he gained a well-deserved reputation as a bloody-minded thug.) Under English control, Bordeaux grew into a city of 30,000 with a new prosperity based on wine; at the height of the trade with England, in 1308, Aquitaine exported almost as much of the stuff as it does today.

Toulouse, under its counts, grew even bigger and richer than Bordeaux, though the city that might have been a natural capital of an Occitan nation instead itself became a victim of imperialism from the north. The French would have made their play for Toulouse in any case, but in the early 1200s fortune provided them with a cause: the presence of the Cathars. This heretical sect, which came from the Balkans by way of north Italy, found a perfect haven in the sophisticated, tolerant atmosphere of the Toulousain and Languedoc. In 1209, a sordid deal between Pope Clement V and the French King Philippe-Auguste paved the way for the Albigensian crusade, supposedly directed against the heretics but in reality a naked grab at the lands of the counts of Toulouse. The troops were provided from Paris, a force under the cruel, lucky and always victorious Simon de Montfort; this army plundered its way through Quercy and the Agenais before the main event, the total subjection of the south. This was clinched by de Montfort's victory at the Battle of Muret, near Toulouse, in 1213; resistance continued, though, giving King Louis VIII an excuse to bring down another army to finish the job in 1224. In 1271, the French crown inherited Toulouse by a forced marriage; long before that, fiefs and offices had been handed out to northerners, and the Inquisition was introduced, not only to incinerate the few surviving Cathars but to ensure that the free culture that made heresy possible would be extinguished forever.

1271–1453: in which the French and the English continue their quarrels and mischief

Despite the vicious way the French had gone about their conquest, with plenty of bloody massacres *pour encourager les autres*, recovery was rapid. The surest sign of the continuing economic boom was the founding everywhere of *bastides*, planned new towns, usually built on lands that had gone back to forest or swamp during the late Empire and Dark Ages; the first of these was Montauban, a creation of Count Alphonse-Jourdain in 1144. Bastides had their political aspect too. Over a score of them were founded by Alphonse de Poitiers, the first French Count of Toulouse, who was King Louis's brother and the man in charge of establishing a durable French control over the new conquests. The English in response founded scores of bastides of their own in Aquitaine. The vigour of society in these times can be read on any map today; hundreds of town and village names show their origins in the 11th–13th centuries: bastides are often named Villeneuve or Villefranche—free towns with their own charter. Many other names end in -*artigues* or -*essart*, words that denoted reclaimed land, a constant necessity in times when the population was increasing rapidly. A village that grew up around a castle is often named *Castelnau*, and the various places called Sauveterre began as *sauvetés*, church foundations that at least in theory were 'safe', exempt from feudal warfare and pillage. The older towns also continued to thrive, notably Cahors, which attracted a number of Italian banking families that fled the disruptions of the Albigensian crusade. The little city on the Lot soon grew into a major financial centre with its own university, and even supplied a pope, John XXII.

England and France, now the only two powers in the region, battled fitfully for a century after the marriage of Eleanor and Henry II, until Louis IX (Saint Louis) agreed to the Treaty of Paris in 1259, formally ceding Périgord and Quercy to the English. From then on the two parties suspiciously eyed one another, in an uneasy truce that occasionally broke out into open hostilities; the French even succeeded in occupying Bordeaux for a decade, until a revolt of the Bordelais threw them out in 1303. But for all the politeness generally shown by both sides, it was a situation that could not last. In an age when nation-states were dawning, feudal logic no longer worked: as dukes of Guyenne (from the English mispronunciation of Aquitaine), the English kings owed homage to the kings of France—a fine position to be in whenever the two nations' interests were in conflict. The inevitable final showdown began with a quarrel over Guyenne in 1337, and went into the books as the Hundred Years' War.

The first decades of the war saw Aquitaine as the major battlefield, without major results until the arrival of Edward of Woodstock, son of Edward III, in 1355. The Black Prince, as he came to be known, ended the war's first round decisively with the Battle of Poitiers (1356), capturing King Jean II among many others. England, now in undisputed control of the southwest, declared their lands a principality free of any claims of French allegiance; the Black Prince ruled it from Bordeaux until his death in 1376. The next round went to the French, under the great Bertrand du Guesclin, who recaptured Quercy and most of Périgord by 1369. The war dragged on, but the two exhausted combatants found it increasingly difficult to maintain control of events. Both sides hired mercenary companies; gradually these got out of hand, and combined with the other desperados shaken loose from society by constant warfare and disruption, they formed the *routiers* ('highwaymen' would be a good translation), armed bands loyal to nothing but their own profit that reduced much of the southwest to anarchy. Coming on the heels of the Black Death (1348–50), which reduced the population by a third in many areas, it caused a time of troubles the region had not known since the days of the Normans.

In the early 1400s, it seemed that France was coming apart once and for all. The English regained all they had lost, and even took Paris in 1420, a time that coincides with the worst ravages of the *routiers* in the southwest. Thanks to Joan of Arc, of course, the French soon recovered and prevailed. They blockaded Bordeaux in 1451, and two years later the climactic Battle of Castillon, near Bordeaux, put an end to the wars and to England's continental empire forever.

1453–1594: in which the lobotomized southwest starts arguing with itself over religion

The French moved quickly to consolidate their hold on the new possessions. Bordeaux got a big new fortress to watch over the citizens, and a *Parlement* to scrutinize their morals and political opinions; the city's wine trade with England was ended by royal decree, sending it—along with most of Aquitaine—into a serious economic decline. For both Aquitaine and the Toulousain, the coming of French rule meant not only general impoverishment, but the enforced death of cultures that had been among the most promising of the Middle Ages. The 1539 decree of Villars-Cotterets mandated the French language in all matters of law and government, the first step along the road to the eradication of the *langue d'oc*, which would not be completed until our own time. Before the French came, the south had its own traditions of literature, architecture and art; under a new rigid authoritarianism, directed from Paris, all this withered away quickly. Southwesterners, when able to build, sculpt or write at all, found themselves forced to ape the fashions imported by their governors from the north, and over the generations it became a habit.

The French grip was strong, and with political opposition impossible, the next wave of southern rebelliousness came in the form of religious dissent. Protestantism first seeped into the southwest from Calvin's Geneva, and it found its most attentive audience among the industrious middle classes and some of the more enlightened courts. The first Protestant communities appeared in Ste-Foy-la-Grande and Agen about 1532. Soon after, the court at Nérac of the Albrets, a powerful noble family of the Agenais, became a centre of humanistic learning and religious heresy (Calvin himself came to visit). This happened in the reign of the learned Marguerite d'Albret—or rather Marguerite of Navarre, for this ambitious family had at the same time, with French help, worked its way to the kingship of that small and woebegone Pyrenean realm.

Protestantism swept across the south, bringing the good news that there was more to life than abject submission to Rome and to Paris. And with the spirit of the time, civil war was inevitable—the Wars of Religion. The conflict gathered steam from 1560, with the massacre of Protestants in Cahors, and the expulsion of the Protestant community from Toulouse two years later. Atrocities went both ways; in Gourdon, for example, it was the Protestants who were doing the slaughtering. Towns and regions chose sides. Cahors, with its powerful bishops, remained steadfastly Catholic, and fought a continuous battle with Protestant Montauban and Figeac; Protestant Bergerac stomped on Catholic Périgueux as early and as often as possible. The religious rebels found a firm pillar of support in Jeanne d'Albret, daughter of Marguerite and a grisly bigot for the new cause, as Protestant and Catholic armies recaptured the spirit of the Hundred Years' War, prowling the region and looking for enemy towns and souls to burn.

In much of the rest of France it was the same story; now, however, for the first time, the southwest stepped up to centre stage in France's history, thanks to the Albrets and Jeanne's son Henri, who by a complicated set of circumstances just happened to be the heir to the French throne. Henri of Navarre was a good Protestant and a hardy warrior; among other things he sacked Cahors in 1580 with more bloodshed than was really necessary. In two decades of campaigning to win his rightful crown, the Protestant lands of the southwest were his solid base. In the end, though, Henri's good sense and good will made him the man to finally put an end to the Wars of Religion—by the conversion of convenience that finally made him acceptable to the Catholics who were controlling Paris. As Henri IV, he ruled well, proclaiming religious tolerance with the Edict of Nantes (1598), and earned a secure place for himself as a national hero in the southwest, particularly in his native Gascony.

1594–1789: in which the French do their best to make everyone miserable, and the southwest fights back and loses

With religious troubles out of the way, the southwest was free to return its thoughts to the joys of rule from Paris. Riots and popular revolts had been common enough in the 1500s, usually over oppressive taxes like the *gabelle*, or salt tax. In the sympathetic Henri's reign, the first of a century-long series of peasant uprisings occurred. The movement of the 'Croquants', in Périgord and Quercy, was more directed at the grasping nobles and their high rents. In 1594 the Croquants formed a peasant army in Périgord; the barons organized and beat them, and punished the survivors with memorable ferocity. Henri's successors in Paris heaped more woes on the common folk: more taxes, more forced labour, and lots of revenue agents and troops to enforce them. The early 17th century would have been rough enough without them. High rents and prices, combined with bad harvests, recurring outbreaks of plague (1629 and 1652) and a climate of hatred and everyday violence, the heritage of the religious wars, made further revolts inevitable. In Toulouse, in 1629, things were so bad that even the royal governor, Montmorency, joined the rebels, and Louis XIII had to lead a big army down from Paris to crush them.

From 1637 to 1642, the Croquants were back in business again. This time they nearly captured Périgueux, though once again the arms of the king and the nobles had the last say. This would be the last revolt on a large scale, though smaller outbreaks were regular features of rural life up until the Revolution. For the nobles, times were never better, as witnessed by the large number of great châteaux built in this period. At the same time, a lot of the old-style castles were disappearing—pulled down on the orders of Louis XIII's minister Cardinal Richelieu, who didn't want any strong places left that could possibly shelter resistance to the national state. If the countryside was in despair, the two large cities weren't doing too badly. Bordeaux found a new prosperity in the late 17th and 18th centuries, based not only on wine but also on the slave trade with the Americas; the city grew enough to become the third-largest in France. Toulouse in the 16th century was still enjoying a modest boom from the manufacture of *pastel*, dyer's woad, and the building by local initiative of the Canal du Midi in Languedoc (1681) made the city the centre of a new trade route that crossed the French isthmus. The *pastel* business dwindled in the face of foreign competition, though, and despite its natural advantages, Toulouse generally continued its long slide into cultural and economic torpor.

For most of the region, hard times continued through the 1700s. If Bordeaux could find no better way to make a profit from the New World than slaving, at least the Americas offered many poor Aquitains a way out: tens of thousands of them emigrated to Canada and the West Indies. Most of the Protestants had already gone, to Prussia and elsewhere, after Louis XIV revoked the Edict of Nantes in 1685. For those who remained, the century was a drowsy era, at least when the peasants weren't revolting. intendants (administrators) from Paris ran everything, and made a few lasting contributions, notably an excellent network of roads (usually embellished with pretty rows of plane trees, as can still be seen in many places today). The intendants also dressed up Bordeaux, remodelling the city into a grandiose provincial copy of Paris.

1789–1940: the southwest helps make a revolution, learns to regret it, and then takes a long nap

In 1789, no people in France were more cheerfully assiduous than the southwesterners in smashing up churches and châteaux, taking special care to find the tax records and rent rolls and burn them. But at the same time, at the National Assembly in Paris, Bordeaux's merchants, and southwesterners in general, were providing most of the voices of moderation and good sense. Their faction, the Girondists, stood for liberal reforms and political decentralization. When the radical, Paris-dominated Jacobin faction gained control in 1792, the Terror began; the Girondists, along with their federalist hopes, became its first victims. A 1793 federalist counter-revolt in the southwest failed largely because Toulouse and Montauban wouldn't have anything to do with it, while stoutly conservative areas like the Lot were against the Revolution from the beginning.

The Lot, ironically, loved Napoleon and contributed more than any part of France to his Grande Armée, including fine soldiers like Joachim Murat, the son of a village innkeeper, who ended up King of Naples. Jean-Baptiste de Bessières of Prayssac, who was in charge of the occupation of Moscow, briefly claimed the title of Duke of Istria. At the end, though, southwesterners were as tired of Napoleon as anybody else. The Duke of Wellington marched through in 1814, on his way up from Spain. When he arrived at Toulouse, the people hailed him as a liberator.

If the Revolution had been a disappointment, nothing that happened in the century that followed it would be any improvement. Paris-appointed prefects replaced the Paris-appointed intendants, and the old regional distinctions and boundaries were destroyed in favour of homogenous *départements*, but through all the 19th-century shifts of the Gallic banana republic/monarchy/empire, no one ever lifted a hand to help the southwest; neither did the region ever show much energy of its own. Aquitaine and the Toulousain had become the most sluggish and listless of all French provincial backwaters, and anyone with any spunk or talent was off to Paris as soon as he could manage it.

The railway arrived in Bordeaux in 1850; seven years later the line from there to Toulouse and the Mediterranean was finished. Instead of catalyzing trade and industry, however, this merely made it easier to leave, and easier for imported goods to flow in and ruin the already hard-pressed southwestern farmers and manufacturers. The farmers did their best, introducing useful new crops such as corn and tobacco, and they managed just barely to survive the 1868 phylloxera epidemic that killed off nearly all their vineyards, but prices stayed low and business stayed bad. And all across the southwest, the villages began to dwindle.

Undoubtedly the biggest event of the last century was one that happened elsewhere—the First World War. Of the millions who died pointlessly for the glory of France, the southwest contributed more than its share. Many towns and village lost a third, or even half their young men; in every one you will see a pathetic war memorial or plaque in the church to remind you of France's greatest catastrophe since the Black Death. Between the war and rural abandonment, the southwest declined in population by almost 25% from 1850 to 1950; in some parts of the Lot and other departments, the figure was as high as 60%.

1940 to the present: a Nazi interlude, followed by the unexpected return of the English

Though the Second World War was less costly and destructive, it was still a miserable and dangerous time for the people of the southwest, however far removed they were from the actual fighting. From the beginning, the Germans seized a strip along the entire Atlantic coast. The 'border' between the occupied zone and Vichy-controlled territory was heavily patrolled, and locals needed special papers to cross it—plenty of people were killed trying to visit their cousins, or sneaking produce over the line to the nearby village market where they had always taken it before. Deportation of men to forced labour in Germany was a terrible burden, and not all who went ever returned. Another strain, particularly in Périgord, was supporting the wave of refugees from Belgium and northern France who had come down in 1940, but this one the people handled ungrudgingly.

The Resistance was not much of a force until 1943, but from then on it operated effectively in the lonely *causses* of Quercy and Périgord, where one of its leaders was the writer and future culture minister André Malraux. In retaliation for their acts of sabotage, the Germans sent the SS *Das Reich* division on a tour of the southwest in May 1944; these distinguished themselves with wholesale massacres of civilians at Mussidan, in Périgord,

Frayssinet-le-Gélat and Montpezat-de-Quercy. Liberation came for most of the southwest in August 1944; Bordeaux's story was much like that of Paris. Colonel Kühnemann, the German commander, was in civilian life a wine merchant with many friends in the city. He had orders to blow up nearly everything on his way out, along with all the bridges as far as Agen, but instead he spent a delicate week dodging the Nazi spooks while successfully negotiating with the Resistance for a peaceful exit. Some German units, trapped at Royan and Verdon on the Gironde, held out almost to the end of the war.

Since the war, the big news has been the unexpected awakening of Toulouse. With considerable assistance from the government planners, the city parlayed its early prominence in aviation to become France's forward-looking City of the Air, home of Aérospatiale and the French space agency, a manufacturer of satellites and supersonic airliners. Striving to become the European 'technopole' of the 21st century, Toulouse has also fixed up its historic centre, now sitting well-scrubbed, pink and pretty on the Garonne. Bordeaux, meanwhile, is still Bordeaux, and oddly proud of it.

There have also been some new faces. Large numbers of refugees from the Spanish Civil War, and a wave of *pieds noirs* (French settlers in Algeria, forced out in 1962) have settled in the southwest, adding a welcome touch of diversity not only to the population but to the cuisine—if there's a dinner on at a village festival, school pageant or whatever, it'll likely be paella or couscous. The British invasion began in Périgord, or 'the Dordogne' as they call it, in the 1960s, when people found out that lovely country homes in that delightful region could be had for a song. *That* particular song is definitely ended, but Périgord today has the largest English ex-pat colony in France, now rapidly spilling over into the *départements* of the Lot and Lot-et-Garonne. The locals joke that the English are trying to buy back what they lost in the Hundred Years' War; so far, though, relations are generally good.

Politically, the only major change of the postwar era was the Socialist government's 1981 decentralization plan, creating the regions of Aquitaine and Midi-Pyrénées. So far the regions have only very limited powers, but as the first reverse in seven centuries of Parisian centralism, it brings at least a hope that the southwest may someday finally regain some degree of control over its destiny.

Topics

The old vans and lorries will start wheezing in sometime after eight, unloading prunes and geese and greens and oysters in the morning fog while the children are passing through on their way to school. The stall-holders in French village markets aren't the sort of people to knock themselves out coming at dawn. That's the whole point. The Friday morning market here has probably taken place since the Middle Ages, and today it is a symbol of liberty, and a refuge for everyone from the clock-driven, bureaucrat-infested life of the cities. Free men and women come and go when they damn well please: there are no receipts, and no VAT that can't be avoided; no advertising, no special discount offers, no styrofoam and no bar codes; just real food, scents, colours and conviviality. Perhaps this is that Free Market they're always chattering about in the newspapers.

The village market is also the reliable country calendar of France, and all of us down here measure the seasons by the asparagus, spring onions, raspberries, wild strawberries, melons, *cèpes* and chestnuts that rise and pass across its firmament, each at its appointed time. It is also the best way to check on the state of the land. Even vendors who are middlemen, and didn't grow the stuff themselves, are willing to discuss the relative merits and demerits of their produce, with a long discourse on the weather responsible for them if they're not too busy. Farmers who bring in chickens will recount their life stories, and tell you to which special fate in the kitchen they think each of them best suited. If you're not in the mood for such discussions, and even if you're not intending to buy anything, you'll come to the market just the same, for the sensual assault that makes it the climax of the week. Best are the fish stands—glistening rainbow trout, pink *rougets* and prawns, inscrutible sea urchins and lithe purple Art Nouveau squids (and a *tielle*, a little Languedocien fish pie, to take home for lunch). Next door are flats of spring flowers, ready for planting, and across the way the green spectrum of the vegetable stand has been arranged with a master's eye for the maximum of colour and effect. There's a touch of colour in the market people too, the rosy flush that comes from spending most of their time outdoors.

The French aren't averse to noise. One thing that distinguishes many villages is the vintage air-raid horns that bellow out from atop the *mairie* to mark mid-day (when the market closes), as if to say '*Bon appétit!*' If they go off unexpectedly, flattening delicate sensibilities for miles around, it's probably to announce a fire; French villages depend on volunteer firemen, that doughty crew that comes roaring up to your house with lights and sirens ablaze just before Christmas with their calendars (if you give them a donation for the calendar, they'll come to your fire). And every village with an alert *syndicat d'initiative* has wired itself for sound, providing a little canned music to regale shoppers at the market in the busy seasons. You may get accordion music, lukewarm rock, or morose Parisian crooners, but in ours, the girls at the SI have grown fond of a tape of Ella Fitzgerald with Chick Webb's band (Ella got her start with Webb; an excellent drummer, his band spent a lot of time in the Apollo and the Cotton Club in the late 1930s. Edgar Sampson provides the arrangements and sax solos). They play it all the time, and under the plane trees at nine o'clock, in a French village market, everyone seems to think it hits just right.

The music isn't the only eclectic element. In our market, there's a solemn Dutchman with dirt under his fingernails who sells his organic *bok choy* and Chinese cabbage, Jerusalem artichokes and spiky African melons. Lots of Dutchmen, passionate gardeners from a space-starved country, come down here for a little tranquility and a little good earth. An Englishman who grew up here provides sweetcorn in late summer—the best you can get in Europe; the seed came from Pennsylvania. Even some of the French have gone exotic. The space cadet at the natural foods stand will sell you popcorn, Canadian wild rice, bulgar or fat-free nacho chips, and just around the corner a lady with a smile like the first sunny day in April is frying Vietnamese *nems* and somozas. Near the *librairie*, next to the fellow who's cooking a gigantic paella in a 4ft-wide pan, is the notorious Brit Van, with a sign portraying a tin of Heinz baked beans. You can get your Marmite and Bisto here, or a can of Guinness or some home-made scones. The friendly fellow who runs it is an English artist who does this to get by; on slow days he comes out and plays his guitar to drum up trade. On the side he's building his own château, from the ground up.

All this may seem a bit disconcerting, if you're the sort given to fantasies about finding a bit of 'unspoiled' rural heaven in deepest France. If that's what you really want, try the Gers or the Aude, fine departments both. But the flagrant cosmopolitanism of many of our village markets has done no harm to their more traditional aspects. One can still pick up live geese, or rabbits and chicks in wooden cages, and farm wives still set up folding tables to sell carefully braided strings of garlic and onions, homemade walnut cakes or delicate-looking but potent disks of *cabécou*. Unless the comet collides with the Earth, you can bet that five centuries from now they'll still be doing it (though maybe by then the list of traditional southwestern specialities will include sweetcorn and *nems*). Not long ago, on a chilly, drizzling market day in early autumn, we saw a thoroughly miserable old farmer, staring blankly out from under a flowered umbrella. A shrewish pinchpenny wife had undoubtedly chased him out in the rain to sell the one treasure he had brought, a sinister-looking courgette the size of a steam boiler, precariously balanced on a wooden box with a sign: *5F/kilo*. Five centuries from now, he'll probably still be there too.

Bertran de Born

East of Périgueux stands the Château de Hautefort, the replacement of the impregnable 12th-century citadel of war-loving troubadour Bertran de Born (c. 1140–1214). Bertran's career makes mincemeat of the romantic/Hollywood stereotype of troubadours as long-haired, love-lorn wimps. Although capable of writing delightfully about love, he liked nothing better than stirring up trouble, which he did through his battle songs and *sirventés*, the topical, satirical songs of the troubadours: 'I want great barons always/to be angry with one another,' wrote Bertran. And elsewhere: 'Peace does not comfort me/I am in accord with war/Nor do I hold or believe/Any other religion.' The minor nobility of Aquitaine listened to his *sirventés*, and agreed; feudal anarchy between overlords offered their only chance for independence and profit. But what assured Bertran's fame is the striking vividness and power of his poetry, capable of enchanting such diverse spirits as St Francis of Assisi, who sang his songs as a wayward youth, and Ezra Pound, who translated many of them so well.

In his day, Bertran was feared by all for his biting satire, so much so that he was blamed for the death of the Young King, Henry Court-Mantel, Henry II's heir to the throne of England and the older brother of Richard the Lion-Heart. The chroniclers tell the story: Bertran through 'ruse and felony' had kicked out Hautefort's co-owner, his brother Constantine, who had appealed to Richard as his overlord for justice. Bertran, resolved to seek aid in other quarters, wrote a series of *sirventés* taunting his friend the Young King, whom Bertran knew was sick with jealousy of Richard; the Lion-Heart already ruled Aquitaine and attracted great renown and money for his exploits, while his older brother chafed with little to do (and a small allowance) while waiting to inherit the throne of England. To every noble court Bertran sent songs of a 'lord of little land' and commented that 'It ill beseems a crowned king to live upon a dole and spend but a Norman carter's tax.' Bertran's satires had their doleful effect in the spring of 1183, when a general uprising against Richard's tyranny broke out across Aquitaine. The Young King joined the rebels, at first reluctantly, and then whole-heartedly when Henry II came down in person to aid Richard. The Young King Henry was now fighting not only his brother but his father too, and he raised money for his mercenaries by plundering; after a raid on the holy shrine of Rocamadour, he sickened along the road, and died at Martel.

Grief-stricken, old King Henry blamed Bertran for his son's death, and sent Richard and Alfonso II of Aragon to besiege Hautefort. Bertran scorched the earth before the enemy, so they would have nothing to eat. But when Alfonso asked him, as an old friend, for sustenance, Bertran offered the Aragonese armies ten days' worth of food, in exchange for the promise that they would not attack the weakened south wall of Hautefort. Of course that was precisely where the Aragonese unchivalrously began their attack, and Bertran surrendered at once, to spare further damage to his beloved castle.

Bertran was carted off before King Henry, who received him furiously, determined to have him put to the sword. Then he said: 'Bertran, Bertran, once you said that you never needed more than half your wits. Surely now you need them all!' 'My lord, what I said is true,' Bertran replied in tears. 'Although since the day of the death of your son, the beautiful and valiant Young King, I lost all my wits, judgment, and mind.' His grief so moved the king that he fainted, and when he recovered he wept and said: 'Ah Bertran, unhappy Bertran, it was only right that you have lost your wits in losing my son, for he loved you more than any other man in the world. And I, for love of him, return to you your liberty, goods, and castle. And I will add 500 marks to rebuild the south wall of your castle. Thanks to this letter from my son Richard, I know of your worthy conduct in the siege of Hautefort. It is as much for your noble acts as a soldier as for your celebrated talents as a troubadour that you have earned today my clemency.'

If Bertran had used his grief to get out of a tight jam, it was nonetheless sincere—his famous *planh* (lament) for the Young King is one of the masterpieces of Occitan literature.

But the experience hardly cooled Bertran's heels; out of Hautefort the volley of *sirventés* continued, now lampooning King Alfonso II for playing Bertran false, now egging Richard to battle with verses as vivid as Villon's:

If both kings are bold and fearless,
we'll soon see fields strewn with bits
of helmets, shields, swords and saddlebows,
and bodies split open from head to foot,
and horses wandering about aimlessly,
and lances protruding from ribs and chests,
and joy and tears, and grief and happiness.
The loss will be great, but the gain yet greater.

As Pound commented, 'This kind of thing was much more impressive before 1914 than it has been since 1920.' Yet for all his love of war, Bertran died in a monastery, from where Dante sent him straight to Hell, inventing for him the interesting punishment of wandering about as a headless trunk, holding his severed head aloft as a lantern. And the head explains to Dante: 'Know that I am Bertran de Born, who gave evil counsel to the Young King and made father and son rebel against one another...Because I parted those who were joined, I carry my brain parted from its roots in this trunk.'

Dances with Bears

Onward the kindred Bears, with footsteps rude,
Dance round the pole, pursuing and pursued.

Erasmus Darwin (grandfather of Charles), in *Economy of Vegetation*

Why do children respond so viscerally to teddy bears? One possible reason is pure atavism: way back in the Middle Paleolithic, or Mousterian culture (*c.* 120,000–35,000 BC) bears often occupied the same cave and shelters as our ancestors, and perhaps not always as dangerous rivals. In the Grotta della Basura on the Italian Riviera, the chamber dubbed the 'Room of Mystery' has fossilized footprints suggesting that bears and people once danced together; in another room a large quantity of bear bones were discovered. And in the 1950s, just above Lascaux at Regourdou, a ritual bear graveyard was discovered; each dead bear had been given 'gifts' of dead animals (*see* p.89).

In the vivid mural art of the Upper Paleolithic in southwest France, bears (like people themselves) are rarely portrayed among the bison, horses, aurochs and other favourite animal subjects: there's a fine one engraved in the Grotte de Bara-Bahau in Le Bugue (in a cave where bears lived for tens of thousands of years) and another at Lascaux, hidden in the body of the bull, almost as if it were part of a children's find-the-hidden-picture game. Other drawings and engravings are accompanied by bear claw marks. Most suggestive of all are the carvings on staffs found at La Madeleine (Dordogne) and at Massat (Ariège)—*see following page*. Few other Paleolithic works are as explicitly, and mysteriously, sexual:

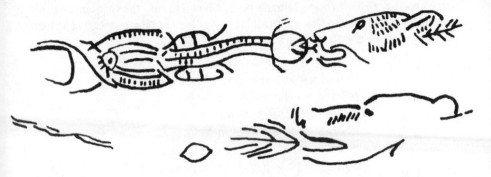

these staffs are the basis for the idea that some of the mysterious symbols in cave art represent male and female principles. Old Eskimo statuettes, from a culture technologically similar to the Upper Paleolithic, demonstrate an intimacy with bears shocking by the nursery standards of Christopher Robin and Pooh.

The evidence suggests that close human relationships with bears are limited to hunting cultures, as in the bear cults that survived into historical times. These were discovered by travellers and scholars in northernmost Japan (the Ainu people) or Siberia, where bears were not only a main source of food and clothing, but were also regarded as the representatives of gods. According to legend, the Ainu descended from the son of a woman and a bear. Ainu hunters apologized profusely when they slew one, and set up bear skulls (where the animal's spirit resides) in a place of honour. When a bear cub was captured, it would be suckled by an Ainu woman and raised with her children until it became dangerous when it played; then for two or three years it would be put in a cage and pampered with delicacies, in preparation for a Bear Festival. Then the bear would be given a huge last meal in a great show of sorrow, as the Ainu apologized and carefully explained to the bear the reasons for sending it to its mountain ancestors. Then it would be ritually strangled and eaten. In commenting on the Ainu in *The Golden Bough*, James Frazer wrote:

> ...the sharp line of demarcation which we draw between mankind and the lower animals does not exist for the savage. To him many of the other animals appear as his equals or even his superiors, not merely in brute force but intelligence; and if choice or necessity leads him to take their lives, he feels bound, out of regard to his own safety, to do it in a way which will be as inoffensive as possible not merely to the living animal, but to its departed spirit and to all the other animals of the same species, which would resent an affront upon one of their kind much as a tribe of savages would revenge an injury or insult offered to a tribesman.

This may explain why Cro-Magnon hunter–artists made animals vivid, flowing and beautiful, and portrayed themselves as inferior, clumsy stick figures.

Our prehistoric ancestors' relationship with bears may also have something to do with the intriguing survival, that 'relic of some primeval association of ideas' that in ancient India and Babylon, in the Book of Job, in Hesiod and Homer and native North American Indian tribes have identified the circumpolar constellation as a bear—the Great Bear, or Ursa Major, which is pursued or watched over by the bright star Arcturus (from the Greek word for bear-keeper). And hence the word for Arctic and Arthur—the early English designated King Arthur's home there, and some speculate that the circle, once known as 'Arthur's Wain' as described by the stars, was the origin of the Round Table. The common English name for the constellation, Charles's Wain, derives from the medieval legendary association of Charlemagne and Arthur.

Which brings us back to southwest France where the Great Bear has since been demoted to a *casserole*, where Charlemagne took his licks at Roncesvalles, and where along the coast of the Landes there are legends of King Arthur galloping to the hunt at night, legends unlike any in Brittany, where one might guess they were common. It is equally fitting that Heinrich Heine's *Atta Troll*, the last great literary Bruin, roved the same land that has preserved our earliest known representations of bears.

Microtourism

We don't have any Eiffel Towers or Chartres Cathedrals to offer you in this book. Famous, familiar sights are rare in the southwest, and anyone who wants great art will have to look for it in unlikely places like Moissac or Souillac, or in the Paleolithic caves of the Périgord. But the hordes of visitors and ex-pats that prowl this part of France hardly feel the lack. Most of them seem content with the area's wealth of pretty villages and châteaux, along with the wine, fresh air and *confits de canard,* and they might spend a slow weekend off in the big towns for a look at a church or a museum.

People who do spend a lot of time down here really need never be bored. Getting the most out of any part of rural France requires learning to look at the country the way the French do—on a small scale. Connoisseurs of every particularity of village and *pays*, the French are passionately interested in the detail of traditional life and local history. For example, painstaking cartographers have compiled maps showing traditional roof styles in France: where they are high-pitched or shallow, and where the boundary is between slate and canal tiles (except in Périgord, this roughly corresponds to the boundary between the *langue d'oil* and *langue d'oc*—it's all connected). Other maps display the types of construction used for *pigeonniers*, or dovecotes, notable features of the landscape in the southwest. In some areas they are round, in others square and set on stone pillars, or attached to the house. Get the locals talking about these subjects and they'll go on for hours, explaining how in some areas only nobles were allowed to keep pigeons, which went out every day and ate all the peasants' grain and so caused the Revolution, which allowed everyone to keep pigeons, and farmers let the poo pile up for their daughters' dowries, but later they planted groves of poplars when a girl was born, because the trees would mature just in time for the girls' marriages, by which time chemical fertilizers had made pigeon droppings less valuable than firewood.... You probably get the idea. And by the way, you've probably noticed how the poplars are always planted in orderly quincunxes, like the Place des Quinconces in Bordeaux, but scholars are divided on whether this fashion, invented by King Cyrus of Persia, came into France in the Middle Ages or in the time of Louis XIV....

If you want to play too, the first thing to do is pick up the *Cartes IGN: Série Bleue* map for the area that interests you. Drawn on a scale of 1:25,000, these are the equivalent of the Ordnance Survey or U.S. Geodetic Survey maps. You'll find them in any good newsagent or bookshop; hunters and mushroom lovers probably account for much of the demand. From the first glance, you'll get a feeling for the traditional life and the slowly evolving fabric of your area: the villages and hamlets, each with its patch of cleared farmland, like islands in the vast green of the forests, along with the works that kept life going: sawmills, remains of old water mills, *pigeonniers*, sandpits and quarries, sources and fountains.

The map will show you some surprises, even if you think you already know the area well. Naturally it will help you find the nearest swimming hole, and some nice places for a walk in the woods, but there will be other surprises too: maybe a dolmen or menhir, a collection of *gariottes* or a fortified tower, or a medieval chapel in an unlikely place that may turn out, like one we found, to have seven devils frescoed on the walls inside. Ruins, by the score, are generally marked on the map—without further detail, so take pot luck; ruins can mean anything from bits of a Roman aqueduct to a *routiers'* stronghold destroyed at the end of the Hundred Years' War, or a barn abandoned by some poor sod who gave up and moved to the city when the phylloxera hit.

Once you get to know the country and its history better, you'll be able to read these maps like a detective. That village surrounded by a circuit of roadside crosses—it must have been a *sauveté* of the Church in the 1100s; the crosses marked the limits within which knights were forbidden to bash each other or molest the peasants. Crosses of all kinds grow thick along the roadsides of the southwest. Around Toulouse people used to believe the Cathars first made them, but in fact many are simply the latest incarnation of markers that go back to Neolithic times (only 200 years ago, a bishop of Cahors was demolishing menhirs and replacing them with crosses, because country people would not stop worshipping secretly at the sites).

Not least among the virtues of rural France is modesty. This doesn't mean a lack of pride in one's region; on the contrary nearly everyone here is convinced that their particular *coin* is Paradise on Earth. But rather, modesty as an outlook, as a way of life. As historian Emmanuel Le Roy Ladurie has noted, France is the country where bars are called *Au Petit Bonheur* or *Au Petit Profit*. Ladurie and others have developed an equally modest and original way of looking at the past. 'Microhistory', studying a single place and time in the minutest detail, not only flushes out unwarranted generalities and clichés, but adds real depth to our understanding. And a little understanding is all the southwest and its people ask of the visitor. Deeply in love with their country, they are concerned that we learn to appreciate it as they do. With understanding, the *petits bonheurs* and sweet surprises begin to add up, secret doors into a part of France where the roots of life are rich and deep.

Art is art. Everything else is everything else.

Ad Reinhardt

Two-thirds of the 115 or so prehistoric decorated caves known in the world are in southwest France. No one will ever know if Upper Paleolithic art was once common everywhere, or if the natives of Lot and Dordogne valleys were especially inspired or gifted between 30,000 and 10,000 BC, or if it is only an accident that conditions here were ideal for the preservation of their art—warm valleys with caves rich in sedimentary deposits, that thanks to rock slides or other accidents were long blocked off from light and air.

Created by ancestors so antedeluvian that they are almost impossible to imagine, it is very difficult to look at the works as art in themselves and not as brief, mysterious encounters with another world. Or as P.M. Grand wrote in *Prehistoric Art*: 'The glamour of the sacred is particularly strong in our epoch, which has almost lost sight of the sources of the supernatural. Not to be deceived by this glamour is a major requirement in any investigation of cultures that present to us vastly more questions than answers.' The fact that there may well have been a ritualistic or supernatural motivation behind the drawings and paintings takes nothing away from their aesthetic value; art has always willingly served religion. Forget, too, the Hollywood view of hairy, grunting brutes dragging Raquel Welch around by the hair when they aren't battling dinosaurs; these people were our intellectual equals, with a keen eye for observations, a capacity for abstract or symbolic expression, and imaginative innovations that would take later artists until the 20th century to duplicate. 'This is the infancy of art, not an art of infancy' as the saying goes.

Prehistory itself is a very recent field. Until the 19th century, Upper Paleolithic artifacts (tools, decorated throwing sticks, carvings in bone or stone, staffs, 'Venuses') were called 'thunderstones', to be dismissed somehow as the 'accompaniments of lightning'. In 1859, the discovery of tools in the same strata as the bones of extinct animals convinced scientists of their great antiquity and led to an increased interest in the field—further fuelled by the publication of Darwin's *On the Origin of Species* the same year. The idea that a stone-tool culture was also capable of the lofty, noble art of painting was much more difficult for many modern intellectuals. When the first extraordinary murals were discovered in the cave of Altamira in northern Spain in 1879, all but a tiny handful of scholars thought they were a hoax.

The Doubting Thomases began to change their minds in 1895, with the discovery of the Grotte de La Mouthe in the Dordogne, where along with the paintings and wall incisions a prehistoric lantern was found. A 23-year-old priest named Henri Breuil was invited to trace the drawings, beginning the career of a man known as 'the father of prehistory'. Now that Breuil and his fellow pioneer Denis Peyrony knew what to look for, important discoveries followed quickly; in 1901, the men discovered Les Combarelles and Font-de-Gaume, both near Les Eyzies. Local children, enthused by the finds in their villages, began to seriously explore the countryside. In 1922 they discovered Pech Merle in the Lot, in 1940, Lascaux, so overwhelming that there's the temptation to stand Breuil's description of the cave as 'the Sistine Chapel of prehistoric art' on its head, and say that the Sistine Chapel is the Lascaux of Renaissance art.

Perhaps the most intriguing thing about the painted caves is that they achieve so many of the aims of art in the last half of the 20th century—they suggest far more than they actually show and invite the viewer to actively participate in their meaning; they admirably make use of their environment and the palette that nature presents (bulges in the stone wall that give forms a three-dimensional feel, the shadows that suggest water, a protrusion that becomes the muzzle of a horse); they are not bound as compositions into the artificial rigueurs of a canvas, much less up and down or north or south; a cave is a natural installation and a natural sanctuary, and it's a shame that Matisse or Joan Miró never had a good crack at one. Most of all, they combine their formal perfection with a function and meaning that, even if the exact nature of it may never be discovered, leaves a powerful and poignant impression even after thousands of years. Nothing means as much or will ever be as immediately close to us as the animal world was to these first artists. The only composition that our century has produced that comes close to the powerful impact of Lascaux is Picasso's *Guernica*, a work about new technological advances in death and horror.

Goose Lore and Livers

In the southwest the national bird, the strutting cockerel, seems far removed, a symbol rarely seen outside the backyard coop. Instead, visitors are confronted everywhere by giant plywood geese, beckoning clients into tiny shops selling foie gras and *confits* in tins.

Although it would be heresy to say so in the southwest, the national dish, *confits d'oie*, may have originated in medieval Venice, where the staple was *bigoli con sugo di oca conservato* (fat buckwheat spaghetti with a goose confit sauce). In fact, for centuries Périgord pâté was made of partridges stuffed with truffles and chicken livers. In 1726 the partridges got a break when a certain Close de Strasbourg discovered that goose liver with truffles tasted much better, and the bigger the liver the better. It had already been noted that pigeons that stuffed themselves silly on corn developed swollen, delicious livers, and the concept was extrapolated to geese and ducks (which are much more amenable to *gavage*, or force-feeding). After spending the life of Riley wandering at will in meadows and walnut groves, the geese are fed a three-week adjustment diet of flour, corn, and meat before being enclosed in autumn for three weeks of *gavage* three times a day—traditionally women's work—each bird downing between 66 and 88lbs of corn to create the perfect creamy pink liver weighing up to 3lbs, all in preparation for Christmas holidays, when half of all France's foie gras is consumed. It was also a hit abroad; one of Talleyrand's secret weapons of diplomacy was his chef, who softened up ambassadors and heads of state with *pâté de foie gras* and a glass of golden Monbazillac.

To the many foreigners (and not a few French citizens as well), *gavage* seems the height of barbarism. They wince at the postcards of geese being force-fed by crafty old women stroking a goose neck with one hand while holding a funnel of corn down its throat with the other; they are horrified that many farms invite visitors to watch, and that many geese willingly waddle over for their corn tipple (they look happier than battery chickens, at any rate). During the Occupation, the Nazis with their delicate sensibilities found the practice offensive and banned *gavage*, with the curious result of making foie gras a proud symbol of the Resistance. In an effort to make *gavage* more humane (but mostly to save the intensive labour involved) attempts have been made to adjust the thymus gland in geese and ducks to make them naturally piggy, but up until now biologically engineered *auto-gavage* has had limited success.

The goose that lays the southwest's golden egg faces an even greater challenge in single market Europe, in the form of importers from Romania, Israel and beyond who are flooding the market with phony foie gras, or foie gras incorporating all kinds of fillers, a scam that threatens to undermine both the traditional producers and confidence in the product; bad enough that such things happen in Paris, but in the sanctuaries of traditional foie gras, such cheating is blasphemy. Yet anyone passing through the region can't help but notice the disparity between the amount of foie gras on offer, and the actual number of geese and ducks. These days connoisseurs and restaurateurs have to know their sources personally.

But the strange attachment of the area to its fetish fowl goes back centuries before anyone thought to tamper with goose livers. The Basques tell of a race of lovely but goose-footed fairies, the *laminak*, and Toulouse was the home of the famous Visigothic queen Ranachilde, wife of Theodoric II, *la reine pédauque* or *pé d'aouco*, the goose foot who could swim better than walk and had aqueducts built in Toulouse so she could paddle from her palace to the city. Her story inspired others, like those of Berthe, mother of Charlemagne (d. 783), who was said to have webbed or at least very large feet, and another goosey Berthe, the wife of Robert the Pious. This couple was excommunicated for a consanguineous marriage, and their incestuous relationship is said to have produced a goose-headed child.

One of the Berthes, at any rate, was customarily represented as a rather domestic queen, telling children tales by her spinning wheel (French tales customarily begin with 'In the time when good Queen Berthe spun...'). Andrew Lang found the first reference to Mother Goose, *la Mère l'Oye*, in a 1650 book called *La Muse Historique*, predating Charles Perrault's 1697 *Les Contes de ma Mère l'Oye*; in English the first reference to Mother Goose appeared in a fairy tale book printed in London in 1729. Perhaps most mysterious of all are the Cagots, a vanished people who lived in the Pyrenees and were said to be albinos, or dwarfs or lepers; in the Middle Ages they were renowned as excellent architects and carpenters, though they were forced to live apart and wear a goose foot around their necks.

The Architecture of Springtime

> *So it was as though the world had shaken herself and cast off her old age, and were clothing herself everywhere in a white garment of churches.*

> Ralph Glaber, an 11th-century English chronicler

On a typically rainy autumn afternoon, we saw an old farmer trudging in the mud alongside the road, so we stopped to give him a lift. It turned out he wasn't a farmer at all, despite the beret, overalls and rough-cut walking stick. He was a retired Swiss teacher, and he had decided to spend the rest of his life walking around Europe, looking at Romanesque churches. That made for some good conversation along the way; we compared notes on buildings in Apulia and the Abruzzo, and Templar chapels along the pilgrimage routes in Old Castile. We told him about one unknown church in a tiny nearby village, one with horseshoe arches derived from Muslim Spain and a Celtic spiral carved over the door. He knew about it already.

Such a devotion may seem eccentric, but this fellow was hardly alone. The Romanesque is a bug that bites unexpectedly; no other art and architecture in the West has the same inexplicable capacity to enchant. At first sight, especially if you've been indoctrinated in the schools, you might think that the products of modern Europe's first artistic urge are mere 'primitives', the first child steps on the way to the Gothic and Renaissance. A closer look reveals an immensely sophisticated art that seems to have sprung, fully formed, out of nothing at the dawn of the Middle Ages. In fact the ideas of Romanesque had been around for a while, breaking out occasionally in unexpected places like Armenia, or Asturias in northern Spain. Only in the tremendous economic upsurge of the 11th century did anyone in Europe really have a chance to build. When they got the chance, they built for the ages, solidly and in good stone. At first sight their works may seem heavy, with the little light that filters through the narrow windows in the afternoon. Not until the late 12th century, with the new Gothic advances, would the technology appear to allow those windows to get bigger. But let your eyes adjust to the shadows for a minute, and you'll see wonders.

'Romanesque', for such a momentous and varied movement in architecture, is as misleading a term as 'Gothic'. Among the few things it has in common with ancient Rome are the use of round arches and a habit of using the basilican plan for churches; large projects, of which the southwest can offer only a few survivors, such as Saint-Sernin in Toulouse or Sainte-Croix in Bordeaux, also often attempt to recapture the monumentality of the Roman manner. But Romanesque has nothing to do with the classical Orders of ancient buildings; rather it depends on a new system of sacred geometry, which probably began with the Hagia Sophia in 6th-century Constantinople, and gradually spread across both Europe and the Muslim world. Anyone with a mathematical bent will enjoy looking over the churches or their plans; every point in the ground plans and elevations can be proved with a compass and straightedge, the same way the master masons designed them.

In the springtime of the medieval world, nearly every large region of western Europe developed its own distinctive style. Freedom and fancy were in the air in the 11th and 12th centuries; standards were high and rules few. Provence had its stiff, heavy buildings and octagonal cupolas; the Catalans built similarly, and accentuated their works with elegant towers and brilliant sculpture, while the Auvergne contributed unique patterned façades perhaps inspired by the caliphate of Andalucía. The basic element in Aquitaine is the *clocher-mur*, a west front that rises above the roofline to make a wide belfry, providing a memorable façade and saving the great expense of building a separate tower. There are some eccentricities, like the cave-churches of St-Emilion and Aubeterre-sur- Dronne, cut out of the rock, while Périgord also came up with the most exotic flower of all Romanesque styles, impressive churches with shallow Byzantine domes, an idea brought back from Syria and Palestine after the First Crusade. Many others in Périgord are fortified churches, a testimony to the roughhouse feudal warfare there, though aesthetics may suffer a bit.

Along with the architecture goes its sculptural decoration—the first great age of sculpture since classical Greece. Early medieval society found not only the resources to raise all these buildings, but to decorate their portals and columns with a wealth of sculpted detail, even in some of the village churches. The southwest contributed more than its share, including the most accomplished of all the workshops, the 'School of Toulouse' that created the vibrant, flowing reliefs on the portals of Moissac and Souillac; many consider Moissac's to be the greatest masterpiece of all medieval sculpture.

And what have the French done with this heritage? The Parisian conquest of the Midi and other lands currently French ensured a calculated devaluation of their art and culture. From the Renaissance Italians, the French first learned a rationale for contempt for their greatest buildings, and set off on a path of slavish imitation of the Romans and a submission to academies and rules—a disaster that plagues the national culture to this day. In the philistine 17th and 18th centuries, the tastemakers in the academies considered anything medieval the artistic equivalent of *patois*, especially if it came from the early centuries when the provinces, not Paris, were the vanguard. They spoilt the interiors of thousands of churches, plastering them over with gaudy Baroque frippery and gilded knick-knacks (most of that has been cleared away in the last few decades). There was more to the world of the Romanesque than the Enlightenment ever dreamt of in its philosophy, and in the first days of the Revolution uncomprehending mobs gleefully smashed up some of the finest of medieval sculpture. Casualties included the School of Toulouse's cloisters of St-Sernin and St-Etienne; you can see the surviving fragments in the Musée des Augustins. After the Revolution, scores of churches and monasteries saw duty as barns, warehouses and barracks; many more were simply torn down for their stone.

When the first attempts at restoration were made, the result was often just as unfortunate—the classic example in all France being Paul Abadie's supremely arrogant job on Saint-Front in Périgueux, in which more was wrecked than restored, while the building was changed out of all recognition. France, surprisingly one of the most backward nations of Europe in historic preservation, has only got its act together in the last few decades. Even in the 1920s, entire cloisters were being sold off or destroyed—a lot of the southwest's best sculpture was purchased for John D. Rockefeller and moved to his Cloisters Museum in Manhattan.

Wandering among the fragments of the early Middle Ages, one often feels like an archaeologist, exploring the enigmatic survivals of a lost civilization. It *is* a lost civilization; we know as little about the inspirations and motivations of early medieval artists as we do about classical antiquity or the Egyptians. The architecture speaks for itself, an inexhaustible vernacular of simple arches, barrel vaulting, pilasters and apses recombined in a thousand different ways. The sculpture is more of a problem; its imagery often reflects concepts that have nothing to do with orthodox religion, or indeed with Christianity at all. Why is the prophet Isaiah dancing at Souillac, and what made the seemingly obscure episode of Daniel in the lions' den the most copied and most significant image in the sculpture of the southwest and Languedoc? And what about the mermaids? In scores of churches around the region, and across Europe, images of mermaids appear in hidden places, sometimes cradling babies, sometimes alone, spreading their forked tails in an unseemly way—any fan of the Romanesque would be reminded of the capital of this strangeness, at Monte Sant'Angelo in Italy, where coiled serpents whisper ancient secrets into the mermaids' ears.

The sculpture is the key, though you'll always have to look carefully to find it. When you visit a Romanesque church, even a simple one in a village, scrutinize every corner, inside and out. The great themes of the Life of Christ and the Apocalypse are portrayed for all to see on the portals, but Romanesque masters stubbornly insist on putting the esoteric bits in places you wouldn't expect, perhaps to hide them from the casual eye, perhaps in their pride to force us to look all around, and so come to appreciate the work as a whole as they did. The faces are everywhere, especially on the *modillons*, or corbel-stones around the roofline: hundreds of faces, grimacing, smiling, interspersed with monsters, cats, dogs, boars, unicorns and all the other inhabitants of the medieval imagination. There may be a giant with a club, a dim memory of ancient Hercules, or a fine lady in a small boat (her name is Phaedria, and she symbolizes Desire). On the capitals inside, hunters and lovers, lions and kings stare down at you. The meaning, and even the identity of the characters is often lost to us, though if you could go back to the 1100s a troubadour poet, or a street singer, or a monk with a little Latin might have explained them all. But you can't, and unless you're willing to cut yourself a walking stick and spend the rest of your life at it, traveling and reading and looking, you'll never know.

The Dordogne: Périgord

St-Front Cathedral, Périgueux

Petra si ingratis, cor amicis, hostibus ensis
Haec tria si fueris Petra-cor-ensis eris

(A stone to the unpleasant, a heart to the friendly, and iron to the enemy/If you're all three, then you're a Périgordin)

Périgord, the *département* of the Dordogne, is at once the gateway to greater southwest France and a region with a strong character of its own. Cross its frontiers and simple words like *vin* and *pain* turn into *vaing* and *pang*, the menu fills up with dishes based on duck, goat cheese, and walnuts, there's a warmth in the air and in the colour of the very stones. To this add Périgord's unique qualities, its truffles, troubadours and love of medieval domes, its lush green colour and forests, carved by a dozen rivers of exceptional beauty, and you have a countryside as Arcadian as an eclogue, 'the nearest thing to Paradise this side of Greece' as Henry Miller wrote. Ironically, this Paradise is the result of long centuries of war and poverty

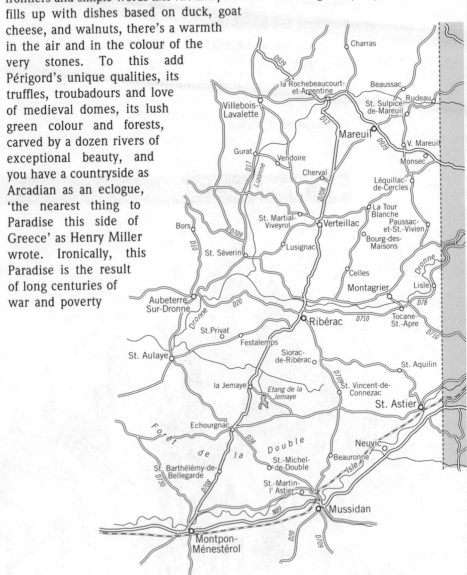

and neglect. So is much of the architecture that so delights visitors today—nearly a thousand castles and fortified churches, and medieval villages with black stone (*lauze*) roofs and farmhouses that never had the wherewithal to improve.

If Périgord could make a tough wiseguy from Brooklyn go sloppy, there must be something to it. In fact, so many people agree with Miller, that the likes of neo-fascist Jean-Marie Le Pen can complain that what the English couldn't conquer in the Hundred Years' War, they are buying up in the 20th century. The truth is

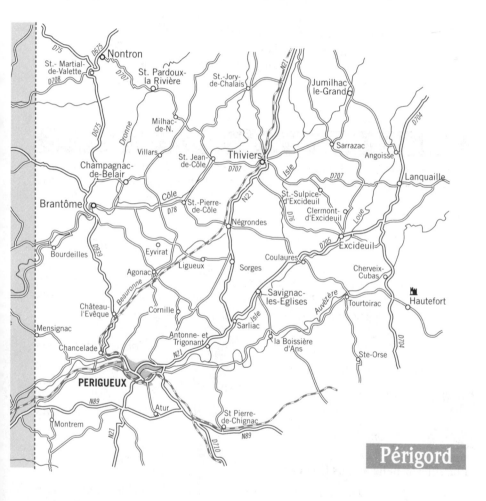

Périgord

that Périgord fulfils a communal dream for a comfortable place, a simpler, rural world of beauty and pleasure. These days the main danger Périgord faces is that of any place that has kept its integrity: of tourism destroying precisely the 'real, authentic' thing it seeks.

The name Périgord comes from the Gaulish nation known as the Petrocorii ('the four tribes'), who according to Caesar sent 6000 troops to aid Vercingetorix in his final defeat against Rome. From the days of the Vikings to the end of the 14th century, it was governed by counts who make Dracula look like a good egg. Under them, Périgord was subdivided into four baronies (Mareuil, Bourdeilles, Beynac and Biron) which survived until the Revolution, when they were combined to form a single *département*, the third largest in France and named after its biggest river, the Dordogne. This first chapter covers the northern section, what is commonly called Green Périgord (after the trees) and White Périgord (after the stones); the next takes in the great valley of the Dordogne—most of Black Périgord (after either its truffles or the deep shadows cast by its oaks) and the recently designated Purple Périgord, purple, that is, after its wine.

Arriving from the North: Périgord Vert

It was Jules Verne who dubbed northern Périgord 'Green' where deep forests, shady rivers and green limestone hills remain luscious even in midsummer; plans are afoot to protect much of it as a natural park. If you're driving down to the southwest, you may find you have no desire to go any further.

Getting Around

Two SNCF bus lines cross this area, one linking Angoulême, Mareuil, Brantôme, and Périgueux four times a day, and the other running between Angoulême, Mareuil and Ribérac. If you're taking the Bordeaux train from Paris, Thiviers (© 53 09 50 50 for information) is the first stop in the Dordogne.

Tourist Information

Mareuil: Place des Promenades, © 53 60 99 85

Nontron: Rue de Verdun, © 53 56 25 50 or 53 56 00 53

market days

Nontron: Wednesdays and Saturdays.

Mareuil-sur-Belle and its Château

If you take the A 10 motorway or N 10 south to Poitiers, continue south through Angoulême and aim southeast for Périgord, you'll enter the *département* of the Dordogne by way of the ancient fief of the barons of Mareuil. These had their seat at the 15th-century **Château de Mareuil** *(open June–mid Nov, 2–6.30pm, adm)*, confidently built on a plain and defended by moats filled by the waters of the Belle; inside is a flamboyant Gothic chapel, the dungeons, and Louis XV furniture.

Mareuil was also the home of the troubadour Arnaud de Mareuil, son of a poor castle workman. Arnaud fell deeply in love with the lovely Countess Adélaïde of Béziers, but kept his passion secret by hiring a *jongleur* to sing his love songs. Eventually one of Arnaud's lyrics gave him away, but rather than scorn her humble-born troubadour, the Countess gave him many gifts—until King Alfonso of Aragón, himself a troubadour and lover of Adélaïde came to call, and made her send Arnaud packing. Dante sent him even further, to Purgatory, although his only sin was to be admired. His poetry, so celebrated in his day, is nearly impossible to translate, 'the result of a technique honed down to the point where all signs of effort vanish, where the words, sounds and rhythms flow past with a mellifluous ease, resulting in a poetry of extraordinarily gentle and delicate beauty' (Anthony Bonner).

You can have your first look at Périgord's famous domed Romanesque churches near Mareuil: just south of Mareuil, **St-Pardoux-de-Mareuil** has a sombre model with an impressive bell tower, while the fortified church at **Vieux Mareuil** to the east has three domes crowning the length of its nave.

Nontron

High on its promontory, Nontron (in Celtic, 'the valley of ash trees') began as a Gaulish *oppidum* over the river Bandiat. It has picturesque old streets to explore, and fine views from the mighty ramparts and from **Place Paul-Bert**. An 18th-century château in Place Fort houses the **Musée des Poupées** *(open 10–12 and 2–5 mid Oct–Mar; 9.30–12 and 2–6 from Apr–June and Sept-mid Oct; 9–12 and 2–7 in July–Aug, closed Jan and Tues, adm)*, a collection of dolls going back to the 16th century, many residing in a fabulous doll's house 22ft long.

On the last Sunday in March, or first Sunday in April, Nontron is invaded by the *souffla-culs* (whistle arses), a hysterical custom dating back to the 13th century. Dressed in nightshirts and nightcaps, the *souffla-culs* march through the streets, squatting here and there to blow their whistles up the nightshirt of the person in front while chanting: 'We are all children of one family; our father was a whistle-maker. No, you're not going to see the colour of my gaiters. No, you're not going to see the colour of my stockings.' The procession ends up with the judgement and fiery death of a dummy symbolizing Carnival.

Around Nontron, on the Limousin frontier

If you aren't around in time for the *souffla-culs*, other peculiarities await in the countryside north of Nontron, all just off the D 675: eroded rock formations like the **Roc Poperdu** 3km north and near a shallow lake in St-Estèphe (7km), the huge **Roc Branlant**, that rocks when touched, and the granite 'Devil's Chapelet'. Further north, the **Donjon de Piégut** still stands as a last memory of the castle wrecked by Richard the Lion-Heart in 1199. Here, in the northernmost tip of Périgord, take the left turn to medieval **Bussière-Badil** to see its beautiful, fortified 12th-century church, a hotchpotch of local Romanesque styles: Limousin features include an octagonal bell tower and the flat pendentives under the dome; the animal and foliage sculptures on the arches of the porch are in the Angoulême style, while the capitals inside are Périgordin.

West of Nontron the main town on the Limousin frontier is **Varaignes**, a village that in recent years has undertaken the restoration of its feudal château, installing inside a museum devoted to the traditional manufacture of cloth in the region *(open 10–12 and 2–6 except Sun am and Mon; out of season closed Tues as well)*. South of Varaignes, the 12th-century church at **La-Chapelle-St-Robert** is, like Bussières, in a mix of styles, with a dome and lovely bell tower. Nearby, in serene **Javerlhac-et-la-Chapelle-St-Robert**, the inhabitants keep their ancestral Occitan alive and suffer cramps from writing their return address. There is a 13th-century abbey church, a château from the 1400s with a great tubby tower, and the Versailles of all *pigeonniers*, with niches for 1500 birds.

Where to Stay and Eating Out

Vieux Mareuil ✉ 24340

> ★★★**Château de Vieux Mareuil**, Rte Angoulême-Périgueux, ✆ 53 60 77 15, is a delightful family-run hotel in a 15th-century castle, set in a 50-acre park. The views from the heated swimming pool are luscious, and the restaurant matches the view, with memorable renditions of classic dishes—save room for the warm apple pie with chestnut liqueur (menus from 130F). ★★★**Auberge de l'Etang Bleu**, ✆ 53 60 92 63, overlooks the local, sometimes crowded swimming hole: a blue lagoon in the woods.

Nontron ✉ 24300

> The lemon-coloured ★★**Grand Hôtel Pelisson et Fils**, 3 Place Agard, ✆ 53 56 11 22, is a comfortable hotel in the centre, with an inner courtyard and pool and the best restaurant in Nontron, with an excellent, filling 100F menu. Six km south of Nontron, another favourite eatery is **La Chouette Gourmande** (The Greedy Owl), in a former presbytery in pretty little St-Front-sur-Nizonne, ✆ 53 56 14 70. Book ahead for the chance to try Périgordin dishes just like grandma used to make, or should have made: *tourin blanchi à l'oseille*; chicken with *tartines de foie gras* and a *charlotte au chocolat* to finish (menus from 170F; a few rooms are available at 230F).

Brantôme and Bourdeilles

The main roads from Mareuil and Nontron lead to Brantôme, a charming town of medieval and Renaissance houses built on an island in the river Dronne. Inhabited since Gaulish times, it has an abbey founded by Charlemagne in 769, who endowed it with the relics of St Sicaire, a slave of Herod who converted to Christianity after participating in the Massacre of the Innocents. Sacked by the Normans in the 11th century, the abbey was rebuilt beside the river against a steep bank. During the Hundred Years' War, the abbey was defended by the barons of Bourdeilles, and it survived the Wars of Religion thanks to one of their descendants, Pierre de Bourdeilles (1540–1614), abbé of Brantôme, known in French literature simply as Brantôme.

Brantôme became abbot at the age of 22, and used the abbey's revenues to finance his escapades as a soldier of fortune and lover of court ladies: he accompanied Mary Stuart to Scotland, visited Morocco, Portugal and Venice, and even planned an expedition to Peru, only to be frustrated by the Wars of Religion. He rendered a genuine service to his abbey by keeping the Huguenots at bay, diplomatically appealing to the Protestant leader—an old companion-in-arms. But Brantôme was never content in his role as a churchman, and when Henri III nixed a promotion, the furious Brantôme decided to go to Spain and fight against France, only to be gravely injured falling off his horse. Thus prevented from committing treason, he spent the rest of his life convalescing while writing gossipy, spicy accounts of the people of his time, especially the *Vies des hommes illustres et des grands capitaines* and the scandalous *Vies des dames galantes*, all so true that he left instructions for his heirs to wait 50 years before publishing them, to make sure all his subjects were dead.

Tourist Information

Brantôme: Pavillon Renaissance, ✆ 53 05 80 52

St-Jean-de-Côle: the Mairie, ✆ 53 55 12 50

Thiviers: Place Foch, ✆ 53 62 14 15

market days

Brantôme: Tuesdays

Thiviers: Saturdays

The Abbey

A charming 16th-century dogleg bridge with a Renaissance pavilion, built by a dreamy abbot to watch the reflections in the water, crosses from the island town to the white pile of the abbey *(10–12 and 2–5, closed Tues; July and Aug daily 9–7, closed Jan; adm)*. The 11th-century church, after suffering a string of bad luck and reconstructions, was given the *coup de grâce* when it was handed over to the 19th-century architect–restorer Paul Abadie, who was never one to preserve when he could rebuild. Only the detached **bell tower** (the oldest in France) with its Merovingian base, pyramid roof and complex tiers of windows and arches attests to the abbey's former grandeur. The church lost its dome back in the 13th century, when the Angevins remodelled it; after the Abadie treatment, only a bas-relief of the Massacre of the Innocents under the porch and a carved capital, used as a font, survives from the original church. Of the cloister, rebuilt in the 16th century, only one gallery remains. The best bits are the curious 'grottes and sacred fountains' carved in the cliff behind the abbey, where the 15th-century monks carved primitive reliefs of the *Last Judgement* and *Crucifixion*.

The abbey buildings contain two museums, one dedicated to prehistoric engravings (including a head of a goose, carved 15,000 years ago), the other filled with the paintings of Fernand Desmoulin, born in Nontron in the 1830s, a friend of Zola and follower of spiritualist Allan Kardec. In this world Desmoulin was known for his portraits of great men like Victor Hugo; in the beyond, painting in complete darkness with the aid of a medium, he produced strange works in a completely different style.

Besides a stroll through the town and a possible canoe trip down the Dronne, don't miss the ivy-covered **Peyrelevade dolmen**, 1km east on the road to Thiviers, the best preserved of many dolmens and menhirs in the area. Brantôme is buried under the epitaph he composed in the chapel of his **Château de Richemont** to the northwest *(open mid–July–Aug 10–12 and 3–6, closed Fri and Sun am; adm)*.

Bourdeilles

From Brantôme, take the lovely D 78 and D 106E2 7km southwest along the Dronne for **Bourdeilles**, seat of Périgord's oldest barony, so old that the first barons lived back in fairy-tale times, when they slew griffons and transported themselves to Jerusalem and back by means of an ointment extracted from a dragon's ear. Their **Château** *(same opening hours as Nontron's doll museum; adm)* stands in a commanding position over the river, by a medieval bridge and quaint boat-shaped water mill. There is magnificent octagonal feudal keep, built in the 13th century, and an adjacent Renaissance château. In the 16th century, Pierre de Bourdeilles's wealthy and widowed sister-in-law, Jacquette de Montbron, designed this herself—she had invited Catherine de Medici to visit, and the old medieval keep simply wouldn't do.

The tour includes both keep and the refined château, richly furnished with 16th- and 17th-century furniture from Spain and Burgundy (donated by the collectors who oversaw the 1962 restoration). Jacquette worked especially hard on her sumptuous **Salon Doré**, painted by Ambroise Le Noble, a member of the Mannerist Fontainebleau school. But when Catherine de' Medici and her notorious Flying Squadron *(see p.137)* swooped through Périgord, she snubbed Bourdeilles, and the furious Jacquette abandoned the building altogether. Amongst the furnishings and paintings, note the gilt bed of Emperor Charles V and a tapestry showing his archrival, François I, with his falconers.

Villars

Another splendid Renaissance creation, the **Château de Puyguilhem** *(same opening hours as Nontron's doll museum)* is northeast of Brântome near **Villars**. Built in 1524 by the first president of the *Parlement* of Bordeaux, Mondot de la Marthonie, it would look more at home in the Loire Valley with its roofline forest of richly carved dormers and chimneys. Saved from total collapse in the 1930s, the interior has been refurnished with period pieces, but the jewel is the chimney, sculpted with the Labours of Hercules.

From Villars, D 82 continues 3km to the **Grottes de Villars** *(open daily Palm Sun–mid Jun and mid Sept–Oct 2–6.30, July and Aug 10–6.30; adm)*. Unlike most caves in the Dordogne, this combines natural art—brilliant white, translucent stalactites and draperies, with prehistoric drawings in magnesium oxide, dating back to the Aurignacian period. The authenticity of the blue outline of a horse and 'sorcerer' was confirmed by the dense layer of concretions formed over the pictures.

St-Jean-de-Côle and Thiviers

To the east, **St-Jean-de-Côle** is as pretty a village as anyone could ask for, sitting on the little river Côle, spanned here by a Gothic humpback bridge, each house crowned by a steep tile roof. It was a busy place in the Middle Ages; the Templars were here, and in the 12th century the inhabitants built themselves a domed church. No one knows how the secrets of dome building were passed on from village to village, but in St-Jean they bungled it so often that they settled in the end for a less precarious wooden roof. The bell tower has some delightful carvings, especially one of God modelling Adam out of clay. In July and August you can visit St-Jean's handsome 12th-century **Château de la Martonie**, remodelled by the same Martonie responsible for Puyguilhem; inside is a museum of paper, ads and posters.

More excellent Romanesque awaits 7km west in the 12th-century church of **Thiviers**. Built over Merovingian foundations, it boasts a Renaissance porch and capitals sculpted with stone monsters and Samson killing a lion, and Jesus giving St Peter the keys to the kingdom; among the statues there's an unusual *Angel and Vagabond*. Thiviers pays tribute to the goose that lays its golden egg, or rather contributes its gorged liver, at the **Musée de Foie Gras, de l'Oie et du Canard** *(open 10–12 and 3–6.30, closed Sun; in winter also closed Mon; adm)*. Opposite the Maison de la Presse newsagent is a plaque commemorating Jean-Paul Sartre, who spent his miserable early childhood and summer holidays here with a grandfather, who for 40 years refused to speak to his wife because she had no dowry. If Sartre hated Thiviers, Thiviers returned the favour, and the plaque was only put up after a bitter fight.

Thiviers fountain

Jumilhac-le-Grand

North and east of Thiviers, the ferny forested frontier of the Limousin is the least populated area in Périgord. And here, like Sleeping Beauty's forgotten castle, stands the **Château de Jumilhac** *(guided tours July–mid Sept 10–12 and 2–6.30, other times Sun and holidays only 2–6pm, closed mid Nov–mid Mar; adm)*. Antoine Chapelle, the brain behind it, was a master of forges who made such fine cannons for Henri IV that the king knighted him and gave him a former Templar stronghold, which Chapelle converted into a fantasia of towers, turrets and chimneys coiffed with blue slate pepperpots, topped with an equally fantastic array of forged iron decorations. Right angles are rare inside as well as out; the **Chambre de la Fileuse**, built into the thickness of the wall, has naive murals imitating tapestries, painted for the lady whose portrait is over the door and who had nothing to do but spin when her jealous husband confined her here. The fairy tale of Rumpelstiltskin comes to mind, and indeed the cellars hold a **Musée de l'Or**, a museum of gold.

Brantôme ✉ 24310

Just outside the centre, the charming, ivy-covered ★★★★**Moulin de l'Abbaye**, 1 Rte de Bourdeilles, ✆ 53 05 80 22, is spread among several buildings—a converted watermill with a working wheel, a carpenter's house and a curé's residence, set in a delightful garden (closed Nov–Apr). The kitchen is the best in the area, serving elaborate but delicious dishes based on local ingredients, topped off with luscious dessert soufflés; weekday lunch menus begin at 185F. Overlooking the river Dronne, ★★★**Hôtel Chabrol**, 57 Rue Gambetta, ✆ 53 05 70 15, occupies a handsome old white building curving with the river (closed 15 Nov–15 Dec and most of Feb). The elegant restaurant is a local favourite, with dishes like *millefeuille de ris de veau au foie de canard et truffe*; menus from 170F. The ivy-swathed ★★**Périgord Vert**, Av. A-Maurois, ✆ 53 05 70 58, is a fine, reliable hotel; near by, in a cave, **Le Vieux Four**, 7 Rue des Cailloux, ✆ 53 05 74 16, serves some of the best pizzas in Périgord. In the same area, there's a very pleasant bed and breakfast Chez Mérillou, Av. A.-Maurois, ✆ 53 05 74 04.

Champagnac-de-Belair ✉ 24530

Near Brantôme, ★★★★**Moulin du Roc**, ✆ 53 54 80 36, offers spacious, beautifully furnished rooms and superb breakfasts; in the kitchen madame performs magic with traditional Périgordin recipes (menus from 200F, closed 15 Nov–15 Dec and 15 Jan–Feb).

Bourdeilles ✉ 24310

The 17th-century **Château de la Côte**, on the road to Biras, ✆ 53 03 70 11, overlooks its huge park, with a pool and horses to ride and rooms from 420F.

Villars ✉ 24530

Le Relais de l'Archerie, ✆ 53 54 88 64, occupies a little 19th-century château, with small but nice rooms and a good restaurant, featuring *magrets* and country omelettes (menus from 60F).

Thiviers ✉ 24800

★★★**Château de Mavaleix**, at Chalais (13km north), ✆ 53 52 82 01, was built in the 13th century and transformed in the 16th into a residence by the same Antoine Chapelle of Jumilhac, but with slightly fewer towers. The swimming pool, set in a 50-acre park, should be completed by 1994 (closed Jan). At Nantheuil, 2km east of Thiviers, **Maurice Debet** is only open for lunch, but what a grand lunch, for a mere 55F; more (from 75F) for the extra-special Sunday lunch, when you'd better reserve.

St-Jean-de-Côle ✉ 24800

Old-fashioned **Le Coq Rouge**, in the main square, ✆ 53 62 32 71 (reservations strongly suggested), is a local favourite, serving sumptuous Périgordin cuisine at reasonable prices (menus from 90F; children's menu for 55F; closed Wed).

Down the Isle and Auvézère

After Jumilhac the river Isle loops down towards to pick up the waters of the Auvézère just before Périgueux. In the 1500s this little mesopotamia was full of iron forges, one of which remains in the wooded gorges of the Auvézère. This is the country of the battling troubadour, Bertrand de Born, and of tubers worth their weight in gold: truffles.

Getting Around

No trains here, but buses linking Excideuil and Hautefort to Périgueux and Brive.

Tourist Information

Excideuil: 1 Place du Château, ✆ 53 62 95 56

Hautefort: Mairie, ✆ 53 50 40 27

Sorges: ✆ 53 05 90 11

market days

Excideuil: Thursdays

Hautefort: Wednesdays

Sorges: Fridays

Excideuil

The busiest market town in the region, Excideuil once belonged to the *vicomtes* of Limoges, who built its vertiginous **fortress** on a butte of Jurassic limestone, a redoubt that on three occasions repelled Richard the Lion-Heart. Its former priory church has a flamboyant portal and a 17th-century retable and overlooks Place Bugeaud, named after the local aristocrat who conquered Algeria in the 1840s. He donated a fountain to Excideuil, and after their war of independence the Algerians made a donation as well—an unwanted statue of Bugeaud.

Excideuil is on the river Loue, which flows into the Isle at **Coulaures**, a pretty village with a double-breasted Romanesque church containing a 14th-century fresco. The best scenery around, however, is along the Auvézère, beginning at **Cherveix-Cubas**, a village with a **Lanterne des Morts** in its cemetery, a slender version of the mysterious towers in Atur and Sarlat (*see* p.121). From here you can drive, ride, or trek along the delicious **Gorges de l'Auvézère**. Highlights along the way include **Génis**, a village of schist houses, the belvedere at the **Moulin du Pervendoux**, and at St-Mesmin the 15-minute walk to the laughing falls of the Auvézère. At **Savignac-Lédrier**, a riverside forge of 1820 and coal warehouse are part of an industrial/archaeological **Eco-Musée** *(open July–Sept 2–6pm)*.

The Château de Hautefort

South of Cherveix and bossing much of the Auvézere valley stand the high-domed towers of one of Périgord's most famous citadels, the **Château de Hautefort** *(open Apr–mid Nov, 9–12 and 2.30–7, other times Sat and Sun 2–6; adm)*. In the 12th century a fortress on this spot belonged to the troubadour Bertran de Born (*see* 'Topics', p.43). In 1640 it was rebuilt by a famous miser, Jacques-François de Hautefort. According to the gossip of the day, Jacques-François was the model for Harpagon in Molière's *L'Avare* (although Molière prudently lowered his miser to bourgeois status); when he fell ill his doctor prescribed English pills, which brought about his death—they cost so much that Jacques-François couldn't bear to swallow them. His sister, Marie d'Hautefort, was the most beautiful woman of her day, nicknamed *Aurore* by the French court. Yet even rarer than her great beauty was her disinterestedness—Marie was both the lover of the melancholic Louis XIII and the best friend of the wife he abhorred, Anne of Austria. Marie's devotion to the queen made her the enemy of Cardinal Richelieu, who went to the extreme of presenting a rival for the king's affections—a handsome young man named Cinq-Mars; when that ploy only resulted in the king having two loves instead of one, Richelieu threatened to leave the king's service himself if Louis didn't dump Marie, and she was only reinstated in court after Louis's death in 1643.

In 1929, the castle passed to the Baron and Baronne de Bastard, who undertook the complete restoration of Hautefort and its gardens. After the baron died, his wife continued alone, finally finishing it in 1968. In the autumn of that same year Hautefort went up in a blaze that could be seen across half of Périgord. But after the shock of losing 39 years of work in one night, the Baronne de Bastard amazed everyone by starting all over again, a job now completed, and open for visits: on view are the terraces and *cour d'honneur*, furniture and tapestries from the Grand Siècle, and a museum dedicated to novelist Eugène Le Roy, born here in 1836 into a family of château labourers and whose most famous novel, *Jacquou le Croquant* (1899) describes the abject poverty that Périgord's peasants lived in so the Hauteforts of the world could afford such dishy spreads. A *croquant* is a southwestern word for a 17th-century peasant rebel; the name invokes a crunching or gnashing of angry teeth.

The **Hospice** of Hautefort, now the parish church, is a Greek cross with a dome echoing those topping the towers. Founded by the parsimonious Jacques-François on his English pill-less deathbed in 1680, the hospital took in precisely 11 old men, 11 boys and 11 young women and was known as the hospital of 33 years, recalling the age of Christ when he died.

Tourtoirac and the Man Who Would Be King

On the Auvézère west of Hautefort lies **Tourtoirac**, with the ruins of an 11th-century Benedictine abbey; the dome of the church survives, along with some delightful carvings on the capitals of the ruined chapterhouse. In the village, a plaque on a small shop notes that His Majesty Aurélie-Antoine Ier, King of Araucania and Patagonia, died here on 17 September 1878. In the cemetery, his tomb is marked with a stele and crown, copied by the stonecutter from a king of hearts on a playing card. Aurélie so wanted the French to establish a protectorate in southern Chile that he went off to do it himself. The Chileans thought he was mad, but he never gave up his claim. He left no direct heir, but the faithful have never failed to produce successors to the throne; the current pretender, Felipe d'Araucanie, runs an 'academy of Araucanian studies'.

Down the Auvézère, in **Auberoche**, a Romanesque chapel with a ruined roof and rain-scoured frescoes is all that is left of a once mighty fortress that saw the very first battle of the Hundred Years' War. In the summer of 1345, the Earl of Derby installed a garrison here to keep an eye on Périgueux. The Count of Périgord, Roger Bernard, besieged it, and when the beset English tried to send an SOS message to Derby, Roger Bernard jeeringly catapulted the message, with the live messanger tied to it, back into the fortress. Nevertheless, Derby somehow got word, and (according to Froissart) surprised the count's 10,000 men while they dined and captured 2000, including Roger Bernard himself. If there isn't much left to see in Auberoche, don't miss the charming watermill downstream at **Le Change**.

Sorges, Périgord's Truffle Capital

North of Auberoche and the river Isle, **Sorges** is the central market for the truffle trade and home of an **Ecomusée de la Truffe** *(daily 10–12 and 2–6; adn)* with a truffle path to walk and all you've ever wanted to know about that little black diamond stud in your foie gras. According to the French, in the year 300, the afflicted St Anthony was clawing at the ground in distress when the angels rewarded him with the first truffles. St Anthony, of course, is the patron saint of animals and in art is usually depicted with a pig, which for centuries was used to root for the delicacy. Nowadays their very uncontrolled pigginess has led many truffle hunters to prefer keen-scented hounds, whose mother's teats were rubbed with truffle juice, or to rely on savvy: in late autumn: the signs are fine soil, looking as if it had been burned bya specially diseased truffle oak, and 'hélomysa' flies circling above. Sorges and the causses de Thiviers are one of the richest sources of the tasty tubor; in the old days there were so many that the favourite way of eating them was to put them under the ashes in the fire, and wolf them down whole. If you aren't in Périgord in truffle season, you can buy them in little jars (look for them preserved in cognac).

Sorges also has a domed Romanesque church and a 13th-century castle to visit, although you may find the 15th-century **Château des Bories** more rewarding *(June–Sept 10–12 and 2–7, other times by appointment, ☏ 53 06 00 01; adm)*. The last castle on the Isle before Périgueux, it is considered the archtype of all Périgordin châteaux, with symmetrical round towers, a Gothic kitchen, huge chimney and monumental stair.

truffle hunters

Excideuil ✉ 24160

Hostellerie du Fin Chapon, 3 Place du Château, ☏ 53 62 42 38, has 10 comfortable old fashioned rooms from 170F and well-prepared menus beginning at 70F. In Génis, the roadside **★Relais Saint-Pierre**, ☏ 53 52 47 11, is a convenient base for exploring the gorges of the Auvézère, with good and filling food to top you up after a long day's rambling (menus from 85F).

St-Mesmin ✉ 24270

Midway up the gorge, **La Ferme des Ages**, ☏ 53 52 71 67 offers delicious farm meals from 85F and horses to hire to take in the superb trails along the gorge (open July–Aug except Tues dinner and Wed; Sat night, Sun lunch the rest of the year; reservations mandatory).

Cherveix-Cubas ✉ 24390

★Le Favard, ☏ 53 50 41 05, in the village centre (4km from Hautefort) is a nice hotel surrounding a round pool; the restaurant serves a very popular 150F menu featuring delicious *tourain*, *pâté de foie gras truffé*, country ham, *confit de canard*, walnut salad, cheese and home-made dessert.

Tourtoirac ✉ 24390

The riverside **★★Hôtel des Voyageurs**, ☏ 53 51 12 29 is a fine old white inn with a garden and restaurant terrace overlooking the river; try the *poulet aux écrevisses* (menus from 65F; closed Jan).

Sorges ✉ 24420

Owned by the same proprietor, **★★Auberge de la Truffe**, N 21, ☏ 53 05 02 05 and **★★Hôtel de la Mairie** in the centre, ☏ 53 05 02 11, both offer fine rooms and a reliable cuisine, with cheaper menus at the Truffe starting at 70F.

Antonne-et-Trigonant ✉ 24420

10km east of Périgueux, **★★★Les Chandelles**, Le Parc, ☏ 53 06 05 10 is a charming little hotel on a 15th-century farm, with tennis, pool, and a pretty garden; try the excellent *pastilla d'agneau* in the restaurant from 150F (closed Jan).

★★L'Ecluse, Route de Limoges, ✆ 53 06 00 04, is a large, recently renovated old inn on the banks of the Isle; most rooms have a balcony.

Le Change ✉ 24640

On the Auvézère, the 19th-century **★★★Château du Roc-Chautru**, ✆ 53 06 17 31, offers luxurious rooms, set in a grove of 100-year-old cedars, as well as a pool, tennis, billiards and bikes to hire; no restaurant, but there are several in the area.

Périgueux

Set in a privileged, fertile valley on the river Isle, the capital of the Dordogne *département* is a cheerful city of 35,000 who produce and market truffles, foie gras and fat strawberries, and print all the postage stamps in France. The old streets around its famous five-domed cathedral have been intelligently restored over the past decades to give the city a lively and lovely heart; another plus is its museum, with its exceptional prehistoric and Roman sections.

History

The first inhabitants of Périgueux, the Petrocorii Gauls, built their *oppidum* on the heights of the left bank of the Isle, by the sacred spring Vesunna. After Caesar defeated their ally Vercingetorix, they settled down to enjoy the *pax romana* and build a brand new town known as Vesunna (or Vésone in French) on the fertile plains of the Isle's right bank. It was the perfect place for a market town. By the 3rd century, Vesunna had 20,000 Gallo-Roman citizens, famous for their ironworking skill.

Vesunna was still in its first bloom when the barbarian Alemanni crushed it under their heels in 275. Raped and pillaged into a state of shock, Vesunna destroyed its own temples and basilicas for the stone to build a wall, contracting itself into the space of a tiny village. As the years (and more barbarians) passed by, this bristling remnant of Vesunna even lost its proud name: it became known as *Civitas Petrocoriorum*, the town of the Petrocorii, or just the Cité, as it's known to this day. Clovis captured the Cité and his successors fought over it; in the Dark Ages, the 24 towers of the wall were converted into donjons by rival factions of gangster-nobles.

The Rise of Puy Saint-Front

As the Cité declined, a new bourg of artisans and merchants grew up around the nearby hill (*puy*), around the tomb of St Front, a 4th-century follower of St Martial. So many tall tales grew around this Front, or Fronto, that the good burghers can be fairly suspected of false advertising to suck in passing pilgrims. Front became no less than a personal acquaintance of Jesus Christ who lived in a state of perpetual virginity. Baptized by the hand of St Peter, he was sent to the Cité, where he converted and baptized 7000 and cured the Count Aurélius of his ulcers. He also managed to be in two places at once, attending the funeral of St Martha at Tarascon whilst saying mass in Périgueux, a miracle proved by the gloves he forgot back in Tarascon. He chased the devils and dragons out of the pagan temple of Vessuna by blasting open an enormous breach in the walls. Thanks to the pilgrims who stopped at this superhero's tomb, bourgeois Puy grew larger and more important than its rival, the noble Cité. In 1182 Puy began its own wall. It also was a firm ally of France against the English.

The English weren't half as much trouble as the counts of Périgord (*see* p.87). One of the worst, Roger Bernard (the same who catapulted messengers), pillaged and partly destroyed Puy in 1246 just to show who was boss. After this outrage, St Louis, with more than human patience, brokered an agreement that united Puy Saint-Front and the Cité into one town and freed it of homage to the counts, with a new motto: *Fortitudo mea civium fides* 'My strength lies in the trust of my fellow citizens.' One can almost hear the counts sneer. Indeed, St Louis's accord made them more ornery than ever; throughout the Hundred Years' War they weaseled from one side to another, and in 1357, when the French were distracted by the capture of John the Good, Count Archambaut V and his brother, Cardinal Hélie de Talleyrand pounced and grabbed Périgueux with English aid. Although Du Guesclin chased the English out in 1369, Count Archambaut managed to stay put by promising loyalty to the crown of France; instead, he took money from England to stir up as much trouble as possible until the exasperated French came back to give him the boot. His castle in the Cité was demolished, his goods confiscated and given to the canons of St-Front.

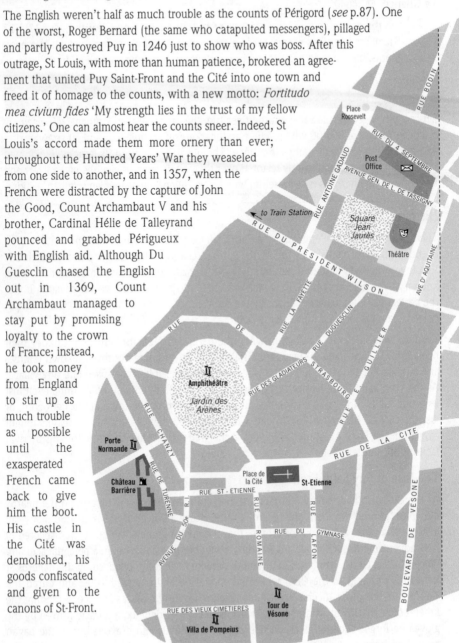

Périgueux

RUE VICTOR HUGO

ALLEES DE TOURNY

RUE LOUIS MIE

Place du Général Leclerc

Palais de Justice

BOULEVARD MICHEL MONTAIGNE

Place Montaigne

RUE MALEVILLE

COURS DE TOURNY

Musée du Périgord

RUE GAMBETTA

RUE MICHEL MONTAIGNE

RUE VOLTAIRE

RUE ST - FRONT

RUE FENELON

PLANTIER

Place André Maurois

COURS MICHEL

RUE EGUILLERIE

Place St-Louis

Maison Tenant

RUE LIMOGEANNE

Place du Marché au Bois

RUE BARBECANE

Place Général de Gaulle

Place St-Silain

RUE DE LA RÉPUBLIQUE

RUE DES CHAINES

RUE DE LA SAGESSE

RUE LONMARY

RUE NOTRE-DAME

DU

RUE MISERICORDE

Maison Estignard

Place Bugeaud

COURS BUGEAUD

RUE A. SAIGNE

Place du Coderc

Galleries Daumesnil

Place Daumesnil

AVE DAUMESNIL

RUE SAUMANDE

Maison des Consuls
Maison Lambert

Place de l'Hôtel de Ville

Hôtel de Ville

RUE TOURVILLE

PT DES BARRIS

RUE TAILLEFER

Place de la Clautre

RUE GEORGES

Tourist Information

RUE CONDÉ

RUE DES FARGES

Musée Militaire

RUE DU CALUIRE

Cathédrale St-Front

Vieux Moulin

Place Francheville

RUE DE LA BRIDE

Tour Mataguerre

Maison des Dames de la Foi

RUE AUBERGERIE

RUE SEGURER

L' Isle

BOULEVARD

Bus Station

RUE LITTRE

COURS FENELON

RUE W. ROUSSEAU

BOULEVARD LAKANAL

N

200 metres
200 yards

Périgord's Bastion of Catholicism

In the 15th century the battered survivors slowly rebuilt, putting the city back on its feet just in time for more trouble in the Wars of Religion. Périgueux was as firmly Catholic as Bergerac was Protestant, but the Huguenots were quicker off the mark: in 1575 they killed the bishop of Périgueux, then, disguising themselves as peasants, entered and captured the city. They held it for six years, wrecking churches and melting down their bells for cannons. Salt was rubbed into Périgueux's wounds when the Treaty of Beaulieu (1576) made the city a safe haven for Protestants; so miserable were the Catholic majority that the triumphal arch they erected for Henri, King of Navarre, read: '*Urbis Deforme Cadaver*'. In pity the Sénéchal André de Bourdeilles offered to buy the town back for the Catholics, and failing that, he captured Périgueux in 1581 by using the same peasant-disguise ruse as the Huguenots.

More Trouble

Since the time of St Louis, the burghers of Périgueux had maintained their privileges. They were exempt from royal taxes and military service; they had their own constitution and elected officials, and to the king owed only 'homage and fidelity'. In 1635, when Louis XIII imposed a tavern tax, the result was a riot. The mayor had to bolt, the tax clerk was murdered and tossed down a well; the Croquants took to the forests and fought the king's men until 1641. Louis XIV cast a cold eye on these goings-on, and by the end of his reign, he had rubbed out all traces of Périgueux's privileges and independence.

In 1790, when the Revolution divided France into *départements*, the worthies of the Dordogne could not choose a capital: as Périgueux, Bergerac and Sarlat all had valid claims, it was decided that the status would be shared on an alternating basis. Périgueux drew the longest straw and got to be capital first, and inertia has done the rest to make sure it never went anywhere else. As a kind of footnote to its beleaguered past, Périgueux gave birth in 1846 to Léon Bloy, France's most curmudgeonly Catholic philosopher and author, who celebrated the sinking of the *Titanic* with a huge party in Montmartre 'because it drowned so many Protestants'.

Getting Around

Daily flights (1½ hours) to and from Paris. The train station, in Rue Denis-Papin (© 53 09 50 50) is 4 hours from Paris, 75 minutes from Bourdeaux, 3 hours from Agen or Toulouse. Buses depart from Place Francheville; the biggest parking lot in the city is up at Place Montaigne, near the Musée du Périgord.

Tourist Information

Rond Point de la Tour Mataguerre, 26 Place Francheville, © 53 53 10 63

market days

Wednesdays and Saturdays.

The Cité

Set back from the river, almost forgotten behind the bus terminal in Place Francheville, the Cité is a quiet place far removed from the days of rabid Count Archambault. Although the 19th century systematically razed its walls, tucked between the modern buildings are a handful of Gallo-Roman and medieval souvenirs, especially the 65ft **Tour de Vésone** in Boulevard de Vésone. Believed to have been originally the central cella of a circular 1st-century AD Gallo-Roman temple, the great cylinder was originally faced with marble and is topped with brick arches; its walls still bear the breach made by St Front's legendary exorcism, although some say the opening in the wall was made intentionally to admit the rays of the rising sun. Excavations in the area found signs of a pair of basilicas that once marked the entrance to Vesunna's forum; just west in Rue des Bouquets are the ruins of the **Villa de Pompeïus,** from the same period *(guided tours run by the tourist office in July and Aug, Tues–Fri at 5pm; adm).* Pompeïus, whoever he was, wallowed in a de luxe set of heated Roman baths; frescoes and mosaics survive as well.

St-Etienne

From here take Rue Romaine up to the centre of the Cité, where St-Etienne, Périgueux's oldest church, was founded on the site of a Temple of Mars by St Front. In the 12th century it was rebuilt in a style that became the prototype of the Périgordin domed Romanesque church, with wide Byzantine cupolas not only over the crossing but cupping the length of the nave. Originally St-Etienne had four of these, culminating in a grand carved portal under a huge bell-tower porch; the Huguenots unkindly tore off the front half, and none too neatly. In 1669 the mutilated structure was no longer deemed worthy to be a cathedral and the status was transferred to St-Front.

The two surviving bays are not only an important lesson in the origins of Périgordin Romanesque but are steeped in shadowy medieval solemnity, an atmosphere so lacking in St-Front. The first dome, from the early 1100s, is solid and primitive, lit only by tiny windows; the second, from around 1160, is elongated, lighter, and supported by twinned columns. The interior has a fine if incongruous 17th-century wooden retable and a 12th-century Easter calendar; the arch from the tomb of Bishop Jean d'Asside (d. 1169) frames the Romanesque baptismal font.

Rue St-Etienne leads from the church to the **Château Barrière,** a *maison forte,* or strong house, built on the walls of the Cité for a loyal retainer of the Counts. Next to the château is a rare 13th-century Romanesque house; across the street the Gallo-Roman **Porte Normande** is a sole survivor of the wall thrown together by the citizens of Vesunna after the invasion of the Alemanni; originally it stood about 35ft high, a jigsaw of columns and temple fragments. The nearby **amphitheatre**, where up to 30,000 spectators cheered gladiators to death is now practically toothless—as the base for the castle of the bloody-minded counts of Périgord, it had been enthusiastically razed in 1391. Only a few stones and an entrance now enclose a pretty garden and playground.

Puy-Saint-Front

On the far side of Place Francheville, once the no-man's land between Périgueux's two rival towns, lies the compact and beautifully restored quarter of Puy-Saint-Front. The tourist office's medieval–Renaissance tour *(Tues–Fri on July and August afternoons)* will get you inside some of the courtyards, and into the last remnant of Puy's walls, the **Tour Mataguerre** in Place Francheville. Decorated with fleurs-de-lys, it was repaired in 1477 with the forced labour of men inflicted with the scourge of 15th-century Périgueux—leprosy.

Just to the left of the Tour Mataguerre, Rue de la Bride/Rue des Farges ('forges') was the main road linking the Cité and Puy-Saint-Front. Some of Périgueux's oldest houses are here, most notably no. 4, the 12th-century **Maison des Dames de la Foi**, built by the Templars, inhabited by Du Guesclin, and in the late 1600s occupied by nuns. At the top of the street is the **Musée Militaire** *(open 10–12 and 2–6, afternoons only Oct–June; adm)*, with uniforms, flags and weapons and memorabilia related to General Daumensil *(see* below). From here, turn right in Rue Taillefer for **Place de la Clautre**, under the looming bell tower of St-Front. This square, site of the Saturday market, was for centuries a graveyard and the theatre for executions; the last walk a condemned criminal would make in this world was up narrow **Rue du Calvaire**.

The Cathedral of St-Front

This is the fourth church built here, on the summit of the *puy* over the Isle. A 6th-century chapel holding the relics of St Front was replaced in 1074 with a much larger church, to suck in pilgrims on the way to Compostella. In 1120, when this new church burned down, it was decided to build one even larger and more extraordinary. Greek architects, it seems, were hired, and they designed a Greek cross plan under five domes. The model was Agii Apostoli in Constantinople (now gone), the same used for another famous church: St Mark's in Venice.

By the 19th century this marvel was a rickety disaster waiting to happen; after the Huguenots had damaged it in 1575 and destroyed the tomb of St Front, a streak of thoughtless restorations exacerbated the typical problems of old age, leaving its domes covered with a sloppy hotchpotch of stones and tiles. The famous medieval re-creator Viollet-le-Duc wanted to have a crack at it but his rival Paul Abadie was given the nod in 1852. Abadie loved Romanesque churches so much that he devoured them whole; he demolished much of St-Front and spent the next 50 years rebuilding it. The result is breathtaking from a distance, especially at night when the cathedral is illuminated and reflected in the waters of the Isle. Close up, it is much harder to overlook its newness, the nakedness, the too precise and orderly cut of the stone. Nor was Abadie above adding improvements to the original, especially the pinnacles on the domes; he liked these so well that he stuck their clones on the bulbous domes of his most famous creation, Sacré-Coeur in Paris.

From Place de la Clautre you can see what survives from the church of 1074: the austere façade fitted with the odd Roman fragment, lateral walls that now form an open courtyard, the bottom two-thirds of the 60m bell tower, two confessions (tomb-shrines of saintly confessors)—one under the bell tower and the other under the west dome—and the haunting little **cloister** with the original Romanesque pine-cone crown of the bell tower as a centre-piece. Inside Abadie's church, the most lingering impression is one of vastness (no wonder—it's one and a half times as long as a football field). In its minimal decoration it looks more like a mosque than a cathedral. Abadie designed the 'Byzantine' chandeliers, which originally hung in Notre-Dame for the pompous wedding of Napoleon III; for a franc you can shed light on the enormous 17th-century walnut retable made for a demolished Jesuit chapel.

Medieval Streets around St-Front

The north door of the cathedral opens onto **Place Daumensil**, the centre of a fascinating web of 15th- and 16th-century pedestrian lanes. The pale stone of their urbane houses was mostly quarried from ancient Vesunna, and residents often leave their gates open to let passers-by admire their beautifully curved inner stairs. Steep, stepped streets descend to the river; houses in Rue du Plantier have terraced gardens (see if you can find the carving of Adam and Eve on one of the stairs), while medieval Rue du Port-de-Graule is lined with tiny boutiques. Down on the quay itself, in a cluster of 15th–16th century houses stands the **Maison Lambert** with its Renaissance gallery and the **Maison des Consuls** with flamboyant dormers. The **Vieux Moulin**, perched on a river wall, is a last relic of the grain monopoly once held by the canons of St-Front.

Back up in Place Daumesnil, enter the picturesque **Galleries Daumesnil** by way of Rue de la Clarté: these are a set of old courtyards opened up to the public, and named after Pierre Daumesnil, born at 7 Rue de la Clarté in 1776.

The Peg-Legged General

Périgueux's feistiest hero fought with Napoleon in Egypt, lost a leg at Wagram near Vienna, and was given what seemed to be the equivalent of a desk job as commander of the Château of Vincennes in Paris. When the Allies took Paris in 1814, they demanded that Daumesnil surrender Vincennes. 'Tell the Austrians to give back my leg or else come in and get the other one,' he replied. They didn't, and Vincennes remained the only part of France never to surrender to the Allies. After Waterloo, Daumesnil was besieged again, and again he held out, refusing to give over the fort to anyone but a Frenchman. Finally the new king, Louis XVIII, came in person to accept the keys.

During the Revolution of 1830, Daumesnil was still on the job. The hated ministers of Charles X were imprisoned at Vincennes, and when a mob came to lynch them, the old general kept them out too, saying that he'd ignite the powder room if they tried to storm the place. In Cours Michel-Montagne, there's a statue of him pointing with pride at his peg leg.

Rue Limogeanne and Around

From the Galleries Daumesnil, continue along pedestrian Rue Limogeanne, Périgueux's busiest shopping street since the Middle Ages. Most of the houses here date from the 16th century. No. 5, the **Maison Estignard** is especially lovely with its dormers, mullioned windows and carvings; no. 3 boasts, in its courtyard, the bas-relief of a salamander, the emblem of François I. Rue de Sagesse, parallel to Rue Limogeanne, boasts other fine Renaissance houses, especially no. 1, **Maison Lajoubertie**, with one of Périgueux's most beautiful staircases, carved with the goddess of Love laying aside her weapons. Rue de Sagesse gives into handsome **Place St-Louis**, created by demolishing a block of slums. It has a fountain decorated with a dumpling lady, who probably overindulged in the offerings of the *marché des gras* (fattened geese, ducks, foie gras and truffles) held in this square on Wednesdays and Saturdays in the winter. The **Maison du Tenant** or du Pâtissier (1518), on the corner of Rue Eguillerie has a sculpted porch and an inscription warning that anyone who speaks badly behind people's backs is not welcome inside, for 'The greatest glory is to displease the wicked.'

Musée du Périgord

Just to the north, at 22 Cours Tourny, the Musée du Périgord *(daily 10–12 and 2–5, closed Tues; adm)* is a cut above the average, with something for every taste. The ethnographic collection in the first rooms, devoted to stone age cultures from around the world (New Caledonia, the Cook Islands, Papua New Guinea and Africa) form a comparative introduction to the extensive **Prehistoric section** upstairs. The prizes here are three extremely rare skeletons: the oldest ever found, the Neanderthal *homme de Régourdou* (70,000 BC), ritually buried with the bears near Lascaux (*see* p.88); *homme de Combe-Capelle* (20,000 BC), founded near Sergeac, and Upper Paleolithic *homme de Chancelade*, a mere whippersnapper only 15,000 years old. The collection of tools ranges from the very first cut stones found in the Dordogne, dating back a cool million years, and Upper Paleolithic carvings and engravings on bone and stone, among them the strange, disembodied *Parade of Bison* from Chancelade and a disc carved with does from Laugerie-Basse. In another room, among the Neolithic and barbarian artifacts are weapons that laid Vesunna low: a bronze Alemanni sword, and Visigothic and Frankish blades.

Downstairs, there are stuffed weasels, snake skins, an Egyptian mummy named Antinoë and a selection of Coptic fabrics, followed by the **Gallo-Roman rooms**, filled with fascinating finds excavated from the original Petrocorii *oppidum* and ancient Vesunna: jewellery, frescoes, mosaics, an excellently preserved wooden pump from 15 BC, items from everyday life, a sculpture of the Celtic 'three-horned god', and a 2nd-century BC altar carved with the head of a ram and bull, dedicated to the Eastern cult of Cybele and Attis.

The cloister is lined with some very intriguing if poorly-labelled stone fragments from Neolithic to medieval times: a 6th-century Visigothic sarcophagus, a lacey fragment of a Carolingian chancel, and strange faces and slatternly mermaids that once adorned St-Front. The **Beaux-Arts section** begins with ceramics and enamels from Limoges, followed by three rooms of paintings, including the *Diptyque de Rabastens* (1286) a rare work painted on leather from the school of Toulouse; a 16th-century Flemish *Excision de la pierre de folie*, a famous Hieronymus Bosch subject, although here we see doctors simply removing the 'madness stone' from a patient's brain; a fine *Portrait of Fénelon* by Bailleul; a

Caneletto, two paintings by the 19th century Paul Guigou, and works by native Périgordins, including sculptures by Jane Poupelet, a student of Rodin.

Around Périgueux: Chancelade Abbey

Six km west of Périgueux, **Chancelade** is an enchanting spot with a natural spring and an 11th-century Augustinian **abbey**. In 1370, the English gave the monks the bum's rush and converted the abbey into a stronghold that only fell when Du Guesclin personally led the attack, storming up the ladder and splitting open the head of the English captain. You can still see the scars of the battle on the Romanesque **Chapelle Saint-Jean**. The main **church**, with its arcaded, three-tiered bell tower, was restored in the 1600s, although 13th-century frescoes of Catholicism's two tallest saints, Christopher and Thomas à Becket have survived the outrages of time and wars. The abbey buildings and abbot's lodge can be visited, along with a **Musée d'art sacré** *(July and Aug afternoons)* in the presbytery. In the 12th century, monks from Chancelade founded the **Prieuré de Merlande**, in a forest clearing 6km north off the D 2. One of the original two domes was smashed by the English; the rest was fortified in the 16th century and wrecked again in the Revolution. Somehow the magnificent capitals on the blind arcading of the choir have survived intact, with interwoven designs of animals and monsters. South of Périgueux, **Atur** (7km on the D 2) has a Romanesque church and a 12th-century *Lanterne des Morts* (*see* Sarlat, p.121); 21km south on the D 8, **Vergt** stands as a rare monument to the seldom-seen constructive side of the counts of Périgord, in this case, Archambaut III, who founded this pleasant bastide in 1285.

Périgueux ✉ *24000*   **Where to Stay**

On the whole Périgueux's hotels are more geared to travelling foie gras salesmen than to visitors. In the centre, **★★Hôtel du Périgord**, 74 Rue Victor Hugo, ✆ 53 53 33 63 offers comfortable rooms and an inner garden around an ancient plane tree. **★★Des Arènes**, 21 Rue du Gymnase, ✆ 53 53 49 85, is a simple little hotel near the amphitheatre, a quiet place to stay with easy street parking; or near the museum, **★★L'Universe**, 18 Cours Montaigne, ✆ 53 53 34 79, has a TV in each room and dining under the arbor in the summer (meals from 90F). **★Du Midi et Terminus**, 18 Rue Denis-Papin, ✆ 53 53 41 06, is your typical budget provincial hotel by the station; all the rooms have showers and the restaurant menus start from 70F.

In Chancelade (24650), next to an 18-hole golf course, the turreted, 19th-century **★★★★Château des Reynats**, ✆ 53 03 53 59 has been converted into a hotel with attractive rooms and a pool and tennis courts; the restaurant, with Empire fittings, serves delicious grilled sole along with a regional menu (menus from 140F). **★★Le Pont de la Beauronne**, 4 Route de Ribérac, ✆ 53 08 42 91 is a friendly, newish hotel near the golf course as well, and there's a good value 90F menu in the restaurant.

In Razac-sur-l'Isle (24430) you can sleep under the mansard roof of the imposing

★★★**Château de Lalinde**, ✆ 53 54 52 30, set in the midst of a 7-acre park with a pool (closed mid Nov–mid Mar); local specialities dominate the menu (100–300F). For other hotels near Périgueux *see* Antonne and Le Change, pp.68 and 69.

Eating Out

Sublime seafood shares the menu with unusual land dishes, such as breast of pigeon with cumin and sesame seeds, at elegant **L'Oison**, 31 Rue St-Front, ✆ 53 09 84 02 (menus from 180F). **Les Berges de l'Isle**, on a terrace overlooking the river at 2 Rue P. Magne, ✆ 53 09 51 50, serves a refined *pavé de boeuf au foie gras* and luscious desserts (menus from 140F, closed Sun). *La Tartine*, 10 Ruet-Silain, ✆ 53 09 87 18, offers a good 50F lunch menu; **Lou Chabrol**, 22 Rue Eguillerie, ✆ 53 53 10 84, also offers a reasonably priced menu of Périgordin dishes in a congenial, warm atmosphere (80F for two main dishes, closed Sun).

West of Périgueux: the Dronne and Forêt de la Double

The name Dronne may evoke nothing as much as a queen bee's studmuffin, but this is one of the most charmingly bucolic rivers in France. Between the Dronne and the Isle are the gentle rolling hills of the Double forest, crisscrossed by streams that feed moody marshes, created by medieval monks to farm fish for Lent.

Tourist Information

Ribérac: Place de Charles de Gaulle, ✆ 53 90 03 10

market days

Tocane-St-Apre: Mondays

Ribérac: Fridays (with a walnut market in October and November and a *marché au gras* from November to March)

Down the Dronne

Tocane-St-Apre, where the D 710 from Périgueux meets the Dronne, is a handsome agricultural village with a good dolmen, the **Pierre-Levée** and Gallo-Roman excavations that suggest folks have long forded the river here. You should, too, following signs for **Montagrier**. The rewards are superb panoramas into the Dronne valley and a 12th-century domed church, **Ste-Madeleine**, with an unusual three-lobed apse and carved capitals; here, on the feast day of the doctor saints Côme et Damien, children with hernias used to gather for a miraculous cure. From here you have a choice of roads up to **Grand Brassac**, with an even more extraordinary 12th-century church, powerfully fortifed, its north portal decorated with sculptures from various periods, while inside three domes hover on pendentives.

As you return to the Dronne and head west for **Ribérac**, keep an eye peeled for the *cluzeaux*, or dwellings cut into the limestone in the Middle Ages. Usually quiet and demure Ribérac jumps on Friday, its market day. It has recently restored its domed Romanesque **Notre-Dame**, but nothing remains of the castle where the Quixotic troubadour Arnaut Daniel was born (active 1180–1210). Dante met his shade in Purgatory, where Arnaut speaks the only line in Provençal in the entire *Divine Comedy*, which, after all, was the language Dante considered using before opting for Italian. Arnaut Daniel's verse is so complex that it is well nigh impossible to translate without losing all of its charm, but he is credited with the most famous of lines ever written by a troubadour:

> *Ieu sui Arnautz q'amas l'aura,*
> *E chatz la lebre ab lo bou*
> *E nadi contra suberna*
> (I am Arnaut, who gathers the wind
> and hunts the hare with the ox
> and swims against the incoming tide).

A Spin around Ribérac

The corner of Périgord north of the Dronne practically bubbles with multi-domed Romanesque churches. Some of the best are at **Bourg-des-Maisons** (with remnants of frescoes), **St-Martial-Viveyrol**, and just north of the latter, **Cherval**, where **St-Martin**, the most beautiful of them all, boast five domes, as many as St-Front itself. Medieval **Lusignac**'s fortified church may be dome-less, but it's a delightful film-set of a village, as is **Vendoire** further north, with a 12th-century church, its façade decorated with sculptures in the style of the nearby Charente. Vendoire also wants to tell you all about peat moss at the **Eco-musée de la Tourbe**, with nature trails and boat rides *(open May–Sept 10.30–12.30 and 2.30–6.30, other times Sun 2–6; adm)*. Lastly, **La Tour Blanche** gets its name from the ruined *Turris Alba*, built in the 10th century over a Gaulish fort. Henri IV lodged here for several weeks, although if he came now he'd be more comfortable in the handsome 1617 **Manoir de Roumailhac** in the centre. The ancient priory of St-Cybard at nearby **Cercles** has excellent Romanesque carved capitals.

Aubeterre-sur-Dronne

West of Ribérac, **St-Privat-des-Prés** has a venerable, formidible Romanesque church wearing a porch and belt of nine blind arches across the façade. St-Privat's delightful **Musée de l'Outil et de la Vie au village** *(daily June–Sept 3–6; adm)* is chock-full of tools and curiosities re-creating a 19th-century village street.

At this point delve 2km into the Charente for **Aubeterre-sur-Dronne**, a hill town with a fascinating underground church, **St-Jean** *(9–12.30 and 2–7, closed Tues; adm)* excavated between the 6th and 12th centuries. If St-Emilion's rock-cut church is the largest in Europe (*see* p.150), Aubeterre's is the tallest at an impressive 65ft; it contains a massive reliquary believed to be a copy of the tomb of Joseph of Arimathea from the Holy Sepulchre in Jerusalem. Next to the church a Merovingian necropolis contains a hundred corpse-size *locali* carved into the walls, similar to the catacombs in Rome. Another of Aubeterre's churches, 11th-century **St-Jacques**, has a magnificent three-arched façade that the

Protestants forgot to smash. The left arch is decorated with a zodiac, while stone monsters writhe on the capitals; one, mysteriously, is said to be a copy of a Chinese Buddah. Inside is an 11th-century statue of the Virgin holding Jesus in her right arm instead of the usual left, a deviation believed to be mystically significant. Not surprisingly, Aubeterre was a popular stop on the road to Compostella, a path rife with diversions from established dogma, just as a pilgrimage was a search for something beyond the daily fare at church.

The Forêt de la Double

Ribérac is the main gateway to the emerald forest of La Double which extends south from the Dronne to the Isle. Take the D 708 for **Vanxains**, a nearly deserted village that was once the seat of the Vicomte de la Double. It has an elegant, domed Romanesque church with fine carved capitals, and a Neolithic line of menhirs at **Sauteranne** that's impossible to find unless you get someone to direct you.

In 1747 Vanxains was the birthplace of Suzette Labrouse, 'the Prophetess of the Revolution' who as a child so wanted to see God that she kept a jar of spiders handy, ready to swallow to kill herself. Then came the day that God told her to go forth, bring down the greats of the world and remedy the ills of the church. She made her way to Paris, where her naiveté was the butt of many jokes; a satirical comedy called her the 'truffled turkey, the patriotic gift of Périgord to the National Assembly'. She met Marat, Dr Guillotin, Desmoulins and, most disastrously Robespierre, who persuaded her to go to Rome to tell the Pope to give up his temporal power. The Pope locked her up in Castel Sant'Angelo the minute she crossed the border. A few years later the French army in Rome liberated her; she returned to Paris and died in 1821, leaving behind a stash of small bottles filled with mysterious liquids, which to the disappointment of alchemists, were never analyzed.

To the east along the D 43, **Siorac-de-Ribérac** has yet another domed fortified Romanesque church, while the fane of **St-Sulpice-de-Roumagnac**, 3km further boasts a beautiful 17th-century wooden retable. The D 43 continues east towards St-Astier on the Isle (*see* below), with grand views most of the way. Alternatively, some of the marshes south of Siorac are actually little lakes suitable for a swim; the largest is the **Grand Etang de la Jemaye**. Near **Echourgnac**, in the very centre of La Double, the nuns at **Trappe de Bonne-Esperance** are known for their cheeses, which you can purchase at the convent along with other goodies; just east of Echourgnac one of the last examples of traditional rural architecture in the region, the **Ferme du Parcot**, is open for tours, and doubles as a Double information centre *[July–Sept daily 2–6, May and June Sat 2–6]*. **St-Michel-de-Double**, further south, has other fine examples of 17th-century rural architecture in its Hameau des Héritiers and the Maisons de Gamanson, close to the Isle.

The Lower Isle Valley

Once past Périgueux, the Isle looses much of its charm; the busy N 89 that skirts the south bank of the river between Périgueux and Libourne/Bordeaux is not going to win any beauty contests either. If you want to stop, there's **St-Astier**, 15km from Périgueux, a lime-quarrying town named after the 7th-century hermitage of St Asterius. Part of this, it is believed, is conserved in the crypt of the massive 11th-century church.

Downriver, **Mussidan** has twice in its history been singled out for disaster: during the Wars of Religion, all the Protestants in the vicinity took refuge there, and fought bravely against the Catholics. They surrendered when their lives were guaranteed, but the Catholics were only joking; many Protestants were hanged, and Mussidan was razed. Henri IV, in honour of the town's sufferings, had it rebuilt. In 1944, the Resistance was very active in the forests that surround Mussidan, and the Maquis were in town on 11 June 1944, when an armoured German train pulled up at the station with a machine gun, and a battle began. In reprisals, 52 people were rounded up and executed, the town was pillaged and was at the point of being razed again when the Gestapo chief—unlike the Catholics—decided Mussidan had suffered enough.

Mussidan is the site of the **Musée des Arts et Traditions Populaires** *(open June-mid-Sept 9.30–12 and 2–6; Mar–Nov Sat and Sun only 2–6; adm)*, a collection of tools and furniture, including a tractor of 1920, built of parts salvaged from a First World War tank. Just north of Mussidan, the 12th-century church at **St-Martin-l'Astier** has a very unusual octagonal choir; the partly medieval, partly 16th-century **Château de Montréal**, 7km east of Mussidan just off the D 38 *(open late June–late Sept, closed Tues; adm)* belonged to Claude de Pontbriand, who accompanied Cartier to Canada and named the new French town on the St Lawrence after his home in Périgord—or so goes one possible explanation for Montréal's name. **Montpon-Ménestérol**, famous for its organs (musical, that is), is also the site of one of several new hatcheries that are trying to revive a fish that used to be king of the southwest's waterways: the sturgeon.

French Caviare

A hundred years ago one of the most abundant fish in the Isle, Dordogne and other tributaries of the Garonne was the *créac*, the native sturgeon (*Acipenser sturio*). Ten feet long, weighing nearly 500lbs each, the luckiest specimens lived to be a hundred. Every June the female with swarms of males would swim up the Gironde in June to lay between 100,000 and 200,000 eggs in its rivers. In 1890, the story goes that a passing Russian prince was shocked to see local farmers feeding the eggs to pigs and chickens. 'But that is the favourite delicacy of the czar of all the Russias!' he exclaimed. The southwest's caviare industry was born.

At first it was a goldmine. After the First World War, 40 tons of caviare a year were sold; by 1940 production fell to 3 tons. In 1979, the last year that sturgeon fishing was legal, only three *créac* were caught—brought to the verge of extinction by over-fishing, pollution, dredging of the sturgeon's spawning grounds for gravel and the hydroelectric works of the national electric utility, EDF. Now a protected species, measures are under way to bring the *créac* back in numbers: EDF has built fish passes to help the *créac* swim up river to lay their eggs, and entrepreneurs are raising the big monsters in tanks along the Isle, Gironde and Garonne. In 1991 a Siberian species, *Acipenser baeri*, that grows up to seven feet in fresh water, was

introduced to river tanks, carefully isolated
from the *créacs*. So far it has
proved a success—both in producing caviare (in an operation called
a 'mini-caesarean') and a million fingerlings
a year, raised for meat and especially delicious if
turned into pricey smoked sturgeon. Experts say it will take at least 15 years before
anyone knows if the *créac* itself will make a comeback in the rivers it haunted of old.

Where to Stay and Eating Out

Tocane-St-Apre ✉ 24350

Auberge à la ferme Maigne, on the D 103 at Fournieux, ✆ 53 90 70 35 is a
tranquil place to sleep (140F), learn how to ride, or dine on fresh products at very
fair prices: menus from 80F.

Ribérac ✉ 24600

**Hôtel de France, 3 Rue Marc-Dufraisse, ✆ 53 90 00 61, a former post house,
is the best and biggest in town, with dining in the garden (from 90F). In nearby
Petit-Bersac, *****Le Mas de Montet**, ✆ 53 90 08 71 offers plenty of R & R in a
beautiful Renaissance château set in a park; all 14 rooms have their own character.

Bourg-des-Maisons ✉ 24320

Book well in advance for a room in the delightful **Domaine de Tinteillac**, ✆ 53
91 12 54, a 13th-century castle with round towers, set in a large park. The huge
rooms, some with balconies all have en suite bath, are a bargain at a mere
270–290F; delicious home-cooked meals are 150F a go.

Sourzac-Mussidan ✉ 24400

Le Chaufourg en Périgord, ✆ 53 81 01 56, is a pretty 17th-century family residence with seven rooms to rent, set in gardens with a heated pool; from 700F.

St-Astier ✉ 24110

La Pomme d'Amour, 9 Place d'Eglise, ✆ 53 07 29 00, is a fine place to dine
overlooking the town's famous tower; delicious salads (menus from 90F; closed
Sun night and Wed).

Montpon-Ménestérol ✉ 24700

Château des Grillauds, at Marcillac, ✆ 53 80 49 71 has seven large, bright
rooms with views for 370F. The best place to eat, **Auberge de l'Eclade**, 2km
north on the D 730, ✆ 53 80 28 64, offers delicious menus at some of the most
reasonable prices in Périgord for the likes of foie gras, served in three different styles
and much more (menus from 70F).

The Dordogne: the Vézère Valley

The Vézère Valley

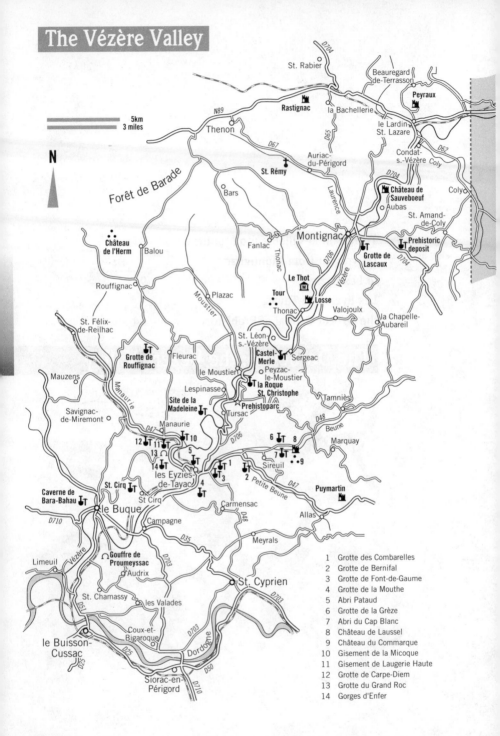

5km
3 miles

N

St. Rabier

Beauregard
de-Terrasson

Peyraux

N89
Rastignac
la Bachellerie
le Lardin
St. Lazare

Thenon

D65

Condat-
s.-Vézère
Coly

D67

Auriac-
du-Périgord

Château de
Sauveboeuf

Colyo

St. Rémy

Aubas

St. Amand-
de-Coly

Forêt de Barade

Bars

Montignac

Prehistoric
deposit

Château
de l'Herm
Balou

Fanlac

Grotte de
Lascaux

D706

Le Thot

Roufignac

Plazac

Tour
Losse

Valojoulx

la Chapelle-
Aubareil

St. Félix-
de-Reilhac

Thonac

St. Léon-
s.-Vézère

Grotte de
Roufignac
Fleurac

Castel-
Merle
Sergeac

Mauzens

le Moustier

Peyzac-
le-Moustier
la Roque

Tamniès

Lespinasse

St. Christophe

Savignac-
de-Miremont

Site de la
Madeleine

Prehistoparc

Tursac

Beune

Manaurie

Marquay

12 T 11 T 10
13
5
Puymartin

St. Cirq

1
3

Sireuil

9

2 Petite Beune

Caverne de
Bara-Bahau

les Eyzies-
de-Tayac

4

St. Cirq

Carmensac

Allas

le Buque

Campagne

D710

D35

Meyrals

Gouffre de
Proumeyssac

Limeuil

Audrix

St. Cyprien

St. Chamassy

les Valades

Coux-et-
Bigaroque

le Buisson-
Cussac

Dordogne

Siorac-en-
Périgord

1 Grotte des Combarelles
2 Grotte de Bernifal
3 Grotte de Font-de-Gaume
4 Grotte de la Mouthe
5 Abri Pataud
6 Grotte de la Grèze
7 Abri du Cap Blanc
8 Château de Laussel
9 Château du Commarque
10 Gisement de la Micoque
11 Gisement de Laugerie Haute
12 Grotte de Carpe-Diem
13 Grotte du Grand Roc
14 Gorges d'Enfer

84

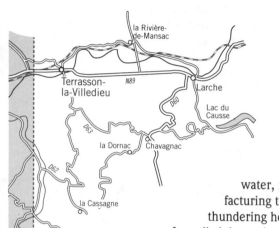

Some 400,000 years ago, when the first people settled on the fair banks of the Vézère, the river had considerably more presence, flowing 100ft higher than it does today. But it was more than gorgeous scenery that attracted these Lower Paleolithic pioneers—the Vézère's bulging cliffs were amenably pocked with caves and shelters, there was fresh water, river pebbles and flint for manufacturing tools, and most importantly, thundering herds of bison and reindeer that funnelled down the valley before the glaciers of the last Ice Age. Over the millennia, the hunters turned to art, and left an extraordinary record of their passing in the valley's most secret caves. When the earth heated up, the big game retreated northwards, somehow taking all the artistic inspiration with them, and leaving the hunters the slow, Mesolithic drudgery of inventing agriculture.

The Vézère valley yielded the first hint of its prehistoric past in 1862, when a deposit of carved flints and bones was uncovered at a place called La Madeleine. The finds suggested for the first time that mammoths and humanity coexisted at one period, henceforth known as the Magdalenian (*c.* 15,000–10,000 BC). This discovery set off a quest for signs of 'antedeluvian man', leading to a torrent of accidental and organized discoveries. One of the most important occurred in 1888, during the excavations for a rail line between Périgueux and Agen, when workers at a hamlet called Cro-Magnon, near Les Eyzies, discovered five Magdalenian-era skeletons, among them a woman, a fetus, and a man over 6ft tall, with a long nose, high forehead and a big brain cavity, a race from then on known as *Homo sapiens sapiens*, or Cro-Magnons. Seven years later the first Magdalenian paintings in France were discovered at Les Eyzies' Grotte de la Mouthe. In 1908, in the caves of Le Moustier, the finding of 70,000-year-old, Neanderthal-like bones of Cro-Magnon's Middle Paleolithic predecessors and their affairs made Mousterian synonymous with Middle Paleolithic culture (*c.* 80,000–40,000 BC). All this remained the fare of scholarly journals until the accidental discovery of Lascaux in 1940 electrified the imagination of the entire world.

To date, some 200 Paleolithic caves, shelters and deposits have been discovered in the valley of the Vézére. UNESCO has short-listed the region for it to be protected as 'the patrimony of humanity'. The sacredness of the place has drawn holy men from the other side of the world—near Le Moustier is one of Europe's most important Tibetan Buddhist monasteries. The Vézère also attracts thousands of more worldly visitors every year, whose fiscal well-being is threatened by a score of recent roadside attractions; even worse, the *département* has spent millions of francs to increase tourist access to the river banks, a project that local property owners translated into bonanza profits for firewood, a chain-saw massacre of the lovely old groves that gave the river its special charm.

Terrasson-la-Villedieu to Montignac

Getting Around

There are daily bus connections between Montignac and Périgueux (𝒸 53 51 82 60) and Sarlat (𝒸 53 59 01 48) and Les Eyzies and Le Bugue are on the rail line, but to see much of the valley you really need a car or bicycle.

Tourist Information

Montignac: In the former hospital, Place Bertrand-de-Born, 𝒸 53 51 82 60.

market days

Terrasson: Thursdays

Montignac: Wednesdays

The Vézère spills down the *causse* of Corrèze towards **Terrasson-la-Villedieu**, a striking medieval truffle and walnut town spanned by a 12th-century bridge. Terrasson is built around an abbey founded in the 6th century by a certain St Sour, who according to the story let his two pet doves decide the exact spot. They flew around and around, and when they finally landed, the cry went up *'Terra sunt!'* ('They've landed!') hence, supposedly, Terrasson. St Sour's church, last repaired in 1889 has some sweet 16th-century stained glass; the church of Villadieu has a Carolingian bell.

Downriver, **Le Lardin-Saint-Lazare** offers the 15th-century **Château de Peyraux** and a 7km detour west to **La Bachellerie**—its name derived, like the English 'bachelor' from *bas-chevalier*, the lowest, youngest order of knights. It is the address of the singular neo-classical **Château de Rastignac** (1811–17) built, not for Balzac's immortal social climber, but for the Marquis Chapt de Rastignac by a Périgordin architect named Mathurin Blanchard. Blanchard studied Victor Louis's works in Bordeaux, but no one knows much else about him, especially how he came up with what looks like the prototype for the rear façade of the White House in Washington. Apparently the resemblance is only a coincidence, but was enough to infuriate the retreating Nazis in 1944, who got symbolic revenge on Roosevelt by burning the original. What you see today is a careful restoration.

Condat-sur-Vézère, a paper-making town, was formerly run as a hospital inn for medieval pilgrims by the Knights Hospitallers. At **Aubas**, the Vézère flows past the classic, severe 17th-century **Château de Sauveboeuf**, built after the 15th-century original was flattened on the orders of Richelieu, to punish the owner for killing a man in a duel. The king's mistress, Marie de Hautefort, was so upset over this scarring of her native Périgord that she had it rebuilt. Her two monumental fountains of 1610 have gone elsewhere, one to New York, another to Clairac (*see* p.293). The village **church** has some fine works, from its 11th-century carved capitals to a pair of 16th-century retables, one in painted wooden and the other in stone fragments. Just before Montignac, the D 67 detours 5 km north to **Auriac-du-Périgord**, with its 14th–16th century **Château de la Faye** built around a medieval keep. The château's chapel of **St Rémy** was famous throughout Périgord; nicknamed St Remédi, the saint was so reputed for his healing juju that all the features of his statue were rubbed off by ill people vigorously rubbing the afflicted parts of their bodies against him.

Montignac and Lascaux

Montignac, once a busy river port, now sits pretty on the right bank of the Vézère, its wooden balconies reflected peacefully across the waters. Although feared for its ferocious counts in the Middle Ages, Montignac rocketed to a sweeter fame in 1940, when a pit used as the occasional dead donkey dump was discovered to house the nonpareil masterpiece of prehistoric cave painting. As extraordinary in its own way is the mutant orange-coloured housing estate that blights the hills south of town.

Château de Montignac and the Counts of Périgord

Montignac had its share of glory and defeats between 15,000 BC and the discovery of Lascaux, most of it centred in the ruined Château de Montignac at the top of Rue de Juillet. Now only vertiginous terraces, vaulted casements and a single square tower out of a dozen that originally punctuated its thick walls remain of what was once the most important military castle in the region.

From the 11th to the 14th century, Montignac was the key to Périgord Noir and the chief citadel of the fierce bad counts of Périgord. Their name Taillefer (later Talleyrand), came from an ancestor who sliced a Viking in two with his sword. They were unique among the vassals of the kings of France in having absolutely no redeeming virtues; even the hawkish troubadour Bertran de Born was in awe of them and wrote that one count, Hélie V, was such a cuss that he slept standing up. Hélie was succeded by his brother Roger Bernard, an ex-priest who thought the best way to govern Périgord was to crush its inhabitants, to 'destroy and pull out their vines' and 'fill their churches with soldiers and pillagers'. Bernard had the support of the king of France for his skill at stomping on lesser barons. But Bernard's even nastier son, Archambault V, swore allegience to England, and took advantage of a truce to surround Périgord with castles. He captured Domme by surprise, burning the church with all the people inside, then hunted down all the women who escaped, forcing them to cut off their dresses at the waist, for easier raping. Archambault attacked even the monasteries and royal officers, declaring himself the absolute sovereign of Périgord, and to show he meant business he destroyed half of Périgueux.

The good folk of Périgord begged Charles VI for relief and in 1394 the king sent down an army to punish Archambault, destroying his fortresses and besieging Montignac for a month. Archambault sued for a truce and offered to pay a huge fine; but as soon as the royal army turned its back, Archambault tortured and hanged the king's commander. Archambault died before the king could punish him again, leaving an heir—Archambault VI—who proved to be even worse, terrorizing Périgord with murder and mayhem, laughing at royal orders to behave. He didn't laugh so hard in 1397, when once again Montignac was besieged by a thousand men, and Archambault was forced to surrender. The king gave Montignac to his brother, Louis d'Orléans (who had to sell it for ransom money when he was captured at Agincourt) while Archambault hightailed it to London, where he connived and made everyone around him miserable until his death in 1430.

The town was the last home of Eugène Le Roy, Montignac's tax collector before he hit the big time with his novel *Jacques Le Croquant* (*see* p.66); hence the local historical exhibits of the **Musée Eugène Le Roy**, adjacent to the tourist office (*July and Aug 9.30–12 and 2–7.30, other times © 53 51 82 60; adm*). Near by, the 18th-century house with columns is by Nicolas Ledoux, the architect of the famous Paris tollhouses. In medieval Rue de la Pégerie is a house Henri IV gave to his mistress, Gabrielle d'Estrées.

Lascaux I and II

One morning in September 1940, two local lads and two young refugees from Paris equipped themselves with lanterns and set off up the hill above Montignac, determined to descend into an old dump to find a legendary secret treasure that their elders believed was nothing more than an old folk tale. With difficulty the boys enlarged the overgrown opening and fumbled down into a treasure beyond anyone's dreams, one that had been virtually vacuum-sealed when the original entrance was blocked by an ancient landslide. Within a week the world's authority on Paleolithic painting, the 73-year old Abbé Breuil, had made his way to Montignac, and was ravished by what he called the 'Sistine Chapel of Prehistoric Art'. He made Lascaux's young discoverers responsible for guarding the cave— which they did vigilantly, with shotguns. But by the early 1960s it had become clear that the Lascaux's worst enemy wasn't something to shoot at, but the 'white disease' caused by carbonic acid from the breath of a million visitors; within 15 years of its discovery, the masterpiece that had endured for millennia was fading under a film of white calcite deposits. On 20 April 1963 Lascaux was closed forever to the public; although the deterioration has completely stopped, admission is limited to five prehistorians twice a week.

Disappointment in the cave's closure was so universal that the Dordogne *département* financed the 15-year-long construction of **Lascaux II** 200 m below the original. This incredibly painstaking reproduction of the two most beautiful chambers, the **Hall of the Bulls** and the long narrow **'Diverticule axiale'** was painted by Monique Peytral with the same colours and techniques used 17,000 years ago. Far better than any photograph, Lascaux II reproduces the exuberant life, movement and the clever use of natural protuberances, faults and shadows of the original, although it hardly explains how an artist limited to a lamp of animal fat and juniper twigs could get the proportions of a 16ft bull so perfectly. For Cro-Magnon artists not only drew with the unerring line of a Matisse, but mastered techniques forgotten until recently (the three-quarter, twisted turn in the animals' heads, the Impressionistic use of perspective in the legs of running horses). Scattered among the animals are mysterious unexplainable symbols reminiscent of a Joan Miró. And what of the Dr Seuss-ish beast dubbed the 'unicorn', the only known 'imaginary' creature discovered in prehistoric art? Was the painting done for a single religious rite and sealed off, never to be revisited? No signs of habitation were discovered here, and the original entrance to Lascaux I has never been found. Humble awe is a common response, or even a sneaking suspicion that LSD guru Terence McKenna might be right (in his book *Food of the Gods*), that Upper Paleolithic culture was built around magic psilocybin mushrooms, a healthy psychedelic experience lost with the climatic changes at the end of the Ice Age *(guided tours—tel 53 51 95 03 to find out when English tours are available; open daily exc Mon and Jan, 10–12 and 2–5.30; from 9.30–7 in July and Aug, when tickets (stamped with a time) are available at a special booth by the Montignac tourist office from 9am on; reservations © 53 53 44 35; adm includes Le Thot).*

Nearly a kilometre above Lascaux, the privately-owned **Gisement du Régourdou** (same hours as Lascaux II; separate adm) has yet to be thoroughly explored—at the time of writing it's a confusion of fences enclosing cavernous pits, five frisky brown bears, and a small museum containing the site's finds. The Cro-Magnon painters of Lascaux ground their red ochres and magnesium oxides here, but the real fascination of Régourdou is its evidence of a Neanderthal bear cult, predating Lascaux by 60,000 years (*see* 'Topics', p.45). In a collapsed cave, 20 ritual bear tombs were discovered: after being ritually cut up, the bear's bones were placed around its skull, sprinkled with red ochre dust and covered with a slab. Around the tombs the fossilized bones of smaller animals were found, presumably funerary gifts to the bear. Fossilized bear turds were found as well. Six feet away from the bear sepulchre, the skeleton of Neanderthal man was found; the flint tools found here and elsewhere suggest he was left-handed.

Around Montignac

Six km southeast of Montignac, by the D 704, stands one of the Dordogne's dreamiest châteaux, the golden limestone lauze-topped **Château de La Grande Filolie** (14th–15th century)—so perfect that, as Périgord novelist Marc Blancpain put it 'one could believe it grew here, as mushrooms grow in the humid sweetness of an autumn night'. Just as visually striking, the fortified church of **St-Amand-de-Coly** looms like a skyscraper over its narrow valley and the rooftops of its hamlet. Built in the 12th century as part of an Augustinian monastery, it is so strong that Huguenots who took shelter in its massive bell tower/keep in 1575 withstood six days of close cannon fire. Defensive traces remain inside as well: just under the roof you can see the path from which the monks and villagers could fire down on their besiegers. All the same, it is stirring, wholesome Romanesque, with a dome hovering 66ft over the nave; some of the capitals are decorated with man-eating monsters *(6km east of Montignac on the D704; open July and Aug 10–7, other times by appointment, ✆ 53 51 67 50).*

Where to Stay and Eating Out

Condat-sur-Vézère ✉ 24570

The luxurious 13th–15th-century ★★★**Château de la Fleunie**, ✆ 53 51 32 74, offers 24 rooms, set in a 106 acre park with tennis courts, pool, driving range, sauna, stables and gourmet meals from 155F.

Montignac ✉ 24290

Montignac can boast two top hotels: ★★★★**Château de Puy Robert**, 2km from Lascaux on the D 65, ✆ 53 51 92 13, a bijou château complete with turrets, immersed in a lovely 20-acre park with a pool; luxurious rooms, decorated with modern fabrics and antiques (700–1200F, closed mid-Oct–May); the restaurant uses local ingredients to concoct innovative dishes from pasta with truffles to smoked Brive pigeon (menus 240–500F). ★★★**Le Relais du Soleil d'Or**, 16 Rue du Quatre-Septembre, ✆ 53 51 80 22, also has a shady park and heated pool, as well as tennis and riding opportunities; recently redecorated rooms (from 340–850F; closed 15 Jan–15 Feb). In the restaurant traditional southwestern cuisine is given a modern, lighter touch; 120–380F. In central Place Tourny, ★**Le Périgord**, ✆ 53 51 80 38 has simple rooms (140–180F) but views and a terrace overlooking the Vézère; reasonably priced Périgordin cuisine (from 85F; closed Nov–Feb). Another inexpensive choice, the little **De la Grotte**, 63 Rue du Quatre-Septembre, ✆ 53 51 80 48 was converted from an old house and offers a riverside terrace, canoeing, and a playground (120–250F, closed mid Nov–mid Jan). The campsite nearest Montignac is **Le Bleufond**, on the D 65, ✆ 53 51 83 95, open April–mid Oct.

For a cheap meal, try the Italian **Les Pilotis**, with tables along the river, good pizzas, lasagne, salads, with luscious ice cream concoctions to finish (around 75F; children 35F).

Around Montignac

Off the beaten track, 7km south of Montignac in La Chapelle-Aubareil (24290), the handsome ★★**La Table du Terroir** farm–hotel–restaurant, ✆ 53 50 72 14, offers panoramic views from its park and hilltop pool, and mini-golf for the kids. In the kitchen there's an emphasis on aromatic morel mushrooms, which attain a kind of epiphany in dishes like *foie gras et cou d'oie farci aux morilles*; menus 85–220F all based on farm products. In St-Amand-de-Coly (24290) the recently renovated, family run ★★**La Gardette**, ✆ 53 51 68 50, offers six quiet rooms and simple meals with menus from 69F (closed Oct and Nov). Coly (24120), 3km north, is the site of the magnificent, ivy-covered 13th-century ★★★**Manoir de Hautegente**, ✆ 53 51 68 03, which has only 10 antique-furnished rooms, but each waits to spoil you in comfort; the shady garden is crossed by a trout stream, and there's swimming in the heated pool. Half-pension mandatory in season (menus from 180F; closed Nov–Apr).

Downriver from Montignac to Les Eyzies

The ticket to Lascaux II includes the **Le Thot Centre de Préhistoire** (same hours), well signposted along the D 706. Inside are audio-visuals on Paleolithic art and on the meticulous creation of Lascaux II, as well as a replica of the tiny chamber at the back of Lascaux, showing a stick man in a bird mask, dropping what looks like a bird decoy as a wounded bison charges and gores him. Another chamber at the back of Lascaux was painted with felines, which fit into the general rule: the artists didn't shy away from depicting dangerous animals, but hid them, either at the back or amidst other drawings (see the bear in the Chamber of the Bulls). Outside are gathered living examples of the subjects of Lascaux—the deer and bulls, and animals that found a last refuge in Poland: European bison and Przewalski's horses, while oxen represent the wild aurochs, which died out in Poland in the 1660s. Even the extinct woolly rhinos and mammoth are animated to wiggle and roar.

Continuing south on the D 706, a signposted lane leads to the riverside **Château de Losse**, associated with the Ophelia of Périgord, the fair Hélène of Château de Sauveboeuf, who drowned on her wedding day rather than marry the horrid old seigneur of Losse. A mix of medieval defensive architecture and Renaissance elegance, Losse has been completely furnished with tapestries, porcelains and other 16th-century pieces from the time of Jean II de Losse, Governor of Guyenne under Henri IV *(undergoing restoration at the time of writing, but should be open July–Sept 10–12.30 and 2–6.30)*. **Thonac**, the nearest village, is dominated by an immense bell tower, but the main attraction is a second, leaning tower 2km away on the Plazac road called the **Tour de Vermondie**; the story goes that a young girl was imprisoned here to keep her away from her lover. When he came and sang at its foot, the tower was so moved that it bent over to allow the two to kiss.

Rouffignac, Mammoths and the Château de l'Herm

Motoring through this corner of the Dordogne, you'll notice that village after village has been twinned with one in Germany. In Rouffignac's case it marks a special act of forgiveness—in 1944, in reprisal for local Resistance activity, the retreating Nazis burned the village to the ground. Only the church of **St-Germain** remained, or at least most of it—the Romanesque apse is rebuilt, but under the bell tower the captivating Renaissance doorway of 1530 survives, its lintel carved with mermaids. If it's open, don't miss the flamboyant Gothic interior, with elaborate vaulting and twisted columns.

Rouffignac has even greater claims to fame. Five km south, off the D 32 is the **Grotte de Rouffignac**, 'the Cave of a Hundred Mammoths' *(open Apr–Oct 10–11.30 and 2–5, July and Aug 9–11.30 and 2–6; adm)*. First off, this is the cave to visit if you have trouble walking: a little electric train waits to trundle you 4km down into the bowels of the earth as the guide illuminates the vivid etchings, drawings of mammoths and woolly rhinoceroses, and niches in the clay floor formed by generations of hibernating bears, restlessly spinning. The ceiling of the innermost chamber is an excellent pastiche of horses, mammoths, bison, and an ibex.

Rouffignac is a lesson in how people only see what they already know. Its entrance has always been open, and for centuries locals would come down and take scary walks or even Sunday afternoon promenades, leaving their names and dates behind on the walls and ceilings. Only in 1956 was it discovered that the graffiti covered vigorous prehistoric masterpieces. When their authenticity was questioned, a description of them dated 1575 was produced; interestingly, the Renaissance author sensed that Rouffignac was a sacred place, but somehow mistook the drawings for erotic 'Love's larcenies' of our 'Idolatrous forefathers'.

Other signs from Rouffignac point 6km northwest to the sinister **Château de l'Herm** *(tours of the interior July and Aug; adm)*, its savage, ruined towers looming over the trees, a remnant of the Fôret de Barade, once Périgord's darkest wood. Few castles in France are so blood-stained: legend tells of the 13th-century Baron de l'Herm, builder of the two heavy round towers, whose daughter Jeanne fell in love with a page. By a freak accident, the young man accidentally cut Jeanne's hand off when they first embraced; a wax one was made in its place, and in remorse the young husband swore to obey her blindly whenever she raised it. Unfortunately he became a violent drunkard, and came home one day to find her listening to a troubadour. In a jealous rage he would have slain the singer, but Jeanne raised her wax hand, and the troubadour made good his escape—only to hear Jeanne's screams as her husband cut the rest of her to bits.

Windows and openings were cut into the round feudal towers when a third tower was added by L'Herm's later owner, an ambassador of François I named Jean III de Calvimont. Calvimont had spent long periods in Italy, and graced his residence with a flamboyant Gothic portal guarded by men-at-arms, a superb stone spiral staircase and carved fireplaces, now surreally suspended over the floorless void. Calvimont died a mysterious violent death and left L'Herm to his 5-year old daughter, Marguerite. His widow immediately married a neighbour, Foucauld d'Aubusson, and married the child Marguerite to his diabolical son, François, to make sure the property stayed in the family. But François was already in love with Marie de Hautefort (aunt of the mistress of Louis XIII), and as Marguerite grew older and François's debts grew larger, he had her strangled, beginning a new 80-year long streak of murders at and around L'Herm involving the Calvimonts, d'Aubussons and anyone remotely connected with them. By 1652, when all the claimants had self-destructed, the château was put up for auction; not surprisingly, no one wanted it. It was eventually converted into a farm and abandoned in 1862.

Peyzac-Le Moustier

Back along the Vézère, **St-Léon-sur-Vézère**, now a charming, sleepy backwater off the D 706, was once a stopping point for pilgrims to Compostella: its handsome, forthright Romanesque church, built on a Gallo-Roman wall, overlooks the willows weeping into the river and a pedestrian bridge. Inside, only some battered frescoes and reliefs remain of the decoration. The village cemetery has a pint-sized version of Sarlat's Lanterne des Morts and some extremely rare *enfeux*, wall niche tombs from the 1200s. St-Léon's bridge leads in a

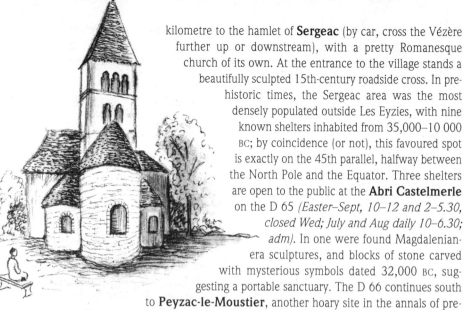

kilometre to the hamlet of **Sergeac** (by car, cross the Vézère further up or downstream), with a pretty Romanesque church of its own. At the entrance to the village stands a beautifully sculpted 15th-century roadside cross. In prehistoric times, the Sergeac area was the most densely populated outside Les Eyzies, with nine known shelters inhabited from 35,000–10 000 BC; by coincidence (or not), this favoured spot is exactly on the 45th parallel, halfway between the North Pole and the Equator. Three shelters are open to the public at the **Abri Castelmerle** on the D 65 *(Easter–Sept, 10–12 and 2–5.30, closed Wed; July and Aug daily 10–6.30; adm)*. In one were found Magdalenian-era sculptures, and blocks of stone carved with mysterious symbols dated 32,000 BC, suggesting a portable sanctuary. The D 66 continues south to **Peyzac-le-Moustier**, another hoary site in the annals of prehistory. Excavations begun in 1908 in the Abri du Moustier have produced such a wealth of material that the last half of the Middle Paleolithic era is known as the Mousterian culture (roughly 100,000 to 35,000 BC). Although you can only visit the shelter by special arrangement, the **Musée du Moustier** *(July and Aug 9–7)* has fossils and other finds.

The bridge from Moustier crosses to the curved prow of **La Roque St-Christophe**, a sheer cliff a half mile long, sliced into five shelves, one of which is the largest natural terrace in Europe *(open all year, Dec–Feb 2–5, July and Aug 9.30–7, other months 10–6.30; adm)*. Inhabited from Mousterian times, the hundred or so caves along the tiers were home for up to 3000 people (the current population of Montignac), who had their own church, cemetery, monastery, and after the 900s, a fort, thrown up against the Vikings sailing up the Vézère and later used by the Protestants. If after all this, you still can't imagine daily life at the dawn of time, Tursac offers its **Préhistoparc** *(daily Apr–mid-Nov, 10–6, July and Aug 9.30–7; adm)*, with life-size outdoor dioramas featuring hunters killing mammoths, woolly rhinos and bears. Downriver, over the Lespinasse bridge from Tursac, the excavations at **La Madeleine** *(Feb–mid-Dec, 10–12 and 2–5, closed Tues; daily July and Aug 9–12 and 2–7; adm)* have produced some 600 pieces of *art immobilier*, giving the name Magdalenian to the greatest age of Paleolithic art. Although the finds are now in Les Eyzies's museum, the path from the parking lot leads to the ruins of a a troglodyte village similar to La Roque St-Christophe: a 10th-century fort carved into the living rock, a 15th-century chapel, and on the promontory, a ruined château.

Eating Out

The **Auberge de Castel-Merle**, © 53 50 70 08 *(open Palm Sun–Oct, closed Wed)* by the museum in Sergeac serves well-prepared specialities of Périgord on a terrace overlooking the Vézère (menus from 70–230F, and a rarity in these parts, a vegetarian menu at 80F). Also near Castel-Merle, the **Auberge du Peyrol**, © 53 50 72 91, offers a picture window overview of the lush Vézère landscape to accompany lush dishes like foie gras in Monbazillac and grilled *magret de canard* with herbs (menus from 70–220F).

Les Eyzies-de-Tayac, the 'World Capital of Prehistory'

The Vézère and Beune rivers meet at Les Eyzies, where the first known bones of *Homo sapiens sapiens* were discovered just above the train station at a place called Cro-Magnon. As the valley's chief crossroads, with an important prehistoric museum and sites in every direction, Les Eyzies is swamped with summer visitors, all watched over by a lumpish creature representing Cro-Magnon man, sculpted in 1930 by Paul Dardé and a grave insult to the painters of Lascaux.

Getting Around

Les Eyzies station has connections with Paris and Agen, and less frequently with Sarlat and Périgueux (© 53 09 50 50). Excursion taxi, © 53 06 93 06. Parking in Les Eyzies in season is notoriously frustrating; excursion buses fill the streets like whales in a goldfish pond. Traffic gets equally congested downriver in Le Bugue, the 'Crossroads of Périgord'; it has a station on the same rail line and a 24-hour taxi service to get you around (© 53 07 22 97).

Tourist Information

Les Eyzies-de-Tayac: in the centre, © 53 06 97 05, daily in summer, winter Tues and Thurs only. Although the hours for the sites are accurate at the time of writing, they are prone to change: pick up the latest list and booking requirements here, as well as info on canoe and kayak hire, horse riding and trails.

Le Bugue: Place de l'Hôtel-de-Ville, © 53 07 20 48

market days

Les Eyzies: Mondays

Le Bugue: Tuesdays and Saturdays

Musée National de Préhistoire

Open daily exc Tues, 9.30–12 and 2 to 5, till 6 in season; adm.

Tucked under the overhanging cliffs that dominate Les Eyzies, and sharing the terrace with the hapless caveman statue, the 16th-century castle belonging to the barons of Beynac was slowly being cannibalized for its stone when it found a new role in 1918 as the Musée National de Préhistoire. It is the perfect prehistory apéritif. Helpful tables and charts put the mind-boggling millennia into perspective. If, technologically, humankind got off to a slow, painstaking start (see the flint blades on Level I) the opposite is true in art: the rooms on Level II form a kind of Louvre of prehistory, with the largest collection anywhere of carved stone blocks. Scholars divide the works here into five chief styles. In the Primitive

(35,000–25,000 BC) figures are very rare, stiff and roughly shaped; in the Archaic (25,000–15,000 BC), animals were drawn in rigid profile on walls (the Abri Pataud Venus, the animal from Abri Cellier) and you find the first sculpture in three dimensions. The final three styles belong to the Magdalenian era (*c.* 15,000–10,000 BC): the Preclassical, marking the beginnings of the great period of cave paintings; the Classical, marked by a scrupulous attention to proportions, movement and detail, gradually marked by a decline of spontaneity until reaching the Final period at the end of the Upper Paleolithic. There are bas-reliefs of shapely Magdalenian women, mammoths butting heads etched on a staff, the famous *Bison licking its Flank* from La Madeleine and the *Aurouchs du Fourneau de Diable*; there are rough carved vulvas and delicate ornate phalluses that make you wonder which sex carved which. Level III has a collection of *art mobilier* casts, of works mostly found along the Vézère in the 19th century, including a case of those first subjects of pre-historic sculptors, the lozenge 'Venuses'—buxom, balloon-bottomed beauties common from the Urals to the Pyrenees. Level IV contains casts of Neanderthal and Cro-Magnon skulls, bones of the animals, and several sepulchres: the remains of bodies covered with ochre and rare seashells. Note especially the Magdalenian tomb from St-Germain la Rivière in the Gironde, where a young woman was laid out in a foetal position under what looks like a dolmen, surrounded with funerary gifts: shells, tools, ornaments and animal bones.

Under a rocky overhang in the centre of Les Ezyies is the equally remarkable **Abri Pataud** (same hours as Lascaux II, *see* p.88) where Upper Paleolithic hunters left 14 layers of inhabitation over a span of 20,000 years. A museum in the nearby shelter, opened in 1990, contains the finds, including one of the oldest known bas-reliefs, an ibex dated 18,000 BC. Near the station, the Hôtel Cro-Magnon marks the site where *Homo sapiens sapiens* was discovered; here, too is the 13th-century **St-Martin-de-Tayac**, an imposing fortified church with antique columns on the porch.

Font-de-Gaume

Although the Grotte de la Mouthe (where the first cave paintings in France were discovered just south of Les Eyzies) has been closed since 1981, a limited number of visitors are allowed into the **Grotte de Font de Gaume**, a 15min walk east along the D 47 *(daily exc Tues, Oct–Mar 10–12 and 2–5, Apr–Sept 9–12 and 2–6; adm. Reservations 10F (essential in summer when only 20 people are let in every 30min), © 53 06 90 80).* After Lascaux and Altamira in Spain, Font de Gaume has the best known polychrome prehistoric paintings, although as in Rouffignac the cave was visited centuries before the paintings were 'discovered' in 1901. A path from the D 47 takes you up to the narrow entrance; inside, beyond a narrow passage called 'the Rubicon' are paintings and engravings that have been dated at 12,000 BC, created with techniques similar to those in evidence at Lascaux, and similarly using natural relief to lend volume to the drawing. Although calcite build-ups and graffiti over the years have damaged the paintings, they remain impressive: friezes of red and black bison on a light background, reindeer, horses and mammoths. And, as at Lascaux, scholars have noted the placement of horses' heads near unusual topographical features. (Font de Gaume is the rendez-vous for visiting Laugerie Haute, *see* below).

East of Les Eyzies, along the Beune Valley

A kilometre up the D 47, the **Grotte des Combarelles** was discovered in the same year as Font de Gaume *(same hours, same reservations as Font de Gaume)*. Some 800 different engravings dated 12,000–10,0000 BC have been distinguished in the cave's last 400ft, including 140 horses and 48 rare human representations—hands, masks, women and a seated person. Many are incomplete, most are superimposed in wild abandon, and others only appear when lit from various angles by a torch. Most beautiful of all is the reindeer leaning forward to drink from a black cavity suggesting water.

A year later and 3km down the road, 100 paintings and engravings were found in the **Grotte de Bernifal**, near the left bank of the Petite Beune *(June and Sept, 9–12 and 2–6, July and Aug 9–7)*. The dominant animal is the mammoth, stylistically similar to the ones in Rouffignac (*c.* 12,000 BC), in the company of many 'tectiform' (roof-shaped) symbols; but the star of the show is a rare, engraved ancestor of the ass.

More prehistory waits around **Marquay**: the **Abri du Cap Blanc** *(daily mid-Feb–Oct, 10–12 and 2–6, July and Aug 9.30–7)* with a remarkable, vigorous, 42ft frieze of nearly life-size horses in high relief, following the natural contours of the cave; the shelter also yielded a Cro-Magnon tomb and tools from the end of Magdalenian age. The nearby **Grotte de La Grèze** has exceptionally ancient engravings, including a bison dated to 20,000 BC (by appointment only, © 53 06 97 03). Just beyond rise the majestic ruins of the 12th–13th-century **Château de Commarque**, a castle betrayed to and ruined by the English in the Hundred Years' War; the elegant keep was added in the 16th century. On the cliff opposite, the much-restored 14th-century **Château de Laussel** sits over the Gisement de Laussel (100,000–17,000 BC), which produced the famous relief of the Vénus de Laussel, holding her bison horn (now in Bordeaux, but there's a cast in Les Eyzies).

North of Les Eyzies

Along the opposite bank of the Vézère from Les Eyzies, the D 47 is chock-a-block with the works of nature and humankind. First, the **Musée de la Spéléologie** *(daily July–Aug, 11–6; adm)*, set in the natural rock fortress of Tayac, offers summer visitors a look at the formation of caves, and the tools and art of potholing. A number of shelters are scattered in the **Vallon des Gorges d'Enfer** *(shelter and park, to reserve © 53 06 90 60, Apr–Sept, 10–6, picnic and lodging and guided tours, 180F adults)*; the most famous, the **Abri de Poisson** (visited in conjunction with Laugerie Haute), has a rare relief of a fish—a salmon over a yard long. It is nearly detached from the ceiling; an enterprising German had sold it secretly to a museum in Berlin, but the French found out just in time and classified the site, saving the fish.

Further along the D 47 is a fairy work by Mother Nature, the stalactite **Grotte du Grand Roc**, halfway up a cliff. This cave is known for its extremely rare triangular formations; others resemble coral, some thumb their nose at the law of gravity *(Apr–Dec, daily 9.30–6)*. Near by, you can visit the **Gisement de Laugerie Basse** *(same hours as Grand Roc, with combined adm available)*, one of the first shelters excavated, in 1863, and a rich source of *art immobilier*. The adjacent Abri de Marseilles was occupied continuously from the Magdalenian to the Gallo-Romans. Although most of the finds have been scattered in museums around the world, a small museum on the site has tools and decorated fragments.

Still along the D 47, at the bottom of another cliff, 42 levels of human habitation have been excavated over the last 120 years at the **Gisement de Laugerie Haute** *(visits daily exc Tues at 11am and 5pm from Apr–Sept, daily July and Aug from 9–12 and 2–6; adm)*. When the massive top terrace of the cliff collapsed *c.* 14,000 BC, it had already been home to people for 11 millennia. There are a number of Solutrean (20,000 BC) engravings as well as a sort of carved gutter, an early attempt to solve a problem that would ever after plague humanity—leaking roofs. Further up near Manaurie, another cave, **Carpe Diem** has lovely coloured stalactites *(late Mar–late Oct, 9.30–12 and 2–6; adm)*. Lastly, the **Grotte de St-Cirq**, discovered in 1956, 5km southwest of Les Eyzies *(daily exc Sat, 12–4, July and Aug 10–6; adm)* is also known as the Cave of the Sorcerer, for its rare engraving of a Magdalenian man with a mask-like cartoon face and a body like that of a deer. It also has a dappled horse among other engravings, and a small museum.

To Le Bugue-sur-Vézère

From Les Eyzies, the D 706 follows the Vézère down to the village and Romanesque church of Campagne, and the 15th-century **Château de Campagne**, given a William Morris neo-Gothic facelift in the 19th century. There's been no tinkering, however, with the magnificent trees in the château's park and its forest stair, the Chemin des Dames. The château is used for archaeological exhibits, but the park is open (© 53 07 44 74).

The Vézère flows broadly past **Le Bugue**, a market town offering a good day of family outings, including a pair of caves. The prehistoric **Grotte de Bara-Bahau**, 2km to the northwest *(Apr–mid Nov, 9–11.30 and 2.30–5.30; July and Aug 9–6; adm)* belonged to the bears before graffiti artists moved in some 35,000 years ago. Its walls, 'as soft as white cheese' as one prehistorian put it, are covered with rustic flint-blade carvings from the Aurignacian culture; among them are animals (including a rare silhouette of a bear), hand or claw marks, and other mysterious signs. The second cave is a chasm, the **Gouffre de Proumeyssac**, 3km south on the D 31E *(Feb, Mar, Oct–Dec 10–12 and 2–5; Apr, May and Sept 9.30–12 and 2–5.30, June–Aug 9–7; wheelchair access; adm)*. For centuries protected by demonic legends, Proumeyssac was explored only in 1907; its nickname, the 'Crystal Cathedral' comes from an extraordinary domed chamber of yellow and white stalactites and draperies. Although freshwater fish lack the bright colours of their salty kin, Le Bugue's **Aquarium du Périgord Noir** *(mid Nov–Feb 2–5; Mar and Apr 10–12 and 2–6; May–Nov 10–7; till midnight Tues, Thurs and Sat in July and Aug; adm)* brings out the charms of pike, sturgeon, eels and turtles in imaginative indoor and outdoor settings; in one hall the fish swim right over your head. Just beyond, the new **Village du Bourant** *(open 10–7, Tues and Fri till 9pm in the summer)* makes a game attempt to re-create Périgord of a century ago with craft demonstrations such as walnut oil pressing and the carving of *sabots*, or wooden clogs—you can see how one of these tossed into a machine could mother a new word—*sabotage*.

From Le Bugue the D 31E follows the Vézère to its confluence with the Dordogne at Limeuil (*see* p.136); becoming the D 51, the road crosses the Dordogne for Le Buisson, from where the D 25 goes to Cadouin (*see* p.134).

Where to Stay and Eating Out

Les Eyzies ✉ 24620

Overlooking the centre of Les Eyzies yet far from the summer brouhaha at Rocher Penne, ***Du Centenaire**, ℭ 53 09 97 18, is a member of the plush Relais et Châteaux, and along with extremely pleasant rooms, offers a pool, sauna and gym (450–950F). What draws the crowds, however, is the Centenaire's award-winning restaurant, where chef Roland Mazère prepares a daringly different menu based on the freshest local ingredients, accompanied with an *embarass de choix* from one of the best wine cellars in the Dordogne (menus from 260F, closed Nov–Mar). Founded nearly a century ago by the discoverer of the first Cro-Magnon bones, creeper-covered ***Hôtel Cro-Magnon**, ℭ 53 06 97 06, is still in the Leysalles family, with the same friendly atmosphere that attracted the first visitors to the Dordogne; the garden annexe near the pool has the nicer rooms (370–570F, closed mid-Oct–Apr). The restaurant, with its old oak beams, is charming both visually and on the palate, where it counts (try the *lotte aux morilles*; menus from 140F). Bang in the middle of Les Eyzies, the family-run ****Hôtel du Centre**, ℭ 53 06 97 13, manages to maintain a modicum of seclusion, thanks to a pedestrian-only square by the Vézère; comfortable rooms 260–300F. The restaurant serves regional specialities, indoors or out under the parasols (from 140F, closed Nov–Mar). Another choice in the centre, the sturdy stone ****Auberge du Musée**, Rue du Musée, ℭ 53 06 90 97, offers the added plus of a shady terrace and pool (230–310F, closed Oct–Easter).

Outside Les Eyzies

There are several places to stay in Marquay (24620), beginning with ****Des Bories**, La Bourg, ℭ 53 29 64 15, a charming family-run country hotel enjoying lovely views, garden and pool (230–440F). The adjacent restaurant makes a brave and usually successful effort to offer a change of pace in its menus ranging from 95–190F: rabbit with curry sauce, thin slices (*aiguillettes*) of duck with raspberry vinegar (closed 15 Nov–Palm Sun). The **Domaine de Lesparre**, on the D 32 between Les Eyzies and Manaurie, ℭ 53 06 94 44, is a British-run country guesthouse, offering cosy bed and breakfast (175F a room, breakfast 25F). The **Ferme Auberge Claude Veyret**, on the D6 overlooking Bardenat, ℭ 53 29 68 44, has a handful of comfortable rooms to let year round (200F with supper), while good home-grown ingredients are the basis for the traditional and more unusual (*tourtière aux salsifis et confits d'oie*) offerings from the kitchen (menu 120F)

In Campagne (24260), the ****Hôtel de Campagne** has 17 tranquil rooms and a good restaurant: try the *escalope de foie gras aux fruits rouges* and fillet of trout (menus from 85F, closed mid Oct–Palm Sunday).

Down the Dordogne I

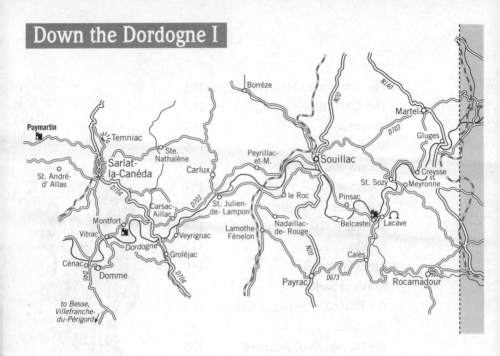

...Laisse, laisse-moi faire, et un jour,
ma Dordogne
Si je devine bien, on te connaîtra mieux
Et Garonne et le Rhône, et
ces autres grands dieux
En auront quelque envie
et possible vergogne

La Boétie

La Boétie, born in Sarlat, didn't live long enough to compose many
rhapsodies after this one, but he may well be smiling up in heaven to see
how famous his Dordogne has become. Its name simply means the Dore
water, *Dore d'eau*; it begins with a waterfall gushing from the volcanic
Monts Dore in the Auvergne, before shooting through the steep, dark
gorges of the Corrèze to the mellower countryside at Argentat and
Beaulieu; by the time it makes its first appearance in Quercy, under the
watchful eye of the mighty feudal castle of Castelnau, the river's queenly
character has been completely formed, and from here on it meanders to
the ocean, dreamily and with a rare elegance, creating melting river-
scapes in hairpin turns, or *cingles*, as it flows through Périgord and

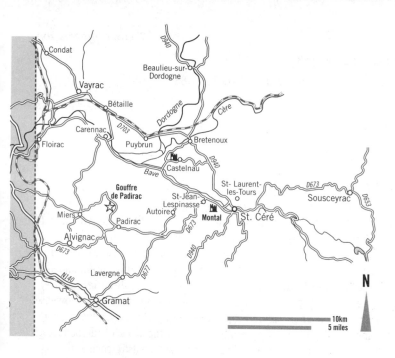

Gironde. At Bergerac, it becomes a wine river, creating the perfect climatic conditions for the likes of Monbazillac and Saint-Emilion. To defend such a prize, enough castles were built along its banks, especially during the Hundred Years' War, to make it the Loire of the Middle Ages.

The Dordogne Quercynois

Before gracing the *département* that bears its name, the Dordogne flows through Quercy, or the *département* of the Lot. Like much of Quercy this is rugged limestone *causse* country, shot with velvet-green valleys and pocked by dramatic cliffs and caves. One of the first is the biggest maw of them all, the Gouffre de Padirac; other five-star attractions here are Rocamadour, which draws in nearly as many visitors as beleaguered Euro-Disney, and the Romanesque carvings in Souillac that outclass anything in snooty old Périgord.

Getting Around

The main SNCF line between Paris and Toulouse stops at Brive and Souillac (information ℂ 55 23 50 50). Get off at Brive to transfer to Bretenoux, Bétaille (4km from Carennac) or Vayrac on the Brive–Aurillac line, or St-Denis-lès Martel, Padirac-Rocamadour on the secondary Brive–Toulouse line. Buses link St-Céré with the Gare Bretenoux-Biars, 8km away.

Bretenoux: © 65 38 59 53

Saint-Céré: Place de la République, © 65 38 11 85

market days

Bretenoux: Tuesdays and Saturdays

St-Ceré: Saturdays

Argentat and Beaulieu-sur-Dordogne

At Argentat the Dordogne suddenly turns from a swift mountain river into a civilized waterway. The Romans founded a port town here, and for centuries the boatmen of Argentat would load timber, cheese, leather, pelts and wine onto their flat-bottomed *gabares* and make their way down to Bordeaux where the *gabares* themselves would be sold for firewood. The old quay at Argentat has several on display; the town itself, under its sloping *lauze* roofs, has the air of a delightful, prosperous pensioner. **Beaulieu**, a lovely town 25km downriver, is even more thoroughly medieval, built around a showcase 12th–13th-century Benedictine abbey church called **St-Pierre**, with a magnificent, complex tympanum of the Last Judgment, stylistically similar to the work of the School of Toulouse in Moissac or Soulliac, although here Christ has his arms outstretched in triumph while a carnival of apocalyptic monsters roll below across the lintel, supported by a strange figure Freda White described as 'flowing upward like a flame of prayer'. The whole inspired abbot Suger, the inventor of Gothic, in his choice of a tympanum for Paris's St-Denis in 1140.

The Château de Castelnau and Bretenoux

The Dordogne bristles with castles of all kinds, but the oldest, the burnished red **Château de Castelnau**, is the most redoubtable of them all, rising high on a conical, 750ft outcropping over the confluence of the Dordogne and the Cère *(guided tours year round, morning and afternoon, closed Tues; adm)*. Begun in the year 1000, building evolved over the centuries, and today it's rated the second military castle in France after Pierrefonds in the Oise. Which is only fair, for its disdainful lords claimed to be 'the second barons of Christendom'. In 1184, when their liege lord the Count of Toulouse put them under the suzerainty of the nearby viscounts of Turenne, they were so insulted that only after the King of France intervened did they agree to pay only the most begrudging tribute to Turenne: one egg, ceremoniously transported by a yoke of four oxen. In 1851 much of the château was damaged by arson, but Jean Mouliéret, tenor at the Opéra Comique, came to the rescue, rebuilding and sumptuously refurnishing one wing. Inside you can see the Grande Salle, where the Etats du Quercy met, fragments of 11th-century sculpture, the chapel, vaulted cellars and the deep, long-forgotten oubliettes, where seven skeletons were discovered. Clustered at the foot of the stone behemoth, the hamlet of **Prudhomat-Castelnau** is worth a stop for its 15th-century **Collégiale**, with Renaissance windows and sculptures.

The biggest urban venture of the lords of Castelnau, however, was the bastide of **Bretenoux** founded on the left bank of the Cère in 1277. The grid plan survives, as do some medieval arcades and houses in Place des Consuls.

St-Céré and St-Laurent-les-Tours

From Bretenoux it's 9km south on the D 940 to **St-Céré**, a charming art-colony town romantically set on the banks of the Bave, 'babbler', which tumbles down the *causse* to join the Dordogne. Pilgrims used to come to see the relics in the church of **Ste-Spérie**, a virgin who refused to marry a pagan and literally lost her head over him. Spérie then picked up her head and gave it a last wash before expiring (794). Her bones are in the Carolingian crypt, along with a curious Celtic altar, but it's only open for 12 days around her feast day in October. **Place du Mercadial**, the main market square, is surrounded by half-timbered buildings; the stone benches on the Rue Pasteur corner were for centuries used by fishermen to display their catch. Other medieval houses line the Rue du Mazel, Impasse Lagarouste and Quai des Récollets.

The first artist to establish himself in the area was Jean Lurçat, whose works are on permanent display in St-Céré's **Galerie du Casino** *(closed Tues)* and up at the craggy medieval towers of **St-Laurent-les-Tours**. These were purchased in 1945 by Lurçat, who had fallen in love with the area while fighting with the Maquis; they now form the **Atelier Musée Jean Lurçat** *(open 15 days around Easter; 14 July–30 Sept, 9–12 and 2.30–6.30; adm)*.

Jean Lurçat and the Renaissance of French Tapestry

After extensive travels in Spain, North Africa and the Middle East, painter Jean Lurçat (1892–1966) spent his first four decades covering canvases with his memories of the colourful designs of the indigenous peoples he had met, marked by a streak of fantasy and interest in natural forms. In 1939, Lurçat was appointed head designer of the Aubusson tapestry factory, a task that marked a turning point both in his career and in French tapestry. For by the 20th century, the proud art of Aubusson, the Gobelins and Beauvais had hit rock bottom, reduced to endlessly reproducing cartoons from the age of the big Louies, themselves servile imitations of paintings. Lurçat's great contribution was to return the art of tapestry to the weavers, creating cartoons that respected the medium and its techniques, combining abstract forms with a return to medieval stylization (see his famous *Apocalypse* of 1948 in Assy, Haute Savoie). His main leitmotiv at this time, a colourful cockerel or *Coq Arlequin*, was a symbol to restore Gaullic pluck after the war.

East of St-Céré: the Ségala

The region to the east of St-Céré is called the Ségala, the 'rye land' (*seigle*), where wheat refuses to grow. Limestone gives way to grey granite here on the frontier of the Cantal—the cold spot of France. There are a few things to see in this far corner of Quercy: the striking 15th-century pilgrimage church of **Notre-Dame de Verdale**, near Latouille-Lentillac, clinging precariously to the rock face high over the Tolerme gorge—take the narrow road off the D 30 to the top and walk down. Further east, old grey **Sousceyrac** is the largest town in the region, once fortified (see the Porte Notre-Dame, topped with a chapel) and ruled by the viscounts of Turenne. They are responsible for the 15th-century **Château de Grugnac**, 1km north, still bearing its charming *lauze* roof.

West of St-Céré: Château de Montal to Autoire

Only 2km from St-Céré, the golden **Château de Montal** was the special project of Jeanne de Balzac, daughter of Robert de Balzac, who had served as governor of Pisa during the wars of Italy. Enraptured by the Italian Renaissance, Jeanne decided to replant some of it in this corner of *la France profonde* as a surprise gift for her son, Robert, while he was fighting in Italy; much to Jeanne' despair, he was killed before ever setting eyes on it. After surviving all subsequent wars and the Revolution, the château fell at the end of the 19th century into the greedy hands of a speculator who spent 22 years stripping it of every decoration. In 1908, when only the frame of the staircase remained, an oil tycoon named Maurice Fénaille stepped in. He bought Jeannne's château, repurchased as many of its original works as he could, and had copies made of the bits the Americans wouldn't sell back. The sculptures purchased by the Louvre were returned when Fénaille donated the whole to the state in 1913.

From the outside, Montal *(open Palm Sun–Oct 9.30–12 and 2.30–6, closed Sat except in July and Aug; adm)* looks like a typical medieval castle, but once you step inside the rough walls a magical courtyard opens up, decorated with lovely façades, ornate dormers and an imaginative frieze over 100ft long, probably carved by the same sculptors who worked in Biron (*see* p.284); note the intertwined initials of Jeanne and her sons Robert and Dordé. Seven of the finest Renaissance portrait busts in France are set in niches between the windows, and are said to accurately depict the features of Jeanne and her family. The decoration around one of the windows, where legend has it Jeanne often sat, watching for Robert's return, sums up her sorrow—a knight holds a scroll reading *Plus d'espoir* (no more hope). Death accompanies a decapitated youth gripping his skull.

The interior is just as beautiful as the courtyard: the meticulously carved stair in golden cream-coloured stone, the grand chimney supporting a heraldic stag with golden antlers, the guard room vaulted with 'basket handle' arches, the walnut table carved from a single tree, the rooms furnished with Renaissance furniture, ceramics, paintings and tapestries. Even the graffiti on the walls is quality—left by Léon Gambetta of Cahors, the hero of 1870.

From here the D 763 ascends past the village of **St-Jean-Lespinasse** with some Romanesque carvings inside its fort-like church, to the **Grotte de Presque** *(open Apr–mid Oct, 9–12 and 2–6, July and Aug 8–7; adm)*, with chambers full of draperies, stone waterfalls and other geological wonders. Another 4km down the D 673 and a right turn will take you to the **Cirque d'Autoire**, where a belvedere overlooks the real, 100ft-high falls of the river Autoire; across the bridge and up the path is a tremendous bird's-eye view stretching from the *cirque* (natural amphitheatre) to the little village of **Autoire** and all the way to the Dordogne valley.

Often picked out as an example of a true Quercynois village, Autoire's steep brown-tiled roofs form an exquisite ensemble around its Romanesque/Renaissance church; even in the 1700s various nobles and bourgeois of Paris chose it to build holiday homes. From here continue along the D 135 towards another exceptionally lovely village, **Loubressac**, a 15th-century eagle's nest overlooking the confluence of the Bave, the Cère and the Dordogne.

The Gouffre de Padirac

A *gouffre* is an immense hole, which is easy to remember if you recall that French trappers named the little burrowing critters they found in America *gaufres*, or gophers. Had a gopher dug the pit in Padirac, it would have to have been the size of the *Titanic*—this chasm plunges down 296ft through the limestone of the Causse de Gramat before forming 13 miles of galleries—or at least that's the length that's been explored so far.

For centuries this great opening, 114ft in diameter, was regarded as the entrance to hell itself. The story goes that St Martin was riding his mule through Padirac, downcast at his failure to convert any pagans on the *causse*, when the Devil happened by, with a squadron of demons, all bearing sackfuls of condemned souls. Satan offered to hand them over to Martin if the saint could get over an obstacle of his creation. Martin agreed, and Satan stomped his foot and opened up a great chasm. Martin said a little prayer and spurred on his mule, which leapt across the abyss (you can still see the hoofprints); the furious Satan gave Martin the souls and leapt with his devils into the pit, which took them straight to hell. In 1889, Edouard Martel, one of the founding fathers of speleology, made the first scientic exploration of the *gouffre*; by 1898 it was opened to the public. Recent investigations have uncovered tools and animal bones from around 50,000 BC, 8km from the entrance.

The 90-minute guided tour of the Gouffre *(open 9–11.30 and 2–5 Apr–mid Oct, all day in Aug; adm exp)* takes you through a subterraean mile and a half, where the temperature is a constant 13°C (55°F). Two lifts and a stair bring you down into the *gouffre*. This immense cavity was formed by water dissolving the limestone over millions of years. The chamber was domed until the weight of the roof grew too great and it collapsed; now the floor is covered by a pyramid of rubble. The tour continues past a spring and down a long underground canyon formed by a river. At the end Padirac's gondoliers await to row you along the Rivière Plane, the 'smooth river', which flows underground into the Dordogne, passing the *Grande Pendeloque*, or Great Pendant, an enormous stalactite that almost touches the water. The gondoliers leave you to carry on by foot up the narrow *Pas du Crocodile*, past a 130ft stalactite pillar into the *Salle des Grands Gours*. A *gour* is a natural limestone dam, and here the *gours* create a fascinating series of basins of clear water, flowing one into the other, with a 20ft waterfall and a green lake at the end. Beyond lies another little lake, the *Lac Supérieur*, fed only by rainwater penetrating the limestone. Last of all is the climactic *Salle du Grand Dôme*—an uncollapsed *gouffre*, as it were, a majestic vaulted space which soars up to 305ft.

If you emerge from the *gouffre* with some francs still jingling in your pocket after the entrance fees and various tips there's exotic flora and fauna to see in the nearby **Zoo le Tropicorama** *(open daily mid-May–Sept).*

Where to Stay and Eating Out

St-Céré ✉ 46400

The ivy-covered ★★★**Le Coq Arlequin et Paris**, 1 Bd. du Dr-Roux, ✆ 65 38 37 27, was the secret headquarters of the British Supply and Intelligence Organization for the local Resistance. The same family, the Bizats, still own the hotel and have recently redecorated the rooms to make them more comfortable than ever. The hotel restaurant (and pool) are 2km down the road at the **Grill du Coq Arlequin**, ✆ 65 38 28 41, where pure Quercy tradition reigns in decor and in the delights that appear on the tables; delicious menus at 100 and 135F. ★★★**France**, Av. F. de-Maynard, ✆ 65 38 02 16, offers cosy modern rooms, a flower garden and pool, and a delicious smoked-salmon salad on the 100F menu; others are at 140–190F. Other choices include ★★**Hôtel du Touring**, Place de la République, ✆ 65 38 30 08, and ★★★**Ric**, 2km south in St-Vincent-du-Pendit, ✆ 65 38 04 08, which has only six rooms but they enjoy marvellous views over St-Céré and a beautiful pool. Out towards Montal, the modern ★★★**Les Trois Soleils de Montal**, Les Près-de-Montal, ✆ 65 38 20 61, is a well-designed modern hotel in a small park, where a fitness room, sauna, tennis and a pool come in handy if you over-indulge in the chef's caramelized pineapple with vanilla cream (menus at 125–280F).

Autoire ✉ 46400

Delightful **Alta-Tarris**, by the church, ✆ 65 38 06 54, has a good selection of menus from 80–140F, with many Quercynois dishes (much the same specialities as you find in Périgord); closed Tues.

Loubressac ✉ 46130

The 17th-century **Château de Gamont**, on the D 30, ✆ 65 38 52 05, an extremely pleasant bed-and-breakfast, offers rooms furnished with antiques (from 280F, to small apartments for 600F).

Padirac ✉ 46500

Not much choice here, but the large white ★★**Auberge de Mathieu**, ✆ 65 33 64 68, has seven comfortable rooms and a pool and menus from 75F.

Carennac to Lacave

This stretch of the Dordogne hugs islets and high cliffs as it flows past several châteaux, a fascinating Romanesque abbey connected with the sweet-tempered archbishop Fénelon, the handsome medieval town of Martel and the splendid stalactite grotto at Lacave.

Carennac: ✆ 65 10 97 01

Martel: Hôtel de la Raymondie, ✆ 65 37 30 03

market days

Martel: Wednesdays and Saturdays

Carennac

From the river Carennac presents a charming higgledy-piggledy cluster of roofs, walls and turrets around its famous honey-coloured **Prieuré St-Pierre** *(open daily July–Sept 10–7.30; at other times, ring the Syndicat d'Initiative, 65 38 58 12)*. Founded in 932 by Frotard, Vicomte de Cahors, the priory was given by the bishop of Cahors to Cluny *c.* 1040. Fortified in the 16th century it managed to repulse Protestant attacks, fortunately preserving some of the finest Romanesque art in the area: the beautiful 12th-century tympanum over the porch, sculpted by the Toulouse school with their favourite scene from the *Apocalypse* (Christ blessing in a mandorla), surrounded by the Evangelists and apostles, divided into registers (as on Cahors cathedral). The frieze below is decorated with an unusual zigzag pattern of animals; in the shadowy interior, capitals carved with primitive birds, animals and monsters add to its atmosphere of archaic mystery. A painting of the Evangelists survives in one 15th-century chapel.

The **cloister**, with its one Romanesque and three flamboyant Gothic galleries, was rescued from its fate as a pigsty in 1928. After the

Revolution, when most of the carvings were hammered, the villagers sold off the priory's art, except a piece they especially loved, the 15th-century *Mise en Tombeau* (in the **Salle Capitulaire** off the closter), a poignant composition of eight intricately detailed figures. The Virgin's arms reach out stiffly in grief; Nicodemus and Joseph of Arimathea, dressed in Renaissance costumes, hold the shroud, while John, Mary Magdalene and the women in biblical draperies mourn (in the folds you can see the original paint). Here too are 17th-century bas-reliefs on the life of Christ and a moving *Pietà* carved from Carennac's stone.

At the south end of the cloisters, the old kitchen, with its monumental fireplace, and refectory have been converted into a conference centre for the commune. During the work a 15th-century mural was uncovered, known as the *Dit des Trois Morts et des Trois Vifs*—three skeletons warning three cavaliers to reflect on earthly vanity. Over one of the fireplaces is a portrait of a dean of Carennac, François de Salignac. In the 17th century, the deanery became a personal fief of the influential Salignac de la Mothe-Fénelon family, whose château is just to the north on the Dordogne (*see* p.118); in 1674, the post was inherited by this dean's nephew, François de Salignac de la Mothe-Fénelon (1651–1715), who went on to further glory as the Archbishop of Cambrai.

Fénelon

Known for his gentle eloquence as the 'Swan of Cambrai', Fénelon was bred for the church from the earliest age and attended the seminary of St-Sulpice in Paris. In 1674, he inherited Carennac from his uncle and was given the special task of bringing Protestant women back to the Catholic fold. Gentle, reasonable, well-spoken and extremely tolerant for his bigoted age, Fénelon was so successful at the task that he attracted the attention of the pious Madame de Maintenon, morganatic wife of Louis XIV and herself a converted Protestant. In 1689 she had Louis appoint Fénelon tutor of his grandson and heir, the singularly charmless Duke of Burgundy. The task took up so much of Fénelon's time that, in spite of tradition, he hardly had time to return to Carennac to compose his celebrated allegory for the duke's instruction, *Télémaque*. This book, a lesson in truth, justice and virtue, follows the life of Odysseus' son Telemachus in Salentum, an aristocratic utopia where seven strictly defined classes lived a simple life and dressed according to their station, hence eliminating one of the banes of his time: luxury born from pride and the need to pay for it by soaking the poor. Tradition has it that Fénelon wrote his romance in Carennac's 'Tour de Télémaque'; Ile Barrade, facing Carennac in the Dordogne, was renamed 'Ile Calypso' after the island in the novel.

It was during this period that the unworldly Fénelon became attracted to the quietist ideals of mystic Madame Guyon, who preached the possibility of abandoning the soul to God's love without any of the outer disciplines or authority of the Church. In 1695, having been recently appointed to the princely post of Archbishop of Cambrai, Fénelon undertook to defend her preachings against the doughty Bishop of Meaux, Jacques Bénigne Bousset, who upheld the authority of the Church. 'It is hard to get a great prelate condemned for trusting overmuch in the love of God,' as Albert Guérard commented, but by 1699 Bousset had succeeded so completely that Fénelon's work had been condemned by the Pope.

With that, the king dismissed him from his tutorial post (his work went down the drain anyway, when the Duke died three years before his terrible grandfather). Even worse, *Télémaque* was published in court without his permission, and was read by Louis as a satyrical comment on his arrogant, bankrupt reign. Fénelon spend the rest of his life as an outcast in Cambrai. Without him, his beloved Carennac fell into ruin and no longer sent him any rents to relieve his poverty. For all that, he asked to be buried there when he died, but the request was denied. As a posthumous apology for Fénelon's treatment from Louis XIV, the Regent had *Télémaque* printed; in the 18th century it went into over 180 editions.

Around Carennac

Taking the bridge over the Dordogne from Carennac, a right turn will take you to **Tauriac**, where the church has some well-preserved 15th-century murals of ladies. A left turn at the bridge will lead you to Vayrac, from which the D 119 leads up a steep hill to a site called **Puy-d'Issolud**, a broad plateau that is one of many possible candidates for the lost site of Uxellodunum, where the Gauls made their last stand against Julius Caesar's victorious legions. Ruins on the plateau have been identified as belonging to Celtic fortifications, camps and temples; there is a small **museum** on the site.

Martel

Proud, staunchly medieval Martel, the 'City of Seven Towers', resolves under the microscope to a rustic village of 1400 souls. Severely depopulated over the last century, today many of its empty houses are being restored as summer homes for people from far away. Still, the population isn't nearly big enough for Martel. However small, this is a real city, and beautiful as it is it wears a melancholy air with so few around to share its beauty.

Martel means 'hammer', like the three hammers the city wears on its coat of arms, and like the hammer wielded by Charles Martel, scourge of the Muslims; a legend credits the grandfather of Charlemagne with founding the city in the 700s. In 1219, Martel received its charter as a free commune, a fief of the viscounts of Turenne; so it remained until 1738, when it was snapped up by the French crown. In central Place des Consuls are the covered market and the huge **Palais de la Raymondie**, begun by the Turenne viscounts *c.* 1300, now the town hall. Its *beffroi* is the first of the 'seven towers'. Another is the bell tower of **St-Maur**, a fortified Gothic church built into the walls that retains a portal from the 12th century with a relief of Christ Pantocrator in the style of Moissac. Inside is some excellent **stained glass** from 1531 with scenes of the Passion, believed to be the work of students of Arnaut de Moles, the master of Auch cathedral. A few sculptural decorations can be seen in the odd corners; for a puzzle, see if you can find the three sleeping monks—the two angels under blankets don't count.

For the other five towers, you'll need to tour the rest of Martel. It won't take long; there are scarcely more than a dozen streets. One of the towers is the **Maison Fabri**, behind the market, where Henri Court-Mantel died from a fever shortly after his pillage of Rocamadour. The **Tour de Tournamire** at the northern gate was used for defence and as a prison.

North of Martel, at the northernmost tip of Quercy, is a sleepy corner called the Causse de Martel, napping under its cover of oak and beech forests. The villages of **Cavagnac** and **Lasvaux** both have simple Romanesque churches.

Gluges and Lacave

The Dordogne is at its scenic best between Martel and Souillac, meandering cheerfully through some dramatic countryside, and often hemmed in by steep cliffs. Directly south of Martel, the riverside village of **Gluges** fairly cowers beneath one of these lofty rock walls. There's an unusual church, half cut into the rock; the local baron, Gérard de Mirandol, built it after his return from the crusades in 1108. A cave, converted to a fortress in the Middle Ages, can be reached from the village by a stairway carved into the cliff. Another cliff across the Dordogne, the **Cirque de Montvalent**, forms a striking natural amphitheatre; the river formed it ages ago before it chose its present course.

From here, the D 23 to **Creysse** follows the river—terrifically scenic, if a bit dangerous; it climbs up and down the cliffs on only one lane. Creysse is an exquisite village built around a Romanesque church, and it attracts more than its share of tourists. Further downstream, well-named **Lacave** can show you one of one of the most spectacular subterranean wonders of France, open to the public since 1905 *(open daily Apr–mid July, 9–12 and 2–6; mid July –Aug, 9–7; Sept–Oct, 9.30–12, 2–5.30; adm)*. It may not be as famous as Padirac, but Lacave offers some unique sights. From the entrance, you'll travel on a miners' train, then up an elevator into the caverns—a mile of them, including the 'Lac des Mirages', where the reflections of stalactites in the water give the illusion of an underwater city. Some of the caverns are illuminated by back light for strange phosphorescent effects. Lacave excels in unusual formations, 'eccentrics' like the pillar in the shape of a *tarasque*, the mythical monster of Tarascon, and the 'column of the spiders' feet'. From Lacave the D 43 continues to Souillac, passing the **Château de Belcastel** in a perfect cliff-top setting over the river *(guided tours of the garden only, in July and Aug)* to meet one of the most graceful iron bridges you'll ever see, at Pinsac; an anonymous engineer of the *Ponts et Chaussées*, France's national public works office, designed it in the 1930s.

Where to Stay and Eating Out

Carennac ✉ 46110

  Auberge du Vieux Quercy, © 65 10 96 59, located in a former post house, has a fair-sized pool, garden and pretty rooms; the restaurant is an idyllic place to linger over a 95F menu featuring *confit de canard à la ciboulette et au jus de* *citron*; there's another menu at 145F (closed Mon). **Hostellerie Fénelon, © 65 10 96 46, at the entrance to the village has authentic provincial rooms and a pool as well; in the garden dining room, try the *feuilleté de morilles au jus du truffe* if you're feeling flush, but the 90–180F menus are a good bet, too. The cheapest rooms of all are in the adequate **Des Touristes**, © 65 38 47 07.

Gluges ✉ 46600

The ★★★**Hôtel des Falaises** enjoys a perfect setting under the cliffs, beautiful gardens and a restaurant (© 65 37 33 59; menus at 95–185–300F; try the stuffed salmon). Creysse is popular and known to all, and so is its hotel, the ★★**Auberge de l'Isle**—but deservedly so: lovely rooms, attentive service, a pool and a terrace over a canal, all at reasonable prices (© 65 32 22 01). At Meyronne, near Gluges, ★★**La Terrasse**, © 65 32 21 60 is an old stone mansion overlooking the river, with modern rooms and an excellent restaurant where you can take the easy way out with a 70F menu or suffer the full force of the foie gras, truffles and *magret* for 270F; alternatively, try one of several compromise choices in between. Meyronne also has a camp site, near the beach along the river; another camp site, the **Vert-Rive** has a beautiful setting on the D 43 just outside Pinsac. Across the river from Meyronne, the ★**Hotel de la Renaissance** on the village square of St-Sozy offers a 55F lunch menu and inexpensive rooms.

Lacave ✉ 46200

Just west of town, on the river, the proprietors of the *Relais et Châteaux* ★★★★**Château de la Treyne**, © 65 32 66 66, have spared no expense to make this the showpiece of the region: stately gardens, antique furnishings, tapestries, luxurious rooms with river views, along with a highly rated—and correspondingly expensive—restaurant (menus from 350F; also 180F for lunch). For less than half the price, you can do well staying at ★★★**Le Pont de l'Ouysse**, © 65 37 87 04; here too there is a formidable restaurant, a bit more adventurous in the kitchen than the Treyne; menus 160–520F. There's also a budget choice, the ★**Hôtel des Grottes**, © 65 37 87 06.

Rocamadour

From Lacave it's 18km of scenery south to the holy village of Rocamadour, which proudly bills itself as the 'Second Site in France' (after Mont-St-Michel). There are a couple of tempting stops on the way—**Calès**, a picturesque little hamlet with a midget château, and a bit further on where the road crosses the blue-green Ouysse, a 13th-century working mill, the **Moulin de Cougnaguet**, fortified against flour thieves and—by the looks of it—against time as well *(open April–Oct, 10–12 and 2–5; adm)*.

You know you're almost there when the road leads up to **L'Hospitalet**, where everyone stops for the picture-postcard view across to Rocamadour, wedged tight under an overhanging cliff, while far, far below the little Alzou cuts deep in its gorge. It is a view that has been enjoyed especially after 1050, when a hostel–hospital was founded by Hélène de Castelnau for pilgrims en route to Compostella. L'Hospitalet was inhabited as early as in the Upper Paleolithic era; its **Grotte des Merveilles** has, besides stalactites, lakes and other subterranean fancies, mostly fantastical rock formations, and some deteriorated art-work (negative hands, animals) that dates back to 20,000 BC *(open Apr, May, June, Sept, Oct 10–11.30, 2–6; July–Aug 9–12 and 1.30–7)*. It suggests that the remarkable site of Rocamadour was a holy place long before any of its stories were written.

Legends and History

The late 11th-century origins of Rocamadour's shrine are murky enough, and coincide neatly with the founding of L'Hospitalet's pilgrimage hostel; if the Benedictines of Tulle, promoters of the cult of the Black Virgin, were at all inspired by the presence of Compostella pilgrims, they certainly weren't the only ones to suddenly find miracles along that great road. The cult was given a big boost in 1166, when a man's body was discovered buried near the altar. Over the centuries, the story evolved that this unknown was none other than St Zaccheus, the publican who climbed the tree to see Jesus. Later, he and his wife, St Veronica (of the holy handkerchief), fled Palestine in an angel-powered boat and lived near Limoges; when Veronica died, Zaccheus came here as a hermit and built the first sanctuaries in the cliff face. The locals called him 'the lover' or *Amator* for his devotion, and hence Roc-Amadour, the rock of the lover or lover of rock. A second attraction was Durandal, the famous sword of Roland; just before he died at Roncesvalles, the hero con-fided his blade to St Michael, and the Archangel hurled it from the Pyrenees like a javelin straight into Rocamadour's cliff.

Yet always the chief attraction was the blackened, goddess-like statue of the Virgin, whose cult, along with that of chivalry, grew by leaps and bounds at the time of the crusades. Rocamadour's first important patron was Henry II of England, who endowed much of its treasure. His wayward eldest son, the Young King Henry Court-Mantel—and companion of Bertrand de Born (*see* 'Topics', p.43)—stole it in 1183 to pay his *routiers* in his war against his own father; he even, some say, replaced the famous Durandel with his own sword. By the time the plunderers reached Martel, the Black Virgin got her revenge, striking young Henry down with a fever. Full of remorse, he asked his father's forgiveness, had a halter put on his neck and laid himself naked in a bed of ashes and died. The Bishop of Limoges refrained from excommunicating the dead man when his grieving father promised to replace Rocamadour's losses.

Rocamadour quickly recovered to become one of the busiest pilgrimage shrines in France. Saints Louis, Dominic, Bernard, Anthony of Padua, Engelbert and the blessed Raymond Lull came, as did the kings of France and countless others, especially on the days of pardon and plenary indulgence, when the chronicles say 30,000 thronged into the village to pick up their Get Out of Purgatory Free Card. Others who came were less willing: thousands of criminals, Albigensian heretics and men who broke the Truce of God by fighting during Lent were ordered by ecclesiastical courts to make the pilgrimage, to climb up the famous steps on their knees, to be bound in chains and led to the Virgin to apologize (*amende hon-orable*) and be purified by the priest. The priest would then strike off the chains, and present the shriven one with a certificate and a little lead medal with a picture of the Virgin to take back home.

Rocamadour suffered a near-fatal setback during the Wars of Religion, when the Huguenot Captain Bessonies came to lay waste and desecrate the shrine, hacking the relics of St Amadour to bits and leaving only the Virgin and her bell intact. After nearly three centuries of neglect, the bishops of Cahors began to restore the shrines in the 1850s—read over-restore in many cases—giving the buildings a Disneylandish air that only increases in the high summer, when Rocamadour is swamped by coaches, and visitors have to queue just to get into the narrow lanes of the village. Arrive early in the morning to avoid the worst; better still, come in the autumn when Rocamadour is at its most magical.

Getting Around

Rocamador's railway station, on the Brive–Figeac line, is 4km from town and connected by taxi; you can hire bikes here, but book them ahead in the summer (✆ 65 33 63 05). Only the cars of visitors with bookings in Rocamadour's hotels are allowed in the village, and in July and August the nearer car parks outside the gates fill up fast, when you should park on top at the château or a 600m walk away at L'Hospitalet (*see* above) and walk or take the lifts into town. The lifts are also handy if you have difficulty walking (the steps aren't steep, but there are 223 of them). You may find the 25F fare, one way, may give you a sudden spurt of energy to tackle them anyway.

Tourist Information

Rue de la Couronnerie, ✆ 65 33 62 59. Stop here for the hours of the guided tour of the shrines *(June–Sept, daily exc Sun)*. At other times, make arrangements in advance through Pélerinage de Rocamadour, 46500 Gramat, ✆ 65 33 63 29.

The Village

The holy road from L'Hospitalet enters Rocamadour by way of the 13th-century **Porte du Figuier**, one of four gates that defended the village's one real road. Once in, past a gauntlet of souvenir stands and a waxworks museum, you'll find the lift near the second gate, towered **Porte Salmon**. Beyond, the 15th-century Palais de la Couronnerie is now the **Hôtel de Ville** and tourist office, where two tapestries of local flora and fauna by Jean Lurçat are on display. The street continues through another gate into the **Quartier du Coustalou**, prettiest and least restored part of the village, with jumbly little houses and a fortified mill.

The **Grand Escalier** into the holy city begins back at Place de la Carretta. The first 144 steps lead up to **Place des Senhals**, where merchants sold the Virgin's lead medals, or *senhals* in Occitan. Rocamadour's oldest street, Rue de la Mercerie, extends from here, with the 14th-century **Maison de la Pomette** at its end. From here, continue up through the gate under the over-restored **Fort**, sometime residence of the bishops of Tulle. Tulle remained in charge of Rocamadour throughout the Middle Ages, despite attempts by Marcilhac and other abbeys to muscle in on the action.

The Parvis de St-Amadour

At the top of the steps the small square, Parvis de St-Amadour, is the centre of the holy city, where the pilgrim could visit seven churches just as in Rome, but in a much abbreviated space. These days only Notre-Dame, St-Sauveur and the Crypt of St-Amadour are open all year; for the other, rather dull chapels of SS. Anne, Blaise and Jean-Baptiste you need to take the guided tour (*see* above).

The 11th–13th century **Basilique St-Sauveur** makes good use of the cliff for one of its walls. Originally built with two equal naves, another was added to cope with the crowd of pilgrims. Over the altar hangs a painted wooden 16th-century *Christ* shown crucified on a tree, His right side pierced by the lance instead of the customary left. A Basque-style wooden gallery runs along the side. Steps lead down into another of the seven churches, the simple 12th-century **Crypt St-Amadour**, where the body of the mysterious hermit was venerated. The Parvis also has the **Musée Trésor Francis Poulenc** *(open Easter–Oct)* with documents and precious works of sacred art— medieval reliquaries from Limoges, stained glass, 17th-century *ex-votos*—all dedicated to the composer Poulenc, whose vision here in 1936 inspired his *Litanies à la Vierge Noire de Rocamadour*.

Parvis Notre-Dame

On the other side of St-Sauveur another 25 steps lead up to the holy of holies, the flamboyant Gothic **Chapelle Notre-Dame**. This dates only from 1479, after a rock crashed off the cliff through the original sanctuary. Inside, darkened by candle smoke, the miraculous Black Virgin still holds court. She is believed to have been carved out of walnut in the 11th century, and sits stiffly on her throne, almost a stick figure; the Christ Child balanced on her knee looks more like Pinocchio than a baby. But the Black Virgin's primitive appearance only heightens her mystic power. The proof is in the pudding, or rather in the *ex-votos*. Many are from Breton sailors, who held the Virgin of Rocamadour in special devotion. And whenever she came through, the miracle would be foretold by the ringing of the 9th-century bell hanging from the roof. Chains from pilgrim petitioners still hang in the back of the chapel. Outside, high in the rock above the door, you can see the supposed Durandal, a rusty sword embedded in the stone, held by a chain to keep it from falling on someone's head.

Sharing this upper square with Notre-Dame is the **Chapelle St-Michel**, with the overhanging cliff for a roof, decorated on the outside with colourful 12th- or 13th-century frescoes representing the Annunciation and Visitation. The patron of travellers, St Christopher, is painted below; to catch a glimpse of him was good luck, so he was always made extra big. To see the faded fresco of *Christ in Majesty* inside you must take the tour.

Further up, a hairpin walk lined with the Stations of the Cross (or the much easier lift from the Parvis de St-Amadour) takes you up to the ramparts of the **Château**, built in the 14th century, offering a vertiginous view high over the *causse (open daily 9–sunset; adm)*. This eagle's nest is also a true one, thanks to the breeding programme for birds of prey at the **Rocher des Aigles** *(open Apr–Oct 10–12 and 2–6, with regular flight presentations orchestrated by an English falconer)*.

Roadside Attractions

Chaucer throws up some clues on what medieval pilgrims did for a good time, which aren't quite the same options of 20th-century man, woman and child: live butterflies in **Le Jardin des Papillons Vivants** and 150 Barbary apes and macaques in the **Forêt des Singes** *(both in L'Hospitalet, open daily Palm Sun–mid Oct)*. Also in L'Hospitalet, there's **La Féerie du Rail**, a huge model 1:87 diorama with 60 trains—the result of 9 years' work by a madman named Robert Housseau *(open Palm Sun–11 Nov, 10–12 and 2–6; sound and light July and Aug 8.30–10.30pm)*. Crocs, snakes and other cold-blooded beasts will slither for you in **Reptileland** between Martel and Gluges *(similar hours)*, while **Quercyland** near Souillac waits to entertain the kids with giant inflatable castles to bounce on, water slides and mini-golf *(July–Aug 10am–10pm, weekends June and Sept)*; for adults they offer canoe and kayak descents down the Dordogne from an hour to a week in length (✆ 65 37 33 51). There are even roadside attractions for geologists just south of Rocamadour—the **Gouffre de Saint Sauveur**, a round, deep, bluegreen pit, and **Gouffre de Cabouy**, the resurgence of an underground river in the canyon of the Ouysse.

Rocamadour ✉ *46500*   ***Where to Stay***

Rocamadour has a vast range of hotels, packed together like sardines and all requiring reservations in the summer. The fanciest place in town, **★★★Beau Site**, Rue R.-le-Preux, ✆ 65 33 63 08 occupies a real medieval house, its decoration a bit too Ye-Olde-Inn-ish to be in perfect taste, but what the hell—this is your chance to sleep in a four-poster bed, if you ask in advance. **★★Sainte-Marie**, Place des Senhals, ✆ 65 33 63 07, is a simple place in the heart of things; the more pricey rooms have superb views, and the restaurant is one of the best in town (menus from 70 to 200F). The least expensive rooms in Rocamadour are at **★★Du Roc**, ✆ 65 33 62 43; **★★Le Lion d'Or**, ✆ 65 33 62 04 and **★Du Globe**, in the medieval centre, ✆ 65 33 67 73. In L'Hospitalet, **★★Panoramic**, ✆ 65 33 63 06 is a small family-run hotel with a pool looking onto Rocamadour.

If you have a car, you may be happier somewhere in the surrounding countryside. **★★★Domaine de la Rhue** is only a few minutes away on the N 140, ✆ 65 33 71 50, a tranquil hotel with comfortable rooms all in stone and exposed beams; there's a pool, good breakfasts, but no restaurant. **★★Les Vieilles Tours**, buried in the countryside 3km from town at Lafage, ✆ 65 33 68 01 occupies a sturdy manor house built between the 13th and 17th centuries and two annexes, with rooms giving onto the garden; there's a pool and choice of breakfasts, including a hearty regional *petit déjeuner* that is hardly *petit*. Six km east in Rignac (46500) there are two worthy and cosy choices, the romantic *Relais et Chateaux* **★★★★Château de Roumégouse**, ✆ 65 33 63 81, set in a pretty park with a lovely terrace and a well-known restaurant, featuring traditional Quercy foie gras and truffle dishes and seasonal dishes (lunch menu at 150F; other at 210 to 300F). The English-run **Auberge de Darnis**, ✆ 65 33 66 84, has completely charmed the French; a beautifully restored old farmhouse with four guest rooms (around 240F) and delicious, generous, reasonably priced menus that put many local places to shame (menus at 75 and 110F, closed Wed).

Eating Out

When it comes to dining, Rocamadour is famous throughout the southwest for its creamy, flat cylinders of goat cheese, *le cabécou de Rocamadour*. Try it after a delicious trout or salmon meal at **Jehan de Valon**, the restaurant of the hotel Beau Site (*see* above; menus from 100 to 230F). For a simple but tasty lunch, try **Anne Maire** or **Château de la Carreta**, both by the Hôtel de Ville, with filling menus from 70 to 100F.

Down the Dordogne: Souillac to Sarlat

Souillac doesn't look like much from the dusty stretch of the N 20 that passes through it, but its church of Sainte-Marie makes it a mandatory stop to see one of the true jewels of Romanesque sculpture and architecture in the Midi.

Tourist Information

Souillac: Blvd Louis Jean Malvy, © 65 37 81 56

market days

Souillac: Wednesdays and Fridays

Souillac

The origins of Souillac are fairly typical: a monastery was founded here in the early 900s and reached its glory days in the 12th century, when there was money to lavish on a great church. A village grew up around its walls and the monastery took some hard knocks in the wars. A fire in the 1570s finished it off altogether, leaving only the church **Sainte-Marie**. The philistines of Louis XIV's time worked some outrageous butchery on it, covering over the stately domes with a fake gable roof, destroying one of the finest carved portals in France, and plastering over everything inside, redecorating it in a way they found more tasteful. All that has been cleared away, and though it may still be hard to imagine Sainte-Marie in its original splendour, the essentials at least remain.

Its denuded state, in fact, might make it easier to appreciate the authority and perfection of the architecture. Sainte-Marie is Romanesque at its most Roman, striving above all for monumental presence. This is best seen outside in the majestic **apse**; one suspects the architect had taken a long look at the palaces and public baths of ancient Rome (some of which were still in good nick in the 1100s). The interior is even better: a single, domed nave, graceful and strong. Of the three domes, the earliest is oddly squared, showing the Islamic origins of the technique; squarish domes like this are rare, though a few turn up in contemporary churches in southern Italy. Sculptural decoration is sparse—some good capitals, including the popular theme of Daniel in the lions' den and a few grimacing faces hidden in unexpected spots.

The surviving fragments of the **portal** have been reconstructed inside the main door. The wild scene on top, showing a fellow with some serious devil troubles, represents *St Theophilus the Penitent*. Archdeacon of Adana (in Turkey), this Theophilus was wrongly thrown out of his office and in revenge sold his soul to the devil; of course the devil got it in writing. Theophilus later repented so sincerely and thoroughly that the Virgin Mary went down to hell and snatched the paper away from the devil for him. The three vignettes in the crowded relief show the signing of the contract, the devil attempting to carry Theophilus away and, above, the Virgin and an angel pulling him up into heaven. Just why this obscure saint should have such a prominent place on the portal is a good question, but then perhaps he isn't so obscure after all—this story is one of the sources for the legend of Faust. Flanking the relief are the two figures without which no French portal would be complete: St Peter (with the keys) and St Paul (with the book).

Outstanding as these reliefs are, the eye is inevitably drawn below to the prophet **Isaiah**. As Freda White rightly noted, 'this statue is alive.' It is commonly called the 'dancing' Isaiah. Poised on one foot, with stone draperies flowing, the composition is unlike anything else produced in the Middle Ages; the carving, in its intricate detail, is a virtuoso display of careful precision. Most striking of all is the extreme stylization: studied and consistent, a vision of form that is the work of a great artist—one of the greatest between the Greeks and Donatello. From this he can perhaps be identified as the same man who did the portal at Moissac, or at least an equally talented member of the School of Toulouse. Besides Isaiah and the ruined statue of the patriarch Joseph, one of the side pillars of the portal was saved, swarming with monsters often (though doubtfully) claimed to represent the seven deadly sins, with biblical scenes like the sacrifice of Abraham cleverly mixed in.

The only other bit of the monastery still standing can be seen just across from the church, the 16th-century bell tower of **Saint-Martin**, with some older fragments of its medieval portal.

Souillac has acquired another attraction of late. Facing Ste-Marie is an ambitious effort called the **Musée de l'Automate** *(Nov–Mar, daily exc Mon, Tues, 2–5; April, May and Oct, daily exc Mon, 10–12, 3–6; July and Aug, daily 10–7; adm)*. Scores of mechanical dolls, some from as far back as 1870, haunt the premises, eating, drinking, playing banjos, jumping through hoops and doing every other trick that clockwork and circuitry can accomplish. They have some modern robots to keep them company, along with exhibits that explain everything you ever wanted to know about the history of automata. (The people who keep them in good repair also make some of their own; you can see these in a fascinating gift shop called Clepsydra, near by on Place de la Nau.) Have a drink in Souillac's **Café de Paris**, the wartime salon for a group of refugee poets and artists—Tristan Tzara, the father of Dadaism and surrealist poet Paul Eluard, among others.

Carlux and Sainte-Mondane

Leaving the *département* of the Lot for that of the Dordogne and, more specifically, the corner known as Périgord Noir (for either its truffles or deep forests—no one seems to ιnow, **Carlux** has a pair of romantic châteaux to look at: a 14th-century castle left ruined by the English in the Hundred Years' War, and on a remarkable site in a holm oak forest, the 16th-century **Château de Rouffillac**. Just across the river, at **St-Julien-de-Lampon** is a Gothic church with 16th-century mural paintings. From there the D 50 continues west to **Sainte-Mondane**.

Mothers are often saints, but few are ever canonized, what with the Church's fantasies about virginity. One who made it into heaven's ranks, however, was Mondane, the mum of Sarlat's patron, St Sacerdos; she spent her later years in a cave in the riverside village that now bears her name. Although the cave is no longer a pilgrimage site, visitors still pour into Sainte-Mondane to see the majestic **Château de Fénelon**, begun in the 13th century and mostly rebuilt in the 1600s *(guided tours Mar–Oct, daily exc Tues 10–12 and 2–6; daily July and Aug, till 7; adm)*. Piled on a set of terraces, defended by a triple ring of walls and gate towers, the roofs are still partly covered with their original *lauze* stones. There's a collection of antique cars in the grounds, and a handful of mementoes associated with Fénelon, who was born here in 1651, a 13th child but one whose brains soon attracted attention *(see p.108)*.

Carsac-Aillac and the Château de Montfort

Downriver on the D 50, **Groléjac** reserves its best features for those willing to get out of the car and walk up its medieval streets, where it conceals a little 18th-century château and a Romanesque church. Near the junction of the Dordogne and the little Enéa stands **Carsac**, a village of 16th–17th century *lauze*-roofed houses with a domed Romanesque **church**, built in the 11th century. Damaged by the English, the nave and chapels were rebuilt in the 1500s with ogival vaults and capitals carved with unusual classical scenes, including a baby Hercules strangling the serpents that crept into his cradle. When the church was restored in 1940, new works were commissioned from Léon Zack: the stained glass and the Stations of the Cross, with texts from Paul Claudel's *Le Chemin de la Croix*.

The **Château de Montfort**, high over its river loop (or *cingle*), is one of the most photographed of all the Dordogne's castles *(no admittance)*. It was named after the ruthlessly effective leader of the Albigensian crusade, Simon de Montfort, although typically for him all he did was burn it to the ground when he captured it in 1214. Still, his name stuck to the spot when the château was rebuilt over the centuries, especially after three sieges by the English in the Hundred Years' War. It is best seen from the road between Carsac and **Vitrac**, the latter village a popular holiday base spread between the crossroads to Sarlat and its medieval core, the old 'Bourg' with a large Romanesque church.

Where to Stay and Eating Out

Souillac ✉ 46200

Lots of people pass through Souillac, and there is a wide choice of places to stay— old two-star inns with a sincere welcome and attractive rooms. Three of these Logis de France places stand out, and each has a swimming pool: **★★Hostellerie La Roseraie**, 42 Av. de Toulouse, © 65 37 82 69; the **★★Bellevue**, 68 Av. Jean-

Jaurès, ✆ 65 32 78 23; and **La Vieille Auberge**, Place de la Minoterie, ✆ 65 32 79 43. In the Vieille Auberge, some of the rooms have TV with video. Less expensive but cosy enough is the *Auberge du Puits, on Place du Puits, ✆ 65 37 80 32; the restaurant here has a wide choice of entrées, from tripe to trout, on menus from 70F; for 125F and up you get *confits*.

Veyrignac ✉ 23470

In a park overlooking the Dordogne, the **Château de Veyrignac**, ✆ 53 28 13 56, began as a Cistercian monastery in the 13th century and was converted to a castle in the 17th. The English owners have 6 rooms and six flats to rent and, besides a pool and tennis courts offer from July–15 Oct hot-air balloon excursions over the valley, piloted by a champion aeronaut; rooms from 375F.

Groléjac ✉ 24250

Grillardin, in the village, ✆ 53 28 11 02, is a simple but pleasant little hotel with a shady terrace and views.

Carsac ✉ 24200

Delpeyrat, ✆ 53 28 10 43, in the village centre may get no stars but it's quiet, well kept and a reasonably priced option, 1km from the Dordogne and 8km from Sarlat (rooms from 100F).

Vitrac ✉ 24200

****Domaine de Rochebois**, Rte de Montfort, ✆ 53 29 36 88, is a refined hotel with lovely views over the valley, and attractive extras—a sauna, *hammam*, 9-hole golf course, swimming pools, an 'English bar' and a restaurant specializing in goose and duck dishes. Relaxing **Plaisance**, Le Port, ✆ 53 28 33 04, has a long garden terrace overlooking the river, canoe rentals, pool and tennis. The nearby **Burg**, Le Port, ✆ 53 28 33 29, is immersed in ivy; it has modern rooms, a heated pool, tennis and views.

Sarlat-la-Canéda

'*Mon Dieu*, there's nothing here but *foie gras, foie gras, foie gras!*' muttered an old farmer, brought by his relatives to Sarlat for a Sunday afternoon promenade. Of course he's right; nearly every other boutique glitters with stacks of tiny shiny tins. But such rich stuff fits Sarlat perfectly well, for cocooned inside its clinking ring of 20th-century sprawl, this golden Renaissance town is architecturally the *foie gras* of southwest France.

History

It was Clovis, they say, who founded the first church at what is now Sarlat, and Charlemagne who stopped here after Roncevalles to give it a fragment of the True Cross and the relics of St Sacerdos, Bishop of Limoges. In the 8th century Pepin, Duke of Aquitaine added an abbey, and Sarlat grew up around it. It was raging with plague when St

Bernard made a memorable visit in 1147, and cured several victims with blessed bread. By the next century, the autocratic rule of the abbot over the increasingly mercantile town had become intolerable to the good burghers, and in 1299, after much strife, the *Livre de Paix* was signed, acknowledging the abbot as boss, but giving the town council-lors the authority to run the show. As compensation, Pope John XXII made Sarlat a bishopric in 1317, elevating the church to a cathedral.

Founded as an abbey town, Sarlat has no natural defences and was constrained to add some formidable man-made ones during the Hundred Years' War. In return for defending itself so well against the English, the French simply handed Sarlat over to Edward III in 1360 as part of the ransom for Jean II, although ten years later, Du Guesclin and the French won it back by arms. As a reward for its loyalty in spite of it all, Charles VII granted Sarlat enough tax concessions in the 1440s to bring about its golden age and a building boom; nearly all of its *hôtels*, or town houses, were built between 1450 and 1500 and grace Sarlat with a rare architectural unity.

In 1574, Catholic Sarlat was captured and pillaged by the irre-pressible Huguenot Captain Vivans, who got in during Carnival by disguising his troops as harlequins. Smarting from the embarrassment more than anything else, Sarlat held tight for three weeks in 1587 when it was besieged by the fanatical Protestant Vicomte de Turenne. When their ramparts were damaged, the Sardalais rebuilt them during the night, and when Turenne offered them terms, they replied: 'We have a good master and don't want any other.' And Turenne went away muttering, ashamed not to have been able by force or ruse 'to take such a town'.

After the Wars of Religion, Sarlat sank gently into the role of a local market town, off the main routes of communications and history. In 1827, the town fathers, hoping to drum up some new business by uncongesting traffic, took a long straight slice out of its heart to create Rue de la République, better known as the *Traverse*. Further 'improvements' were prevented after 1963, when Sarlat was chosen as one of the first towns to be restored and protected by the state under the *Loi Malraux*.

Getting Around

Direct trains to Bordeaux, Les Eyzies, Bergerac, Souillac from Av de la Gare, © 53 59 00 21. Taxi: © 53 59 02 43 or 53 59 00 49. One bus each morning to Périgueux (Laribière, © 53 59 01 48). Bike hire from the station, or from 52 Av. Gambetta, © 53 59 03 60.

Tourist Information

Place de la Liberté, © 53 59 27 67

From Place de la Grande Rigaudie to the Cathedral

Parking is the first hurdle confronting any motorist arriving in Sarlat; the largest and most convenient places are south of the Traverse, in and around vast **Place de la Grande Rigaudie**. Here, in 1892, Sarlat erected a statue to its famous son, Etienne de La Boétie, although it unfairly makes the young thinker look like a wimp (*see* below). On the hill beyond him and the courthouse is the **Jardin Publique**, offering a good overview of Sarlat and its many steep *lauze* roofs.

The urban scale becomes immediately more intimate and richly detailed once you walk up Rue Tourny, just north of Place de la Grande Rigaudie. A lane on the right leads into the **Cour des Fontaines**, with its age-old fountain. Clovis founded Sarlat's first church in the second courtyard, a site now occupied by the 12th-century **Chapelle des Pénitents Bleus** *(open July and Aug only)*. Follow the narrow passage to the **Ancien Cimitière**, where 12th–15th-century tombstones have been excavated and arranged on terraces.

A stair from here leads up to Sarlat's great oddity, the **Lanterne des Morts**, a stubby stone rocket built at the end of the 12th century. Its original use has been forgotten—it may have commemorated the miracle of St Bernard, or have been used as a funerary chapel, or perhaps a lantern was lit here during wakes and vigils on the ground floor (there's an upper floor, but it's completely, mysteriously inaccessible). There may even be a confusion over its original name; sometimes it was described as the *lanterne des Maures*, refering to its marked resemblance to Turkish *türbes* and other Muslim mausolea that the crusaders surely saw.

Below stretch the flying buttresses and bulb-topped steeple (locally known as the 'scarecrow') of the **Cathédrale St-Sacerdos**, dedicated to the 6th-century, leper-curing Bishop of Limoges. The first church was built at the same time as the Lanterne des Morts and had to be concecrated twice, the second time in 1273, after Sarlat's abbot was shot down while saying Mass by a disgruntled monk with a crossbow. This church was demolished (except for its Romanesque *clocher-porche*) by Bishop Armand de Gontaut-Biron in 1504 in order to construct a much grander cathedral. Unfortunately the project took until the dull 17th century to complete, and although the result is roomy enough, it holds nothing as artistic as the Bishop Armand's own effigy tomb in Biron (*see* p.285).

Place du Peyrou and La Boétie

Adjacent to the cathedral in Place du Peyrou is the former bishopric or **Ancien Evêché** (now a theatre), with handsome, mullioned windows and a top-floor gallery in brick that looks like it escaped from Italy—not surprising, as it was built by a Florentine cousin of Catherine de' Medici, Cardinal Niccolò Gaddi, who added bishop of Sarlat to his titles in 1533.

Opposite the Cathedral stands the most lavishly ornate town house in Sarlat, the **Hôtel de**

La Boétie (1525). The modern entrance is through the wide round arch of a former shop; richly ornamented mullioned windows dominate the upper three floors, squeezed between a vertiginously steep gable. The decoration reaches a curlicue frenzy in the dormer window, in frilly contrast with the sombre *lauzes* of the roof. The *hôtel* was built by the father of the precocious Etienne de La Boétie, who was born here in 1530. A student of the classics, Etienne was aged 18 when he wrote his most original essay, *Discours de la servitude volontaire*—asking why people willingly give up their liberty to support tyrants, when such tyrants could never exist without people willing to give up their freedom, the most precious thing of all. These were radical ideas in the 16th century, and even when Montaigne published La Boétie's papers after his premature death at the age of 33, he discreetly omitted the *Discours*. It only appeared in 1576 in a collection of 'libellous' Protestant writings, and even then its influence remained dormant until the advent of Rousseau. But most of all, La Boétie is remembered as Montaigne's perfect pal in the latter's beautiful *Essay on Friendship*.

Place de la Liberté and Rue des Consuls

From Place du Peyrou, duck through the medieval alleyway of the Passage Henri-de-Segogne to another of Sarlat's architectural gems, the **Hôtel de Maleville** (now the tourist office). A 16th-century combination of three older houses, with two distinct Renaissance façades—one French, one Italian—it belonged to Jean de Vienne, a local boy who owed his rise to national high office by Henri IV (see the portrait medallions of the king and a woman—either Henri's wife, Marie de' Medici, or favourite mistress Gabrielle d'Estrées). It was later owned by the family that produced Jacques de Maleville, one of the prime authors of the Napoleonic *Code Civile*.

The *hôtel's* French façade overlooks elongated **Place de la Liberté**, Sarlat's main square and favoured café stop. Next to its 17th-century Hôtel de Ville, Rue de la Salamandre leads up past 15th- and 16th-century mansions to the handsome **Présidial** and its garden (visible through the gate). Now a private house, the Présidial was originally the seat of a royal court set up by Henri II in 1552 in defiance of local wishes to administer local justice; note the curious little polygonal lantern on the loggia. More delights—gabled houses and carved portals—wait along Rue du Présidial and Rue Fénelon, which brings you back to the northern extension of Place de la Liberté, the **Place du Marché**.

Here stands the sad carcass of a church with a massive bell tower, **Sainte-Marie**, begun in 1365 and completed in 1507. After being used for storing saltpetre during the Revolution it was sold for a pittance to a speculator who lopped off its chancel and converted its chapels into shops; before the First World War it served as a post office. Now it forms part of the permanent stage for Sarlat's summer theatre festival, starring Paris's Comédie Française. The picturesque **Rampe Magnanat**, ascending to the right, has been used by a score of French film directors for their climactic duel scenes, with the brooding backdrop provided by the 16th-century **Hôtel de Gisson** and its hexagonal tower.

On the other side of the Hôtel de Gisson is the old goose market, **Place du Marché aux Oies**, and the narrow Rue des Consuls. Among the magnificent hôtels here, the **Hôtel Selve de Plamon** (nos. 8–10) stands out; it was owned by a prosperous family of drapers, who added a new floor every century or so—early Gothic on the ground floor, flamboyant Gothic on the first and Renaissance on the second. Opposite is a curious cave-like fountain from the 15th century; the river Cuze passed openly under the Hôtel de Plamon as a pestilent sewer until it was covered over in the 19th century.

Across the *Traverse*

The *Traverse* cuts the wealthy Sarlat of splendid town houses from the steeper, more popular and piquant neighbourhood to the west, where some alleys are scarcely wide enough to walk arm in arm. In its intimate scale, the **Chapelle des Pénitents Blancs** in Rue Jean-Jacques Rousseau seems like a walrus; originally part of a convent, it now houses a worthy little **Museum of Sacred Art** *(Easter–Oct, 10–12 and 3–6, closed Sun mornings)*. Rue J.-J. Rousseau continues to the lovely, nearly intact 16th-century **Abbaye Sainte-Claire**, occupied until the Revolution and generally open in July and August. Further south are Rue du Siège and a stretch of Sarlat's walls that survived demolition; here too is the **Tour du Bourreau**, the executioner's tower. In Rue Rousset there's a second tower, the 15th-century crenellated **Tour de Guet**.

Just beyond the boulevards on this west side of Sarlat, there's a **Musée Aquarium**, in Rue du Commandant-Maratuel, with all you've ever wanted to know about creatures that swim and slither in the Dordogne and how Périgordins have traditionally nabbed them in their flat-bottomed *gabarres (open 10–12 and 2–6, June–mid-Sept 10–7)*.

Sarlat ⬜ *24200*   **Where to Stay**

As the capital of Périgord Noir, Sarlat with its many small hotels provides a convenient base—as long as you book in advance in the summer. A traditional stone manor house, set in a landscaped park at the west entrance to Sarlat has been recently converted into the ★★★**Relais de Moussidière**, © 53 28 28 74; it has a pool, and near by are riding stables, golf and tennis courts. Near the medieval centre, ★★★**De la Madeleine**, 1 Place de la Petite Rigaudie, © 53 59 10 41, was converted from a 19th-century town house; rooms are air-conditioned and soundproof, while a private garage conveniently solves Sarlat's parking problems. Owned by a chef, the main focus at La Madeleine is in the restaurant, where regional specialities (*civet d'oie* in vin de Cahors, and such) share the menu with lighter, more modern dishes (menus from 140F). Also in the centre but open all year round, ★★★**La Salamandre**, 2 Rue de l'Abbé Surguier, ✆ 53 31 22 32, began life as a distillery before becoming a comfortable hotel with a garden and pool; 30 (mostly Louis XV) rooms and five flats.

Less expensive choices include the modern ★★**Saint Albert et Montaigne**, with fresh, colourful rooms at the south entrance of the old town in Place Pasteur, ✆ 53 31 55 55; the enthusiastic chef offers delicacies on the order of stuffed goose neck and duck liver in *verjus* (from 130F). ★★**La Couleuvrine**, 1 Place de la Bouquerie, ✆ 53 59 27 80, has unusual antique-furnished rooms in the 14th–18th century ramparts of Sarlat's walls; the restaurant prides itself on its market-fresh produce (menus at 100 and 220F); closed part of Nov and Jan. ★★**De Compostelle**, 18 Av de Selves, ✆ 53 59 08 53, has modern rooms with private terraces and TV, not far from the centre. The little, family-owned ★★**Hostellerie Marcel**, 8 Av. de Selves, ✆ 53 59 21 98, has pleasant rooms in a stone house, the cheapest in this category.

Just Outside the Centre

Within a radius of a few kilometres of Sarlat you'll find nearly as many places to choose from, with the added plus of peace and quiet. A former hunting lodge, ★★★**La Hoirie**, 2km south from Sarlat near La Canéda, ✆ 53 59 05 62, has 15 rooms fitted with minibars, pool and tennis; the restaurant is one of the best near Sarlat—try the *coquilles Saint-Jacques* with *cèpes*. The hilltop ★★★**Hostellerie de Meysset**, at Argentouleau (2 km on the Les Eyzies road), ✆ 53 59 08 29, offers smallish but pretty rooms with country furnishings to go with its views over its park, pool and the Sarlat valley; it's equally pleasant from the restaurant terrace, dawdling over delicious *confits* served with a garlic cream sauce and other treats. Less than a km from Sarlat, set in a 4-acre park, ★★**La Verperie**, at La Verperie, ✆ 53 59 00 20, is a rambling old house converted into a peaceful, cosy hotel especially suitable for families (pool, games, etc; closed Dec and Jan). New, but traditionally styled ★★**La Mas de Castel**, at Sudailissant, 2½km towards Souillac, ✆ 53 59 02 59, offers bright pastel rooms around the pool in the midst of a large garden (closed mid-Nov through Palm Sun). The best camping around is at the luxurious **Les Périères**, 1km from Sarlat on the D 47, ✆ 53 59 05 84, in a beautiful shady park, open Easter–Sept.

Eating Out

Despite the tons of foie gras, central Sarlat isn't exactly graced with culinary epiphanies. The best are in the aforementioned hotels; otherwise try the **Rossignol**, near the Mairie at 15 Rue Fénelon, ✆ 53 31 02 30, serving good-value, regional cuisine (menus from 90F, closed Wed), or west of the Traverse, **Au Bon Chabrol**, 2 Rue des Armes, ✆ 53 59 15 56, with a tiny terrace, perfect for lingering over a *soupe paysanne* and walnut salad (menus from 70F, closed Wed). The Périgordin menus are even cheaper (from 55F) at **Criquettamu's**, 5 Rue Armes, ✆ 53 59 48 10.

Note that reservations are essential for all the following: the charming **La Sanglière**, 6km south at Vitrac, © 53 28 33 51, specializing in regional 'bourgeoise' cuisine (stuffed pigeon, trout in warm flaky pasty) with gastronomic menus from 100F; closed Oct–Mar). **Ferme-Auberge du Barry**, on the D 704, © 53 59 07 69, serves crisp salads with breast of duck, mushroom dishes and other local favourites (menus from 100F, also a few rooms available, open Easter–Oct). Further afield, at **Lo Cobano en Périgord**, Le Breuil, © 53 29 66 23 in the countryside around St-André-d'Allas (4km west of Sarlat) you can dine on home cooking in a unique, intimate setting—in a handsome *borie* (menus from 70F; camping and gîtes available).

North of Sarlat: the Plateau of Périgord Noir

Two km north of Sarlat, Pepin the Short built the first citadel on the natural belvedere at **Temniac** in the 8th century (access off the D 704, or by way of a marked walking path beginning off Av. Brossard). In the 1200s the bishops of Sarlat used the site for a palace; it was rebuilt in the 15th century, and today stands in evocative, romantic ruins. The bishops' tower and the pure Périgordin Romanesque **Chapelle de Notre-Dame**, with its pair of domes and vaulted choir, are nearly intact.

From Temniac, take the D47 east from Croix d'Alon for 8km, then follow minor roads for another 3km to the 17th-century **Manoir d'Eyrignac**, where the current owner has won prizes for his immaculate restoration of the 18th-century French gardens, a perspective of hedges cut into cubes, triangles, circles, and spheres *(guided tours 10–12.30 and 2–7; Nov–Mar 10–12.30 and 2–5; adm)*. From here continue northeast to the D61 for **Salignac-Eyvigues**, a picture postcard Périgord town spread below the 12th–17th-century pepperpot towers of the **Château de Salignac-Fénelon** *(open Apr–Aug, 10–12 and 2.30–6.30, closed Tues; adm)*. Built by Archbishop Fénelon's feudal ancestors, the château was hotly disputed in all the region's wars. Terraces now replace the once bristling ramparts; among the highlights inside are two floors of vaulted cellars, the chapel and a Renaissance fireplace.

Eight km northwest of Sarlat, off the D 47, the twin-turretted 15th–16th century **Château de Puymartin** *(open 15 Apr–Oct, 10–12 and 2–6.30; adm)* was Turenne's headquarters when the Protestants besieged Sarlat, but for better or worse has had little to do with history since then. Rooms are fitted with 17th-century furnishings, some with Aubusson tapestries. Then, for something completely different, make your way south to **St-André-d'Allas** (4km west of Sarlat); at the stately **Château du Roc**, take the narrow road to the right for the **Cabanes du Breuil** *(open 10–12 and 2–6, in July and Aug 10–7, with a nocturnal spectacle at 9.30 pm Tues–Fri in the summer; adm)*, a hamlet of tiny, dry-stone huts and breast-shaped stone roofs, the kind of place where Asterix or Obelix would feel perfectly at home. Similar villages of *bories*, or *gariottes*, exist in Provence. No one knows who built them, or how long ago; the most likely answer is shepherds, who kept them in good repair over the centuries.

Lovely, honey-hued Domme is the bastide town from the Hundred Years' War, but one whose grid plan was remarkably transplanted onto a bluff-top eyrie over the Dordogne. Philippe III the Bold built it in 1281, and although he bestowed many favours on it, he had to resort to threats to get the local peasants to build and settle his baby—only to pay the workers in black leather coins 'minted', or rather cut out, at the Mint in Place de la Rode, Domme's oldest building.

Despite its lofty site and walls, Domme was captured several times: by the English, the counts of Périgord and, in 1588 during the Wars of Religion by Henri of Navarre's invincible captain, Geoffroy de Vivans—although only on the fourth try, after he laboriously established a secret ammunition depot in a cave halfway up the precipitous, undefended cliff. Then one black night, laying coats on the bare rock to muffle the noise, his troops sprung with a thunderous roar upon the unsuspecting town.

Tourist Information

Domme: in the *place*, © 53 28 37 09, mornings only in the winter. Buy cave tickets here. To hire a canoe from the little port under Domme, © 53 28 22 01.

Villefranche-du-Périgord: in the centre, © 53 29 98 37

market days

Domme: Thursdays

Cénac: Tuesdays

A Roam through Domme

If you approach Domme from the east by way of the D 46E, you'll enter the town walls through the best preserved of its three gates, the 13th-century **Porte des Tours** *(afternoon guided tours; see the tourist office)*. The narrow gate is framed by two fat guard towers built by Philip the Fair, which were converted into prisons in 1307 when the king ordered the arrest of the Knights Templars; some of them lingered here until 1318, engraving crucifixes and other graffiti you can still see on the wall. Domme's other two gates are equally worth a look: the arched **Porte de la Combe** to the south and the **Porte del Bos**, still grooved for its portcullis.

As with any bastide, the focal point of Domme is its central market square, here called **Place de la Halle**, although no other bastide square is quite like this: one side, beyond a statue of the Dordogne's literary hero, Jacquou le Croquant and the church, gives onto the **Belvedere de la Barre**, with panoramic views from

Monfort to Beynac. It's also easy to see why the locals hadn't bothered to defend the bluff, even from Vivans. Vivans took care to destroy the church, which is why the current one offers little interest.

However, Place de la Halle boasts other fine buildings: the turreted, asymmetrical Governor's House from the 1500s (now the tourist office) and the Maison Garrigou containing the **Musée Paul-Reclus**, with a mammoth tooth, prehistoric and historical collections, traditional arts and crafts *(open Apr–Oct, 10–12 and 2–6)*. In the middle, the charming 17th-century stone and timber market offers more than the usual turnips and carrots—the entrance into Domme's very bowels, through the **Grotte de la Halle** *(open Mar and Oct 2–6; Apr–Sept 9.30–12 and 2–6; July and Aug 9.30–7; adm)*. Although the lower part of the cave was used as a refuge for the inhabitants during the Hundred Years' War, the upper part, where fossilized bison and deer bones were found, was discovered only in 1954; beyond is a well-lit stalactite phantasmagoria that ends with a ride in a glass lift up the sheer cliff, depositing you near the Jardin Publique, with the option of walking back to the Belvedere along the cliffside walk.

Le Mai

One last thing that may or may not be in Domme when you visit is a tall pine pole in Place des Halles, decorated with hoops and *tricolores* and a sign reading *Honneur à Notre Maire*; if it's gone down in Domme you may well spot similar poles in other villages or towns, or even next to private homes, reading *Honneur au Patron* or *à Notre Elu*, or with the names of a newly married couple, or perhaps even a newborn baby. They are called *les Mai*, or maypoles, and are erected at boozy confabs known as *la Plantation de Mai*. Once up, they are meant to rot away rather than ever be taken down. The Périgordins apparently have been planting their maypoles ever since Gallo-Roman times, when a newly elected official would be honoured with a similar pole crowned with a garland. Since the Liberty Trees put up during the Revolution, they have taken on an added republican virtue.

Cénac

Just below Domme, some exceptionally lively Romanesque sculpture is concentratred in Cénac's early 12th-century priory of **Saint-Julien**, located on the edge of town *(open summer only; at other times Sundays before 11am)*. The Huguenots who smashed it fortunately gave up before reaching the apse: the exterior *modillons* depict carvings of a man-eating pig, grimacing faces and other oddities, while the interior capitals are vigorously sculpted with a bestiary, Daniel in the lion's den, Jonah and the whale, a monkey-trainer, a naked woman with a snake, and more.

South of Domme to Besse and Villefranche

All is rural tranquillity south of Domme, especially along the D 60, fringed by chestnut forests and meadows. The Brigadoon stillness that reigns here (except during the autumn mushroom hunts) makes the few 'sights' somehow more magical for being unexpected: the elongated old village of **Daglan** with—to the north—its curious, fortified, cross-shaped Château de Peyruzel from the 1600s; medieval **St Pompont**, with a pair of châteaux and a mini-maze of medieval houses huddled beneath the fortified church; and further south, remote **Prats-du-Périgord**, with an even mightier 12th-century church and 16th-century château.

From Prats (Occitan for 'meadows'), follow the signs for **Besse**, an even tinier hamlet, with yet another château and an overbearing fortified church, although this one is special: not only has it held on to its *lauze* roof, but also a vigorous sculpted 11th-century porch, a rarity in these parts. French books claim the figures represent the 'Mystery of Redemption'—there's a Garden of Eden scene, possibly an Annunciation (under the six-winged angel), a midget Crucifixion and seven deadly sins although the hunter on horseback, St Michael killing the dragon, and the waltzing horses seem to belong to another story altogether. To guard Périgord's southernmost marches, Alphonse de Poitiers founded the bastide of **Villefranche-du-Périgord** in the 1260s. Although the grid plan and a fountain survive from Alphonse's day, Villefranche's central square has taken a lot of licks, leaving only one row of arcades facing the stone-pillared *halle*. The church sharing the square is a more maladroit than usual 19th-century rebuilding of the original; adjacent to the tourist office, a small **Eco-Musée** is devoted to mushrooms and chestnuts.

Domme ✉ *24250*   ***Where to Stay and Eating Out***

Up in the centre of Domme by the belvedere, the tranquil, renovated *****L'Esplanade**, ✆ 53 28 31 41, offers cosy rooms, some overlooking the Dordogne far below. Half board (*demi-pension*) is mandatory in season—not a terrible penance in the charming restaurant or on its terrace, especially when asparagus is in season (in a flaky pasty with *morels*); menus from 150F, but much, much more if you splurge with the truffles. In pedestrian-only Grand Rue, English-owned ****Le Pré Mondain**, ✆ 53 28 33 88, offers eight comfortable rooms with exposed beams in a 15th-century town house. In the same street, the slightly larger ***Lou Cardil**, ✆ 53 28 38 92, offers an attractive inner courtyard to go with its rooms.

La Clé des Champs on the D 710 in Mazeyrolles (5km southwest of Prats), ✆ 53 29 95 94, offers bright rooms in a former goose barn, a swimming pool and tennis, and good home cooking in the restaurant, featuring a flaky apple *tourtière* for dessert (menus from 100F). In Villefranche, the **Petite Auberge** 'Loin de Bruit' is well signposted from the centre, on a hill up a country lane. Don't be put off by the corny courtyard: the food is delicious.

Down the Dordogne II

West of Domme and Sarlat the Dordogne bends below celebrated belvederes and beauty spots, some elbow to elbow: from the château of Beynac you can count six other châteaux rising along the river. The Vézère kicks in at Limeuil, and the newly swollen river whiplashes two more times before you see Bergerac and the first vineyards, which will keep it company all the way to the Gironde.

The Central Dordogne: Beynac to Bergerac

Getting Around

The Sarlat–Bordeaux railway line runs through here five or six times a day, with stations at Beynac, St-Cyprien, Siorac, Le Buisson, Trémolat, Mauzac, Lalinde and Bergerac; Le Buisson is also on the main Paris–Agen line

Tourist Information

Beynac: Parking de la Balme, ✆ 53 29 43 08. Ask about walking paths in the area.

market days

St-Cyprien: Sundays

Belvès: Saturdays

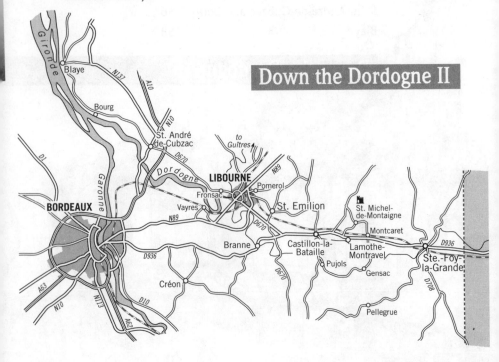

Down the Dordogne II

The car park along the river is five times as large as the entire village of **La Roque-Gageac**, heightening the effect of a two-dimensional stage set. In truth, there isn't room for much depth, when you build into the face of an overhanging cliff; the warm stone houses and their brown roofs are piled against it so harmoniously that they hardly seem real. Facing the sunny south, La Roque Gageac is sheltered enough that an exotic garden of cacti and palms thrives by the little 16th-century **church**, set on a throne of rock. Reality does intrude occasionally, when bits from the huge cliff break off and fall like meteors through the roofs.

At the eastern end of La Roque stands the manor house belonging to the village's most famous native son, the 16th-century canon Jean Tarde, a humanist scholar and friend of Galileo who left a moving chronicle of the devastation wrought by the Wars of Religion in the area. At the the the western end, the **Château de la Malartrie** is a convincing reconstruction of the 15th-century original. Flat-bottomed *gabarres* on the village quay offer hour-long tours of the cliffs and châteaux that mark this stretch of the Dordogne *(daily between 10 and 6; discounts for morning cruises)*.

It's a few minutes from La Roque-Gageac to **Beynac-et-Cazenac**, although you may have already seen its overpowering **Château de Beynac** from a number of points along the Dordogne *(open Mar–mid Nov, 10–12 and 2.30–4.30, summer until 6; adm)*. Barons of Périgord, the Beynacs were as daunting and fierce as their castle. When Richard the Lion-Heart made it known that he meant to give their castle to his devoted Captain Mercadier, the Beynacs joined forces with Fortanier of Gourdon, whose father and brothers had been killed by Richard, and who had vowed to seek revenge. In March 1199, when Richard and Mercadier came down with a band of *routiers* to besiege Châlus (a castle just over the border in the Limousin), Fortanier shot an arrow that caught the king in a gap in his armour. Richard died a few days later, and not long after that the Beynacs liquidated Mercadier. In 1214 Simon de Montfort attacked Beynac and its lord, who was nicknamed the 'arca satana' (Satan's Bow) for being a devoted friend of Count Raymond VI of

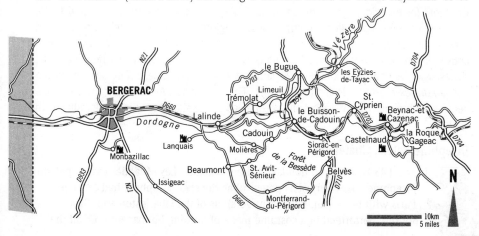

Toulouse; although he spared Satan's Bow for his loyalty to the King of France, Simon destroyed the château's most imposing towers. During the Hundred Years' War, Beynac fought a constant war against English Castelnaud, just over the river.

The interior was often restored: there's a monumental 17th-century stairway, a Grand Siècle salon with a sculpted wooden chimney carved with mythologies, a *Sacrifice of Isaac* done with provincial panache, and late 15th-century frescoes in the Oratory (stylistically only about 400 years behind Tuscany) of the Last Supper, the Pietà and the Man of Sorrows; in the Last Supper note the rare portrayal of the Maitre D'—St Martial, the apostle of Limousin and Périgord, and a fitting patron saint for a people in love with food.

Behind the castle, the **Parc Archéologique de Beynac** *(open 15 June–15 Sept, 10–7; adm)* evokes the area's roots from Neolithic to Gaulish times, with reconstructed huts, demonstrations and various workshops such as tool making.

Castelnaud-la-Chapelle and its Three Castles

Opposite Beynac, the powerful hulk of its eternal nemesis, the **Château de Castelnaud** stands arrogantly on the limestone cliffs at the confluence of the Dordogne and Céou rivers. First mentioned in 1214, when its Cathar owner was chased out by Simon de Montfort, Castelnaud's later rulers, the Caumonts, stuck with the English, who built the keep as a base from which to terrorize the surrounding countryside. The Caumonts let the Huguenot Captain Vivans use Castelnaud for similar exploits, but by that time the family had moved out of their feudal fort into Les Milandes (*see* below). Now open for visits *(end of Mar–mid-Nov, 10–6, till 7 in the summer; adm)*, Castelnaud's stark, dark little rooms and narrow stairways suggest why the Caumonts upped sticks. There are audiovisual displays explaining various aspects of medieval warfare, including how to shoot a catapult.

A wooded lane north of Castelnaud follows the river past the privately owned **Château de Fayrac**, built between the 14th and 17th centuries and romantically restored in the 19th century. Further on, in its own hamlet, is Castelnaud's third château, **Les Milandes** *(open Palm Sun–Sept 10–11.30 and 2–6; adm)*, a Renaissance beauty built by François de Caumont for his bride, Claude de Cardaillac. They decorated it with frescoes and sculptures, while the chapel filled up with elegant effigy tombs. Unfortunately, François and Claude's grandson, raised as a priest, took his conversion to Protestantism with such righteousness that all these lovely, worldly things were smashed to bits. He married one of the richest widows of his day, and in 1571 fathered a daughter, Anne, before being slipped a few *anamites mortelles* in his mushrooms. The King made Anne a marquise, and she became such a marriage prize that she was hauled to the altar three times before her 18th birthday.

Josephine Baker, Châtelaine

In the 1930s, while on holiday in the Dordogne, Les Milandes cast a spell on Josephine Baker almost as powerful as the spell Josephine had cast over Paris with her joyful, exuberant versions of the Charleston and Black Bottom, performed in a costume made of nothing but bananas. Of all the black Americans who came to France to escape racism at home, she was the most successful, becoming the highest paid performer in Europe. She purchased her dream castle and 600 acres to go with it, and used it during the war to hide people wanted by the Nazis, earning a medal for her work in the Resistance. In the late 1940s, after spending millions on the restoration of Les Milandes, she adopted 13 children of every race and creed, her 'Rainbow Tribe'; but her ambitions (which included a 120-acre pleasure garden and amusement park) were unfortunately bigger than her purse, and she and her husband Jo Bouillon fell so deeply into debt that Josephine—it broke her heart—had to sell Les Milandes in 1964. Today the attractions are more National Trust than interracial trust, but are well worth a visit nevertheless—the panelling and woodwork inside and carved windows that survived the Reformation fervour, and the lovely flamboyant Gothic **Chapel**, where Josephine and Jo were married. Just down the lane from the château, a house has on its corner a statue of the Virgin Mary with children, the Virgin bearing the features of Josephine. If you take the road down behind Les Milandes you can see the quaint and wistful remnants of her amusement park.

St-Cyprien, Belvès and Walnut Country

To the northwest, across the river from Castelnaud, **St-Cyprien** overlooks the fertile alluvial plain that has long been the source of its fat, contented air. In the Middle Ages the Romanesque church with its bulky 12th-century bell tower had an important relic-magnet for pilgrims—the *Sainte-Epine*, or holy thorn, which monks rubbed against the clothes of sick people. The next river town, **Siorac-en-Périgord** is a busy market and holiday centre (complete with a 9-hole golf course) that uses its 17th-century château as a *mairie*.

From Siorac, take a 5km detour south on the D 710 for the ancient hill town of **Belvès**. Inhabited for donkey's years thanks to its lofty position, it was a fortified Roman *castrum* and a walled English town in the Middle Ages; a ring boulevard circles the site of the walls. In the ring, the old plan remains intact, as a kind of proto-*bastide*, the straight narrow lanes lined with Gothic and Renaissance buildings. In the central Place d'Armes stands a last relic of Belvès's defences, the **Tour des Fillols** and a 15th-century *halle*, supported by 23 pillars, one still bearing the chains from pre-Revolutionary days, when it doubled as a pillory.

Belvès is best known for its nuts; **Doissat**, some 7km to the southeast, off D 54, has the most extensive walnut plantations in the Dordogne, which produces more of them than any other *département* in France. Doissat's partially-collapsed château, the last resting place of the dashing Captain Vivans, has a little **Walnut Museum**, open in the summer.

Where to Stay and Eating Out

Beynac ✉ 24220

**Bonnet, ✆ 53 29 83 74, is a traditional hotel between the château and river; the restaurant, with a riverside terrace, is famous for its *truffe en croûte*, a warm pastry containing truffles, smoked bacon and foie gras; menus from 120F. Tranquil

★★Du Château, ✆ 53 29 50 13, on the road up to the castle, has a restaurant that makes good use of quality ingredients (menus from 90F). Halfway up the village, **Hôtel de la Poste**, ✆ 53 29 50 22, offers a warm welcome and rooms, some with a view, from 150F.

La Roque-Gageac ✉ 24250

★★La Belle Etoile, ✆ 53 29 45 63, is a modest family hotel with pretty views of the river and village. Try the *ravioles de langoustines* in the restaurant; menus from 125F. The gastronomic awards in the village, however, go to **La Plume d'Oie**, ✆ 53 29 57 05, where excellent, light renditions of Périgordin specialities are served in a charming dining room (menus from 100F). There are also four pretty rooms to rent, from 280F.

Siorac-en-Périgord ✉ 24170

Lots to choose from here, beginning with the **★★★Relais du Périgord Noir**, Place de la Poste, ✆ 53 31 60 02, a handsome stone building with pleasant if old-fashioned rooms. Relaxing **★★L'Escale**, ✆ 53 31 60 23, overlooks a little beach; **★★Auberge de la Petite Reine**, ✆ 53 31 60 42 is more expensive but offers just about every possible sport, including golf lessons.

Belvès ✉ 24170

Le Belvédère de Belvès, 1 Av. Crampel, ✆ 53 29 90 50, is an elegant hotel in the centre of town, all rooms with bath and TV (from 220F); meals from 80F. **★Le Home**, Place de la Croix-des-Frères, ✆ 53 29 01 65 is simple but adequate and open all year; good-value menus from 55F.

Buisson-le-Cadouin to Bergerac

Continuing down the Dordogne, **Buisson-le-Cadouin** with its river beaches and camp sites is an important crossroads, where you can catch the D 710 for Le Bugue and the Vézère valley or Périgueux, or continue west along the river (*see* below), or take the D 25 south along the Compostela pilgrimage route into the Forêt de la Bessède, to the once-famous Abbey of Cadouin.

Tourist Information

Beaumont-du-Périgord: Rue Romieu, ✆ 53 21 30 24 and 53 22 39 12

market days

Lalinde: Thursdays

Cadouin

In 1115, a holy man named Géraud de Salles and a group of canons from Périgueux's St-Front founded a monastery at the end of a wooded valley. Four years later they affiliated themselves to the Cistercians and built a vast Romanesque church and cloister in the Norman style; at the end of the 15th century the cloister collapsed and was lavishly rebuilt by masons from Languedoc and the Rouergue. Why such an ambitious enterprise in the middle of nowhere? Because in 1117, the abbey got hold of a precious gift that put it square on the pilgrimage map of France—the *Saint Suaire*, the cloth used to wrap the head of Christ, a lesser Shroud of Turin.

Christ's Turban

The legend goes that in the year 68, during the persecutions in Jerusalem, a converted Jew hid the relic to keep it from coming to harm. After he died his two sons—who hadn't converted to Christianity—inherited it, the younger buying the elder's share, after which he enjoyed a famous streak of luck, while the elder knew nothing but misfortune. The cloth remained in the family as a lucky charm, and when the last member died in 660, Christians and Jews in Jerusalem quarreled over it and put their case before a Muslim judge. He separated the two parties with a bonfire, and threw the cloth in; it proved itself the real McCoy by miraculously not burning, and when it blew over to the Christians' side, they got to keep it.

In 1100 Hugues, brother of King Louis the Fat of France, purchased the cloth, and when he died he gave it to his confessor. He in turn passed it on to a priest from Périgord, who returned home with it hidden in a vat of Communion wine. He could not help blabbing his secret, however, and it wasn't long before the newly arrived monks at Cadouin got it off him—in return for the job of watching over the relic. Pilgrims en route to Compostela poured in, until the Hundred Years' War, when the monks desposited the holy relic in Toulouse's Eglise du Taur for safekeeping. Toulouse, however, refused to give the cloth back, and the Cistercians of Cadouin had to spirit it out of the city by stealth (1456). In 1935, a scientific examination of the cloth showed it to be a fine Egyptian weaving from the 11th century. An even greater embarrassment was discovering that what for centuries had been considered a decorative border, was in fact an Arabic inscription in praise of Allah.

The Abbey Church and Cloister

The centre of the village is a sturdy, flamboyant **halle** supported on stone pillars, facing the **abbey church**, consecrated in 1154. All the austere decoration of the asymmetrical façade is in triplicate: three flat buttresses, three doorways, three windows and nine blind arches, while the interior, with its three naves and domes has been stripped naked by Cadouin's 19th-century restorers to reveal the vigorous architecture in all its purity. The reliquary holding the *Saint Suaire* originally hung behind the altar in the choir; only the dangling chains remain.

The entrance to the lovely, flamboyant Gothic **Cloister** is just to the right of the church *(open 10–12 and 2–5, closed Tues; July–Aug open daily 9–12 and 2–7, closed Jan; adm)*. It took so long to build that even a remote spot like Cadouin fell under the spell of the

Renaissance before its completion; while the first, eastern galleries have pinnacles carved with curly kale leaves and thistles, the west gallery, built in the 1500s, is entirely Renaissance. A hand-out in English explains the scenes carved on the columns, ceiling pendants and doorways, an altogether hearty mix of sacred and the profane—an Annunciation, scenes from the Last Judgment, Lazarus and Job keeping company with merchants fighting over a goose, an odd four-eyed, three-headed creature, and an anti-feminist trilogy—Samson and Delilah, a scene from the Lays of Virgil, and a courtesan straddling Aristotle (her name is Phyllis; this is from a medieval legend warning against the vanity of scholars). The debunked *Saint Suaire* is displayed with its copper gilt reliquary in the little museum in the Salle Capitulaire.

A Circular Detour around Cadouin

From Cadouin, consider a little circuit through the woods to the minor but interesting sights in the area: along the D 27 to the unfinished English bastide of **Molières**, then south in the valley of the river Couze (site of several prehistoric *abris*) to charming **Saint-Avit-Sénieur**, a tiny medieval hamlet around an immense fortified **church** from the 11th century, built by Augustinian monks. Despite the terrifying aspect of its towers, the abbey was sacked during Simon de Montfort's crusade; the church's wrecked domes were later replaced with ogival vaulting. Of the abbey, only sections of the cloister, dormitory and *salle capitulaire* survive; tours are offered in July and August.

From Saint-Avit, keep a lookout for signs to **Montferrand-du-Périgord**, a graceful medieval hilltop village to the southeast, dominated by the ruins of a medieval castle. It has a pretty 16th-century **halle** and a little Romanesque church by the village cemetery, although even better is the Romanesque church at **Sainte-Croix** (take the D 26E), with a stern *clocher-mur* and good carved capitals inside.

Some astute navigation on the wiggly narrow lanes, heading northwest of Sainte-Croix, will eventually reward with you with the D 660 for **Beaumont-du-Périgord**, a bastide founded in 1275 by a lieutenant of Edward I, Lucas de Thaney, who honoured Edward's father, Henry III, by laying out Beaumont's wide straight streets in the form of an H. One mighty gate remains of the old ramparts, the **Porte de Luzier**, as well as the 13th-century fortified church, **Saint-Laurent et Saint-Front**, which could probably lick even Saint-Avit's church in a pitched battle. Yet for all its military features, an effort was made to embellish the west front, with a carved porch and frieze depicting the four Evangelists, a hunt, a king and a mermaid. One of the southwest's most impressive Neolithic sights, a megalithic gallery known as the **Dolmen du Blanc** can be seen just over 3km to the south along the D 676, on the left side of the road. From Beaumont, the D 25 will take you back to Cadouin.

Back along the Dordogne: Limeuil and Trémolat

Before settling down in the western plains around Bergerac, the Dordogne pierces through a last stretch of glorious scenery between Le Buisson-de-Cadouin and Lalinde. From Le Buisson, follow the D 51 north 3km, then turn left for lofty **Limeuil**, where the Vézère flows into the Dordogne. The lords of Limeuil defended this important junction with bristling walls, in part intact, along with three mighty gates; the snug village inside, with cobbled streets and stone cottages laced with ivy and roses is almost too cute to be real. There's a Renaissance statue of the Virgin to look at in the church, and outside the village on the road to Le Bugue, the domed Romanesque **Saint-Martin** was jointly financed in 1194 by King Richard the Lion-Heart and King Philippe Auguste of France as an expiatory chapel for the murder of Thomas à Becket by Richard's dad (see the Latin inscription over the door, asking for God's mercy).

La Douce Limeuil

In the 16th century, Isabelle de Limeuil, daughter of the *seigneur* of Lanquais (*see* below), put the little town's name on the tip of every tongue in Paris. Rhapsodized by Brantôme as 'La Douce Limeuil', she was one of the loveliest of Catherine de' Medici's bevy of ladies-in-waiting, jokingly known as the 'flying squadron'. As Queen Mother, Catherine employed astrologers and sorcerers to get her way, and like the wicked witch in Snow White once sent a poison apple to an enemy; nor was she above using the virtue of her 'flying squadron' to seduce great Protestant nobles of France, in the hope that a conquest in the bedroom would translate somehow into a conquest for the Faith. Catherine sent the delightful Isabelle to charm one of the most powerful—the Prince de Condé. When a growing waistline betrayed the fact that she succeeded only too well, Catherine sent her home in disgrace. After the baby's birth, Catherine had a change of heart, and gave Isabelle in marriage to a social-climbing Italian banker to whom she owed money.

West of Limeuil the Dordogne's most majestic loop is followed by a scenic corniche road called the *Route du Cingle*. Along the way are a pair of belvederes and **Trémolat**, a charming village whose boundaries exactly match the outlines of a 6th-century estate owned by the parents of Trémolat's patron, Saint Cybard. Signs of a Carolingian chapel, built to mark the miracles Cybard performed at home, can still be traced in the nave of the 12th-century church. Trémolat may look distinctly familiar if you've seen Claude Chabrol's thriller *Le Boucher*, filmed here in 1970. Don't miss the spectacular views from the **Belvedere de Trémolat**, just to the west.

Lalinde and Lanquais

The *Route du Cingle* descends through Mauzac to the busy market town of **Lalinde**, which stretches between the Dordogne and the canal built to avoid the Saut de la Gratusse, a dangerous stretch of rapids. Before the canal was built, boatmen from Lalinde made a good living navigating all the flat-bottomed barges on the river through the rapids, warning of a great serpent that gobbled up anyone who foundered. A waterside **Chapelle de St-Front** was built over the worst stretch for heavenly aid, just opposite Lalinde's river terrace. Although founded in 1267 as an English bastide, only Lalinde's street plan and central square have survived the vicissitudes of time.

West of Lalinde, cross the Dordogne at **Couze-et-St-Front**, where the river water is so clear that from the 15th to the 19th century the village became the area's chief paper-maker, producing a fine-quality product sold throughout Europe; along the river you can see vestiges of nearly a dozen old mills. From here, the D 37 leads to the delightful **Château de Lanquais** *(open Apr–Oct 9.30–12 and 2.30–6, closed Thurs; adm)*. The stout medieval towers were built in the 15th century, and in the 1570s a pavilion modelled on the Louvre was added; the whole is furnished with antiques and chimneys believed to have been carved by itinerant Italian craftsmen. The 16th-century **Grange** to the right of the château hosts summer Baroque music concerts. Lanquais is also a great place to go riding, with scenic paths in every direction: Norwegian mounts can be hired at **La Crabe**, near the château, ✆ 53 24 99 13.

To continue west towards Bergerac, recross the Dordogne for the D 660, which heads straight and fast across the comparatively dull, flat landscape. It is here that you'll see the first of the vineyards that the river wears like a green sleeve down to the sea.

Pécharmant

A great comeback after decades of decline, this pocket wine region is located on the northeastern outskirts of Bergerac, on a south-facing amphitheatre (literally the 'charming hill') of granite sand and rubble topped with clay. Pécharmant is limited to four communes, producing a sumptuous, fra-grant, tannin-rich red wine that is one of the finest of Bergerac's 13 AOC wines. Made from Cabernet-Sauvignon, Cabernet-Franc and Merlot, with a touch of Malbec for smoothness, it needs at least four years in the cellar before drinking. On the road to Ste-Alvère, Colette Bourgès at **Clos Les Côtes**, ✆ 53 57 59 89, won a gold medal for her Pécharmant in 1992; compare it with the prestige, raspberry-scented wines aged in oaken casks at the 17th-century **Château de Tiregand** in Creysse, ✆ 53 23 21 08, especially the '88; the estate also bottles a fine white AOC Bergerac.

Where to Stay and Eating Out

Le Buisson ✉ 24480

***Manoir de Bellerive**, Route de Siorac, ✆ 53 27 16 19, is a completely reno-vated Directoire manor house in a 7-acre park, endowed with such creature comforts as air-conditioning, 12 TV channels, sauna, tennis and pool; breakfast available, but no restaurant.

Cadouin ✉ 24480

Auberge de la Salvetat, 2½km east of Cadouin on the D 54, ✆ 53 22 92 08, is a well-restored old farm in a pretty garden setting; rooms at 250F include use of the pool and other activities. Delicious menus from 90F (closed Wed).

Beaumont ✉ 24440

*Des Voyageurs, Rue Romieu, ✆ 53 22 30 11, has pretty little rooms, some with balconies, and a restaurant, **Chez Popaul**, a great place to fill up on masses of good, solid food—including a well-endowed buffet table of *entrées*—with menus from 80F; book. Another alternative is a farmhouse bed-and-breakfast 4½km south-east, at Labouquerie, just off the Monpazier road (**Chez Laparre**, ✆ 53 22 40 22). Beaumont is also endowed with an award-winning camp site: **Les Remparts**, ✆ 53 22 40 86, with plenty of shade, tennis, pool, and more.

Trémolat ✉ 24510

The utterly sybaritic *****Le Vieux Logis**, by the church, ✆ 53 22 80 06, is an old inn with an intimate garden and pool; the restaurant (in a former tobacco-drying barn or on the terrace) serves the best meals for miles around: heavenly *salade du terroir* and *languoustes*, with an excellent wine list, from 300F (closed Tues). Enjoying one of the prize views over the Dordogne, ****La Panoramic** is perched atop the Cingle de Trémolat, ✆ 53 22 80 42; rooms are quiet and cosy, and the restaurant features local dishes with menus beginning at 95F.

Limeuil ✉ 24510

**Les Terrasses de Beauregard, Rte de Trémolat, ✆ 53 22 03 15, is another panoramic hotel-restaurant overlooking the Dordogne with a good restaurant, with a better-than-average selection of non-meat dishes (*terrine de légumes* and *soupe aux fruits au Pécharmant*; menus from 110F.

Lalinde ✉ 24150

High over the river, the ****Hôtel du Château** 1 Rue de la Tour, ✆ 53 61 01 82 was begun in the 13th century, and has a pool and eight simple but comfortable rooms with TV in each. Its restaurant enjoys a wide reputation for its rich duck dishes; in the mushroom season, try the *fricassée de cèpes au beurre de Monbazillac* (closed Fri). The tranquil *****La Métairie**, east of town in Mauzac, ✆ 53 22 50 47, has nine rooms spread through a row of traditional Périgordin houses, and a kichen specializing in Périgordin treats with a light, modern touch (menus at 110–260 F).

Bergerac

Bergerac, known far and wide as the name of a poetic cavalier with a big nose who never even set foot in the town, is a fine little city where swans swim in the Dordogne and a tidy cluster of medieval, half-timbered houses basks by the old river port. It has also been recently christened the 'Capital of Purple Périgord', rectifying the hitherto unfair colour-lessness of this corner, in a *département* elsewhere divided into Green, White and Black. The purple is, of course, for *le vin*: this is the only wine-growing part of *département* number 24, where 93 communes produce a wide variety of vintages. Perhaps back in the days when Humphrey Bogart could seduce Lauren Bacall by blowing smoke in her face, it would have been dubbed nicotine Brown Périgord: tobacco is still a force to be reckoned with, and the city is not only the home of the national *Institut du Tabac* but also boasts a unique museum on the much-maligned weed, first popularized in France by Catherine de' Medici, who used it to cure her migraines.

History

Medieval *Brageira*, or modern Bergerac, grew up around a feudal castle, but really took off as a town with the construction of a bridge in the 12th century—at that time the only one on the river. As a result Bergerac became the chief crossroads on the Dordogne, and the town naturally evolved into a commercial centre and river port. Like most of France's self-reliant mercantile communities, the Bergeracois converted to Protestanism with gusto. During the Wars of Religion it was known as the 'French Geneva' for its ardour.

The convictions of its merchants spelt the slow death of Bergerac as a prosperous commercial city. First the walls of the city were destroyed by Richelieu in 1620; in 1681 dragoons forced the Calvinists to convert to Catholicism; in 1685 Louis XVI revoked the Edict of Nantes, denying Protestants the right to worship. By the end of the 17th century, an estimated 40,000 inhabitants of Bergerac and its surrounding *pays* had emigrated to England and Holland. The city only revived at the end of the 19th century thanks to tobacco, wine and the national gunpowder works.

Getting Around

Bordeaux's airport, Roumanières, lies 10km to the south, with daily air connections to Paris and Lyon (© 53 57 76 03). The railway station (© 53 57 26 71), north of the centre, is on the Bordeaux–Sarlat line; to get on the main Paris–Périgueux–Agen line, you have to go by way of Le Buisson. There's convenient parking by the river at Place du Port.

Tourist Information

97 Rue Neuve d'Argenson, 24100, © 53 57 03 11

market days

Although the stalls in the modern covered market are open daily, Wednesdays and Saturday mornings are Bergerac's big shopping days, with additional stalls outside the market and around Notre-Dame church.

The National Tobacco Museum

Open Tues–Fri 10–12 and 2–6, Sat till 5, Sun 2.30–6.30; adm—but no smoking!

Although Bergerac occupies both banks of the Dordogne, all the interesting points for visitors are concentrated in the pedestrian area on the north bank. Here restoration work in the last 15 years has uncovered a handsome set of buildings from the 14th to the 17th century—Bergerac's heyday. Some of the finest are in Place du Feu, especially the handsome, turretted, **Maison Peyrarède** (1604), now the National Tobacco Museum. The museum is chock-full of curiosities on the herb, beginning with documents on its role as the sacred medicine of Aztec gods and a binder of peace agreements among North American tribes (the Sioux calumet, or peace pipe is one of the museum's prize exhibits). As other items in the first room show, widespread use in Europe came only after the whole west coast of Africa had adopted the vice by the end of the 1500s, thanks to the slave ships that brought it across the Atlantic to trade for their human cargoes. Among the astonishing variety of African pipes displayed is a bowl from the Cameroons that seems to be an intricately carved biography of the smoker.

The upstairs rooms trace the use of tobacco in Europe, beginning with snuff—the most popular way to take tobacco in France from the late 16th century until the Revolution, when clay and porcelain—and later briarwood pipes, with bowls shaped like the heads of famous men—became the rage. There are paintings by Teniers, Meissonnier and others, showing happy snuff-takers and puffers, but it was the 19th-century invention of the cigar (from the Spanish *cigarra* or cicada, for its resemblance to the insect's body) and cigarette that awoke the masses to the delights of smoking. Among the cigar and cigarette holders, see especially the 1850 Viennese meerschaum cigar holder carved with a Sicilian wedding. One of the last exhibits is a curious machine capable of carving a dozen pipe bowls at once.

The rest of the museum covers the history of Bergerac. Not much has survived all the troubles—some 14th-century ceramics, pharmaceutical jars and other titbits.

Cloître des Récollets

Behind the tobacco museum in Place du Dr-Cayla is Bergerac's 19th-century Protestant Temple, where only occasional services are held for the last die-hard Calvinists. Just behind it is the picturesque 16th-century **Cloître des Récollets**, with its wooden gallery and lone tree *(free entry, through the glass door)*. The Récollets were a Franciscan order founded in Spain in the late 1400s, named, according to the *Catholic Dictionary* 'from the detachment from creatures and a recollection in God which the founders aimed at.' Louis XIII charged the Récollets with the task of bringing the burghers of Bergerac back to the Catholic fold; after the revocation of the Edict of Nantes their methods of persuasion included book burnings. Today their cloister serves as headquarters of the regional wine council: the Cellier de Récollets offers a wide selection of Bergerac vintages and other regional products.

From Place du Dr-Cayla it's a few steps up to charming, tree-filled Place de La Myrpe and the town's biggest photo opportunity, its statue of swashbuckling **Cyrano de Bergerac**. Cyrano owes his appearance here to Edmond Rostand's tremendously successful 1897 play *Cyrano de Bergerac*. Rostand based much of his character on the

CYRANO DE BERGERAC

real Savien Cyrano (1619–55) born in Paris of Italian parents. A swashbuckling extrovert and poet (the records say nothing of his olfactory appendage), he was appointed as a musketeer in a company of Gascons; to better fit in with that boastful lot, he added Bergerac to his name. He was a celebrated duellist, and published tragedies, comedies, letters and a humorous essay called *Le Voyage dans la Lune*. Until the early 20th century, all of the real Cyrano's biographers took the Bergerac in his name as fact; but if he is not a literally a native son, he will always be one in a literary sense, and anyway Bergerac is grateful for the free advertising.

At the end of Place de La Myrpe is the **Musée du Vin et de la Batellerie**—an interesting collection of models and tools used by vintners, coopers and boatmen in the days of yore—installed in a half-timbered boatsmen's tavern from the 1700s *(open Tues–Fri 10–12 and 2–5.30, Sat 10–12 and Sun from 15 Mar–15 Nov 2.30–6.30)*. Just up Rue des Conférences, the little **Musée d'Art Sacré** occupies a 17th-century Catholic mission *(open Easter week, July and Aug daily exc Mon 3.30–6; other times Wed and Sun only 3.30–6)*. It displays typical Counter-Reformation church paraphernalia and the strange Gallo-Roman *Buste Acéphale de Lauzerte*, a white half-bust of a female—reminiscent in its stylization of ancient Cycladic sculpture—holding its severed head to its abdomen, just like St Denis, the patron saint of Paris. Way before the French Revolution, the Gauls were always chopping off heads, tying them to the tails of their horses or impaling them on stakes in their temples, where they were perhaps used as intermediaries with ancestors in the underworld. Female figures, however, are rare.

Rue des Conférences continues to Rue des Fontaines, with two important buildings: **Maison Doublet**, where the future Henri IV and the agents of Henri III negotiated a truce between Protestant and Catholic forces in 1577, and the 14th-century **Vieille Auberge**, at 27 Rue des Fontaines. Rue de St-James leads from here to long Place Pélissière and the church of **St-Jacques**, which began in the 12th century as a pilgrim hostel, but was completely rebuilt in the 17th century after the Catholic victory. At the same time the chief Protestant temple, a block up Grand Rue, was demolished; in 1885 a metal market pavilion was built on the site. Further up the Grand Rue stands the lofty neogothic bell tower of **Notre Dame**, a creation of those two busy 19th-century re-creators of the old, Viollet-le-Duc and Paul Abadie. It does boast two 16th-century Italian paintings, donated from the collections of the Duc d'Orléans: *Adoration of the Magi* by Pordenone and *Adoration of the Shepherds* by Godenzio Ferrari, a pupil of Leonardo da Vinci.

Around Bergerac

Just outside the city, on the D 660 towards Lalinde, are the laboratories and botanical gardens of the Institut du Tabac at the **Domaine de la Tour**. The institute was created in 1927 to improve the product of the region's nearly 300 growers, who have moved away from brown tobacco to the lighter, low-tar blond. Over a thousand varieties of *Nicotiana* (named after the 16th-century French diplomat Jean Nicot, who introduced tobacco to France) are grown here, and cigarettes aren't their only use—to find out more, ring ahead to vist, © 53 63 66 00.

Six km south of Bergerac is the foursquare **Château de Monbazillac** *(open June–Sept 10–12.30 and 2–7.30, Oct–May 10–12 and 2–5)*, erected by Charles d'Aydie, seigneur of Bergerac, in 1550 and—miraculously—essentially the same as the day it was built, undamaged and unimproved: a nice compromise between the necessities of defence, with its dry moat, machicolations, towers and parapet walk, and beauty, in its array of rooflines covered in flat brown tiles, dormers and mullioned windows, and graceful fleur-de-lis weather vanes that even managed to escape the Revolution. The owners were Protestants after 1607, made vicomtes by Henri IV, and they used the castle as a venue for theological discussions and as a refuge for persecuted pastors, until the Vicomtesse neatly recanted the day she heard of the revocation of the Edict of Nantes.

The grounds and two lower floors of the castle are open to the public. There are rooms filled with old Périgordin cupboards and dressers, antique maps of the area, Flemish tapestries, rare Huguenot books that escaped the book-burnings, prints by engraver Jacques Callot, who presaged Goya's series on the horrors of war, and the flamboyant dining room made for the flamboyant Comédie Française actor Mounet-Sully. As Monbazillac is also the namesake and headquarters for the cooperative of one of Bergerac's most famous vintages, you can also visit and taste in the cellars.

Another famous spot in the area is the **Moulin de Malfourat**, just west on the D 14E, a ruined windmill with a bird's-eye view and orientation table; nor should lovers of the Romanesque miss the church at **Sadillac**, due south, with a dome and excellent animal carvings.

Monbazillac, and the Other Wines of Bergerac

Although overshadowed by the elite vineyards of nearby Bordeaux, Bergerac has produced wines since the 12th century and began exporting them to England in 1250. Although quality controls in the 1300s had already strictly defined the planting area, or *vinata*, and set the date of the harvest, Bordeaux used its position downriver to give priority to its own wines until 1511, when the Parlement of Guyenne granted Bergerac a charter guaranteeing access to the Atlantic.

By that time, however, Bergerac with its Protestant connections had built up an alternative overland trade with Holland and Scandinavia. And in the 18th century when the Dutch developed a taste for sweet, heavy wines, or *vins liquoreux*, the best vineyards on the chalky clay hills of **Monbazillac** were converted to the production of a strong white dessert wine using mostly Sémillon grapes, with small quanities of Muscadelle and Sauvignon. Unusually, the vines are planted on the steep, north-facing slopes to take advantage of a microclimate similar to that of the Sauternes and Barsac areas, where autumnal morning mists help to incubate *Botrytis cinerea*, the 'noble rot' that withers the grapes but adds an extra, distinctive sweetness and fragrance that tastes so good when served icy cold with *foie gras*, melon (with a dash of Angostura bitters) and desserts.

In the 19th century, the reputation of Monbazillac slowly sank, becoming 'the poor man's Sauternes' and then simply cheap plonk. In the 1960s, with the change of fashion to drier wines, Monbazillac's growers rooted up much of the old stock and replanted new vines, especially Sauvignon, to produce dry white wines and drier, lighter *vins liquoureux*. The result is a lovely golden colour that deepens with age, and a scent of wild flowers mellowing into a distinct 'roasted' flavour when aged. Monbazillac averages 13 degrees, but goes up to 15 degrees in good years—1988, 1989 and 1990 were all superb and may be safely kept, they say, for 30 years.

Some Monbazillac growers also produce a selection of Bergerac's other AOC vintages, in red, rosé or white. The reds are bright and robust when drunk young, while the whites are the perfect summer drink and an accompaniment to seafood or hors d'oeuvres. Fine **Côtes de Bergerac Rouge** is produced at **Château La Borderie**, © 53 57 00 36, and **Château Theulet**, © 53 57 30 43 (the 88 is especially fine). To the west, in the minute AOC region of Saussignac that separates Monbazillac from the vineyards of the Bordelais, **Château Court-les-Muts** in Razac-de-Saussignac produces a singular *moelleux* wine, but only in the best years; the estate also bottles a good dry red and elegant white AOC Bergerac.

Bergerac ✉ *24100*   **Where to Stay**

The modern ★★★**De Bordeaux**, 38 Place Gambetta, © 53 57 12 83, offers a chance to relax in the centre of Bergerac, with its garden and pool; its restaurant, **Le Terroir**, serves unusual delicacies—the most upriver version of *lamproie à la bordelaise and aiguillettes de canard au miel* (menus 90–160F). Just to the north, ★★**Le Cyrano** (there had to be one!), 2 Bd Montaigne, © 53 57 02 76, has 11 fine rooms and the best restaurant in town, where succulent meat and fish dishes are grilled as you watch; also try the delicious *lasagne au fumet de cèpes* (menus from 95F). For something less expensive, but central and friendly, ★★**Le Family**, 3 Rue du Dragon near Place du Marché Couvert, © 53 57 80 90; parking is available in a nearby garage.

Around Bergerac

Especially designed for family vacations, the 17th-century ★★★**Manior Le Grand Vignoble**, amid woods and meadows at St-Julien-de-Crempse (12½km north of Bergerac), © 53 24 23 18, has three monitors to entertain the small fry with pony rides, dance lessons, playground, minigolf, pool, bike rides and tennis. Three km from Bergerac on the Périgueux road, *****La Flambée**, ✆ 53 57 52 33, is noted for its kitchen's delicious southwest specialities (200F); stay in the hotel, and you can work off that *feuilleté de truffes* in the pool or tennis court, or rambling about the panoramic park. The hospitable **Ferme de Séjour Marie-Jeanne Archer**, (La Barabie D 30, 24520 Lamonzie-Montastruc, ✆ 53 23 22 47 or 53 23 22 26), is a wonderfully seductive place to linger and reasonably priced to boot; delicious breakfasts and meals, bikes to borrow, and Périgordin cooking workshops Nov–May. Two nights minimum stay.

Eating Out

The aforementioned hotels are at the top of the list, but alternatives near the Tobacco Museum include tasty Moroccan *tajines* and couscous at **Le Sud**, 19 Rue de l'Ancien Port, ✆ 53 27 26 81, where a full meal runs between 95 and 100F, or **Le Poivre et Sel**, 11 Rue de l'Ancient Port, ✆ 53 27 02 30, with a wide variety of salads and desserts, and menus at 70 and 200F.

Monbazillac (24240) is home to the celebrated **Les Ruines**, Route de Mont-de-Marsan, ✆ 53 57 16 37, in a contemporary building incorporating 12th-century fireplaces, with a terrace in the garden where you can linger over an *escalope de foie gras au vin de noix* or *écrevisses* with artichoke hearts; lunch menu from 75F, dinner around 200F. Closed Mon, Sat lunch, Sun night (unless you book a day in advance) and Sept. The restaurant at the **Château de Monbazillac**, ✆ 53 58 38 93, serves traditional cuisine of Périgord, with a long wine list; in the summer inexpensive quick lunches are available on the terrace (from 140F, closed Mon).

At Lamonzie-Saint-Martin, on the road to Bordeaux, the **Ferme-Auberge Le Monteil**, ✆ 53 24 07 59 (book ahead), offers well-prepared farm dishes beginning with *tourain à l'ail* and ending up with a home-made dessert, from June–Aug, menus from 90F. Best of all, however, is **La Vieille Grange**, a pretty country restaurant with a terrace and Louis XIII décor at La Petite Forêt in Saint-Nexans, just southeast of Bergerac, ✆ 53 24 32 21, where the cuisine of Périgord meets Italy to produce some luscious surprises (menus from 110F, closed Wed).

West of Bergerac to Saint-Emilion

The main D 936 drives relentlessly west towards Bordeaux, more or less following the route of the Dordogne. If this is your first trip, leave yourself a good day to dawdle on the way—especially in the haunting medieval lanes of Saint-Emilion. The first stop on the way is **Sainte-Foy-la-Grande**, a bustling market town that was founded as a bastide by Alphonse de Poitiers in 1255. Like Bergerac it was a Huguenot stronghold, and to this day it retains a sizeable Protestant population. Although none of the architecture is out of the ordinary, there are some fine old houses along the main street, Rue de la République, and in the arcaded Place Gambetta.

The next large town, **Lamothe-Montravel** on the north bank, produces its own fine AOC wine as does **Castillon-la-Bataille**; just east of the village, along the D 936, is a signpost for the 'Monument à Talbot'. This marks the spot where the last battle of the Hundred Years' War was fought on 17 July 1453. The English commander, John Talbot, Earl of Shrewsbury, was at Mass when a spy told him that the French, camped near the Dordogne, were retreating. Talbot, still in his bright Sunday clothes, hopped on a horse to see for himself, only to learn that if the French were retreating, it was only to attack—*reculer pour mieux sauter*; and because he was so conspicuous, Talbot was one of the first of 4000 to die. The monument in a field marks the spot where he was axed down.

There are fine views from points north of Castillon: north, from **St-Philippe-d'Aiguille** and its water tower (*château d'eau*), with an orientation table, although the main reason for heading this way is to continue up to **Petit-Palais-et-Cornemps** to see its lovely and magnificent 13th-century Romanesque church, **St-Pierre**. Though simple in form, the façade is lavishly covered with sculptures of animals and birds. On either side of the main door are figures inspired by antique models, especially the relief of the man pulling an arrow or spine from his foot.

Moncaret and Saint-Michel-de-Montaigne

Just north of the D 936 is **Moncaret**, where in 1887 workmen digging the foundations for a bathhouse next to the church struck their shovels on the rock-hard mosaic floors of the luxurious baths of a 2nd–4th century AD **Gallo-Roman villa**. The presence of the villa must have been known to the builders of the church, who incorporated a funerary stele into the apse (along with a primitive Carolingian relief of Adam and Eve) and reused some Roman capitals for its columns; other items (vases, tombs, etc) discovered in the area are now in the **museum** flanking the excavations.

North of Montcaret, swathed in vineyards, the hamlet of St-Michel-de-Montaigne stands on the outskirts of the **Château de Montaigne**, purchased by the philosopher's great-grandfather, merchant Raymond Eyquem in 1477. In 1533, it saw the birth of Michel Eyquem de Montaigne, who was baptized in the village church. In 1885, the château went up in flames, but by good fortune the fire spared Montaigne's home within a home, the round tower where he wrote his famous *Essays (guided tours daily 9–12 and 2–7, closed Mon and 6 Jan–6 Feb; adm)*. There's a minute chapel on the ground floor, its altar painted with a scene of St Michael stabbing the dragon, of which the tolerant Montaigne said: 'I like to light a candle to St Michael, and to his serpent, too.' Stairs wind up to the bedroom on the next floor, equipped with a handy toilet, while upstairs the philosopher installed his famous inner sanctum, a library, where he could sit at his desk surrounded by bookshelves and windows, with a stone armchair niche in the wall for quiet readings. The books are all gone now, but the beams still bear the Greek and Latin maxims Montaigne inscribed on them to ponder; you can see a few scratched out when he tired of them. He died here after a long illness in 1592, and his heart is buried in the village church.

Michel de Montaigne

Few men at any time have had the wise and gentle upbringing of Michel de Montaigne, the eldest of eight children raised 'without whip or tears' by a Catholic father and Jewish mother. They brought in a tutor to teach him Latin as his first language, and he learned Greek as a child's game. As a young man, he followed the legal and public career destined for him as a court counsellor in Périgueux and Bordeaux; in the latter he met his dear friend La Boétie of Sarlat (*see* p.122). He married in 1565, his wife providing him such a large dowry that in 1571, despairing over the hypocrisy of the law and the violence of the Wars of Religion, Montaigne could afford to retreat from the world to his château above the Dordogne. He was 39 at the time, and vowed to spend his life doing nothing at all; instead, he wrote three volumes of *Essays*.

The freest French thinker of the 16th century, Montaigne was also the most sceptical, the product of sober, heartfelt sorrow at the dogmas, cruelty and fanaticism of his day. In his writings he reasoned that if human beliefs throughout history have fluctuated so violently, if one age's reason and common sense inevitably seemed ridiculous to the next, then the only sane response to the world was to not believe in its external things and smilingly accept constant mutability and chaos. *Que sais-je?* ('What do I know?') was his motto, and he had it inscribed over the château door. In such a world one could only be true to oneself and live as tranquilly as possible. 'To live properly is our great and glorious masterpiece' he wrote. In 1580 he went to Italy, where he heard to his surprise that he had been elected Mayor of Bordeaux. He reluctantly returned, and was re-elected for another term, an unusual honour, in recognition of his moderation and justice, and his efforts to bring about a reconciliation between Catholics and Protestants.

Where to Stay and Eating Out

Gensac ✉ 33890

Gensac, 2km south of Pessac on the south bank of the Dordogne, is the site of **Les Remparts**, 16 Rue du Château, ✆ 57 47 43 46; the site offers lovely views across the valley, the perfect accompaniment to the delights on your plate: try the *médaillon de veau à la crème de thym*; menus from 95F (closed Mon lunch and Tues). Closer to the river on the D 130, **Le Belvédère**, near La Tourbeille, ✆ 57 47 40 33 has more lovely views and generous, good-value menus (closed Tues night and Wed).

Castillon ✉ 33350

Le Bateau Ivre, ✆ 57 40 30 30, a small boat restaurant near the bridge, serves filling meals of traditional southwest specialities, accompanied with a bottle of Côte-de-Castillon, one of the finest Bordeaux Supérieur wines; 90F (closed Mon).

St·Michel·de·Montaigne ✉ 24230

Le Jardin d'Eyquem, ☎ 53 24 89 59 has five very nice flats in a restored building with a pool in the middle of a vineyard (from 480F).

Saint-Emilion

Set in a natural amphitheatre surrounded by its famous vines, Saint-Emilion is a gem of a town mellowed to the colour of old piano keys. A favourite of medieval popes and English kings, it has been restored to much of its old elegance, but leave your high heels at home; lanes called *tetres*, unevenly paved with granite blocks from Cornwall (the ballast of England's wine ships) are so steep that handrails have been installed down their centres. For all that, the town keeps its greatest secrets underground—not only the ruby nectar in its cellars, but Europe's largest subterreanean church, where chthonic fertility cults are covered with a thin veneer of medieval Christianity. Come late in the day to avoid the crowds of day-trippers, stay overnight, and see the sights first thing in the morning.

History

Known simply as Ascumbas, or 'hill' in Gallo-Roman times, the town's destiny was set in motion in the 8th century with the arrival of a Benedictine hermit named Emilion. His piety attracted a number of companions, and they enlarged the natural shelters and caves on the site. The largest one was used as a church, slowly excavated until the 11th century to become the Eglise Monolithe. When the founder died, the monastery took his name: *Sent-Melyon* in *langue d'oc.*

As Libourne was not yet founded, the walled town that grew up around the monastery controlled this section of the Dordogne. It received its first charter in 1199 from John Lackland, who also set up a new civil authority of a hundred peers from the bourgeoisie known as the Jurade. The Jurade was responsible for everything from tax collecting and the local militia to maintaining the quality of the wine up until the time of the Revolution—wine that was imported by the *tonne* to the English court, for unlike Bergerac just upriver, Saint-Emilion enjoyed the same export privileges as Bordeaux. English interest was so keen that in 1289 Edward I set the limits of the production area—the same limits used to this day.

Getting Around

There are two railway stations nearby: St Emilion's on the Bordeaux–Bergerac–Sarlat line and Libourne, 7km away, on the Bordeaux–Paris TGV line. There are several Citram buses daily for Bordeaux and Libourne. The country lanes around St-Emilion make for a fun spin on a bike; hire one at the *Logis des Remparts* hotel.

Tourist Information

Place des Créneaux, © 57 24 72 03, the place to book and start the 45min guided visits of St-Emilion's subterranean monuments; open daily 9.30–12.30 and 1.45–6.

market days

Sunday mornings at Porte Bouqueyre

St-Emilion, On Your Own

Four of the town's principal sights can only be seen on the tourist office's guided tour (*see* below); but don't fail to take a wander on your own. If you're staying the night, save the tour of the well-preserved town walls for dusk, when the views are most romantic.

Entering Saint-Emilion from the south on the D 122, you'll pass a public park built around the **Masion Gaudet**, home of the Girondin deputy, Marguerite Elie Gaudet, who managed to flee Robespierre's executions in Paris with seven other Girondins. They hid out for nine months in Saint-Emilion, in a dark damp tunnel under the garden of Gaudet's sister-in-law, Marie-Thérèse Bouquey. All but one were captured by Robespierre's henchmen and guillotined—ironically only a few days before 9 Thermidor, when Robespierre himself got the chop. Across the road, rising abruptly out of a vineyard, the **Grandes Murailles** is a single 65-ft wall with ogival arches that belonged to the Dominican monastery of 1287; as it was outside the town walls, it was destroyed by a marauding French army in 1337.

Just beyond is the main entrance to Saint-Emilion, the **Porte Bourgeoise**. Take the first left to see the more substantial remains of the once-sumptuous **Palais Cardinal**, built in 1316 by the Cardinal de Sainte-Luce, nephew of Pope Clement V. Continue up Rue Gaudet, where just beyond Place du Chapitre the Dominicans rebuilt their monastery, or **Couvent des Jacobins**, after a donation in 1378 by the English Lieutenant of Aquitaine, Jean de Neville—a donation that had to be reconfirmed several times in the face of opposition by the Jurade, who didn't think Saint-Emilion *intra muros* had room for any more monks. Nevertheless, until the Revolution, this church held the town's main pilgrimage attraction: a statue of St Valéry, patron of Saint-Emilion's vintners (now in the Collégiale). New brides would gently wipe the statue with their handkerchiefs while wishing to become pregnant; Valéry's exact role in the matter was the cause for many pleasantries.

Continue straight up Rue Gaudet, passing the 14th-century **Maison Gothique** on the left. The streets fork here: take Rue des Cordeliers for the **Commanderie**, an old Templar post, and the ruined, partially overgrown Romanesque **Cloître des Cordeliers** *(open 10–12.30 and 2–6.30)*, built in 1383 by the Franciscans who had to get a bull from Pope Gregory XI to be able to build in the town. In the adjacent chapel, note the carving of two snakes entering a jar, a symbol that goes back to the ancient Greeks; snakes were commonly used to portray the *daimones*, or genius and identity of a family or tribe. Twins were a symbol of fertility; read the jar as a cornucopia. The Franciscans must have copied it from the Eglise Monolithe, where it appears twice.

Backtrack to Rue Gaudet and Rue de la Cadène, which soon passes under the 16th-century arch of the **Porte et la Maison de la Cadène**, 'of the chain' suggesting that the street could be quickly closed off in case of emergency. Note the half-timbered house on the left, decorated with a pair of grotesque heads and dolphins. Further up, Rue Gaudet runs into **Place du Marché**, a magnificent urbane stage set built over St-Emilion's first cemetery, its cafés shaded by a Liberty Tree from the Revolution of 1848. Built into the flank of the cliff here is the strange Eglise Monolithe, a misnomer, for it's not built out of a single stone, but dug into the rock. It can only be visited on the guided tour *(see* above for hours).

The Guided Tour

The **Eglise Monolithe** was excavated by the Benedictines between the 8th and 11th centuries, until they attained a cavity measuring 38 by 20 m; then they gave it up to construct the Collégiale. It is a primitive, sombre and uncanny place, its nave supported by ten rough, ill-aligned pillars, its colourful 12th-century murals nearly completely obliterated during the Revolution, when it was used as a saltpetre factory; the only decoration that remains are bas-reliefs: four winged angels, signs of the zodiac, and a dedicatory inscription. Bell ropes from the original bell tower hung through the hole in the ceiling.

Next to the Eglise Monolithe is the entrance to the round **Chapelle de la Trinité**, built in the 13th century by Augustinian monks to the memory of St Emilion, and converted into a coopery during the Revolution. Bring your specs to see the interesting but faded wall paintings between the ribs of the apse. An 8th-century sarcophagus and knight's tomb have been placed here, a preview of the adjacent 8th-century **catacombs**, excavated when the Place du Marché cemetery was filled to overflowing with the dearly departed who longed to be near the holy relics of Emilion. Bones were deposited through the funnel-like cupola connecting the catacombs with the cemetery of the canons: around the vault you can make out the engraved figures of three corpses with upraised arms, weird zombies supposedly symbolic of the Resurrection. Lastly, the tour takes in the **Grotte de l'Ermitage** where Emilion lived, a cave that over the centuries has evolved into a little chapel in the form of a Latin cross. He had running water from a natural spring, worshipped since pagan times and reputedly good for what ails you, especially eye diseases; young women who could drop two hairpins into the water in the form of a cross were sure to be married within the year. Carved in the stone are the hermit's 'armchair', where sterile women would sit, hoping for offspring, and his bed, which probably doubled as his tomb.

The Collégiale

From Place du Marché, walk up steep Tertre de la Tente to Rue du Clocher. To the left opens up Place des Créneaux, where the 11th–15th century **bell tower** rises up 173ft, the second highest in the Gironde after St-Michel of Bordeaux; for a small fee you can climb the 198 steps for a superb view of all St-Emilion. Here, too, is the entrance to the **Eglise Collégiale**, a hotchpotch of a church built over a number of periods, begun in 1110 (the period of the west portal, the Byzantine cupolas, and frescoes of a devil, St Catherine and the Virgin on the right wall of the nave). The north portal has a tympanum adorned with a Last Judgment from 1306, with niches that once held high reliefs of the Apostles; in the choir are 15th-century stalls and the treasure, with the relics of Saint-Emilion. From the nearby tourist office you can visit the Gothic **Cloître de la Collégiale** *(open in the summer 9.30–12.30 and 2.45 and 7; adm)*, while opposite the church in Rue des Ecoles is the **Musée du Logis de Malet** *(open June–Sept)*, with a small archaeological and historical collection. Follow Rue des Ecoles to Rue du Couvent and the austere Norman **Tour du Roi**, the donjon of the castle built by Henry III *c.* 1237, with more grand views *(open daily 9.30–12.30 and 2.30–6.45; adm)*.

Saint-Emilion and Saint-Emilion Grand Cru

The most annoying problem facing the Gallo-Roman inhabitants of Aquitaine was the fact that they had to import wine from the Mediterranean. Every year new varieties of grapes were tried, but none grew well in the climate until sometime around the year 20, when the local druids came across vines called *basilica* with wide-grained wood and fairly loose fruit that the Greeks in Marseille had imported from Epirus (modern Albania). The Biturige druids of Burdigala (Bordeaux) planted them around what is now Saint-Emilion, where they took so well that the Biturgies, never known for their modesty, renamed the vines *biturica*. Just south of Saint-Emilion's walls at Château Belair, you can still see where they grew in ancient 'flower pot' rows gouged into rock and filled with soil; adjacent to Château Belair are the ruins of an Imperial Roman villa believed to have belonged to the poet and governor Ausonius, whose grandfather and father were said to be druids, and who lent his name to the greatest, most rarefied—and smallest—of the Saint-Emilion estates, Château Ausone.

The reputation of Saint-Emilion soared in the Middle Ages. The French praised it as the *vin honorifique*, the English as the 'king of wines'. No one can really explain why it's so good; the growing area on the north bank of the Dordogne enjoys no special microclimate, and the soil has no prominent characteristic besides its complexity, with clay present in most places; hence the predominant variety (over 60 per cent) is Merlot, which does well in clay, mixed with Cabernet Franc (or Bouchet, as it's called here), Cabernet Sauvignon and/or Malbec. A substantial factor in the creation of this ruby nectar has been some of the strictest quality control in France. Estates are remarkably small compared to others in the Bordelais (the Grands Crus are only 10 to 20 hectares). In 1921 it was decided to limit the growing area to that decreed by Edward I in the 13th century. In 1948 the Jurade of Saint-Emilion was reincarnated, complete with the swish scarlet caps and robes trimmed in ermine for special occasions; the members announce the *Ban des Vendages*, or beginning of the harvest, with a fête the night before and a procession to the top of the Tour du Roi with a resounding blast of trumpets over the countryside. The Jurats also gather for the crucial *Jugement du vin nouveau* in June, to taste each new wine to see whether or not it merits its *appellation*. You can make your own tests the first weekend in May, when a dozen châteaux open their doors for free tastings of the previous year's harvest.

What is especially confusing about Saint-Emilion is the often changing classifications within the *appellation*. The last revision in 1985 divides the châteaux into *Premiers Grands Crus Classés A* (of which there are only two, Ausone and Cheval-Blanc), followed by nine others distinguished by *Classé B*, followed by 63 *Grands Crus Classés*, all of which have to undergo a second tasting two years or so after the harvest to merit their labels. Below these come the simple Saint-Emilion and its eight satellite communities, which came under the authority of the medieval Jurade (St-Laurent-des-Combes, St-Hippolyte, St-Christophe-des-Bardes and St-Etienne-de-Lisse are considered the best).

The **Maison du Vin**, Place Pierre-Meyrat, © 57 74 42 42, has the most up-to-date information on the châteaux open for visits and their visiting hours. Few have any architectural distinction; very few offer tastings for individuals—unless you go on one of the tourist office's afternoon tours *(June–September, English translation available)*. Take the road to Pomerol to ogle two of St-Emilion's greatest vintners, Cheval-Blanc and Figeac, the latter with a handsome 18th-century manor house.

In the Environs of St-Emilion

Nearly every little village in the area has a Romanesque church worth a look. One of the best, **St-Martin-de-Mazerat** (1137) is less than a kilometre west; its bell tower stood several storeys higher until the Jurats ordered it cut down to size to keep Huguenots from using it to bombard Saint-Emilion. Note, too, the richly carved south portal. Due west of Saint-Emilion, overlooking the Dordogne on the D 19 is the largest menhir in the Gironde, the 16-ft **Pierrefite**. Unlike most menhirs, it gets a big summer solstice party—no druids, but old jazz, bonfires, floating candles in the Dordogne, games, food and wine.

Three km north of Saint-Emilion, the 18th-century **Château Saint-Georges** is the most beautiful estate in the area, incorporating several towers from the original castle and a magnificent garden stair reminiscent of the one behind Bordeaux's Grand-Théâtre. Inside is the **Ecomusée du Libournais** *(open Mar–Nov, 10–12 and 2–6.30, July and Aug 10–1 and 2–7.30; adm)* a historical and wine museum with an educational path through a vineyard. The village of St-Georges's 12th-century church has bizarre heads carved on the capitals around the door. **Lussac**, another 4km north, produces excellent Lussac-Saint-Emilion, which you can learn all about in the village's Maison du Vin.

Don't expect to find any bargains in St-Emilion, either regarding wine or hotels. Up at Place du Clocher, the handsome stone ★★★★**Hostellerie de Plaisance**, ✆ 57 24 72 32, is the most luxurious, and the only one with facilities for the disabled; it has an elegant gourmet restaurant and terrace featuring the likes of *langoustines royales* and *mignons de boeuf aux girolles* (closed Jan, good-value menus from 140F). The stately classic ★★★**Palais Cardinal**, Place du 11 Novembre 1918, ✆ 57 24 72 39, has the advantages of a heated pool; ask for a room overlooking the garden terrace. The sweet and pretty ★★★**Le Logis des Remparts**, 18 Rue Gaudet, ✆ 57 24 70 43, has a little inner courtyard and rooms complete with bath and TV. Least expensive, the little ★★**Auberge de la Commanderie**, on pretty Rue des Cordeliers, ✆ 57 24 70 19, has 18 rooms; alternatively there's an excellent camp site with a pool and tennis courts, **La Barbanne**, 3km north from St-Emilion on the Montagne road, ✆ 57 24 75 80. In Lussac you can stay amid the vineyards at **Château de Roques**, a bed-and-breakfast, ✆ 57 74 69 56, with good, copious country cooking (at around 100F), bikes to rent and free wine tasting, too; open all year.

Eating Out

Besides the aforementioned Plaisance, you can dine old-fashionedly well at **Le Tertre** on Tertre de la Tente, ✆ 57 74 46 33, a classic provincial restaurant serving a choice of menus from 130F (mussels with saffron, coq au vin, etc) and a special low-calorie, 170F menu; closed Sun dinner except in the summer, and from Nov–Jan. In Place de l'Eglise Monolithe, **Amelia Canta**, ✆ 57 74 48 03 is a reliable brasserie, with a strategically located terrace and menus from 75F. Local gourmets will tell you that St-Emilion's wines go with everything except strong cheeses, and especially well with that Bordelaise favourite, lamprey. If you'd rather stick to the wine, St-Emilion has a wine bar, **L'Envers du Décor**, Rue du Clocher, ✆ 57 74 48 31, where you can try a wide variety of local labels by the glass, with a snack or light meal (around 70F, closed Sun). In town you'll see many signs for *Macaroons de Saint-Emilion*, a traditional sweet dating back to the town's long-gone Ursuline nuns; the best are made at **Mady Moulierac** in Rue du Clocher.

The Libournais and the Haute Gironde

In 1269, Sir Richard de Leyburn, of Leybourne, Kent, undertook to build the bastide port decreed by Edward, son of Henry III and Duke of Aquitaine. Edward wanted to double the export capacities of Bordeaux, and found the perfect site: a languishing hamlet founded by Charlemagne called Fozera, located on the deep tidal waters of the Isle just before its confluence with the Dordogne. The new bastide was named Leyburnia after its founder, gradually gallicized to Libourne as the town grew into a major river and sea port, shipping wine and wood west and sea salt east. To this day it remains an important commercial and wine centre.

Libourne is on the main line from Paris to Bordeaux, with occasional TGV stops; it also has connections to Périgueux and Thiviers, © 56 92 50 50. Buses for the surrounding villages depart from the *gare routière* next to the station, © 57 51 19 28. Hébrard (© 57 42 11 61) and Citram (© 56 43 04 04) run buses from Bordeaux to Blaye, stopping at Saint-André and Bourg. There's also a ferry from Blaye to Lamarque in Médoc, © 57 42 12 09.

Tourist Information

Libourne: Place Abel-Surchamp, © 57 51 15 04

Saint-André-de-Cubzac, © 57 43 64 80

Bourg-sur-Gironde: Hôtel de la Juarde, © 57 68 31 76

Blaye, Allées Marines, © 57 42 12 09

market days

Libourne: Tuesdays, Fridays and Sunday mornings in Place Abel-Surchamp

Bourg: Sunday mornings

Blaye: Wednesdays and Saturdays

Libourne

A Walk Around the Town

After the French sacked Libourne in 1294, the English surrounded the town with high walls and towers; the large cylindrical **Tour Richard**, named after the son of Edward III, still overlooks the Isle at the **Grand Port**. Here and there you can see old wine warehouses and merchants' houses, mostly from the 18th century, especially in Rue Victor Hugo and Rue Fonneuve. Both lead into the central square of the bastide, **Place Abel-Surchamp**, with its arcades, covered market, 16th-century houses and the **Hôtel de Ville**, built in 1429 and restored when the 19th-century infatuation for neogothic was at its peak. Under its pointy clock tower, you'll find the entrance to the **Musée des Beaux-Arts et d'Archéologie** *(open Mon–Fri 10–12 and 2–6)*, featuring the lively landscape and animal paintings of Libourne native René Princeteau (1844–1914), the first teacher of Toulouse-Lautrec, and a sprinkling of minor works by Le Brun, Bartolomeo Manfredi, Jacopo Bassano, Picabia, Foujita and Dufy. Don't miss the goofy statue on the landing of the monumental stair: *La France* embracing a bust of the worst Bourbon wastrel, Louis XV.

Libourne's public library, or *'Médiatheque'*, is installed in the 17th-century cloister of the Récollets *(open Tues, Wed, Fri and Sat)* and contains a rare survivor: *Le Livre Velu* (the 'hairy book', because of its calf-hide cover), a manuscript of 1476 transcribing the charters and privileges given to Libourne by the kings of England since its foundation.

Pomerol

Tiniest of all the Bordeaux's great red-wine districts, a mere three by four kilometres, Pomerol produces some of the most distinctive wines in France, noted for their power and bouquet. As in adjacent Saint-Emilion, the soil is very complex, but its cold, even more clayey nature makes for a more intense and tannic wine; its best vintages take decades to come into their own. Merlot is the predominant grape, making up 95 per cent of Pomerol's most celebrated *cru*, Château Pétrus, considered the best Merlot wine in the world by wine lovers lucky enough to experience it; the 82 and 83 are said to be among the greatest ever. Unlike Saint-Emilion and its confusing, constantly changing classifications, Pomerol is simply Pomerol: after legendary Pétrus, the consistently best wines come from La Conseillante, L'Evangile, Trotanoy, Lafleur, Gazin and Vieux-Château Certan. Wines from the gravelly vineyards of nearby Néac and Lalande come under the *appellation* AOC Lalande-de-Pomerol; the best are close to the minor Pomerols and are certainly more reasonably priced as well. Les Hauts-Conseillants and Les Hauts-Tuileries, Moncets, and Siaurac are among the top châteaux in the district.

North of Libourne

From Libourne, D 910 follows the course of the river L'Isle north to **Saint-Denis-de-Pile**, a village named after its 12th-century **church**, with a decorated apse and a painting of *The Visitation* by Le Nain. Two companies offer barge excursions from St-Denis upstream to Abzac during weekends and holidays from May–15 October: © 57 74 29 63 or 57 69 01 47, with a stop at **Notre-Dame-de-Guîtres**, a church the size of a cathedral begun by the Benedictines in 1080 and finished in the 15th century. Despite fortifications added during the Wars of Religion, it was damaged on a number of occasions and only restored in 1839. The 13th-century grand portal is especially good.

If it's a Sunday or holiday afternoon between May and October and you're not on the barge, you can hop on another transport antique at Guîtres: a narrow-gauge train, pulled by a locomotive of 1924, that chugs 15km west to **Marcenais** and back in three hours. On Sundays in August there's a morning departure as well (© for info: 57 69 01 47). The old station at Guîtres has a small train museum. In this same area, on the D 10 west of Guîtres, **Saint-Ciers-d'Abzac**'s Romanesque church used to attract pilgrims with weak, stunted children, who came under the special jurisdiction of St-Cyr. Specially venerated here is a massive block of sandstone called La Feyra that once formed part of a Neolithic monument; it turns three times at the ringing of the midday Angelus.

West of Libourne

Over on the south bank of the Dordogne, **Vayres** is the centre of its own little AOC wine region, Graves de Vayres. It boasts a crenellated castle that once belonged to Henri IV, the **Château de Vayres** *(daily July and Aug, at 3, 4 and 5; other times Sun and holidays only; adm)*. Built on a partially artifical terrace, the château is endowed with a magnificent monumental stairway descending gracefully towards the Dordogne and its riverside park. The buildings, essentially 16th and 17th century, are built around a grand court; the refined, decorative east gallery is attributed to Louis de Foix, architect of the famous light-house of Cordouan. The 17th-century gardens were restored in 1939. Downriver, the little bastide town of **Saint-Loubès** gave the world one of its first silent film comedians and one of Charlie Chaplin's inspirations, Max Linder (1883–1925, born Gabriel Leuvielle). He shot three of his films in St-Loubès before shooting himself in the head, and is buried in the village cemetery.

West of Libourne, the wine district of Fronsac begins along the north bank of the Dordogne. The village church of **La Rivière** has a tall 14th-century alabaster statue of the Virgin and Child and the grand 14th-century **Château La Rivière**, producer of some of the finest Fronsac, aged in huge limestones cellars that open to the public on weekdays 8–11 and 2–5. **La Lande-de-Fronsac**, further west, has a minor architectural jewel in the façade of its church of **Saint-Pierre**. The tympanum is carved in a rough, oriental style with a scene from the Apocalypse: St John with the Seven Churches and his vision of 'someone resembling the Son of Man', with seven stars in his right hand, with a double-edged sword coming out of his mouth. There is nothing else like it in France, making the date a matter of guesswork.

Fronsac

Just west of Libourne, high on a limestone plateau separated by the river l'Isle from Saint-Emilion and Pomerol, are the two *appellations* of Fronsac and Canon-Fronsac. In the 18th and early 19th century, the fresh, generous, supple red wines of Fronsac were pricier and more reputed than those of Saint-Emilion. After a century of near oblivion, they have been making a comeback in the past decade, thanks to a greater care in their elaboration.

Merlot again is the dominant grape, with high proportions of Cabernet Sauvignon and Cabernet Franc. Although the best vintages can be aged for decades, they are also delightfully fruity and ready to drink after four or five years, and go well with chicken dishes. Visitors are welcome at the loveliest estate, the aforementioned Château La Rivière, and at Château Cassagne Haut-Canon in Saint-Michel-de-Fronsac, © 57 51 63 98, on a former hunting estate of Cardinal Richelieu, bottlers of a wine called *La Truffière*, recommended with truffle dishes. The handsome white 18th-century Château Dalem at Saillans, © 57 84 34 18, has led the way in the rebirth of the wine, exporting it to 16 countries.

Saint-André-de-Cubzac and Bourg

There are two last towns to visit along the Dordogne before its waters merge with those of the Garonne. **Saint-Andrè-de-Cubzac** is an important crossroads near the Paris–Bordeaux autoroute and in 1910, the birthplace of Jacques Cousteau. Just north of town, in the centre of its vineyards, stands the 16th-century **Château de Bouilh**, partially rebuilt to include a pavilion and hemicycle by Victor Louis beginning in 1787; these were left unfinished when the owner was guillotined. There's a neo-Greek chapel, an 18th-century kitchen and rooms with their original panelling *(guided tours July–Sept, on Thurs, Sat and Sun from 2.30–6.30; adm)*. The two iron bridges at **Cubzac-les-Ponts** were designed by Eiffel in 1882 and 1889, and later restored by his grandson.

From Saint-André, the D 669 follows the scenic green banks of limestone that characterize this last stretch of the Dordogne. For centuries this was the most sought-after building stone of Bordeaux, especially from the old quarries at **Marcamps**, photogenic enough to be used as a set in Robert Hossein's *Les Misérables*. Other old quarries are now used as mushroom farms. **Tauriac** near Marcamps has a 12th-century church with Merovingian capitals and two carved tympanums, illustrating the Angus Dei and a knight. Earlier residents—from the Aurignacian period—decorated the **Grotte de Pair-non-Pair**, just north of the D 669 in Prignac-et-Marcamps *(open 10–11.30 and 2.30–5, closed Tues and October; adm)*. The cave's name, 'Even-odd' is derived from a village that once stood near by, lost by its seigneur over a game of heads-or-tails. Today you can see some etchings and black marks, all that survive of the extremely rare Aurignacian paintings discovered in the last century, only to be tragically washed away in 1899 by an imbecile who wanted to clean them off using a hose from a vineyard pump. The etchings, dated 30,000 BC, in places scratched one over the other, include mammoths and bison, and most notably, a horse in flight, head turned dramatically back towards an unseen pursuer.

Despite its name, medieval **Bourg-sur-Gironde** is still on the banks of the Dordogne, its river port crowded with pleasure craft. There are fine views over the town and river from Bourg's **Terrasse du District**. You can also visit the **Château de la Citadelle** and its historical museum *(open 10–12 and 2–7, closed Mon)* originally a home from home for the archbishops of Bordeaux, reconstructed as a folly in the 18th century and restored, complete with its gardens of magnolias and pistachios, after the retreating Germans set it on fire in 1944. Pick up the key at Bourg's tourist office to visit the fascinating Romanesque crypt at **Libarde**, 1km to the north, with primitive 11th-century carved capitals.

Côtes de Bourg and Premières Côtes de Blaye

The attractive wooded hills around Bourg give way in places for the vineyards of AOC Côtes de Bourg, a lesser-known but worthy red wine. Limestone dominates the soil, and Cabernet Sauvignon and Merlot are the two leading varieties. Like most minor *appellations*, Côtes-de-Bourg wines mature earlier than Bordeaux's *grands crus*, and are often good value: names to look for are Château de Barbé, Château Plaisance, and Château Mendoce (the 15th-century property of Diego de Mendoza, François I's maître d'hôtel and cousin of the Mendoza grandees of Spain), all at Villeneuve, and especially the powerful yet supple wines from Château Guerry at Tauriac. All of the above are open for tastings and sales; in the centre of Bourg, the Maison des Côtes de Bourg, Place de l'Eperon, © 57 68 46 47 has a list of others.

AOC Premières Côtes du Blaye is the northern extension of Côtes de Bourg and produces mainly red wine and a less significant quantity of white. There is even more limestone in the soil here, and the wines are fruity with some body, yet very drinkable when only three or four years old. Among the most notable estates are Château Bertinerie at Cubnezais and Château L'Escadre in Cars.

Bourg to Blaye

From Bourg, the delightful **Corniche de la Gironde** winds between the limestone cliffs and the tail end of the Dordogne before it joins the Garonne to create Europe's largest estuary, the Gironde. There are impressive views of the great confluence and estuary islands from **Pain-de-Sucre**, the local version of Rio's Sugarloaf Mountain. Further up is **Gauriac**, with troglodyte houses built into the limestone, while at **Plassac** you can visit the excavations of three Gallo-Roman villas dating from the 1st–5th century AD and the **Musée Gallo-Romaine** *(open June–Sept, 9–12 and 2–7; other times, © 57 42 07 05)*. It is interesting to note the development of the Aquitaine style of Roman villas, along with that of their polychrome mosaics; the museum contains wall paintings, bronzes, coins, ceramics and other finds.

Blaye

Occupying a limestone spur overlooking the narrowest, most defensible part of the Gironde estuary, Blaye entered history as a camp of Roman legionaires called *Blavia* and grew into a town sung by Ausonius. Today the site is dominated by a massive 22-hectare **Citadelle**, built to defend Bordeaux from the English in 1686 by Louis XIV's famous engineer Vauban, along with two other less important forts, on the Ile Pâté and at Fort Médoc. As was so often the case in that era, defending the town entailed its partial destruction—250 houses were razed to make room for the walls. The greatest loss was the Romanesque Basilique de Saint-Romain, founded in 350, where Roland, lord of Blaye and nephew of Charlemagne, was buried in the 8th century after blowing his brains out at Roncesvalles. The foundations of the basilica have recently been excavated.

Leave the car outside the 146-ft high walls of the Citadelle to walk through the little town within, now filled with arts and crafts shops. The best views are from the **Tour de l'Aiguillette** overlooking a cliff. A small history and art museum has been installed in the former commander's quarters, the **Pavillon de la Place** *(open June–mid Sept 10–12 and 2–7; adm)*. The Pavillon received an unexpected 'guest' in 1832: Marie-Caroline de Bourbon-Sicilie, Duchesse de Berry, arrested in Nantes while trying to overthrow Louis-Philippe for her son, a pretender to the throne. The flamboyant Marie-Caroline was a political hot potato for Louis-Philippe until the next year, when as a widow of 12 years, she gave birth to a daughter. Once she was neutralized by the scandal, Louis-Philippe packed her off to Palermo.

Jaufre Rudel

Blaye was firmly marked on love's map even before Marie-Caroline, thanks to the extraordinary passion that fired the heart of the handsome troubadour Jaufre (or Geoffroi) Rudel, the Prince of Blaye. Although his triangular castle was engulfed and mostly destroyed by Vauban's citadel, two towers and low walls remain north of the Place d'Armes to give at least some physical credence to his strange and mystical story, well known in the Middle Ages: in 1147 the dreamy Jaufre fell in love with Melisande, Countess of Tripoli, merely on the hearsay of her beauty. He composed many fine songs for her, and begged his sovereign lord, Count Alphonse Jourdain of Toulouse to let him accompany him on the next crusade. Seeing how pale he was for love, Alphonse Jourdain reluctantly took him along, but as they approached the Holy Land, Jaufre became feverishly ill and the crusaders left him to die alone in a poor fisherman's hut. Suddenly a lovely damsel entered and tenderly took Jaufre's head in her hands, and said: 'You were right to seek me, Jaufre, even if it has cost you your life. I am she whom you have long sought. Rest assured that you will find me as you dreamed.' At that the troubodour smiled and died, and the Countess of Tripoli buried him with the Knights Templars. In grief, she entered a convent and was never seen again. The story inspired writers from Petrarch to Rostand (*La Princesse lointaine*) and Heine, who has the lovers reunited as tender ghosts in a poem from *Romanzero* (1851):

> *'Melisande! Was ist Traum?*
> *Was ist Tod? Nur eitel Töne.*
> *In der Liebe nur is Wahrheit,*
> *Und dich lieb ich, ewig Schöne.'*

('Melisande! What is a dream? What is death? Just empty sounds. In love alone is truth, and I love you, eternal beauty')

Where to Stay and Eating Out

Libourne ✉ 33500

Libourne is well equipped with hotels and restaurants geared more towards business travellers than tourists; three that stay open all year are ***Loubat**, 32 Rue Chanzy, near the station, © 57 51 17 58; **Auberge Les Treilles**, 11 Rue des Treilles, © 57 25 02 52; and *France**, 7 Rue Chanzy, © 57 51 01 66.

St-Andrè-de-Cubzac ✉ 33240

In Saint-Gervais, 3km north of Saint-André on the same road as the Château de Bouilh, **Au Sarment**, © 57 43 44 73, is an old-fashioned country inn, and one of the best places to take the plunge and order lamprey, both succulent and reasonably priced, or else opt for the delicious *paupiettes de sole*, served in a warm rustic interior or out in the summer garden; menus from 120F, weekends a bit more (closed Wed and Aug).

Bourg ✉ 33710

Eight km northwest of Bourg, tranquil **★★La Closerie des Vignes**, at Saint-Ciers-de-Canesse, ✆ 57 64 81 90, is a charming modern house surrounded by vineyards, with a park and pool; the restaurant serves a delicious smoked salmon quiche and homemade desserts (menus from 120F). In the centre, **Le Croque-sel**, 1 Place Jeantet, ✆ 57 68 30 67 is reputed for its well-prepared seafood, menus from 95F, closed Mon. Between Bourg and Blaye, **Le Rigalet** in Gauriac, ✆ 57 64 87 69, is a great place to refuel in a big way, on a terrace overlooking the Gironde; try the grilled fillet of trout (five-course menus from 100F).

Blaye ✉ 33390

Stay in Blaye not faraway but in the centre of the citadel, **★★La Citadelle**, ✆ 57 42 17 10, most of the rooms overlooking the swimming pool and the Gironde; the restaurant specializes in locally farmed sturgeon cooked in *Premières Côtes de Blaye* (menus from 100F). The small municipal camp site is inside the walls of the citadel, overlooking the Gironde, ✆ 57 42 00 20. **Le Caneton d'Argent**, 31 Rue St-Roumain, ✆ 57 42 81 00, offers simple, classic cuisine—*fricassée de langoustines*, or leg of lamb with garlic, in a pleasant rustic atmosphere (menus from 95F, closed Mon). In bakeries you can find the speciality of the town, the *Praslines de Blaye*, or pralines of burnt almonds, invented by the chef of the Maréchal de Plessis-Praslin, governor of the citadel in 1649.

Bordeaux

*...Bordeaux, squatting in the depths of the Gironde, could be
London, Carthage, Rotterdam or New York, could have been
Occitan but is only Bordeaux, capital on paper, capital of
provincial paper, former satellite of London, and today of
Paris...a port that only discovered America at the moment of the
slave trade.*

Yves Rouquette, *Occitanie.*

It's true that Bordeaux, that warm, magic, generous name on the bottle,
evokes more than it delivers in the urban flesh. It is a mercantile city that
has lost its port; it is both terribly grand and terribly shabby and monotonous, a hallucinatory city of long flat vistas tinted in a thousand nuances
of white, from golden cream to unwashed tennis socks. Nearly all of its
proudest monuments, its squares, its uniform quayside Grand Façade and
its proto-Haussmannian boulevards—the very features that confirm to the
French mind that this is The Most Beautiful City After Paris—were
rammed down Bordeaux's throat by its royal governors, the intendants.
The Bordelais screamed and kicked about every one—because they had to
pay for them, a terrible imposition even though at the time money was
rolling in, thanks to the slave trade.

Bordeaux offers a meaty comparison to Toulouse, the other large city in
this book. Toulouse is confident, rosy, and resolutely southern, medieval
brick and modern glass, and rather in love with its river front and canals;
Bordeaux is Gothic and 18th century, splenetic, nostalgic and funky, a
stone necropolis that has always looked to the north for tutelage while it
made a living from its port. Today it seems uncertain, wondering what to
do with itself, divorced from the wide Garonne by a furious funnel of
traffic. Like Toulouse, it owes its new aeronautics industries to the
largesse of Paris; Bordeaux's portion, however, is dominated by the military, and cranks out ballistic missiles instead of glamorous Airbus jets.

In 1857 a Bordelais named Paul-Ernest de Ratier published a pamphlet
called *Preuve évidente que Bordeaux n'existe pas*. It is a 'whitened sepulchre' a phantom city of phantom beings. 'It has created nothing, it
receives everything. It thinks nothing, it hears all, but never listens. It has
nothing, it seems to have everything. It is a magnificent scaffold of
appearances, of *faux-semblants*, of colours, of pretexts, of reflections, of
illusions.' In response to Ratier's jibes, Bordeaux has in fact finally created
something of its very own—*GERTRUDE*, an acronym for a system that
electronically times stop lights to facilitate the flow of traffic. The idea
was to save energy; the mentality is very American, to see the heart of a
city as an obstacle to pass through as quickly as possible. Or is it because,
as Gertrude Stein once said of Oakland, that 'there's no there there'?

History

The Greek geographer Strabo was the first to mention the Gironde estuary: in the 3rd century BC, a Celtic tribe from Bourges called the Bituriges Vibisci was 'the only foreign people to settle among the Aquitains. They paid them no tribute and they occupied Burdigala as an emporium. 'Bituriges translates as the 'kings of the world', a big bold title for a band of tin traders; the crescent-shaped Burdigala, founded at the confluence of the Garonne, the Dévèze and the Peugue was the 'Port of the Moon'—reflecting not only its crescent shape but also the lunar influence over the tidal changes of the Gironde estuary, 'with its river filled with the boiling tide of the ocean', as Ausone, Bordeaux's famous Gallo-Roman poet described it. Besides tin, Burdigala helped initiate the barley-beer-swilling Gauls into the joys of wine—imported from southern Italy and the Mediterranean colonies of Greece and Rome by way of Toulouse.

Burdigala knew which side its bread was buttered on, and had no objection to being captured in 56 BC by Crassus. Quickly Romanized, the Bituriges soon tidied up their helter-skelter trading centre to conform to the basic Roman town plan, with a north–south *cardo* (Rue Sainte-Catherine) and east–west *decumanus* (Cours de l'Intendance). To slake the Gaulish thirst, the traders of Burdigala attempted to grow their own vines, but it took until the year 20 AD to discover the right variety of grape suited to the humid climate—Basilica from Epirus (*see* p.151).

Although Vespasian acknowledged Bordeaux's increasing prestige by making it the capital of Aquitaine in place of Saintes (Civitas Santonum), the city had hardly begun to make a name for itself when it was severely mutilated in the barbarian invasion of 276 and retreated into a more defensible *castrum*. Much of the reconstruction was by Christians, devoted to the cult of St Seurin (Severinus), bishop of Bordeaux (d. 420). Not only is his name confusingly similar to Toulouse's St Sernin, but his tomb equally became the focal point of one of the most desirable burial grounds in the early Middle Ages.

Medieval Bordeaux

In the 7th century Dagobert made Bordeaux capital of the duchy of Aquitaine. The son of one of his dukes, Huon de Bordeaux, shares a *chanson de geste* with Charlemagne and the 'Elf Oberon'; he was followed by ten Duke Guillaumes (as in Toulouse, again, there was a wretched lack of originality in given names), who ruled an Aquitaine that stretched from Poitiers to the Pyrenees. The most famous was Guillaume IX (d. 1126), the first known troubadour, and one of the bawdiest. He was the grandfather of great Eleanor, only child of Guillaume X. She inherited the duchy and gave Bordeaux first to France when she wed Louis VII (1137), then to Anjou and England when she divorced the pious and dour Louis and married the more amusing Henry Plantagenet.

Bordeaux blossomed under the English and grew so much that the walls had to be rebuilt twice. The reason for this affection was simple: the Bordelais paid fewer taxes and had an eager guaranteed market for their wine, or claret as the English called it, a corruption of the French *clairet*—a once popular blend of white wines. Their beloved duchess Eleanor granted the wine growers special privileges, confirmed by her son John Lackland in 1206, after Bordeaux was besieged by his brother-in-law the king of Castille. The siege revealed John's inability to defend the city; to keep it loyal he granted it considerable municipal power—a mayor and *Jurade*, and in 1214 he went even further with letters of patent that gave the bourgeoisie of Bordeaux the right to sell their wine and other goods duty-free. Under Henry III, Bordeaux's Château de l'Ombrière became the seat of the Seneschal of Aquitaine. Another plus in Bordeaux's eye was the powerful English fleet, able to protect the city's all-important sea trade; among the many things brought back by the English crusaders was the ancient law of the sea from Rhodes, which they re-established in Bordeaux.

Medieval Bordeaux was a tough town that produced some tough hombres. One was the archbishop of Bordeaux, Bertrand de Got, elected Pope Clement V in 1305, after an 11-month conclave. Between earning himself the everlasting hatred of Rome by moving the papacy to Avignon, and helping King Philippe le Bel put an end to the powerful order of the Knights Templars he did much for Bordeaux, Aquitaine and his relatives—suddenly there are 11 Gascon cardinals in the Curia, who if nothing else kept electing popes from southwest France. However, to pay for his extravagances, Clement V soaked Bordeaux so badly that he had to avoid it when he travelled in the area.

In 1360 Edward III renounced his claims on the crown of France in exchange for sure title to the quasi-independent principality of Aquitaine, extending from Poitou to the Bigorre; to rule it, he sent his eldest son, Edward of Woodstock, the Black Prince (so called for his swish black armour). The Black Prince made Bordeaux his capital from 1355 to 1372 while he campaigned to recapture the rest of the 'old duchy of the Plantegênets' and when the French tried to say *non*, he captured their King Jean, his grand captain, Du Guesclin, and a bouquet of the flowers of French chivalry; in Bordeaux he set up his autonomous Exchequer and minted his own leopard coins. But cash, or rather the lack of it, soon dealt a death blow to his ambitions; in spite of the Black Prince's string of victories, money was withheld by the *Jurade* and aristocrats of Aquitaine—especially the Armagnacs and the Albrets who, rather than pay their taxes to the Black Prince turned to France and Charles V. With their encouragement, Charles began another round of the Hundred Years' War in 1369; the Black Prince, ill and exhausted, died in 1376.

The French finally took Bordeaux in June 1451, an event known in the city annals as the *male jornade*, the rotten day, that saw 10,000 Bordelais massacred in the marshlands near the present Pont d'Aquitaine before Bordeaux's archbishop Pey Berland was able to negotiate an honourable surrender. The final French conquest in 1453 was so unpopular that the Bordelais rebelled off and on until the end of the 17th century, never forgetting their old rights and trading privileges, and their say in the taxes imposed on them. The French monarchy responded by building three fortresses to police Bordeaux, all of them now vanished: the enormous Château Trompette (now Place des Quinconces), Fort du Hâ and Fort Louis. The machinery of French power over Bordeaux included a *Parlement* of royal appointees and an intendant, also appointed by the king.

Thanks to its position near the Gironde estuary, Bordeaux controlled the export of wines from the *haut pays* (Bergerac, Cahors, Gaillac, etc.) which were greatly preferred back in the days when all wines were drunk young. To mollify Bordeaux, in the 16th century a law was passed to block the sale of wine from the hinterlands—until all the wine from Bordeaux was sold first. Frustrated English drinkers turned to port and sherry. A happier event was the welcome that Bordeaux gave in 1540 to hundreds of Jews chased out of Portugal by the Inquisition; by 1753 Bordeaux had seven synagogues.

Bordeaux Booms Again

At the beginning of the 18th century, Bordeaux still made much of its living as it had since the Middle Ages, exporting its claret to thirsty northerners and selling supplies to passing ships. After the death of Louis XIV, new markets opened up in the New World, especially in the Caribbean, and merchants from Britain, Germany, the Netherlands, Portugal and elsewhere were on hand to help the Bordelais make fortunes in the triangular trade: glass, fabrics, weapons, and gimcracks from Bordeaux were shipped down to slave counters in west Africa in exchange for a human cargo (one ship, with a nice touch of irony, was named the *Contrat Social*), which was in turn sold in America and the Caribbean for cotton, tobacco, indigo and, most importantly, sugar. Sugar, literally worth its weight in gold in the Middle Ages, was so fashionable in 18th-century Europe that, imported raw, refined in Bordeaux and re-exported, it brought in as much money as wine. The local glass industry took off when it was discovered that wine in bottles survived the journey to America better. By the end of the century, Bordeaux was the first port of France.

To create a city equal to all of its sweet, intoxicating ambition, Bordeaux's indendants started demolishing its poky, crowded medieval streets to give the city light and air—in the face of fierce local opposition. Begun by Intendant Boucher, who laid out the Place Royale (now Place de la Bourse), the destruction and re-creation of central Bordeaux was enthusiastically continued under his successor, Louis Urbain Aubert, the Marquis de Tourny (1743–57). 'Bordeaux being one of the cities in the kingdom where one meets the most foreigners, it is fitting to try to give them a favourable opinion of France...I will make you the most beautiful city in the realm, if you will only have confidence in what I shall propose and help me in the execution.' Tourny laid out wide *cours* or *allées* planted with trees linking his new squares and the first public gardens; to adorn them, 5000 new buildings went up, including those of the river-front Grand Façade. Tourny's taste was confirmed in the next century by Stendhal, who called Bordeaux 'undeniably the most beautiful city in France.' And who could argue with Stendhal, a novelist so known for fainting at the sight of beauty that in Italy he gave his name to a syndrome that scores of tourists are treated for every year?

By the beginning of the Revolution, Bordeaux was the third largest city in France, with a cosmopolitan population of over 100,000. The connections between its port and the new United States and the influence of Montesquieu and the Philosophes combined to make the local Girondin party a moderate, decentralizing force at the Convention. In the Commune they clashed with the Jacobin fanatics who believed in a centralized dictatorship; in 1793, suspected of fomenting a federalist insurrection, 20 of their leaders were arrested by Robespierre and died on the guillotine after an all-night fling in the Conciergerie. In

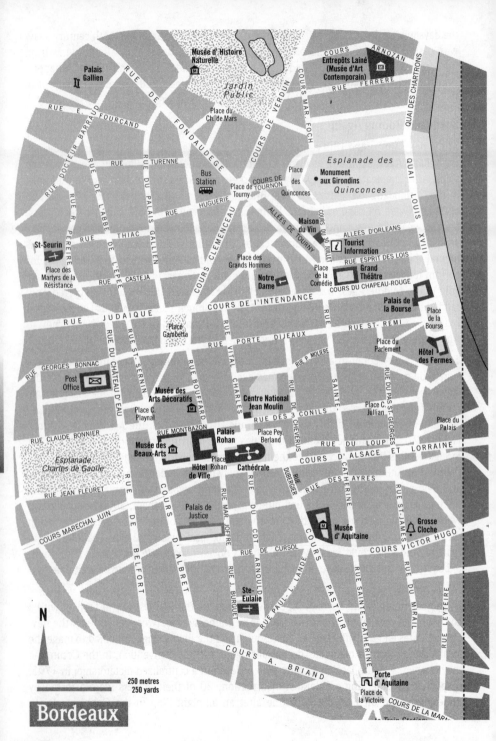

Bordeaux the only surviving sign of the Revolution are the quaint, enthusiastic street names engraved into the buildings (Rue de l'Amour d'Egalité, Rue du Peuple Souverain).

Bordeaux in the 19th and 20th Centuries

During and immediately after the Napoleonic wars, Bordeaux hit one of its lowest ebbs: the continental blockade destroyed the city's commerce, the slave trade was abolished in 1815 and the competition of sugar beets undercut its sugar refineries. Ships from the North and Baltic seas began to sail across the Atlantic without stopping to be provisioned in Bordeaux. The grand urban plans of the intendants ground to a halt. It was only with Louis XVIII (and the demolition of the hated Château Trompette, symbol of the king) that Bordeaux began to get on its feet again and build its first-ever bridge over the Garonne (1822). Although it had one of the first railroads in France (1841) and greatly improved its quays, little new industry came its way. Inexorably port traffic moved to the north.

Bordeaux, so proudly and grandly moulded to fit the French idea of a capital, actually served as one three times, in circumstances France would rather forget: in 1870, 1914 and 1940. Bordeaux remembers 1914 most fondly, when it hosted *tout Paris* and became one of the chief debarkation points for the American army, while June 1940 leaves the bitter memory of World War I hero Philippe Pétain negotiating the armistice with Hitler, announcing to France over the radio: *'Je fais don de ma personne à la France'* before moving the government to Vichy, because the Germans wanted the Atlantic coast for themselves. The four years and two months under the Occupation left deep scars that were covered up, in Bordeaux as elsewhere, by the political class that runs France today. The infamous case of Maurice Papon is only the most notorious: Papon served as general secretary of the prefecture of the Gironde from 1942–44 and deported hundreds of Jews. Although there were enough members of the Resistance around to prevent him from becoming *préfet* of the Landes in 1945, from 1958 to 1967 he served as police prefect in Paris, and in 1979 became minister of the Budget under Giscard d'Estaing. His bloody past, though

Garonne

QUAI DE LA DOUANE

Porte Cailhau

PONT DE PIERRE

Place de Bir Hakeim

Porte de Bourgogne

QUAI DES SALINIERES

QUAI DE LA GRAVE

RUE DES FAURES

RUE SAINT-FRANCOIS

La Flèche

Place Canteloup

St Michel

QUAI DE LA MONNAIE

RUE G. PHILIPPE

RUE C. SAUVAGEAU

to Ste-Croix

known by his bosses, was only exposed to the public in 1983; now, over a decade later, the chances of his ever coming to trial remain slim.

The postwar years in Bordeaux have been dominated by the presence of Mayor Jacques Chaban-Delmas, a 31-year-old general in the Resistance when de Gaulle sent him down to sort out Bordeaux in 1946. That same year he became a deputy, the next year, mayor; from 1969 to 1972 he served as Pompidou's prime minister and has played a role in national politics ever since. Pragmatic, dynamic, foxy, and a brilliant manipulator of his own image, the Paris-born Chaban acted an updated version of the intendants, radically changing the face of Bordeaux with the urban-renewal project of Mériadeck and the new Quartier du Lac, the congress and leisure complex north of the centre. At the same time, the application of the Loi Malraux in 1966 safeguarded 370 acres of 18th-century Bordeaux (especially in the Quartier Saint-Pierre); organized by the energetic Renaissance du Vieux Bordeaux, the rehabilitation of old port buildings and warehouses into new cultural centres continues today. In spring 1994 Chaban announced his retirement, and Bordeaux waits to see if his successor will carry out his projects for a métro and the construction of La Bastide, designed by Catalan neo-neoclassical architect Ricard Bofill on the hitherto neglected right bank of the Garonne. On a scale similar to Bofill's work in Montpellier, this would include a new Musée des Beaux Arts, an auditorium, luxury flats and an international business centre.

For all Bordeaux's urban renewal efforts, people continue to drain away from the centre. Nevertheless, the 220,000 remaining Bordelais manage to take up more room per capita than other city dwellers in France, many living in single-storey terrace houses known as *échoppes*. Since the 1900s the suburbs (pop. 450,000) have burgeoned out in every direction, a situation compared by one Bordelais writer to the universe of Pascal, where 'the centre is everywhere and the circumference nowhere'. The insatiable concrete mixer devours even the vineyards that have provided Bordeaux's fermented lifeblood for centuries.

One feather in Bordeaux's cap, although one often begrudged by the feather himself, was François Mauriac (1885–1970), 1952 winner of the Nobel prize for literature. At the age of 22 he fled for Paris, where, at a distance, he could exorcize an unhappy provincial childhood in books like *Le noeud de vipères* (*The Nest of Vipers*) which didn't exactly gild his relationship with the folks back home. Even during the official reconciliation of Bordeaux with its native son in 1965, in a ceremony in the Grand Théâtre honouring his 80th birthday, Mauriac shocked them by saying: 'The honour that you do me at the very evening of my life gives me a great joy, but a grave joy. Dare I say, a sad joy? I love and I hate Bordeaux like myself.'

Getting to and from Bordeaux

By air: Bordeaux International Airport is 12km west of the centre at Mérignac, ✆ 56 34 50 50; there's a coach linking the airport to the railway station, less frequently at weekends. Air France: 29 rue Esprit-des-Lois, ✆ 56 44 64 35. Air-Inter: 44 Allées de Tourny, ✆ 56 44 80 70. British Airways: 37 Allées de Tourny, ✆ 56 52 65 11. TAT: ✆ 56 34 89 96.

By train: All trains arrive and depart from Bordeaux St-Jean station in Rue Charles-Domerq, ℂ 59 92 50 50, reservations ℂ 56 92 60 60. TGVs from Paris-Montparnasse take 3 hours; regular trains from Paris-Austerlitz take 4½ hours. Other connections are Périgueux (2hrs); Sarlat (3hrs) by way of St-Emilion and Bergerac; Tarbes by way of Orthez, Pau and Lourdes; TGVs or regular trains to Hendaye by way of Dax, Bayonne, Biarritz and St-Jean-de-Luz or to Toulouse (2hrs), by way of Agen and Montauban; other trains 3hrs with additional stops in Marmande, Aiguillon and Moissac. Also local lines to Mont-de-Marsan, Pointe de Grave and, roughly once an hour, to Arcachon.

By bus: The station for Citram buses serving most towns and villages in the Gironde is at 14 Rue Fondaudège, ℂ 56 81 18 18. For information on international bus connections to London, Portugal and Spain, contact Eurolines, ℂ 56 92 50 42.

By car: Paris has its *périphérique*; Bordeaux has a great ring highway called the *rocade*, which sucks up all the autoroutes and national roads to Bordeaux and spins them around the city, making it sometimes easier to circumvent the city than penetrate its centre.

Getting Around

The city's CGFTE buses (ℂ 57 57 88 88 for information) are frequent, convenient and huge, prowling the long straight streets like links of metal sausage. Buy blocks of 10 tickets at kiosks or pay on the bus; from the station, bus 7 will take you to Place Gambetta and the Chartons; bus 1 follows the river. Bus maps are free at the tourist office or railway station.

You can hire bikes at the station, ℂ 56 92 50 50 or 56 91 34 20. Cabbies are not allowed to ply for hire in Bordeaux, but there are 24-hour taxi ranks at the railway station and Place Gambetta, and during the day ranks in key locations. Parking is easiest in the vast Place des Quinconces.

Tourist Information

Bordeaux's main city office is at 12 Cours du 30-Juillet, ℂ 56 44 28 41; branch offices open from June–September are in Gare St-Jean (ℂ 56 91 64 70) and at the airport (ℂ 56 34 39 39). For information on the Gironde, contact the Maison du Tourisme de la Gironde, 21 Cours de l'Intendance; for all of Aquitaine, the Comité Régionale de Tourisme d'Aquitaine, Rue René-Cassin, ℂ 56 39 88 88.

Post office: 52 Rue Georges-Bonnac

Money exchange: Thomas Cook, at the station, every day from 8am to 9.30pm, ℂ 56 91 58 80. American Express: 14 Cours de l'Intendance, ℂ 56 81 70 02, open Mon–Fri 8.45–12 and 1.30–6.

UK consulate: 15 Cours de Verdun, ℂ 56 52 28 35

US consulate: 22 Cours Maréchal Foch, ℂ 56 52 65 95

Sainte-Croix and Saint-Michel

Taking the railway station at the south end of Bordeaux as the point of departure, spare yourself the urban anomie of the long, straight, endless Cours de la Marne by proceeding up Rue de Tauzia. The first monuments that beckon in this genteelly dilapidated neigh-bourhood are around the former monastery church of **Sainte-Croix**. Built in the 12th century, this once had a remarkably exuberant Old Curiosity Shop of a façade that was sadly entrusted in 1860 to Paul Abadie (*see* p.61) who, with the destructive self-confidence of his time, completely dismantled it and put it back together all wrong. The south tower, portal, figures of Avarice and Luxury, and some carved capitals in the transept survived the Abadie touch; the relics in the parish chapel were reputed in the Middle Ages to cure mad-ness. An abbey building of 1672 now houses the school of fine arts while the new monster along the Quai Sainte-Croix goes to show that Abadie had no patent on dubious taste; this 1980s bunker housing the national conservatory is called the **Centre André Malraux**, a backhanded compliment to the Minister of Culture in the 1960s who passed the national preservation law and surely deserves better.

In nearby Place Pierre-Renaudel, an 18th-century sugar refinery was converted in 1990 into the **Théâtre du Port de la Lune**. A stone's throw away you can learn all about printing and publishing before the advent of computers at the **Musée des Métiers de l'Imprimerie**, 8–10 Rue du Fort Louis *(open Mon and Wed 2–6 and Sat 9–1)*.

Since the time of Charlemagne a church has stood at the site of **Saint-Michel**, in what is now a lively, piquant Portuguese–North African neighbourhood. Its denizens hold a morning flea market under the detached hexagonal bell tower, the 'arrow' or **Flèche** as the Bordelais call it, built between 1472 and 1492 and shooting up 377ft, the highest mon-ument in southwest France. It was financed in part by Louis XI, a devotee of St Michel, and overrestored in the 19th century by Abadie; unfortunately you can't visit the once-cele-brated crypt beneath the tower, where Victor Hugo and other 19th-century tourists came to gape at the naturally mummified bodies (as tourists still do in Palermo). The grimy, flam-boyant Gothic St-Michel was a product of Bordeaux's medieval prosperity, largely built by the city's guilds. It is missing one of its most remarkable features—the original stained glass, blasted away by Allied bombers in the last war. Inside *(open 9–12 and 2–6)*, the chapels belonged to the various, local artisan guilds and contain the best art: the Chapelle Ste-Ursula in the right aisle with a rare 15th-century sculpture of *St Ursula and the 11,000 Virgins*; in the left aisle, note the Chapelle de St-Sépulchre with a beautiful *Descent from the Cross* carved in 1492; the Chapelle Notre-Dame with a Flemish painting of the *Annunciation* (1500); and the Chapelle St-Joseph with the nine alabaster Renaissance bas-reliefs on the altarpiece. In 1994 these were rather embarrassingly discovered for sale at an auction in New York; ten years earlier thieves had made off with them, leaving in their place some not terribly skilful plaster copies that completely fooled everyone.

From behind St-Michel, Rue de la Fusterie (once lined with coopers' shops) leads to the **Porte des Salinières**, the 'salt' gate built in 1755 by Jacques-Ange Gabriel, although money ran out before it could be festooned with statuary. This overlooks the **Pont de**

Pierre, the city's oldest bridge, built only in 1842 and prettily lit at night by a necklace of street lamps.

From here continue up busy Cours Victor-Hugo. The corner at Rue Saint-James is often mobbed with bargain hunters at a branch of Paris's famous Tati department store, has been bustling since the Middle Ages—this was the road to Compostela, and the gate that defended it is known as the **Grande Cloche**. Built next to and dwarfing the odd little church of Saint-Eloi, this gate was part of the second wall built by the English in the 1400s. They were so pleased with it that they put it on their coat of arms; here the Bordelais would come to check the time, and each year a great bell would ring out at the start of the *vendange*. Across Cours Victor-Hugo, the continuation of Rue Saint-James had, until 1840, a well, where a serpent dwelt that was so horrifying that a mere glance at it meant certain death. One day a soldier, covering his own face and taking a mirror, went down a rope into the well and made the serpent look at itself. It keeled over, the local water problem was solved and the street had a new name, Mirror street, or Rue du Mirail.

Musée d'Aquitaine

Open daily exc Tues 10–6; adm.

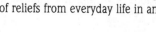

Although from the outside it looks like a hard slog, don't be deterred: the Musée d'Aquitaine at 20 Cours Pasteur is one of the most compelling and beautifully arranged in southwest France. Its subject is the history of Aquitaine, and one of its first works is the unique, utterly mysterious 25,000-year-old bas-relief of the *Venus with a horn* from Laussel in the Dordogne. The horn she holds curves like the moon; her hair appears to be in 'corn rows' and the stone she's carved on still bears traces of red ochre, used in Upper Paleolithic tombs and sacred sites. She keeps company with two other 'Venuses' from Laussel: one an even fatter, saggy-breasted fertility figure with prominent hands, the other a slender dancing form. Another evocative, if less clearly defined, relief has two figures holding hands, one above the other, their arms forming the shape of an egg. Among the Neolithic artifacts is a treasure horde—of flint slices—and burials from the Grotte aux 80 Morts at Coux-et-Bigoroque, with a double trepanned skull. There are pots, swords and jewels from the Metal Ages, and a curious face carved on a wooden post from Larrau in the Pyrénées-Atlantiques, and the golden Celtic treasure of coins and a torque from Tayac.

The excellent Gallo-Roman section has another treasure, of 4000 coins from the time of Claudius found in the Garonne, as well as mosaics, sculptures (note the highly stylized fragment of a relief of horses pounding through water) and a fascinating set of reliefs from everyday life in ancient Burdigala. Ironically enough it's the funerary steles that really bring the dead to life: thin-faced Tatiana gazing at eternity with a wry look and wrinkled brow, and especially the little child Laetus, clutching a kitten the way toddlers do, while a rooster at his feet nips at the kitten's dangling tail. The inscription notes that it was dedicated by his father, who despite his sorrow created this charming memorial so that the child who delighted him would still delight us 2000 years later.

Further on is a legless but still impressive life-size bronze Hercules, and a room dedicated to finds from a Mithraeum discovered in 1982 during the construction of an underground car park in Cours Victor-Hugo: in the 2nd and 3rd century Mithrasism, an all-male, monotheistic religion from the east posed serious competition to Christianity. A small statue shows the birth of Mithras, rising from earth with the cosmic globe in one hand and a knife to slay bulls in the other; there are statues of Cautes and Cautopatès, his two companions in Persian costumes, and a rare *Leontocéphale*, a lion-headed man holding keys, his legs entwined with chicken-headed snakes.

Beyond the Early Christian sarcophaguses and mosaics are a few strange 11th-century capitals from the Abbaye de La Sauve Majeur, and La Brède, along with English alabasters, traded in exchange for wine. Montaigne's centotaph with its Greek inscription stands among the section devoted to French rule. Upstairs are rooms devoted to Aquitaine's last 300 years: its agriculture, industries, port and wine, with the copy of a letter from Thomas Jefferson to the count of Lur-Saluces praising his Sauternes—and a letter from Ronald Reagan to his descendant, thanking him for hosting a banquet celebrating the bicentennial of the Battle of Yorktown.

South of the museum, Cours Pasteur leads down to Place Victoire and another museum, the **Musée Ethnographique** *(open Mon–Fri 10–7; adm)*, devoted to artifacts from around the world, and especially from France's former colonies. The gate, the **Porte d'Aquitaine** (1753) guarded by a pair of sea gods, closes the south end of pedestrian-only **Rue Sainte-Catherine**, Bordeaux's main street since Roman times, and often swarming with bargain hunters from end to end. Lastly, fans of Art Deco in its morose, idiosyncratic French version, might like to stroll briefly from Place de la Victoire up Cours Aristide-Briand to see the **Bourse du Travail** (1934–8), commissioned by Bordeaux's Socialist mayor Marquet, and decorated with reliefs on the outside and frescoes inside.

Cathédrale Saint-André

Bordeaux's Gothic cathedral is the fourth church erected on this site since the 6th century, the successor of the church where Eleanor of Aquitaine married Louis VII in 1137. What you see today was built under English rule between the 13th and 15th centuries; in 1440, as the ground was marshy and the architects were reluctant to add more weight to the church, it was given a detached tower, the **Tour Pey-Berland**, a model followed a few years later by St-Michel; this was used as a lead ball factory from 1793 to 1850, when it was repurchased by the archbishop, truncated and crowned with a shiny Virgin Mary.

The cathedral itself, at the time of writing undergoing a long-awaited cleaning, is built in the form of a Latin cross and supported by an intricate web of buttresses. There are fine tympanums over the north transept door (a 14th-century scene of the *Last Supper*, *Ascension of Christ* and *Triumph of the Redeemer*) and on the nearby Porte Royale, used by visiting kings and dignitaries and decorated with a throng of saints and a serene 13th-century Last Judgment, where the lids of the open tombs on the lintel add a nice rhythmic touch. The west front, which originally formed part of the city wall, is strikingly bare. The south portal, dedicated to the Virgin, lost its tympanum to make room for carts rumbling in and out when the church was converted into a feed store during the Revolution, but carvings of the Wise and Foolish Virgins, angels and apostles have survived. Often the doors are left wide open, as in the Middle Ages, admitting both worshippers and pedestrians making a short cut. The nave is single and nearly as long and wide as Notre-Dame in Paris, measuring 410 by 145ft, large enough to hold the tremendous pageant on 6 April 1364 when 1,447 nobles came to pay homage to the Black Prince, 'the most magnificent lord of his time', as Froissart called him. The wrought-iron grille in the choir is 18th century, and there are some fine statues in the seven chapels radiating from the ambulatory, especially the 16th-century alabaster *Notre Dame de la Nef.*

Just north of the cathedral, Mayor Chaban-Delmas created the **Centre National Jean Moulin** in 1967 *(open weekdays 2–6; free)*, with a collection devoted to the Occupation, Resistance, and Deportation, from posters (one with a mother telling her daughter 'Hard Times are Over. Papa's Gone to Work in Germany!') to a folding motocycle (part of a parachute drop to the Resistance). Upstairs the office of the courageous resistance leader Jean Moulin has been reconstructed, containing a collection of his drawings—his cover was running an art gallery in Nice.

Musée des Beaux-Arts

Open 10–6 exc Tues; adm; free on Wed.

There's talk of moving it across the river some day, but when you read this Bordeaux's cache of paintings will still be in a wing of the large and luxurious **Palais Rohan** at 20 Cours d'Albret, built in the 1770s by the Prince Archbishop Mériadeck de Rohan to replace an insufficiently princely medieval archbishop's palace. To make space for this ecclesiastical bachelor's pad, Rohan got permission from the king to knock over several acres of medieval Bordeaux, and to finance the building by selling off the archbishopric's properties. He kept a close eye on the construction, assuring the most fastidious fittings, but before he got a chance to move in he was made Archbishop of Cambrai. Since the mid 19th century, most of the palace has been Bordeaux's town hall.

The rest is the **Musée des Beaux-Arts**. It has paintings by artists rarely seen in French provincial museums—works by Titian (*Lucretia and Tarquin*); a serene Perugino *(Virgin and Child, with SS. Jerome and Augustin)*, in need of a cleaning; a portrait of a senator by Lavinia, a rare 16th-century female painter from Bologna; a chubby *Magdalen* and chubby *Marie dei Medici* by Van Dyck; Rubens' *Martyrdom of St George*; and the jolly *Fête de la Roserie* by Jan Breughel le Velours. Amid a room of 17th-century, rosy-cheeked portraits and mythologies are a pair of paintings of the cruel world of galley slaves (*Arrivée des*

Galériens dans la Prison de Gênes and *Débarquement des Galériens dans la Port de Gênes)* by the Genoese Alessandro Magnasco (1667–1749), that singularly uncanny 'painter of phantasmagorias' completely out of synch with his time, in both his choice of subject matter (you can't help but wonder who would have commissioned these disturbing scenes) and his technique of quick, nervous, impromptu brush strokes that give his works their strange light, and his often tormented figures their peculiar phantom-like unreality.

Later paintings from the 18th century include the portrait of *Baron Rockeby* by Reynolds, Dutch landscapes by Ruysdael and co. (a favourite of Bordeaux's nouveau-riche merchants), and a *Nature Morte* by the inimitable Chardin. The next room has representatives of all the grand -isms of the 19th century, from the neoclassical—*L'Embarquement de la duchesse d'Angoulême* by Gross and antiquating neoclassical (Guérin's *Hippolytus and Phaedre*, the funniest painting in the collection, where both protagonists have the same face, although Phaedra looks as if she's just sucked a lemon) to the highly charged Romanticism of Delacroix (the famous *Grèce sur les ruines de Missolonghi*) and Isabey (the huge *Incendie du steamer Austria*). There are several glossy snicker-nudge-nudge nudes that first became popular in the decorously porno Second Empire, including Henri Gervex's notorious *Rolla*, inspired by a poem by Alfred de Musset and the source of a tremendous scandal at the 1878 salon (the fact that the naked girl on the bed was neither a goddess nor an allegory, and had left her mussed-up clothing piled to one side was considered indecent according to the magnificently hypocritical taste of the time). There are paintings by proto-Impressionist Boudin, and Bordeaux's own Odilon Redon (1840–1916), introspective precursor of the Surrealists.

Bordeaux produced two other influential artists, whose paintings are displayed in the last room: Albert Marquet (1875–1947), who was a fellow student of Matisse and co-founder of Fauvism before going on to paint his simple landscapes, and André Lhote (1885–1962), represented by his hallmark colourful, geometric compositions on various planes. A lesser known Bordelais is Impressionist Alfred Smith, whose best works resemble early Monets. Here too are a selection of minor paintings by major 20th-century artists—Matisse, Bonnard, Renoir and Seurat. Temporary exhibitions, including a prestigious May Show, are held near by in the **Galerie des Beaux-Arts** in Place du Colonel-Raynal.

Behind this, and on one of the *axes* so beloved by French urban planners (in this case, aligned with the Palais de Rohan) is the **Nouveau Quartier Mériadeck**. Mériadeck, named after the aforementioned slum-busting cardinal, was a fragrant slum flattened in 1954 by Mayor Chaban-Delmas, clearing 30 hectares to create the largest single urban renovation scheme in France. Seven hectares were set aside for greenery and fountains and the buildings facing this central mall were designed in cruciforms (as in the reflecting-glass Préfecture) by planner J. Willerval, to spare pedestrians the sight of Mériadeck's plain-jane skyscraper. As corporate bosses haven't been beating down the doors for office space here, most of Mériadeck is occupied by government bureaucracies, and it shrivels to a desert after dark. However run-of-the-mill post modern, Mériadeck earned itself an environmental gold star as the first major project in Europe to make large-scale use of geothermal heating (1981).

Around the corner from the Musée des Beaux Arts at 39 Rue Bouffard, the neoclassical *hôtel particulier* built in 1779 by Bordelais architect Etienne Laclotte is the perfect setting for the **Musée des Arts Décoratifs** *(daily exc Mon and holidays 2–6, adm; free on Wed)*, with three floors of furniture, ceramics, paintings, gold and silverwork, glass and costumes that evoke the good life in Bordeaux in the 18th and 19th centuries.

Rue Bouffard continues up to **Place Gambetta** (originally Place Dauphine), laid out with uniform façades by Tourny in 1743 and soon after given a simple gateway, **Porte Dijeaux**. During the terror in the autumn of 1793 a guillotine was installed that parted the heads from the rest of 300 Bordelais, including the Girondins who hid out in Saint-Emilion; their last words here were muted by the beating drums. The chief revolutionary in Bordeaux was the fiery redhead Tallein, former editor of the *Ami du Citoyen*. Tallein would have given many more the chop had it not been for the gentle pleadings of his Spanish mistress, Teresa Cabarus, the Dame de Fonteni. When Tallein was recalled to Paris and Teresa was imprisoned by Robespierre, he freed her—by boldly toppling Robespierre himself on the 9th of Thermidor. Legend has it that Tallein's name was among those on a hit list found in Robespierre's pocket when an acquaintance just happened to be rifling through his famous sea-green coat, looking for a piece of paper to answer to a bodily need. Tallein and the others realized it was a case of us versus them, and Robespierre's head rolled.

Saint-Seurin

West of Place Gambetta, **Place des Martyrs-de-la-Résistance** marks the site of a famous cemetery in the Middle Ages. Consecrated, according to legend, by Christ himself in the company of the first saints of Gaul, it was one of several supposed burial places of the paladins from Roncevaux. It was linked to Bordeaux's oldest church, **Saint-Seurin**, named after the city's 5th-century bishop Severinus. Its antiquity allowed its medieval canons to concoct a number of pretty stories, most famously that Charlemagne chose it as the last resting place for Roland's great horn Oliphant after the hero's brain popped from blowing on it too hard. Although Oliphant seems to have gone missing, there are other things to see at Bordeaux's oldest—though often remodelled and expanded—church: the 14th-century porch with lavish sculptures of the Last Judgment and Resurrection; an unusual 11th-century porch, with capitals depicting the sacrifice of Isaac and the tomb of St Severinus, hidden behind the undistinguished main façade of 1828; and inside, a 7th-century sarcophagus, used as an altar in the Chapelle St-Etienne, and a pair of beautiful 15th-century alabaster works, namely, the retable in the Chapelle of Notre-Dame-de-la Rose and 14 panels in the choir, on the lives of St Severinus and St Martial, the apostle of Gaul. Note, too, the magnificent 15th-century episcopal throne, curiously made of stone imitating wood.

The 11th-century crypt (you may have to ask the sacristan to open it) has a fine collection of 6th- and 7th-century sarcophaguses, medieval tiles, Merovingian plaques and the tomb of Saint Fort, supposedly the first bishop of Bordeaux, way back in the 1st century; the Bordelais would sit their young sons on his tomb, to make them strong *(fort)* by mystic osmosis. Excavations under the crypt have revealed the 4th-century **Paleo-Christian** crypt *(open Apr–Sept Tues and Sat 2–6; adm)*, which goes back to the 4th-century origins of Christianity in Bordeaux: sarcophaguses, amphoras and frescoes.

Ausonius

Near St-Seurin was the Pagus Novarus, city address of Decimus Magnus Ausonius (*c.* 310–94), scion of one of Burdigala's most noble families. After his studies in Toulouse, he returned to Bordeaux as a professor of rhetoric, with such a reputation that he was appointed tutor of Gratian, son of Emperor Valentian; Emperor Gratian in turn appointed him prefect of Gaul (377). A familiar of St Ambrose of Milan and Emperor Theodosius, Ausonius managed to live blithely through the golden twilight of the Roman Empire, an empire overextended and attacked from all sides, but cosy enough for a patrician to retire in a choice of villas sprinkled across the Gironde, to hunt, fish, grow grapes for wine and write elaborate, bland poetry; he could have left us something more interesting for the interesting times he lived in. His correspondence with his Bordelais disciple, the poet-saint Paulinus de Nola, has proved more illuminating; the two broke their long friendship towards the end of Ausonius's life, when the austere Paulinus rejected his master's conviction that the new religion could be reconciled with the Olympian muses and the sweet worldly life he loved.

Quartier Saint-Pierre

From the 3rd to the 12th century, Saint-Pierre was its own walled quarter outside the city walls, built around the Palais de l'Ombrière, home of the dukes of Aquitaine and kings of England, and later, the Parlement of Bordeaux. Although destroyed in 1800, its triumphal arch-gate, the **Porte Cailhau** still overlooks the river with its asymmetrical turrets and tower. It was begun in 1493 to celebrate Charles VIII's draw at the Battle of Fornovo, in which the nobility of Guyenne played a prominent role. Inside are displays and a film devoted to the history of the port, the architecture and urban planning in Bordeaux, past, present and future (especially Bofill's project for the right bank) *(open 15 June–15 Sept, 10–1 and 2–6)*. From here you can observe the effect of the 18th-century **Grande Façade** project conceived by Jacques Gabriel and Intendants Boucher and Tourny to create a homogenous kilometre of architecture from Cours du Chapeau Rouge to Porte de la Monnaie, a regular row of pale stone houses, all the same height, with arcades on the ground floor, each arch with a *mascaron* at its key, topped by two floors of large windows, then a slate mansard roof with stone dormers.

Although in the Middle Ages the parish of Saint-Pierre was inhabited by English merchants and artisans remembered only in the street names—Rue Maucoudinat ('badly cooked'—the address of the tripe butchers), Rue des Bahutiers ('cabinet-makers') and Rue des Argentiers ('silversmiths'), the presence of the Parlement of Bordeaux from the 15th century on led to the construction of a number of stately 18th-century *hôtels particuliers*, now restored for the most part by the Association pour la Renaissance du Vieux Bordeaux (12

Rue des Faussets). You can see the best of them by walking straight through Porte Cailhau to Rue du Loup (note especially No. 71); then cross busy Rue Sainte-Catherine, and turn right in Rue de Cheverus (note No. 8, now the offices of the *Sud-Ouest*, Bordeaux's paper), and from here turn up Rue Poquelin-Molière. In 1656 Molière and his troupe performed at a *jeu-de-paume*, a walled court for court tennis, located at No. 9, replaced after a fire in 1728 by a handsome *hôtel*. From here find Rue Grassi and turn right in Rue Saint-Rémi.

This leads right into the centre of Bordeaux's neoclassical showcase, Jacques Gabriel's **Place de la Bourse**, commissioned by Intendant Boucher in 1735, who wanted to give the city a touch of Parisian class in spite of Bordeaux's nay-saying nabobs. Originally called the Place Royale, it had for a centrepiece a bronze equestrian statue of Louis XV that was gleefully pulled down and melted into cannons to fire at other kings in the Revolution; today a fountain of the three Graces (1864) holds pride of place, the Graces said to represent Empress Eugénie, the Queen of Spain and Queen Victoria. On one side stands the **Palais de la Bourse**, or stock exchange (now the Chamber of Commerce), enlarged in 1862 and 1925, and repaired after bomb damage in 1940; one the other, the **Hôtel des Douanes**, which must be the most grandiose customs house in the world. Installed in its grand, vaulted clearance halls of the former Fermes du Roy is a museum devoted to a subject that infuriates people to this day—French customs. The **Musée des Douanes**, at 1 Place de la Bourse *(open 10–12 and 1–5, closed Mon; adm)* traces the history of taxes on imports from the days of the ancient Gauls to displays of more recent uniforms, weapons, weights and measures (including a grand 200-year-old scale) of France's *douaniers*, as well as examples of the forgeries and contraband they've nabbed. Among the originals: Monet's *La cabanne des douaniers, effet d'après-midi* (1882).

The Golden Triangle and Esplanade des Quinconces

Bordeaux's Golden Triangle of good taste and luxury shops is formed by Cours de l'Intendance, Cours Georges-Clemenceau and Allées de Tourny. Amid the glitter, at 57 Cours de l'Intendance, the **Casa de Goya** *(open Mon–Fri 1–6)* was the last address of the painter, who in 1824 asked permission of Ferdinand VII to settle in Bordeaux with his former nursemaid and mistress. At the time Goya was still the official painter of the Spanish court, but serious illnesses, deafness and political disillusionment had made him ever more reclusive. In his last four years, in the company of his fellow exiles, he turned to a new medium, lithography (*The Bulls of Bordeaux* and *La Laitière*) and evolved a nearly Impressionistic freedom in his handling of paint. He died suddenly in 1828, age 82, while painting a portrait of his friend Molina, and was buried in Bordeaux until 1889, when his remains were transferred to Madrid. You can visit Goya's rooms; there are copies of his works and exhibits put on by the Spanish cultural centre.

Just off the Cours in Place du Chapelet is Bordeaux's chief Baroque church, **Notre-Dame** (1684–1707), directly inspired by the Gesù in Rome. Originally a Dominican chapel, its luxurious altar, organ and paintings show a marked change in the Order's taste since the days of Les Jacobins in Toulouse (*see* p.354). Behind it, in the centre of the Golden Triangle, is the iron and glass **Marché des Grands-Hommes**, rebuilt in 1991 and soon nicknamed the *bouchon de carafe* (the 'carafe stopper') The east end of the Cours de l'Intendance opens into **Place de la Comédie**, a space cleared of its 300 houses, a church and a remarkable Gallo-Roman palace called the Piliers de Tutelle by order of Louis XIV, who, after the uprising of the Fronde, wanted nothing to stand in the way of uppity Bordeaux and his cannons pointed at the city from the Château Trompette (*see* below). In 1773, the Maréchal-Duc de Richelieu, great nephew of the famous cardinal, governor of Guyenne and a famous libertine who fathered scores of Bordelais (at one of his dinner parties the only guests were the 29 most beautiful society belles of Bordeaux, masked to permit every indiscretion), felt he wasn't being properly entertained in Bordeaux and commissioned the **Grand Théâtre** from neoclassical master Victor Louis. If he forced the theatre down the city's throat by making the Jurats pay for it, it is now Bordeaux's proudest showcase, and in 1992 underwent a thorough restoration. From the outside it resembles a Greek temple, fronted by a row of mighty Corinthian columns and crowned with statues of goddesses and muses. Louis came up with a number of innovations, especially the great metal tie-beam (the '*clou de M. Louis*') that supports the entablature of the peristyle (shades of Soufflot's Pantheon in Paris; France's technically incompetent 18th-century architects had a hard time making their neoclassical stone confections stand up, and by necessity became leading innovators in the use of iron—a habit that culminated in the Eiffel Tower). If it looks fairly restrained from the outside, all sumptuous hell breaks loose within. Louis's vestibule has more columns, Doric this time, supporting a magnificent coffered ceiling, lit by a 62ft cupola; his bold grand stair was copied by Garnier for the Paris Opéra; the auditorium has golden columns and a domed ceiling (repainted in 1919) hung with a massive crystal chandelier weighing 2860lbs. From the day it opened, this high temple of illusion answered a deep-felt need in business-oriented Bordeaux; every single night it was thronged with merchants who paid a king's ransom to bring down the best players and dancers from Paris.

On the same theatrical note, just down the Cours 30 Juillet rises the irresistably overblown 19th-century **Monument aux Girondins**, a lofty column crowned by Liberty over a fountain mobbed by Happiness, Eloquence, Security, a crowing cockerel and a host of other fine allegories. Originally statues of the Girondins themselves were planned, but financial troubles kept them from even coming to their own party, as it were. In the fountain basin, two remarkable quadrigas of bronze horses violently rear their sea-monster paws to the sky while expressive figures of Falsehood (holding a mask), Vice (with pig ears) and shameful Ignorance, cower under the utterly vacuous gaze of the Republic. The Nazis stripped the fountain of its bronzes in 1943; to everyone's surprise they were later found squirreled away in Angoulême, although they had to wait in storage until the hotly contested mayoral election of 1983, when Chaban suddenly pulled the money out of a hat to restore the fountain.

Stretching out endlessly from here to the river is Europe's largest, and one of its least interesting squares, the **Place des Quinconces**. When speculators purchased the hated royal Château Trompette and began dismantling it just before the Revolution, their intention was to lay out new streets and build 1800 new houses. Now half of the square is a parking lot, and in the rest you're hard put to find any quincunxes at all (What's a quincunx, you ask?

Coat-of-arms on a hôtel particulier

A pattern like the five on a dice; all French farmers plant their trees in rows like this. Supposedly the fashion was started by the granddad of all gardeners, King Cyrus of Persia). At the river end, the Place is closed by two columns, the **Colonnes Rostrales**, erected in 1829, decorated with the prows of ships and topped by allegories of Commerce and Navigation.

Tourny laid out a tree-lined promenade now called the Allées de Tourny to give the Bordelais a place to stroll, along with the city's first patch of greenery, the **Jardin Public** (1756), which the Intendant had to promote as something practical to make it palatable to Bordeaux's conservative business class: 'In a commercial city, one must look at such public gardens as very useful, where merchants, often meeting one another there, transact much business. It is like having a second Exchange.' Originally laid out by Jacques-Ange Gabriel in the various perspectives of a *jardin à la française*, it was destroyed by Napoleon's troops, who used its trees and statues for target practice. When it was finally replanted in 1856, it was in the English style popularized by Napoleon III. The Cours de Verdun entrance to the garden has a bust of Bordeaux's greatest 20th-century writer, François Mauriac, by Zadkine; the 18th-century portico inside the garden sees a Sunday morning stamp market. At the west end of the garden, a *hôtel particulier* of 1778 has housed since 1862 the **Musée d'Histoire Naturelle** *(open daily exc Tues, 2–5.30; adm)*, containing an important collection of quaternary fossils, many from the Grotte de Pair-non-Pair near Bourg-sur-Gironde, as well as a selection of stuffed animals from around the world, and mineralogy and geology sections.

Two streets behind the musuem in Rue du Docteur Albert-Barraud, a monumental entrance and a few arches known as the **Palais Gallien** is all that remains of the 15,000-seat Roman amphitheatre of Burdigala built in the 3rd century AD. The barbarians, not as keen on gladiator sports as the civilized Gallo-Romans, burned it soon after its construction. Its name comes from a tangled tale that Charlemagne built it as a palace for his wife Galliene; old engravings show that the arena remained fairly intact until the 18th century, when its walls were incorporated into the surrounding buildings; today you need to be in an aircraft to trace its oval shape.

The Chartrons

In the 14th century, Carthusians chased out of Périgord found refuge in the swamp north of Bordeaux's walls and drained the land henceforth known as the Chartrons. The presence of the massive Château Trompette kept the neighbourhood apart from the rest of Bordeaux, and in the 17th century Flemish wine merchants (then known as *courtiers*), feeling discriminated against by the pro-English Jurats, set up their own business and quay here, soon to be followed by German, Dutch and Irish traders affiliated with the Hansa of Bruges, and then by the English themselves. The most successful of these merchants, brokers and shippers bought their own vineyards and evolved into fabulously wealthy wine dynasties, the *aristocratie de bouchon*. Their smug, closed social circle—the source of Anglophile Bordeaux's reputation for snobbery, clubbiness and affected mannerisms (as in replacing many French words with English)—first suffered with the Revocation of the Edict of Nantes. This sent the Protestants among them abroad, although they kept up their commercial ties with Bordeaux and helped enlarge the market for its wine across Europe.

The decline of the Chartrons began with the Revolution, when many Chartrons merchants were guillotined and many others moved abroad. Under Napoleon commerce came to a standstill—for 30 years the Chartrons lived only by fitting out corsairs. Although Chartrons commerce revived, it was never the same; if in the 1950s the brokers still had their offices in prestigious if shabby waterfront buildings along the quay, by the 1960s the relocation of port activities to the north, to Bassens and Ambès, and the switch to land transport of wine had made even this vestige of the past irrelevant. Ever since then the city has sought a new role for the Chartrons while maintaining as much of its original wine business as possible in the shiny new (if utterly sterile) **Cité Mondiale du Vin** on the Quai des Chartrons, concentrating hotels and an ultra-modern conference centre, with exhibitions and shops open to the general public.

The snobbiest of the Chartrons nobility lived on the Pavé des Chartrons (now Cours Xavier-Arnozan) paved by Tourny and planted with trees at the same time as he laid out the nearby Jardin Public. Where it meets the quay stands the **Hôtel Fenwick**, built in 1790 for Joseph Fenwick, who managed to combine his duties as the first American consul in Bordeaux with his mercantile activities—represented in the ship's-prow decoration.

One of the success stories of the Chartrons is the restoration of the austere neoclassical **Entrepôt Lainé**, around the corner from Hôtel Fenwick at 7 Rue Ferrère, built in the 1820s where spices and other goods imported from France's colonies were unloaded, exempt from duty; now its vast spaces are used for the giant-scale exhibitions and installations of the **Musée d'Art Contemporain** *(open 11–7, closed Mon; adm)*. Not far from these displays of the newest contemporary art are shops dealing in fond old things: antique dealers line Rue Notre Dame on all sides of the austere Protestant Temple, its only ornament the relief of a Bible exploding out of the clouds.

The old wine trade is remembered in the *hôtel* of Irish broker Francis Burke (1720), now the **Musée des Chartrons**, 41 Rue Borie, between the Quai des Chartrons and Cours Balguerie *(open Tues–Sat 10–12.30 and 2–5.30)*, with a collection of lithographs, wine labels and bottles going back to the 1600s. You can also learn about the long-lost wine of the islands—in the old days brokers would load Caribbean-bound ships with 900-litre casks of the finest Bordeaux *crus*, accompanied by a vintner to keep an eye on the evaporation and top up the casks when necessary. This precious cargo was not for the likes of the colonies, however; when the ship arrived in the Antilles, wine and vintner stayed on board, and sailed back to Bordeaux. The journey improved the wine so much that as *Bordeaux retour des îles* it commanded a premium price in the restaurants of Paris. When steamers took over the route, it was found that the wine didn't improve at all; the secret had been the gentle rolling motion of a sailing ship, and *retour*, as it was known by its lovers, went the way of the dodo.

Further north, at 60 Quai des Chartrons, visitors are welcome aboard the retired battleship **Colbert** (bus 1 or 91; *open daily Apr–Sept 10–6; other times closed Mon and Tues; adm exp*). In the same area, at 40–50 Cours du Médoc (just off Quai des Chartrons), the **Musée Goupil** *(open Tues–Sat 2–6; adm)* displays works from the archives of the Parisian printer and editor Goupil from 1827 to 1920.

For fifty years, Bordeaux's old docks along Boulevard Alfred Daney (bus 9 from the station or boulevards) have been disfigured by sinister Nazi U-boat pens, encased in vast indestructible bunkers with walls 5.6m thick. In 1993, these pens were converted into a unique museum of pleasure boats, the **Conservatoire Internationale de la Plaisance de Bordeaux** *(© 56 11 11 50; open 1.30–7, weekends 10–7, closed Mon, Jan and Feb; adm 45F)*. Among the 60 craft displayed are a replica of the *Simon and Jude*, a catamaran of 1662 built by Cromwell's physician, Sir William Petty; one of the first petrol-run pleasure motorboats, built by Daimler in 1889 for Bismarck; and the world's fastest sailboat, Sir Timothy Coleman's *Crossbow II*. To the west the last swamps of the Chartrons were concentrated in 1960 into an artificial lake, the centre of the **Quartier du Lac**, with Bordeaux's trade fair buildings, congress centre, golf courses, an arboretum and recreational facilities.

Pessac

Pessac (bus P from Saint-André) may be one of many victims of Bordeaux's 20th-century transformation into an octopus, but it is also the site of a landmark experiment to meet the need for new housing and create something architecturally new: Le Corbusier's first project, the **Cité Frugès** in Avenue Henri Frugès. The name commemorates the Bordeaux industrialist whose desire to transform a tract of land he owned near the railway line into healthy, light and airy affordable housing for 300 families led him to give the young Swiss architect Le Corbusier a crack at practising his theories of urban housing for the post-Cubist era. In 1926 Le Corbusier and his co-builder Jeanneret produced 51 houses for Henri Frugès. The result: geometric modules with rough concrete skins, with hanging gardens on terraces and brightly coloured paint. The houses had many comforts the old *échoppes* of Bordeaux lacked: central heating, running water and adequate sewerage, but the sight of them drove the Bordelais bananas. Frugès was dismissed as a loony, and when people reluctantly moved in, the first thing they did was try to make Le Corbusier's modules fit their idea of houses. In his dismay Frugès never finished the project, although up in heaven he must be gratified to see that his cité is now classed as a historic monument and is slowly being stripped of later additions to restore the architect's original intention.

Pessac-Léognan

Since 1987 the northern third of the traditional Graves growing area has been given its own *appellation*, Pessac-Léognan. Its worst enemy is urban sprawl; at the turn of the century, the four closest communes to Bordeaux (Pessac, Gradignan, Mérignac and Talence) had 119 vineyards. Today there are nine. Yet these, especially in Pessac, only 6km southwest of central Bordeaux produce some of the greatest wines in the entire *département*, beginning with the prestigious **Château Haut-Brion** (on the P bus route, in Avenue Jean-Jaurès) founded in 1550. The elegant finesse of its reds (50 per cent Cabernet Sauvignon, 35 per cent Merlot, 15 per cent Cabernet Franc) were rewarded in 1885, when the property became the only non-Médoc wine to be granted Premier Grand Cru status. But Haut-Brion was famous even before then, especially in London. As far as anyone knows, this was the first wine sold under the name of the estate that produced it, rather than under the name of the parish; 17th-century Londoners called it 'Ho-Bryan' and made it such a success that the original owners, the Pontacs even opened one of London's first luxury restaurants, called the 'New Eating House', with a French grocer and wine cellar on the premises. Later owned by Talleyrand, the estate was purchased in 1935 by American banker Clarence Dillon, whose granddaughter, the Duchesse de Mouchy, now runs the company. In 1983 she purchased the equally celebrated **Château La-Mission-Haut-Brion** across the street—which until the Revolution belonged to a mission founded by St Vincent de Paul—and produces a powerful wine equal to the finest from Médoc. Today the two vineyards are green islands in Bordeaux's postwar sprawl, which creates an urban climate that protects the vines from spring frosts and accelerates the harvest, a plus in years of heavy autumn rains. A third vineyard in Pressac (Avenue Pasteur) is the one with the longest continuous history of them all, planted in 1300 by Bordeaux archbishop Bertrand de Got before he became pope, and hence known as **Château Pape-Clément**, producing a *cru classé* famous for its intense wines that pack an extraordinarily aromatic tobacco bouquet (visits possible, but no sales).

Markets and Shopping

Bordeaux has five covered markets open every morning exc Sun (Cours Victor-Hugo, Place des Capucins (the most fragrant), Place des Grands Hommes, Place des Chartrons and Place de l'Erme) and a bric-à-brac antique market in Place Meynard on Tues, Wed, Thurs and Fri 8–6. A bottle is the obvious souvenir of Bordeaux; there are wine shops and all kinds of vinous paraphernalia in the Cité Mondiale des Vins on the Quai des Chartrons. For free tastings, information and a list of wine châteaux that welcome visitors without reservations, stop by the **Maison du Vin SNCM/CIVB**, opposite the tourist office at 1 Cours du 30 Juillet, ✆ 56 00 22 66. Pedestrian Rue Sainte-Catherine is Bordeaux's favourite shopping street, especially for clothes. English books are available at **Bradley's Bookshop**, 32 Place Gambetta, ✆ 56 52 10 57. Bordeaux has two streets devoted to antiques: Rue Bouffard around the Musée des Arts Décoratifs and Rue Notre-Dame in the Chartrons, with two-score shops and galleries. Quartier Saint-Pierre is another good place to look for old things and curiosities, in particular along Rue de la Devise. For an unusual gift, choose from 600 different packs of cards or pick up antique postcards at **Au Bonheur du Cartophile**, 4bis Rue de Cursol.

You can tour the Garonne and its ports aboard the *Ville de Bordeaux*, © 56 52 88 88 or 56 32 32 50 or the Grands Bateaux d'Aquitaine, © 56 86 50 65. Besides the Jardin Public, Bordeaux has another lung further west in the **Parc Bordelais** (buses 18 or 14). Golfers have a choice of two courses on the outskirts of town: the 27-hole **Golf de Pessac**, 5 Rue de la Princesse, © 56 36 24 47, and the less expensive 36-hole **Golf de Bordeaux-Lac**, Av. de Pernon, © 56 50 92 72. Mériadeck has a bowling alley and indoor skating rink (both at 95 Cours du Maréchal Juin, © 56 24 40 39). Bordeaux's beloved rugby team plays in Bègles just to the south; the Girondins football team play in the Art Deco Stade Municipal (1938) in Bd. du Maréchal Leclerc.

Bordeaux ✉ 33000   **Where to Stay**

expensive

There are a clutch of pricey new chain hotels at Bordeaux Lac easily reached off the *rocade* ring road, and a pair of worthy non-chain hotels in the centre. The 19th-century façade of the ★★★★**Château Chartrons**, 81 Cours St-Louis, © 56 43 15 00 conceals Bordeaux's most comfortable ultra-modern lodgings, complete with garden terraces and a wine bar; the plush rooms are soundproofed and air conditioned, and there's private parking. In a handsomely restored 18th-century *hôtel* near the Grand Théâtre, ★★★**Sainte Catherine**, 27 Rue du Parlement, © 56 81 95 12, is the most comfortable hotel in its class, with exceptionally nice rooms.

moderate

On the corner of the Allées de Tourny, ★★★**Bayonne**, 4 Rue Martignac, © 56 48 00 88, has recently been redecorated—exactly as it was originally in the Art Deco '30s. All rooms have TV and shower. At ★★★**Les Quatre Soeurs**, 6 Cours 30-Juillet (near the Quinconces), © 57 81 19 20, you can sleep where Richard Wagner slept, before he was run out of town for dallying with the wife of a local politician; rooms, overlooking the street or courtyard, are cosy and furnished with mini-bars. ★★★**Royal Médoc**, 3 Rue Sèze (just off Place Tourny) © 56 81 72 42, has very comfortable up-to-date rooms and a garage.

inexpensive

In the quiet Chartrons quarter ★★**Notre Dame**, 36 Rue Notre-Dame, © 56 52 88 24, is a pretty little hotel in a 19th-century building, recently given a complete face-lift. Centrally located, on a pedestrian-only lane off Cours de l'Intendance, the ★★**Hôtel de la Tour Intendance**, 16 Rue Vieille-Tour, © 56 81 46 27 is simple and sweet and run by a friendly family. Near the station, the best choice has the silliest name: ★★**One Star**, 34 Rue Tauzia, © 56 94 59 00, a welcoming hotel with shipshape decor.

If possible, give the hotels near the station a miss for the old-fashioned **Amboise**, 22 Rue Vieille-Tour, ✆ 56 81 62 67, or the slightly more expensive ***Studio**, 26 Rue Huguerie, near the bus depot off Place du Tourny, ✆ 56 48 00 14, where the larger rooms come complete with shower and WC. Masochists can check into the ugly concrete, surly and inconvenient **Auberge de Jeunesse**, 22 Cours Barbey (bus 7 or 8 from the station), ✆ 56 91 59 51. The nearest camp site to Bordeaux is to the south at Villenave-d'Ornon (33140): the pleasant, well-equipped **Les Gravières**, ✆ 56 87 00 36, but really only practical if you have wheels of your own.

Eating Out

Unlike most folks, who pick a bottle to go with their meal, the Bordelais tend to choose a vintage first, then create a menu that will enhance the wine. This concern, and Bordeaux's choice setting between land, river and sea, has led to the invention of a wide choice of specialities from the famous *entrecôte à la bordelaise* to the more rarefied pleasures of lamprey.

Lamprey (*Lamproie à la bordelaise*)

This is not a recipe for the squeamish, nor one that would have survived Brigitte Bardot's animal rights squads if the beast in question weren't a remarkably uncuddly, ugly, blood-sucking parasite that missed the evolutionary boat back in the night of time, probably because it doesn't seem to have any eyes. Nail a live lamprey to the wall and cut it across the tail, carefully catching all the blood that drains out (for thickening the sauce). Next cut off the poisonous dorsal cartilage (ingesting some by mistake is said to have killed Henri I) and plunge your lamprey into boiling water to make it easier to remove the skin. Slice the delicate white flesh into rounds and add it to a mixture of leeks, onions, chunks of ham and a bottle of Saint-Emilion that has been stewing for three days. Poach the lamprey in the wine mixture, and add the blood and a touch of chocolate. It comes in tins in delicatessens if you don't feel like doing it yourself.

Although Bordeaux suffered a post-war slump in the kitchen along with its post-war blues in other fields, a new school of chefs in the 1970s have brought about a remarkable revival. Best of all, prices have remained reasonable; to dine as well in Paris or along the Côte d'Azur would cost an arm and a leg. Note that you could starve on Sundays in Bordeaux, when the city's beaneries shut down as tight as a clam.

The oldest restaurant in Bordeaux (since 1800) is still one of the best, **Le Chapon Fin**, 5 Rue Montesquieu, ✆ 56 79 10 10. During Bordeaux's periods as capital of

France it was packed with *tout Paris*, and Sarah Bernhardt and Edward VII stopped in whenever they were in town. Its sumptuous Rococo decor, unchanged since 1901, and inner garden are a perfect match for the likes of the *marbès de ris de veau et fois gras* and *marmite* of fish and crustaceans with pistou—Provençal pesto, prepared by Francis Garcia; long lists of *grands crus* (menus from 170 to 400F; closed Sun and Mon). At the north end of town near the Parc Bordelais, **Pavillon des Boulevards**, 150 Rue Croix-de-Seguey, ℂ 56 81 51 92, is in a simple, tastefully designed house with a veranda in the back garden, the stage where chef Régis Franc presents delicate, sophisticated dishes based on the absolutely best and freshest ingredients; for a real splurge order the lobster au Sauternes (menus from 200 to 400F, closed Sat lunch and Sun). **Le Rouzic**, 34 Cours Chapeau Rouge, ℂ 56 44 39 11, offers a sumptuous combination of classic and imaginative dishes (including a famous *gelée d'huîtres à l'eau de mer*) prepared by a Maître Cusinier de France; menus from 195 and 280F.

moderate

If you stick to the 160F or 230F menus, you can dine moderately and memorably at one of Bordeaux's best and classiest restaurants, **Jean Ramet**, 7 Place Jean-Jaurès, ℂ 56 44 12 51, where chef Ramet prepares both old-fashioned (braised veal knuckle) and original dishes (*gratin de figues*) to the delight of his fashionable customers. In the Quartier St-Pierre, **Les Plaisirs d'Ausone**, 10 Rue Ausone, ℂ 56 79 30 30, has a most delicious, imaginative 150F menu and a 'Taxi-Gourmand' menu designed for people who hate the hassle of parking: for 250F, you have a choice between four entrées, main courses, desserts, wine and coffee and a taxi ride to and from any point in Bordeaux (closed Sun, Mon and Sat lunch). Near St-Michel, **La Tupina**, 6 Rue Porte-de-la-Monnaie, ℂ 56 91 56 37 is the baliwick of Jean-Pierre Xiradakis, one of the pioneers in the great Bordelais restaurant revival, and a good place to fill up on hearty delights like *émincé de canard* with shallots (lunch menu 110F, dinner 160F, closed Sun). For a delicious beef filet with a creamy mustard sauce or poached pineapple with kirsch sorbet, get a table at **L'Alhambra**, 111bis Rue Judaïque, ℂ 56 96 06 91; lunch menu 100F; others at 150 and 200F, closed Sat lunch and Sun.

inexpensive

A new restaurant in the Chartrons, **Gravelier**, 114 Cours Verdun, ℂ 56 48 17 15, offers very toothsome cuisine, especially seafood, prepared with an exotic touch (couscous with tuna and spices, or *saint-pierre* with ginger); 90F lunch menu, others at 120 and 185F (closed Sat lunch and Sun). This same neighbourhood recalls a bit of its cosmopolitan past in **La Petite Sirène**, 28 Quai des Chartrons, ℂ 56 51 22 60, a delightful Danish smorgasbord featuring a wide variety of herring, salmon, ham and other goodies (menus from 100 to 170F). A paradise for mice, or anyone who loves cheese and wine, **Baud et Millet**, 19 Rue Huguerie, ℂ 56 79

05 77 offers 850 wines from around the world to go with its farm cheese and *raclettes* (many menus, from 95 to 185F, closed Sun). At cosy **La Cave de Bigoudy**, 36 Rue Tourat, ✆ 56 51 69 43, a fine choice of wine and beef grilled over vine cuttings and other regional dishes keep its clients coming back (closed Sat lunch and Sun, menus at 95 and 120F). If it's Sunday (or any other day of the week), **La Cave à Jules**, 56 Rue du Mirail, ✆ 56 91 44 69 offers generous menus from 89 to 130F, and for 30F extra, ostrich tournedos with morel sauce (ostrich has become trendy in recent years; they raise them in the Tarn).

cheap

Seafood lovers on a budget can indulge in fish soup and filet of red mullet with walnut oil at the new **Bistrot du Chalut**, 59 Rue du Palais Gallien, ✆ 56 81 43 51; menus at 60 and 75F, closed Sun and Mon. **Mably**, 12 Rue Mably, ✆ 56 44 30 10, has been Bordeaux's classic brasserie for 60 years, where the little blackboard lists the day's dishes: try the *poêlée de Saint-Jacques et pétoncles* if it appears (menus at 70 and 100F, lunchtime *plat du jour* 39F), closed Sun. For delicious fresh pasta and homemade desserts on a 55F menu, get yourself to **La Rital**, 3 Rue des Faussets, ✆ 56 48 16 69, closed weekends and September; **Malabar**, 7 Rue des Ayres, ✆ 56 52 18 19, is one of Bordeaux's better Indian restaurants, with one of the city's widest choices of vegetarian dishes (menus from 43 to 120F, closed Sun and Mon).

around Bordeaux

Bouliac ✉ 33270

In Bouliac, to the southeast, 4km from the right bank of the Garonne, ★★★★**Hauterive Saint-James**, 3 Place Camille-Hosteins, ✆ 56 20 52 19, is an ultra-screwy post-modern hotel designed to look like a local tobacco drying barn by Jean Nouvel of Périgord (architect of the wonderful Institut du Monde Arabe in Paris) and Jean-Marie Amat, the hotel's owner, celebrated chef and local celebrity. The sombre rooms, designed for people who never take their sunglasses off, come complete with embarrassing bathrooms by Philip Stark and electric beds that take some practice to master; but you can escape them in the gym, sauna, jacuzzi, squash courts or pool. The hotel's restaurant, **Amat** is another story altogether, where the eponymous chef prepares the best meals in the entire Gironde, based on a wide variety of farm-raised poultry, wild mushrooms and fresh seafood, accompanied by a magnificent wine list (menus 250F with wine, and 450F, lunch 180F, closed Sun and Mon out of season only). Amat, who doesn't at all mind going over the top, also runs the adjacent **Bistrot**, ✆ 56 20 52 19, where you can dine well for less (à la carte for under 200F) in carefully cultivated 'destroy'-style surroundings meant to evoke the fall of the Berlin Wall and urban decay.

Mérignac ✉ 33700

Near the airport at Mérignac, 10km west of Bordeaux, you can dine on perfectly prepared fish dishes and reasonably priced wines at **L'Iguane**, 127 Avenue Magudas, ✆ 56 34 07 39; the Bordelais make the trip even when they don't have a flight to catch (menus at 110, 150 and 240F, closed Sun night).

Pessac ✉ 33600

In Pessac, 6km southwest, ★★★**La Réserve**, 74 Av. de Bourgailh, ✆ 56 07 13 28, is the only hotel in the greater Bordeaux area in a park with a lake and swans, along with tennis courts and a pool to go with comfortable if pricey rooms—from 600F.

Gradignan ✉ 33170

In Gradignan, 12km south of Bordeaux, ★★**Le Chalet Lyrique**, 169 Cours Général de Gaulle, ✆ 56 89 11 59 is an exceptionally comfortable hotel over-looking a terrace more Mediterranean than Bordelais; good restaurant, with meals from 135F.

Carbon Blanc ✉ 33560

In Carbon Blanc, to the northwest just over the Garonne, **Marc Demund**, 5 Av. de la Gardette, ✆ 56 74 72 28, prepares dishes based on traditional, bourgeoise recipes from the past, that perfectly match the country mansion in a park setting; the menu changes every six months (menus at 100, 250 and 350F, closed Sun night and Mon).

Entertainment and Nightlife

The premier stage of Bordeaux remains Victor Louis' **Grand Théâtre**, ✆ 56 90 91 60, followed by the **Théâtre Femina**, 8 Rue de Grassi, ✆ 56 52 45 19. Concerts and ballets frequently show up on the bill at the above, and at the **Palais des Sports**, Place de la Ferme Richemont, ✆ 56 79 39 61, and **L'Espace du Pin Galant**, 34 Av. du Maréchal de Lattre de Tassigny in Mérignac, ✆ 56 97 82 82.

Bordeaux doesn't have as much nightlife as Toulouse, but there are a few places to check out for a drink or a dance before hitting the sack. University students hang out in the bars around Place de la Victoire, especially at **Chez Auguste** or **El Bodegon**, with rock music and videos daily until 2am. **El Alguacil**, near the station at 84 Quai de Paludate, ✆ 56 85 32 90 is a lively, often overflowing tapas bar (Tues–Sat 10pm–2am); **Le Chandelier**, 9 Quai de la Douane, near Place de la Bourse, ✆ 56 79 14 94 offers more central tapas and concerts on Saturday (open 11pm–2am, closed Sun). **Le Boeuf sur le toit**, 15 Rue de Candale, ✆ 56 91 41 14, open daily 7pm to 2am serves a selection of beers and other drinks in a tropical island setting, with occasional free rock concerts.

In several places, Bordeaux's former port buildings have been converted into discotheques: **Caesar's**, Quai Louis XVIII, ✆ 56 51 99 41, is the most grandiose—a complex including a cabaret revue, Russian-Gypsy piano bar and top-of-the-pops disco in an Imperial Roman atmosphere (daily 10pm–4.30am). **Le Chat Bleu**, 122 Quai de Bacalan, ✆ 56 29 19 67, plays house, rock, rap, French pops, etc., with occasional concerts at weekends (daily exc Sun 10pm–4am); for techno music from 11pm until dawn, there's the **Ubu Club**, 135 Quai des Chartrons, ✆ 56 39 77 25, closed Sun; free entrance during the week. Out in Mérignac, **La Macumba**, Rte du Cap Ferret, ✆ 56 34 05 48 has four rooms with a variety of pop music, and dancing in the garden in the summer (daily exc Mon 10.30pm–4.30am).

To top off a late night in Bordeaux, finish up at the Marché des Capuchins near St-Michel for a bowl of onion soup with the workers unloading the produce. Bars here open from 1 to 5am; try **Chez Rhodes** or the **Bistrot de Joseph**.

The Gironde

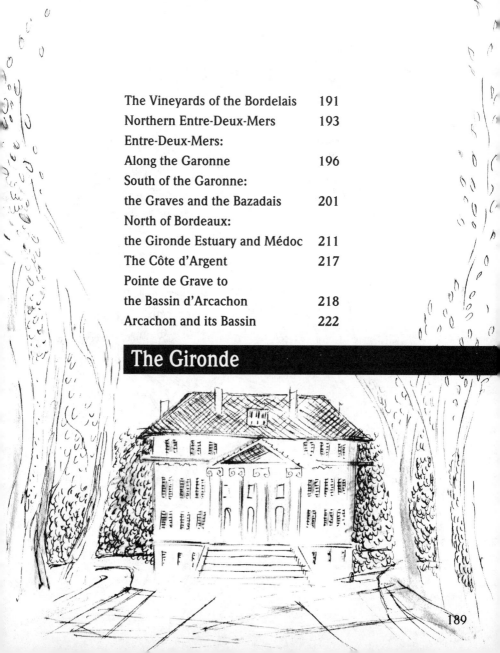

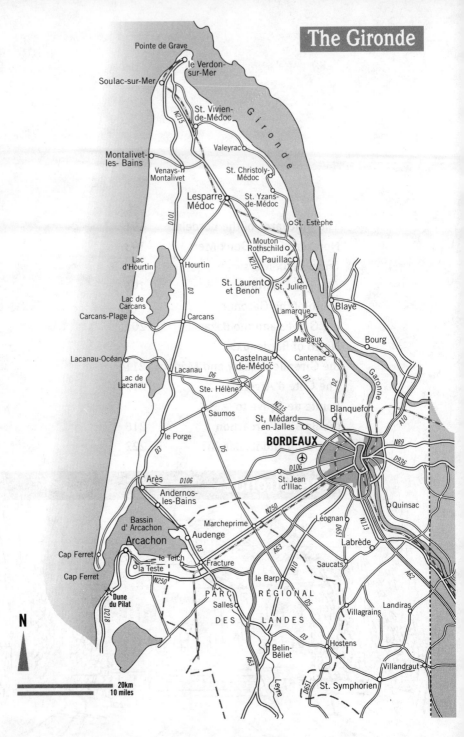

The Gironde

Pointe de Grave

le Verdon-
sur-Mer

Soulac-sur-Mer

St. Vivien-
de-Médoc

Gironde

N215

Valeyrac

Montalivet-
les- Bains

Venays-
Montalivet

St. Christoly-
Médoc

Lesparre
Médoc

St. Yzans-
de-Médoc

D101

St. Estèphe

Mouton
Rothschild

Lac
d'Hourtin

Hourtin

N215

Pauillac

St. Laurent
et Benon

St. Julien

D3

Lac de
Carcans

Carcans-Plage

Carcans

Lamarque

Blaye

Margaux

Bourg

Lacanau-Océan

Lacanau

Castelnau-
de-Médoc

Cantenac

Garonne

D6

D1

D2

Lac de
Lacanau

Ste. Hélène

Saumos

N215

Blanquefort

le Porge

D3

D5

St, Médard-
en-Jalles

BORDEAUX

A10

N89

D936

Arès

D106

D106

St. Jean
d'Illac

Andernos-
les-Bains

N250

Léognan

Quinsac

N113

Bassin
d' Arcachon

Marcheprime

Audenge

A63

Labrède

Arcachon

D3

Cap Ferret

le Teich

la Teste

Fracture

Saucats

A62

Cap Ferret

W250

le Barp

N10

Landiras

D218

N

PARC

RÉGIONAL

Salles

D5

Villagrains

Dune
du Pilat

DES

LANDES

Leyre

D3

Hostens

A63

Belin-
Béliet

Villandraut

D651

20km
10 miles

St. Symphorien

Bordeaux's *département*, the Gironde, is one chock-full of superlatives. It is the largest in France (6650 square miles), contains 2170 miles of rivers and 72 miles of Atlantic coast, the whole lined with fine silver sand scarcely touched by development. In the Gironde, you'll find France's largest two lakes, Europe's largest estuary, its oldest lighthouse, its highest sand dune and the northern fringes of Les Landes, its largest forest. Not to mention the largest and, by most criteria, the best vine region in the whole wide world.

The Vineyards of the Bordelais

The nuances and names of the numerous vineyards, *appellations*, growths and other classifications of Bordeaux's wines are befuddling enough even before you go careening off on a wine tour. A look at the map reveals that you can divide the Bordeaux vineyards into four main regions: the Libournais along the north of the Dordogne, encompassing the superb *appellations* of Pomerol and Saint-Emilion, Côtes de Blaye and Côtes de Bourg (*see* pp.148–58); the Entre-Deux-Mers, between the Dordogne and Garonne; the Graves, south of the Garonne; and the Médoc, along the south bank of the Gironde estuary north of Bordeaux.

In the 18th century, much of the best land for growing grapes was consolidated into the hands of Bordeaux's political and legal movers and shakers, the *noblesse de robe*, who built themselves splendid manor houses by their properties. These became the basis for the châteaux system that characterizes Bordeaux's vineyards and gives its wines their prestigious reputation in the consumer's mind (although no one can keep 4000 names of châteaux straight, and you can bet that wine sellers are well aware that any Bordeaux château that incorporates magic words like Biron and Mouton in its name will be a big seller). Outside of Médoc and Sauternes, wine tours also reveal that many glorious sounding châteaux are not only insignificant but also non-existent— most surprisingly in fancy-pants Saint-Emilion.

The market for Bordeaux red wine, or claret, was always big in England (*claret* originally meant white or rosé, but somehow around 1600 the word got twisted into a name for Bordeaux red wine). After 1853, with the construction of the railway to Paris, the market began to expand in France as well, especially after the 1855 Paris Exhibition that saw the famous classifications of Bordeaux's Médocs and Sauternes. Bankers (most famously, the Rothschilds) and investors, both French and foreign, bought up estates just in time for the outbreak of phylloxera in 1878. Vines were replanted, grafted on phylloxera-resistant American roots, and good wine was produced again in quantity in 1893. After a brief revival and a few good years, the economy and weather went sour. Excellent wines were produced again in the 1920s, but the prices went out from under them and the market collapsed.

It wasn't until after the Second World War that the vineyards of Bordeaux began to turn in a profit again; in the late 1950s enough confidence had returned to allow the experimentation and technological improvements in winemaking that revolutionized Bordeaux in the 1960s and '70s—sprays against rot and adjustments in the temperature of fermentation to an even coolness, especially important for white wines. Even mechanical harvesters are now used in over half the vineyards, enabling vintners to get all the grapes in at the peak moment of ripeness.

An ideal introduction to all Bordeaux wines is offered at **La Maison de la Qualité**, halfway between Bordeaux and Libourne on the N 89, near Beychac-et-Caillau *(open to the public Mon–Fri 8.30–12.30 and 1.30–5; also Sat in the summer)*. This modern building is the fief of those wizards of the nose and taste bud who sniff and gargle each estate's wine every year to see whether it merits the proud name of Bordeaux or Bordeaux Supérieur; for visitors there's a film, free tastings of select wines, commentaries and advice on visiting the châteaux. *See also* p.19 for a guide to vintages.

Entre-Deux-Mers

The name comes from *inter duo maria*, 'between two estuaries' (the Dordogne and the Garonne) and by the flat Gironde's standards we're talking highlands—an undulating plateau of soft limestone occasionally reaching over 320ft in altitude, pocked with natural cavities. Its fine, blond stone was quarried to build Bordeaux, leaving behind tunnels converted into mushroom farms that keep the metropolis in fungi. On the whole, however, Bordeaux regards the Entre-Deux-Mers as its backyard Ruritania, a natural base for microtourism, where any village over 2000 souls seems downright urban.

Entre-Deux-Mers AOC

Bordeaux's largest producer of dry white wines, to the tune of 18 million bottles a year, much of Entre-Deux-Mers is a rolling emerald sea of vineyards. Of its 92,600 acres of vines, a tenth belong to one of ten different *appellations*, most of which are located in the south and along the Garonne valley. The wide diversity of altitudes, soils and influences from its two great rivers make this mesopotamia a patchwork quilt of microclimates, but for many long years Entre-Deux-Mers was considered second-rate. Pride, perhaps more than anything else since the late 1970s has stirred the winemakers (most of whom are natives of the area) to improve the quality and bring out the distinct character of the wines, and lift the *appellation* back up to snuff. As for all white Bordeauxs, Sauvignon is the dominant grape, blended with one or more of the following—Sémillon, Colombard, Ugni Blanc, Merlot Blanc, and Muscadelle. Some

60 per cent of the production is sold abroad. Along with white wine, a number of estates produce reds under the *appellation* Bordeaux or Bordeaux Supéieur. At La Sauve, **Château Turcaud**, ✆ 56 23 04 41 produces a delightful, floral wine; the cooperative **Les Vignerons de Guyenne** in Blasimon, ✆ 56 71 55 28 does a fresh, classic pale Entre-Deux-Mers. Or for a hint of the vast range of this *appellation*, try the elegant cold-fermented wines of the vast 18th-century **Château Bonnet**, further north in Grézillac.

Northern Entre-Deux-Mers

In the Middle Ages, this great wedge of land belonged to the Benedictines, headquartered at the great abbey of La Sauve-Majeure, and they sprinkled the countryside with good Romanesque churches. A century or two later, this peaceful region found itself on the front lines in the Hundred Years' War, which caused such devastion that in the 15th century the French kings repopulated it with northerners speaking the *langue d'oïl*, the *gavaches* as the Gascons called them, who settled in tiny hamlets or lone farms that to this day appear regularly every mile or so. The less said about the peninsula of Ambès (the northern corner of Entre-Deux-Mers) the better, unless you hanker after grey urban dilation, modern port installations and defunct petroleum refineries.

Tourist Information

Sauveterre-de-Guyenne: 1 Rue Saint-Romain, ✆ 56 71 53 45

Blasimon: Hôtel de Ville, ✆ 56 71 52 12

Monségur: Place Darniche, ✆ 56 61 60 12

market days

Créon: Wednesdays

Sauveterre-de-Guyenne: Tuesdays

To the Abbaye de La Sauve-Majeure

As you drive east from Bordeaux along the D 10/D 10E there are a handful of places discreetly bidding a detour: **Lignan**, a hamlet once owned by the Knights of St John, who left behind a little Romanesque church with carved capitals and some unusual 11th-century tombs, carved out of a single rock; **Sadirac**, an old pottery village to the east, has a pair of Renaissance châteaux and a pair of new potters firing up their kilns. Further to the southeast lies the Gironde's 'Little Switzerland', a green region sliced by a score of valleys, with **Créon** as one of its chief towns, a bastide of 1316 founded by and named after the English seneschal Amaury de Craon, who hoped to dilute the power of the Benedictines at the nearby Sauve-Majeur. Créon retains three sides of arcades in its central square and a church rebuilt in the 16th century, as described in the ornate Gothic inscriptions on its wall of its pentagonal apse. Inside, see the curiously disproportionate 13th-century statue of the Virgin that for long time stood in the niche of the 17th-century *clocher-mur*. Just south of Créon, the church at **St-Genès-de-Lombaud** is built over a Roman villa, with a Romanesque portal sculpted with animals and odd little figures.

Continue 3km east of Créon for the remarkable ruins of the Benedictine **Abbaye de La Sauve-Majeure** (*silva major*, the great forest) founded in 1079 by St Gérard de Corbie, who was granted the power of sanctuary and justice by the troubadour Duke Guilhem IX of Aquitaine. By the 1200s it had chapters as far away as England and Aragon. The great Romanesque church dates from this golden age; it was damaged in the Hundred Years' War and Wars of Religion, and picked apart piece by piece by carrion salvagers from the days of the Revolution until 1882, leaving only the skeleton behind. Few skeletons, however, command such presence: three of the twelve massive pillars that supported the triple nave still stand, culminating in a row of five 'bread oven' apses, while the lofty hexagonal bell tower with ogival windows still rises with panache from the fourth bay, fitted with a viewing platform on top. Two carved Romanesque capitals (sacrifice of Abraham, beheading of St John) are in the second bay, but the most spectacular are the capitals in the choir and apses, the eyes and hair of the figures lovingly detailed: there are scenes of drinking griffons, fighting centaurs, a battle between an asp and basilisk, and in the apses scenes from Genesis, Daniel in the Lion's Den and Samson. A pair of others are in the Musée d'Aquitaine in Bordeaux. To see the rest (and the *modillons*, carved by the same hand) you'll have to go the Cloisters Museum in New York. La Sauve has an interesting **museum** of its own, located in the former monastery *(open daily exc Tues, 10–12 and 2–5, July and Aug 9–7; adm)*, containing a fine statue of St Gérard in a style reminiscent of Chartres, medallions, 13th-century carved keystones, and documents relating to other religious foundations in the Entre-Deux-Mers.

The statue of St James on the flat chevet of La Sauve's parish church of **St-Pierre** is one of the first known to depict the saint in pilgrim's garb, with cockleshells, staff and broad-brimmed hat; next to him stand SS. Peter, Michael and the Virgin and Child. Inside, a Roman capital does duty as a holy water font, and there are some simple 13th-century frescoes.

Sauveterre-de-Guyenne and Blasimon

The bastide of **Sauveterre-de-Guyenne**, founded by the English in 1283, has kept its arcaded square and its four fortified gates but not much else of interest; from here, however, the D 230 heads west to **Castelviel**, where the portal of the 11th-century church is one of the gems of the region, carved with Virtues and Vices and the Labours of the Months and a bevy of other figures; Deadly sins and saints appear on the capitals.

From Sauveterre it's 7km north on the D 17 to **Blasimon**, site of another Benedictine abbey, prettily isolated in the little valley of the Gamage. Part Romanesque, part Gothic and gracefully ruined, the church itself has somehow managed to survive in good nick, complete with a charming Romanesque façade that takes on a magical golden patina at sunset. The sculptures on the portal (1170) are exceptionally finely chiselled—scenes of Vices and Virtues, animals and scenes from the hunt. In contrast, the interior of the church is simple and pure to the point of austerity; the cloister has a handful of good Romanesque capitals. The village museum, housed in the Mairie, has a small collection of antiquities and *ex-*

votos from the abbey. Just to north (on the D 17) don't miss the 14th-century **Moulin de Labarthe**, built by the abbots of Blasimon and one of the most picturesque fortified water mills in southwest France.

Northwest of Blasimon in **Rauzan**, the **Château des Duras** *(open July–15 Sept 2–7, other times Sat and Sun only, 2–5; adm)* originally belonged to John Lackland before passing to the Duras family. Hotly contested during the various wars, the castle was rebuilt and expanded several times between the 12th and 15th centuries, and has mullioned windows and other details, and a pretty church from the 1200s. Its centrepiece, an impressive 100ft cylinder of a keep pierced with narrow slits for archers, offers lovely views over the village and valley.

East of Sauveterre-de-Guyenne to Monségur

Medieval **Castelmoron d'Albret**, just east of Sauveterre-de-Guyenne, is the smallest commune in France (it's not even 10 acres), squeezed behind its walls on a rock overlooking a little valley. Further east is the fortified 11th-century Benedictine abbey of **Saint-Ferme** (a corruption of St Fermin—he of the bull-running in Pamplona). Although the façade has taken a beating, the interior has an excellent, lively set of capitals illustrating the Old and New Testaments, especially a David and Goliath, a Daniel thrown to a pair of snarling lions, along with two giant heads apparently ready to swallow a squatting man; you may have to ask the sacristan to turn on the lights. The *mairie* is installed in the handsome abbey buildings of 1585 (open for visits), a complex that forms the heart of the peaceful village.

Monségur is the capital of la Petite Gavacherie, where the inhabitants, brought in from the north in the 15th century, are to this day called *gavaches* or *gabots*. Originally the word meant uncouth mountainmen, or hillbillies, although in the 20th century, realizing that in this world one is always someone else's hillbilly, the little enclave of northern French descendants living among the twanging Gascons take their nickname in their stride. Monségur is still a walled bastide, this one founded in 1265 by Eléonore de Provence, wife of Henry III, and it has kept its arcaded central *place* with a 19th-century covered market, several lanes of old houses and a simple Gothic church. Monségur overlooks the river Dropt, and like the *pays de Duras*, just to the east in Lot-et-Garonne (*see* p.308), it busies itself with plums, prunes, and prune eau-de-vie.

Where to Stay and Eating Out

Créon ✉ 33670

> ★★★**Hostellerie Château Camiac**, 3km northeast of Créon on the D 121, © 56 23 20 95, has a score of rooms in a delightful castle in a park with a pool and tennis court, and meals served out on a magnificent garden terrace in fair weather; try the *barbue* (barbel, a freshwater fish) with leeks and truffle juice (closed Tues and Wed lunch; menus from 160F to 200F). In the centre of Créon, the charming **Le Prévôt**, 5 Rue Charles-Dopter, © 56 23 08 08, serves tasty home cooking, with menus beginning at 90F and going up to 200F.

Sauveterre-de-Guyenne ✉ 33540

★De Guyenne, ✆ 56 71 54 92, is simple but one of the least pricey hotels in the region. In the centre of Targon, southeast of La Sauve, **Le Lion d'Or**, ✆ 56 23 90 23 has a solid local reputation for its abundant fare served in informal, dogs-sleeping-under-the-table surroundings; a wide choice of menus from 55F all the way to an overwhelming 140F feast.

Blasimon ✉ 33350

In Ruch (33350), just to the northeast near Blasimon, you can sleep sweetly in the lovely 17th-century **Château Lardier**, just off the D 232, ✆ 57 40 54 11; many of the charming rooms are furnished with antiques, and there's a pretty park to stroll in (from 230 to 330F a double). The restaurant isn't bad, either, whether you dine inside or out; menus begin at 95F and go up to 280F.

Saint-Ferme ✉ 33580

The **Château du Parc**, the stately Italianate 18th-century residence of the abbots of Saint-Ferme, has five delightful rooms from 400F, open all year, and a restaurant with candlelight dinners (190F menu).

Monségur ✉ 33580

The 18th-century **Château de la Bûche**, 10 Av. de la Porte-des-Tours, ✆ 56 61 80 22, offers three charming, recently renovated guest rooms for a bargain 270F for two, with breakfast, and good home-cooked meals for 80F. Overlooking quiet Place Darniche, the **★★Grand Hôtel**, ✆ 56 61 60 28, is not so grand, but charming and unaffected and open all year; good regional cooking in the restaurant with menus from 60 to 160F.

Entre-Deux-Mers: along the Garonne

The most beautiful and dramatic scenery in the Entre-Deux-Mers overlooks the Garonne. Here, there are many vineyards of AOC Premières Côtes de Bordeaux instead of white wine. Medieval Cadillac, Saint-Macaire and La Réole are the chief towns to aim for, and there is plenty of fine scenery along the way.

Tourist Information

Cadillac: Hôtel-de-Ville, ✆ 56 62 12 92

Saint-Macaire: 8 Rue du Canton, ✆ 56 63 32 14

La Réole: Place de la Libération, ✆ 56 61 13 55

market days

Cadillac: Saturdays

La Réole: Wednesdays and Saturdays

Bordeaux to Sainte-Croix-du-Mont

From Bordeaux, take the D 10 towards **Quinsac**, birthplace of Rosa Bonheur (1822–99), one of France's finest animal painters, an outspoken cigar-chomping, trouser-wearing feminist and the first woman to be awarded the Grand Cross of the Légion d'honneur. **Cambes**, a small pleasure port to the southeast, has a good Romanesque church with 15th-century English alabasters inside. On the D 240 towards Tabanac, you can have a look at the elegant Palladian **Château de Plassan,** generally attributed to Victor Louis and architecturally one of the finest wine châteaux in the Bordelais, the residence and the *chais* (an outbuilding where the new wine is stored) built as a harmonious ensemble.

Just after **Langoiran**, the next village upriver, stands the half-ruined medieval **Château de Langoiran**, a d'Albret property put to the sack in the Hundred Years' War and again in the Fronde; carved chimneys and some murals survive *(guided tours daily July–Aug 9–12 and 2–6; other times Sun only, same hours; adm)*. If you have the kids in tow, there's a small zoo with plenty of snakes and birds of prey in Langoiran's pretty Parc de la Peyruche. Little **Rions** was originally peaceful Gallo-Roman Riuncium, but found itself square on the frontier between the French and English in the Middle Ages, hence the heavy fortifications—especially the Porte du Lhyan (1304) defended by an 80ft tower, ruins of the citadel and a watchtower.

Cadillac, a riverside bastide of 1280, gave its name to America's biggest dream cars but only by an extremely devious route. A local boy from Saint-Nicolas-de-la-Grave, named Antoine Laumet, went off to seek his fortune in America, where he adopted the grander alias of Lamothe-Cadillac. After a busy career up in the Great Lakes country, where he founded Detroit in 1702, he ended up as governor of the Louisiana territory. In 1902, a Detroit car-maker took the name Cadillac; it was merged with General Motors in the 1920s, and the rest is history. A fullsize Caddy would look like Moby Dick in the main square of Cadillac, and trying to squeeze it under the pretty, lantern-topped 18th-century **Porte de l'Horloge**, the main river gate, would be asking for trouble. But this village does have something even bigger than its eponymous car: the **Château de Cadillac** built between 1598 and 1620 by Henri III's favourite *mignon* ('cutie-pie', roughly), the fabulously wealthy Nogaret de La Valette, Duc d'Epernon *(open daily, 9.30–12 and 2–6; adm; guided tours at 12, 3, and 5)*. The story goes that when Henri IV inherited this proud, dangerous and ruthlessly ambitious toyboy from his predecessor, he made him governor of Guyenne and went out of his way to encourage him to spend as much of his time and fortune as possible building himself this palace. The result is architecturally a meld of the styles popular in the time of Henri IV and Louis XIII, but after damage in the Revolution and a century of duty as a women's prison (until 1928) it has lost some of its original sparkle. Purchased by the state in 1952, the château has great vaulted guard rooms below and elaborately painted ceilings above, tapestries from the 13th and 17th centuries (the latter, showing scenes from the life of Henri III, were made here) and, best of all, eight monumental chimneypieces, beautifully sculpted in part by Jean Langlois and decorated with rare marbles, cascades of flowers and fruits, cupids and armour. Also on display are fragments of the grand Mausoleum of the ducs d'Epernon, bashed in the Revolution and originally set in a rich marble chapel in the nearby church of St-Blaise. One wing of the château holds the Cadillac wine confraternity's Maison du Vin.

Wine is also the name of the game in **Loupiac**, the next village (with ruins of a Gallo-Roman villa that may have belonged to Ausonius) and **Sainte-Croix-du-Mont**, which sits on an enormous fossilized oyster reef like a great pearl. One of its two châteaux belonged to Pierre de Lancre, a psychotic witch-hunter who terrorized the Basque lands in the 1600s on behalf of the Parlement de Bordeaux. The square in front of the church enjoys a wide-ranging view of the Garonne valley, and a cave excavated in the petrified oysters offers tastings of Sainte-Croix's golden nectar.

Premières Côtes de Bordeaux

This *appellation* begins in the suburbs of Bordeaux and extends along the hills on the north bank of the Garonne to Ste-Croix-du-Mont. Although in the 1970s most of the wine produced here was white, fashions have changed and a very pleasant, fruity red wine made from Cabernet Sauvignon and Merlot is now the main product. Conditions vary widely, but in general the wines made to the west are lighter, with less capacity for ageing. Some of the best red wines come from the sun-soaked, well-drained vineyards of the 14th-century **Château de Pic** at Le Tourne in Langoiran, © 56 67 07 51, and **Château Puy-Bardens**, in Cambes, © 56 21 31 14, and the panoramic **Château La Roche** at Baurech, © 56 21 31 03—one of the few Bordeaux vineyards run by a woman, Martine Palau.

Within the Côtes de Bordeaux area, facing Sauternes-Barsac are three small communal *appellations*: Superior AOC Cadillac, Loupiac and Sainte-Croix-du-Mont—all sweet, white dessert wines rated just a notch below Sauternes-Barsac, although they tend to be lighter and fruitier. They are grown on pebbly clay soil on steep hillsides, some 300ft above the Garonne; look for Loupiac's **Château de Ricaud**, producer of a beautifully perfumed sweet wine and a dry white (as well as red Premières Côtes) and **Château Loubens** at Sainte-Croix.

Saint-Macaire

Perched on its rock over the Garonne, Saint-Macaire is one of the Gironde's medieval gems, a busy port called *Ligena* in Roman times. In the Middle Ages it assumed the name of its 4th-century hermit Macaire and got a big boost when the kings of England designated it a coin-minting *ville royale d'Angleterre*. In the 18th century the Macariens woke up one morning to find their quays left high and dry when the Garonne slightly altered its course; this in effect took away any economic impulse to modernize its narrow lanes and medieval houses, leaving Saint-Macaire a village of considerable charm. Another plus is the village's white wine, AOC Côtes de Bordeaux Saint-Macaire.

Three fortified gates still defend the town, including the **Porte de l'Horloge**, equipped with a watch tower, the town bell and a clock. Best of all is the irresistible, irregular **Place du Mercadiou**, or 'God's marketplace', lined with Gothic arcades and houses in a picturesque variety of styles from the 13th to the 16th centuries. A Renaissance building called 'Henri IV's Posthouse', with an attractive spiral stair and painted chimneypieces, now holds the **Musée Régional des PTT** *(open 9–12 and 2–6.30, closed Tues; from 15 Oct–1 Dec, open Sun only 2–6.30; adm)*, with a collection of post-office memorabilia, stamps, postmen's uniforms, models and a lesson on Louis XI, who set up the first state postal service in the 15th century. On top of the village ramparts, the church of **St-Sauveur** originally belonged to a Benedictine priory built in the 12th century on the site of St Macaire's hermitge. St-Sauveur has an interesting carved portal and tympanum, and a curious interior plan, ending in a choir shaped like a cloverleaf. Painted murals from the 1400s, wrecked by bumbling over-restorers in the 1850s, decorate the crossing with ghostly memories of their glory: the Wise and Foolish Virgins, St John the Evangelist and the Christ of the Apocalypse. St-Sauveur's priory buildings, with their wide-ranging views over the countryside, are a favourite setting for summer fêtes.

François Mauriac's beloved summer home, **Malagar** (3km northwest, in Saint-Maixant), belonged to his great-grandfather, and since 1985 to the Conseil Régional d'Aquitaine, who have set up a museum related to the author's life, and allow visitors to ramble in its park *(open July–Sept 2–7 closed Tues, weekends only in June and Oct)*. **Château de Malromé**, 6km northeast of St-Macaire in St-André-du-Bois, was where Toulouse-Lautrec came to pass his summers with his mother, only to die here in 1901 at the age of 36, burned out from alcoholism and syphilis. The château, now the seat of a foundation in his name, is open for visits *(Sun and holidays from Easter–1 Nov; also daily 15 June–15 Sept, 2–7; adm)*; on view are reproductions of his works in a plush Second Empire setting, and the vineyards. 'I'll drink milk when the cows start eating grapes,' Toulouse-Lautrec would thunder at his doctors, and the château's red Bordeaux (unusually, made of 70 per cent Merlot) was one of his favourites; now his posters adorn its labels. Toulouse-Lautrec is buried, rather uncomfortably one imagines, for a hard-living, keen-eyed observer of Parisian lowlife, in the prim and proper Basilique de Notre-Dame at nearby **Verdelais**, to the south-west. Further up the Garonne, **Saint-Pierre-d'Aurillac** has a nice river beach and a Merovingian sarcophagus in front of its church, but the most tempting stop between St-Macaire and La Réole is **St-Martin-de-Sescas**, to see the excellent portal of its 12th-century church, with lively carvings of birds, rabbits, trees, leaves and people.

La Réole

In 977, the Benedictines received a charter from the Duke of Gascony to refound a Carolingian-era priory at Squirs on the Garonne, which had been left in ruins ever since the Normans hooliganned their way through in 848. The Benedictines renamed the priory after their Rule (Regulam in Latin). The name was later corrupted to La Réole, and Richard the Lion-Heart gave the priory a set a walls to match its strategic position over the river and to defend its river trade, especially in wine from the *haut pays*. Pilgrims coming from the Limousin brought additional wealth, and until the English created its rival port of Libourne on the Dordogne, La Réole could proudly claim to be the second town in Guyenne after Bordeaux. Even today it presents a stately river façade, especially with the mass of the 18th-century **Prieuré des Bénédictins** on its riverside terrace. Now used for various municipal services, you can easily wander about the old priory—the panelled and stuccoed Louis-XV *salle d'honneur* is now the mayor's office, and the impressive vaulted cellars house the library and a little museum of religious art and archaeology *(open Sat and Sun 3–5)*. In nearby Place Rigoulet, the old Benedictine priory church of **Saint-Pierre** was rebuilt in 1230; it has a pair of pretty Gothic chapels and a painting of the *Marriage of the Virgin* by Valdés Leal of Seville (1666). Look for the mermaids carved on the capitals in the nave.

Among the old boutiques and houses in medieval La Réole is the oldest **Hôtel de ville** still standing in France, built in the early 1200s by order of Richard the Lion-Heart, pierced with irregularly placed mullioned windows, and below, a *halle* on Romanesque columns with capitals naively imitating antique models. Rue Peysseguin is a charming street, with La Réole's synagogue and medieval houses; Bordeaux's *parlement* met between 1653 and 1678 in a handsome 15th-century *hôtel* on Côte Saint-Michel. In 1230, an English archi-tect under Henry III Plantagenet designed La Réole's **Château des Quat'Sos** ('of the four sisters'), its name referring to the massive round towers at each angle, of which only one is still intact; this castle suffered 12 different sieges, lastly in 1629. It remained a personal property of the kings of England and was always heavily garrisoned; the Black Prince spent a good deal of time here.

Just north, on the river Dropt, you can visit a pair of attractive water mills: the fortified, 14th-century **Moulin de Bagas**, built by the Benedictines of La Réole, while 2½km fur-ther up is the Romanesque **Moulin de Loubens**. Remains of Gallo-Roman villas have been regularly discovered, about every 2km in the valley.

Where to Stay and Eating Out

Langoiran ✉ 33550

> **Le Saint Martin**, by the port, ✆ 56 67 02 67, is a luminous restaurant–tearoom with huge windows overlooking the Garonne. Eels, shad and lamprey hold pride of place in the spring, *magrets* and *confits* and foie gras the rest of the year; menus 60F lunch, others from 75 to 150F, closed Sun night.

Cadillac ✉ 33410

> There's a good camp site near the Lac de Laromet, 3km away, ✆ 56 62 17 72.

St-Macaire ✉ 33490

> There's not much in the centre of St-Macaire (but a good riverside camp site, the **Camping des Remparts**, ✆ 56 62 23 42) and some good choices outside of town. In St-André-du-Bois there are eight Napoleon III-era guest rooms in Toulouse-Lautrec's **Château de Malrome**, ✆ 56 76 44 92; prices range from 320 to 770F. In Verdelais, the ***Hostellerie Saint Pierre**, ✆ 56 62 02 03, has nine basic rooms, half with *en suite* bath, and a restaurant serving well-prepared *cuisine de terroir* (and plenty of it) for 100F. East of St-Macaire, just off the N 113, **L'Abricotier**, ✆ 56 76 83 63, is a charming place to dine, with innovative menus

and regional specialities from shad to lamprey, depending on the season (menus at 70F on weekdays, also 110, 160 and 190F; closed Tues night).

La Réole ✉ 33190

One little Logis de France hotel here, ★**De l'Abbaye**, 42 Rue A. Caduc, ✆ 56 61 02 64, open all year, and a good restaurant, **Les Fontaines**, 24 Rue André Benac, ✆ 56 61 15 25, named after the fountain in the middle of the restaurant, which adds a refreshing touch to the garden-fresh cuisine; try the bass roasted with potatoes, or the *pot-au-feu* with foie gras (menus from 95 to 240F, 75F plat du jour; closed Sun and Mon). There's a good *ferme-auberge* near by, **Les Barthes**, just east of La Réole off the N 113, ✆ 56 61 70 39, serving an abundant 110F menu, including soup, *mousse de foie gras*, omelette, *confit de canard*, vegetable and dessert (closed Mon, Tues, Wed and Aug). In Gironde-sur-Dropt, 4km west of La Réole, ★★**Les Trois Cèdres**, N 113, ✆ 56 71 10 70, is a nice but no-frills hotel with 14 rooms, open all year; its restaurant serves grilled bass with superb fresh pasta and other delicacies under three cedars on the terrace (menus from 90 to 200F). In Bassanne (just over the Garonne, on the Canal Latéral) the **Moulin de Flaujagues**, ✆ 56 71 08 62, is in a 17th-century mill on the gurgling little Bassanne, where you can try variations on local themes—*pétoncles* in cream, *magret de canard* in *vin de cassis*; in winter a crackling fire makes the mill especially cosy (menus 60, 110 and 170F; *menu dégustation* 210F; closed Sun night and Mon winter only).

South of the Garonne: the Graves and the Bazadais

Graves is not exactly the name a public-relations firm would choose to sell a region, but it isn't so sombre when you remember that here it has more to do with gravel than old boneyards; the greatest vineyards in the *appellation* look as if they're growing out of gravel pits, and in some areas, there is a deep rivalry between gravel merchants and vineyard owners, each waiting their chance to pounce when any land comes up for sale. The gravel forms a wedge between the river and the deep ferny Landes forest and is endowed with several special microclimates that make it perfect for wine—most famously Sauternes.

Vin de Graves: Bordeaux's Rive Gauche

A 55km gravelly, sandy ribbon between Bordeaux and Langon, varying from 15 to 20km in width, is the fief of the *appellation* of Graves, a household word in England long before anyone heard of Médoc. As an area it is extremely disparate, but one basically known for its soft, full-flavoured wines. The cheap quality and sulphur stink of the whites produced here for many years gave Graves such a mediocre reputation that many wine buffs learned to dismiss the lot; nor did anyone protest too loudly when Bordeaux's planners concreted over vineyard after vineyard. Improvements began with the new Graves classification in 1953, when 13 red wines were given their cru (growth) credentials. In 1959 they were joined by eight white Graves. As all of these most prestigious crus are concentrated in the north near Bordeaux, in Léognan, Pessac and Talence, a vinous civil war of prestige erupted that resulted in 1987 with a secession of the *crus classés* from the common Graves, in an *appellation* of their own called Pessac-Léognan. The *ne plus ultra* here is Haut Brion, bang in the middle of Bordeaux's suburbia, along with Mission-Haut Brion and Pape-Clément (*see* p.182). Other noble names here are Haut-Bailly, Chevalier, Carbonnieux, Fieuzal and Olivier. Visits to these citadels are only possible by elaborate rendez-vous; the place to buy them are the **Caves de Léognan** in Léognan, ✆ 56 21 17 63.

Most of the southern Graves vineyards are concentrated in five communes, Langon, St-Pierre-de-Mons, Landiras, Illats and Cérons; the last two also produce wine called AOC Cérons—the demi-sweet intermediary between the dry whites and sweet Sauternes that isn't quite as popular as it used to be. In the past 20 years growers here have changed over in a big way to red wines (mostly Cabernet Sauvignon, which has a surprisingly different character here than in the Médoc) with help from Merlot and Cabernet Franc. While the reds of AOC Pessac-Léognan are famous for their nearly infinite capacity for ageing, those in the southern Graves are light and fruity, generally best drunk after three or four years. Graves *blancs* (Sémillon and Sauvignon, in various proportions) have greatly benefited from the techniques of cold fermentation and work by the Institut National des Appellations d'Origine, which has researched vine cloning in Langon. Among Graves to look out for are **Château Rahoul**, in Portets, ✆ 56 67 01 12 (especially the '89 red and their elegant whites); the well-structured reds and aromatic whites of **Château Chantegrive**, in Podensac, ✆ 56 27 17 38, owned by Henri Lévêque, who bought his first patch of Graves by selling his stamp collection in 1968; **Château Beauregard-Ducasse**, in Mazères, ✆ 56 63 41 70, located on the highest part of the Graves, home of a good Sauvignon white and an easy-going red, and **Château d'Ardennes**, in Illats, ✆ 56 62 53 80, that uses a variety of traditional and novel techniques to produce a remarkable gamut of exceptional, reasonably priced whites and reds. The **Maison des vins de Graves**, 2 Rue François-Mauriac, in Podensac, ✆ 56 27 09 25, has tastings, sales and reams of advice *(open Mon–Fri 8.30–12.30 and 1.30–5.30, daily from May–Oct)*.

Tourist Information

Langon: Allée Jean-Jaurès, ✆ 56 62 34 00

Villandraut: Place du Général-de-Gaulle, ✆ 56 25 31 39

Bazas: 1 Place de la Cathédrale, ✆ 56 25 25 84

market days

Langon: Fridays

Villandraut: Thursdays

Château de La Brède

Open April–June, weekends and holidays 2–6; July–Sept daily 2–6, exc Tues; Oct–11 Nov, weekends 2–5, adm.

One Graves estate has been producing good wine since the days of its most celebrated owner, Charles-Louis Secondat, baron of Montesquieu; from Bordeaux, take the N 113 and turn off at La Prade for his ivory tower, the Château de La Brède. Montesquieu, currently starring on the 200F banknote, described it as 'one of the most pleasant places in France, where Nature puts on her dressing gown as she rises from bed'. Montesquieu wore a number of hats in his life, not only as a successful wine grower who sold his vin du Graves in England but also as a magistrate in the parlement of Guyenne and, most memorably of all, as a clear-thinking philosopher of the Enlightenment and the author of the best-selling *Lettres persanes*, a satire of French society, and the *De l'Esprit des Lois* (1748), a work that proposed the separation of power into legislative, executive and judiciary branches that became the basis for the Constitution of the United States. His descendants still own the stern Gothic castle he was born in, defended by wide moats and preserving Montesquieu's magnificent vaulted library with over 7000 of his books. His bedroom, left as it was, doubled as his study; Montesquieu sat writing by the fireplace for so long that one of the firedogs is worn down from his foot resting against it. He created the château's park, its pride and glory, shaded by cedars planted at the time of the American Revolution, which Montesquieu influenced. After La Brède the N 113 passes through or very near a collection of villages synonymous with wine but little else: **Portets, Podensac, Cérons, Illats** and **Barsac**. At the last-named, we pass into the magic kingdom of noble rot.

Sauternes-Barsac

Celebrated, simply, as the world's finest dessert wine, or by southwestern autochthones as the only proper drink to wash down a foie gras, Sauternes and its twin appellation Barsac are golden in tone but bring out the purple prose latent in many a French pen; give them a glass of Château d'Yquem, the closest thing on earth to the nectar of the gods, and you get:

Yquem pushes our sense of taste to the limits of the inexpressible...To taste the apotheosis of taste! The lips make their acquaintance (never a rediscovery, but an endless procession of rebeginnings) with that bewitching freshness. And then, words fail. There doesn't exist, in any language, a way to express the infinite pleasure it consents to offer. Your palate (palais in French), suddenly merits its name. It welcomes the sovereign of beverages. The supreme offering of nature dazzles your mouth. You look across at your friend experiencing the same sensations. The force of communion binds you. A kind of complicity is at work. You read your own

expressions on his face. He has become the mirror that reflects
your ecstasy.

The nectar descends on you.
Close your eyes for an instant
And there you are on the other side of life.

Frédéric Dard

Sauternes and Barsac owe this inimitable quality to the excellence of their *pourriture noble*, or noble rot, or *Botrytis cinerea*, nurtured by the autumnal morning mists formed when the waters of the icy little stream Ciron meet the warmer Garonne. Botrytis is a fungus that feeds on overripe grapes, dehydrates them, enhances their sugar content, and puffs them up until they look like brown turds. Unfortunately for the growers of Sauternes-Barsac, it doesn't happened uniformly. The most traditional châteaux (like Yquem) harvest the berries, literally one by one, selecting each by its degree of noble rot; some years the pickers will go around the vineyard as many as ten or eleven times. Add to the high cost of labour the risk: because the grapes are picked late in the year, a good rainstorm could make the overripe grapes pop and replace all the carefully cultivated noble rot with common old rot. Another factor is the low density of growth; a good Médoc yields 40 hectolitres per hectare; a Sauternes is allowed 25 maximum. Château d'Yquem averages a mere seven and should be at least 10 years old before drinking. Because of the noble rot, the vinification requires three grape pressings; during fermentation, the wine needs special attention to maintain a balance between sugar and alcohol, which must be a minumum 12.5 per cent—many are over 14. Hence the extraordinary prices for the finest Sauternes and Barsacs. Conditions in 1989 and 1990 were so superb that in this century you have to go back to the legendary Sauternes of 1928 and 29 to find their match; 1983, 86 and 88 were classic years as well.

The five communes of the Sauternes *appellation* lie on the left bank of the Ciron, while Barsac is all by itself on the right bank, where the soil has more limestone and clay, enough to create a subtle difference noticeable to the lucky few who can afford to drink these classiest of dessert wines more than just on special occasions. Like Médoc, Sauternes-Barsacs were classified in the Paris Exhibition of 1855, and have kept their cru classifications ever since, although in many cases quality has noticeably gone up or down. While some of the châteaux listed below welcome visitors, prices are too prohibitive for casual tastings; persistence, however, may well be rewarded with a fine Sauternes in the 100F region, to put aside for your daughter's or granddaughter's wedding.

The Barsac-Sauternes Circuit

This is a pretty tour of immaculately kept vineyards and castles from every period; on a fine day, consider hiring a bike at Langon's railway station and doing the trip in reverse. Beginning in **Barsac**, you can pay your respects to St Vincent, patron saint of wine growers, whose church dates from the 16th to the 18th centuries, its Baroque interior a sumptuous combination of woodwork, stuccoes and wrought iron with a wowser of a high altar, carved in 1742. The story goes that up in heaven St Vincent became terribly thirsty for the good French wine he loved, and looked so woebegone that the boss gave him permission to return to earth for one last wine tour if he agreed to return to paradise at a certain time. After drinking himself across the country, Vincent's time ran out, but there was no sign of him. The angels found him in the cellars of La-Mission-Haut-Biron (*see* p.182) drinking everything in sight, and so drunk that he was in no state to go anywhere at all, much less to heaven, so they turned him into stone on the spot. And they say he's still there, with his mitre awry and grapes in hand.

From Barsac, head south to the handsome neoclassical **Château Nairac** (1776, 2nd *cru classé*), with its fine park. Over the railway line stands the fortified, 17th-century **Château Menota**, which is fairly easy to visit; next is an 18th-century *gentilhommière* (country seat), **Myrat**, whose owner in 1975 could no longer afford the astronomical costs of making wine and pulled out all the vines, although the new owner has since replanted them. Beyond is **Château Coutet**, a *gentilhommière* built around a medieval tower in the 17th–19th centuries; and a former charterhouse, the **Château Climens**. The last two are Barsac's two *premiers grands crus classés*, and many oenophiles rate Climens as second after Yquem, although they have very different personalities—Climens is fresh and elegant whereas Yquem is above all luscious *(visits Mon–Fri 8.30–11 and 2–4)*. Beyond is **Château Doisy**, a property now divided into three estates, all of which are excellent 2nd *crus classés*, especially Doisy-Daëne.

Follow the D 114 along the Ciron and under the A 61 towards Pujols-sur-Ciron. Before crossing the Ciron into the Sauternes, you can look at two non-wine châteaux, the handsome 16th-century **Château de La Salle**, set in a large walled park, and 4km south, the **Château de Budos**, built in 1308 by a nephew of Pope Clement V, and now a striking ruin enjoying a lovely view of the Ciron valley.

If you cross the Ciron at Pujols, the first Sauternes vineyard belongs to the spectacular 17th-century **Château de Lafaurie-Peyraguey**, set in 13th-century walls. It's a *premier cru classé*, as is the adjacent **Château Rabaut-Promis**, attributed to Victor Louis. Follow the Ciron and D 109/E5 up to Bommes and Château de Haut-Bommes, and turn right on the D 125E for the hamlet of **Sauternes**, which snoozes away without a care in the world. It has a disdainful Maison de Vin which you should avoid, but a couple of new wine shops have opened to sell and tell you about Sauternes. Continue south to the 19th-century Italianate **Château Filhot**, a *premier cru classé*. The stunning park, with its *pigeonnier* from the 1600s, is open for visits.

North of the village of Sauternes, take the D 125 to the D 8 and turn right for the hilltop **Château Rieussec**, a *premier cru* recently purchased by the Domaines Rothschild, and the **Château de Fargues**, a *cru bourgeois* that has long been as good as a *premier cru*, owned for 500 years by the same Lur-Saluces who own Yquem, and who sell nearly all of it in the USA. The magnificently positioned **Château d'Yquem** itself is just north of Sauternes on the D 125. It's the one château everyone longs to visit, but can't—although you can certainly ogle it from the road. In the same family for over four centuries (the Sauvage-Yquems, who in 1785 married the counts of Lur-Saluces), the building dates from the 15th to the 17th centuries. The pale gold wines produced on Yquem's 250 acres have been the quintessence of Sauternes since the 18th century, a position confirmed since the 1855 classification that put it in a class all its own. In some years a rich, dry and more affordable white wine is produced as well, simply called Y (Ygrec).

From Yquem carry on to the north, turning right on the D 116, then left on the D 8E for **Château de Suduiraut** (an excellent *premier cru*), built in the style of Versailles, complete with a garden by Le Nôtre. From here continue past the 18th-century **Château Bastor-Lamontagne** and turn right for the one Sauternes bailiwick open regularly for visits, the 17th-century **Château de Malle** *(open Easter–15 Oct daily exc Wed 3–7; adm)*. Originally the country house of a Bordelais judge, and later of the Count de Lur-Saluces, Malle has kept much of its original furnishings, as well as an Italian garden and nymphaeum decorated with a pebble mosaic depicting figures from the commedia dell'arte. Wine tastings (Malle is a 2nd *cru classé*) are included in the price of admission.

The port at **Langon**, the largest town and capital of the southern Graves, is the highest on the Garonne to feel the tide. For centuries, until the advent of rail, it was important in shipping wine and other products from the hinterland. Trains between Toulouse and Bordeaux still stop here, and it even boasts a new 18-hole golf course at St-Pardon de Conques and a somewhat atypical Zurbarán (the *Immaculate Conception*, showing the Virgin floating in russet clouds on the heads of two cherubs, her dark mantle flowing all around like a bat-winged storm cloud) in its Gothic church of **St-Gervais**. But unless you're stopping to look in the wine shops or dine at Claude Darroze, there's no really compelling reason to linger.

South of Sauternes: a Detour into the Landes

Landes in French means moors, sand and maritime pines, and once they begin south of the Garonne they don't stop until the foothills of the Pyrenees, constituting the largest single forest in Europe. South of Sauternes or Langon you can dip into the pines; for more, head up the river Leyre from the Bassin d'Arcachon to Belin-Béllet (p.229–30).

There is already a definite Landaise air about **Villandraut**, the birthplace of Bertrand Got, who went on to become Pope Clement V in 1305. The papacy then wasn't quite the plummy job it is now—in 1305 Rome was in the throes of all-out gang warfare and not a very safe place even for the boss of the syndicate; Clement V's predecessor, Boniface VIII, usually avoided the city, but a rival faction eventually caught up with him and delivered the famous 'Slap of Anagni', a good slap across the Pope's mug that symbolically put an end to the power of the medieval papacy. The slapper, Sciarra Colonna, was acting for Philippe

IV of France, and when this same wily king invited Clement to move to France in 1308, he jumped at the chance. Before moving the papal court to Avignon and the Comtat Venaissin (a piece of French territory that was the papal spoils for the Albigensian crusade), Clement spent a year here, in his strong, moat-belted **Château de Villandraut**, built without a castle keep, a style made popular in Wales under Edward I *(open daily June–Sept, 9.30–12.30 and 3–7; the rest of the year, Sat and Sun only, 2–5; adm)*.

Saint-Symphorien, west of Villandraut, claims another summer residence of Mauriac, but unless you're a fervent fan of the writer there isn't any real reason to stop. Just east, however, in the church of **Saint-Léger de Balson**, there are some unusual medieval frescoes of labourers, with comic-strip-like captions over their heads, while further south **Bourideys** awaits as a perfect and utterly tranquil example of a Landes village. **Préchac**, to the northeast, has a late Romanesque church and, 4km east, overlooking the river Ciron, the irregular polygonal **Château de Cazeneuve** *(open daily July–Aug 2–7, weekends only the rest of the year; adm)* was originally a medieval castle, converted into a pleasure palace in the 17th century by the d'Albrets; Henri IV and his dishy Queen Margot spent a holiday here, and it has a number of interesting features—the *salles troglodytes* cut into the central court, a Greek nymphaeum, and sculpted chimneypieces.

The Pope Clement V tour continues, however, east of Villandraut in the little town of **Uzeste**, founded by Clement's Got (or Goth) ancestors in the 13th century. In 1312 Clement began to pour money into Uzeste for the construction of a small but dignified **collegiate church**, and the next year declared his intention of being buried there, although not quite as soon as he thought. Being in France obliged Clement to go along with Phillipe IV's scheme of abolishing the Templars in 1312 and confiscating their enormous wealth to fill the empty French treasury. In 1314 the Grand Master of the Templars, Jacques de Molay, was burned alive at the stake in Paris, but not before he cried out that both king and pope would follow him to the grave that same year, as indeed they did—the pope from indigestion after eating a plate of ground emeralds, prescribed by his doctor. Unfortunately for Clement's monument to himself, the Protestants took some really good whacks at his church and **tomb** (1315–59): the white marble effigy atop the black slab no longer has a face, although the embroidery of the vestments and anatomy of the dragon at his feet show a great attention to detail. Until the Protestants came, the tomb also sported a black marble baldachin, decorated with alabasters, precious stones and all the sumptuous pomp required by a dead medieval pope. The church's 14th-century *Virgin and Child* was once the object of a local pilgrimage. These days Uzeste is especially zesty around 15 August, when a four-day festival of all kinds of music fills its streets.

Bazas and its Cathedral

Since anicent times, **Bazas** (Gallo-Roman *Cossio*) has been the natural capital of a little region of fertile hills south of the Garonne, known as the Bazadais. From the 5th century until the Revolution it even had its own bishop, thanks in part to a unique relic—the blood spilled at the beheading of St John the Baptist, supposedly wiped up in a cloth by a pious woman of Bazas, who brought it and the new religion back home with her. To shelter the precious relic, a triple church was built on the town's most prominent site, dedicated to SS. John the Baptist, Peter and Stephen. When this threatened to fall over, the present **cathedral** was begun in 1233 by the seneschal of the King of England. Completely contrary to usual practice, the building began with the triple portal (echoing the original triple church) and ended with the choir, and this last bit was only completed thanks to subsidies sent over from Avignon by Clement V. When the rampaging Huguenots turned up to wreck Bazas's pride and joy in 1578, the bishop, Arnaud de Pontac, saved the façade by buying it from the Huguenots for 10,000 écus.

It was worth it; you certainly don't get such jammy pieces of theatre in many other places in the Gironde. Around the year 1500, a flamboyant rose window (the petals of which contain the 64 names of the bishops of Bazas), pinnacles, buttresses and a gallery were added to set off the three great 13th-century Gothic doorways. The **central portal** is devoted to the Last Judgment, showing the dead climbing out of their tombs, the good souls blithely heading off to the New Jerusalem as some nasty-looking devils corral the wicked into the maw of hell, while stacks of virtues, prophets, angels, martyrs and confessors rocket up vertiginously in the five archings. Along the lintel are scenes from the life of Bazas's patron saint, John the Baptist. The **north portal** is dedicated to the Mission of the Apostles, especially that of St Peter; here too are Adam and Eve, Cain and Abel and the Wise and Foolish Virgins. The **south portal** belongs to the Virgin, showing her coronation, Dormition and Assumption. The finely detailed archings here are sculpted with signs of the zodiac, scenes of the Virgin's life, and the tree of Jesse. The interior, completely destroyed by the Huguenots in 1578, was carefully repaired by Bishop Pontac, his nephew and great-nephew, only to be devasted again in the Revolution. To fill the space, furnishings, paintings and an 18th-century high altar in coloured marbles were brought in from deconsecrated churches in the area. South of the cathedral you can visit the pretty chapterhouse garden, overlooking the valley of the Beuve.

Part of the cathedral's charm is its magnificent setting, atop the vast, gently sloping **Place de la Cathédrale**. This is bordered by arcades and some fine 16th- and 17th-century houses, most strikingly No. 3, the **Maison de l'Astronome** (1530), with ogival arcades and carvings of stars, planets, a blazing comet and a wizard astronomer in a pointy hat. Things get very hot indeed here every 23 June, when strings of bonfires are lit in honour of St John, and the Bazadais leap over the flames and take embers home for good luck, just as everyone in Europe did a few centuries ago. A bull is symbolically offered to the mayor, for Bazas means beef as much as Sauternes means wine; the town is home of its very own race of cattle, the *bazadaise*.

Entrecôte à la Bordelaise

Although nowadays a juicy two-inch-thick rib steak from Bazas is practically synonymous with this dish, until the end of the 18th century this method of cooking was reserved for another kind of meat: rats, namely the big fat ones caught prowling the vineyards, their bellies gorged with grapes. Obviously just what you'd expect of a people who lust after lamprey in blood-thickened sauce, but, keeping in mind the Belgian restaurant that has thrived serving rat fricassée for a century, it may have tasted better than it sounds. Add to that the peculiar peasant pleasure of eating your enemy, like those pesky escargots.

In most restaurants, what passes for an *entrecôte à la bordelaise*—a slice of beef with a sauce of shallots and wine—was invented by Parisian chefs in the 19th century (obviously before the 1870 siege of Paris, when rat—and cat—were considered great delicacies). To make the real McCoy, grill your *boeuf de Bazas* over a barbecue of vine cuttings (*sarments*): Cabernet Sauvignon for the heat, and at the last moment, Merlot, which spreads out the smoke and give the meat its special taste. Top it with finely chopped shallots and serve it with a side dish of *cèpes* cooked with garlic and parsley.

Besides *entrecôtes*, Bazas also offers visitors a **Musée d'Histoire Locale** in Rue St-Antoine with a small archaeological and decorative arts collection, and a pharmacy from the time of Louis XV. In the Allées Clemenceau you can pick up the pretty **Promenade de la Brèche** along the top of the ramparts, a walkway lined with shade trees with views over the valley.

Around Bazas

North of Bazas towards Langon, the last of the Graves vineyards are in **Mazères**, where you have a chance to visit the amazing **Château de Roquetaillade**, high on a spur that has had some kind of fort on it since prehistoric times *(open daily 2.30–7 Easter–1 Nov; daily 10.30–7 in July and Aug; other times, Sun and holiday afternoons only; adm)*. There are actually two castles, one built in the 12th century and partly ruined, and the other built in the 14th century by a nephew of Pope Clement, given the complete Viollet-le-Duc restoration treatment inside in the 19th, and unabashedly kitsched in the 20th; the costumed dummies seem to be patiently waiting for the next Hollywood remake of *Robin Hood*. There's a farm museum as well, the **Métairie de Roquetaillade**, with a 12th-century dovecote, farm animals, and 100-year-old farmhouse interiors. The wine that bears the château's name belongs to another family and has recently won medals for its reds—especially the '83, '85 and '86.

Where to Stay and Eating Out

La Brède ✉ 33650

La Maison des Graves, in the village centre, © 56 20 24 45, serves regional dishes that bring out the best of the Graves at kind prices. Lunch menu at 75F, closed Sun night and Mon.

Barsac ✉ 33720

★★★**Château de Rolland**, N 113, © 56 27 15 75 incorporates part of a 14th-century monastery; large, comfortable rooms in a peaceful setting, surrounded by vineyards.

Sauternes ✉ 33210

In the middle of a sea of vines, the **Château de Commarque**, 2km from the centre, ☎ 56 76 64 30, has comfortable rooms with baths in its courtyard for 200–400F a double, a swimming pool and a nice little restaurant serving dishes such as leg of lamb braised in a *cèpe* sauce (menus from 85 to 185F). In the village centre, there are a pair of restaurants that make fine intermissions along the wine road: **Le Saprien**, ☎ 56 76 60 87, with well-prepared fish and other dishes, topped off with Sauternes by the glass (menus from 100 to 250F; closed Sun dinner and Mon). For an entrecôte, properly cooked over *sarments*, omelettes with *cèpes* and other *bordelais* treats, try **Les Vignes**, a charming little country inn at Place de l'Eglise, ☎ 56 76 60 06 (60F lunch menu, also 100 and 130F, closed Mon).

Langon ✉ 33210

There are quite a few choices here, with the top of the list firmly filled by ★★★**Claude Darroze**, 95 Cours du Général Leclerc, ☎ 56 63 00 48, a hotel in a formal 18th-century building, with beautiful and sumptuous rooms for sweet dreams. But Claude Darroze is best known for his delicious terrace under the plane trees, where some of the best traditional Girondin dishes appear—crayfish salads, foie gras, lamprey with leeks and game dishes prepared with a light modern touch, accompanied by a perfect wine list (menus at 195 and 320F, à la carte at least 400F). The other hotels are more reasonable, if less grand: among them ★★**Horus**, 2 Rue des Bruyeres, ☎ 56 62 36 37 and ★**Le Chantilly**, 24 Rue Pasteur, ☎ 56 63 11 95, or out in the country on the Bazas road, ★★**Auberge Domaine de Moleon**, ☎ 56 62 38 94. All are open all year.

Bazas ✉ 33430

Just south of Bazas, the ★★★**Domaine de Fompeyre**, ☎ 56 25 98 00 is a bright, modern hotel with 35 rooms, set in a quiet four-acre park, with a pool, lit tennis court, and billiard room. There are three very comfortable bed-and-breakfast rooms just outside Bazas at the **Château d'Arbieu**, ☎ 56 25 11 18, with a pool (from 400F a double). For the most succulent entrecôte in town, get yourself up to the panoramic **Les Remparts**, overlooking the Jardin de Sultan in the Espace Mauvezin, Place de la Cathédrale, ☎ 56 25 95 24; if you aren't a beef eater, try the delicious Grignols capon with *cèpes*, game or fish specialities; expect to pay around 140F. At Cudos, just south of Bazas, the *ferme-auberge* **Houn Barrade**, ☎ 56 25 44 55, offers farm home cooking on its 70 and 100F menus, and a *menu gastronomique* for 130F; be sure to leave room for the *tourtière bazadaise* for dessert (open weekends or by reservation all year round, and daily July–15 Sept).

Villandraut ✉ 33730

★★**De Goth**, Place Gambetta, ☎ 56 25 31 25, is a typical provincial hotel; dine at the pond-side **La Vallée du Silence**, ☎ 56 25 33 91, with a charming terrace and local specialities from land and sea (menus 100, 150 and 200F).

Great freighters and tankers promenade along Europe's largest estuary, along with rather dainty fishing boats, with nets extending from the sides and skimming over the water like giant dragonflies, nabbing lamprey, shad, eels and crayfish; smaller nets manned from the Gironde's banks catch elvers, or *pibales*, which traditionally must be eaten with wooden forks. Islets in the estuary come and go with the tide; refineries and port installations come and go with the economy, and even the vineyards of Médoc took some hard knocks in the 1920s and '30s, only to rebound—the first great year was 1945, in time to celebrate the end of the war.

Médoc, Haut Médoc, and Other Médocs

Geographically a continuation of the Graves, Médoc is a 10km-wide ribbon between the Gironde estuary and the sands of the Landes forests, a thick Quaternary terrace of pink and blue gravel and sand. Although its '61 *grand crus classés* are today the celebrities of Bordeaux wines, protectionists in the Graves prevented anyone from planting vines in this ideal wine region until the late 17th century, when wealthy Englishmen, insisting on better quality wines and increasingly buying port, madeira and malmsey instead of claret, became a force in the market that the Bordelais couldn't afford to ignore. The secret behind Médoc's success and consistency is the unusual depth of its poor, gravelly ridges, which forces the vine roots to go deep in search of water and nourishment; the older the vine (10 years is the minimum age for a Médoc cru), the stronger and deeper the roots, and the greater its ability to withstand drought. Equally, in soggy years the perfect drainage of the gravel keeps the roots from getting waterlogged. Because the gravel absorbs heat during the day, damage from spring frosts can often be avoided; the vines are pruned quite short as well. Even in the worst years, a *grand cru* usually comes shining through.

Climate, as always, is another important factor. The vast Gironde estuary regulates the temperature, keeping the Médoc from extremes (the great estates all 'see the water'), while the rains and winds off the Atlantic are tempered by the screen of pine forests of the coast. If away from the waterfront, Médoc's great gravel ridges overlook *jalles*, the wide gullies that drain the Landes and also serve to moderate temperatures. Another factor is the vast size of the estates—enabling the *maistre des chais* to adjust the blending and proportions of the grape varieties, depending on the vagaries of the weather. Slow-ripening Cabernet Sauvignon is the chief here, accounting for half the vines grown in Médoc, and forming up to 80 per cent of the *grands crus*; Merlot Noir (around 35 per cent of most Médocs) gives the wine strength and suppleness; a dollop of Cabernet Franc adds its characteristic bouquet.

Médocs have been classified and reclassified more than any wines on this planet. The Paris Exhibition of 1855 classified 60 Médoc vineyards and divided them into five crus that, thanks to vested interests, have become fixed in concrete like the handprints of the movie stars in Hollywood; when Mouton-Rothschild at last moved up into the first division *premiers crus* in 1973 it was a major event. Although Premier Crus shatter the price barriers, the amounts asked for the other four growths tend to reflect current quality rather than the 1855 classifications; hence superior fourth growths that cost more than second.

In 1920 Médoc estates left out of the Paris rating created a syndicate of their own, the *cru bourgeois*, which, unlike Paris, has undergone a number of adjustments, lastly in 1978. A *cru bourgeois* has to come from a property with a minimum 17 acres, be bottled on the estate and not in a cooperative, and pass the syndicate's taste test; a *cru grand bourgeois* has to be aged in wooden casks; a *cru grand bourgeois exceptionnel* has to be château-bottled in a commune of Haut Médoc, i.e. the half of the region closer to Bordeaux. Besides all these, there are eight small communal *appellations* in Médoc. For all the fussiness, there's more than enough to go around: the average production of the whole Médoc area is 24 million bottles a year. Last but not least, recent studies demonstrate that it's good for your health—Médoc contains bactericidal ingredients that can knock certain viruses cold, it speeds up digestion, and has a natural beneficial effect on arteriosclerosis. So drink hearty! Below we've mentioned only the most famous châteaux, but there are scores of others that welcome visitors; pick up lists, maps and suggestions at the Maisons du Vin, either in Margaux or Pauillac.

Getting Around

Trains from Bordeaux on the Soulac line stop in many of the Médoc villages. If you're driving from the north, there's a convenient ferry across the Gironde between Blaye and Lamarque near Fort Médoc; from Blaye crossings are at 7.30 and 10am and 3, 4.30 and 6pm; from Lamarque at 8 and 10.30am and 3.30, 5 and 6.30pm.

Tourist Information

Pauillac: For wine and tourist information, the Maison du Tourisme et du Vin du Médoc, La Verrerie, © 56 59 03 08

Lesparre: Place Docteur-Lapeyrade, © 56 41 21 96

market days

Pauillac: Saturdays

Haut-Médoc: Margaux and Saint-Julien

Haut-Médoc begins just beyond the northern suburbs of Bordeaux; aim for Blanquefort and get on the main *route des châteaux*, the D 2, off which the great plantation houses are nearly all easy to spot. These mostly date from the 18th and 19th centuries and lend Médoc its patina of distinction and big money. Yet resident proprietors are increasingly rare; corporations and foreign consortiums, looking for sound investments, have bought up some of the most prestigious Médoc vineyards, although foreign ownership is nothing new here—in the 18th century three of the finest châteaux belonged to Irishmen named Kirwan, Dillon, and Lynch (the last was once mayor of Bordeaux).

The first village of vinous renown is **Macau**, which also produces AOC artichokes and has a little estuary port, where the Bordelais come at weekends to gobble down *bichettes* (little fresh shrimp). At **Labarde**, the next hamlet north, the **Château Siran** and its ample *chais* contain some of the best *cru bourgeois* in the Haut Médoc—the very best is stocked in a nuclear fallout shelter (head there if the sirens start to wail). Visitors are welcome on guided tours every day of the year; Siran's park is famous for its cyclamens, and several rooms of the château, once owned by the ancestors of Toulouse-Lautrec, contains works of art—a *Young Bacchus* by Caravaggio, engravings by Velázquez, Rubens and Daumier as well as 19th-century furniture and ceramics. Another highly rated vineyard in Labarde, 19th-century **Château Giscours**, welcomes summer visitors to its *chais* and pretty wooded park *(open 9–12.30 and 2.30–6).*

The wines of Siran and Giscours are in the prestigious communal *appellation* of **Margaux**, noted for the magnificent finesse and delicate perfume of its wines. The **Maison du Vin** in the little square dispenses information and sells bottles *(open 9–12 and 2–6, closed Sun and Mon am)* and you can visit the cradle of its celebrated Premier Grand Cru, **Château Margaux**, just outside the village *(hour-long tours of the* chais *weekdays 10–12.30 and 2–5 exc in Aug and during the harvest; book the day before, © 56 88 70 28).* Here are some of the oldest, most wizened vines in the Médoc, and one of the most severely neo-classical châteaux, designed in 1802 by a student of Victor Louis, set in a pretty English garden. While in the area, have a look at the lovely early 17th-century **Château d'Issan**, set amid the moat of its medieval predessor ('For the tables of kings and the altars of the gods', reads the inscription on the gate), and the adjacent **Château Palmer** (1860), founded by one of Wellington's generals and still partly British-owned; its wine is often rated just under Château Margaux.

Moulis-en-Médoc (inland from Margaux and to the northwest) is the smallest communal *appellation*, where the top wine has had the delightful name of **Château Chasse-Spleen** ever since Byron commented that a glass of it chases away ill-humours. It is closely rivalled by **Château Poujeaux**, both of which are *cru grand bourgeois exceptionnel.* Just opposite the Moulis station, the **Musée des Arts et Métiers de la Vigne et du Vin** pulls out all the stops to initiate you into the cult of the 'blood of the vine', including an optional heli-copter ride over the vineyards *(open every day of the year, 10–12 and 2–6).* Moulis also has a fortified Romanesque church with an ornate apse (carved *modillons* outside and cap-itals inside, one showing Tobias carrying a fish); the holy water stoup built into the façade was set aside for lepers.

Adjacent to Moulis is another tiny communal appellation, **Listrac**. Both Moulis and Listrac are distinguished by their powerful wines, although the fact that they don't 'see the water' prevented them from being classified in 1855; the Rothschild-owned **Château Clarke**, one of the rising stars of Listrac, is open to visitors between June and September. From

Listrac, take the D 5 down towards the Gironde to see the **Château de Lamarque**, a medieval castle that defended Bordeaux from raiders down the estuary until the 17th century, when the task was taken over by nearby **Fort Médoc** *(open daily 10–12 and 1–7; adm)*. Designed by Vauban, Louis XIV's crack fortifications expert, the fort was begun in 1689 and completed only in 1721, owing to the difficulty of building on a marshland. Besides the heavily sculpted Porte Royale, complete with Louis's sun symbol, you can visit the fort installations and take in the view across the estuary to Médoc's sister citadels, at Blaye and the island Fort Pâté.

North of Fort Médoc, signposted off the D 2, the eclectic neo-Tudor-Spanish **Château Lanessan** (1870) is the seat of an estate that has been in the same family since 1790; its *chai* was considered the paragon of modernity in the 19th century, and it produces an excellent Haut-Médoc *cru bourgeois supérieur* famous for its long ageing capacity. In the stables (complete with marble mangers), a **Musée du Cheval** displays an interesting collection of early horse-drawn vehicles from the beginning of the century, saddles and other antique horsey gear *(hour-long guided tours of the* chais *and museum, closed Sun in the winter; adm)*. The Duc d'Epernon, governor of Guyenne and admiral of France (*see* the Château de Cadillac, p.197), inherited by marriage the next estate on the grand Médoc tour, which became known as the **Château de Beychevelle** because every ship that passed in the estuary paid its respects by lowering its sails (*becha vela* in Gascon) before paying the admiral his toll. The current handsome white building bearing the name was originally a charterhouse, adapted to its new use in 1757 and decorated with a sculpted pediment *(tours of the* chais *May–Sept, Mon–Fri 9.30–12 and 2–5)*. Nearby Château-Talbot is believed to have belonged to John Talbot, earl of Shrewsbury, loser in the last battle in the Hundred Years' War at Castillon (*see* p.146). Both of these are in the *appellation* of Saint-Julien, wines distinguished for their fruitiness and original character; it has the highest density of *crus classés* of any in Médoc, especially the several riverside vineyards of Léoville that once formed the estate of the Marquis de Las-Cases, in the 18th century the most famous property in all Médoc. The most distinctive châteaux here are the 19th-century **Château Ducru-Beaucaillou**, home of a 2nd *cru classé* and the 18th-century **Château Langoa-Barton**, which unusually for Médoc has its *chais* under the château.

Pauillac

Before settling into the comfortable position of capital of Médoc wines, with more *premiers grands crus classés* than any other commune in the Bordelais, the pleasant town of Pauillac was an important estuary port; before the 1930s, when the estuary was dredged, steamers from France's colonies in the Americas, Africa and Asia would call at the île de Patiras, in the middle of the Gironde, where passengers would be transferred to and from Bordeaux by smaller craft. Nowadays instead of exotic steamers, the view over the estuary takes in the looming silhouette of the Braud nuclear power plant.

But what people come to ponder at Pauillac is another source of power altogether: the most famous wine châteaux in France, where the purest gravelly ridges produce an astonishing 7 million bottles a year of the most powerful Médocs of all, full-bodied, presumably nonradioactive wines laced with a distinctive blackcurrant bouquet. Approaching from the south, don't miss the **Château Pichon-Lalande**, built in the 19th century by the Grande Dame of Bordeaux wine in the 1800s, the Comtesse Lalande, complete with a magnificent view over the riverside vineyards. Further up, the legendary **Château Latour**, owned by Allied-Lyons since 1989 (purchase price a record 10,000,000F an acre, for 200 acres), has rarely failed to live up to its *premier grand cru classé* status, nor to lead the way in innovation; in the 1960s it revolutionized the storage of wine in the Bordelais with the introduction of stainless steel vats.

Just north of Pauillac, **Château Mouton-Rothschild** was purchased by Baron Nathaniel de Rothschild in 1853, who was simply devastated when his wine was not selected as a *premier grand cru classé* in 1855—an omission corrected in 1973, thanks to the enthusiasm of his descendant, the legendary Baron Philippe de Rothschild. In the 1920s Baron Philippe took over a property no one else in the family cared much for and made it his life until he died in 1988. One of his first moves in the '20s was to bottle all of his wine at the château, an idea that seemed eccentric at the time. The neo-Tudor château, while not terribly interesting in itself, has an exquisite English garden. For oenophiles, the guided tour must be the equivalent of obtaining a private audience with the pope, but is rather easier to obtain *(weekdays exc in Aug; ring 56 59 22 22 to make an appointment)*. It begins with the awesomely perfect *grand chai*, Baron Philippe's 'theatre of wine' with its immaculate blond wood barrels lined up with military precision and the château's collection of wine labels by famous artists (Dalí, Picasso, Warhol, etc), a tradition begun in 1945. Perhaps because it belongs to the Rothschilds, the bank vault atmosphere is unavoidable. The tour continues to a rich museum of art devoted to wine—the oldest pieces are from ancient Mesopotamia—and finishes with a climactic descent into the cellar, the holy of holies, where bottles worth as much as your house and car put together do their silent alchemical work.

The big Mouton's eternal rival, the 120-hectare **Château Lafite-Rochschild** (owned by the Baron's cousins), broods over the Pauillac-Lesparre road from its height, in Gascon *la hite*, hence Lafite. Only a tower survives of the medieval castle, whose lords were in charge of dispensing justice in Pauillac, while the present château dates from the 18th century. In 1868 it was bought by James de Rothschild; his descendants hired the fashionable Catalan Ricardo Bofill to design their extraordinary new round *chais*. Lafite's cellars have bottles going back to 1797 (visits by appointment only, © Paris (16 1) 42 56 33 50 and wait for an invite in the post).

To the north lies **Saint-Estèphe**, the last communal *appellation* and one that produces vigorous, deeply coloured wines that differ from Pauillac and other Médocs in their need for extra long periods of bottle-ageing. This is due to their large quantity of Merlot, which can reach as much as 40 per cent of the vintage, as in Saint-Estèphe's leading producer, **Château Cos d'Estournel**, just north of Lafite along the D 2. This is the most striking landmark along the *route des châteaux*, with its *chais* designed in the 19th century as a replica of the palace of the Sultan of Zanzibar. In this *appellation* you'll also find **Château Calon-Ségur**, dating back to the 12th century and given its heart-shaped device in the

18th century by the Marquis de Ségur because he loved it so much. **Vertheuil**, 6km west of Saint-Estèphe has an 11th-century abbey church endowed with not one but two bell towers and a portal carved with the Elders of the Apocalypse and peasants pruning the vines. The interior, if you're lucky to catch it open, has three naves and was redesigned in the 15th century with a striking and unusual barrel-vaulted ambulatory, rib-vaulted choir and choir stalls carved with scenes from monastic life.

North of Loudenne in Saint-Yzans-de-Médoc, one last wine stop: the riverside **Château de Loudenne**, a handsome 18th-century charterhouse in a stunning setting with a museum of old winemaking tools and guided tours and tastings in English *(open daily 9.30–5.30, closed Sat, Sun and holidays; June–Sept, also open Sat afternoons 2–5.30)*. The main town in the area is **Lesparre**, which until the end of the 14th century was the seat of the *seigneur* of lower Médoc. His castle crumbled away over the centuries, leaving only an impressive foursquare keep known as the **Tour de l'Honneur**, housing a local-history museum *(open July–15 Sept daily exc Sun, 10–12 and 3–7; adm)*.

Where to Stay and Eating Out

In the old days, one of the spin-offs of winemaking in the Médoc was sucking-lamb. All large vineyards had sheep whose task it was to graze between the rows and keep the weeds down. Lambs, because they bounced around too much and damaged the vines, were confined to the sheepfold, and fed only their mother's milk until they were slaughtered two months later. Their tender pearly meat was a delicacy that died out when chemical herbicides stole the sheep's job. Since 1985, however, *agneau de Pauillac*, raised the old-fashioned way, has made a comeback in local butchers shops and on restaurant menus. Another speciality is a refined tripe sausage called *grenier médocain*, rarely seen outside of the region.

Margaux ✉ 33460

Where do Médoc buyers go to swan around and deduct it all as a business expense? The luxurious ★★★★**Relais de Margaux**, Chemin de l'Ile Vincent, ✆ 56 88 38 30, with lush gardens, park and a lovely pool; the equally beautiful restaurant serves a succulent *agneau de Pauillac* as well as other land and sea food, accompanied by a wine list and wine prices that could melt a credit card; lunch menu 130F, others at 230 and 350F (closed Sun night and Mon in winter, and most of Jan). Also in Margaux, **La Savoie**, 1 Place Trémoille, ✆ 56 88 31 76, is rare in these parts for offering good food, a warm welcome *and* a reasonable bill. Menus at 80 and 120F; closed Sun and holidays.

Moulis ✉ 33480

The 19th-century **Château de Foulon**, set in the woodlands south of Castelnau, ✆ 56 58 20 18 offers five dreamy, perfectly tranquil rooms and the chance to watch swans fluttering across the lawns (around 400F for a double, large breakfast included).

Listrac ✉ 33480

Château Cap-Léon-Veyrin Donissan, at Donissan, ✆ 56 58 07 28, produces an excellent *cru bourgeois* and runs a small bed-and-breakfast in its comfortable guest-house in the middle of a vineyard. You can visit the *chais* and order a nice bottle to go with a well-prepared meal (doubles with breakfast are 250F, meals around 100F).

Pauillac ✉ 33250

Set in a sea of vineyards, the lovely little ★★★★**Château de Cordeillan-Bages**, Rte des Châteaux, ✆ 56 59 24 24, has 18 charming rooms in the Relais et Châteaux tradition and the best restaurant in Médoc, where the best local ingredients are enhanced without muss or fuss by a true master chef, Pascal Charreyras; the ragoût of asparagus and morels is heavenly. Even for a restaurant patronized by wine merchants and wine lovers, the selection from the cellar is astounding, thanks to one of France's best sommeliers, Pierre Paillardon, who loves to share his knowledge (menus 150F for lunch, 180–375F for dinner, closed Mon lunch, Sun, and 15 Dec–Jan). For half the price (but still dear for two stars), the ★★**De France et D'Angleterre**, 3 Quai Albert Pichon, ✆ 56 59 01 20, has pleasant riverside rooms, near stands selling *bichettes*, little shrimp lightly flavoured with aniseed.

Lesparre-Médoc ✉ 33340

★★★★**Château Layauga**, 2km from the centre in Gaillan-en-Médoc, ✆ 56 41 26 83, has seven very pretty rooms in a lovely château, with a pond and lawns set among the vineyards, and a restaurant with a solid emphasis on the best ingredients the southwest can offer—*cèpes*, truffles, foie gras, game and fish—but combined in rare fashions. Save room for one of the chef's excellent desserts (menus at 200 and 350F).

The Côte d'Argent

From Médoc's Pointe de Grave to the Basque lands in the south runs a nearly straight, wide 228km ribbon of silver sand, with the giant rolling waves of the Atlantic on one side and deep green pine forests on the other. Dubbed the Côte d'Argent, the Silver Coast, by a Bordeaux newspaperman in 1905, there is so much sand here that it can be a nuisance (see Soulac-sur-Mer), but what the rocky French Riviera wouldn't do for a dune or two! Although we only go as far down as the Bassin d'Arcachon, the oldest resort in the northern half of the Côte d'Argent, it's enough to get a taste of the coastline, offering broad sweeping vistas of empty space rare in Europe. If that weren't enough, just on the other side of the dunes are a score of lakes and ponds for calmer water sports, which also happen to lie on one of the Continent's major flyways for migratory birds. The whole is France's greatest outdoor playground: the pleasures of surfing, sailing, fishing, birdwatching, delta-planing, canoeing, golfing, cycling or building sand castles on the beach and slurping oysters draw more summer visitors every year.

A 'pinasse' in the Bassin d'Arcachon

Pointe de Grave to the Bassin d'Arcachon

Getting Around

Three trains in the winter and six in the summer link Bordeaux St-Jean or Bordeaux St-Louis to Soulac-sur-Mer, Le Verdon-sur-Mer and Pointe de Grave; some trains are replaced by SNCF bus from Pauillac (*℄* 56 09 85 56). Ferries from Le Verdon Port to Royan in the Charente-Maritime run roughly every hour and a half, with more frequent crossings in the summer (*℄* 56 09 60 84 for hours). At Soulac you can hire quality bikes by the week, from April to September at Cyclo Star, 9 Rue Fernand-Lafargue, *℄* 56 09 71 38.

From June to September, *La Bohème II* sails out from Le Verdon-sur-Mer to visit the Phare de Cordouan, offers low- or high-tide fishing excursions, or cruises along the Gironde estuary. For times and bookings in English, *℄* 56 09 62 93.

Getting to the lakes by public transport is feasible and not too difficult, at least in the summer: Pullmans Médocains, *℄* 56 59 57 05 link Bordeaux to Castelnau-de-Médoc, Carcans and Hourtin, and there are five Ouest-Aquitaine buses a day from Bordeaux to Sainte-Hélène, Lacanau, Moutchic and Lacanau-Océan, *℄* 56 05 06 33. Among the patrol routes laid out by the Germans, now converted into cycling paths, is a 70km trail from Bordeaux (beginning near the Pont d'Aquitaine) to Lacanau; from Lacanau south along the Atlantic to Cap Ferret it's another 40km. You can hire decent bikes in Mérignac at Ecocycle, 47 Av. Aristide Briand, *℄* 56 96 07 50.

Saint-Vivien-de-Médoc: in the centre, ℭ 56 09 58 50

Soulac-sur-Mer: Rue de la Plage, ℭ 56 09 86 61

Le Verdon-sur-Mer: Rue François-le-Breton, te 56 09 61 78

Vendays-Montalivet: 64 Av de l'Océan, ℭ 56 09 30 12

Carcans-Maubuisson: 127 Av. de Maubuisson, ℭ 56 03 34 94

Lacanau-Océan: Place de l'Europe, ℭ 56 03 21 01

market days

Saint Vivien: Wednesdays

Soulac: daily

To Soulac-sur-Mer

As you continue north of Lesparre, the vineyards begin to give way to coastal plains at Queyrac. Just before St-Vivien, you can visit one of the last working windmills in the southwest, the 1858 **Moulin de Vensac** *(open Sun afternoons, or by ringing ahead, ℭ 56 09 45 00)*. After a few decades of inactivity, the mill has been on the job again since the 1980s, stone-grinding flour—on sale at the mill. From St-Vivien, the D 2 leads to the village's small oyster ports. The oyster industry began by accident in 1868 when a captain, bringing oysters from Portugal to Arcachon, was waylaid here during a storm for several days and jettisoned his cargo, believing all the oysters had croaked. Enough of the bivalves survived and proliferated to create a profitable cash crop that employed 700 people before 1970, when the Portuguese oyster parasite struck and the new port at Verdon went into full polluting gear.

Legend has it that **Soulac-sur-Mer** is the descendent of Noviomagus, the fabled ocean port of the Bituriges, which one cataclsmic day in the 6th century sank into the sea. The fact that recent explorations have proved the legend real surprises no one here; Soulac itself is known as 'Jeune Soulac', since it replaces the original Soulac that underwent a slower cataclysm of being methodically swallowed up by sand in the 18th century. As a result of these roving sand piles, little remains of the medieval port where English pilgrims to Compostela would disembark, except for the **Basilique de Notre-Dame de la Fin des Terres**, Our Lady at the End of the Earth, and even this was buried twice by the voracious dunes, in the 13th and 18th centuries; in 1859, it was exhumed again, just before the top bit of the tower vanished forever, and it now sits tidily in a sand-lined hollow.

Our Lady at the End of the Earth was founded according to fond legend by St Veronica (*see* Rocamadour, p.111). It became a popular pilgrimage site—Louis XI personally made the journey three times—and it was always the first shrine that English pilgrims visited after disembarking at Soulac. It has a remarkable apse from the 13th century; inside is the polychrome wooden statue of the Virgin worshipped by the pilgrims. Seated with the Child, she holds a lily in one hand and a ship with a wind-swollen sail in the other. The carved capitals show Daniel in the lion's den, St Peter in prison, and the tomb and reliquary of St Veronica, who is said to have been buried here before her body was moved to Bordeaux. Three marble columns from the pre-Romanesque church survive in the apse; the stained glass dates from 1954.

Soulac also has a small **Musée d'Archéologie** with some interesting prehistoric and Gallo-Roman artifacts, at 28 Rue Victor Hugo *(open daily May–15 Sept, 3–8pm; free)*. On Boulevard du Front-du-Mer you can see the lighthouse of Cordouan, 8km away, or play the slots at the casino; just south is Soulac's small resort of **L'Amélie-sur-Mer**, named after a ship that was wrecked here decades ago. A popular sport along this shore is *char à voile* (sand yachting); learn how from Ubatuba, © 56 73 62 16, which also has surfboards, kayak surf, body board and speed sail equipment.

Le Verdon and The Phare de Cordouan

From Soulac, the road continues up to the little resort of **Le Verdon-sur-Mer**. Verdon was one of the last places held by the Germans in France in the Second World War; ordered to dig in here, to keep the Gironde and its ports from being used by the Allies, they held out until the April 1945 Battle of La Pointe de Grave. Just before the end they destroyed all Verdon's port installations for ocean liners. In 1967 these were replaced by the rather less glamorous petroleum and container terminals; further up, at **Port Bloc**, is the ferry terminus for Royan (and for the vedette boat for the Phare de Cordouan). Here an ancient forest of holm oak has managed to survive the war to become a popular picnic spot.

Europe's oldest lighthouse, the **Phare de Cordouan** sits on a limestone bump between the Gironde's two shipping lanes. In the 11th century the first tower was built; and in the 14th, the Black Prince contributed the first lighthouse, manned by a hermit whose job was to feed the fire on the top platform. By 1582 this was falling over, and Louis de Foix, an engineer who had already made himself famous for relocating the mouth of the river Adour, was given the task of erecting a new lighthouse. When good King Henri IV came to power, Louis de Foix decided to add a second dimension, that of monument to the glory of the monarchy. The result, set on a 24-foot pedestal, was an extraordinary Renaissance confection that was completed only in 1611 under another monarch, Louis XIII. Unfortunately in 1788 this most froufrou of all lighthouses was truncated in order to add a 130-foot, no-frills utilitarian white cone. To prevent further depredations, Cordouan was designated a historic monument in 1862; in 1981 it even became obsolete as a lighthouse, and was just spared demolition. Inside, the first of seven floors houses the king's apartments, and the second a chapel, with a pretty cupola and 17th-century windows and an inscription from a time that often seems a bit warped in retrospect: 'Un Dieu, un Roy, une Foy, une Loy.' From here you can climb up another 250 steps to the look-out and lantern for a bird's-eye view of the estuary.

La Pointe de Grave, and Down to Montalivet

At the end of the road and the northernmost tip of the Gironde is La Pointe de Grave (or de Médoc), marked by another lighthouse, the **Phare de Grave** (1852), which you can climb for the view; one room is dedicated to the history of the Phare de Cordouan *(July and August daily, 2.30–6.30)*. Near the lighthouse, a stele commemorating Lafayette's departure for America in 1777 replaces the one destroyed in 1942 by ill-tempered Germans who didn't like people remembering such things.

Most of the Germans who come down to the Médoc coast these days couldn't be more harmless; most of them don't even have any clothes on, but leave them at the gate at one of Europe's largest naturist resorts, the **Centre Hélio-marin** set up in 1950 at the modest seaside resort of **Montalivet-les-Bains**. Along with the Germans, Scandinavians, Belgians, Dutch, and increasingly the French, come to strip down, usually with the whole family in tow; unlike the posy beautiful bodies of St Tropez, the emphasis at Montalivet is good clean fun among sand, sea and pines. There's another naturist centre on the nearby beach of Dépée; if you're not quite ready to let it all hang out, there are designated beaches for '*textiles*' at Montalivet and to the north at a place that sounds like a gaseous belch, **Le Gurp**. Just in from the beaches, dotted here and there along the coast you can see the crumbling blockhouses and pillboxes from the Germans' Atlantic Wall. Many were originally hidden by the dunes; occasionally you'll find one licked by the tide, covered with barnacles and algae and inhabited by little sea creatures.

Lacs d'Hourtin-Carcans and Lacanau

One of the great selling points of the Côte d'Argent is the proximity of its calm, safe lakes to the Atlantic breakers, popular with windsurfers and sailors who don't want to get too wet. **Lac d'Hourtin** and its contiguous twin **Lac de Carcans** stretch 16km from north to south, making it the longest lake in France. There's no road, but a cycle track runs between the Atlantic and the lake, ideal if you want to seek out your own private acre of sand between **Hourtin-Plage**, a small family resort in the north, and **Carcans-Maubuisson**, the sports-oriented resort at the southern end of the lake, with a 15km sandy beach. A museum here, the **Maison des Arts et Traditions Populaires** *(open Easter, and 15 June–15 Sept, 3–7; adm)*, evokes life in the Médoc at the beginning of the 20th century.

The southern part of the lake, around the dunes and the lovely **Etang de Cousseau** has 13km of marked paths reserved for cyclists and walkers, who if they're lucky may see a wide variety of migratory waterfowl, such as *balbuzards* and water rails, along with boar, deer, tortoises, genets, and European mink. Further south, **Lac de Lacanau** has been a favourite weekend escape of the Bordelais since the early 1900s. They built pleasant summer villas at **Lacanau-Océan**, never guessing that the huge rollers that smacked the beach would in the 1960s begin to attract a new breed of tourist—the cream of Europe's surfing fools. You can rent boards at Surf City, Résidence Casino, Bd de la Plage, © 56 26 33 92. Don't come any where near Lacanau in mid-August without a firm reservation in hand, when the place is packed to the gills for Europe's surfing championships.

Soulac-sur-Mer ✉ 33780

★★Dame de Coeur, Place de l'Eglise, ✆ 56 09 80 80, has pleasant rooms, open all year. Also open all year, **★De la Gare**, Routes des Lacs, ✆ 56 09 85 60. At L'Amélie, **★★Des Pins**, ✆ 56 09 80 01, offers nothing fancy, but pines and sea views; the beach is 100m away (open Mar–Dec). There are a slew of camp sites along the ocean, from the four-star **Camping Palace**, Bd Marson de Montbrun, ✆ 56 09 80 22, with a capacity of 1750 campers to the more rustic **Des Pins**, two minutes from the beach at L'Amélie, ✆ 56 09 82 52.

Le Verdon-sur-Mer ✉ 33123

If you're waiting for the ferry, **Chez Arlette**, 66 Route de la Pointe-de-Grave, ✆ 56 09 60 42, offers tempting seafood platters that help make time whiz by (menus at 90, 155, 180 and 200F, closed Sun night and Mon).

Montalivet-les-Bains ✉ 33930

Besides the bungalows at the **Centre Hélio-Marin**, ✆ 56 09 30 47, you can camp in your altogether a few km inland at Grayan-et-l'Hôpital to the northeast, site of the largest naturist camp site in France. You can keep your clothes on at the ocean-front **★★De l'Océan**, ✆ 56 09 30 05, a simple place open all year.

Lacanau-Océan ✉ 33680

At **★★★Du Golf-Latitudes**, ✆ 56 03 23 15, golfers couldn't be any closer to their beloved links; it has a pool to cool off in after a hot round. On the seashore, **★★L'Oyat**, Front de Mer Ortal, ✆ 56 03 11 11, is a good bet, and a place where the usual half-board terms is a delight—the restaurant has some of the best food in town (closed Nov–Mar). Decent sleeps and eats are also on tap at **★★L'Etoile d'Argent**, Place de l'Europe, ✆ 56 03 21 07, open all year except for half of January; count on 250F a person half board.

Arcachon and its Bassin

The straight line of the Côte d'Argent is broken by Gascony's inland sea, the 250 square kilometre Bassin d'Arcachon. Not only does it sound like something in your bathroom, but like that fixture the actual amount under water in it varies greatly, when the tide sweeps through twice a day—at low tide large sections turn into sandy mud pies. The Bassin managed to stay out of history most of the time; the Romans and Rabelais wrote admiringly of its oysters, and in the Middle Ages it belonged to the redoubtable Captals de Buch, English allies in the Hundred Years' War. In the 18th century Louis XVI thought to make the Bassin into a military port and sent down an engineer of the Ponts et Chaussées, Brémontier, to fix the shifting sands. Brémontier built tall palisades 80yds in from the high tide, stopping the wind-borne sand to create barriers dunes between 30 and 40ft high, which he anchored with a long-rooted grass called *oyat*. To stop the dunes from wandering inland, he spread a mix of seeds of gorse, broom and maritime pines under a network of branches. The gorse sprouted up quickly, and helped hold down the soil as the slower pines established themselves.

For all that, the Revolution intervened before the military port project ever got under way, leaving the Bassin to daydream to the ebbs and flows of its tides until the mid 19th century, when it discovered its double destiny as a massive nursery for oysters and a summer resort for the Bordelais; these days the gargantuan Dune du Pilat, just south of Arcachon, alone attracts a million visitors a year. Yet mass tourism has left many corners untouched: the little villages in the back Bassin could be part of 17th-century Dutch landscape painting, with their ports sheltering the Bassin's distinctive small, shallow-keeled sailing boats called pinasses (or *pinassayres*, in Gascon), painted the colour of the owner's house, usually green, light pink or straw yellow.

Getting Around

There are trains nearly every hour from Bordeaux to Arcachon, and in the summer, TGVs direct from Paris Montparnasse (© 56 92 50 50). Several CITRAM buses a day from Bordeaux (from 14 Rue Edouard-Maybon, © 56 43 04 04 or from the station coinciding with the TGVs) serve Andernos, Arès and Cap Ferret. Bicycles are a convenient way to get around, and the Bassin has many cycle-tracks; you can hire bikes in all the villages, and in Arcachon at Judlin, 104 Cours Lamarque, © 56 83 11 88; Locabeach, 326 Bd de la Plage, © 56 83 39 64; and Dingo Vélo, Rue Grenier, © 56 83 44 09.

Arcachon

Arcachon was a small fishing village until 1841, when its life was turned upside down by the building of a railway line from nearby La Teste de Buch to Bordeaux. This new link neatly coincided with the new fashion for sea-bathing launched by the Duchesse de Berry. Private villas went up here and there, but the resort really took off after 1852, when a pair of brothers, Emile and Isaac Pereire, took over the railway line and extended it to Arcachon. The Pereire brothers were descendents of Spanish Jews who found a safe haven in Bordeaux during the Inquisition; their grandfather, Jacob, was famous for inventing the first sign-language alphabet for deaf-mutes in the 1700s. The Pereire brothers proved just as inventive, but as property speculators, and laid out their new resort with cute winding lanes according to the anglophile tastes of Napoleon III. They divided the residential sections into four subdivisions, each named after one of the four seasons. Although Spring and Autumn never really caught on, the **Ville-d'Hiver**, the area best sheltered from the ocean winds and always 3°C/7°F warmer than the rest of Arcachon, attained full fashion status by the 1860s—Gounod, Debussy, Alexandre Dumas, Napoleon III, Marie Christine of Austria and her future husband Alfonso XII of Spain (who came incognito) were all habitués. For a centrepiece, the Ville d'Hiver has the **Parc Mauresque** named after its fabulously outlandish pseudo-Moorish casino (1864), inspired by the Alhambra and the Great Mosque of Cordoba—but tragically destroyed by a fire in 1977. Inspired by its fantasy, the usually staid 19th-century Bordelais who built second homes in the Ville d'Hiver let their hair down, indulging in neogothic, Tyrolean, Tudor, pseudo-mediéval and other fond fancies; some 200 of these lacy gingerbread villas survive, many now owned by wealthy retirees. Don't miss the fine overall view of the Bassin from the Parc Mauresque gardens, its **Passerelle Saint-Paul** (over adjacent Allée Pasteur), built by Eiffel in 1862 and the observatory, reached by a 19th-century lift.

The **Ville d'Eté**, facing the Bassin and cooler in the summer, has most of Arcachon's tourist facilities, seaside promenades, sheltered sandy beaches and the **Musée-Aquarium** in Rue Professeur-Jolyet *(June–Aug 9.30–8, the rest of the year 10–12 and 2–7; adm)*, with a pretty collection of tropical fish, tortoises, seashells, stuffed weasels and shark skeletons. The Ville d'Eté's most notorious resident was Toulouse-Lautrec, who had a house by the ocean and liked to swim in the nude, offending the sensibilities of his neighbours. To pacify them, he erected a fence between his house and the beach—then mischievously covered it with obscene drawings. The furious neighbours eventually bought the house and gleefully burned the fence. Their descendents have never really forgiven them. (They should consider the chagrin of the heirs of the young man in the Marquesas Islands, charged with tidying up Gauguin's hut after the painter's death. Finding it cluttered with sculptures and paintings, he loaded everything onto his boat and dumped the lot into the Pacific.)

Since 1950, a new crop of villas went up on the ocean front in **Parc Pereire**, overlooking Arcachon's best beach, Plage Pereire. As incredible as it seems, in 1922 someone had the chutzpah to drill for oil right in the middle of the park, but instead of black gold discovered, at 1600ft down, a natural spring of mineral water, known as **Les Abatilles**, which is exploited and bottled in the spa. Further south, along Boulevard de la Plage, a new **casino** has been installed in the more Disneylandish than outlandish Château Deganne, with a brand-new congress centre, the Palatium, to keep it company.

The Dune du Pilat

As the afternoon draws to a close in Arcachon, the thing to do is drive or cycle 8km south, through the resorts of **Moulleau, Pyla-sur-Mer** and **Pilat-Plage**. In the pine trees, there's a pay car park to leave your vehicle, and beyond that, the awesome, terrible, extraordinary sight of the Moby Dick of dunes, the **Dune du Pilat**, at 347ft the highest pile of sand in Europe, at 2.7km the longest, and at 550yds the widest. Excavations in this little chunk of the Sahara have found that Pilat began to form 8000 years ago, and more or less reached its present dimensions in the 17th century. Like all dunes, it's in a constant state of flux, and every year it inches a little further inland, consuming the pines and forcing the camp sites and cafés at its rim to move a bit further inland. A wooden stair with 190 steps helps you get to the top of the steep behemoth for an unforgettable view—especially at sunset. If you can't resist the urge to roll and slide and scamper down the ocean-side slope, be prepared to face the torturous return trip back up the slippery sands. Often included in the sundown view are schools of bottlenose dolphins and porpoises, who like to frolic just offshore. South of the sand-monster there's a beach called **Petit Nice** and beyond that a naturist beach, both with lifeguards and snack bars.

Excursions and Activities

The UBA, Union des Bateliers Arcachonnais, from the Thiers and d'Eyrac jetties (© 56 54 60 32 or 56 54 83 01) make frequent half-hour crossings to Cap Ferret in the summer (*see* below) and two hour-long excursions to the **Ile aux Oiseaux** at 3.30pm, all year long. The Bassin's only island, the Ile aux Oiseaux is government-owned and given over to sea birds as well as oyster farms and sailing boats. In the old days, herdsmen in boats would have their horses swim over to the sweet islet pastures. The Ile aux Oiseaux's landmarks are its picturesque *cabanes tchanquées*, huts perched on stilts.

In July and August the UBA offers days on the shadeless, hot and sandy **Banc d'Arguin**, a wildfowl refuge at the entrance of the Bassin; in June sandwich terns by their thousands nest here (bring a picnic). Guided tours of the oyster beds are also offered, and 4-hour trips up the cool, forested river Leyre (*see* below). The **Pinassiers du Moulleau**, departing from Arcachon's Moulleau jetty (© 56 54 04 88) also cross to Cap Ferret, and make summer excursions to the ocean, up the Leyre river *bayous* and to the Banc d'Arguin.

Among the daredevil sports practised off the Dune du Pilat are deltaplaning (contact **Les Ailes du Delta**, in Pyla-sur-Mer, ℂ 56 32 97 09), hang-gliding and *parapente*, a cross between hang-gliding and parachuting (contact **Locarêve**, 210 Bd de la Côte d'Argent, in Arcachon, ℂ 56 83 62 83 and **Sport Passion**, at Les Gallouneys, La Teste de Buch, ℂ 56 32 97 09). In the 19th century Arcachon had a sizeable British colony, to which it owes its passion for golf; there are three courses and a practice course in the area and closest is the beautiful **Golf Club d'Arcachon**, 35 Bd d'Arcachon, ℂ 56 54 44 00. Sailing is popular and a challenge, with strong currents, sandbanks, channels and occasional high winds, and over the course of the year there are a number of races, including the **18 heures d'Arcachon** sail race, that takes place every 3 and 4 July. The tourist office has a long list of places to hire your own craft, as well as listings for horse-riding, tennis, diving, water-skiing, fishing, cycling and nearly every other sport you can imagine.

Arcachon ✉ 33120   **Where to Stay**

Hotels in fashionable Arcachon are in general more expensive than any place else in this book. If you plan to stay a week or more, you'll go less broke in a furnished room, studio or flat—pick up the fat list at the tourist office. Book months in advance for anything in July or August.

expensive/moderate

All of the below have rooms in both price categories; if you plump for a sea view, rates rise considerably. The most charming choice is the ★★★**Semiramis**, 4 Allées Rebsomen, ℂ 56 83 25 87, your chance to stay in a 19th-century Arcachon summer villa in the Ville d'Hiver, complete with painted ceilings and ceramic decorations of the birds likely to be seen at Le Teich. It has a potpourri of 17 rooms, no two alike, and a pool set in a garden of palms, mimosas and acanthus; open all year. ★★★**Arc-Hôtel sur Mer**, 89 Bd de la Plage, ℂ 56 83 06 85, is a moderate-sized, modern but stylish hotel where the rooms, all with balconies, overlook either water or garden; heated pool, sauna and jacuzzi are among the other amenities, and it's open all year. ★★★**Grand Hôtel Richelieu**, 185 Bd de la Plage is an old-fashioned hotel dead in the centre of town, right across from the beach (closed Nov–mid Mar). You can't stay much closer to the ocean than at ★★★**Les Vagues**, 9 Bd de l'Océan, ℂ 56 83 03 75, decorated with a fresh, light touch and with rooms looking right down on the waves (open all year).

inexpensive/cheap

★★**Le Nautic**, 20 Bd de la Plage, ℂ 56 83 01 48, has recently been renovated with a Spanish touch and has some of the nicest rooms in this category; open all year. ★★**Les Mimosas**, 77bis Av. de la République, ℂ 56 83 45 86, has tidy if somewhat bland rooms not far from the sea in the Ville d'Eté. The municipal camp site, **Des Abatilles**, ℂ 56 83 24 15, is nothing fancy, but clean and cheap (open Easter–Oct).

Pyla-sur-Mer (33115)

Among the nicest here are the ★★★**Haitza**, Place Louis-Gaume, ✆ 56 22 74 64, set in the pine woods, a stone's throw from the beach (closed Oct–Mar); by the beach and at the foot of the mighty dune, ★★**La Corniche**, 46 Av. Louis-Gaume, ✆ 56 22 72 11, is a neo-Basque wood and brick hotel built in 1932 with spacious balconies and a stairway down to the beach. The restaurant has not only good seafood but also a selection of southwestern duck confections as well (menu at 150F; closed mid-Oct–Mar). ★**Côte Sud**, 4 Av. de Figuier, ✆ 56 83 25 00, is in a 1940s villa in the pines, a 5-minute walk from the beach (closed Jan). There are two excellent camp sites south of the dune, both with pools: **Camping La Dune**, ✆ 56 22 72 17, and **Pyla Camping**, ✆ 56 22 74 56, closer to the beach; both open May–Sept.

Eating Out

Arcachon's classiest garden terrace, **L'Ombrière**, 79 Cours Héricart-de-Thury, ✆ 56 83 42 52, serves delicious seafood platters as well as duck and veal dishes, and a good selection of wine (menu 127F, closed Sun night and Wed). **Le Patio**, 10 Bd de la Plage, ✆ 56 83 02 72, surrounds diners with bright clutter, a waterfall and delicious aromas from specialities such as lobster salad, oysters in flaky pastry, hot stuffed crab and *bouillabaisse océane* (menu 160F, closed Tues in winter). In La Teste, **La Varangue**, 67 Av du Général de Gaulle, ✆ 56 66 77 43 specializes in duck in nearly every possible form known to the southwest, served in a park with a pool in the centre; for something different try *carpaccio de magret* with foie gras and *vert jus* (menu 150F, closed Wed). **Restaurant du Port**, 2 Av. des Ostréculteurs, ✆ 56 54 64 81, is known for its *bouillabuche*, a bouillabaisse served with *aïoli* (garlic sauce) instead of the traditional *rouille*; the shellfish, tapas and meat dishes are also tempting (average 140F, closed Mon night and Tues).

For under 100F you can fill up on *gambas à la plancha* and other Spanish-style seafood treats at **La Plancha**, 17 Rue Jéhenne, ✆ 56 83 76 66 (closed Sun in winter). For just a bit more, you can get a vast seafood platter at friendly **Chez Dubern**, 78 Bd de la Plage, ✆ 56 83 12 15; for a wide choice of Chinese and Vietnamese dishes, find a seat on the terrace overlooking the fishing port at **Le Dragon de Jade**, 66 Bd de la Plage, ✆ 56 83 13 11 (menus 60 and 100F).

Around the Bassin

Ten communes, a score of picturesque little ports with wooden oyster shacks, beaches, a river delta and a bird sanctuary, a trip up the Leyre river into the Landes and a score of rather more commercial amusements await to be savoured around the rim of the Bassin. Try at least once to cross the water the traditional way, in a *pinasse*—promenades are offered from the ports of Arcachon, Arès, Andernos, and Lège-Cap-Ferret.

La Teste de Buch: Place Jean Hameau, ✆ 56 66 45 59

Gujan-Mestras: 41 Av. de Lattre de Tassigny, ✆ 56 66 12 65

Andernos-les-Bains: Place du Broustic, ✆ 56 82 02 95

Arès: Esplanade G. Dartiguelongue, ✆ 56 60 18 07

Lège-Cap-Ferret: 214 Rte du Cap-Ferret, ✆ 56 60 86 43

market days

La Teste de Buch: Thursdays and Sundays, in the covered market

La Teste de Buch to Le Teich

East of Arcachon, pines line the Bassin at **La Teste de Buch**. Its name recalls the Captals de Buch who lorded it over the Bassin in the Middle Ages, although in those days pine resin rather than oysters was the cash crop. La Teste has some handsome houses dating back to the 18th century, and includes in its municipal boundaries not only the Dune du Pilat and a racetrack, but also the **Lac de Cazaux**, the second largest in France.

Since 1969, arts and crafts from the days of the Captals have been displayed at the reconstituted **Village Médiéval** at **La Hume** (just east of La Teste), where 50 craftsmen and craftswomen demonstrate their skills, from bookbinding to jewellery-making *(open mid-June to mid-Sept, 10–12 and 2–7; adm)*; there's even a **Mini-Golf Médiéval**, for putt-putting as in ye knightly days of yore. In the same area, La Hume has sprouted three other roadside attractions to keep mom and dad in the poorhouse: a 'zoo' of domestic animals, the **Parc Animalier La Coccinelle** *(end May–mid Sept; adm)*, where children can feed the baby lambs and goats; **Aquacity**, for a day splashing around in rivers, pools with waves, and every kind of water slide imaginable *(June–mid-Sept, 10–7; adm)* and **Marinoscope** *(May–Aug, 10–7, rest of the year 2–7; adm)*, a museum of models of every kind of ship put to sea since 1947, made perfectly to scale by master model-maker Bernard Foueré.

Next to La Hume, the Bassin's oyster capital, **Gujan-Mestras**, has seven little ports crowded with *oustaous* (oyster huts), which provide the perfect backdrop for ordering a plate of oysters to *déguster*, as the French say. The critter on Gujan's coat-of-arms, however, is the ladybird beetle, the *barbot* in Gascon, a name that goes back to the early days of the phylloxera epidemic, when the locals noticed that their infected vines invariably swarmed with ladybugs. They accused those helpful insects of spreading the plague, while in fact they were gobbling down the real culprits as fast as they could; the priest at Gujan even held *barbot* exorcisms in the vineyards. When the real, much tinier lice-like pests were discovered, the villagers of Gujan became the butt of jokes from their neighbours, who called them the *barbots*. By the 1920s, Gujan learned to laugh at itself, and adopted the ladybug as its own, even naming its rugby team the *Barbots*.

The Oyster's their World

Oysters from the Bassin were popular among rich Romans of Burdigala, who would set up relays to have them brought to their tables in a few hours, where they would slurp them raw with *garum*, the prized and mysterious fish gut sauce that culinary archaeologists guess was something similar to Vietnamese *nuoc nam*. By the Middle Ages, when the old Roman roads were full of mud and potholes, tastes turned to dried oysters put up in barrels, eaten in a sauce or fried. The Bassin's industry remained small and local, however, until 1850, when once again speedy transport—in the form of the railway—allowed the tasty bivalves to chug posthaste to Bordeaux, and then on to Paris in 1857—at a time when restaurant diners thought nothing of beginning a meal with 10 or 15 dozen. Twice, however, Arcachon's bread-and-butter industry was devastated by oyster parasites; the first, in 1922, wiped out Arcachon's flat, native *gravettes*. These were replaced by *portugaises*, which in turn fell prey to a new parasite in 1970. Since 1972, the oysters farmed in the Bassin belong to two different species—a new *gravette*, a flat hybrid of Charente and Breton oysters, and a parasite-resistant, elongated Japanese oyster, the *huître creuse*, or *gigas*.

Today the Bassin d'Arcachon is the fourth-largest oyster producer in France, but the first in Europe in 'trapping' microscopic oyster embryos and larvae swishing about the sea in search of a home—they simply can't resist stacks of Roman roof tiles, bleached in a mix of lime and sand. After eight months clinging to a tile, the baby oysters are moved into calm nurseries in flat cages; the next year, they are moved once more to oyster parks, in fresh plankton-rich waters, where the oyster farmers defend them the best they can against greedy starfish and crustaceans, who will nevertheless devour 15 to 20 per cent of the crop over the next three years. In the parks, the oysters are constantly turned, to encourage them to develop a nice shape and a hard shell. When at long last they're ready to go on the market, they are placed for up to four days in special pools that trick them into no longer trusting the tide, and to remain sealed tight while they are shipped and sold by size, from 6 (the smallest) to 0 (the largest and best).

'Now if you're ready, Oysters dear/ We can begin to feed' as the Walrus said. To prepare the little rascals *à la mode d'Arcachon*: count on a dozen oysters per person (or more if you're really greedy), four (or more) *crépinettes* (small flat sausages cooked in white wine), plenty of thinly sliced rye bread and butter and glasses of dry white Graves, properly chilled at 6–8°C (44°F). Open the oysters and keep cool, fry or barbecue the sausages just before serving and eat—slurp down a cold oyster, take a bite of hot sausage with a bit of buttered bread and wash it down with a swallow of wine.

Le Teich, the Leyre, and a look into Les Landes

At Le Teich, the Leyre (or L'Eyre), one of the most important rivers of the Landes, drains into the Bassin d'Arcachon, forming the kind of marshy delta beloved of migratory waterfowl. In 1972, Le Teich's rare environment of saltwater and freshwater *bayous* was set aside as the **Parc Ornithologique** *(open daily 10–6 Mar–Oct, other times weekends only; adm; bring your binoculars, or rent them on the site)*. The delta is a favourite stop on the great migration route between Africa and Scandinavia, and a nesting ground for several species, especially grey herons, black cormorants, white storks, black and white oyster-catchers, egrets, kingfishers, dabbling garganeys and spoon-billed shovelers. Altogether some 280 different species have been sighted. One of the big success stories has been the return of the mute swan, which vanished from France at the time of the Revolution.

The park is divided into four sections: the vast **Parc de Causseyre**, with a path for visitors and several hides and observation posts; the **Parc de la Moulette**, where the geese, swans and ducks are concentrated; the small **Parc des Artigues**, with a collection of ducks from around the world, at liberty, and large aviaries; and the inaccessible **Parc Claude Quancard**, for wading birds (although there are two observation posts). There's an information centre in the **Maison de la Nature du Bassin d'Arcachon**, and a fine viewpoint over the delta from the **Observatoire du Delta de Leyre**. Next to the park you can visit our smaller winged friends at the **Serre aux Papillons**, a live butterfly zoo *(open mid Apr–Sept, 10–7.30; adm)*.

Le Teich lies in the northern confines of the **Parc Naturel Régional des Landes de Gascogne**. The great pine moors of the Landes may seem monotonous from the car window while you're zooming down the autoroute to Spain, but close up they are striking, especially when the heather, gorse or honeysuckle is in bloom and the heady scent of resin fills the air in an aromatherapy overkill. The nearest place to learn about the secrets of the Landes is **Belin-Béliet**, 30km up the river Eyre from Le Teich. There's a park information office in Place de l'Eglise, © 56 88 06 06; canoe and kayak and bicycle hire at the Centre d'Animation du Graoux, © 56 88 04 62. Belin is a tranquil place, but it can claim a mention in nearly any medieval history book as the birthplace of Eleanor of Aquitaine in 1122, and (some say) of her favourite son, Richard the Lion-Heart (in a now ruined castle on the outskirts of town, marked by a stele). The church of **St-Pierre-de-Mons**, on the outskirts of Belin, was built during Eleanor's reign, although its bell tower was only fortified a century later, during the Hundred Years' War, that time bomb left by her French and English marriages. Inside are four archaic capitals, carved with scenes of mysterious import; legend has it that St-Pierre's cemetery, like St-Seurin in Bordeaux and the Alychamps in Arles, has the tombs of Charlemagne's paladins.

The Back Bassin, around to Cap Ferret

At **Biganos**, north of the Leyre delta, many of the old picturesque oystermen's *cabanons* have been converted into holiday homes, while the oystermen, one presumes, now work in the local paper mill. The next town, **Audenge** is a sleepy fishing village where the day's catch is trapped in reservoirs left by the retreating tide—a method of fishing that inspired someone to dig similar tide-fed reservoirs for humans; if the tide is out you can join the locals in the public seawater pools. Next to the north is **Lanton**, with a long beach and a 12th-century church, the oldest on the Bassin. **Andernos-les-Bains**, a lively summer resort with splendid views across the water, and **Arès** both have beaches safe for children.

The northwestern curve of the Bassin is sprinkled with little oyster port-resorts set between the calm waters and rough Atlantic, and all belonging to the commune of **Lège-Cap-Ferret**. The prettiest port is **L'Herbe**, an intimate hamlet of wooden houses on tiny lanes, founded in the 17th century. The commune's 35km of ocean beaches culminate in the sandy tail of Cap Ferret, which has long been doing its damnedest to close off the mouth of the Bassin; in the past 200 years the cape has grown 4km and gobbled up several fashionable villas in its wake. A path leads around to the tip of the cape, with splendid views of the Dune du Pilat, most breathlessly from the top of the 255 steps of the lighthouse *(open 15 June–15 Sept, 10–11 and 2–3)*. The cute little **Tramway du Cap-Ferret** links the end of the road to the ocean beaches, where surfers ride the big rollers expedited by the Bay of Biscay.

Where to Stay and Eating Out

La Teste ✉ 33260

> **★★Auberge Basque**, 36 Rue du Maréchal-Foch, ✆ 56 66 26 04, in one of the oldest buildings in La Teste, a Landais-style house of 1776 with a pretty terrace covered with rhododendrons. A family of oyster farmers also owns **Chez Diego**, Centre Captal, ✆ 56 54 44 32, guaranteeing the freshest of oysters and other delicious seafood in a south-of-the-border decor (menus from 90 to 130F).

Gujan-Mestras ✉ 33470

> The light-filled dining room and terrace of **Les Viviers**, Port de Larros, ✆ 56 66 01 04, offers a wide selection of shellfish and other denizens of the deep, as well as a tasty beef *brochette* with *cèpes* (menu 120F, open daily).

Le Teich ✉ 33470

> The **Maison de la Nature**, ✆ 56 22 80 93, doubles as a hostel, with 36 beds, kitchen and bikes and canoes to hire. There's a good camp site, **Ker Helen**, near the port on the D 650, ✆ 56 66 03 79, with caravans or bungalows to hire, open all year.

Bélin-Béliet ✉ 33830

> **★★Aliénor d'Aquitaine** occupies an old post house in the village centre at Rue Ste-Quietterie, ✆ 56 88 01 23.

Biganos ✉ 33380

> Two refreshingly cheap choices here in the village, both open all year: **★Chez Marie**, 57 Av. des Boïens, ✆ 56 82 60 37, and **★Hôtel de France**, 99 Av. de la Libération, ✆ 56 82 61 08.

Andernos-les-Bains ✉ 33510

L'Esquirrey, 9 Av. Commandant-Allègre, ✆ 56 82 22 15 is a haven for oyster-lovers—the freshest of bivalves served in a real *cabanon* at friendly prices—along with the freshest, tastiest fish the Bassin has to offer; from 60 to 130F (open summer only).

Lège-Cap-Ferret ✉ 33970

Cap Ferret is the trendiest spot on the Bassin these days, and there are plenty of bars, restaurants and camp sites, but only a handful of hotels; quite a few people sack out under the stars. Taking the hamlets from north to south: in Le Petit Piquey, **Chez Auguste**, ✆ 56 60 52 12, is the local oyster bar to see and be seen in, with a terrace overlooking the Dune du Pilat. The best ice cream on the whole Bassin is the homemade creations of **Pat-à-Chou**, in Le Grand Piquey, ✆ 56 60 51 38. Just south in Piraillan, in a traditional Basque house, **Chez Pierrette**, 9 Impasse des Sternes, ✆ 56 60 50 50 has a good reputation for unfussy dishes, based on the market and the day's catch, but there are meat specialities as well (closed Mon in winter, menus 80 and 150F). ★**De la Plage Chez Magne**, in the Port de l'Herbe, ✆ 56 60 50 15 is a delightful simple eight-room wooden hotel by the beach, with a good restaurant, although the menu is rarely committed to paper (open 15 June–15 Oct). The nearby **Rond-Point**, ✆ 56 60 51 32 has an equally simple decor but more pretentions in the kitchen, preparing abundant portions of seafood (monkfish sautéed in Vieux Médoc, for instance) as well as land food, served inside or out on the terrace (menus 120F, lunch only, closed Thurs).

Down at Cap Ferret, there's the little duneside and seaside ★★**Des Dunes**, 119 Av. de Bordeaux, ✆ 56 60 61 81 (open mid-June to mid Sept) and ★★**La Frégate**, 34 Av. de l'Océan, ✆ 56 60 41 62, complete with a pool (open April–Aug). The very popular **Auberge de Jeunesse** at 87 Av. de Bordeaux, ✆ 56 60 64 62, open July and Aug only, gets so many customers that many end up under tents. The best restaurant in this corner is **Chez Hortense**, Av. du Sémaphore, ✆ 56 60 62 56, offering a wide variety of seafood, prepared in a wide variety of styles (à la carte only; around 130F, open 25 June–12 Sept).

The Lot: Quercy

Connoisseurs of tourist slogans will find the current 'The Lot: A Surprise at Each Step' a limp noodle when the *département* is blessed with a name so full of potential. Possibilities come racing to mind: 'Take the Lot, will you?' 'We have a Lot to answer for' 'A Whole Lot to Love' 'A Lot like Arkansas' 'What a Lot of ★★★★★', or whatever. The truth is, the Lot needs a lick of PR. Outsiders often lump it together with the neighbouring Dordogne, when in fact the Lot's heartstrings have always pulled it in the other direction—to the south. Instead of the lush, tidy, green-shire beauty of the Dordogne, the Lot is more cowboy rough-and-tumble, its landscape tossed up in wild and arid limestone plateaux. What soil it has is said to be the worst in France (the vines don't mind that at all). The Dordogne belongs to Aquitaine, the Atlantic and Bordeaux; the Lot occupies half of the ancient province of Quercy, the northernmost possessions of the counts of Toulouse, and to this day it belongs to Toulouse and the Midi-Pyrénées region.

'Quercy' may evoke oaks (as in the Latin *quercus*), the tree that covers much of its territory, but the name is really derived from its Gaulish residents, the never-say-die Cadurcii, who are also remembered in the name of their capital, Cahors. In 51 BC, after Caesar's defeat of Vercingetorix, the feisty Cadurcii still refused to surrender to the Romans and holed up at an *oppidum* with a wonderful, ululating nursery-rhyme of a name, Uxellodunum. Julius Caesar was niggled enough to come in person to sort out this last pocket of resistance, and got the Cadurcii to surrender by diverting the physical manifestation of their goddess—their water supply. Now no one remembers where Uxellodunum was, but most scholars agree this lost Alamo of the Gauls is somewhere in the Lot: Puy d'Issolud north of the Dordogne river, Mursens, Luzech or Capdenac-le-Haut all have supporters to their claim.

What the Lot doesn't have a lot of is people. So many have migrated in

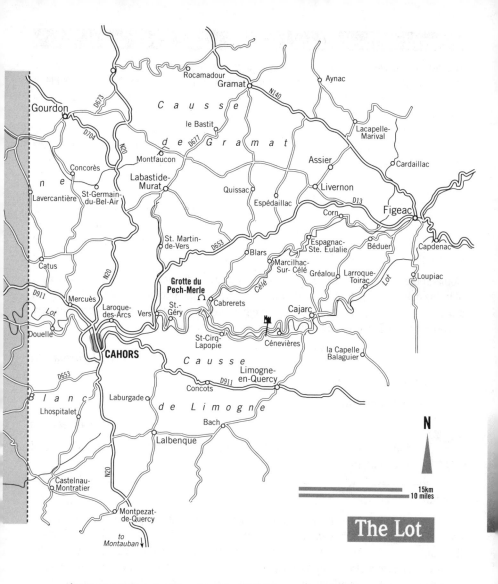

the past century looking for jobs that Quercy's present population is equal to that of Roman times, and the old stone houses they left behind have either tumbled into ruins or have been restored as holiday homes—a full half of all the houses in the department are secondary, which has proved to be the kiss of death for everyday life in many smaller hamlets. There are serious noises about running a motorway to Cahors to improve access, introduce some industry, shake loose some jobs. The idea is anathema to the arcadian faction. Stay tuned.

Between the Dordogne and Lot Rivers: the Causse de Gramat

The largest and wildest of Quercy's rocky arid limestone plateaux, the Causse de Gramat is the upper crust of an extraordinary subterranean world of lakes and rivers, accessible to earth-dwellers through caverns, little canyons and *gouffres*, including the spectacular pit of Padirac (*see* p.105). The *causse* itself has a peculiar fascination in the spring and early summer, when the scrub oak and juniper, wild flowers, wild rose and honeysuckle soften the deserted landscape; the odd-looking flocks of the *causse*—a local breed of sheep called the *caussenarde* whose eyes are protected from the sun by natural black spectacles—forage in the shade, butterflies flutter by and the dark shadows of buzzards and kestrels slowly make their loops across blue-grey horizons. The limestone soaks in the sun as it soaks in the rain, and the heated scent of juniper in a clearing is like inhaling from a vat of gin. Holiday people boost the meagre native population, and the cafés and restaurants are open, which can be a welcome sight after you've travelled miles without passing a sign of human life.

Come in the winter, and the *causse* becomes a study in desolation, the colour drained out of it, the oaks clinging dismally to their brown leaves in the sodden mists. The villages seem sad and empty, or locked up altogether; the buzzards and kestrels are still there, but now they seem sinister as they circle over the silent, overcast ridges.

Tourist Information

Gramat: Place Four, © 65 38 73 60

Labastide-Murat: Place Mairie, © 65 21 11 39

market days

Labastide-Murat: Sundays 9–12, and a huge fair on the second Monday of each month

---

Gramat

Gramat on the river Alzou is the pleasant if not very remarkable capital of the *causse*, with only a 15th-century clock tower and a watchtower that recall the town before the Wars of Religion; Gramat's baron, Gontaut d'Auriolle was an ally of Henri IV, but unfortunately for the town everyone else in the vicinity remained Catholic. These days Gramat serves as Rocamadour's tourist overflow tank, but also as a base for the many potholers who come to explore the pocked *causse* and, surprisingly, for police-dog trainers—the Gendarmerie's national kennels are here, and on Thursdays at 3pm from April to October you can watch the cops and their best friends do their stuff. Besides dogs, you can see a thousand other European animals and birds in semi-liberty as well as a botanical garden at Gramat's **Parc Animalier de Gramat** *(open 9–7, Sun and holiday mornings only Nov–Feb; adm)*.

The environs of Gramat are full of little wonders, easily explored by bike (on hire at the station). One of the most important tumuli in the Lot, jokingly known as the *Etron* ('turd') de Gargantua is just east (on the D 15) and covered with flowers that don't grow anywhere else. There are good dolmens at Pech-Farrat (east off the N 140), Ségala (up the Alzou from Gramat) and at Les Aspes, to the west on the D 39. Les Aspes is also near a sizeable *gouffre* at Ligue de Biau (inquire about access at the Gramat tourist office); at **La Pannonie**, off the D 39, the vast Mansart-roofed **Château de la Pannonie** was begun in the late 1400s as the pleasure dome of a Rocamadour merchant, and has a fine set of windows and dormers. Northeast of Gramat, **Lavergne** has an impressive *pigeonnier*, unusually built over a gate; the apse of the village's Romanesque church has *modillons* carved with lively human and animal faces. Another 2½km to the north is **Thégra**, with a harmonious 15th-century château.

South to Labastide-Murat

Further afield (10km south on the D 6477) **Le Bastit**, once an important Templar commandery serving passing pilgrims, has one of the *causse*'s most impressive *avens* (natural wells), the **Igue de la Vierge**. **Montfaucon**, to the southwest, is a charming hilltop bastide, erected by Edward II in 1292 on the English front line as a foil to the new French town of Labastide-Murat. The fine *causse* country all around is at the time of writing threatened by the construction of the A 20 motorway to Cahors, a deathly project that nearly all Lotois vigorously oppose, knowing well that one of the great charms of the area is precisely its lack of motorways. It means to cut off minor gems like **Séniergues**, 2km north of Montfaucon, a picturesque rural hamlet with a 12th-century Romanesque church and splendid views all around, and **Vaillac**, 3km south, seat of a formidable feudal castle and Romanesque church, where recently a medieval relief of the Virgin of Rocamadour was discovered.

The agricultural centre of the south *causse* is **Labastide-Murat**, founded in the 13th-century by Fortanier, the seigneur of Gourdon and named after him until 1852, when the town decided to rename itself to honour hometown boy Joachim Murat.

The King of Naples

Born in 1767, the son of the local innkeeper, the young Murat began his career by being kicked out of the army for unruly behaviour. The advent of Napoleon gave him a second chance in the wars of Italy and Egypt, where as Bonaparte's aide-de-camp Murat distinguished himself with gut-busting courage and bravado, giving substance to Napoleon's saying that each of his soldiers carried a marshal's baton in his knapsack. Murat nudged his destiny along by loyally supporting Napoleon at the *coup d'état* of 18 Brumaire (a gesture rewarded with his marriage to Caroline Bonaparte in 1800); in 1808 he crushed the May insurrection in Madrid with a brutality immortalized in Goya's paintings of the French firing squads. Pleased, Napoleon gave him the throne of Naples, which he clung to until his master's fall in 1814. The next year, like Napoleon, he attempted to regain his realm; when he landed in Italy the first peasants he met tried to kill him. Soon after the Bourbon army arrested him and shot him on the spot.

While all this was going on, Murat never forgot the folks back home, as seen by the neo-classical château he built for his brother André and the letters he sent to his mum displayed in the **Musée Murat** (in his father's auberge); amongst the memorabilia is a giant family tree showing Murat's relationship with most of the crowned heads of Europe *(open mid June–Sept 10–12 and 3–6; adm)*.

Around Labastide-Murat

To explore the wildest, most desolate part of the *causse*, the Braunhie, take the small roads between Labastide-Murat and Espédaillac, to the east; or just take a look from **Soulomès**, 3km southeast of Labastide-Murat. This was one of several Templar commanderies in the region, and the village's 14th-century Gothic church has a Templar baptismal font and highly unusual frescoes on the *Life of Christ*: the scenes of Jesus taking a stroll with Mary Magdelene, Doubting Thomas, and the Resurrected Christ with a knight (either a Templar or a Knight of St John, a member of the Order that inherited most of the Templars' property when the latter were dissolved on charges of heresy in 1308). **Caniac-du-Causse** to the east has, under its modern church, a 12th-century crypt containing the 11th-century reliquary of St Namphaise, a friend of Charlemagne who fought against the Saracens in Quercy and returned to live as a hermit, wandering about hollowing out drinking holes for the flocks of the *causse*, earning himself the devotion of the shepherds. East of Caniac, you can visit the **Gouffre de Planegrèze**, a pit descending 890ft, watered by an underground river; there's a dolmen just over the stone wall.

From Labastide-Murat the D 32 heads south through the narrow valley of the little river Vers, its clear waters reflecting the deep, steep greenery of its banks. It was favoured by those most picky of water connoisseurs, the Romans; the valley's gem of a village, **St Martin-de-Vers**, has remains of the ancient aqueduct carved in the rock that once slaked the thirst of Cahors. Downriver and to the west, **Cras** is the beginning of the road up to the haunting, slender ruins of the **Oppidum de Mursens**, a possible Uxellodunum, while the main Vers valley road continues down the Lot.

East of St-Martin-de-Vers you can hook up to the dull D 653, the fast road linking Cahors to Figeac. There are, however, possible stopovers on either side of the road: **Blars**, near the midway point, has a domed Romanesque church with carved capitals and reliefs. **Quissac** and **Espédaillac** are picturesque, sleepy villages, the former with a *Pietà* in its church from the 1600s. Just northwest of **Livernon**, one of the larger towns on the *Causse de Gramat*, you can see the biggest dolmen in the entire Lot, the **Pierre Martine** (off the D 2; walk through the scrubby trees to the end of the field). Its table stone stretches nearly 22ft long, but as massive as it is, it would wiggle at the touch of a finger until 1948, when it cracked; now concrete blocks support it. You can scramble over the stone wall near by to see a second, slightly smaller dolmen in the next field. If you aren't afraid of getting lost, leave the path between the road and the Pierre Martin to see what must have been the quarry of a score of megalithic monuments—the bare limestone gouged out and still scoured bare after millennia. From Livernon the stately D 653 leads to Assier (*see* below).

Gramat ✉ 46500

No lack of small hotels here at this touristic crossroads, beginning with the central ★★★**Le Lion d'Or**, 8 Place de la République, ✆ 65 38 73 18; solid and comfortable, with one of Gramat's best-known restaurants, and a cellar full of vin de Cahors (menus from 100–300F, with a special 220F Sunday lunch). For charm (and a pool), the prize goes to the completely renovated ★★**Le Relais des Gourmands**, 2 Av. Gare, ✆ 65 38 83 92, with cheerful rooms and a restaurant with a growing reputation for the chef's tasty versions of cassoulet; delicious duck *confits* with potatoes fried with *cèpes* on the 165F menu (other menus at 100–180F; closed Mon, and Sun in the winter). If you're just staying overnight, ★★**Du Centre**, Place de la République, ✆ 65 38 73 37, has simple modern rooms; or there's the less expensive, creeper-covered ★★**La Roulage**, 1 Av. Louis-Mazet, ✆ 65 38 71 69 and ★★**De Bordeaux**, 17 Av. du 11 Novembre, ✆ 65 38 70 10, serving a good, filling 70F menu. There are five pleasant rooms in the **Moulin de Fresquet**, a bed-and-breakfast in a 17th-century water mill less than a km from the centre, ✆ 65 38 70 60 (240–340F for two, with breakfast).

In Carlucet (14km southwest of Gramat on the D 50) the **Pizzeria Rigalou**, ✆ 65 33 17 89 serves tasty pizzas in a rustic setting, as well as other meals all year (menus from 60F).

Labastide-Murat ✉ 46240

★★**Hôtel Climat de France**, Place de la Mairie, ✆ 65 21 18 80 is a member of a small, reliable chain of hotels and has 20 rooms in a handsome stone house.

Gramat to Figeac: the Limargue

The main N 140 between Gramat and Figeac rather neatly separates the *causse* from a lush micro-region of chestnut forests and meadows called the Limargue. It has a pair of charming villages, and the remains of one of the most blustering castles ever built by man.

Tourist Information

Lacapelle-Marival: Place Halle, ✆ 65 40 81 11

Assier: Rue Lacapelle, ✆ 65 40 50 60

market days

Lacapelle-Marival has a farmers' market on Tuesdays (10–12.30 July and Aug, 5–7pm the rest of the year)

Aynac and Lacapelle-Marival

The N 140 traces an important pilgrim route, remembered in places like **L'Hôpital** (named after a hostel run by the Knights of St John, of which a chapel survives). Further southeast, tiny **Thémines** is noted for its fine *halle* with a *lauze* roof; **Rudelle** is a rather dilapidated 13th-century bastide, defended by an astonishing battlemented church built by Bertrand de Cardaillac that looks more like an overgrown rook from a chessboard than a house of God. For a scenic detour, take the D 40 north from Thémines to **Aynac**, site of a 16th-century château built by the bastard son of the Vicomte of Turenne, its four corner towers crowned with breast-shaped slate-coated cupolas; the delicate bas-relief over the door fits in perfectly, even if it was carved in 1895. Aynac's Romanesque church is also worth a look, with its octagonal tower and carved capitals. The most extraordinary thing about Aynac is the average height of its inhabitants—in the 1980s five out of 710 measured at least 6ft 6in. A skeleton found near the château was just short of 8 feet.

The capital of the Limargue, **Lacapelle-Marival** grew up around an 11th-century chapel, and was defended after the next century by the Cardaillacs' **Château de Lacapelle-Marival**, one of that powerful family's principal residences, located smack in the middle of the village; although still undergoing restoration, you can stroll along its parapet walk and take a look at its medieval frecoes *(daily July–Sept 10–12 and 3–7; adm)*. The tiny *halle* on sandstone pillars squeezed into the village centre dates from the 1400s. There's another good Romanesque church with interior carvings at **Le Bourg** at the N 140 crossroads.

Assier and its Cannonballing Egomaniac

The pleasant, tidy commune of **Assier** straddles the dramatic division between the Limargue and the Causse de Gramat. In the 16th century, much of what you see, or at least 2500 acres of it, belonged to the irrepressible braggart Galiot (Galahad) de Genouillac (1465–1546), François I's Captain General of Artillery, Master of the Horse, and Lieutenant General of Guyenne. In 1515 Galiot helped the king beat the redoubtable Swiss pikemen at the Battle of Marignano by blowing them away with cannons—the first time anyone ever employed them so in battle. As he bought up the largest property in all Quercy, he made two rich marriages to help finance a building programme that was pharaonic for 1526: a Loire Valley-style château in an immense quadrangle, numerous windmills and barns, a vaulted, 180ft stable (still standing in the village), a forge, a church, the Rockefeller Center of *pigeonniers*, and a *jeu de paume* for court tennis matches. The pile was inherited by the dukes of Uzès, who cared little for it, and by 1786 it had reached such a state of decay that the owners let builders cannibalize it for a small fee; wherever you see a carved stone incorporated in a local house, you can bet it came from the château. When Prosper Mérimée, inspector of historical monuments, came to Assier in 1841, he was touched by the romantic ruin of Galiot's pride and put it on his register to prevent the rest from going to hell. Only the relatively simple west wing of the quadrangle, the guards' quarters, remains of the once enormous **Château d'Assier** *(open daily exc Tues; Oct–Mar 10–12 and 2–5; 2–6.30 other months, July and Aug without a break; adm)*.

The exterior façade of this wing is framed by two of the château's original four towers, one sheathing Galiot's humble medieval birthplace. The once ornate dormers have all been stripped off, except for one on the left; the niche over the entrance once held an equestrian statue of Galiot. The interior façade, however, is still a handsome Renaissance work; large stone windows and walls bearing medallions of Roman emperors alternate, while bands of a frieze show swords and cannons relating to Galiot's deeds or those of Hercules, with whom Galiot fancied a resemblance. The interior, described by Brantôme as 'the best furnished in France with its vast piles of silver, tapestries and silks', now contains the sole survivor of a score of grand stairways, this one decorated with a handsome pilaster carved with grotesques, Hercules and the Nemean Lion and Galiot's trophies. A pendant in the vault showing Hercules wrestling with Ateneus is inscribed with Galiot's motto: *J'aime fortune* (a play on words, meaning either 'I love fortune' or 'I love one very much'). There's an exhibit on Galiot's career, and a hologram of his armour sent over by the Metropolitan Museum in New York.

The man's overweening self-esteem is most manifest today in Assier's **church**, built by Galiot between 1540–49 as a personal shrine to himself and his weaponry. Although Gothic in form, the decoration is Renaissance: a frieze that girdles the exterior is devoted to cannons and artillery, with nary a Christian symbol in sight (reminscent of Venice's Santa Maria Zobenigo) although in the tympanum over the door we see the Virgin—looking quite pleased to accept Galiot's military insignia from an angel—while two other angels unfurl banners reading *Vivit d. Jac. Galeotus!* ('Long live Galiot!'). Inside, under the lovely star vaulting, is Galiot's tomb, topped with a statue of you-know-who in his battle gear, leaning nonchalently against a cannon, with a braggart's epitaph and his *J'aime fort une* motto. According to the dictates of his will, 500 priests were gathered together to give him a rousing send-off at his funeral. On the Lacapelle-Marival road, you can still see Galiot's 38ft-high pigeon tenement with 2300 varnished nests, each one representing an acre of his land.

Cardaillac

Eponymous cradle of one of the oldest and most powerful families of Quercy, **Cardaillac** is a delightful old *village perché* just 3km off the N 140. Only traces of its mighty 12th-century fortifications have survived Richelieu's destruction squads of 1629, sent to punish Cardaillac for being a Protestant safe haven—Jeanne de Cardaillac, mother of Madame de Maintenon and future mother-in-law of Louis XIV, was an important Reformation figure. Another important member of the family was Hugues de Cardaillac, who wrote a code on the use of cannons in warfare (1346)—a code that his neighbour Galiot probably broke at Marignano. You can climb up to the fort's **Tour de Sagnes** for the grand views. Cardaillac also has the unique **Musée éclaté** (July and Aug 3–6), a collection of items related to Cardaillac's history and traditions not confined in the walls of a single building, but *éclaté* ('burst open') and displayed where they belong—in the old school, bakery, farm buildings, etc. The villagers founded the museum and provide an enthusiastic narration.

Lacapelle-Marival ✉ 46120

★★La Terrasse, Rte de Latronquière, ✆ 65 40 80 07, has 16 adequate rooms in a fairly nondescript building, with an equally dullish dining room. The food, however, is far from boring—try the *ris de veau au jus de cèpes* (menus from 90–200F).

Assier ✉ 46320

The **Ferme Auberge de Badouli** on the D 653 towards Le Bourg, ✆ 65 40 87 62, offers downhome Quercy cooking in a modern building (for a change); book in advance and arrive with a good appetite to do justice to the delicious *potage*, homemade terrine, *crudités*, lamb grill with garden vegetables, cheese, homemade dessert, coffee and wine—all for 100F (or plump for the even grander 150F menu).

Cardaillac ✉ 46100

Chez Marcel, ✆ 65 40 11 16 has been a local institution for decades—one that could almost be part of the village museum. The secret, time-tried formula: copious, well-prepared authentic cuisine at the best prices around—four menus all under 180F (closed Mon); there are six simple rooms to rent for 130–160F.

Figeac

Figeac, the metropolis of the Célé valley, has more than one feather in its cap. It gave the world Jean-François Champollion, the linguistic wizard who cracked Egyptian hieroglyphics, and Charles Boyer, the archetypical French lover of the silver screen (and the inspiration for Warner Bros' cartoon skunk, Pepe le Pew). Figeac is the second city of the Lot, with all of 11,000 people; it has more obelisks than Paris, and lays fair claim to flexing the *département's* industrial muscle, thanks to the aeronautics manufacturer Ratier. But for the casual unsuspecting visitor, it's Figeac's heart of golden sandstone that comes as the most charming surprise of all—if none of the individual buildings make the architectural textbooks, some 700 have been intelligently restored in the past decade to create a delightful ensemble.

History

The story goes that Pepin the Short was resting on the banks of the Célé in 753 when he saw doves suddenly fly up in the form of a cross. He founded a church (the ancestor of St-Saveur), which, the legend continues, was consecrated two years later by Pope Stephen II himself. The abbey that grew up around it linked itself with Cluny, and drew in its share of pilgrims en route to Rocamadour or Compostela. As was so often the case, the 11th and 12th centuries saw the hamlet around the abbey expand into a sizeable town that chafed at being bossed around by an abbot, and in the late 1200s Philip the Fair liberated it, replacing monastic rule with that of seven consuls, one for each quarter.

As in many mercantile towns, Protestantism made many converts in Figeac, although the Calvinists only took control in 1568 when their captain bribed the wife of a consul to steal her husband's keys while he slept and toss them over the gate. In 1598 the Edict of Nantes made Figeac a Protestant safe town; Henri IV's brilliant minister, the duke of Sully, took refuge here after the king's assassination. Sully had remained Henri IV's right-hand man (and a Protestant) even after the king decided that Paris was worth a Mass; as the powerful superindentent of finances he performed the seemingly impossible task of filling the king's war chest, promoting agriculture and building roads all across France while lowering taxes and balancing the budget. In his retirement he wrote the *Memories of wise and royal economies of the state of Henry the Great*, which subsequent superintendents of finances would have done well to study, rather than abet France's kings down their extravagant road to ruin and revolution.

If the Calvinists damaged much of Figeac's ecclesiastical patrimony, the Nazi SS in 1944 cruelly struck at the inhabitants themselves, deporting nearly every able-bodied man not employed by Ratier, which at the time made parts for the Luftwaffe. Of the 540 who went, only 395 returned from the labour and concentration camps at the end of the war.

Getting Around

Figeac's railway station is on the Brive–Toulouse line, with direct connections to Gramat, Rocamadour and Capdenac (© 65 34 10 37). The SNCF runs regular buses from Figeac to Capdenac, Toirac, Cajarc, St-Cirq-Lapopie, St-Géry and Cahors.

Tourist Information

Figeac: at the Hôtel de la Monnaie, Place Vival, © 65 34 06 25

Capdenac-le-Haut: © 65 34 17 23

market days

Figeac: Saturday mornings, and a fair on the 15th of each month

Place Vival and Around

There is something vaguely Venetian about Figeac, beginning with its medieval street plan, full of curving lanes and irregular, asymmetrical little squares, offering a wealth of visual surprises for the pedestrian. The stone houses are so tall and densely built that many are topped with covered rooftop terraces that the Venetians call *altane* and the Lotois call *soleihos*, which not only offered city dwellers a breath of fresh air but came in handy for drying clothes, fruit and other foods. Figeac has no grand central piazza like Venice, but a dozen smaller ones that form the focal points of its old neighbourhoods, like Place Vival, site of the elegant 13th-century **Hôtel de la Monnaie**. Philippe le Bel granted Figeac the privilege of minting its own coins, a dandy boost to commerce in those days; the ground floor with its pointed arches was used as a bank, while on top is a typical *soleiho*. Sharing the hôtel with the tourist office is the little **Musée du Vieux Figeac** *(open July–Aug*

10–12.30 and 3–7; other times 3–7, closed Sun; free), an eclectic collection including the beautiful Renaissance door from Sully's mansion, a set of stocks, a carving of a monk playing a drum, and more.

Just west of Place Vival runs **Rue Caviale**, one of Figeac's prettiest streets, where you can still see the house where Louis XI lodged in 1463 (no. 30). Rue Caviale gives into **Place Carnot**, Figeac's ancient market square, although sadly lacking its 13th-century grain *halle*, destroyed in 1888. Note the 15th-century house in the corner, with a turret: this was the residence of Protestant Pierre de Cisteron, master armourer of Louis XIV. Just before revoking the Edict of Nantes, Louis sent down a special safeguard for Cisteron, to keep him from the persecutions he had in store for Protestants who weren't so dear to his heart. Adjacent **Place Champollion** was long the site of the market for chestnuts—until the 19th century a staple in the local diet. The butchers had their stands under the ogival arches, and the Templars a commandery in the building with little columns on the windows, on the south side of the square. In nearby Rue Séguier is the **Musée Champollion** *(open 10–12 and 2.30–6.30, or 2–6 Nov–Feb; adm)*.

Champollion and the Rosetta Stone

Jean François Champollion, born in this much-restored 14th-century house in 1790, astonished all his teachers with his precocious aptitude for languages—by age 14 he could rattle away in Latin, Greek, Hebrew, and Arabic. While still in his teens he began studying hieroglyphics—at the time commonly believed to be mere decorations—and began a serious study of Oriental languages.

In 1799 the huge corps of scholars accompanying Napoleon's expedition to Egypt began the first systematic study of that country's antiquities (as well as scouting out the possibility of a canal through the Suez and inventing the lead pencil). It's a good thing they were around when French soldiers uncovered a fragment of polished black basalt at Rosetta, covered with inscriptions in hieroglyphics, Greek and a cursive demotic script. In 1814 the Rosetta stone ended up in the British Museum, where attempts by Thomas Young to translate it were frustrated until Champollion got hold of a copy of the text and made the essential discovery that the hieroglyphics were not only phonetic, but figurative and symbolic (described in his *Précis du système hiéroglyphique*, 1824). He spent the rest of his abbreviated life as the curator of the Egyptian section in the Louvre, translating texts in Egypt and in Paris, and leaving behind a posthumously published dictionary and grammar of hieroglyphics.

In the museum, audiovisual displays tell you exactly how Champollion cracked the code, and show the resulting translation; there are three mummies and other Egyptian arts, while outside the museum in the **Place des Ecritures** Champollion's bicentenary was celebrated with the installation of a giant facsimile of the Rosetta Stone in the pavement and the planting of a papyrus garden, all designed by American artist Joseph Kosuth.

Notre-Dame du Puy and Saint-Saveur

Figeac's churches haven't withstood the trials of time as successfully as its secular build-ings, but are nevertheless worth a look. From Place Champollion, Rue de Colomb passes some of Figeac's most aristocratic houses (note especially the fine courtyard off the pedes-trian lane, Rue Malleville), while to the right other lanes or steps lead up the hill to **Notre-Dame du Puy**. This much-tampered-with 12th-century church replaces an ancient chapel built where the Virgin made a rose bloom on Christmas day; the church's 14th-cen-tury portal retains its carving of animals, and inside there are some carved capitals from the same period. Perhaps best of all are its views over Figeac's medieval roofscape.

The most picturesque descent from Notre-Dame is by way of narrow medieval Rue Delzhens, past the **Hôtel du Viguier** (1300s), seat of the king's judge, to Rue Tomfort, where Galiot of Assier had his town house. This street continues to **Saint-Sauveur**, encased in a forgettable 19th-century façade and bell tower crowned with a giant bread box; only the large size and some much knocked-about bits on the north and south flanks hint at Figeac's once great medieval church. In the 17th century, to repair some of the damages caused in the Wars of Religion, a local sculptor decorated the former chapter-house (now a chapel off the right aisle) with naive painted reliefs of the Passion; don't miss the *Last Supper*, where the Apostles are confronted with a platter of roast hamster, or the scene of baby Jesus sleeping sweetly on a cross, dreaming of his future torments. In the nave are medieval capitals from the original portal, transformed into holy-water fonts. In the adjacent riverside Place de la Raison stands a small obelisk, a monument to Champollion.

Just before the river, Rue du Balène winds past the **Hôtel du Balène** with its huge ogival door and flamboyant windows, a building now used as a theatre and cultural centre. From here Rue Orthabadial, once the realm of the medieval abbey gardener, returns you to the Hôtel de la Monnaie.

Around Figeac: Obelisks and Capdenac

The classic Figeac excursion is to its mysterious 26ft obelisk-needles or *Aiguilles*, erected in the 12th century on the summit of two nearby hills—the **Aiguille de Lissac** to the west and the **Aiguille du Pressoir** to the south, on the colline du Cingle. Their original pur-pose has long been forgotten, but they may well have been set up by the abbey of St-Saveur to mark boundaries or to lift the spirits of pilgrims approaching over the *causse*, or to set the limits within which fugitives were guaranteed the abbey's asylum.

After the death of Henri IV, Sully divided his time between Figeac and his 14th-century castle 8km south at **Capdenac-le-Haut**, a perched, medieval town fortified with ramparts; this was one of the keys to Quercy, and was constantly besieged throughout its history. Capdenac-le-Haut lays claim to the Uxellodunum title; digs have revealed artefacts dating back to Neolithic times, most notably the torso of the *Lady of Capdenac*, from *c.* 3000 BC, one of the oldest statues ever found in France. You can see a cast of her (the original is in Cahors) as well as Roman coins and other odds and ends in the little municipal **museum** *(open Easter and from June–Aug, 10–12 and 3–7)*. Capdenac's Gallo-Roman spring/ fountain is claimed to be the very one cut off by Caesar. But Uxellodunom or no, Capdenac is a charmer, with a pair of Gothic gates, medieval lanes of sunny limestone houses and a belvedere, enjoying a bird's-eye view of the Lot and the village's own ugly stepsister, the industrial railway junction of Capdenac-Gare. East of here the corniche road leaves the Lot to wind into the chestnut forests of the Aveyron.

Figeac ✉ *46100*   ***Where to Stay***

Modern, motel-like ★★★**Des Carmes**, Enclos des Carmes, ✆ 65 34 20 78, is close to Figeac's historic centre; in the summer enjoy delicious poolside meals based on Quercy ingredients (mushrooms, lamb, vin de Cahors); good-value menus from 100 to 275F. The older, but more stylish ★★**Hostellerie Champollion Europe**, 51 Allées Victor-Hugo, ✆ 65 34 10 16, offers full en-suite baths, a winter garden and an Art Deco-kitsch touch in the public rooms. Other less expensive hotels in Figeac include ★★**Les Bains**, 1 Rue du Gruffoul, ✆ 65 34 10 89, with simple rooms directly over the waters of the Célé; the tidy provincial ★**Paramelle**, 59 Av. du Faubourg du Pin, ✆ 65 34 21 82, and perhaps nicest of all in the cheap category, ★**Le Terminus St-Jacques** by the station at 27 Av. Georges-Clemenceau, ✆ 65 34 00 43, with a bit of a garden; the restaurant serves a tender slice of beef with Roquefort sauce (menus at 80 and 120F). Basic bungalow accommodation, a beach, artificial lakelet and pool are available at the Camping Municipal Les Rives du Célé, a km from Figeac, ✆ 65 34 59 30 (open mid May–mid Sept).

Eating Out

Rivalling the aforementioned Carmes for Figeac's best food, **La Puce à l'Oreille** (flea in the ear, an expression meaning an awakened suspicion) in a 15th-century mansion at 5–7 Rue St-Thomas, ✆ 65 34 33 08, offers both traditional menus featuring snails in flaky pastry and duck *confits* as well as unusual dishes such as duck with *sabayon* (syllabub) and honey; menus from 75 to 210F (reservations suggested; closed Mon, exc in July and Aug). **Chez Marinette**, the restaurant attached to Hotel Champollion Europe (*see* above) does wonderful things with mushrooms and other traditional Quercy ingredients (menus at 80 and 120F, the latter being excellent value). Other places in the historic centre include the intimate **La Draisine**, 41 Rue Emile-Zola, ✆ 65 34 65 34, with good menus from 60 to 120F (closed Sun lunch and Wed) and the **Pizzeria del Portel**, 9 Rue Orthabadial, ✆ 65 34 53 60, for a good selection of fairly authentic Italian pizzas, good salads and pasta dishes (pizzas 30–40F, closed Mon).

The Célé Valley

The Lot's merriest river, the Célé (from the Latin *celer*, or rapid) is born in the harsh lands of the Cantal, but once past Figeac this clear and shallow stream takes on a softer quality as it splashes through gentle valleys and steep colourful gorges protected by cliff forts, the so-called *châteaux des Anglais* left over from the Hundred Years' War. In the off-season the tiny hamlets along the river are almost deserted; come before the first tourist wave of Easter and you may think you've landed in a Quercy Brigadoon. Until the 1700s the valley was famous for its saffron, grown mostly as a dye and marketed by German merchants. Not a trace of a saffron remains, in spite of the local appetite for paella—a dish introduced by the many refugees from the Spanish Civil War who settled in southwest France. This is ideal walking country: pick up a copy of the *Randonnées pédestres entre Lot et Célé* available at Figeac and other area tourist offices.

Tourist Information

Marcilhac-sur-Célé: ✆ 65 40 61 43

Cabrerets: ✆ 65 31 27 12

From Figeac to Espagnac-Sainte-Eulalie

Six km west of Figeac, leave the D 13 for the picturesque riverside D 41 near the much restored, fat-towered 15th–16th century **Château Ceint d'Eau**. Soon to the right, just beyond a ruined Romanesque chapel is a road leading up to tiny **Camboulit**, a charming medieval hill village as yet not given over to holiday homes. The valley narrows once past Boussac, where overhanging cliffs similar to those along the Vézère in Périgord were used as shelters or fortresses in the Middle Ages. In and around **Corn**, an old farming village, are fortified caves from the Hundred Years' War as well as a pair of 17th-century chateaux on either side of the river.

Espagnac-Sainte-Eulalie, another 9km downstream, is perhaps the most photographed beauty spot along the Célé, a tiny hamlet watched over by a striking *clocher*, a slender tower crowned by an open-work timbered chamber with a bell from the 1500s and a pointy octagonal roof, the whole almost too quaint to be real. This belongs to a convent fittingly named **Notre-Dame-du-Val-Paradis**, founded in the 12th century but greatly expanded in the next by its benefactor, Aymeric d'Hébrard of Carjac, a member of the area's leading family and bishop of Coimbra in Portugal. The convent, which survived until the Revolution, incorporated all the buildings within the towered gateway, including the pleasant communal *gîtes*.

Once you've gone this far, chances are you will have met Madame, the guide to the little church of **Notre-Dame** (her house is marked with a sign). The bell tower isn't the only quaint thing about it; note how the pentagonal apse rears up abruptly, a full storey higher than the rest of the church. The portal, decorated with carved ivy and fig leaves, leads into an interior half rebuilt after fires in the 15th century. There are

A pigeonnier

three tombs: those of Aymeric d'Hébrard, the knight Hugues de Cardaillac-Brengues (d. 1342) and his elegant wife, Bernade de Trian, niece of Pope John XXII. The choir is decorated with the arms of the Cardaillacs and little mitred heads. On the high altar, a gilt wooden retable from the 1700s displays a badly restored copy of an altarpiece by Vouet, showing Louis XIV's mum, Anne of Austria, floating up to heaven in the guise of the Virgin of the Assumption.

The next village, **Brengues** is an old Cardaillac fief, built on a bluff over the river that conceals a *château des Anglais*. The Hébrards came from the next village, **Saint-Sulpice**, partially built into the curve of its cliff, where the much restored 12th-century château is still in the family. In the Middle Ages this was a cradle of bishops, soldiers and diplomats who served in important posts across Europe; the Hébrards owned so much of the Célé valley that it was nicknamed the 'Hébrardie'.

Marcilhac-sur-Célé

With a population of 240, **Marcilhac-sur-Célé** is one of the larger villages in the valley. It owes its existence to a powerful Benedictine abbey founded by Pepin the Short, which by the 12th century possessed over a hundred properties, including Rocamadour. Its abbots, however, had failed to foresee Rocamadour's potential—unlike the bishops of Tulle, who made it a prestigious pilgrimage site. When the pilgrims (and profits) starting piling in, Marcilhac naturally wanted it back, leading to an unseemly conflict that saw each side booting out the other's monks. In the end, Marcilhac surrendered its claim in exchange for cash. Badly pillaged in the Hundred Years' War, the Hébrards of Saint-Sulpice took the abbey under their wing in 1451 and rebuilt the damaged bits in the Gothic style; this was in turn destroyed by the Protestants. A few monks hung on until the Revolution.

There are more ducks than people here now, but along the Célé they are still defended by the thick medieval buttreses topped with little carved figures mysteriously called 'conspirators' heads'. The path from Place des Platanes leads past the curious capitals on the outside of the Romanesque chapterhouse, carved with scenes of heaven and hell in two distinct styles. The lofty, grandiose ruins of the bays and narthex of the abbey's Romanesque church form a kind of courtyard around what is now Marcilhac's parish **church**, rebuilt by the Hébrards in the Gothic style to replace the once-vast Romanesque apse and ambulatory. The interior is decorated with Hébrard coats-of-arms and 15th-century frescoes, 17th-century panelling and a copy of a Van Dyck *Virgin and Child* in the retable. Note the angel's head with a teasing smile on the pew with the heraldic carvings. Step outside what was the Romanesque church's south portal to see the rare Carolingian tympanum, a triangular composition of bas-reliefs. Christ on top is framed by symbols of the sun and moon, while two angels below grip instruments of the Passion, and at the bottom stand SS. Peter and Paul.

Two km northwest of Marcilhac, a steep hairpin road zigzags up to the **Grotte de Bellevue**, discovered in 1964, full of curious red and white stalactites and stalagmites; one is called the 'jellyfish' *(open Palm Sun–Oct; © 65 40 63 92 for hours)*.

Beyond the old village of **Sauliac-sur-Célé** (a lovely place for a riverside picnic, over-looking a dilapidated château) is the narrow but well-signposted road up to Cuzals and the **Musée en Plein Air du Quercy**. This re-creates with original buildings two traditional farms, one pre-Revolution and one from the early 1900s, along with 25 little museums of crafts, agriculture, water and natural sciences; examples of rural architecture, a dentist's surgery from 1900, an antique carousel, and more; there's also a picnic ground and snack bar *(© 65 22 58 63, open 1 Apr–1 Nov: Apr Mon–Fri guided tours at 10.30 and 3; May Mon–Sat tours at 10.30 and 3, Sun and holidays unguided visits from 10–7; June, Sun–Fri, unguided visits 9.30–6.30; July–Sept, Sun–Fri unguided visits 10–5; Oct, Mon–Fri, guided tours at 2.30, Sun unguided visits from 1–5.30; adm exp, but ticket good for a week).*

Cabrerets and Pech Merle

Set back against the cliffs of the Célé, **Cabrerets** is the site of a dramatic *château des Anglais* known this time as the *château du Diable* (devils and Englishmen were often syn-onymous in the Middle Ages). Downstream, on top of a high bluff is the much restored 14th-century **Château de Cabrerets**, owned by the Gontaut-Birons until the Revolution. The main reason for visiting, however, is 4km up the road from Cabrerets, the **Grotte du Pech Merle**, the finest prehistoric painted cave still open to visitors since the closing of Lascaux *(open Palm Sun–1 Nov 9.30–12 and 1.30–6; adm)*. The original entrance had been blocked up at the end of the last Ice Age, and the cave was only rediscovered in 1922 by 16-year-old André David, son of the owner of Pech Merle, and his fried Henri Dutertre. Inspired by the exploration of caves by Abbé Lemozi, a native of Cabrerets, they wormed and scrambled their way through a narrow 120m passage and found exactly what they dreamed of finding—a magnificent work of nature that inspired and suggested magnificent works of art back in the dawn of time.

Some 80 drawings of animals and humans and hundreds of symbols decorate a third of Pech Merle's mile of passageways, spanning three distinct artistic styles from the Solutrean to the Magdalenian periods (20,000–15,000 BC). The tour begins with the **Chapel of the Mammoths**, an arched gallery carved by an underground river with a great spiral frieze of mammoths, horses and bison outlined in black around a horse; one artist took advantage of the bulge in the rock to paint a mammoth in natural relief—a fine example of 'non-polar-ized' art, void of any north–south or up–down orientation. The frieze is believed to date from the Aurignacian or early Magdalenian age (15,000–14,000 BC), while the traces of red date back from the first cave users. Here too is the **Ceiling of Hieroglyphs** (what Abbé Breuil called 'macaroni'), covered with finger drawings of female and animal figures and mysterious circular signs dating from all periods.

From here the cave descends to the **Hall of Discs**, named after the rare calcite concentra-tions in upright concentric circles caused by water dripping slowing through hairline fissures in rock. Even more extraordinary are the footprints in the upper gallery, left by a woman and her 12-year old child in the muddy clay of a natural dam at least 12,000 years ago. The next drawing is known as 'the wounded man'—a long figure hidden along the ceiling, pierced by arrows, with a bull and mysterious red signs, all from the Magdalenian age. Beyond are the famous white or red cave pearls (pisolites), part of the upper **Geological Network**, culminating in the magnificent **Red Hall**, with stalactites and columns formed by dripping limestone and oxides. Near a batch of cave pearls are curious figures, believed to be an artistic synthesis of female forms and racing bisons.

The visit re-enters the prehistoric section by way of the **Bear's Gallery**, with signs of claw marks and a bear's head carved faintly in the wall. Beyond is Pech Merle's best known work, the two beautiful **spotted horses**, fat yet graceful beasts reminiscent of ancient Chinese figures, one with its delicate head drawn on a natural protuberance in the rock. The spots spill out of the outlines while six feminine 'negative hands' (made by blowing paint over hands) seem to be yearning to stroke or hold the horses. Over the horses is a rare picture of a fish—a large pike. Lastly, the **Combel Gallery** has the extraordinary root of a living oak for its ceiling; bears' lairs are hollowed out in the floor and a cache of bear bones was discovered here.

The **Musée Amédée-Lemozi** (same hours as Pech Merle) is near the entrance to the cave. Devoted to the study of Quercy's prehistory, it has a collection ranging from the Lower Paleolithic to the Iron Age: engraved pebbles, tools, Bronze Age swords, pots and small works of art discovered in over a hundred sites, as well as photos of decorated caves and a film.

Where to Stay and Eating Out

Boussac ✉ 46100

Between Figeac and Corn, the *ferme-auberge* **Domaine des Villedieu**, ✆ 65 40 06 63, is a duck farm offering meals in its apple orchard: garnished duck dishes (*confit de canard*, *magret* grilled or on the spit) for 50F, or you can order the whole whack with foie gras (175F) or the house speciality, *magret Rossini*, duck breast with truffles, foie gras and Madeira sauce.

Marcilhac-sur-Célé ✉ 46160

In the centre, ★**Hôtel des Touristes**, ✆ 65 40 65 61, offers four simple tidy rooms and inexpensive meals in the 60F range. Book early for a chance at a room in **Les Tilleuls**, ✆ 65 40 62 68, a superb bed-and-breakfast in a Quercy house with a shady lawn; pretty rooms for 200F for two, including breakfast (closed Nov–Dec). Near the church is a communal *gîte*, with a dozen beds and kitchen facilities, open Easter–Oct.

Cabrerets ✉ 46330

★★**Des Grottes**, ✆ 65 31 27 02, a simple hotel with a pool. There's a friendly **bed-and-breakfast** opposite the Mairie, ✆ 65 30 25 46, with rooms for 150F for two with breakfast. Near the entrance to Pech Merle, the tranquil ★★**Auberge de la Sagne**, ✆ 65 31 26 62, is a charming old inn set in lovely gardens.

Sometime in the deep dark past the letters in the Celtic name *Olt* were jiggled to create the Lot, a river with more bends and curls in it than Goldilocks' ringlets; if you stretched it out from its source in the Lozère to Aiguillon, where it flows into the Garonne, it would measure 471km—all that, to travel a mere 270km as the crow flies. Taking its own sweet way, the Lot wanders through three distinct landscapes. Above Vers it is closed in by colourful limestone cliffs that the feudal lords of Quercy found convenient to carve out as nearly inaccessible *châteaux des Anglais* or to use as bases for their castles.

Beyond Vers the cliffs have been worn down into *cévennes*, rounded but arid rocky hills covered with scrub oak where vineyards were planted in the Middle Ages; in the rich alluvial soil of the meanders are tobacco and walnut farms. From Cahors down to Fumel, the typical Lot valley landscape is asymmetrical—*cévennes* on one bank, spacious valley on the other, cut by seemingly wayward loops, or *cingles*, similar to those of the Dordogne. Beyond Cahors, where the Ice Age glaciers dumped gravel, grow the postwar Cahors vineyards. The scene changes again downriver at Fumel; the *cévennes* give way to isolated hills, locally called *pechs*. The river gives up its sharp bends in the wide valleys; the vines give way to plum orchards, the source of the renowned prunes of Agen.

Getting Around

By bus: Since the train has been discontinued (but *see* p.259, 'Getting Around, Cahors') the SNCF runs several buses a day between Cahors station and Figeac stopping at Vers, St-Géry, Conduché, St-Cirq-Lapopie, Cajarc, Montbrun, Toirac, Capdenac and Figeac.

By boat: In 1990 the Lot was made navigable again between St-Cirq-Lapopie and Luzech, thanks to the repair and installation of 14 locks. The pleasure-boat season runs from April to 15 Nov; three firms offer day and half-day excursions: Safaraid at Cahors and Vouziès, © 65 30 22 84 or 65 31 26 83; Coche d'Eau (with a restaurant) at Cahors, © 65 22 67 80 or 53 66 74 43; Navilot at Caix, near Luzech, © 65 20 13 31. Antinéa-Loisirs at Douelle has excursions on wide-bottomed *gabares* by the hour, © 65 30 95 79. You can also hire your own boat in Bouziès from Safaraid (*see* above); in Cahors from Baboumarine, © 65 30 08 99 or Lot Plaisance, © 65 35 36 87; in Douelle from Blue Line, © 68 20 08 79 or Port de Douelle, © 65 30 95 85; in Luzech from Locaboat Plaisance, © 65 30 71 11.

Tourist Information

Cajarc: Tour de Ville, © 65 40 72 89

St-Cirq-Lapopie: Place du Sombral, © 65 31 29 06 or 65 31 23 22

Capdenac to St-Cirq-Lapopie

To follow the Lot west of Capdenac, you'll have to cross over the bridge at Capdenac-Gare and follow the scenic D 86 along the south bank as far as the bridge to **Saint-Pierre-**

Toirac, a pleasant village named after its 12th-century Romanesque church. In the 1300s, this doubled as the base for the town's defensive tower; the walls were thickened, and an upper rooom was added over the vaults. There are rustic carved capitals inside, and some recently-discovered Merovingian sarcophaguses outside.

Larroque-Toirac is spread under the lofty donjon of its singular **château** *(open for guided tours daily from 9 July–9 Sept at 10, 12, 2 and 6; adm)*. Dating from the 12th century, it passed to the Cardaillac family, whose fidelity to France in the Hundred Years' War invited numerous sieges before the English succeeded in taking it in 1372. It burnt down soon afterwards, was rebuilt in the next century and considerably restored in the 1920s. The high, pentagonal donjon, now cut off with a sloping roof, originally stood an incredible hundred feet higher until it was cut down to size in the Revolution; in the lofty manor house, served by a spiral Romanesque stair, are some fine chimneypieces and furnishings. Prettily situated **Montbrun** has the ruins of another Cardaillac castle, overlooking the grand belvedere on the south bank, known as **Saut de la Mounine** (Monkey's Leap). The cruel lord of Montbrun, furious at his daughter's choice of lovers, had ordered her to be tossed off the cliff; a kindly hermit dressed up a monkey in the girl's clothing and hurled it off in her place. The sight made the lord of Montbrun deplore his cruelty, and when he found out he had been duped, he immediately forgave his daughter. What she thought about him wasn't recorded.

Next downriver, spread across a loop of the Lot is **Cajarc**, a pleasant riverside resort with a beach and extremely popular *plan d'eau* (manmade lake). Georges Pompidou had a holiday home in the village, and served on the town council when de Gaulle insisted that his ministers hold posts in local government to keep in contact with the people. Pompidou's strongest influence on Cajarc was an abiding passion for contemporary art, expressed in the temporary exhibits in the **Centre d'Art contemporain européen** *(open daily except Tues, Apr–Oct, closed 12–2)*. There are many fine medieval houses in the teardrop-shaped boulevard (especially the 13th-century Maison de Hébrardie) and, less than a kilometre north, a pretty 90ft waterfall that, alas, dries up in the summer.

Château de Cénevières

Perched on a lofty cliff over the river, the **Château de Cénevières** *(© 65 31 27 33, open daily Easter–1 Nov, 10–12 and 2–6)*, marks a strategic point that has been fortified since the cows came home. Here in 763 Pepin the Short came, hunting down Waiofer, the last Merovingian duke of Aquitaine; in the 13th century, the lords of Gourdon constructed the first castle to spite the English. In the 1500s its lord was yet another master of the royal artillery, this one ripely named Flottard de Gourdon, who served François I with his buddy Galiot de Genouillac and married Marguerite de Cardaillac. The château was embellished and enlarged in the Renaissance style; Flottard's son Antoine converted to Protestantism, and in 1580 the future Henri IV stopped here, to plot his attack on Cahors. During the Revolution, local sans-culottes arrived to burn this symbol of feudalism to the ground. The custodian open the door and invited them in—to the wine cellar. They were soon drunk as skunks; afterwards they half-heartedly vandalized a bit here and there and staggered home, and Cénevières stands to this day.

Near the entrance to the château is the little Protestant temple added by Antoine. Of the medieval castle, only the donjon remains, although it's hardly recognizable behind the ornate dormers and windows that stylistically meld it to the Renaissance sections added by Flottard and son. These are richly appointed with period furnishings and tapestries; there's an ornate chimney, a complex stair, charmingly painted coffered ceilings, a vast kitchen and an unusual *Salle d'Alchimie* decorated with 16th-century frescoes; never fully explained, the paintings seem to express some alchemical allegory.

Saint-Cirq-Lapopie

Saint-Cirq appeared to me, embraced by Bengal fires—like an impossible rose in the night...I no longer have any desire to be any-where else. I believe the secret of its poetry is related to certain of Rimbaud's inspirations, the product of the rarest balance in the most perfect gradiation of relief. The enumeration of its other qualities can never exhaust this secret...

André Breton

If a hard-nosed urban surrealist like Breton melts at the sight, you can gather that the prettiest village in Quercy must be quite a looker. The setting is spectacular; St-Cirq (pronounced Sain-Seer) hovers 330ft above the Lot, overlooking the kind of dramatic, sheer cliffs beloved of Romantic poets. Its architecture is pure, harmoniously medieval—and rigorously preserved and protected. In season parking is nearly as difficult as at Rocamadour—there's a car park just west of St-Cirq, next to the belvedere. In the summer, get there early to avoid the disgorging coachloads; on the other hand, in winter you may well have it all to yourself.

St-Cirq began as a Gallo-Roman villa called Pompéjac, owned by the 7th-century bishop of Cahors, St Didier. It was the last possession of Waiofer of Aquitaine to be conquered by Pepin, and gave its name to the La Popie family who made it their bailiwick. In the 13th century, its strategic importance was such that the site was shared by the lords of Gourdon, Cardaillac and La Popie (later succeeded by the Hébrards), each of whom had their own castle, linked together at the top of the town. Such rare cooperation failed to keep the English out in the Hundred Years' War: not once but three times in the 14th-century they scaled the sheer cliff and surprised the French barons. In 1471 Louis XI ordered the contiguous castles to be destroyed to punish the Hébrards for siding with the English. Enough, however, remained intact to cause trouble in the Wars of Religion, until the future Henri IV ordered the site razed to keep out the Catholics, leaving only a few crumbling but wonderfully panoramic **walls** above the church; many of the cut Gothic stones were incorporated into the houses of St-Cirq.

The **church**, built by master mason Guillaume Capelle between 1522–40, is now the most prominent building in St-Cirq, its buttressed apse high on the bluff, its turreted watchtower running up the side of the stout bell tower. To the left of the portal are two medieval grain measures; inside, the church incorporates a Romanesque chapel, with carved capitals of Judith and Holofernes. The font is held up by a Gallo-Roman capital. Near the church you'll find St-Cirq's most medieval and picturesque lane, **Ruelle de la Fourdonne**, and the main street, the Grand-Rue, lined with 15th- and 16th-century houses; along the way look out for the lampholder with a head carved on it. The Château de la Gardette holds the **Musée Rignault** *(open Apr-Oct 10–12 and 2–7)* and a collection of art from Africa and Oceania. The names of Rue de la Pélissaria and Rue de la Payrolerie recall two formerly important trades in St-Cirq: skin dressing and copper cauldron making. Another was wood turning, and from 1810 to recently, the village was known for the manufacture of box-wood taps for barrels. These days most of the residents are artists, following in the footsteps of Man Ray and Foujita, who came to stay with André Breton.

St-Cirq Lapopie to Cahors

One scenic way to continue downriver is to walk the towpath cut in the rock below St-Cirq that runs 5km west to **Bouziès**; it's part of the GR 36, and is marked with red and white signs. On the way note the relief carved into the cliff. Little Bouziès is the chief pleasure-boat port on the Lot; here in the cliffs is another fortified cave, or *château des Anglais*. Opposite is the little medieval hamlet of **Bouziès Bas**, while Pech Merle is just to the north (*see* p.249). **Vers**, where the little Vers river ripples down to meet the Lot, has grooves cut in the rock left by the Roman aqueduct that follows the pretty Vers valley; the church under the cliffs, **Notre-Dame-des-Velles** ('of the sails') was long a boatman's chapel and has a 12th-century apse decorated with *modillons*.

On the south bank, **Arcambal** has a castle, restored in the 19th century; the town marks the eastern limits of the region producing vin de Cahors (*see* below). The name of **Laroque-des-Arcs** on the north bank recalls the arches of the Roman aqueduct where it crossed the Lot. It had three storeys, like the Pont du Gard, but was demolished in 1370 by the consuls of Cahors to keep the English from seizing it. Nowadays Laroque's chief land-mark is its little chapel of St-Roch on a bluff, with the wall of a *château des Anglais* below. Laroque-des-Arc's castle, **Château de Polminhac**, with its great round 13th-century donjon, began as a *borie*, or fortified country farm, built by a branch of the Gourdon family.

From Laroque-des-Arcs, you can make a scenic detour 8km north on the narrow D 22 to visit the even more imposing **Château de Roussillon** (also visible off the main N 20 north of Cahors). Surrounded by a dry moat, it was begun in the 12th century and rebuilt in subsequent centuries as one of the city's chief defences. Cannibalized for its stone in the 19th century, the still-mighty remnants house a swell place to spend the night (*see* below).

St-Cirq-Lapopie ✉ 46330

Built in the 13th century, intimate and friendly ★★★**La Pélissaria**, ℂ 65 31 25 14 has eight wonderful rooms in the lower part of the village, two rooms housed in tiny houses of their own; for the best views, request no. 4 (open April–mid Nov); the restaurant has only a few tables, so reserve for a chance to try its delicious canapés and fresh homemade pasta (around 150F, dinner only, closed Thurs). Also in a medieval house in the centre of St-Cirq, ★★**Auberge du Sombral**, ℂ 65 31 26 08, also has eight charming rooms under its steep-pitched roof (open Apr–mid Nov); the restaurant serves a delicious *gratin aux cèpes* and trout in old Cahors wine à la carte, but also good food on its 100 and 150F menus (closed Tues night and Wed). There are also two camp sites to choose from, both of which fill up fast, so book ahead: **Camping de la Plage**, at Porte Roque, ℂ 65 30 29 51, by the river, with kayaks and bikes to rent, and up on the *causse*, **La Truffière**, Rte de Concots, ℂ 65 30 20 22, open year round with plenty of trees and a pool.

Bouziès ✉ 46330

★★**Les Falaises**, ℂ 65 30 23 87, is a large country hotel overlooking the cliffs of the Lot; a heated pool and tennis court will keep you fit, and the hotel hires out motor boats and mountain bikes (closed Dec and Jan, exc Christmas holidays). The restaurant serves good, reasonably priced Quercy cuisine (menus at 75, 95, 125 and 240F).

Vers ✉ 46090

Vers is endowed with a pair of moderate hotels: modern but attractive ★★**Les Châlets**, ℂ 65 31 40 83, with balconies overlooking the charming Vers river; it also has a pool and good restaurant specializing in fresh trout (menus from 70F; open Mar–Nov). In an old stone farmhouse, ★**La Truite Dorée**, ℂ 65 31 46 13, offers good rooms and an amoeba-shaped pool (closed Dec).

Lamagdelaine ✉ 46090

The gourmet star on this stretch of the river is **Marco**, in Lamagdelaine, just east of Laroque-des-Arcs, ℂ 65 35 30 64, where Claude Marco performs magic with local ingredients—*canette aux pêches de vigne* (duckling with rustic vineyard peaches), or tender titbits of *causse* lamb prepared with parsley and truffles; excellent-value menus at 120 and 200F (closed Sun night and Mon outside of season, and Jan and Feb).

Laroque-des-Arcs ✉ 46090

Near the river, ★★**Beau Rivage**, ℂ 65 35 30 58, is a classic French inn with big cedars in the garden; ask for a room at the back (closed Nov–Mar).

In the still-intact section of the **Château de Roussillon**, ℂ 65 36 87 05, are vast bed-and-breakfast rooms (from 320–520F) and a gîte for 4–5 people let weekly.

South of the Lot: the Causse de Limogne

South of the Lot rises the dry, sparsely populated Causse de Limogne. More wooded and less dramatic than the Causse de Gramat, its rocky emptiness is dotted with dolmens, magnificent *pigeonniers*, abandoned walls and stone huts. Lavender is grown commercially here, and most of the Lot's truffles hide out near the roots of its twisted dwarf oaks. From November to February you can watch men with little baskets under their arms, dickering at what is modestly claimed to be 'the world's biggest truffle market' at **Lalbenque** (Tuesday afternoons). Lalbenque is south of Arcambal and has a fine carved 18th-century wayside cross by the fire station, but otherwise holds little of interest when the aromatic tubers aren't in season. Five km to the northwest are the pretty farms and full-sailed windmill of **Cieurac**, as well as the ruined priory of Pauliac, a daughter of the abbey of Marcilhac, and the 15th-century **Château de Cieurac** *(open daily exc Thurs, July–mid Sept, 10–12 and 4–6; adm)*, which has retained its sculpted portal, carved stair and mullioned windows, in spite of being put to the torch by the retreating Germans in the last war. The other main 'sight' in the area is the exceedingly vast public wash basin (*lavoir*) of **Aujols**. Are the locals laundry-proud, we asked; or do they overindulge in too many salads of dandelion greens (*pissenlits* in French)? 'No, no, that's just the way it is,' the little old lady assured us.

There's another seasonal truffle market on Fridays in **Limogne-en-Quercy**, the capital of the *causse*, but a town as dull as Lalbenque. It does have a pair of old-fashioned mills: a working windmill at Promilhanes with demonstrations on summer Sundays, and a walnut-oil mill, the Moulin de Varaire, operated daily by donkey power. **Beauregard** to the south is a bastide founded by the abbot of Marcilhac with a very pretty 14th-century market coiffed with a gorgeous *lauze* roof; you can still see the original grain measures cut into the stone. Lavender-scented **Laramière** to the east has the département's second largest dolmen (off the D 55), the **Dolmen de la Borie du Bois** as well as a charming 12th-century priory, restored by the Jesuits after damages in the Wars of Religion. There are sculptures from the 1300s in the chapel, a room to put up pilgrims en route to Compostela, and a lovely chapterhouse, decorated with geometric designs and effigies of St Louis and his wife, Blanche de Castille *(tours on request, closed Tues)*. To continue south of here into the Valley of the Bonnette, *see* p.315.

Where to Stay and Eating Out

Lalbenque (46230) is the resort centre of the *causse*, with two hotels: modern white ★★★**L'Aquitaine**, west of town on the N 20, ℂ 65 21 00 51, with a pool, tennis and restaurant (80–160F, closed Sun lunch, Sun night and Mon) and in the centre, ★**Lion d'Or**, ℂ 65 31 60 19, a Logis de France with eight simple rooms and a little restaurant (70–110F, closed Sat).

> *Towards Cahors the country changes, and has something of a savage*
> *aspect; yet houses are seen everywhere, and one-third of the area is*
> *under vines. That town is bad.*

Arthur Young, *Travels in France* (1787–89)

The immediate surroundings of Cahors are some of the most discouraging landscapes in all France. In winter, the hardscrabble grey *causse* hills that glower over the town appear desertlike and eerie, and in summer they do not significantly improve. The anomic clutter of the newer parts of town matches them well, but persevere—in the middle you'll find a medieval city of surprising subtlety and character; its star attraction is the Pont Valentré which, as any Frenchman will tell you, is the most beautiful bridge on this planet.

History

A man from Cahors is a *Cadurcien*, just to remind us that the capital of the Lot department began its career as *Divona Cadurcorum*. Divona was the name of the sacred spring that still flows under the riverside cliffs, or perhaps of the Celtic goddess who presided over it. Cadurcarum refers to the Cadurcii, the local tribe who probably had their capital here before the arrival of the Romans. Under Roman rule, Divona Cadurcorum was famous for exporting linen; the town boasted an aqueduct, well-appointed public baths, and a theatre with room for 1000. It isn't known whether any of these were still working when the town became embroiled in a civil war among the Franks in the 570s and got thoroughly trashed. Fortunately, not long after, a strong-willed bishop named Desiderius took matters in hand; even more fortunately, this Gallo-Roman gentleman, later to be declared Saint Didier, was also royal treasurer to King Dagobert, and he found enough loose change to resurrect Cahors at a time when very little was being built anywhere else in Gaul. By the time he died, *c.* 650, Cahors's first cathedral was well under way, and its Roman bridges and aqueduct were restored.

Further insults were in store—unwelcome visits by Vikings, Magyars and Arabs—but Cahors survived to find a brilliant and surprising career in the Middle Ages. The bishops still ruled, and did quite well for themselves, gradually gaining control of most of the Lot valley and becoming a factor that even the French and the counts of Toulouse had to take into consideration. Under their stable rule, the town began to learn to make money. The founders of Cahors's great foray into modern capitalism seem to have been Italians, 'Lombard' merchants who fled north to the relative safety of the bishops' domains from the terrors of the Albigensian Crusade in the early 1200s; among the old palaces of Cahors you will find family names like Dominici, Issalda and Grossia.

Throughout the 13th century these families and their native colleagues perfected their skill at merchant finance and moneylending. They became familiar figures in all the trade fairs and business centres of Europe, so prominent—and so predatory—that *Caorsin* became a common French word for a usurer. Dante mentions them in the *Inferno* (canto XI, 50); he put the Caorsins down with the people of Sodom in the third circle of hell. No doubt they laughed all the way to the bank. The king of France needed them, whenever he was in the mood for a campaign; the noblemen and the Church needed them too, and they got on just fine with the town's bishops. In 1270, the bishop granted the merchants a proper city charter, establishing rule by elected consuls.

As their wealth piled up, the merchants translated it into impressive palaces along the main streets. Cahors's golden age, which lasted until the Hundred Years' War, produced not only these, but a new set of fortifications, magnificent bridges, a university and the completion of the cathedral. Even more money flowed in after 1316, when a Cahors merchant's son named Jacques Duèze became Pope John XXII. John reigned from Avignon, where he acquired a somewhat sinister reputation as an alchemist. One story has him bewitching the cardinals with a magic knife to secure his election. Another account has him quarrelling with a competitor in sorcery, another bishop of Cahors no less, and eventually having the man burned at the stake for trying to do him in with wax voodoo dolls and potions made of spiders and toads.

Cahors suffered from the Hundred Years' War only indirectly. Its new walls were good enough to keep the English out, but the disruption of trade meant a slow but inexorable strangling of its business affairs. The refined little city carried on, making a modest living off its rents and the wine trade and devoting its energies to higher things. During the Renaissance Cahors had a reputation as a cultured city, full of academies and libraries; its university lasted until 1751, when the jealous scholars of Toulouse succeeded in having it merged into their own.

During the religious wars, Cahors with its still-influential bishops remained stoutly Catholic. In 1560, there was a bloody massacre of Protestants; 20 years later, Henri IV stormed the city, and in retaliation the future king allowed his troops to give the place a thorough sacking. Not much has happened since; after 600 years of decline, Cahors is comfortable enough in its somnolence, a town with no industry, no economic base to speak of save the paper-stampers of the prefecture and departmental council.

The Poet of the Nipple

Cahors gave birth to several exceptional, obstinate men, with Pope John XXII and Léon Gambetta (*see* below) at the top of the list. A third was the poet Clément Marot (1495–1544), son of a Cadurcien mother and the Norman poet Jean Marot, *valet de chambre* of François I. Sent to Paris at age 11, Clément went into the service of the king's sister, Marguerite d'Angoulême, and soon made a mark at court for his elegant verse, if not for his personal charms; contemporaries described him as looking 'like a skinned rat'.

Marguerite was known for protecting Protestants, and Clément Marot was often suspected of being one, especially in 1526 when he was chucked into prison for eating bacon during Lent. His eloquent plea to the king, the *Epître au roi* got him out of the calaboose overnight, and the next year he succeeded his father as *valet de chambre*.

Although Marot remained faithful to the medieval forms of his father in his ballads and rondels, he was the first French poet to write in sonnets. When he got into trouble again in 1534, and was forced into exile in Italy, he regained favour with the invention of the *blason* (a short poem eulogizing an attribute of a lady) with his *Blason du beau tétin* ('to the beautiful nipple'). It was an immediate success: Clémont, 'the Prince of Poets', was welcomed back to court in 1536. But he was too honest to take much comfort in fashion; bored by his vast number of imitators that cropped up, he wrote the *Contre-blason du laid tétin* ('anti-blason to the ugly nipple')—setting a new fad for indelicate satires. Then he published *L'Enfer*, inspired by his stay in prison and today considered his greatest work. At the time, however, it caused such an uproar that he was forced to leave France yet again, and for the last time; he died alone in Turin in 1544.

Walking Cahors

Cahors's charms are discreet, and most tourists have little time for them. But a bit of knowledge and a careful eye can make this well-preserved and genteel medieval town come alive. First, pay no attention to the broad and leafy Boulevard Gambetta, pretending to be the centre of town. This is merely the course of the city's old walls; everything of interest is squeezed between it and the river. Instead, for a panorama of Cahors's medieval skyline most people never see, start from across the river, over the Pont de Cabessut.

Long and narrow Cahors had a single main thoroughfare (Rue du Château du Roi north of the cathedral, Rue Nationale south of it). Along this are most of the merchants' palaces; to each side, the ranks of tiny alleys crowded with tall houses give an idea of how dense and urban the medieval town must have seemed. Many of these alleys are partially covered; if so they are not called *ruelles*, but *botes*, a word meaning 'vaults' that is peculiar to Cahors. The medieval palaces, built in grey stone, are spare and squarish, with big arches facing the street for the business façades and elegant twinned windows on the family quarters upstairs; less imposing buildings were made *en colombage*, in half-timbering, and scores of these survive. In the 1400s, Cahors developed a distinct style of decoration, surrounding doors and windows with carved rosettes and *bâtons écotés* (raised mouldings). Another feature is the *soleiho*, a Venetian-style sun porch on the top storey (as in Figeac); in Renaissance palaces they are often made of brick arches and called *mirandes*.

Getting Around

Cahors is on Eurolines' coach route from London to Toulouse, an uncomfortable 20hr journey that beats the train in that you don't have to go through Paris and change stations; in Cahors get tickets at Belmon, 2 Bd Gambetta, © 65 35 59 30. The railway station (© 65 22 50 50) is near the centre, with frequent connections north towards Gourdon, Souillac and Paris, and south towards Montauban and Toulouse; this is the base of SNCF buses towards Fumel and Figeac. Although the Cahors–Capdennac tracks along the Lot are no longer used for regular service, the 1950s omnibus *Micheline* now rides the rails again on Saturdays and Sundays from May–Oct at 8.30am; return at 6pm. The price includes a brief boat excursion from Cajarc. Tickets (170F adults, 85F children) are on sale at the tourist office.

Place Aristide-Briand, © 65 35 09 56. This office continues Cahors's fine medieval traditions of financial savvy; when you write to ask them for information, they send it along with a request for payment.

market days

Place de la Cathédrale, Wednesday and Saturday mornings, though the covered market is open daily exc Sun. Every second Saturday there is a big *foire* spread all along Boulevard Gambetta and the Allées Fénelon with clothes and hand-crafted items; in the same place on Saturday mornings from Nov–Mar there's a fattened duck and goose and truffle market. Finally, there's an antiques and bric-à-brac fair in Place Rousseau on the fourth Sunday morning each month.

St-Etienne Cathedral

Begun in the 10th century on the site of St Didier's original cathedral, this is the second of the domed churches of Périgord and Quercy, directly inspired by St Etienne in Périgueux. Not completed until the 1400s, its western and eastern ends were completely rebuilt, resulting in a not unlovely architectural mongrel, a kind of Romanesque-on-Gothic sandwich. The severe façade, the typical broad tower-façade of a Quercy church writ large, was redone in the 14th century, and the original entrance was moved around to the side. Now the **north portal**, this is one of the finest in southern France, though regrettably much eroded. In the centre, Christ in a mandorla is flanked by angels tumbling down out of the heavens and scenes of the martyrdom of St Stephen; below are the Virgin Mary and 10 apostles (there wasn't room for 12). Of greater interest are the borders and *modillons*, with a full complement of monsters, scenes of war and violence, and unusual decorative motifs of roses that seem to prefigure the trimmings on Cahors's Renaissance palaces.

Once inside (through the main portal), turn around to see the colourful, finely drawn frescoes (*c.* 1320) high above the west door, a series of scenes from Genesis including the *Creation* and *Adam and Eve*. The other surviving original paintings are in an equally inconvenient spot, under the first of the two domes in the nave. These include figures of eight *prophets*, and in the centre the '*14 lapidateurs*' with their stones, ready to lapidate poor Stephen and ensure his status as first Christian martyr.

In 1330, the original east end was replaced with a Gothic apse, an odd structure built on the plan of a pentagon that from the outside looks like a separate building. Inside, it contains some of the best of Cahors's sculptural work in its side chapels, done 1484–91. More of the same can be seen in the **cloister** (1509), lavishly spread with flowing flamboyant decoration. Tragically, Henri IV's boys did a thorough job of smashing this up in 1580, but enough remains, or has been restored, to appreciate one of the finest sculptural ensembles of the south. Note in one corner the winsome carved *Vierge des Litanies*. The carvings around the arches in the cloister's grassy centre have an M.C. Escher quality, metamorphosing from a curling leaf of lettuce, to an ocean wave, to a dog licking its hind legs. If

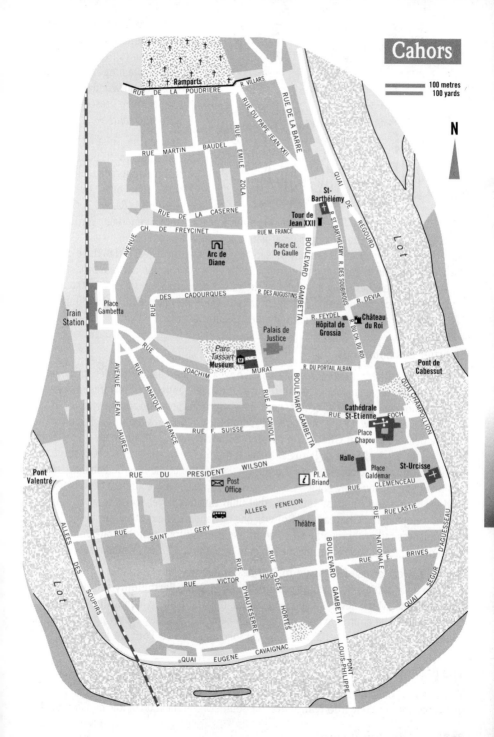

Cahors

100 metres
100 yards

N

RUE DE LA POUDRIÈRE
R. VILLARS
Ramparts
RUE DE LA BARRE
RUE DU PAPE JEAN XXI
RUE ÉMILE ZOLA
RUE MARTIN BAUDEL
QUAI DE REGOURD
Lot
St-Barthélémy
Tour de Jean XXII
R. ST-BARTHÉLÉMY
AVENUE CH. DE FREYCINET
RUE M. FRANCE
Arc de Diane
Place Gl. De Gaulle
BOULEVARD GAMBETTA
R. DES SOUBIROUS
RUE DES CADOURQUES
R. DES AUGUSTINS
R. DEVIA
RUE
Place Gambetta
R. FEYDEL
Hôpital de Grossia
RUE DU CH. DU ROI
Château du Roi
Train Station
AVENUE JEAN JAURÈS
RUE ANATOLE FRANCE
RUE
JOACHIM
Parc Tassart Museum
M
MURAT
Palais de Justice
R. DU PORTAIL ALBAN
Pont de Cabessut
QUAI CHAMPOLLION
RUE J. F. CAVIOLE
BOULEVARD GAMBETTA
Cathédrale St-Etienne
RUE FOCH
Place Chapou
Pont Valentré
RUE DU PRÉSIDENT WILSON
RUE F. SUISSE
Post Office
Pl. A. Briand
Halle
Place Galdemar
RUE CLEMENCEAU
St-Urcisse
ALLÉES DES SOUPIRS
RUE SAINT GÉRY
ALLÉES FENELON
Théâtre
RUE LASTIE
QUAI SÉGUR D'AGUESSEAU
Lot
RUE VICTOR HUGO
RUE D'HAUTESSERRE
RUE DES HORTES
BOULEVARD GAMBETTA
RUE NATIONALE
RUE E. BRIVES
QUAI EUGENE CAVAIGNAC
PONT LOUIS-PHILIPPE

you're lucky, the flamboyant entrance to the **Chapelle Saint-Gausbert** will be open (off the east colonnade), containing the cathedral treasure and wonderfully vivid 15th-century frescoes of the *Last Judgment*.

Across the square from the cathedral, you'll notice a bank that has restored an old painted shop sign over its modern façade: *Bazar Genois—Gambetta Jeune et Cie*. This Italian immigrant grocer earned his immortality for being the father of Léon Gambetta, Cahors's great native son. As a lawyer and politician, Gambetta was a strong opponent of the tyranny of Napoleon III. After the defeat of 1870, he declared the Third Republic in Paris, and then dramatically escaped from the city in a balloon while the Prussians were besieging it. After that, he raised new armies in the south (though the Prussians whipped them too), and eventually became premier; all France mourned in 1882, when he accidently killed himself while cleaning a gun.

Quartier des Soubirous

North of the cathedral extends what was the wealthy merchants' quarter in medieval times; **Soubirous** means superior, for the way the area climbs uphill towards the citadel. Neglected for centuries, only recently have the Cadurciens begun to restore some of its old mansions, and a few of the old bankers' counting houses now hold swish shops and antique dealers. **Rue du Château-du-Roi**, the spine of the neighbourhood, is an elegant street reminiscent of Siena or Perugia. Its most impressive façade is at no.102, the 13th-century **Hôpital de Grossia**. Take the alley to the right of it, the Bote de Fouilhac, which will bring you to a typically hidden Cahors surprise, a tiny, lovely courtyard decorated with modern murals and a musical fountain (that unfortunately never seems to work). Across from the Hôpital, the **Château du Roi** was one of Cahors's grandest palaces in the 1300s, though it was rather thoroughly wrecked in the last century when the state converted it into a prison; the tall donjon inside, visible only from the riverfront, is all that survives.

Here the street changes its name to Rue des Soubirous, and continues its way to the northern edge of the city, with the austere church of **Saint-Barthélemy** and the adjacent **Palais Duèze**. Much degraded by the centuries, this was built by John XXII for his family; he also rebuilt the church, where he had been baptized. The best surviving parts can be seen from Boulevard Gambetta, including the solid and graceful **Tour de Jean XXII**.

The Badernes

This was the popular quarter of the city, south of the cathedral, though it too had its share of palaces, mostly along **Rue Nationale**, the southern continuation of Rue du Château-du-

Roi. For one example, at the beginning of the street, there is the lovely Baroque carved door at the **Hôtel de Marcilhac** (no. 116). The streets to the left off Rue Nationale are worth a digression, with a large number of well-restored half-timbered houses, and a few medieval palaces, along Rue Lastié. The neighbourhood's church, **Saint-Urcisse**, stands at the end of Rue Clémenceau near the river. The 13th-century statue of the Virgin on the façade is one of the oldest sculptural works in Cahors; if the church is open, don't miss the set of carved capitals with fond naive scenes of Adam and Eve and the life of Christ.

Pont Valentré

If anything is a sign of opulence in medieval cities it's bridges. Cahors had three, where one would have sufficed, and the two that have disappeared were almost as good as this one. The city demolished them in 1868 and 1907. Cahors in its decadence cared very little for its ancient monuments; the Roman theatre of Divona Cadurcorum survived to the last century, but the city fathers destroyed it to make way for the railroad.

The **Pont Valentré** survived because it was out of the way (at the end of Rue du Président Wilson, ½km west of the cathedral) and carried little traffic. But it was built well enough that cars can and do still cross over it. Begun in 1308, and financed with the help of Pope John, the bridge nevertheless took nearly a century to complete. With the Hundred Years' War in full swing, it isn't surprising that defence became the major consideration. The three towers that look so picturesque are three rings of defences to keep the English out; each had its portcullis, and slits for archers and boiling oil.

Wherever in southern France you find a medieval bridge, you can be sure the Devil had something to do with it. Here, according to the legend, this master engineer made a deal for the soul of the Pont Valentré's builder in return for his aid. The builder tricked him, of course, by giving him a sieve with which to fetch water, but the Devil got his revenge by coming back each night to steal one of the corner stones of the central tower, which had to be replaced every following day. In the 19th century, restorers added the stone with the Devil carved on it to remind us of the tale (on the east side of the tower, near the top). The bridge's central **Tour de Diable** is open July and Aug, with a diorama of the Lot, an exhibition on 19th-century Cahors, and the story of the bridge. Near the top of the steps, the nasty metal cage was used to lock up adultresses and plunge them into the river.

From the bridge, on the upstream side you may see the **Sainte-Catherine**, permanently moored here. This is a reconstruction ('5200 hours of work!') of a medieval mill-boat, the only one in France, though we must report, with sadness, that it sank during a storm in 1994; they're not sure if they'll ever be able to raise it. Near by, on the riverbank, you can see the **Fontaine des Chartreux**; this source, fed by the underground streams of the *causse*, is probably Divona, the spring of ancient times around which Cahors grew up.

There isn't much else to see in the newer quarters of town. On Rue Caviole, just north of Rue du Président Wilson, the **Musée Henri Martin** *(open only July and Aug; ask at the tourist office)* contains archaeological finds from Divona Cadurcorum to medieval times, as well as colourful canvases of the Lot by pointilliste painter Henri Martin, a native of Toulouse who lived and painted in Labastide-du-Vert, a village to the west of town. The only other reminder of the Roman town is the **'Arch of Diana'** in a school ground, visible from Avenue Freycinet; this fragment of stone and brick was a part of the municipal baths.

Cahors ✉ *46000*   ***Where to Stay***

Cahors's luxury hotel is 6km northwest of the city in Mercuès (*see* p.271), while in town there's the charming, resolutely retro ivy-covered ★★★**Le Terminus**, opposite the station at 5 Charles de Freycinet, ✆ 65 35 24 50, in business for at least a century; it also has a garage, disabled access, TV in each room, and Cahors's best restaurant (*see* below). Less expensively, the modern ★★★**La Chartreuse**, St-Georges (overlooking the Lot by the spring of the same name, not far from the Pont Valentré), ✆ 65 35 17 37, has the same facilites as the Terminus, and a pool. ★★**Le Clos Grand**, ✆ 65 35 04 39, 3km from the centre off the D 8 at Labéraudie, in the suburb of Pradines (46090) is the pick of the two-stars, a country inn with cosy rooms, a large garden and pool; the restaurant serves hearty meals for around 175F (closed Sun night and Mon). Budget choices include the functional ★★**Le Melchior**, Place de la Gare, ✆ 65 35 03 38, opposite the station; tidy ★**De La Paix**, above a restaurant bar overlooking the market (30 Place St-Maurice, ✆ 65 35 03 40); and **Le Coq et La Pendule**, 10 Rue St-James, ✆ 65 35 28 84, the closest to an old-fashioned inn in Cahors, with pleasant rooms and obligatory half-pension— inexpensive and guaranteed to fill you up, even if it's not exactly cordon bleu.

Eating Out

Long gripping the gourmet gonfalon of Cahors, **Le Balandre** in the Terminus hotel, ✆ 65 30 01 97, has an elegant dining room, serving delectable Quercy dishes with a twist (try the *magret de canard* with the French version of green tomato chutney); the restaurant's famous starter is poached eggs with an escalope of foie gras and truffles (menus from 120–300F, à la carte easily much more; closed Sunday night and Mon in winter, Sat lunch in summer). If you have a car, it's 5km north on the N 20 to St-Henri and **La Garenne**, ✆ 65 35 40 67, installed in a country manor where you can feast on imaginatively well-prepared land and sea dishes such as the delicate sole in puff pastry or duck with *cèpes* (menus at 90, 150, 175F and up, closed Tues night and Wed, exc in July and Aug). For a romantic evening on the Lot (literally), try the well-prepared regional and fish dishes aboard **Au Fil des Douceurs** anchored off Quai Verrerie, ✆ 65 22 13 04 (from 150F, closed Tues).

Cahors is blessed with an excellent Chinese restaurant, **Le Mandarin**, 216 Av. Jean-Jaurès (just south of the station), ✆ 65 22 22 93; newly open and eager to please, and especially good at soups and starters, about 110F, and a 50F lunch menu. There are plenty of chances for a 50–60F lunch in the centre, though none really stand out. The best is tucked in a corner of Place Chapou across from the Halles: **Le Trouquet des Halles**, ✆ 65 22 15 81, where the long communal tables are usually packed for lunch. There are two daily specials, along with soup, dessert and a half bottle of wine, all for 40F (closed Sun).

South of the River: Quercy Blanc

Quercy shows a markedly different, drier face south of the river, less hilly and forested, with fewer villages and farms. Conspicuous in the open countryside are the slopes where the poor soil has been washed away to expose the pale limestone underneath; this is also used to build the characteristic houses and simple Romanesque chapels, giving 'White Quercy' its name. Beyond the sunbaked grandeur of its white hills, its fields of sunflowers and vineyards of Chasselas table grapes, attractions are few; if the sun isn't shining, it can be haunting, impatiently waiting for the Lot to give birth to a Thomas Hardy to give it justice.

Tourist Information

Montpezat-de-Quercy (82270): at the *mairie*, © 63 02 07 04

Castelnau-Monratier (46170): Rue Gisbert, 65 21 94 21

Montcuq (46800): Les Boulevards, © 65 22 94 04

market days

Castelnau-Monratier: Sundays

Montcuq: Sundays

Montpezat-de-Quercy

Montpezat-de-Quercy, a half-hour due south of Cahors and west of the N 20, may be the most rewarding destination in this area. This thoroughly medieval village retains its gate and arcaded square, as well as plenty of half-timbered houses, many of which are finally getting a long-overdue restoration.

Montpezat grew up in the 10th century. In 1257, its lord Alphonse of Poitiers granted it a charter as a free town, with rights to its own mill, a pigeon-house and an oil press. In the 1300s, Montpezat was home to a dynasty of churchmen named Des Près. Well-connected at the papal court at Avignon, they brought one of the popes' architects home to build the **Collégiale Saint-Martin**, set on a shady promenade at the edge of town. The wealth of the Des Près is evinced from their Carrara marble tombs inside, and especially from the church *trésor*, with glittering medieval reliquaries and some lovely carved alabaster plaques from England. The collégiale's real prize, however, is the series of tapestries hung around the apse, perfectly preserved 16th-century Flemish works commissioned by Jean Des Près that tell the *Life of St Martin of Tours* with the colour and vivid directness of a comic strip. Woven to fit the very spot where they are displayed, each of the 16 scenes is accompanied by an Old French quatrain. A few minutes from Montpezat, off the D 38 towards Castelnau, the woodland church of **Notre-Dame-de-Saux** has 14th-century frescoes of the legends of saints George and Catherine, the childhood of Jesus and the Crucifixion (the key is at the Montpezat mairie).

Castelnau-Monratier and Montcuq

Northwest of Montpezat, **Castelnau-Monratier** had the honour of being razed to the ground in 1214 by Simon de Montfort during the Albigensian crusade. Rebuilt soon after as a bastide, it has an unusual, triangular arcaded market square. Castelnau's pride and its symbol, however, are the three venerable stone **windmills** on the hilltop above the village. Two centuries ago, when these were built, almost every village without a dependable river had its windmills; Castelnau's are very rare survivals. You can also poke around the ruins of a Roman villa at the Moulin du Souquet. Don't miss **Flaugnac**, a striking medieval hilltop village just east of Castelnau.

North of Castelnau is an open, strangely empty part of Quercy Blanc. It was probably busier in Neolithic times; a number of tumuli can be seen, as at Lhospitalet and Villesèque. The people of **Montcuq**, on the D 653, claim that their village's name comes from the Latin *Montis Cuci*—Mount Cuckoo (and *do* pronounce the Q, unless you want to see the French giggle). Montcuq's landmark, visible for miles around, is the **Tour Comtale** *(guided tours in July and August; see the tourist office in the mairie)*. Impressive as it looks, the donjon wasn't strong enough to keep out Simon de Montfort; he called here too, and sacked the village. Just to the north on the D 28 is the huge stalactite **Grotte de Roland** with an underground lake. Montcuq plans to open it to the public in spring 1994.

Where to Stay and Eating Out

Castelnau-Monratier ✉ 46170

A pair of choices here: modern **★★Les Trois Moulins**, ✆ 65 21 92 95, with tidy rooms, pool and wide view, or no-star **Les Arcades**, in central Place Gambetta, ✆ 65 21 90 22, with rooms from 120–190F and a wide variety of tasty menus from 60F to 170F (with foie gras). Closed Jan.

Flaugnac ✉ 46170

When you can't face another *confit de canard*, **Le Piquemil** ✆ 65 21 05 83 serves dishes hard to find elsewhere in Quercy—the German chef not only prepares his national cuisine, but hot spicy Thai dishes as well, open all year (120–200 F).

Montcuq ✉ 46800

★★Du Parc, Rte du Fumel, ✆ 65 31 81 82, is a sun-drenched country inn in a pretty garden; meals from 95F (closed Oct–mid Apr).

Down the Lot: Cahors to Duravel

Abruptly leaving the cliffs and *causse* behind, after Cahors the Lot valley becomes lush and fertile, the heart of the Cahors wine region. Among these landscapes, the river suddenly decides it is in no particular hurry to get to the sea, and winds around in big lazy loops. It contains more than its share of modest attractions, as well as plenty of wine châteaux and country inns.

There is a regular SNCF bus service from the railway station in Cahors through Luzech and Puy-l'Evêque to Monsempron-Libos, ✆ 65 22 50 50 or 56 92 50 50 for schedules.

Luzech: Maison des Consuls, ✆ 65 20 17 27

Prayssac: Blvd de la Paix, ✆ 65 22 40 57

Puy-l'Evêque: on the D 911, ✆ 65 21 37 63

Duravel: in the centre, ✆ 65 24 65 50

Luzech: Wednesdays

Prayssac: Fridays

Puy-L'Evêque: Tuesdays

Duravel: Saturdays

Mercuès to Prayssac

The river's transition is marked by the **Château de Mercuès**, prominent on its hilltop 5km northwest of Cahors; begun in its present form in the 15th century as a stronghold and pleasure dome of the bishops of Cahors, this castle suffered sackings by the English and the Protestants. In 1563, the latter smoked the bishop out, and he was caught climbing out of a window. He was made to ride backwards on a donkey dressed in mock papal regalia before being rescued, and his embarrassment was so acute he died shortly after. The bishops gave Mercuès up in 1909, and since then it's settled down to its present career as the poshest hotel in the Lot (*see* below). It owes much of its present storybook appearance to 19th-century restorations; any bishop would be proud of the vast wine cellars.

From the centre of Mercuès, take the D 72 south for **Caillac** and its handsome Renaissance château, **La Grézette**, beautifully restored down to the *pigeonnier*, overlooking a prestigious vineyard. **Douelle**, across the river, is a favourite port and certainly the most colourful one, ever since artist Didier Comizo painted the 120m quay wall with a mural on the Creation, wine and humankind.

Luzech, further west, enjoys the most striking setting of the river villages, on a sort of narrow isthmus where two loops of the Lot nearly meet. Luzech's Gallo-Roman original can be seen on the steep hill above the village, where some remains of a wall and buildings survive at the site called the **Oppidum d'Impernal**. This is yet another Uxellodunum contender and, from the description of the site given in Caesar's *Gallic Wars*, it probably has the soundest claim of all. Below, medieval Luzech gathers itself under the stout **donjon épiscopal** (sometimes called the Tour Impernal), another fortress of the Cahors bishops, with ruins of its castle all around. In the village centre, the 13th-century **Maison des Consuls** now houses the Syndicat d'Initiative and the small **Musée Municipal**

(open Easter week, and May–Sept, 9–12 and 3–7) with finds from Impernal. The wide square that carries the main road, the D 8 through the village, was once a canal, cutting off the loop of the river and dividing the village from its *bourg*. From here, you can walk up to the teardrop-shaped hill that forms the river loop. At the top, the flamboyant Gothic church of **Notre-Dame-de-l'Isle** was begun in 1505, in the same style as the Cahors cathedral cloister. Queen Margrethe of Denmark, who married a local boy, Henri de Montpezat, comes down every summer; she stays at the family château at **Caix**, a village just outside Luzech. The surrounding vineyards produce the wine served at the royal table in Copenhagen; there's also a little wine museum (✆ 65 20 13 22). Caix also has an early Romanesque church with interesting naive carvings, and a small recreational lake.

Albas, just to the west, occupies an exceptionally picturesque spot on a cliff over the river. The tiny fortified centre includes a church and yet another Cahors episcopal palace. Its most famous citizen is Comte André de Montpezat, father of Henri, who was a rice planter in Vietnam before becoming a founding member of the Côtes d'Olt Vin de Cahors Cooperative in nearby Parnac, which still bottles the count's label. **Castelfranc**, a few km west on the opposite bank, is an austere bastide of the 13th century, with die-straight streets and a central square with a spare, elegant church, typical of medieval Quercy architecture, with its great front tower, as wide as the church itself, serving as much for defence as for decoration. The village's small but elegant suspension bridge is typical of the structures the *Ponts et Chaussées* erected all around this area in the early 1900s.

The long ridge to the northwest of Castelfranc was an important Neolithic site. Leaving the village on the D 911 west, take the first turn right, which climbs up the hill for a fine view over the valley, and then a marked *circuit des dolmens*; there are only two dolmens, but in addition an unusual 'double' *garriote*, a rock-carved niche called 'Caesar's armchair', near an ancient well, and at the summit of the hill, a circle of three huge menhirs amidst jumbles of rocks the locals call 'Chaos'.

Prayssac, like Castelfranc, started out as a bastide—only a round one, a mere circle of houses around a marketplace; it has grown greatly since the 19th century, as the biggest producer of the *Vin de Cahors* region. Prayssac is worth a mention for its addiction to marble statuary, starting with the quite unforgettable nude **Venus** on Venus Square, the vernal nymph in the lobby of the cinema, and the well-endowed sphinx-like creatures in the fountain by the post office. Also in marble is Jean-Baptiste Bessières, the 'Duke of Istria', across from the *mairie*. One of Napoleon's henchmen, this son of Prayssac oversaw the military occupation of Moscow, and died with a cannonball in his brain at Lützen in 1814. On the south bank, opposite Prayssac, **Bélaye** stands perched on the cliffs overlooking the valley. This ancient fortified place was one of the most important towns in the area before the English *routiers* raided it—several times—during the Hundred Years' War. The ruins of its episcopal castle remain, along with a strong-looking fortified church with a retable brought back by the souvenir-hunting Maréchal Bessières.

Vin de Cahors

Wine historians rate the deep crimson, full-bodied 'black' wine of Cahors as one of the last 'real' French wines, not drastically changed since the day

Julius Caesar sent amphorae back to Rome after his victory over the Gauls at Uxellodunum. It went down so well in Rome that by the next century, Italian vintners were whining about the competion, which in those pre-EU days resulted in an order from Emperor Domitian to uproot Cahors's vineyards, in 96 AD. The vines were restored in 276 by a prince named Probus; they prospered, and in 1152 they became part of Eleanor of Aquitaine's dowry when she wed Henry Plantagenet. When John XXII of Cahors become pope at Avignon, he further boosted the reputation of the wine by declaring it the papal communion wine. François I planted Cahors vines at Fontainebleau, and Peter the Great, finding vin de Cahors soothed his ulcer, planted vines in Azerbaijan, along the Black Sea, which to this day produces its very own Caorskoie.

Knocked out in the 1870s by a phylloxera epidemic, Cahors wasn't replanted as quickly as other French wines. In 1947 a slow revival began with the founding of the Côtes d'Olt Cooperative in Parnac, although it wasn't until after the vines froze in 1956 and 57 that the wine growers seriously began to replant the Cahors of yesteryear, at least 70 per cent Malbec (also called Cot or Auxerrois) mixed with Merlot and Tannat. Their efforts were rewarded in 1971 with AOC status—partially thanks to the good offices of the then president Georges Pompidou who had a summer residence in Cajarc. The immediate result brought the wine a flitting popularity, soon tarnished by greed and local feuds that produced many a dire bottle of plonk. In the 1990s, however, the wine is enjoying a comeback, thanks in part to Cartier head and Cahors winegrower Alain Dominique Perrin (owner of the medal-winning **Château La Grézette** in Caillac; ring ahead, ✆ 65 20 01 70), who formed an association of châteaux-vineyards known as Les Seigneurs du Cahors.

A leading member is the **Château de Haute-Serre** , just south of Cahors, where Georges Vigouroux laboriously has revived a famous medieval vineyard—planted not in the Lot valley as other post-phylloxera vines, but on the traditional limestone *causses.* His gamble paid off: Haute Serre today is one of the top wines of the appellation, and he's even built his own huge shop at the south end of Cahors at Roc de Lagasse, **L'Atrium** (✆ 65 20 80 90), as well as adding the Château de Mercuès to his empire. Also in Mercuès, Bruno and Christine Guichard's elegant **Château les Bouyesses** *(✆ 65 30 91 85, open 10–12 and 2–6, call ahead outside of season)* is in a Cistercian priory converted into a winery, where besides wine, you can take in a collection of ancient agricultural tools.

The oldest of the Cahors dynasties is headed by Jean Jouffreau at Prayssac's **Clos de Gamot,** ✆ 65 22 40 26. Jouffreau's family was first recorded here in 1290—a history traced in the frescoes in the cellars. The Jouffreaus have in their cellars the oldest known vin de Cahors, with bottles from the turn of the century; they have also conserved Cahors stock predating the phylloxera scourge, and have just planted an entire vineyard in the hills over Labastide-du-Vert; the first results of this venture are due to hit the shelves in 1996. Besides the Clos de Gamot, the Jouffreaus also welcome visitors at the elegant, early 17th-century **Château de Cayrou,** ✆ 65 21 32 70, by the river in Puy-l'Evêque, where a botanist planted redwoods and other exotic trees 200 years ago. The Jouffreaus's wines are all organic and, unusually, 100 per cent Auxerrois. Another Cahors thoroughbred is south of the river, the neatly kept vineyards of the 17th-century **Château de Chambert** at Floressas, © 65 31 95 75.

Nearly every vin de Cahors producer welcomes visitors and the less hoity-toity ones sell the last few *millésimes* (vintages) by petrol pump (*en vrac*) if you bring your own container. Try the vin de Cahors or refreshing rosé at **Delbru et Fils** just north of Prayssac on the road towards Pomarède (© 65 22 42 40), or at the Japanese-owned **Domaine de Kanijo Maleta**, at Labrande in Puy-l'Evêque (© 65 21 34 75). In the same village, **Château La Reyne**, © 65 30 82 53, must produce the jumpiest vin de Cahors—it is the official wine of BAC Mirande, France's top women's basketball team.

Puy-l'Evêque to Soturac

The hills close in on the river again at **Puy-l'Evêque**, giving this village its exceptional riverside setting, best seen from the new bridge over the Lot. By now, you should be able to guess to which *evêques* this *puy* (an Occitan word for 'hill' or 'mount') belonged. The Cahors bishops picked up this property in 1227, and soon after built the **donjon**, similar to Luzech's, at the highest point of the town. Though small, Puy-l'Evêque is worth a look around, for its quiet medieval streets, the battered flamboyant Gothic portal of its church, Saint-Sauveur (near the top of the town), and views over the valley. To the north, the church of the pretty village of **Martignac** has remains of 16th-century frescoes, including large allegories of the Seven Deadly Sins (not well preserved), some Italianate chiaroscuros, and in the apse a strange, looming figure like the king on a playing card that seems to be a pope, or God the Father himself. South of Puy l'Evêque, the great square **Château de Grézels** squats on its hillside like a fortified bunker. Restored in the 1960s, it now serves as home to the *Confrérie du Vin de Cahors* and the *Université du Goût* sponsored by the Ministry of Culture. Its small museum is dedicated to the wine and cuisine of Quercy, and it puts on a summer calendar devoted to food, music and drink, with long-winded guided tours of the château daily at 4.30.

The next village is **Duravel**, dominated by its massive 11th-century church atop a terrace, one of the most interesting pieces of Romanesque architecture in Quercy, but unfortunately one of the most restored in the 19th century. The outside of its apse is decorated with perforated metopes—openings under the roofline, usually round, alternating with *modillons* or other carvings, a conceit popular in this corner of the Lot. The occasion of this vast building project was the arrival in Duravel of an 11th-century sarcophagus containing 'three holy bodies' brought back from Palestine, by a crusader who perhaps bought them off some sharpsters with less imagination than the ones who peddled Geoffroi de Hardoin the Crown of Thorns. You can see their relics once every five years on the last Sunday in October (next display, 1995); at other times they are stored in the church's rare Carolingian crypt, with primitive but finely carved capitals, one showing a peacock. Bring a light to pick out the other carved capitals in the nave (scenes of misers in hell, St Michael pinning down the dragon) and a Gallo-Roman relief of—aptly for this wine village—bunches of grapes.

From Duravel you can take the pretty back road by way of St Martin-le-Redon to the Château de Bonaguil (*see* below). Alternatively, continue along the river until the signs point you back over the bridge to **Touzac**, site of a lovely deep-blue spring and 12th-century mill, the Moulin de Leygues (*see* below). The road from here continues south up to the villages of Lacapelle-Cabanac and Mauroux. Between the two, to the right of the D 5, is the striking Romanesque **church of Cabanac**, with a bell tower rebuilt in the 13th century. It stands at the highest point of the lost medieval city of **Orgeuil**. Orgeuil means 'pride', and an overweening insolence was the reason for its fall: in the 13th century the knights of Orgeuil, sworn enemies of the bishop of Cahors, terrorized the Lot valley, burning, pillaging and raping as far south as Moissac. Although the King of France took Orgeuil into hand by putting it directly under his rule, the Hundred Years' War brought new troubles. The lords of Orgeuil sided with the English, and when they were banished the town became a robbers' den, occupied by English *routiers*. By the time the count of Armagnac paid the *routiers* to go away in the mid 1300s, the town was already partly ruined, and has since crumbled. You can pick out bits of the ruins; the current owner of the site is determined to wreck the rest as a cross-country-motorbike playground.

Where to Stay and Eating Out

Mercuès ✉ 46090

Sitting on a spur high above the valley, the ★★★★**Château de Mercuès**, ✆ 65 20 00 01, has been sumptuously renovated into the last word in luxury. Rooms (two are in the towers) are fitted with large marble baths, canopy beds and other creature comforts; hanging gardens with a pool, and tennis courts are included in the lofty price (closed Nov–Mar). The restaurant is equally classy; the young Michel Dussau does delicious things with the ducks and lamb of Quercy, as well as seafood—rare in these parts (menus at 200, 295 and 395F).

Nuzéjouls ✉ 46150

Ten km northwest of Cahors on the D 12, **L'Oasis**, ✆ 65 30 98 44, offers the only chance we know of in the Lot to pretend you're really in the Sahara desert; you can dress up like a Touareg and ride a dromedary, by the hour or by the day, and order a complete nomadic feast consumed in a genuine Touareg tent. Otherwise, you can just camp here—there's a pool as well.

Caillac ✉ 46140

★**Le Relais des Champs**, ✆ 65 30 91 55, has simple, well-kept rooms 10km west of Cahors, near the river and vineyards.

Douelle ✉ 46140

★**Auberge du Vieux Douelle**, in the centre, ✆ 65 20 02 03 offers quiet rooms with TVs all year—except the last three weeks of Dec. Menus from 70F.

Pontcirq ✉ 46150

At the D 911 crossroads at Rostassac, ★**Auberge de Vert**, ✆ 65 36 22 85 is an old stone country inn with seven rooms and economical meals and 60F lunches (closed part of Nov).

Labastide-du-Vert ⊠ 46210

For one of the best meals around, ring Mme Lasfargues at the village café-tabac, ✆ 65 36 21 86; tell her how many you are, how much you want to pay per head, and she will suggest a meal using seasonal ingredients.

Puy-l'Evêque ⊠ 46700

There are three pleasant little hotels here: the ★★**Bellevue**, on the D 911, ✆ 65 21 30 70, with a pool is the most expensive and enjoys the best views, although the bar-restaurant below is trying a bit too hard to go upmarket; across the street with a wide stone arch for an entrance is ★★**La Truffière**, ✆ 65 21 34 54, with a TV and full bath in each soundproofed room. Both close in the winter, while the cheapest of the three, ★★**Henry**, at the bottom of Puy-l'Evêque, 23 Rue du Docteur Rouma, ✆ 65 21 32 24, has a garden at the back, TVs, a good-value restaurant, and is open all year.

Grézels ⊠ 46700

A valley favourite in the village centre is **La Terrasse**, ✆ 65 21 34 03; ring ahead to book a delicious country lunch under the oak beams, with as much wine as you can drink for 65F or 115F for a huge Sunday lunch.

Duravel ⊠ 46700

Signposted, 1km from the centre, **Ferme-Auberge La Roseraie**, ✆ 65 24 63 82, is a bit newer than the typical farm in the region, but lays down as delicious and traditional a Quercy spread as any, with menus including vin de Cahors at 100 and 150F (with foie gras); open daily mid June to mid Sept exc Mon, at other times by reservation only (it also has four *chambres d'hôte* and a pool). Book early for a room at one of Quercy's most delightful and friendly rural bed-and-breakfasts, the **Domaine de Barry-Baran** (signposted off the D 911 between Duravel and Puy-l'Evêque), ✆ 65 24 63 24. Meals 110F, evenings only and only by booking in advance (open Easter–Oct).

Touzac ⊠ 46700

Next to the spring and bamboo forest, in a 12th-century mill, ★★★**La Source Bleue**, ✆ 65 36 52 01, was once owned by actress Marguerite Moreno, who used to host her friend Colette. Colette had an insatiable appetite for truffles cooked in the ashes (the way the locals used to eat them 50 years ago, when the annual harvest was 25 times what it is now). The 15 rooms are charming (try to get one of the large ones in the mill), and a sauna, pool, and gym come with the deal; and you can still get truffles in the restaurant on occasion, along with foie gras and other regional delights (menus at 140 and 200F; closed mid Nov–Jan). Right on the Lot,

Le Clos Bouyssac, © 65 36 52 21, is a delightful, shady camp site, with bunga-lows to rent, pool, boats and bikes.

Mauroux ✉ 46700

**Hostellerie Le Vert, on the D 5, © 65 36 51 36, has seven lovely rooms in a country manor house; the elegant restaurant serves delectable variations on local delights—try trout in Sauternes or warm *foie gras de canard* with pears (menus at 100 and 200F, closed Thurs and Fri lunch; the whole place closes Dec–mid Feb).

North of the Lot: Gourdon and La Bouriane

Bories in Provence are dry stone huts, or what the southwest calls *cazelles* or *gariottes*; in this most Périgordian corner of Quercy *borie* means a 'farmhouse', especially a fortified medieval country retreat of Cahors's merchant elite; they give this mini-*pays* its name. Scattered farmhouses amid lush landscapes of chestnuts, pines and meadows are indeed the order of the day in the Bouriane, but there are some surprises, too: frescoed churches and a painted cave near the region's capital, Gourdon.

Getting Around

Gourdon has a railway station (© 65 41 02 19) with connections to Cahors, Souillac and beyond; ring ahead to hire a bike.

Tourist Information

Gourdon: Rue du Majou, © 65 41 06 40. For information on Gourdon's July and August Festival de Musique, contact the Comité d'Animation culturelle, 8 Bd du Docteur-Cabanes, © 65 41 06 40.

Saint-Germain-du-Bel-Air: Place Mairie, © 65 31 09 10

Cazals: Rue Notre-Dame, © 65 22 88 88.

Catus: Av. Lac, © 65 21 20 06

market days

Gourdon: Tuesdays and Saturdays in front of St-Pierre (fair first and third Tuesdays of each month)

Catus: Tuesdays

Gourdon

Harmoniously piled on a lofty bluff, rose-coloured Gourdon is easily spotted from miles around. Its strategic position attracted inhabitants very early on. In 961 Count Raymond I of Toulouse gave the city to the Gourdon family; one branch, the Fortanier de Gourdon, was nearly wiped out in 1189 when Richard the Lion-Heart captured the town. The story goes that the son who survived the massacre got his revenge with his crossbow ten years later at the siege of Châlus, when he shot Richard a fatal arrow in the shoulder. Gourdon in its medieval heyday had four monasteries, although one of its lords, a troubadour named Bertrand I, had a run-in with the Inquistion for protecting the Cathars. The monasteries also made a juicy target in the Wars of Religion for the fierce Protestant captain Duras, who spent a month razing them to the ground and slaughtering their inhabitants. Gourdon's once mighty castle suffered a similar fate in 1651 when the lord of Gourdon foolishly supported the cause of Marie de' Medici over her son, Louis XIII. In the 18th century the city walls went down to form a circular boulevard.

Start your tour of Gourdon at the top and the massive church of **Saint-Pierre**, begun in 1302, its façade flanked by two 100ft towers, linked by a gallery over the rose window. The portal has some delicate carving on the capitals; inside, the vast single nave is the most important venue of the town's summer music festival. For a view from Gourdon equal to the view of Gourdon from the distance, climb the stairs by the church for the esplanade that once formed the base of the castle: you can see the Dordogne valley, the green Bouriane and just about every roof in town.

Narrow little streets, like the famous Rue Zigzag leading up to St-Pierre, are lined with well-restored medieval houses. Near the church, the 13th-century consulate was converted in the 1700s into the **Hôtel de Ville**, with graceful arcades on the ground floor that shelter the farmers' market. Behind St-Pierre in Place des Marronniers, note the fine Renaissance portal and carved door of the **Cavaignac house**. The Cavaignacs were nationally prominent in the Revolution and 19th century; the father, Jean-Baptiste, served on the National Convention and ended up as a counsellor of Napoleon. His eldest son, a Republican journalist, created a society dedicated to the rights of man, while the younger personally led the massacre of the Parisians in the revolt of 1848. The main street, **Rue du Majou** is lined with relics of the Middle Ages—handsome houses, a fortified gate and chapel.

On Gourdon's ring boulevard, the Gothic church of the **Cordeiliers** survived Duras's monastic destruction. Although it's not much from the outside, the honey-hued interior is pure and lovely (open for festival concerts; otherwise ask at the tourist office) and has a beautiful 14th-century baptismal font carved with the figures of Christ and the twelve apostles. While there, check the opening hours of **Notre-Dame-des-Neiges**, 1km from the Hostellerie de la Bouriane (*see* below). Built near a water mill, the church stands on the site of a miraculous spring; the snow in its name refers to one of the Virgin's 4th-century miracles in Rome, when she caused a summer snowfall on the site of Santa Maria Maggiore. Although only the apse survives from the Romanesque church, the whole is simple and charming and contains an altar by Tournier.

Around Gourdon

North of Gourdon are the two **Grottes de Cougnac** *(open Palm Sun–Nov 1, 9–11 and 2–5; July and Aug 9–6; adm)*, one cave full of stalactites and stalagmites; the second, 300yds away, was discovered in 1952. Its entrance was blocked millennia ago, preserving inside the *département*'s second most important collection of prehistoric paintings, black and red outlines of goats, deer, mammoths, symbols and a number of humans, some pierced by lances. The cave walls around them look like trees and mutant cauliflowers. Amongst them, palaeontological detectives have found fingerprints believed to be 20,000 years old.

From the caves, the D 17 continues north to **Milhac**, a delightful medieval village that was the cradle of the lords of Gourdon; another charmer is **Masclat** further north, built around a pretty château and church, only a few km from Lamothe-Fénelon. **Le Vigan**, 6km east of Gourdon, is a busy village built around a massive **abbey church** with a giant belfry, founded by the canons of St-Sernin in Toulouse and especially favoured by the popes in Avignon, who gave it the relics of St Gall, uncle of St Gregory of Tours. The English in the Hundred Years' War so thoroughly pillaged the abbey that it never recovered, although stained glass was added to the church in the 15th century. Le Vigan is also the home to one of the Lot's newer museums, **Musée Henri Giron** *(open daily July–Aug 10–7, May, June, Sept and Oct daily exc Mon 10–6; adm)*, where you can examine the landscapes, still lifes and nudes of the *inclassable* Giron, who has lived in Brussels since the 1930s.

Further east, **Saint-Projet** has a naive pilgrims' cross, in which the serpent represents evil; the heart, triumphant love; the skull and crossbones, unredeemed humanity; while on the top Christ is crucified. The cross has an identical twin just to the east near **Graules**, on route to Rocamadour; the Graules cross has preserved its mysterious stone pendants. For a grand bird's-eye view, cross the N 20 to Reilhaguet. **Payrac** to the north is a pleasant town unfortunately sliced in two by the big road, but the kids might like its **Aqua Folies** with slides, pools and mini-golf (15 June–15 Sept).

Just off the scenic D 673, 8km west of Gourdon, stand the romantic ruins of the **Abbaye-Nouvelle** at Léobard (© 65 41 13 74). A Cistercian abbey (the 'old' one was at St-Martin-le-Désarmat), it was founded in 1242 on a rock overlooking the valley of the Céou on lands donated by Guillaume de Gourdon-Salviac, anxious to get back into good graces with the Inquisition. The Gothic church (1274–87) was damaged in the Hundred Years' War and never properly repaired, and by 1658 the abbey was abandoned. In 1950 it was dynamited by the farmers who owned it; the once elegant stairs were dismantled for a barn. Now only the lofty, ruined walls of the church stand, originally 90ft high—Abbaye-Nouvelle was the only known Cistercian church in France without a transept, and one of the few built with two storeys; the wooden upper floor has long since vanished. A local organization is dedicated to bringing the ruins back to life in some way.

One of the many pretty routes to follow in the Bouriane is the D 12 along the Céou valley, dotted with ruined castles at Clermont, Concorès and St-Germain-du-Bel Air. The D 673 to **Salviac** has its scenic merits as well; Salviac has a Renaissance château, some old houses, and a Gothic church built by Jean Duèze of Cahors, the future John XXII, and preserves some of its original stained glass. From Salviac a good navigator can get you through the narrow lanes to **Rampoux** to the southeast (or, easier, head south on the D 6 from Dégagnac); the reward is a 12th–14th century Benedictine priory decorated with naive frescoes and a statue of St Peter from the 1200s.

Cazals and Les Arques

Back on the D 673, the most important town in the area is **Cazals** next to a pretty *plan d'eau*. The town was a bastide laid out for the King of England by Guillaume de Toulouse in 1319. Only the main square serves as a reminder of its bastide origins, and the church (with some good capitals inside) is said to be built over a Roman temple. Cazals gave the world Hugues Salel (1504–53), one of the poets who drove Clément Marot crazy by imitating his *blasons*, preciously dedicated to pins and the like. **Montcléra**, the next village, has a most beguiling fat 14th-century château at the south end of town, best viewed when you head north up the D 673.

At Les Gunies, turn east for **Les Arques**, a sleepy village that's always had an artist or two ever since the Cubist sculptor Ossip Zadkine of Smolensk bought a home here in 1934. The works left by his widow to the city of Paris have been transferred here to create a little **Musée Zadkine** *(open daily Easter week and May–Sept, 10–7; weekends and school holidays 2–6; adm)*. Zadkine is best known for his 1947 *Destroyed City* in Rotterdam, and in peaceful Les Arques his works—several are on public display—seem almost too searing and painful. Next to the museum is the superb 11th-century church of **Saint-Laurent**, which Zadkine loved; he initiated the restoration and contributed three sculptures. Once a priory of Marcilhac, the interior has been stripped down to its mellow ochre stone to reveal its essentials: a single nave ending in three tiny apses, divided by columns with primitive carvings and divided by little Mozarabic horseshoe arches, while below is a tiny, ancient crypt; on one of the exterior portals, note the carved Celtic spiral. At the museum, pick up the key for Romanesque **St-André-des-Arques**, 4km on the other side of the D 45 (signposted). In 1954 Zadkine discovered its 15th-century frescoes under the plaster in the apse, interesting but damaged by the wet: Christ in Majesty, the Annunciation, and the Apostles. St Christopher is painted on one pillar, and baby Jesus, waiting to be carried, on the other.

The Southern Bouriane

Little **Frayssinet-le-Gélat** occupies the crossroads between Gourdon and Fumel, Cahors and Villefranche-du-Périgord. The only thing striking about it, besides its attractive medieval church, is the little monument next to it, with the inscription *TO THE MARTYRS OF GERMAN BARBARISM*, in letters big enough for everyone to notice. On 21 May 1944, a detachment of soldiers who had been attacked by the Resistance took their revenge on Frayssinet, rounding up villagers and shooting them; the old folks in the village still talk about it.

The D 678 to Fumel follows the valley of the Thèze, passing under **Montcabrier**, a little bastide founded in 1297 by and named after Guy de Caprari, the seneschal of Quercy. Its church of **St-Louis** with its arcaded *cloche-mur* was given a pretty flamboyant portal and rose window in the 14th-century; inside its prize is a reliquary of St Louis, one of the few to give the king a beard. The steep heights on the opposite side of the D 678 once held the town of **Pestilhac**, Montcabrier's bitter rival; some of its outer fortifications can still be seen from the valley. For three centuries, the two towns fought each other like Kilkenny cats; Pestilhac finally succumbed and disappeared in the 1500s. In its day it must have been one of the most important centres in the region. If you want to see the most evocative ruins in Quercy, climb up and make the acquaintance of the pleasant woman who lives in the smaller of the two houses on the site. The path leads through her back garden, up a wild, forested jumble of stones that includes parts of the walls and bastions, various buildings and best of all the church of Notre-Dame, still substantially intact, with some lovely carvings and an oak tree growing right through one of its Romanesque windows.

If you take the D 660 east from Frayssinet-le-Gélat, you'll pass through the golden village of **Goujounac** where the Romanesque church has a tympanum on its south side, carved with Christ and the four Evangelists. **Les Junies**, in the lush valley of the Masse, has a picturesque 14th-century château in the centre (and one of the few you'll see that hangs the washing out on the line). This was given by the bishop of Cahors as a thank-you-for-stomping-on-the-Cathars present to Bertrand de Jean. The de Jeans built a nuns' priory near by; the church has lovely 14th-century stained glass showing the founders, along with scenes of Christ and St John. The name de Jean was corrupted to form the village's name, Les Junies. Downstream, at **La Masse**, it's worth your while to patiently seek out (and tip) the woman with the key to see the liveliest frescoes of any Bouriane church, before the whole thing falls over: religious scenes on one wall, and on the other frisky devils and goaty satyrs scampering off with sinners in tow.

At La Masse tiny roads wiggle east towards St-Médard and **Catus**, site of another very popular *plan d'eau* and a buttressed priory church with a polygonal apse, all that remains of a 10th-century priory. The star attraction here is the 12th-century chapterhouse with 12 magnificent capitals and column bases, carved by the same school as Moissac. The farms around Catus are especially photogenic, some retaining their *lauze* stone roofs, which are pretty rare in the Lot. Legends say that Roland clobbered the Saracens at **Montgesty** to the northwest, in revenge for a town they had destroyed on the site; all that digging has produced, however, is bits of a Gallo-Roman villa at Mas-de-Rieu.

Where to Stay and Eating Out

Gourdon ✉ 46300

★★★Hostellerie de la Bouriane, Place du Foirail, ✆ 65 41 16 37, is a large country inn that has long been *the* place to stay in Gourdon, on the very edge of town; rooms are lovely, the food—including some fish dishes—delicious (menus from 80 to 250F, closed mid Jan–Feb, and Mon outside the season). Even more tranquil, the Relais et Châteaux **★★★Domaine du Berthiol**, D 704 towards Cahors, ✆ 65 41 33 33 occupies a large stone manor house in the woods, with a pool and tennis and games for the kids; here, too, the restaurant will win you over with a delectable seasonal menu (from 100–260F, closed Nov–Mar). Of the cheaper places, the nicest is **Bissonnier**, in the medieval town at 51 Bd Martyrs, ✆ 65 41 02 48, with rooms from 160–320F, and a good *coq au vin* on the 80F menu (closed Dec). Fairly new to Gourdon, **A l'Arbre Rond**, 69 Bd Galiot de Genouillac, ✆ 65 41 18 00 offers a mellow *ambiance* to accompany its buffet of hors d'oeuvres and main courses (150F).

Salviac ✉ 46340

La Casserole, Rue Haute, ✆ 65 41 57 87, has become a local favourite for its well-prepared dishes by two amiable Dutchmen, who occasional regale the Bouriane with Indonesian evenings (menus at 85 and 110F, closed Jan and Feb). If you want to stay, there are eight simple rooms in the ***Hôtel de la Poste**, Grande Rue, ✆ 65 41 50 34.

Frayssinet-le-Gélat ✉ 46250

Signposted from the centre of Frayssinet, the ferme-auberge **La Serpt**, ✆ 65 36 66 15 (ring ahead), serves some of the best duck and goose *confits* and *magrets* in the Lot; for 110F you get an apéritif, soup, pâté, choice of entrée, *pommes de terre sardalaise*, salad, homemade cheese, dessert, wine and coffee. Order ahead to try traditional dishes like *mique levée*, or goose cooked in Cahors wine, or *pastis*, apple pie smothered in lighty flaky pastry like a pile of autumn leaves.

Goujounac ✉ 46250

In the village centre, the **Hostellerie de Goujounac**, ✆ 65 36 68 67, offers a handful of recently remodelled rooms and generous menus, seasoned just right and priced at 60, 100, and 120F. Closed Sun night and Mon, exc July and Aug. In Pomarède, 4km southwest, **Jeanne Murat**, ✆ 65 36 66 07, lays down one of the most popular spots around for a filling 60F lunch, using mostly homegrown ingredients. On Sunday, when it goes all the way up to 75F, you have to book.

Montcabrier ✉ 46700

Buried deep in the countryside, *****Relais de la Dolce**, ✆ 65 36 53 42, is a modern motel with swimming pool, although the restaurant dates back to the 12th century. Good traditional dishes, but also special consideration for vegetarians (150F, closed Nov–Mar). **La Ferme de Cuzorn**, in the chestnut groves just east of Montcabrier ✆ 65 36 57 16, offers *chambres d'hôte* and Quercy farm cooking, specializing in semi-domesticated boars (arrive at 5pm to watch the bristly porkers being fed); menus from 90F. Another rural address, **Chambres d'Hôte chez les Lemozy**, ✆ 65 36 53 43, offers an Arcadian bed-and-breakfast on the farm in the hamlet of Mérigou, on the D 68 west of Montcabrier.

Saint-Médard, near Catus, ✉ 46150

Le Gindreau, ✆ 65 36 22 27, is the Bouriane's gourmet haven, in a building that originally served as the village school, with a pretty terrace overlooking the countryside. Here Alexis Pélissou prepares *elegantissimo* dishes with authentic ingredients—lamb from the *causse*, the freshest vegetables in season. There's a sommelier to help you select the correct wine, with Cahors naturally at the top of the list (menus at 150, 225 and 330F, closed Mon outside of season, Sun night).

Barbaste

Lot-et-Garonne

Lot-et-Garonne

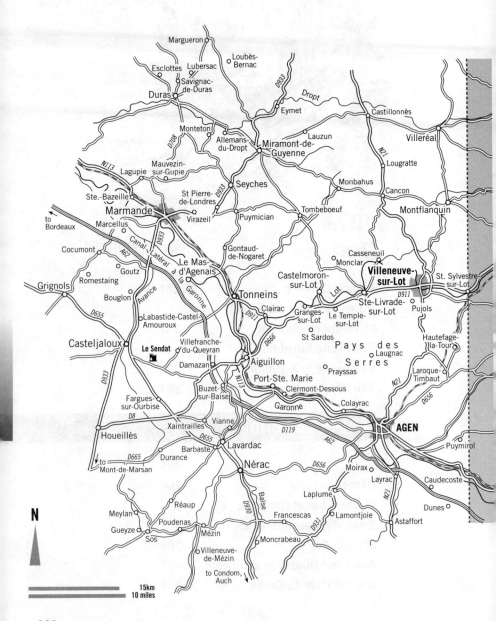

N

15km
10 miles

West of the Bouriane a similar landscape of rolling hills, woodlands and meadows continues into the *département* of Lot-et-Garonne and the southern bit of the Dordogne. Stendhal described these landscapes as the 'Tuscany of France'; it has not only a superb collection of bastides, but two of the finest castles in the southwest, the Châteaux de Bonaguil and de Biron.

Bastide Country

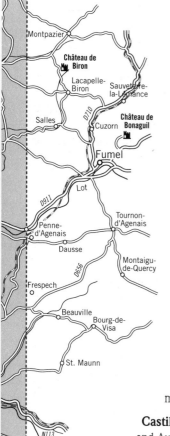

Getting Around

The train station at Monsempron-Libos is on the Paris–Agen line, with connections to Les-Eyzies and Périgueux (© 56 92 50 50).

Tourist Information

Fumel: Place Georges-Escande, near the *mairie*, © 53 71 13 70

Monflanquin: Place des Arcades, © 53 36 40 19

Villeréal: © 53 36 09 65

Castillonnès: Grand Rue, © 53 36 87 44

Issigeac: © 53 58 79 62

Monpazier: © 53 22 60 38

market days

Monsempron-Libos: huge market on Thursdays

Monflanquin: Thursdays

Villerèal: Saturdays, also a farmer's market on Wednesdays

Castillonnès: Tuesdays, and a farmers' market on Fridays in July and August

Monpazier: Saturdays (only in season)

Lacapelle-Biron: Mondays

Fumel and Monsempron-Libos

Just west of the last Cahors vineyards is **Fumel**, the Lot's own rust belt, or rather, little rust garter. The barons of Fumel, first recorded in the 11th century as protectors of Moissac, were in the Wars of Religion ardent Catholics and buddies of Catherine de' Medici; François de Fumel (Catherine's ambassador to Constantinople) was so unpopular locally that in 1562 his Protestant subjects rose up and slaughtered him in his château. Bitter reprisals and mass executions followed, and Fumel only recovered in 1848, when it was chosen to have the first industry on the Lot, a small steel mill. The one sight in town is the **château**, now the *mairie*; François of Fumel was responsible for converting the medieval donjon into an Italianate villa, and it was completed in the 1700s, with immaculately kept garden terraces overlooking the river.

In recent years Fumel has reached out to touch its neighbours with its super- and hyper-market sprawl. If you can get past the parking lots of **Montayral** across the Lot, look for its fortified mill built directly in the river, or its château, a 13th-century residence of the pirate lords of Orgueil, with bits added over the centuries. **Monsempron-Libos**, on the far side of the steel mill, is spread around a medieval *castrum* on a hill with the exquisite 12th-century church of **Saint-Géraud**. The exterior is decorated with perforated metopes, while the unusual plan inside has innovative vaulting and a special entrance under the choir to accommodate pilgrims who once flocked to see the relics displayed there. The capitals in the nave (redone in the 14th century) are carved with masks and monsters.

The Château de Bonaguil

It's so perfect that it seems ridiculous to call it a ruin.

Lawrence of Arabia, 1908.

Of all the castles bristling across France, few are as useless and as photogenic as the great prow-shaped Château de Bonaguil, 'the swan song of feudalism', born 200 years behind the times. Begun in the 13th century by a family of knights from Fumel, it passed in the 1460s to the hunchback Brengon de Rocquefeuil who liked to be called 'the noble, magnificent and most powerful lord' of his assorted little possessions. Brengon was a perfect cartoon baddie, a proto-survivalist, as nasty and paranoid as he was vain. When Charles VII fined him for brutality towards his vassals, Brengon ensconced himself at Bonaguil, in a massive donjon reminiscent of the Flatiron Building in New York, filled with years' and years' worth of provisions and weapons, and surrounded it with a moat, surging walls and towers, designed to deflect cannon fire from all sides (at the same time, all the other nobles of France were abandoning their medieval castles for elegant Renaissance châteaux). 'I will raise such a castle that my villainous subjects will never take it, nor the English, nor even the most powerful soldiers of the King of France,' he boasted. Never mind that none of the above ever showed the least interest in Bonaguil (although the Huguenots partially wrecked it in 1563, and it was rebuilt in 1572 by another Rocquefeuil). By the 18th century Brengon's lair was such a white elephant that it once sold for a hundred francs and a bag of walnuts. Partially demolished in the Revolution, it was purchased by the town of Fumel in 1860.

Whether you approach it from Fumel or from above, via St-Martin-le-Redon (*see* p.277), it is as stunning as a Hollywood set; on summer nights it's illuminated until midnight. The interior *(guided tours in French only Mar, May and Sept at 10.30, 2.30, 3.30 and 4.30; June, July and Aug at 10, 11, 3, 4, 5, and 6; Feb, Oct, and Nov, Sun and holiday afternoons only; ring the Fumel tourist office for details)* can't match the exterior: there are fireplaces suspended in the void, objects found in the castle midden, graffiti (Rocquefeuil names, games, dirty doggerel and the magic square SATOR ROTAS), and views from the walls. The adjacent castle chapel, St-Michel, has an unusual cinquefoil window.

Monflanquin, Villeréal and Around

Monflanquin is a convenient starting point for exploring the bastide country, whether you approach from Fumel to the east or Villeneuve-sur-Lot to the west. Strategically planted atop a 181m hill with views from miles around, the bastide of Monflanquin, 'one of the most beautiful villages in France', was founded in 1256 by St Louis's brother Alphonse de Poitiers. Alphonse's interest in these marches had much to do with his marriage to Jeanne, the only child of Raymond VII of Toulouse, which was part of his brother's strategy to solidly frenchify the lands recently devasted by the Albigensian Crusade; Alphonse and Jeanne further obliged by dying childless and leaving Toulouse to the crown. Monflanquin has preserved most of its original bastide elements: the central square bordered with wide arcades, or *cornières*, a fortified church still bristling behind its original façade, its grid street plan and blocks of medieval houses. Monflanquin's most recent vocation is art, and it fills the summer with events and exhibitions; in winter it's as dead as dogmeat. The late Robert Maxwell's château on the outskirts of Monflanquin is up for sale, in spite of local rumours that the fat man is alive and well and hiding inside from his creditors.

It's a beeline 13km north up the D 676 to another foundation of Alphonse de Poitiers, the 1269 bastide of **Villeréal** alongside the river Dropt (or Drot). Villeréal, with its agriculture (mostly orchards and tobacco) and commerce has a more solid air to it than artsy Monflanquin; the shop-filled arcades of the main square overlook the 14th-century *halle*, which has an upper storey added in the 16th century; the façade of the church is framed by two towers and retains the loopholes in the apse, from where the citizens shot at the rampaging English. A decade before Villeréal, Alphonse had founded the handsome bastide of **Castillonnès** (13km west), down the Dropt and midway between Villeneuve and Bergerac, on the N 21. Castillonnès has conserved its *cornières* and narrow medieval lanes, and, on Rue du Petit Paris, a fine 17th-century house. If the church is open, pop in to see its 17th-century gilded retable. In mid August, its bell tower and the turret of the house across the *place* are used to support a high wire, where acrobats perform their acts while the hearts of everyone below go pit-a-pat. The tiny village of **Douzains**, just to the southwest, is famous for its enormous oak tree that figures in several local legends.

Picture-postcard **Issigeac**, north of Castillonnès and Villeréal, has changed so little over the centuries that it's a favourite location for films; among its charms are a late Gothic church with a good porch, a bishop's château, and the half-timbered **Maison de Têtes**, decorated with leering faces.

Monpazier

Monflanquin, Villeréal and Castillonnès held the front lines against the English at Beaumont and **Monpazier**, 'the most perfect bastide', 15km up from Villeréal on the Dropt. Founded by Edward I in 1284, Monpazier had a perfectly rotten 14th century, when the town was a football kicked from side to side in the Hundred Years' War—even the Baron of Biron got into the act and put it to the sack—*routiers* pillaged it, and a streak of bad harvests were followed by a typhoid fever epidemic. The local lepers were blamed, and a few burned alive. Then in 1350 came the Black Death.

Amid the terrors of the next round of warfare, over religion, the duke of Sully recorded a story about Monpazier worthy of Monty Python: by sheer coincidence Monpazier decided to raid Villefranche-du-Périgord, the next bastide to the east, on the same night that Villefranche decided to do the same to Monpazier. By chance each militia took different paths; each was delighted to find their goal undefended and easy to plunder, and carried its booty back—to ransacked homes. An agreement was struck, and both sides gave back everything they stole.

Despite all the troubles, Monpazier has held itself together remarkably well, from its fortified church (still bearing its Revolutionary slogan, that 'The People of France believe in a Supreme Being and the Immortality of the Soul') to its 16th-century *halle*, complete with its original grain measures. Note that the regulation *cornières* around the square are irregular, and that narrow spaces were left between the houses—not to give the residents air or light as much as a place to throw their rubbish. In 1637 crowds stood under the arcades to watch Buffarot, the leader of the Croquants, broken on the wheel.

The Château de Biron

From Monflanquin or Villeréal you may have already sighted the superb **Château de Biron**, largest of all Périgord's castles *(open daily July–Aug 9–12 and 2–7; at other times, 10–12 and 2–5, closed Tues and Jan; adm)*. The steep hill was a natural stronghold, and the first castle was built in the 11th century to command the northern approaches to the

Agenais. In 1189 Gaston de Gontaut, chief of the four barons of Périgord (and an ancestor of Lord Byron) got his hands on it, and they were like glue—the Gontauts held on to the castle for 24 generations, until the early 20th century. Over the centuries the family created one of the most charmingly eclectic castles in France. The first Gaston built the square 12th-century keep, or *Tour Anglaise*, while Romanesque walls and the Tour du Concierge (with Renaissance dormers) date from after the 1212 siege of Biron by Simon de Montfort; Gaston de Gontaut was tainted with heresy after wedding his daughter to the Cathar captain, Martin Algaïs, England's seneschal of Gascony. Agaïs led a brave defence against the crusaders, but de Montfort only agreed to go away when the young man was handed over for execution. The next important building spree was initiated by Pons de Gontaut-Biron, who accompanied Charles VIII on his invasion of Italy in 1497. Pons returned to Biron, determined to add some *quattrocento* grace to his muscular feudal domain with the delicate Pavillon de la Recette and a two-storey chapel—the ground floor built as a parish church for the villagers of Biron, and the upstairs reserved for the nabobs. This chapel long held two 14th-century masterpieces, a *Pietà* and *Mise au Tombeau*, which to the great outrage of many were sold by the Gontaut-Birons in the early 1900s to the Metropolitan Museum in New York; of the tombs, only two were priced too high for the New Yorkers, those of Pons de Gontaut-Biron (carved with the *Resurrection of Lazarus* and *Christ Appearing to his Disciples*) and his brother, Armand, bishop of Sarlat (d. 1531, with three dignified feminine Virtues).

A third round of building was begun by Baron Armand de Gontaut, a Maréchal de France (1524–92), who died fighting the Catholic League at the side of Henri IV. His hot-headed son Charles continued the fight, receiving 32 wounds in battle. Henri rewarded him by raising Biron to a duchy, and making Charles ambassador to England; but Charles found peace boring, and in 1602 he was un-duked and beheaded at the Bastille for conspiracy against the king (hence Biron's story of a headless ghost). The moat was filled in under Richelieu, who didn't like great lords feeling safe. Work was taken up again in the 18th century, but left incomplete at the time of the Revolution.

From the castle take the D 150 south to **Lacapelle-Biron**, a village founded on the orders of Biron's baron to host the Monday market that used to take place under the château—the baron hated to be awakened by the noise. Lacapelle-Biron stands near the head of the sweet leafy valley and mini-gorge of the Lède, a little stream that not only sounds like the mythological river of oblivion, Lethe, but really does make the cares of the world seem far away. There's a striking 12th-century six-storey donjon at **Gavaudun**, and just above Gavaudun, at **Saint-Sardos-de-Laurenque**, a small **Musée de la Préhistoire** *(open Easter, July and Aug afternoons, or © 53 40 82 29)* documenting the dense habitation of the valley from the Mousterian to the Magdalenian era. Saint-Sardos itself was a bastide founded in 1323 by pro-French monks connected with Sarlat. This founding angered the pro-English contingent at Monpezat, who attacked the new town, put the monks to the sword and hanged the French seneschal from the maypole set up to celebrate the founding of the bastide. Sorting out the incident caused the king of England to delay his homage to Charles IV for the duchy of Aquitaine, giving Charles sufficient reason to send in an army to confiscate Aquitaine, igniting the Hundred Years' War. Another, more peaceful relic of the past is the old mill near **Salles** that spins wool the traditional way; visitors are welcome between 9–12 and 2–6.

Alternatively, you can head east from Lapcapelle-Biron to **Sauveterre-la-Lémance**, dominated by a large castle, built by Edward I in the 13th century, with a medieval hamlet at its skirts. Sauveterre was another popular prehistoric residence, and gave its name to the early Mesolithic period, the *Sauveterrien*; you can visit the excavations in the summer, or visit the little **Musée Préhistorique** *(open Mon–Fri mornings)* at the *mairie*.

Where to Stay and Eating Out

Fumel ✉ 47500

If it's charm you want, book a room at the 16th-century ***La Petite Auberge**, up in medieval Monsempron, ✆ 53 71 05 48, with seven adorable rooms, garden and little pool; the menus, from 95F will fill you to the gills. Some of the best seafood in the area is served up to the steelworkers at **72nd Avenue**, 72 Av. de l'Usine, just across from the mills, ✆ 53 71 80 22 (from 110F).

Bonaguil ✉ 47500

Just below the castle, **Auberge Les Bons Enfants**, ✆ 53 71 23 52, with its terrace lined with weeping willows has put on reliably good meals for the tourists for a long time; menus at 60, 90, 130 and 180F. The inn also has three rather pricey rooms beginning at 230F (all closed 15 Nov–15 Feb).

Monflanquin ✉ 47150

You can stay very pleasantly in a restored mill on the road to Villeréal, the ****Moulin de la Boulède**, ✆ 53 36 40 27, or just enjoy one of its good menus from 60F to 175F. On the same road, the **Ferme-auberge de Tabel**, ✆ 53 36 30 57 (book) offers lunches and dinners prepared from home-grown products from 75–135F; they also have three rooms to rent.

Villeréal ✉ 47210

Le Lac, Rte de Bergerac, ✆ 53 36 01 39, is a fine un-gussied-up little hotel by a little lake, popular with swimmers and fishermen (closed Oct–Apr). ***Europe, 1 Rue Mirabeau, ✆ 53 36 00 35, has simple rooms in the centre of the action.

Castillonnès ✉ 47300

***Des Remparts, Rue Paix, ✆ 53 36 80 97, offers handsomely furnished rooms in a 19th-century house, overlooking the ramparts; dine out on the terrace around a fountain and plump for the superb 140F menu (closed Wed and Sun night in winter, and mid Jan to mid Feb).

Douzains ✉ 47330

Located by a country pond, the **Ferme-auberge du Bois de Mercier**, ✆ 53 36

81 97, has lovely rooms at lovely prices open all year (135–200F for two, including breakfast). In the kitchen, Denise Bousquet, the owner, waits to convert you to the charms of prune sauces (dinner only, under 100F).

Monpazier ✉ 24540

****Edward 1er**, 5 Rue Saint-Pierre, ✆ 53 22 44 00 occupies a 19th-century mini-château that the French call a bachelor pad (*gentilhommière*), with an attractive swimming pool added to where the moat might have been. The rooms are fitted out with every comfort—some with steam baths and jacuzzis—all have satellite TV and mini-bars; but no restaurant (closed mid Nov to mid Apr). You won't starve, however, thanks to **La Bastide**, 52 Rue St-Jacques, ✆ 53 22 60 59, which serves up the likes of *poulet au verjus* and trout with almonds in an attractive setting (menus from 80 to 250F, closed Mon and Feb).

Gavaudun ✉ 47150

In the bucolic Lède valley, between Gavaudun and Lacapelle-Biron, the **Auberge du Vezou**, ✆ 53 40 82 12, has a handful of bed-and-breakfast rooms (160F), the perfect cure for stressed-out urbanites (open all year).

Sauveterre-la-Lémance ✉ 47500

*Du Centre**, ✆ 53 40 65 45 is a blessing for the budget traveller, with good, cheap rooms and a generous 85F menu.

Down the Lot from Fumel to Villeneuve-sur-Lot

At Fumel the Lot moves into the 20th century, shedding its ringlets along with its pristine lack of industry, car parks and commercial sprawl as it meets flatter country on route to its confluence with the mighty Garonne at Aiguillon. From the valley road the scenery might seem unexciting, but take a short detour anywhere to the south and you'll find some of the most remarkable landscapes anywhere in the southwest: rank upon rank of flat-topped mesas, cut out of the limestone by little streams over the past few million years—the northern extremity of the Agenais *pays de serres* (the overlook at the top of Penne is a good place to see the whole of them). However dramatic, it is still a green and pleasant land, especially in the spring when its orchards burst into blossom.

Tourist Information

Montaigu-de-Quercy: 7 Rue de la Fontaine, ✆ 63 94 41 63

Penne-d'Agenais: Rue du 14–Juillet, ✆ 53 41 37 80

Villeneuve-sur-Lot: Blvd Georges-Leygues, in the left wing of the theatre, ✆ 53 70 31 37

Villeneuve: Tuesdays and Saturdays; farmers' market Wednesdays; also fair first and third Tuesday of each month

Pujols: Sundays

Tournon-d'Agenais, Montaigu-de-Quercy and Penne-d'Agenais

Before leaving Fumel, there are two hill towns just to the south that merit a detour: **Tournon-d'Agenais**, the first, is a pretty mesa-top bastide, founded by the indefatigable Alphonse de Poitiers in 1270; there are several half-timbered houses, and arcades around the central Place du Marché; the second, **Montaigu-de-Quercy**, which looks more Italian than French, has an especially nice *plan d'eau* with a beach if you need a swim or a doze. The vineyards in the area produce red *vin de pays Thézac-Perricard*, which was served to Nicholas II of Russia. Won over, Nicholas immediately ordered a thousand bottles for a family party, and ever since then the wine has been known as the *Vin du Tsar*; try it at **Les Vignerons de Thézac-Perricard** in Tournon, © 53 40 72 76.

On the river itself, **Lustrac**, 9km west on the D 911 from Fumel, is a charming spot marked by one of France's most impressive fortified mills, the **Moulin de Montnavés**, founded in 1296; the adjacent château was a glorified river tollbooth. Further downstream, on the south bank, **Penne-d'Agenais** grew up around its pilgrimage church **Notre Dame de Peyragude** (from *pierre aigue*, or sharp stone), first built around the year 1000 on a 500ft crag overlooking Penne. In 1182, Richard the Lion-Heart added a castle near by, making Penne his headquarters on the Lot; he is locally recalled in name of the medieval gate, the **Porte Ricarde** and in the town's old nickname, *Penne la sanglante*, for the massacres and general bloodletting that marked the Lion-Heart's footsteps across Europe. The chapel was rebuilt in 1653, after a plague killed half the population of the Agenais, then again in 1842 after the Revolution sold it off for building stone. So many pilgrims turned up that in 1896 the local prelates built what you see now—a huge basilica in the kitschy neo-Byzantine taste of the time, but with a superb view in every direction. Beautifully restored medieval Penne has enough summer crafts shops to make sure pilgrims don't go home empty-handed.

Villeneuve-sur-Lot

The bustling market city of **Villeneuve** grew out of yet another bastide, founded by Alphonse de Poitiers in 1264. Although Villeneuve now spreads every which way, it has retained its simple medieval bastide heart. Enter by way of the 13th-century **Porte de Paris** crowned with a 100ft tower, the bottom third stone, and the top two-thirds brick. The central market square, **Place Lafayette** is still framed in its *cornières*, rebuilt in the 17th century after the riots of the Fronde. Near by, the elaborate brick **Sainte-Catherine** was completed in the 1930s, replacing the original Gothic church which was in danger of collapse. The magnificent Gothic and early Renaissance stained glass of the latter were incorported in the modern church, depicting the Life of Christ and a bevy of saints associated with the city, including St James the Greater, who appears three times. St James is there of course because of the many pilgrims who passed through en route to Compostela because Villeneuve had a bridge, the **Pont Vieux**. This takes the Périgueux–Auch road, first tramped out in Neolithic times, and it made Villeneuve's fortune when the English built it in 1282, with three fortified towers similar to those of Cahors's Pont Valentré. Unfortunately these tumbled down when the bridge partially collapsed in a flood—hence the asymmetrical wide arch. Further evil has since been averted thanks to a frilly, dolled-up statue of Our Lady of Joy in the chapel overhanging at the north end, rebuilt in 1642.

Across the Vieux Pont, Rue de Pujols leads to the **Musée Gaston Rapin** *(open daily exc Tues, 2–6)* with a collection of archaeological finds, church art, local paintings from the last two centuries, and a room devoted to prunes. Some artefacts hail from **Eysses**, originally the Roman Excisum, a pretty place with the remains of a tower and a villa (2km to the north on the Monflanquin road). Further north at **Castelnaud de Gratecambe** is a new golf holiday complex, with 27 holes and a driving range.

Pujols, and Two Caves

The main attraction around Villeneuve is white, walled, medieval antique-dealing **Pujols**, 2km from the Vieux Pont. To enter Pujols, pass under the arch of the tower of 15th-century flamboyant Gothic **Saint-Nicolas** that leads into the ancient market square. The church has star vaulting inside, and curious tribunes with little fireplaces so the barons of Pujols could attend Mass more snugly. A chapel on the left contains bits discovered and moved here during various remodellings—Gothic tombstones and a Renaissance mausoleum, originally in the choir. A second church, **Sainte-Foy la Jeune** dates from the 1400s and contains some excellent murals from the period, one showing Ste Foy (Faith) of Agen, a 3rd-century maiden whom the Romans burned on a gridiron, just as they did to St Lawrence. Although her cult centre is up at Conques (Aveyron), some of her relics were taken to Glastonbury and a number of English churches were named after her.

Ten km south of Pujols are the **Grottes de Fontirou**, with extraordinary limestone formations *(open April and mid Sept 3–5.30; June–Aug 10–12.30 and 2.30–6.30; adm)*; in the adjacent prehistoric zoo *Jurassic Park* fiends can check out the life-size concrete dinosaurs ('Their noises will surprise you', as their brochure promises). About 7km northwest, the **Grottes de Lestournelles** are just as splendid *(July and Aug 10–12 and 2–7, at other times, weekends and holidays only, 2–7; adm)*.

Where to Stay and Eating Out

Tournon-d'Agenais ✉ 47370

In the medieval centre, you'll find the family-run **★Le Midi**, ✆ 53 40 70 08, with simple rooms and filling menus. Tournon prides itself on its *tourtiéres* (flaky apple or prune pie), and this is a good place to try it. Menus at 70, 90 and 120F, closed Fri eve and Sat exc in July and Aug.

Montaigu-de-Quercy ✉ 82150

★★Le Vieux Relais, 3 Place Hôtel-de-Ville, ✆ 63 94 46 63, has pleasant rooms in a half-timbered 15th-century post house; the dishes served in the rustic dining room venture beyond southwest traditions, the vegetables being especially well pre-pared (menus from 110–210F, closed Mon). An 18th-century *gentilhommière*, the **★★★Château de l'Hoste**, 10km west at Saint-Beauzeil, ✆ 63 95 25 61, has well-restored, guaranteed peaceful rooms in the midst of a large park with a pool (closed Oct); the kitchen specializes in seafood and lavish desserts. Menus at 110, 230 and 275F, book.

Penne-d'Agenais ✉ 47140

Chez Bonnet, ✆ 53 41 22 17, has a wide terrace in the central square, run by an outlandish Dutch artist and her husband, who is fond of cooking up lavish but mod-erately priced Indonesian feasts ordered a couple of days in advance (about 110F a head, closed Feb). Below Penne, in Saint-Sylvestre-sur-Lot, the striking 13th–18th century **★★★★Château Lalande**, ✆ 53 36 15 15, has recently been given a com-plete overhaul and fitted with all the mod cons and heated swimming pools cascading into one another. The restaurant, manned in the kitchen by chef Jean-Luc Rabanel, is one the tops in the region, although beware—you can easily drop 500F at a meal.

Villeneuve-sur-Lot ✉ 47300

Hotels here are geared to prune merchants, but **★★★Les Chênes**, on the hillside at Bel-Air in Pujols, ✆ 53 49 04 55, will charm you with its refined rooms and heated pool. In Villeneuve, **★★La Résidence**, 17 Av Lazare Carnot, ✆ 53 40 17 03, and **★Les Remparts**, 1 Rue E. Marcel, ✆ 53 70 71 63, are both functional but pleasant; golfers can stay near the links, pool and tennis courts at the **★★Golf Hôtel de Castelnaud**, 12km north at La Menuisière, Castelnaud-de-Gratecambe (47290), ✆ 53 01 60 19.

Pujols ✉ 47300

For lunch or dinner, Pujols' **La Toque Blanche**, ✆ 53 49 00 30, wins hands down in altitude and cuisine. Accompany the panoramic views with some of the most delicious, delicately prepared duck dishes you've ever had, from the most tra-ditional to the most innovative (especially the *magret* grilled with preserved pears); extensive wine list; delicious 190F menu, others 275 and 450F (closed Sun night and Mon exc in summer). For less budget-busting prices, try La Toque Blanche's annexe, **Auberge Lou Calel**, ✆ 53 70 46 14, in a handsome medieval house, with a great view over the valley and delicious menus from 85–200F (closed Tues night and Wed exc Aug). Otherwise, dine under the wisteria by the river at **Aux Berges du Lot**, 3 Rue Hôtel-de-Ville, ✆ 53 70 84 41, where the fish dishes are especially good (menus from 75–200F, closed Sun night and Mon).

The prunes of Agen are known around the world. As it happens, though, most of them do not come from Agen at all, but from the rich lands of this last stage of the Lot valley. It isn't a touristy area, but a businesslike, well-off agricultural paradise, packed tightly with not only plum orchards but also strawberries, asparagus and all the other *primeurs* that decorate France's markets around the year.

Tourist Information

Aiguillon: Av. J. E. Bazin, ☏ 53 79 62 58

market days

Casseneuil: Wednesdays

Sainte-Livrade: Fridays

Clairac: Thursdays

Castelmoron: Tuesdays

Aiguillon: Tuesdays and Fridays

Monclar: Wednesdays and Saturdays

After Villeneuve, the first village on the Lot is medieval **Casseneuil**; since good stone was lacking in this part of the valley, nearly everything is made of brick, including most of Casseneuil's houses and its church. The same goes for **Sainte-Livrade-sur-Lot**, where there is an odd brick fortification called the Tour du Roi, the *roi* being Richard the Lion-Heart, who built it according to the local legend. The bricks of Ste-Livrade's church are half eroded away, giving the building a strangely outlandish air. This was the church of an important priory, around which the village grew up, and the ambitions of its founders far outran the resources of those who followed. Look inside for some fine carvings in the 'Romanesque Chapel', now housing the main altar: on the capitals, a mermaid and her baby, a satyr, and a monster or two.

Next down the river on the south bank, **Le-Temple-sur-Lot** was the site of a Templar commandery that oversaw all the order's holdings in the Agenais; the commandery building survives, along with its chapel, now the village church. Near the village, the century-old botanical gardens of the **Latour-Marliac** firm have a vast array of lotuses, water lilies and other water-loving plants *(open daily mid Mar–Sept)*.

In the hills to the south, off the D 13, you can find your way to a delightful place called **Saint-Sardos**, a tiny, sleepy hamlet decked with flowers and sleeping dogs. The 12th-century church on its green has a lovely, well-preserved portal carved with beasts and floral designs, which is lit up at night. Where the D 13 meets the river is the unfortunately named **Castelmoron-sur-Lot**, where the Lot is backed up by a dam to make a little lake for swimming and boating; there's a beach along the river. The hills to the north of Castelmoron are quite pretty, though there is nothing to detain you there except another typical bastide of Alphonse de Poitiers, **Monclar**. West of here, at Brugnac, you can visit **Le Chaudron Magique**, where you can learn about raising angora goats and rabbits and natural plant dyes; there are baby goats for the kids to bottle-feed and a shop selling yarn, mohair cloth and pullovers *(tours at 3, 4.30 and 6 in the summer holidays, 3 and 4.30 on Sat and Sun only the rest of the year; adm)*.

In **Granges-sur-Lot**, just downstream from Castelmoron, one of the largest plum farms in the valley has created the **Prune Museum** *(open daily 8–11 and 2–6, Sun 3–7; adm)* for the curious and the constipated; a 35-min prune video, old drying ovens, local costumes, a prune jammery and *chocolaterie*, free tastings and the plummiest shop in the hemisphere are only some of the attractions.

Pruneaux d'Agen

We all remember the episode in *Le Tour de Gaule d'Astérix*, where a treacherous Agenais innkeeper tries to capture Astérix and Obelix by slipping a Mickey into their prunes. And you will be as shocked as we were to learn that this is a flagrant anachronism. It seems that the first plums in the area were brought over from Damascus by the crusaders in 1148; they took at once to the local soil and climate, and people soon learned to dry them out for the famous *pruneaux d'Agen*, the prunes of Agen, which as every French gourmet knows are the finest in the universe. Most come from a fast-drying plum called *prune d'ente*, named after the special graft given to the tree. Go to any local market to discover the extraordinary variety of prunes. The Lot-et-Garonne produces, on average, 30,000 metric tons a year. You'll see a considerable portion of them prettily displayed in the purple shop windows of Agen: boxes of *pruneaux fourrés* (prunes stuffed with chocolate, etc) jars of prune cream, and prunes in Armagnac. There are also some really excellent prune liqueurs and *eau de vie* made by small local producers—you'll see them on sale occasionally in patisseries. Local cooks bend themselves over backwards to come up with new ways to employ prunes in cuisine; recipes combine them with quail, rabbit, pork and even fish.

Alose aux pruneaux (shad with prunes) from the Marmande tourist office: Clean and cut 1.5kg of shad into sections. Soak 20 Agen prunes in warm water for 5mins, drain and stone them and cook for 8mins on low heat with a clove and orange peel in a cup of Côtes du Marmandais. Quickly brown the shad sections in a little oil in a large saucepan, sprinkle with Armagnac, set alight and remove the fish. In the same pan sauté 150g of chopped shallots, 50g of thinly sliced carrots, 50g of thinly sliced celery, and garlic, thyme, parsley and bay leaf. Add the sauce from the prunes and two cups of red wine (minus a small glass), and when it's a quarter boiled down, add a half cup of *fumet de poisson* (or fish boullion). Cook for another 5mins, then add the fish and prunes and cook for 20mins. When the fish is done, remove fish and prunes, strain the sauce and put back on the heat, add the glass of wine and season. Remove skin and bones of shad, arrange on a plate with the sauce ladled on top, sprinkle with chives, and then give it to the cat.

Clairac presents a beautiful panorama from the riverfront; from the inside, it is perhaps less beautiful, and has little to show from a busy history. Clairac's great abbey was wrecked in the Wars of Religion, leaving only a bit called the *tour ronde*. Near by, the village's dubious attraction is the **Abbaye des Automates**: dozens of clockwork monks working, praying and illuminating manuscripts, and dozens of other figures illustrating favourite fairy tales. Clairac also has a museum of village history and life on the farm in the old days, the **Musée du Vieux Clairac**. East of Clairac on the D 911, follow the old blue historic marker signs and with luck you will find your way to one of the most remarkable monuments of the region: an ornate monumental stone **fountain** most likely the work of Jean Goujon, France's master sculptor of the Renaissance, standing at the edge of a broad lawn *(private property; ask at the house to visit)*.

The Lot meets the Garonne at **Aiguillon**, a town that began as a Roman encampment but knew its greatest fame as the residence of the wealthy Duc d'Aiguillon, a political figure of the last days of the *ancien régime* whose little court and decadent parties here made Aiguillon the hot spot of the Agenais in the summer, when lots of swells (including the duke's friend Madame du Barry) came down from Versailles. It is to him that the town owes its landmark **château** (1765), a stately work of early neoclassical architecture.

The Pays des Serres

Ever since the Middle Ages, the triangle between the Lot and Garonne has been called the *pays des Serres*. It is a fitting word: *serres* means an eagle's talons (the limestone looks as if it has been clawed by a huge bird, leaving gashes between its limestone 'tables'); coincidentally the word also means greenhouses, and there are plenty of these too—or more likely plastic tunnels for fruit and vegetable *primeurs*, which farmers have lately added to supplement their wheatfields. Many of the villages here haven't changed much since the *pays des Serres* was given its name, places like **Hautefage-la-Tour**, south of Villeneuve, with a flamboyant Gothic church, hexagonal Renaissance bell tower and a village *lavoir* in the centre; nearby **Laroque-Timbaut** has a 12th-century *halle* and tiny medieval lanes, especially the Ruelle de Lô, entered under the clock tower. To the northeast, **Frespech** is a delightful little hilltop hamlet, where old gates and houses, and an 11th-century church with a partial *lauze* roof, still stand intact.

Further east are two baby bastides: **Beauville**, complete with its arcades, vestiges of its walls and Gothic church with a pyramidal bell tower, and **Bourg-de-Visa**, near a sacred Gaulish spring now known as the Source de Saint-Quirin. South is the moated, four-towered **Château de Brassac**, begun in 1180 by Raymond V of Toulouse *(guided tours July–Oct, 2–6)*. In the same area you'll find **Castelsagrat**, another bastide (vintage 1270), with its old communal wells in the irregularly arcaded *place* and a church with a wonderfully overripe Baroque retable, and half-timbered **Montjoi**, just west, which could win a prize as the tiniest bastide of all. **Saint-Maurin**, further west, is a charming, half-timbered village near the impressive ruins of an abbey founded by Moissac. There's a model of it in the church, as well as some carved capitals telling the story of Maurin's martyrdom. The inhabitants of St-Maurin have put together a small but intriguing **Musée de la Vie Agricole et Artisanale** in the abbey cellars *(open July and Aug 3–7, closed Tues; at other times contact the* mairie, © 53 95 31 25).

Towards Agen is the bastide of **Puymirol**, built by Count Raymond VII of Toulouse in 1246. Located on a bluff, with a citadel and deep moat at its weakest point, Puymirol was believed to be impregnable until the Protestants seized it in 1574. Much of medieval Puymirol has surived—the counts' residence, the *cornières* and *halle* (now the village *salle de fêtes*), the 13th-century Gothic porch of the church, and the views from the Champ de Mars, site of the citadel before Richelieu had it razed. The most interesting part of the western *Serres* is around **Prayssas**, a market town and Chasselas grape grower. Medieval **Clermont-Dessous** offers fine views down the Garonne valley. Catherine de' Medici and her daugher, Marguerite de Valois spent time hiding out from the Protestants at **Port-Sainte-Marie**, and met Henri of Navarre there—Marguerite's future husband.

Where to Stay and Eating Out

Ste-Livrade-sur-Lot ✉ 47110

For lunch if you're passing through, try **La Belle Epoque** on the main street; confits and seafood on menus 70–145 F.

Beauville ✉ 47470

*Hôtel du Midi in the centre, © 53 95 41 18 is a sweet little place, with good home cooking (menus at 55 and 80F).

Bourg-de-Visa ✉ 82190

In the centre, the terrace of **Chez Maria**, © 63 94 24 22, is a fine place for a country lunch for under 100F (closed Sept). On the D 7 south of Bourg, **Ferme-auberge de Lasbourdettes**, © 63 94 26 75, offers a delicious variety of menus including wine and coffee, featuring locally raised duck, goose and rabbit dishes (from 90–200F).

Castelsagrat ✉ 82400

There are five peaceful bed-and-breakfast rooms at the **Ferme-auberge de Pachot**, 1km from the village (follow the signs), © 63 94 23 50; menus with local rabbit or duck dishes from 90–170F.

Puymirol ✉ 47270

This little bastide, 17km east of Agen, has something few one-horse towns ever dream of in their brightest moments: one of the top-rated restaurants in France. The beautifully medieval/modern ******L'Aubergade**, 52 Rue Royale, © 53 95 31 46, is run by master chef Michel Trama, who takes local ingredients—foie gras, *cèpes*, duckling, snails and so on—and combines them with the sure art, imagination and magic of an early Renaissance master. Everything is superb, but Trama's desserts are legendary—warm chocolate cake with an exquisite sour sauce, or the *larme de chocolat* with tiny morello cherries (reservations mandatory; weekday lunch menu 180F; also menus at 270 and 480F, easily much more à la carte or with a fine Bordeaux; closed Mon exc in summer, and the first half of Mar). L'Aubergade is also a Relais et Châteaux hotel, with 10 gorgeous rooms, all opening onto a garden courtyard.

Agen

Caesar made the first known mention of the future prune capital, then the humble hilltop *oppidum* of Aginnum, in his *Gallic Wars*. In the *pax romana* that followed, Aginnum relocated down into the Garonne valley, where it suffered the usual barbarian and Norman invasions. In the 13th century Agen found itself smack on the front lines between French and English territory. It changed hands 11 times in the Hundred Years' War, but it could have been worse—each new ruler would try to make the Agenais happy to see him by granting the town new privileges.

Even after becoming a commune in the 13th century, Agen was under the influence of its noble bishops. During the Renaissance many of these were Italian, and they gave the little provincial town a jump-start in art appreciation and the humanities. A booming textile trade, begun in the 17th century when Agen grew by leaps and bounds, was snuffed out by the Continental Blockade. These days it owes much of its prosperity to its location midway between Bordeaux and Toulouse; transport depots, fruit packing and bureaucracy are the things that keep the money coming in. Admittedly these aren't big tourist magnets, but this shapeless and rather staid departmental capital does have an ace up its sleeve: one of the finest provincial art museums in France. Or come when the Agenais show their wild and crazy side, when their beloved rugby squad is thumping some hapless opponent. You'll know if they're doing well: all the shops in the town centre will have team photos and banners in their windows, next to the displays of prunes.

Getting Around

Agen's airport is to the southwest, ✆ 53 96 21 77. There are several trains a day to Paris (change at Limoges), with stops in Monsempron-Libos, Penne, Périgueux, Les Eyzies, and TGVs to Bordeaux and Toulouse from the station at Place Rabelais, ✆ 56 92 50 50, reservations 56 92 60 60. For a taxi, ✆ 53 66 39 14.

Tourist Information

107 Boulevard Carnot, ✆ 53 66 50 50. For information on nearly every conceivable aspect of the Lot-et-Garonne, contact the Maison du Tourisme, 4 Rue André Chenier, B. P. 158, Agen, ✆ 53 66 14 14.

Wednesdays and Sundays in the Place du Pin; Saturdays in Place Jasmin; annual prune fair in mid-September in Place 14-Juillet.

Musée Municipal des Beaux Arts

This, the one great reason to visit Agen, is located in the centre of the city at Place du Docteur-Esquirol, on the corner of Rue des Juifs *(open 10–12 and 2–6, closed Tues; free on Wed)*, where its vast hoard occupies four beautifully restored 16th- and 17th-century *hôtels particuliers*. The collection begins with the Middle Ages—tombstones and effigies, goldwork, carved Romanesque and 'Gothic capitals and a 16th-century tapestry on the *month of March*. The star of the Gallo-Roman section is the *Vénus du Mas*, a 1st-century Greek marble dug up by a farmer at Mas d'Agenais in 1876, who, despite her lack of a head and part of an arm, is still a helluva tomato, a Venus de Milo in her early 20s; the special lighting perfectly shows off the exceptional cut of the drapery. Don't miss the fine small bronzes in the glass case—a Gaulish helmet, a Celtic horse head and a pawing horse. The next room, with a Renaissance chimneypiece, is devoted to hunting and warfare, with another fine tapestry and a Renaissance dagger carved with an intricate *danse macabre*. Prehistoric finds are kept downstairs where Agen used to keep its criminals—in the dungeon.

A beautiful spiral stair leads up to the 16th- and 17th-century paintings: two striking Renaissance portraits by Corneille de Lyon, a *Portrait of a man* by Philippe de Champaigne and a *Virgin and Child* by the school of Raphael. There's a reconstruction of a pharmacy, and the ceramic works by philosopher Bernard Palissy, born in 1510 near Monpazier, who desperately sought the ancient secret of enamel, burning even his furniture to light his kilns. Here too are brightly coloured plates from the same period by the Italian masters, especially from Urbino.

Beyond minor works by Tiepolo and Greuze are **five Goyas**, left to the city by Chaudordy, French ambassador to Madrid, which form a complement to the more important collection of Goyas at Castres. There's a powerful *Self Portrait* painted by the artist in his 40s; one of the *Caprichos*, with a donkey, elephant and bull flying over a crowd of people. Another crowd follows the ascent of the *Mongolfière*, recording the 1793 launch of a hot-air balloon in Madrid; a royal commission, the *Study for an Equestrian Portrait of Ferdinand VII*; and *La Misada Parida*, a picture of the first Mass of a newly-delivered young mother, which Goya painted on top of an old painting that is slowly but surely leaching through. There's also a copy of Goya's *La Promenade* said to depict Goya and the Duchess of Alba. Other works here include *Le Conteur* by Watteau.

The last rooms move on to the 19th century, first with ceramics, including those of Agen's own Boudon de Saint-Amas (1774–1856), who introduced English glazed-ware techniques to France. There's a fine landscape by Corot, another by Sisely, and seascapes by proto-Impressionist Eugène Boudin, the master of Monet and one of the first French painters to paint out-of-doors.

And the Rest of Agen

Agen's cathedral, **St-Caprais** (north of the museum, a block from the station, in Rue Raspail), is named after a local boy who hid out during Diocletian's persecutions until he heard of the courageous martyrdom of Ste Foy (*see* p.287), when he outed himself as a Christian, only to get his head chopped off. There isn't much to see inside (just as well, because it's often closed) but the Romanesque tri-lobe apse with *modillons* sculpted with heads of humans and animals. In the northwest corner of Agen an impressive 23-arch aqueduct, the **Pont Canal** carries the Canal Latéral (*see* below) over the Garonne. You can hire canal boats to explore it further; contact the Maison du Tourisme.

Besides a stroll around Agen's prune-laden *patisseries* and *confiseries*, walk over to the banks of the Garonne and the city's favourite promenade, the Esplanade du Gravier. It offers a fine view of the Pont Canal, while just up Av. du Général de Gaulle stands the **Monument to Jasmin**, honouring Agen's favourite poet.

Jasmin, the 'Hero of the Occitan Renaissance'

Jacques Boé (1798–1864), son of a humble tailor of Agen, was a wig-maker who liked to recite the poems he wrote in his native Occitan to his customers. In 1830 he published the fruits of his labours, the *Papillotos*, under the name of his grandfather, Jacques Jasmin; by chance the book was picked up by Charles Nodier, the author of *Trilby*, who made them the toast of Paris. The capital was then in the midst of a fervent, slightly retarded Romantic era and the wigmaker-poet of Agen caught its fancy. Fellow poet Lamartine dubbed Jasmin 'the Homer of the Proletariat'; the Académie Française honoured him; he was received by Louis Philippe and Napoleon III, and embarked on a lecture tour across France, reciting his poetry and donating all the proceeds to charity. Provençal poet Frédéric Mistral (who went on to become the only Nobel prize winner in literature in a minority language), idolized Jasmin and in 1854 asked him to lead his Occitan literary movement, the Félibrage. But Jasmin preferred to devote the rest of his life to poetry and charity. Perhaps his finest lyrics were love songs to Agen: *Me fas troubà, pel sero de ma bito/Sourel del mèl et cami del belour...* (You found for me in the evening of my life/A sun of honey and velvet way...).

Agen ✉ 47000   ***Where to Stay***

****Château-hôtel des Jacobins**, Place des Jacobins, ℭ 53 47 03 31, offers 15 very comfortable rooms in central Agen, in a beautifully restored, ivy-covered *hôtel particulier*. ***Le Provence**, 22 Cours du 14-Juillet, ℭ 53 47 39 11, is a pleasant little hotel in the centre, with spruce, soundproofed rooms. Of the cheaper places, **Les Ambans**, 59 Rue des Ambans, ℭ 53 66 28 60, is one of the nicest, recently remodelled, with showers in every room. There's an **Auberge de Jeunesse**, 17 Rue Léo-Lagrange, Cité Léon-Blum on the road to Cahors, ℭ 53 66 18 98, open all year.

Agen's best restaurants are all outside of town (*see* below), but in the centre try **Michel Latrille**, 66 Rue C.-Desmoulins, ℰ 53 66 24 35, with lots of seafood on the menu (from 85 to 260F, closed Sat lunch and Sun); **Le Bouchon**, 78 Bd Carnot, ℰ 53 66 33 94, with a cool, pastel dining room upstairs serving meals with a light touch—rare in these parts; landfood menu at 90 F, seafood menu 165F (closed Sat lunch and Sun). Another good choice, **Le Petit Vatel**, 52 Rue Coeur-de-Lion, ℰ 53 47 66 00, also does lovely things with seafood; the *soupe de crabe en croûte* is absolutely delicious (menu at 105F, more à la carte, closed Sat lunch and Mon).

For half that you can have a filling lunch at the popular **Bistrot Apicius**, 8 Rue E. Sentini, ℰ 53 66 07 81, with typical bistrot food (closed Sun and Mon eve) or at the **Crêperie des Jacobins**, 3 Place des Jacobins, ℰ 53 66 33 94, serving both flour and buckwheat (*sarrasin*) crêpes with a long list of fillings and side salads (closed Sun and Mon). And don't be shy about dining in the café of Agen's railway station; at lunchtime it's one of the most crowded places in town, and they make the best 39F *steak bordelaise* you'll find anywhere.

Around Agen

****Château Saint-Marcel**, 3km south on the N 113 towards Toulouse, at Boe (47550), ℰ 53 96 61 30, belonged to Montesquieu, who may have given the order to plant the majestic cedars that line the entrance. Recently restored, there are very sumptuous suites furnished with antiques in the castle, or more modern (and far less pricey) rooms in the annexe; there's a pool and tennis courts in the park. The restaurant serves imaginative, delicate combinations of local ingredients. The 160F menu is exquisite (also at 250F, closed Sun dinner and Mon).

At suburban Bon-Encontre (47240) ****Le Parc**, 41 Rue République, ℰ 53 96 17 75, has 10 cosy country rooms opposite the pilgrimage shrine of the Virgin of Bon-Encontre and another top restaurant, **Mariottat**, named after its chef, who works wonders with the best the daily market provides; menus at 98 and 150F, and a special 200F Friday menu (closed Sun night and Mon). *****Renaissance de l'Etoile**, Rte de Mont-de-Marsan, at Brax (47310), 6km west of Agen, ℰ 53 68 69 23, offers peaceful, well-furnished rooms in a park and a lavish spread at the table, accompanied by one of the longest wine lists in the *département* (menus at 105, 165 190 and 290F, closed Sun night, Sat lunch and Mon). *****La Corne d'Or**, on the N 113 towards Bordeaux, at Colayrac-St-Cirq (47450), ℰ 53 47 02 76, is a pleasant place to stay, with prices low for the category.

South of Agen: the Brulhois

Vines take over from plums between Agen and the Gers in the hills of the Brulhois. **Layrac**, 11km south of Agen, is the main town here, a pleasant hilltop bastide built over a Roman villa. Don't miss the 17th-century *fontaine-lavoir*, or the roadside cross, carved with indecipherable symbols. Its 12th-century church, **St-Martin** has capitals on its façade adorned with intertwined demons and a striking Roman-Byzantine apse; the dome was added in the 18th century. **Dunes** and **Caudecoste** to the east are other picturesque bastides to visit; **Moirax** to the west has a delightful 11th-century church with more than its share of fine carvings both outside and inside.

Côtes de Brulhois

South of the Garonne, on the borders of the Gers, AOC Côtes du Brulhois is perhaps the least-known wine from the Lot-et-Garonne. Grown on the alluvial pebbles atop a clay and limestone bed, this well-structured, dark-red wine is made from malbec, tannat and fer-savadou, as well as merlot and cabernet franc. A favourite tipple of the Templars, it can be aged up to ten years and goes well with game, rich meat dishes and cheeses. Best of all, it's much cheaper than Madiran and Cahors. Try it at the cooperative cellars at Dunes-Donzac or Goulens, south of Layrac.

Nérac

There's a pretty little river called the Baïse that starts up in the mountains near Lannemezan and bubbles down the Hautes-Pyrénées and Gers through rather unappreciative countryside; it doesn't pass anything particularly edifying until it gets to **Nérac**. This fat village counts scarcely more than 7,000 inhabitants, but its association with the d'Albret family in the 1500s has given it some fine monuments and the air of a little capital, if you see it from the right angle.

Tourist Information

Avenue Mondenard, off Place de l'Hôtel de Ville, © 53 65 27 75

The Marguerite of Marguerites

It was no accident that the d'Albret family came into such spectacular prominence in the 15th and 16th centuries. They were in fact the agents of the French crown. Their loyalty assured Paris an important ally in a Gascony that had few natural ties to France, made up of regions that had become accustomed to a large degree of independence under English sovereignty and the feudal anarchy that had preceded it. In return, the French kings showered every sort of prize on the family, not the least of which were advantageous marriages to increase the d'Albret's wealth and influence. With their help Henri d'Albret became king of Navarre, at which point King François I found him a fitting match for his sister, Marguerite d'Angoulême (1492–1549).

Already a widow at 35, it was Marguerite's second go. Everyone at the time counted her the most eligible lady of France—not just for being the king's sister, but for a wit, charm and intelligence that stood out even in Renaissance courts. Henri d'Albret was no match for her, but he had sense enough to take care of political business and stay out of the way while Marguerite turned their favoured residence of Nérac into a brilliant court where poetry and the new humanistic learning were the order of the day. Though they never converted themselves, Henri and Marguerite welcomed many of the new Protestant thinkers to Nérac, including John Calvin; dissenters circulated bibles and preached openly. Among the poets who enjoyed Marguerite's favour was Clément Marot of Cahors, who wrote some fulsome lines in her honour, describing her as *plus mère que maistresse*. Marguerite had literary ambitions of her own. Best known among her works, and widely popular throughout France, was the *Heptameron*, a collection of stories with a frame tale of travellers snowbound at Sarrance in the Pyrenees, inspired by Boccaccio's *Decameron*.

Marguerite and Henri had a cute little daughter, known to everyone in France as *Mignonne*, the nickname her uncle, King François had given her. Sitting in at her parents' table, Jeanne must have been much more impressed with the fiery preachers than the poets. She grew up to be the redoubtable Jeanne d'Albret—'nothing in her of a woman but the sex'—a dour, intolerant Protestant who enforced her theological opinions on most of her subjects, including the Néracais, and contributed as much as anyone in keeping the flames of the religious wars burning. As evidence for the argument that traits and qualities skip generations, consider Jeanne's son, the fellow who was brought up a good Protestant and fought across France for the cause, but finally found a way to use good sense and tolerance to put an end to the troubles—King Henri IV.

The Château

On a height over the Baïse, this is quite the most elegant thing in Nérac—at least what's left of it. Vengeful demolitions ordered by Cardinal Richelieu in 1621 have left only one side of what was once a stout, old-fashioned castle, hiding inside of it a magnificent Renaissance courtyard built by Henri d'Albret's grandfather Alain. The side that remains has a lovely loggia of twisted columns. Inside is Nérac's **museum**, largely devoted to explanatory exhibits of the town in its heyday, with models of the château as it originally looked; downstairs is the archaeology section, with everything from a mammoth's molar to scraps of Roman pottery with their manufacturers' trademarks.

A walk from here around the old centre of Nérac won't take long: it only covers some 15 blocks. Rue de l'Ecole was the old main stem; on it you can see the 17th-century (former) town hall and a fine Renaissance palace, the **Maison des Conférences**. Nérac's church of **St-Nicolas**, like most French churches of the 18th century, hardly rates a notice in most books, but this one is a cut above the norm, a restrained neoclassical façade that is probably the better off for never having been able to afford the statuary that was intended for it, and a clean, airy interior with some 19th-century stained glass that impresses in the way such windows are supposed to impress: the whole story, from Abel and Noah up to Jesus himself behind the altar. Entering Nérac along the Allées d'Albret, you have probably already noticed the obligatory statue of 'Our Henry', Henri IV, with a twinkle in his bronze eye.

Henri spent much of his time in Nérac before he became king; he especially enjoyed hunting boar in the pine forests of the Néracais. Even then the common people were fond of him, and it didn't bother Henri at all to learn that everybody in town called him 'Big Nose' (*Grand-nas*). The statue may not do it justice.

La Garenne

From the back of the château, an elegant stair descends to the Baïse, leading to the Pont Neuf and Nérac's cross-river *faubourg*, Petit Nérac. Henri's father, Antoine de Bourbon, laid out a royal park here for his family called **La Garenne**, stretching for over a mile along the riverfront and which has survived to become the town's outstanding civic embellishment. Everyone in Nérac comes here in the afternoon, to stroll along the Baïse, to fish, or just to take the kids to the playground. Near the entrance on Avenue Georges Clemenceau, a small brick shelter covers a bit of **Roman mosaic**, excavated in an important villa that once stood near by. Further on you'll come to the **Fontaine de Fleurette**. According to the local legend, Fleurette was the daughter of Antoine and Jeanne d'Albret's gardener, and Henri's first love—when he abandoned her, she drowned herself in the river. If you like, you may take La Garenne as the setting for *Love's Labours Lost*; most of the action of the play takes place in 'the king's park at Navarre'.

Petit Nérac's streets are as old as the town centre; the best part is along the river: picturesque **Rue Séderie**, the site of the tanneries that were Nérac's main business in the old days. Now most of its houses have been restored (there's even an art gallery). Around the corner on Rue Sully is the 16th-century **Vieux Pont**, and the **Maison de Sully**, a 16th-century house where Henri IV's great minister stayed when Henri was in Nérac.

On Sunday and holiday afternooons at 4.30, weather permitting, there are **river tours** from the Quai de la Baïse.

The Néracais

Tourist Information

Mézin: Place Armand Fallières, ✆ 53 65 77 46

This very pleasant *pays*, tucked between the Armagnac and the pine forests of the Landes, is also often called, along with parts of the neighbouring Landes, the 'Pays d'Albret'; its long history as the feudal domain of the d'Albrets has given it an identity that lasts to this day. South of Nérac on the D 656, where the road crosses the river Osse there is a pretty medieval bridge called the **Pont Romain**. The next village, **Mézin**, was the home of Armand Fallières, president of France from 1906 to 1913. Fallières's presidency caused no embarrassment to Mézin, and consequently the villagers have honoured him by naming their main square after him. There is a small **museum**, with exhibits on Fallières's life and on corks—cork oaks being one of the area's traditional crops—and also a Roman statue of Jupiter *(daily exc Mon, 10.30–12, 2.30–7 from July–Sept, otherwise 2.30–5.30; closed Oct to 14 April)*. Mézin grew up around an important Cluniac abbey, and it retains the church of **St-Jean**, Romanesque in the apse and the rest strong and graceful Gothic—though the builders may have botched it; currently there are cracks in the vault and iron girders holding up a tilted column. On the vault over the altar, note the whimsical carving of a grimacing giant and pot of flowers. The tympanum on the north door must have been destroyed in the Revolution; replacing it you can still barely make out some Revolutionary slogan about the 'Supreme Being'. These are common enough in French village churches; the radicals in Paris were telling the peasants that it was still all right to believe in God, though not necessarily the god of the Christian Church—it's a mystery, though, that so many of these inscriptions survive.

You could get lost for a long time in the lush, delightful countryside around Mézin and never mind it. On the stretch of the D 656 that follows the valley of the Gélise, you'll pass pretty things like a country chapel and a traditional Agenais *pigeonnier* on stilts, and plenty of farmers hang signs out to sell you asparagus and *cèpes*, foie gras and *floc*, the sweet apéritif wine of the neighbouring Armagnac. At **Poudenas**, there is a fine Italianate **château** to visit; built largely in the 17th and 18th centuries, it has some period furniture and paintings *(guided tours daily 3–5 pm, 14 July–1. Sept, and Sundays only from Pentecost to 1 Nov; adm)*. There are Romanesque churches at **Sos** and **Gueyze**, and a fortified church from the 1200s at **Villeneuve-de-Mézin**, south of Mézin. **Meylan**, just inside the pine forest of the Landes, is a tiny village that seems to consist of a swing set, a *mairie* in a shed, a picnic table and a war memorial, yet it contains so many curiosities that the Meylanais have drawn out a little itinerary for them, posted in front of the *mairie*. The circuit includes the château and unusual Romanesque church of Saint-Pau, a small cromlech hidden in the pine woods, called Las Naous Peyros, and the **Lac Sans-fond**. As the name implies, no one has yet found the bottom of this mysterious little lake. There are a number of legends: about the phantom that haunts it, and about the church that once stood on its bank; the lake swallowed it up one Sunday, parishoners and all.

East and south of Nérac, the landscapes are much the same. You can visit the attractive bastide of **Lamontjoie** (they've got Saint Louis's hand in a reliquary in the church), or else swap some lies with the experts at **Moncrabeau**. Over 200 years ago, a jolly, tale-telling monk founded the Académie des Menteurs here, and ever since its 40 members (just like the Académie Française) have met every year on the first Sunday in August to throw the bull around and elect the King of Liars, consecrated in a solemn ceremony at the 'stone of truth'. Every three years this droll village also claims to host a competition for the World Championship of Grimacing.

North of Nérac, the D 930 takes you to **Barbaste**, and one of the famous sites of the southwest, the **Moulin de Henri IV**. If it looks more like a castle, it is that too; fortified mills are not uncommon in France, built in feudal times when grain was precious and there were plenty of enemies ready to try to grab it. This one, along with the bridge in front of it, is from the 1200s. The story has it that the nobleman who built it had four daughters of different ages, and made the mill's four towers different heights in their honour. In later times the mill belonged to the d'Albrets, and it passed from them to Henri IV, who liked being called the 'Miller of Barbaste', at least, better than he liked being called 'Big Nose'. To the west, on the D 665, **Durance** is a 13th-century bastide surrounded by forests that were the hunting preserve of the d'Albrets and King Henri; the village has ruins of the castle they used for their hunting lodge.

Northeast of Barbaste is another bastide, **Vianne**, founded in 1284 by Jourdain de l'Isle, seneschal of King Edward I. Vianne still has most of its walls and gates, along with the church of Notre-Dame and its austere tower, and a pretty churchyard full of cypresses. Today the village makes its living from faience and crystal; there are some lovely things for sale in the shops on the main street, and at Faïence des Remparts, built into the village's wall. The **Cristalleries et Verreries d'Art** factory offers tours: ✆ 53 97 55 05. In the hills above Vianne is the **Château de Xaintrailles** *(tours by appointment)*, once the home of Maréchal Poton, a companion of Joan of Arc.

Where to Stay and Eating Out

Nérac ✉ 47600

Nothing special here in accommodations; the **★★Du Château**, ✆ 53 65 09 05, on Avenue Mondenard will put you up for a night you won't remember, but much better, they can also fill you up royally with a good 60F menu and others up to 150F, including salmon in *millefeuille* pastry, a roast duck laced with strawberry vinegar and other recherché dishes. There's also the simple and proper **★★Hôtel d'Albret**, 40 Allées d'Albret, ✆ 53 65 20 26 (closed Sept). The d'Albret has one of the better restaurants in town, a typical southwest *confit* and foie gras palace with an outside terrace and a choice of menus 60–260F. There are two inexpensive choices: the **★De la Paix**, Loc. Bourg, ✆ 53 65 41 41, and the **★Du Pont**, at the end of Avenue Mondenard by the Pont Neuf, ✆ 53 65 09 76; some rooms overlook the river.

Nérac also runs a pleasant, shady **municipal camp site** in the park of La Garenne, ✆ 53 97 02 66. If they're full, there's a municipal camp site just as good by the river in Mézin, ✆ 53 65 70 01.

Poudenas ✉ 47170

The star accommodation of the Néracais is here, in a 14th-century mill on the banks of the Gélise. **★★★La Belle Gasconne**, ✆ 53 65 71 58: seven beautifully decorated rooms, a pool and garden, and above all an excellent restaurant with the best of fresh local ingredients, wines and recipes on a 165F menu. The bargain choice, just down the D 656, just happens to be a lovely, half-timbered 17th-century post house: **★Roi Henri**, with cheap, basic rooms and a 50F menu. If you don't care for mills or stage stops, try **★Le Postillon**, Place Delbousquet, ✆ 53 65 60 27, in nearby Sos; this one's in a restored smithy, with a few cosy rooms, and nice fat *magrets* and *confits* with *cèpes* out on the terrace (menus 95–210F).

In fact, it isn't just the Garonne; you have a choice of either following the river or the **Canal Latéral Garonne**, the 19th-century waterway that parallels the river, providing a complement to Languedoc's Canal du Midi and providing boats with a direct passage from the Mediterranean to the Atlantic.

Tourist Information

Casteljaloux: ✆ 53 93 00 00

Le Mas-d'Agenais: ✆ 53 89 50 58

Tonneins: ✆ 53 79 22 79

Marmande: Boulevard Gambetta, ✆ 53 64 44 44

market days

Marmande: Tuesdays, Thursdays and Saturdays; flea market on the second Sunday of each month

From Aiguillon to Marmande

Starting from Aiguillon (*see* p.293), just across the river and the canal is **Buzet-sur-Baïse**, a village near the confluence of the Baïse and the Garonne, dominated by its castle, high on a hill with tremendous views. There are two things to do here: take a 2-hour ride along the Baïse or the canal in a modern houseboat or a traditional boat called a *capucine* (Aquitain Navigation, ✆ 53 84 72 50) and seek out a bottle of guess what.

Côtes-de-Buzet

A cousin of Bordeaux, red Buzet is a mainly Merlot wine that owed its AOC status in 1973 to the tireless work of the Cave Coopérative de Buzet (now called the Vignerons Réunis), created in 1955 in Buzet-sur-Baïse to bring back the winemaking traditions that made the wine important in the Middle Ages. Although the growing area stretches all the way down the Baïse beyond Nérac, the vineyards only exist in pockets among other crops, on the best drained, pebbly land—many old mediocre family vineyards have been pulled up in the last two decades in favour of the more favoured modern varieties—Merlot, Cabernet Franc, Cabernet Sauvignon and Cot. Dedication, discipline and a unique interest in just the right type of oak cask (the cooperative has a coopery attached that makes 850 to 900 barrels a year, each with a five-year life span) have resulted in a fine, structured aromatic wine that goes beautifully with the region's rich dishes in prune sauces. At the top of the list of reds is the superb Château de Gueyze (especially the '87 or '88, which are almost ready to drink), followed by Cuvée Baron d'Ardeuil, named by Napoleon after the Gascon soldier who offered him some from his gourd (he too, was known henceforth as Baron). The whites have improved lately: the '89 is especially fine. Get them at the Vignerons Réunis, which markets over 90 per cent of the wine and offers tours of its vast cellars *(open Mon–Fri 9–12 and 2–6, Sat 9–12; © 53 84 74 30)*.

Damazan, another bastide of the 13th century, has creaky, leaning half-timbered houses, a little *mairie* over the market *halles*, and some of its walls and towers intact. Damazan, like Buzet, is one of the main centres for canal tourism, and there are cruises and boats to rent in season. North of Aiguillon, the large village of **Tonneins** advertises itself as the 'City of Free Parking'. But it needn't be so modest. Tonneins offers a wonderful panorama over the Garonne valley from the top of the town, and it can claim the annual production of some ten billion of France's distinctively stinky home-grown cigarettes at the **Manufacture**, the plant of the national tobacco monopoly. *Gauloises* and *Gitanes*, smokeable only by Frenchmen and masochists, are made largely from Aquitaine tobacco; the factory here cranks them out at the rate of 8000 a minute. You can watch them roll out at the Manufacture by ringing ahead, © 53 84 11 00.

Le Mas-d'Agenais

You'll reach this village by an elegant modern suspension bridge that crosses both the Garonne and the canal. Though the customary red-bordered sign announces the village, along with a floral arrangement of Mas's coat-of-arms (three gold hands on a red field), not a house is to be seen. Mas is up in the clouds, on a hill above the Garonne, a village closed into itself; Mas is special, and it knows it.

Known as *Velenum Pompeiacum* in Roman times, Mas was still one of the most important centres of the area in the Middle Ages; it isn't a large village, just a few lovely streets and squares with many restored houses, a brick medieval gateway, a wooden market *halle* from the 1600s, and a beautiful view over the Garonne from its little park on the edge of the cliffs. It also has one of the region's most interesting churches, **Saint-Vincent**, begun in 1085, replacing an ancient church (*c.* 440) that itself was built on the site of a Roman temple. Tinkered and tampered with over the centuries, it isn't much to look at from outside; Viollet-le-Duc gave the main entrance its present appearance, and at about the same time the tall steeple over it was demolished. The interior, however, contains a wealth of excellent sculptural decoration, mostly on the capitals (nearby shops or the tourist office sell tokens for the lighting: in the south aisle, Old Testament scenes including *Samson, David and Goliath, the Sacrifice of Abraham* and *Daniel in the Lions' Den*. The capitals in the north aisle and choir are mostly New Testament vignettes, along with *St Michael and the dragon* and the *Martyrdom of St Vincent*, while those high up in the nave itself have some surprising subjects: one is claimed to be the *Race of Atalanta* from Greek mythology and apparently the *Hunt of the Calydonian Boar* from the same story.

The church contains two ancient relics; one is an early Christian sarcophagus, said to be that of the obscure martyr St Vincent, which was on prominent display in Mas's original church. Hidden in the cemetery during the Norman invasions, it was only rediscovered in 1785. The other, a Roman *cippus* with a confusing inscription, may have originally been the base for the statue of a pagan god. Note also the beautifully carved **choir stalls**; these are believed to be a gift of Mary Stuart, originally intended for the church at La Réole. Mas's claim to fame, a painting by Rembrandt, is in the chapel to the right of the altar. originally, this scene of *Christ on the Cross* was part of a series of six on the Passion; all the rest are now together in Munich. For anyone who thinks Rembrandt only painted portraits, it will be a revelation (there are photographs of the others in the church); these are intense, remarkable paintings, where Jesus goes up on the cross a man and comes down a god.

South of Mas, the D 6 passes through the lovely Forest of Mas d'Agenais, another old hunting preserve, on the way to **Casteljaloux**, a former possession of the d'Albrets and the gateway to the great piney Landes. The name sounds as if it should mean jealous, but really comes from *gelos*, meaning perilous, a reality confirmed by the state of the castle itself, now a ruin. There are a few 15th-century buildings around the centre, but that's about it. However, it has the pretty sand-bordered Lac de Clarens just southwest, and just southeast down the D 11, the striking multi-towered **Château du Sendat**, first built in the 12th century, set amidst a tidy French garden. Among the Romanesque churches in the area, there's a good one at **Villefranche-du-Queyran** due northeast on the D 120, with a score of carved capitals; **Labastide-Castel-Amouroux** to the northwest has another one, with some good monsters on the capitals.

Further northwest, **Romestaing** has the 12th-century church of **Saint-Christophe** with more mysterious capitals. **Cocumont**, a main centre of the Côte de Marmandais growing area (*see* below) is just northwest of **Goux** (or Goutz) with a remarkable Romanesque church built on top of a 2000-year-old tumulus; deep below is the circular tomb of a local chieftain, never excavated. **Marcellus** is the site of a handsome 16th-century château, cradle of the counts who bought the Louvre's Venus de Milo from the Greek farmer who dug her up, and was determined to keep her from the Turkish occupiers. Further downstream, **Meilhan-sur-Garonne** sits atop a natural balcony, overlooking the hills of the Entre-Deux-Mers and their famous vineyards.

Marmande

Marmande, the most important market town between Agen and Bordeaux, is currently on its third name. Originally it was Marmande-la-Royale, when it received its charter in 1182 from Richard the Lion-Heart. After being used as a kind of revolving door in the Hundred Years' War (when it changed hands eight times) and Wars of Religion, it was Marmande-la-Sainte; now it has settled down on Marmande-la-Jolie, the queen of tomatoes.

Marmande has just redone its centre, Place Clemenceau, and in honour of its big red tomatoes has a statue called *La Pomme d'Amour*, referring to the old belief that tomatoes were an aphrodisiac. This overlooks the lofty fountain of Europa; near by is the **Musée Municipal Albert Marzelles** *(open 2–6, Sat 3–6, closed Mon)* with a hotchpotch of local items, especially from the 19th century; don't miss the lavish firemen's helmets, which perhaps explain why pre-Impressionist French historical paintings were called *pom-*

piers (firemen). Rue Léopold Faye, lined with half-timbered houses, leads back towards the 13th-century **Notre-Dame**, where you can inspect a pretty rose window, a Baroque *Mise en tombeau*, a 16th-century retable dedicated to St Benedict and a fine Renaissance garden cloister. From here Rue de la Libération leads up to the **Chapelle St-Benoît** with an impressive 17th-century ceiling painted to imitate coffering.

Côtes du Marmandais

Rather unusually, Marmandais has two very distinct growing areas divided by the wide valley of the Garonne; the northern area has the same limstone-clayey soil as Entre-Deux-Mers, the south is an extention of the sandy, gravelly Graves region just to the west. In the 18th and 19th centuries the lusty red and dry white wines grown here were in great demand in the Netherlands, but this century saw a decline only halted in the last few decades. Like neighbouring Buzet, Marmandais owes its rise in status again to the cooperative efforts of its vintners, who after years of work achieved AOC status in 1990 for their bright, merry red wine that they promise 'will re-animate chagrinned spirits and save an ordinary meal from insipidity'. One major change was the move from the somewhat obscure traditional grape varieties of the region (Boucalès, Abouriou, Fer-servadou). The reds, by far the majority, are now made from Merlot and Cabernet Franc; the whites are mostly Cabernet Sauvignon. As in Buzet, most of the wine is produced in cooperatives like **Beaupuy**, just north of Marmande, a village with grand views in every direction (© 53 64 32 04) or the **Cave de Cocumont**, at Cocumont, south of the Garonne and A 62, © 53 94 50 21, *(open daily 8–12 and 2–6)*.

Around Marmande

Down the Garonne, **Sainte-Bazeille** was a Roman town, named after the daughter of a proconsul who was martyred for her faith; decapitated, her head bounced nine times, each bounce bringing forth a spring—now known as the nine fountains, *neuffonds* (St Paul suffered a similar fate in Rome, but his head, being full of weighty theology, bounced but thrice). On a stream called the Gupie, **Mauvezin-de-Gupie** has a 13th-century church covered by a remarkable roof shaped like a ship's keel. **Lagupie** has a 12th-century church with a sculpted tympanum; there's another, carved with Christ and the Elders of the Apocalypse, to the east of Marmande at **Saint-Pierre-de-Londres**, an English bastide project that never got further than this church. **Virazeil**, between Marmande and Saint-Pierre-de-Londres, has a neoclassical château built by Victor Louis, architect of Bordeaux's Grand Théâtre, in 1774.

Where to Stay and Eating Out

Damazan ✉ 47160

Right by the landing on the canal, the **★★Hostellerie du Canal**, © 53 79 42 84, offers rooms overlooking the water and a restaurant with imaginative menus featuring trout, duck and, *mais oui*, lots of prunes, at 65–150F.

Le Mas-d'Agenais ✉ 47430

For lunch here, you won't do better than the 55F menu at the **Restaurant Champon**, ✆ 53 89 50 06, right in the centre by the market stalls: four honest courses with maybe Bayonne ham for a starter, and for the main course maybe a choice of a *boeuf en daube* or a *confit de poulet* (for 55F did you expect duck?).

Marmande ✉ 47200

★★★**Le Capricorne**, just outside town on Rte de Tonneins, ✆ 53 64 16 14, is a modern motel with a pool, home to a good restaurant, **Le Trianon**, with local seafood dishes (poached oysters, salmon, etc; menus from 80–200F). Near Notre-Dame, ★★**Le Lion d'Or**, 1 Rue de la République, ✆ 53 64 21 30, has adequate modernized rooms. The best meals in town come from the kitchen of **Thierry Arbeau**, 10 Av. Charles Baylac, ✆ 53 64 24 03, who does wonderful things with grilled pigeon and Garonne lamprey; in good weather you can dine out on the pretty patio (menus from 120–260F; closed Sun night and Mon). Another popular eatery just outside Marmarde is the **Auberge du Moulin d'Ané**, 4km east by the river Trec in Virazeil, ✆ 53 20 18 25, where good country ingredients and fresh seafood create a delicate cuisine; sit on the terrace and let the apricot mousse with redcurrant sauce melt in your mouth (menus from 100–290F).

Along the Dourdèze and Dropt, and the Pays du Duras

The low, rolling hills of this northwest corner of the Lot-et-Garonne department hold some of its most unusual sights, and some of its best wine. The French come here for *douceur de vie*, and the English, perhaps remembering Duras as one of the most pro-English corners of Aquitaine, have returned to buy large sections of it back.

Tourist Information

Allemans-du-Dropt: in the centre, ✆ 53 20 25 59

Duras: Maison du Pays de Duras, Bd Jean-Brisseau, ✆ 53 83 82 76

Saint-Sernin-de-Duras: in the centre, ✆ 53 94 76 94

market days

Lauzun: Saturdays

Duras: Mondays, Thursdays and Saturdays

Lauzun

Il n'était pas permis de rêver comme il a vécu

La Bruyère, on the Duc de Lauzun

Lauzun owes its fame to Antonin Nompar de Caumont, born the younger son of an impoverished local baron in 1633 but so endowed with natural talent and charm that he quickly become Louis XIV's favourite. The Sun King made him a marshal and duke; one of his missions was to help James II's queen, Mary of Modena, and her son flee from England to France during the Glorious Revolution. On another occasion Lauzun hid under the king's bed to hear what Louis and his mistress were saying about him. Women loved him, most overwhelmingly, the Big Miss herself, the *Grande Mademoiselle*—Louis's headstrong cousin—who fell head over heels for Lauzun, much to the astonishment of the court and to the fury of Louis, who sent Lauzun to the Bastille. Most accounts say that he secretly married the *Grande Mademoiselle* anyway, then proceeded to be terribly unfaithful to her. When she died, the spunky duke married a 15-year-old (he was 62), then to her horror lived to the ripe age of 90. One thing he did was add the domed pavilion to his golden half-medieval, half-Renaissance château. The Gothic **church**, next to an 11th-century tower, has a retable by Tournié of Gourdon, an elaborately carved altar, and two wooden statues of the Virgin from the 13th and 15th centuries.

Just northwest of Lauzun is another bastide, **Eymet**, founded by Alphonse de Poitiers, with its arcades intact and a donjon containing a small **Musée d'Archéologie**, with prehistorical items from the area *(open afternoons July–Sept)*. Eymet's chief rival, just to the south, **Miramont-de-Guyenne** was founded as a bastide by the king of England, but after grave damage in the Hundred Years' War and the Fronde it only retains some old houses; even the church is brand new, with stained glass by modern master Emile Wachter. You can, however, take a unique trip back to the world of medieval bookmaking thanks to a pair of unabashed enthusiasts at the **Musée Vivant du Parchemin et de l'Enluminure**, 33 Rue du Temple *(open 2–6, closed Tues and Jan; summer and school holidays 10–12 and 3–7; adm)*, who demonstrate step by step how parchment was made from sheepskins, bound into books and illustrated with goose quills in the time of St Louis.

Allemans-du-Dropt

Supposedly named after the barbaric German tribe that pushed and shoved its way through in the Dark Ages, **Allemans** has an ancient church given a neo-gothic face-lift in the 19th century. The choir has a Mozarabic horseshoe arch, but best of all are the 15th-century frescoes in the nave, rediscovered in 1935 by the church bell-ringer. These are lively, colourful paintings—especially of the devils, one carrying off souls like a grape-picker in a basket on his back, another impaled by the armoured archangel in charge of separating baddies and goodies. All the damned appear to be either women or priests.

Nearby **La Sauvetat-du-Dropt** was yet another bastide, and one that saw a terrible bloodletting in 1637, when the Duc de la Valette put down a peasant uprising by massacring 1500 *croquants*. From the 13th century there's St-Gervais, a church with an ornate portal and choir that survived a cyclone in 1242, and a charming seven-arched bridge over the Dropt. Don't miss the beautiful Renaissance house on the main street.

Southwest at little **Monteton**, the delightful Romanesque **Notre-Dame** sits high on a terrace where the keen of eye should be able to pick out 13 bell towers on the horizon. One of the few churches to escape damage over the centuries, it has unusual interior buttresses, fine vaults, and a triumphal arch with carved capitals.

Duras

Spread out along a spur overlooking the emerald valley of the Dropt, **Duras** is said to be the only town in France that never built a Catholic church; the current one began as a Protestant temple. Having the same name as a famous French novelist hasn't hurt it, nor has the renown of its excellent wines. It is the home of a little English-language newspaper and has some fine old houses and arcades along its main street, Rue Jauffret.

But the main reason to stop is a visit to the great prow-shaped **Château de Duras** *(open 10–12.30 and 2.30–8 in season, at other times © 53 83 77 32)* was first built in the 1100s, only to be completely redone in 1310 by Bertrand de Goth, nephew of Pope Clement V in Avignon. His niece married a Durfort, and from 1325 the castle belonged to that powerful pro-English family. In 1345 Duras was occupied by the English; in 1389 it was besieged by Du Guesclin, then razed by Charles V. This did not keep the Durforts from returning and rebuilding what you see today. Jeanne d'Albret holed up here when Catholic Catherine de' Medici sent down the troops. In 1794 the castle's surviving towers were cut down to size, and by the 20th century, it was abandoned and falling to bits; the town purchased it in 1969.

After a 20-year restoration, it has been brought back to life, and not only in its architecture—the grand halls, kitchen, the 'room of secrets', the oratory, the prison and moats, the tower with views that on a very clear day stretch to the Pyrenees—but also its troubadours, knights, and ladies and music and boiling pots, thanks to lasers, video, sound and light and other high-tech gimcracks by the same wizards who created Futuroscope in Poitiers.

Côtes de Duras

Born during the Hundred Years' War, Côtes de Duras was one of France's first AOC wines, receiving the prized designation back in 1937. Of its gently rolling hills, only the sunniest slopes with the proper soil are under vines and they produce a mere 100,000 hectolitres of wine—a drop in the bucket compared to the various Bordeaux wines next door.

Côtes de Duras reds are often made from either 100 per cent Merlot or Cabernet Sauvignon; the whites are from Sauvignon, Mauzac, or Sémillon. **Domaine de Laulan** in Duras, ✆ 53 83 73 69 offers an expressive white wine and a great red Duc de Laulan '89.

The pride of the **Cave Coopérative de Duras**, ✆ 53 83 71 12 *(open Mon–Sat 8–12 and 2–6)*, is its standard-bearer, Duc de Berticot, both red and white (try the '92, 60 per cent Sauvignon and 40 per cent Sémillon). Among the sweet *blancs moelleux*, the soft, rich '90 Château La Moulière is outstanding, the perfect accompaniment to foie gras (from **Blancheton**, in Duras, ✆ 53 83 70 19).

Around Duras

Romanesque churches share the *pays de Duras* with the grapes, and one of the best is to the north in **Esclottes**, built in the 13th century, it has an unusually short nave, a false transept and skilfully carved capitals, one with a fish. Others are at **Savignac-de-Duras**, **Lubersac** and **Loubès-Bernac**. This last church has two doors; the one on the north was known as the **Porte des Cagots**. Loubès-Bernac also has a 14th-century château, completely redone in the 17th century.

Where to Stay and Eating Out

Allemans-du-Dropt ✉ 47800

⋆⋆**L'Etape Gasconne**, Place de la Mairie, ✆ 53 20 23 55, is open all year, with pleasant, reasonably priced rooms, a pool for the weary and good food for the hungry; even the 60F weekday menu includes hors d'oeuvres and wine (closed Fri night except in July and Aug).

Monteton ✉ 47120

There are a pair of good places to eat: **Auberge des Treize Clochers** next to the church, ✆ 53 20 24 50, with a tasty 120F menu (closed Mon; open weekends only in winter) and the 18th-century **Château de Monteton**, ✆ 53 20 26 96. In the summer ring ahead to book a table; the food is delicious and based on fresh ingredients (with several vegetarian dishes). Menus start at 60F. The château also has popular, inexpensive full board for families and individuals.

Agnac ✉ 47800

West of Eymet, on the D 933, the 16th-century château **Clos Saint-Georges**, Le Bout du Pont, ℂ 53 83 05 18, is one of the finest places to eat in the area, from first course to chocolaty desserts (menus 80–210F, closed Mon).

Miramont-de-Guyenne ✉ 47800

*La Poste, 31 Place Martignac, ℂ 53 93 20 03, has 14 rooms in an old post house and the best restaurant in town; try the *éventail* (fan) of salmon and asparagus (lunch menus at 55F, others at 90, 120 and 170F, closed Sat outside of season).

Duras ✉ 47120

You can stay amongst the vines at the ****Hostellerie des Ducs**, Bd. Jean-Brisseau, ℂ 53 83 74 58, pleasantly located in a former convent. For less, the ***Auberge du Château**, Place Jean-Bousquet, ℂ 53 83 79 58, has 10 simple rooms.

Moissac abbey

Tarn-et-Garonne

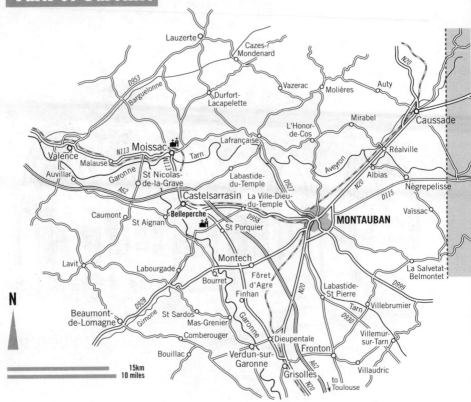

South of the Lot lies Bas Quercy, the region's lost half. Although the Revolutionary bureaucrats in Paris originally left Quercy together as a single *département*, Montauban was absolutely mortified to find itself a mere spot on the map while rascally Cahors got to be a capital. All of the city's protests in Paris fell on deaf ears, but in 1808, it saw its chance when Emperor Napoleon and Josephine just happened to be passing through on their way between Spain and Paris.

Montauban rolled out the red carpet, the mayor was ever so flattering and Napoleon, his imperial ego aglow, promised to give the Montaubanais a *département* of their very own. He was as good as his word. He sliced off the south end of the Lot, and gathered in the corners from several other neighbouring *départements*, and No. 82, the Tarn-et-Garonne was born.

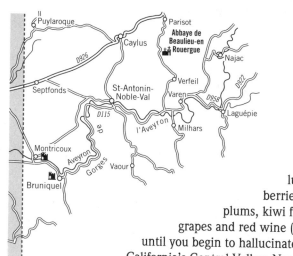

The resulting kaleidoscope of landscapes, regional architecture and allegiance, all crisscrossed by the Garonne, Tarn and Aveyron rivers, contains a bit of everything, but orchards most of all—in the summer the *département*'s main roads are lined with wooden stands and shacks overflowing with luscious peaches, pears, strawberries, apples, apricots, nectarines, plums, kiwi fruits, melons, white table grapes and red wine (VDQS Lavilledieu, St-Sardos) until you begin to hallucinate that you're driving up California's Central Valley. Napoleon also gave the Tarn-et-Garonne another superlative: Moissac.

Northeast Approaches: down the Bonnette and Aveyron Valleys

The Tarn-et-Garonne's most scenic corner is the northeastern bulge Napoleon gouged out of the Rouergue and the Tarn. Its rolling hills mark the transition in landscapes between the Massif Central and the Aquitaine Basin, sliced through by the gorges of the languorous Aveyron and its tributaries, beginning with the Bonnette that descends from the north. This is the best walking area in the whole *département*, crossed from north to south by the GR 46, with numerous small paths winding off through fine scenery, medieval villages and ancient abbeys.

Getting Around

Public transport exists on a limited scale. From Montauban there are four buses daily to Caylus, two to St-Antonin-Noble-Val and a mere one a day from most of the other villages to Montauban.

Tourist Information

Caylus: Rue Evariste-Huc, © 63 67 00 28

Laguépie: Place du Forail, © 63 30 20 34

Saint-Antonin-Noble-Val: at the *mairie*, © 63 30 63 47

Bruniquel: Promenade du Ravelin, © 63 67 24 91

Caylus: Tuesdays and Saturdays

Laguépie: Wednesdays and Saturdays

Varen: Saturdays

Caussade: Mondays

Caylus and the Abbaye de Beaulieu-en-Rouergue

From Montauban, the N 20 north to Caussade then the main D 926 will take you straight to Caylus; if you're coming from the north, find Beauregard and the Causse de Limogne (*see* p.256) and drive south by way of **Lacapelle-Livron**, a village with a Templar commandery (rebuilt in the 15th century) and a church so fortified that it looks more like a little castle. For a less bristling house of God, continue south a kilometre to 15th-century **Notre-Dame des Grâces**, a miniature Flamboyant Gothic gem with a bird's-eye view across the *causse*; 4km south is another, built in 1302 called **Notre-Dame de Livron**, 'Our Lady of Liberation' in Occitan—a nearby cave was inhabited by a pesky dragon until a bold knight axed it and liberated the neighbourhood.

Caylus, the most important and prettiest town on the Bonnette, is built in an amphitheatre, most strikingly viewed from the west on the D 926. The counts of Toulouse built a castle here in the 1200s, the ruins of which still dominate the region. The medieval town, below the main road, is centred on the Place du Marché, with some arcades and a very sturdy *halle* with octagonal pillars. The church with the mighty stone steeple is **St-Jean Baptiste**, endowed with an elegant seven sided choir of 1470 and the *Christ Monumental* by Zadkine, carved in 1954 from the trunk of an elm. Don't miss the 13th-century house near by, with gargoyles shaped like wolves—as if to get back at these terrors of the Middle Ages, they were made to do duty as rain spouts.

West of Caylus, the 13th- and 14th-century hilltop bastide of **Puylaroque** is a miniature version of the famous hilltown of Cordes near Albi. Southeast of Caylus, **Beaulieu-en-Rouergue**, like most Cistercian abbeys, is prettily isolated at the bottom of a wooded valley *(open Palm Sun–Sept daily except Tues, 10–12 and 2–6, © 63 67 06 84)*. Founded in 1144 by 12 monks from Clairvaux, the present buildings were begun in the late 1200s; in the Wars of Religion, the whole was stripped and the cloister devastated. The *parlement* of Toulouse had much of it rebuilt in the 17th century, and the last Italianate stuccoes and marble chimneypieces were just put in place in time for the Revolution. Viollet-le-Duc had the idea of taking the church apart piece by piece and rebuilding it in St-Antonin-Noble-Val, a plan that fell through when St-Antonin couldn't come up with enough money for the job. Used as barns until 1960, the abbey was restored after 1974 and now houses a regional centre for contemporary art and music, with a permanent collection of late 20th-century works and annual summer art exhibitions. Although much-rebuilt over the centuries, Beaulieu is an excellent example of the development of Cistercian architecture (and of the monks' increasing concern for their physical comforts, a far cry from the original austerity of St. Bernard of Clairvaux). The early 14th-century church is harmonious, with a beautiful portal and rose window. In the north crossing, a *porte des morts* survives—a door each monk went through but once in this vale of tears.

Down the Aveyron: Laguépie to Saint-Antonin-Noble-Val

From Beaulieu the D 33/D 20/D 958 will take you down to **Laguépie** at the very corner of the Tarn-et-Garonne, a pretty village with a ruined castle at the junction of the Aveyron and Viaur rivers. Like **Varen**, the next village west, it's popular with riverside campers, but Varen has the added attraction of a 10th-century Benedictine priory, with a barrel-vaulted, single-naved church from the late 1000s with no door on its west front—originally the façade formed part of the town wall. The sculpted capitals on the north come from Varen's parish church, demolished in the 1700s, while the capitals in the choir, closed off by three mini-aspes and two crypts, are among the most important from the period, decorated with sturdy knots, symmetrical face-to-face animals and biblical scenes. The adjacent 14th-century tower was the residence of the dean of the priory.

After Varen, the Aveyron flows below one of the oldest towns in the *département*, a medieval charmer called **Saint-Antonin-Noble-Val**. Its setting delighted the Romans, who named it *Nobilis Vallis*; the Saint Antonin was tacked on when the body of the apostle of this area floated downstream in a boat and a monastery was founded to hold the relics. In the Middle Ages the village was a Cathar stronghold; in the Hundred Years' War, it was occupied by the English, who left their name behind in the tremendous cliffs of the Rocher d'Anglars that looms over the village. The monastery was wiped off the face of the earth by the Protestants, who were themselves clobbered in 1622 by Louis XIII; the king had failed to take Montauban after an 86-day siege, and in his pique came here to pick on someone smaller.

What it lacks in sacred architecture, Antonin more than makes up for in the secular, beginning with the lovely Gothic **Place des Halles** and the **Maison des consuls** of 1120, unhappily Disney-fied by Viollet-le-Duc, who not only over-restored this rare example of Romanesque civic architecture, but added an incongruous Florentine belfry. On the first-floor gallery, note the pillar sculpted with Byzantine Emperor Justinian holding his famous Code. The hollowed-out spaces on the second floor originally held Hispano-Moorish ceramic plates. Bits of these are now in the building's **Musée du Vieux Saint-Antonin** *(open July–Sept 10–12 and 3–6, other times by appointment, © 63 30 63 47)*, along with tools, furniture and prehistoric items. The *halle* in front has a curious 15th-century *Crucifixion*, carved on a stone disc.

Antonin's labyrinthine lanes have such a rare assortment of medieval houses that the town has been called an outdoor museum of secular architecture, untouched by any recent attempts at restoration, much less the Viollet-le-Duc treatment. Even the streets have pungent names like Rue Bombecul (what an American would call 'Shelf-butt street'). Down by the river along the Promenade des Moines are the remains of the tanneries which once made Antonin's fortune, along with a working walnut-oil mill. Further along the river is a slate-roofed spa of 1913; the mineral spring here, rich in copper, has been a popular cure for urinary infections since the 18th century.

The well-marked paths around Antonin make for exceptionally fine walking, especially along the Aveyron and up to the mighty 660ft Rocher des Anglars with its wide-ranging belvedere. Another place to aim for is the **Grotte du Bosc**, 3km northeast *(open Easter–Sept, 10–12 and 2–6, adm)*, formed by a subterranean river; there are remarkable formations and a little museum of prehistoric finds. Further northeast, the D 75 leads to **Château de Cas Espinas** *(open July and Aug 10–12 and 2–6, or by appointment at weekends Apr–Oct, © 63 67 07 40)* a rather austere citadel that defended the Bonnette valley, with a Merovingian chapel. It was the seat of a Templar commandery, and has been restored and refurnished after damage in the Revolution and the Second World War.

The D 5 from Antonin leads west to **Septfonds**, home of a good set of dolmens (including a jauntily tilted proto-Baroque model) and an austere Spanish Republican cemetery of 1939, near a vast camp set up for refugees of the Civil War. The largest town in these parts is **Caussade**, a pleasant, bustling place on the main Cahors–Montauban road, surrounded by small industries, including one that produced Maurice Chevalier's famous boaters and other straw hats. Just south, still on the main road, is a little bastide with a delightful name—**Réalville**—and a popular Basque restaurant (*see* below).

Bruniquel and Montricoux

After St-Antonin, the Aveyron cuts off a corner of the *département* of the Tarn, passing through a dramatic gorge near the striking medieval village of **Penne**, with its castle hanging over the cliffs. Next down the river is **Bruniquel**, a hill town and artists' colony built under a large fortress. This, according to Gregory of Tours, was founded by Queen Brunehaut (d. 613), a Visigoth married to Siebert, the grandson of Clovis. She was as fierce as a queen on a chessboard, fighting a relentless war with the neighbouring queen Fredegunda, personally eliminating ten members of Fredegunda's family, until her own nobles tired of her cruelty and handed her over to her son, who tied her by the hair to a wild horse.

Story or not, the **château** *(open daily July and Aug 10–12.30 and 2–6, June and Sept, afternoons only, adm; other times © 63 67 27 67)*, rising 300ft over the confluence of the Vère and the Aveyron, dates back only to the 12th century—the tour includes the keep, called the Tower of Brunehaut, the knights' room and chapel, and an elegant Renaissance gallery. The nearby **Maison des Comtes Payrol**, in Rue du Château, is a rare example of 13th-century civic architecture, with murals and a coffered ceiling *(open 15 June–15 Sept,*

3–7; adm). Two of Bruniquel's medieval gates are intact, including the picturesque ivy-swathed **Porte de l'Horloge**, at the top of a winding lane.

The gorge of the Aveyron begins (or peters out) at **Montricoux**, a town founded by the Templars. It has a 13th-century church, topped with a 16th-century Toulouse-style bell tower; inside is a fresco from the 1920s by Marcel Lenoir. Marcel Lenoir? The name doesn't ring a bell? Then find out more in the **Musée Lenoir**, housed near by in Montricoux's château, built around the Templar keep and given a Tuscan facelift in the 18th century *(open 10–12 and 2.30–7, closed Tues; adm; in winter © 63 67 26 48 for hours).* Briefly, Lenoir was born in Montauban in 1872 and died in Montciroux in 1931, although he spent most of his career in the artistic whirl of Paris, where his work was admired by Braque, Matisse and Rodin. Since then, however, few artists have been more forgotten, partially because Lenoir refused to accept honours or compromise at all with critics, dealers or even his own peers. Nor is he easy to pin down with an easily recognizable style—like Picasso, he had an endless capacity and need to change styles, from his early days under the Symbolist influence of Gustave Moreau and Mucha, to Cubism, Surrealism and abstraction, but approaching each new phase in his career with religious intensity, sometimes in religious subjects, such as his surreal *Descent from the Cross.*

Where to Stay and Eating Out

St-Antonin-Noble-Val ✉ 82140

> ★★**Le Lys Bleu**, Place de la Halle, © 63 68 21 00 is a little *Logis de France* hotel in a medieval house. The ferme-auberge **Bas de Quercy**, on the D 926 towards Caylus, © 63 31 97 61, has four comfortable bed-and-breakfast rooms (240F for two) and menus from 90 to 190F, based on chicken, duck or guinea fowl (closed Mon and Sun night). For a lunch to beat all lunches, reserve a table at the vast farmhouse dining room of **La Bergerie**, 5km east of Antonin off the N 19, © 63 30 60 58; expect the best country cooking, and loads of it, especially if you order the 170F *menu gastronomique.*

Réalville ✉ 82440

> The **Eskualduna**, on the N 20, © 63 31 01 58 is packed every day at lunchtime; stop by for a tasty foray into Basque cooking (lunch menu around 70F).

Bruniquel ✉ 82800

> The no-name **Chambres d'Hôte**, Promenade de Ravilin, © 63 67 26 16, has four rooms complete with baths in a grand old house with fine views; count on paying 230F for two with breakfast.

Montricoux ✉ 82800

> The modern ★★**Terrassier**, in Vaïssac (to the southwest), © 63 3094 60, is pleasant, has a pool and is open all year; it has good food in the restaurant, especially in the autumn when most dishes include wild mushrooms (menus from 75 to

165F). The **Relais du Postillon** on the east edge of town, ℂ 63 67 23 58, offers simple rooms for 140F a double, and delicious meat and fish dishes in the restaurant—leg of lamb, salmon with sorrel, chicken with morels and more, on menus ranging from 70 to 175F (closed Fri night and Sat lunch).

Montauban

Originally covered with silvery willows, hence *Mons Albanus* ('white hill'), Montauban prefers to be known as 'the pinkest of the three pink cities' (pink, that is, as in brick; the other two are Toulouse and Albi). The capital of the Tarn-et-Garonne, it was cast in an original mould from its foundation, a successful medieval experiment in city planning, a new possibility that caught on in dozens of baby Montaubans—the bastides. Not many have evolved into such pleasant medium-sized cities, or can claim a collection of art as prestigious as Montauban's Musée Ingres.

History

Montauban owes its origins to a crew of oversexed monks. These were the brethren of Montauriol, a monastery founded in 820 by St Théobard, who claimed the *droit de cuissage* (the right to select their bedfellows from the local population). The monks abused their privilege to such an extent that the people of Montauriol asked Count Alphonse-Jourdain for a new town. He complied, and in 1144 laid out the grid plan of the first new town in the southwest, essentially a bastide a hundred years before the others began sprouting up like autumn mushrooms on the battle lines of the Hundred Years' War.

The counts allowed Montauban to elect its own consuls, and gave it so many privileges that it soon sucked up all the loose ends in the area. In spite of being punished for loyalty to Toulouse during the Albigensian crusade, Montauban quickly rebounded; as a new town with a relatively free, new population it had something of the enterprising spirit of an American frontier town. By the mid 14th century it was bustling with the import and export of textiles—just when the Treaty of Brétigny (1360) ceded Montauban to England. John Chandos came in person to take it for the Black Prince, who spent many months here, plotting and fighting on the frontiers of French territory.

After the Hundred Years' War Montauban's commerce quickly picked up again, and like other mercantile towns (Bergerac, Nîmes, La Rochelle, for instance) it was especially receptive to the new doctrines of Calvin. After a good deal of simmering, the pot boiled over on 20 December 1561; the Montaubanais en masse broke down the cathedral door, pillaged the building and burnt it to the ground, then did the same to all the other churches and convents in town, except for St-Jacques, which they converted into a Protestant temple. All the brick and stone of the churches immediately went into building walls, which were unusually efficient, twice repelling the concerted Catholic attacks.

The future Henri IV spent much time here, and when he became king his Edict of Nantes made Montauban a Protestant place of safety. His less tolerant and less capable son, Louis XIII, marched down in 1621 with an army of 25,000 and besieged Montauban for weeks, setting the outskirts on fire, but he found the Protestants too tough for his taste and went home, feeling sorry for himself. Richelieu, however, waited until the fall of La Rochelle in 1629, which left Montauban isolated as the last Protestant stronghold in France, and diplomatically convinced it to surrender.

No dummy, Richelieu's first act was to demolish Montauban's walls. His second was to cajole the enterprising inhabitants to stay by offering them plums—money and job-generating bureaucracies, their own intendants and a regional bureau of finances; Richelieu may have been a cardinal but he knew well enough that it was the mercantile Protestants who generated much of the national wealth. His plan worked so well that by the 18th century Montauban could proudly claim to be the third city in the southwest. Its weavers produced a thick wool fabric called *cadis* that sold like hot cakes in France's American colonies. The intendants drew out new broad avenues and laid out the first parks.

Montauban's contribution to the Revolution was a woman about two hundred years ahead of her time: Olympe de Gouges, born in 1748, daughter of the obscure poet-magistrate Lefranc de Pompignan. Defender of the rights of of all people, even women, to live without oppression, she wrote a brochure called *Les Droits de la femme et de la citoyenne*, declaring that 'if a woman has the right to mount the scaffold, she has the right to ascend to the seats of justice'. For trying to obtain political rights for women and 'forgetting the virtues of her sex' she was guillotined in 1793. If the Revolution denied women's rights, the new Napoleonic code really put half the population of France in its place by ending rights (especially property) that even medieval women had enjoyed. Only since the 1970s have French wives been able to open bank accounts in their own names.

Another setback was in store for Montauban—much of its *cadis* trade declined, thanks to the loss of Canada and Louisiana and competition from the new industrial mills in the north. Napoleon's intervention, making Montauban a departmental capital, assured at least a bureaucratic vocation that kept the town from complete economic decline in the 19th century, although it was a century burnished by the reflected glow of the international fame of its native sons, Ingres and Bourdelle, Rodin's chief assistant. Since the last war, Montauban has typified the turn-around of a *ville moyenne*—the proximity of dynamic Toulouse and its key location on the southwest railways and highways, has attracted numerous small enterprises and led to, among other things, the thorough restoration of its old brick charms.

Getting Around

Montauban's station on Rue Solengro, at the northeast end of town (© 63 63 50 50, reservations © 63 63 05 14), is well served by trains between Paris and Toulouse and between Toulouse and Bordeaux (with stops at Moissac and Agen). Autocars Barrière, 16 Rue du Châteauvieux, © 63 93 34 34, has buses twice a week direct to Barcelona, Valencia and Morocco. Buses depart from Place Lalique (© 63 63 88 88) for Castelsarrasin, Montech, Lavilledieu and Beaumont-de-Lomagne; others (© 63 63 43 43) go to Agen, Caussade, Lauzerte, Toulouse, Bruniquel, and Albi. You can hire bikes at Gury, 26 Av. Gambetta, © 63 63 19 10.

Private boats (*pénichettes*) to explore the Canal Latéral à la Garonne (just west of the city) can be rented by the day, weekend or week from Loisirs-Acceuil Tarn-et-Garonne, Place Foch, © 63 63 31 40. Larger boats also make regular excursions: the *Baladine* (© 63 03 54 20) and the *Jennifer* (© 63 63 31 92).

Tourist Information

2 Rue du Collège, © 63 63 60 60. Also, information for the whole of Tarn-et-Garonne is available at the Comité Départemental du Tourisme, Hôtel des Intendants, Place du Maréchal-Foch, © 63 63 31 40.

market days

Farmers' market, Saturdays in Place Prax-Paris. In the winter, *Marché au gras* in Place Nationale every Wednesday and Friday mornings.

Place Nationale

The finest gift bestowed by old Alphonse-Jordain on the new town of Montauban is its central square, the Place Nationale. It is the prototype for the central bastide market square, yet none can match its innovative, urbane sophistication. First off, it isn't even a square at all, but a more subtle, visually interesting irregular trapezoid with covered chamfered corners. The whole plan of the new town echoes this slight distortion of the plain, monotonous square grid. Its unique 'double cloister' arcades date from 1144 and were originally built in wood; after a fire in 1614, they were slowly rebuilt exactly as they were in warm brick, even though the style of vaulting was considered archaic at the time (you can see the year when each bay was completed, inscribed in the keystones of the vaults—the last reads 1708). The interior galleries functioned as covered lanes, the continuation of the streets that come into the angles of the Place National; the outer galleries were given over to displays of merchandise. In the central square the Montaubanais bought their food, hanged their thieves, and issued their proclamations

In the 17th-century fashion for homogenous squares, the city ordered that all the façades of the buildings facing the square should be rebuilt in the same style, with the attic storerooms lit by openings called *mirandes*. Note the sundial on the north side, with the legend *Una tibi* ('Your hour will come!'); the metal metre bar set vertically in the southwest corner of the square was put in place to instruct the locals when the Revolution standardized French measures.

St-Jacques and the Pont-Vieux

If you leave Place Nationale by the metre corner, you'll soon find yourself in Place Victor-Hugo, site of **St-Jacques**, a combination church, assembly and voting hall built by Montauban's consuls in the 13th century. During the repairs following the Hundred Years' War, it was given an octagonal bell tower, which, like St-Sernin in Toulouse, has a curious change in design halfway up and still bears scars from Louis XIII's cannonballs. The neo-

Roman portal with its coloured-tile decoration dates from the 19th century; the interior is typically southern Gothic, with a large single nave.

Down from St-Jacques, **Place Bourdelle** is named after Bourdelle's dramatic 1895 **Monument to the War Dead of 1870**, an early major work, showing the influence of Rodin. Here the neoclassical Tribunal de Commerce now houses two museums: the **Musée d'Histoire Naturelle** upstairs *(open 10–12 and 2–6, closed Mon and Sun morning)*, with an immense collection of birds and minerals, including pieces of a meteorite that fell in the Tarn-et-Garonne in 1864 and excited much speculation about aliens from outer space; and, on the ground floor, the **Musée du Terroir** *(same hours)* devoted to country life in the good old days and southwest ethnography in general. The interesting section on regional prehistory *(same hours)* is near by in the former library at 8 Square du Général-Picquart (a street, incidentally, named after the army intelligence officer who went to prison for defending Dreyfus in 1898; Montauban is still a progressive town).

From Place Bourdelle the Tarn is spanned by the **Pont Vieux**, a bridge planned from Montauban's foundation by Alphonse-Jourdain, though financial and technical difficulties prevented its erection until King Philippe le Bel was passing through Montauban in 1303, and the consuls (as they would later buttonhole Napoleon) got the king to promise his assistance in raising taxes and providing wood for the brick kilns, in constructing their long awaited bridge, promising to name its towers after him. Construction on the 677ft structure began in 1311 and was a technological *tour de force*; its seven uneven arches stood up to the worst floods the unruly Tarn has sent down, including water so high in 1441 that it washed over the top of the bridge. Originally it resembled the Pont Valentré in Cahors, with Philippe le Bel's three fortified towers; these were demolished at the turn of century to let more traffic through.

The Musée Ingres

The museum is housed in the pretty bishops' palace at the eastern end of the bridge, built over the foundations of a medieval castle that had been the local headquarters for English rule. The palace, begun in the 1640s—a decade after the King's troops marched in—made a conscious symbol of the new political and religious order. After the Revolution the building became Montauban's *mairie*, though later the mayor gave way for what seemed to be a more fitting use: a monument to the city's favourite son, Jean-Auguste-Dominique Ingres (1780–1867).

This painter, whose donations to his home town make up the core of the museum's collection, was tremendously popular in his time, a technical virtuoso whose icily perfect religious and mythological works fitted the mood of Napoleonic neoclassicism; in fact many of his first paintings were kitsch-propaganda pieces for the emperor. Ingres was an Academic artist from head to toe, the sort of dedicated conformist who believed in rules and precepts, and measured his success by the medals he won at competitions. His battles with the younger generation of Romantic painters, especially Delacroix, were legendary. The earlier paintings on display here were done when Ingres was still in the workshop of his master, the even more indigestible Jacques-Louis David.

The collection includes thousands of sketches and drawings, some of which are displayed in a way that shows up the contrast between the Academic painter and the suppressed artist within, as in the *Jesus among the Doctors* (painted when Ingres was 82), where a lovely, almost Pre-Raphaelite study is juxtaposed with the stiff and silly finished work. Ingres did much better at portraits, of which several are offered here, and also in mythological scenes such as the *Dream of Ossian*, a colossal canvas of ghostly figures in the sky, painted for Napoleon's bedroom (Ossian was the supposed medieval Scottish bard whose 'rediscovered' works, all fakes, nevertheless made a great impression on poets at the dawn of the Romantic era).

The Salle Ingres, the bishops' bedchamber, was partially decorated by Ingres's father, also an artist. It houses a little shrine to Ingres, with the great man's desk, his paints, a view of his studio in Rome, and his violin—all arranged the way Ingres himself planned it.

Not all the works present are by Ingres. From his personal collection are archaeological items—an Etruscan burial urn and a black-figure Greek vase with the *Battle of Centaurs and Lapiths* that may be the best work in the museum—as well as a few Italian paintings: a Masolino predella panel and a *Nativity* by Carpaccio, and one from Spain, a striking *St Jerome* attributed to Ribera. And a flatulent historical echo is supplied by Ingres's spiritual ancestor, Charles Lebrun, the first director of the Académie: *Louis XIV in the Chariot of State*. Montauban's other famous son, the sculptor Antoine Bourdelle (1861–1929), gets a room full of works, with portrait busts of figures as diverse as Ingres himself and Krishnamurti; Bourdelle's most acclaimed work, however, stands out in front of the museum on the square, the *Dying Centaur*.

Down in the bishops' cellars, the museum keeps a small archaeological collection, including a Roman mosaic, and some medieval items, among them a nasty torture contraption subtly called the *banc à question*.

The Cathédrale Notre-Dame

From the Musée Ingres, Rue de l'Hôtel de Ville leads up to Montauban's cathedral, rebuilt between 1692 and 1739, when Louis XIV sent down his own architects to build a church worthy of the Counter-Reformation, celebrating the victory over heresy and as always his own glory. Unlike the warm red brick that epitomizes Montauban, the cathedral shows its foreign, Parisian origins in its white stone and frostily perfect classicism (not many cathedrals were built during this period in France; Versailles's is the most famous one).

The vast interior is full of equally frigid 18th–19th-century furnishings, and one of Ingres's major works, the enormous *Vow of Louis XIII*, commissioned for the cathedral and painted in Florence between 1820 and 1824. He exhibited the painting in the 1824 Paris salon, where it hung next to the *Massacre of Chios*, the Romantic masterpiece of Delacroix. To the neoclassical heirs of Jacques-Louis David, Delacroix's work was 'the massacre of painting' and Ingres was declared the champion and upholder of Academic values; Delacroix sniffed that Ingres's 'painting was pure Italian', and a lifelong rivalry was born. It is certainly easy to see what Delacroix meant: the Virgin, Child and angels seem to have come straight out of Raphael's sketchbooks. Louis XIII is seen offering the Virgin his crown and sceptre, symbolizing the kingdom of France. The subject could only have been suggested by a rabid Catholic (or a Parisian), as Louis XIII certainly didn't do Montauban any favours.

Around Montauban

In 1679, Montauban's intendant Foucault initiated the greening of the pink city by planting thousands of elms on the banks of the Tarn, along the broad street that now bears his name, **Cours Foucault**. Enjoying a fine view of the historic centre, it has been the city's most popular promenade ever since. Its focal point, closing the view between the long alleys of trees, is Bourdelle's *La France veillant sur ses morts*, a First World War monument inspired by the temples and sculpture of ancient Greece, typical of the sculptor's later career, when he moved from Rodin's romanticism to a more classical style. South of the centre, the **Jardin des Plantes**, created in 1860, has several rare species of tree, while to the east of Place Prax-Paris (with the mushroom-roofed market) is **Parc Chambord**, created in 1972; in May and June, the thousands upon thousands of roses from around the world planted in its rose garden burst into intoxicating bloom.

Montauban ✉ *82000*   ***Where to Stay***

The prettiest place to stay in Montauban is 3km west of the city, ★★★**Hostellerie Les Coulandrières**, on the D 958, ✆ 63 67 47 47, a modern inn under a superb cedar tree, with a pool and park and bright rooms; the restaurant is one of the best, featuring delicious seafood. Opposite the station, ★★**D'Orsay**, Rue Salengro, ✆ 63 66 06 66 has very comfortable rooms, several air-conditioned. ★★**Des Trois Pigeons**, 4 Av. du 11ème R.I., ✆ 63 66 46 46, is out near the hospital, but has a pool and sauna and nice rooms. ★★**Prince Noir**, Place Prax-Paris, ✆ 63 63 10 10, is a reliable, conveniently located town hotel; if you're driving, there's the modern motel ★★**Le Relais des Chênes**, Pont Chaume, off the east ring road (*Rocade Est*), ✆ 63 20 20 88, with a pool, tennis and soundproofed rooms. ★**Du Commerce**, Place de la Cathédrale, ✆ 63 66 31 32, is well kept and full of old fashioned charm. The **Centre Equestre de St Hilaire**, just off the D 927, ✆ 63 66 46 89, offers a pair of rooms for 180F a double, as well as the chance to ride and dine at the table d'hôte (meals, featuring *cèpes* in the autumn, 80F)

Eating Out

Ambrosie, 41 Rue Comédie, ✆ 63 66 27 40, is a fair name for the delicious dishes served in this up-to-date restaurant—the 110F menu is good value and offers alternatives for both seafood lovers and fish haters—try the duck in an onion fondue (closed Sun and half of July). The warm and welcoming restaurant in the Orsay hotel (*see* above), **La Cuisine d'Alain**, takes local ingredients and traditions and gives them an original slant on the menus (100, 160 or 200F); among the à la carte is the local version of *cassoulet*. Save room for a choice from the fabulous dessert cart (closed Mon lunch and Sun). In a prettily restored 17th-century dyeworks, **Le Ventadour**, 23 Quai Villebourbon, © 63 63 34 58, serves an aromatic dish of beef with morels and other delicacies (menus at 85 and 240F; closed Sun and Mon night, and most of Aug).

For a special meal, the Montaubanais drive 10km south on the N 20 to Brial and the white villa of **Jacques Depeyre**, © 63 23 05 06, where the eponymous chef produces the most delightful, sunny, innovative dishes in the whole *département*—for instance, the country pigeon with ginger and grapefruit that sounds iffy but tastes absolutely divine (lunch menu 145F, dinner 220–500F, book; closed Sun night and Mon).

Moissac

There's only one reason to make the trip to Moissac, but it's a solid five-star reason: the Romanesque Abbaye de Saint-Pierre, one of the crown jewels of medieval French sculpture. The town of Moissac, washed clean of most of its character in a tragic flood in 1930 that killed over a hundred people and wiped out over 600 buildings, now busies itself growing aromatic pale golden *chasselas*, France's finest dessert grapes, first cultivated in the Middle Ages by the abbey's monks.

Getting Around

Moissac is on the railway line between Bordeaux, Agen, Montauban and Toulouse, © 63 63 50 50

Tourist Information

Place Durand-de-Bredons, © 63 04 01 85

market days

Sunday mornings

The Abbaye Saint-Pierre

The first Benedictine monastery was founded here by Clovis in 506, commemorating his victory over the Visigoths. The battle had cost him a thousand men, whom Clovis declared would be remembered by an abbey of a thousand monks. Exactly marking the spot of such an important religious foundation being a very serious matter, Clovis, as the legend goes, climbed a hill and hurled his trusty javelin, telling God to guide it where he saw fit. Gshshloop! went the javelin as it struck the gooey muck of a marsh. Never questioning God's peculiar choice, Clovis ordered his builders to get to it. He had to order them three times. In the end they had to sink deep piles to support the structure. No one knows if the story has a germ of truth in it, or if the monks made it up to explain their annoying moisture problems.

One of Clovis's successors, King Dagobert, put the abbey under royal protection, thanks to the influencial bishop of Cahors, St Didier (630–55) who according to some accounts was the true father of Moissac. Although royal protection was promised into the 9th century, the Merovingian and Carolingian kings proved to be too far away to be of much help when the abbey was sacked by the Arabs in 721 and 732 (the year of their defeat at Poitiers), then by the Normans in 850 and by the Magyars in 864. Fed up with royal protection, the abbots henceforth placed themselves under the counts of Toulouse. After a roof cave-in in 1030 and a fire in 1042, the monastery was in such spiritual and material disorder that the counts put it under the control of Cluny, which, noting its key position along one of the main pilgrimage routes to Compostela, sent money for its restoration and a new abbot, Durand de Brendon, who was also bishop of Toulouse and who consecrated the new church on 6 November 1063.

Because of Moissac's close links with Toulouse, Simon de Montfort sacked it during the Albigensian crusade in 1212; although Raymond VII managed to recapture the abbey in 1222, he was helpless to save the 210 heretics burned by the Inquisition here in 1234. These human bonfires seem to mark a turning point in the abbey's popularity; in 1466 a papal bull stripped the abbey from Cluny's jurisdiction and put it under absentee *abbés commanditaires* who sucked up most of the rents due to the abbey for their private pockets. By 1626 the monks had been replaced by a chapter of canons. Louis XIV's finance minster, Colbert, purchased its library and moved it to Paris, and much was demolished on the eve of the Revolution, which as usual could find no better use for the monastery than as a saltpetre works, after taking care to surgically guillotine the carved figures of the greatest Romanesque cloister in France.

In 1847 Viollet-le-Duc was summoned by the then superintendent of historical monuments, Prosper Mérimée, to restore the majestic porch. He had hardly begun in 1850 when along came a cohort of philistines who made the sans-culottes look like schoolboys—the builders of the Bordeaux–Toulouse railroad—who announced that the cloister was dead smack in the way of the line someone in Paris had drawn for the tracks. A huge battle ensued with the preservationists, and although at the last moment the tracks were realigned, the railway men had their evil way with the splendid refectory and kitchens. A century and a half later, opinion has turned 180 degrees; now there are plans to cover up the railway tracks to enhance what's left of Moissac's medieval atmosphere.

The Porch

Given Moissac's record of trouble, the great abbot Ansquitil decided in 1115 to fortify the church's tower-porch. The tower is 12th century up to its first floor chapel; Viollet-le-Duc restored the brick steeple and crenellations. Sheltered underneath is the sublime porch, one of the most powerful and beautiful works of the Middle Ages, and the men who commissioned it are remembered in the two statues on pilasters off on either side, abbot Ansquitil on the left (or, some say, St Benedict) and on the right abbot Roger (1115–35) who completed the work after Ansquitil's death.

The **tympanum**, originally vividly painted, rests on a lintel recycled from a Gallo-Roman building, decorated with eight large thistle flowers and enclosed in a cable or vine, spat out by a monster at one end and swallowed by another monster at the other. The main scene represents one of the key visions of the Apocalypse (Rev. 4:2–8), of Christ sitting in the Judgment of Nations, with the Book of Life in his hand ('And he who sat there appeared like jasper and carnelian, and round the throne was a rainbow that looked like an emerald'...'and before the throne there is as it were a sea of glass, like crystal'). You might notice that this Christ has three arms, one on the book, one raised in blessing, and another on his heart, but please don't ask for an explanation; no one's come up with a convincing one yet.

The four symbols of the Evangelists twist to surround him, and two Seraphim as well, carrying scrolls representing the Old and New Testaments, are squeezed under the rainbow. The rest of the tympanum is occupied by the 24 Elders, no two alike, each gazing up from their thrones at Christ, 'each holding a harp, and with golden bowls full of incense, which are the prayers of the saints'. Most writers describe the fear and awe in the Elders' eyes, but in actual fact they don't look frightened at all; bemused might be a better word (and in place of harps they all play the medieval proto-violin, the rebeck). The whole wonderfully rhythmic composition could just as easily be an old-timers' band raising their glasses in an intermission toast to a stern, but respected and beloved bandleader.

But that's not all. The central pillar of the door, the **trumeau**, is sculpted with three pairs of lions in the form of Xs symbolically guarding the church (others prowl about the capitals of the tower). Note the scalloped edges of the doorway, a Moorish idea picked up from Spain. On either side of the door are tall, relief figures of *St Peter* with his keys, stepping on a dragon (left); *Isaiah*, whose scroll prophesizes the coming Messiah (right); and on the outer sides of the porch are a severe *St Paul* and a gentle, dreamy-eyed *Jeremiah* (also holding a scroll), elongated, stylish supple figures that sway and almost dance, most probably from the same anonymous chisel that sculpted the wonderful Isaiah at Souillac. To the right of the portal are scenes from the life of the Virgin—the *Annunciation*, *Visition*, and *Adoration of the Magi*; to the left, poor Lazarus' soul is taken into the bosom of Abraham, while below the soul of the rich, feasting Dives is carried off in the other direction. Below him, you can make out a miser with demons on his shoulder as he refuses alms to a beggar, while to the left is Lust, serpents sucking at her breasts while an amused, very Chinese demon looks on.

Jeremiah

Up above the porch on the cornice—hiding in plain sight—is a large figure blowing a horn, perhaps Gabriel. Few visitors ever notice him.

The Church

Inside the porch, the vaulted square of the **narthex** has some excellent Romanesque capitals, carved with voluptuous vegetation playfully metamorphosed into animals; one shows Samson wrestling with a lion. Above it is the mysterious **upper chapel**, built of a dozen arches linked in a central oculus. This has been interpreted as a symbolic representation of heaven, or more specifically the New Jerusalem. As in other, similar constructions around Europe, whatever ceremonial or liturgical functions it might have had are lost in time. There are two ways to enter it, the broad door for the many, and a narrow one leading into the cloister, for the monks.

The **interior** of the church had to be rebuilt in 1430 and can't begin to compete with the fireworks on the portal. You can see the foundations of the single-naved 1180 church (along the bottom of the Gothic nave), which like Cahors was crowned with a row of Byzantine domes; unlike Cahors they collapsed and have been replaced with flamboyant Gothic vaults in brick. Only one chapel has managed to retain its 15th-century geometrical murals, which inspired the restoration on the other walls. Some of the church's excellent polychrome sculpture survives, especially a 12th-century *Christ*, and from the 15th-century, the *Flight into Egypt*, with a serious-minded burro, the beautiful *Entombment* and a *Pietà* (the figure with the swollen head is Gaussen de la Garrigue, consul of Moissac). Note the Baroque organ consul, bearing the arms of Cardinal Mazarin, *abbé commanditaire* from 1644 to 1661 and one of the most successful grafters of all time.

The Cloister

Open 9–12 and 2–6; adm.

Behind the church is the abbey's serenely magnificent cloister, built by abbots Durand de Bredons and Ansquitil. After Simon de Montfort sacked Moissac, the arches had to be rebuilt, and were given a gentle hint of a Gothic point (1260), but all of the 76 magnificent capitals, set on alternating paired and single slender columns of various coloured marbles, come from the end of the 11th century; they are the oldest *in situ* in France. They also mark a major artistic turning point, away from the immobile, rather stiff, hieratical figures of the great Guilduin (as in Toulouse's St-Sernin) towards more fluid, stylized poses with a sense of movement, exquisite modelling, and a play of light and shadow hitherto unknown in Romanesque sculpture. The capitals are carved with foliage inspired by Corinthian capitals, but with luxuriant virtuosity; others have birds and animals, intricately intertwined.

Some 46 capitals tell the lives of the saints—don't miss the dynamic martyrdoms: St Lawrence burning on the grill, while two Romans blow on the flames; St Martin dividing his cloak with the beggar; St John the Baptist and the feast of Herod; St Stephen being stoned; St Peter upside down on his cross next to St Paul's beheading, a capital set near a little niche that once contained some of their relics. Other scenes are rare—the city of Jerusalem vs. unholy Babylon, the story of Nebuchadnezzar, and Shadrach, Meshach and Abednego in the furnace. At the corners and in the centre of each gallery are square pillars, covered with recycled tops of Roman sarcophaguses; the corners are carved with bas-reliefs

Moissac Abbey Cloister

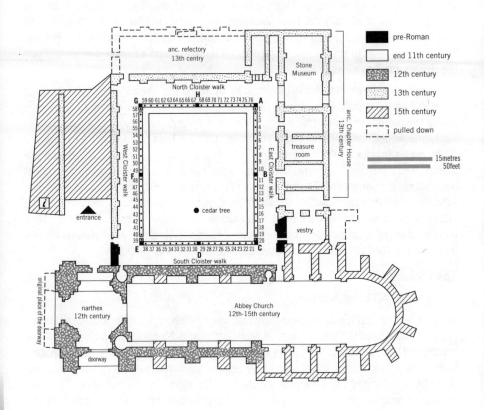

Legend:
- ■ pre-Roman
- □ end 11th century
- ▨ 12th century
- ▨ 13th century
- ▨ 15th century
- ⸬ pulled down
- ▬▬▬ 15 metres
- ▬▬▬ 50 feet

anc. refectory 13th centry

North Cloister walk

Stone Museum

West Cloister walk

East Cloister walk

anc. Chapter House 13th century

treasure room

cedar tree

vestry

entrance

South Cloister walk

narthex 12th century

Abbey Church 12th–15th century

original place of the doorway

doorway

A.	Corner pillar: SS John and James	B.	Central pillar: Abbot Durand of Bredons
1.	Annunciation	11.	Decoration of eagles and human figures
2.	Martyrdom of SS Fructorosus, Eulogius and Augurius	12.	The rich man Dives and the beggar Lazarus (as on the portal)
3.	Acanthus and vine decoration	13.	Decoration of palms and birds
4.	Martyrdom of St Sernin	14.	Jesus and the Apostles
5.	Acanthus decoration	15.	Martyrdom of St Lawrence
6.	Decoration, griffins and eagles	16.	Acanthus decoration
7.	Adoration of the Magi; Massacre of the Innocents	17.	Adam and Eve
8.	Palm and vine decoration	18.	Decorations, alphabet and inscriptions
9.	Wedding at Cana	19.	Martyrdom of SS Peter and Paul, with Nero
10.	Decoration of eagles and human figures		

330

of eight apostles, the 'pillars of the church'; the central pillar in the east gallery has an effigy of Abbot Durand de Bredons, while on the west you can see the dedication inscription of the cloister: 'In the year of the Incarnation of the eternal Father 1100, this cloister was completed in the time of Lord Ansquitil, Abbot, Amen.'

Off the cloister, the 13th-century **chapel of Saint-Ferréol** has faint frescoes of its eponymous saint curing the ill; it now contains a museum of other capitals and the original reliefs from the lower part of the portal, damaged by the damp and replaced by copies. Near the entrance, a narrow stair leads up to the Upper Chapel.

Other Sights

Just behind the church, in the old abbots' palace, the **Musée d'Art et Traditions popu-laires** *(open 9–12 and 2–6, closed Sun morning)* has a bit of everything from bonnets to bed-warmers in old-fashioned settings. South of the abbey is Moissac's market square, **Place des Récollets**, created in the early 19th century with the demolition of its convent. From here Rue J. Moura leads to the deconsecrated church of St-Jacques, now a small **Municipal Museum** *(open 3–7, closed Mon)*, with tools and other odds and ends donated by the Moissagais. The Canal Latéral à la Garonne passes just to the south, spanned by a mobile bridge that permitted canal barges to pass. Upstream, an impressive bridge, similar to the one in Agen, takes the canal over the river Tarn.

On the western outskirts of Moissac, the medieval church of **St-Martin** was also threat-ened by railroad cretins in 1850, and when it too escaped demolition, it was given a restoration. Founded in the 7th century over a Gallo-Roman villa, it was given a new nave in the 10th century, and was partially destroyed by Simon de Montfort and rebuilt again. Pick up the key at Moissac's *mairie* (in Place Delthil, next to the abbey) to see the Gothic murals of the Childhood of Christ and scenes of the Passion.

Moissac ✉ *82200*   ***Where to Stay and Eating Out***

Occupying a huge water mill on the Tarn (which was burned down in 1916 and rebuilt), the ★★★**Auberge du Moulin**, 1 Promenade du Moulin, ✆ 63 04 03 55 has a wide choice of rooms at various prices and a good restaurant, with menus from 80 to 170F. The old-fashioned ★★**Le Pont Napoléon**, 2 Allées Montebello, ✆ 63 04 01 55, is named after the bridge commissioned by Bonaparte in 1808, although it had to wait for Napoleon edition no. III, in 1852, to actually be built. It has both nice rooms and some of the best food in Moissac, served on a terrace over-looking the Tarn, with menus from 90 to 250F; in season try the salmon stuffed with tiny leeks that only grow between the vines, on the 170F menu. In Moissac centre, ★**Le Relais Auvergnat**, Bd Delthil, ✆ 63 04 02 58, has adequate rooms for an overnight stop. The municipal camp site is on the Tarn as well at **Ile du Bidounet**, ✆ 63 32 29 96 (open April to Sept). Across from the market on Place des Récollets, the **Bar de Paris** serves up pizzas and other dishes (including a fine plate of frogs' legs); menus 60–150F.

Around Moissac

North of Moissac lies the realm of Quercy Blanc, with its sunflowers, vineyards of Chasselas grapes and striking dovecotes (*see* p.264). The Tarn-et-Garonne is said to have more of these bird hotels than any other *département* in France, and if rural architecture tends to follow traditional forms, when it came to building the dovecote, or *pigeonnier*, the farmer let his imagination stray a bit—they come in all forms and all postdate the Revolution. Before then, only the nobility were allowed to have them, and there was nothing the peasants could do if the seigneur's bird gobbled down his corn. Pigeons or doves had several very practical purposes: they kept down insects on the vines, they provided food for the table, but most of all, they made a lot of guano, considered the best of all fertilizers and so precious that many a girl was married off with a dowry of pigeon poop.

Tourist Information

Lauzerte: Rue de la Mairie, © 63 94 61 94

Castelsarrasin: Place de la Liberté, © 63 32 14 88

Beaumont-de-Lomagne: 3 Rue Fermat, © 63 02 42 32

market days

Castelsarrasin: Marché de Gras, winter Thursdays

Beaumont-de-Lomagne: Tuesdays and Saturdays

Lauzerte and Cazes-Mondenard

Above the road to Montcuq hovers the memorable site of the bastide of **Lauzerte**, founded by Raymond VI of Toulouse in the 12th century and nicknamed 'the Toledo of Quercy' for its proud profile on the hill; it has charmingly irregular *cornières* around its central square, but one corner of the cobblestoned pavement looks as if it's been turned up, like the page of a book, with coloured tiles underneath. There's a fine selection of 14th- and 15th-century residences made from the white, sunbleached Quercy Blanc limestone. Below Lauzerte, visit the church of the **Carmes** for its extraordinary high altarpiece dated 1689. All Baroque is theatrical, but this is a veritable stage set: the figures of the Virgin handing rosaries to St Simon Stock and St Teresa of Avila, while the prophet Elias and St John of the Cross stand by, all under God stage-managing from above.

Even more surprising is the museum to the east in **Cazes-Mondenard**—the only one in France dedicated to hearses, the **Musée des Corbillards**, on the D 16 *(privately owned, ring Yvan Quercy, © 63 95 84 02)*. Odds are that it would be someone's hobby to take rusty old hearses out of junkyards and lovingly restore them; there are old tractors and carriages and more. South of Cazes-Mondenard, and east of Moissac on the Tarn is a French bastide of 1271. By that time they had run out of names for them and simply called this one **Lafrançaise**. It has a grand panoramic view over the Tarn, but good food is the main reason to stop by (*see* below).

Auvillar

Just west of Moissac where the Tarn flows into the Garonne is a region called La Lomagne—the bit Napoleon nicked off the Gers; it was also known, after its hills, as *Gascogne bossue*, hunchbacked Gascony. This is melon country, and the town to aim for is the lovely village of **Auvillar**. Auvillar's strategic location on the Garonne saw it badly battered in the Hundred Years' and Religious wars, but it recovered nicely, and in the 18th century enjoyed a little economic boom based on goose quills for pens and painted ceramics, which you can see in the **Musée du Vieil Auvillar** *(open daily on request from the mairie)*. This is located in Auvillar's very fetching **Place de la Halle**, which, already defying the usual bastide geometry with its triangular shape, goes a step further in its unique circular market, rebuilt in 1828, with Tuscan columns and a tile roof. From the **Promenade du Château** are fine views down the Garonne, unfortunately including the cooling towers of the nuclear plant at Golfech. Auvillar's war-scarred church of **St-Pierre**, by its sheer size, hints at the town's importance in the Middle Ages, when it produced the cantankerous Marcabru.

Marcabru

The courts of love of Eleanor of Aquitaine in Poitiers had a role in changing European attitudes towards women, which until then had been influenced by the Church's opinion that women were the source of Original Sin and deserved to be nothing but the property of men. With an astute mix of what we might call today 'politically correct' translations of Ovid, Arthurian legend and Occitan troubadour poetry, Eleanor and her daughters (especially Marie de Champagne, her firstborn with Louis VI) formulated a startling alternative, that men were the property of women. The queen and her ladies were the judges of the new standards of behaviour of a knight towards his lady.

Auvillar's troubadour Marcabru (active 1129–1150) offers the opposing view, to put it mildly. A foundling raised by Aldric d'Auvillar, he fought the Moors in Spain and had for a patron Eleanor's father, Guilhem X of Aquitaine (himself son of the first known troubadour, the bawdy Guilhem IX). Marcabru was a great innovator in rhymes, rhythms and new metrical schemes and used language in ways no one had ever done before, his vocabulary ranging from the most vulgar—even gross—realism to elegant, noble lyrics. Of his 41 surviving poems, a few are in a tender mode, especially *A la fontana del vergier*, beautifully depicting a young girl's sorrow for her lover crusading in the Holy Land; the majority lambast women as fickle adulterous whores in language unfit for travel guides. 'He was one of the first troubadours within memory...and he spoke ill of women and of love' said one of his biographers. Eleanor must have frowned to hear his songs—or perhaps she laughed. Marcabru's *Dirai vos senes duptansa*, at any rate, is the medieval version of Louis Jordan's *Brother, You Better Beware*:

> *...Don't you think I know*
> *when Love's cross-eyed or blind?*
> *His words are sweet and polished*
> *Listen!—*
> *and his bite is gentler than a fly's,*
> *But the cure is far more painful.*

Men who follow women's wisdom
Will surely come to ill,
as the Scripture tells us.
Listen!—
Misfortune will bear down on you,
all of you, if you don't beware.

Translated by Anthony Bonner, in *Songs of the Troubadours*

Valence, a rather pretty town on the Garonne, started as an English bastide of 1283; today it gets on as best it can in the shadow of the steaming concrete towers of the nuclear plant at **Golfech**. A typical imposition of the EDF, the national electric monopoly, and its nuclear industry allies, Golfech was built to meet a demand that does not exist. Currently the EDF is trying to spin a new web of high-tension lines across the region to sell Golfech's power elsewhere, and the project has become the environmentalists' public enemy number one in the southwest. The EDF is responding with a publicity campaign on several fronts. On television they're trying to convince everyone to convert to expensive electric heating (while the government makes sure that all new public housing for the poor has it); at Golfech, they've opened a visitors' centre *(open daily 9–1, 2–6pm; Sun 10–6, free! Ring 63 29 39 06 if you want to tour the reactors)*.

Up the Garonne Valley: Castelsarrasin and Belleperche

East of Auvillar, the confluence of the Tarn and the Garonne at **Saint-Nicolas-de-la-Grave** forms a large lake that's the local swimming hole for the whole region. The other main attraction of this area is south of the motorway, at **Le Pin**: an extraordinary 19th-century folly called the **Château Saint-Roch** *(open 2–7, daily mid-July to mid-Sept; Sun only Easter–1 Nov, © 63 95 95 22)*, a precursor of Disneyland's Sleeping Beauty's Castle built by a disciple of Viollet-le-Duc for an art lover who wished he had inherited a château on the Loire.

Although the Arabs never built a castle here in their 8th-century thrust into France, **Castelsarrasin** did have a famous six-towered 12th-century stronghold built by the counts of Toulouse, who picked up a few stylistic tips during their many journeys to the Middle East, and hence its name. The defenders were so terrified of Simon de Montfort in 1212 that they gave up without a fight; after stalwartly standing up to the Huguenots of Montauban in the Wars of Religion, the castle was razed in the 1600s. Castelsarrasin has kept the grid plan laid out by the counts of Toulouse, and more unusually, the Revolutionary names of its streets, reinstated in 1876 by a mayor in the Third Republic who had shared Victor Hugo's exile on Jersey. At 6 Place Lamothe-Cadillac lived the founder of Detroit, Antoine de Lamothe-Cadillac (b. 1658 at St-Nicolas-de-la-Grave), who was so unimpressed with his new settlement that he sold his title of *seigneur de Détroit* in order to purchase the governorship of Castelsarrasin (*see* p.197). Castelsarrasin's main sight is **St-Sauveur**, a church founded by the monks at Moissac in 961 and rebuilt in 1260 in the southern Gothic style. The magnificent Baroque woodwork, especially the elaborate organ console, carved choir stalls, and the pair of prayer-stools, one carved with a virgin and a unicorn, were originally at Belleperche.

The **Abbaye de Belleperche** *(usually open summer Saturdays—ring the Moissac tourist office for information)* overlooks the Garonne, 5km south of Castelsarrasin. Founded in the 1140s, in the revival fervour ignited by St Bernard's preaching, the abbey was built by 200 monks and noted for its magnificence. Nearly all was destroyed in the Wars of Religion, except for the vaulting in the library, the entrance to the refectory, and sections of the 13th-century painted tiled floor (partly removed to the Musée Ingres in Montauban). The church was rebuilt at the end of the 16th century; and the last work was done in 1760, just in time for it to be sold to speculators in the Revolution, who completely dismantled it (other bits in the vicinity are the stalls at nearby Cordes-Tolosannes and two inlaid marble altars at St-Sauveur-de-Castel). The enormous monastery, however, has survived intact and includes many fine details; there is talk of restoring it.

South of Castelsarrasin

The pleasant bastide of **Beaumont-de-Lomagne** was founded in 1276 by the French and has kept its original fortified church, coiffed with an octagonal 14th-century Toulousain bell tower, a handful of old houses, and an even rarer survivor—the wooden *halle* from the 14th century. The statue here of a 17th-century gentleman is of native son Pierre Fermat (1601–65), a jurist by profession and a mathematician for pleasure who invented differential calculus (*see* p.355).

Further south, pretty much in the middle of nowhere, the village of **Bouillac** has a rare treasure: the reliquaries from the 13th-century Cistercian abbey of Grand-Selve, secreted out before the abbey was smashed and burned in the Revolution. Now in a case in Bouillac's 17th-century **St-Sulpice**, a church with an unusual arcaded *clocher-mur*, are beautifully worked caskets and mini-churches of gold and precious stones from the 13th century. To the north begin the vineyards of **St-Sardos**, a pleasant *vin de pays* (tastings in the cooperative in the centre), while on the other bank of the Garonne, a velvety red wine called **La Ville-Dieu-du-Temple** has been produced ever since the Templars planted the first vines.

Between the two is **Montech**, the centre of the Tarn-et-Garonne's only forest, the **Forêt d'Agre**, which in the Middle Ages stretched from Castelsarrasin to the edges of Toulouse. Donated by a wealthy couple to the abbey of Moissac in 680, this mostly oak forest became the source of the abbey's prosperity; although now rather diminished in size and split by the railway and motorway, there are riding and walking paths to explore. Montech was an old stronghold of the counts of Toulouse and has a fine 15th-century church with an enormous bell tower. Montech is proudest these days of the world's first **Pente d'eau** on the Canal Latéral à la Garonne, a slope that replaces five canal locks.

Lauzerte ✉ 82110

La Luzerta, in an cosy old mill at Vignals, ✆ 63 94 64 43, serves good southwest food with a nouvelle cuisine twist (menus from 95 to 220F, closed Wed, and Dec–Feb); there's a pair of hotel rooms, too, at 240F a night.

Cazes-Mondenard ✉ 82110

★**L'Atre**, Place Hôtel de Ville, ✆ 63 95 81 61, is an especially nice little village inn, where the good cooking brings in a regular local clientele (lunch menu 60F, others 100 and 140F). Or dine at the hearse museum (*see* above), which is not only much better than it sounds, but a pleasure, whether you opt for the traditional or classic menus: **Restaurant Yvan Quercy**, ✆ 63 95 84 02 (70–140F).

Lafrançaise ✉ 82130

★★**Le Fin Gourmet**, ✆ 63 65 89 55, is a little *Logis de France* hotel in the centre, with good dining, as its name promises (menus from 75 to 170F, closed Mon in winter). Just north of town, on the D20, follow the signs to the **Ferme-Auberge des Trouilles**, a huge farm with six delightful guest rooms and a pool (220–70F a double with bath and breakfast) and superb farm meals (book ahead): for 130F fill up on an apéritif, soup, pâté, Quercy salad or leek tart, grilled *magret* or lamb or stuffed chicken, vegetables, cheese, homemade dessert, wine and coffee.

North in Molières, on the D22 towards Caussade in Espanel, the old-fashioned **Ferme Auberge de Coutié**, ✆ 63 67 73 51 (book ahead), features a choice of five menus from 90 to 190F.

Auvillar ✉ 82340

Bacchus, on the road to Valence, ✆ 63 29 12 20 offers a traditional, good-value menu at 90F.

Castelsarrasin ✉ 82100

The local postman runs a charming old farm bed-and-breakfast with a pool called **Les Dantous Sud**, 3km south off the N 113 on the D 958, ✆ 63 32 26 95; doubles 230F, and exquisite home-cooked meals, open all year. For something more up-market, head south to Labourgade for the ★★★**Château de Terrides**, ✆ 63 95 61 07, which has 53 rooms in a 16th-century castle, near a golf course, pool and tennis courts.

Le Pin ✉ 82340

★★★**Château Saint-Roch**, ✆ 63 94 85 54, has 14 rooms to spend the night in, as well as a bar and restaurant.

Beaumont-de-Lomagne ✉ 82500

*Du Commerce, 58 Rue Maréchal-Foch, ✆ 63 02 31 02, is a reliable hotel-restaurant in the centre of the town, with good, filling 100 and 140F menus. **L'Arbre d'Or**, 16 Rue Despeyrous, ✆ 63 65 32 34 is a luxurious bed-and-breakfast and table d'hôte in a garden setting run by a friendly English couple (rooms 280F, menus from 60 to 160F).

For a decadently overwhelming feast of delicious duck dishes, reserve a table at the **Auberge de la Gimone**, Av. du Lac, ✆ 63 65 23 09, bring 170F, go to gastronomic heaven, then pop like a balloon.

Montech ✉ 82700

**Notre-Dame, Place Jean-Jaurès, ✆ 63 64 77 45, has comfortable rooms and puts on a good spread in a bright and pretty dining room (menus from 85 to 200F).

South to Toulouse

There is little to detain you here, or to make any road besides the autoroute worth pursuing—unless you're feeling like a tipple.

Côtes-de-Frontonnais

This is another ancient district, dating back to the 4th century BC, and made AOC in 1975. The predominant use of the local Negrette grape (from 50 to 70 per cent of most vintages) gives it its unique character; grafted onto sturdier stock grown on tiered terraces between the Garonne and Tarn rivers, Negrette thrives on the kind of soil the French call *boulbènes*, silty pre-glacial soil on top, red clay subsoil, and at two or three feet under that, pebbles that provide good drainage. A second factor is the local wind, the *autan* that usually assures fine weather in September and October. The resulting ruby red wine, with a redcurrant fragrance, is either drunk quite young or after a few years in the cellar, when it is the perfect accompaniment to *cassoulet*; the rosés are a fruity summer drink.

The two centres of the *appellation*, Fronton and Villaudric, both have cooperatives; the **Domaine de Joliet**, Route de Grisolles in Fronton, ✆ 61 82 46 02 produces some of the more interesting Frontonnais, especially the 100 per cent Negrette *Vin de Printemps* with a violet bouquet.

On the south side of Toulouse itself, a very respectable red, rosé and white *vin de pays de la Haute-Garonne* comes from the Domaine de Ribonnet in Lagardelle-sur-Lèze (✆ 61 08 71 02). This vineyard used to be air pioneer Clément Ader's hobby-horse, and has recently been revived by a Swiss owner. The commune of Toulouse, unique among the great cities of France, owns an 85-acre vineyard, the Domaine de Candi, that provides wine for its hospitals—although only the most manic oenophiles would consider having their tonsils out to try some.

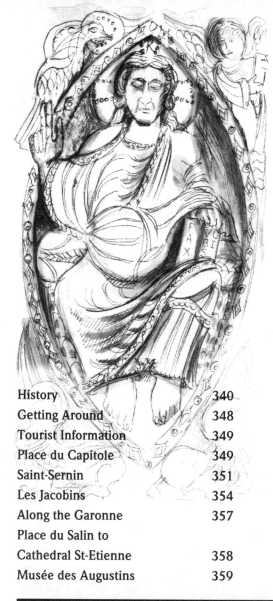

Toulouse

One thing that keeps southwest France from nodding off in its goose fat and wine is this big pink dynamo on the cutting edge of the 21st century. Toulouse, *La Ville Rose*, has 650,000 inhabitants, counting 86,000 students (one out of eight Toulousains), and 70 per cent of the industry in the Midi-Pyrénées region, much of it high tech, related to aeronautics and space. It is the only provincial city in France with its own radio, Sud Radio, and the first to have its own TV station (1988).

Toulouse should have been the rosy capital of a nation called Languedoc, but was knocked out of the big time in the 1220s by the popes and kings of France. Seven and a half centuries later, the Toulousains are getting their rhythm back. No star is too high, as the city's promotional board declares: 'Italy, Florence, Tuscany . . . Toulouse!' What they could be thinking is hard to fathom; in fact it's really Spain that extends her cape here, distilling enough passion to give the heirs of Toulouse's merchants a dose of madness. Toulouse is above all *une ville émotion*'; listen to the Toulousains chant their national anthem, which they do at every possible occasion: *'O moun païs, Toulouse, Toulouse! O moun païs, Toulouse, Toulouse!'* over and over again. There aren't any other verses; according to the natives, there's nothing else to say.

History

The history of Toulouse is detestable, saturated with blood and perfidy.

Henry James

Toulouse was founded at a ford in the Garonne called the Bazacle, at the centre of what the ancient Greek geographer Strabo called the 'Gallic isthmus', the crossroads between the Mediterranean and the Atlantic, the Pyrenees and the Massif Central. Yet confusingly, the original Toulouse (the name means 'elevated place') was on a hill, 10km from the modern city, at a spot now called Vieille Toulouse. The first Toulousains with a name came from the north: a Celtic tribe known as the Volcae Tectosages after their woollen cloaks (*tectus sago*). Because they controlled the roads through the Gallic isthmus, the Tectosages creamed profits from the silver mines to the south and from the trade in Italian wines. They mined the gold of the Ariège, but looked upon it as something too sacred to be minted into coins, and stored most of it at the bottom of a sacred swamp. Despite their wealth, the insatiable Toulousains ranged far and wide ever searching for more; in 279 BC they even participated in the sack of the sacred treasuries of Delphi.

In 125 BC, Ligurian tribes in Provence asked Rome to protect them from the fierce Tectosages. This was all the sneaky Romans needed to muscle in on their own account: they made Toulouse a 'new ally' and sent a garrison to Toulouse to 'collaborate'. In 107 BC when the Tectosages dared to give their allies the boot, the Senate sent General Servilius Caepio to crush them and confiscate their fabulous swamp treasure—110,000 pounds of silver and 100,000 pounds of gold. But only a fraction of this horde ever made it to Rome.

Caepio claimed his convoy was held up by Teutons near Massalia (Marseille); the Senate, suspecting embezzlement, confiscated Caepio's goods, sent him into exile and his women-folk to the brothels. Hence the Roman expression *habebat aurum tolosanum* (to have the gold of Toulouse), meaning that ill-gotten gains seldom prosper.

If Rome cleaned out Toulouse's sacred swamp, it also brought years of peace. The Tectosages felt safe enough to come down from Vieille Toulouse to the plain of the Garonne, and by all accounts they were soon doing well enough again as one of the most important cities in the province of Gallia Narbonensis, with a population around 20,000. The city became known as *Palladia Tolosa* after its protector, the goddess of wisdom Pallas Athena. Yet because it was all made of brick, next to nothing has survived.

The Capital of the Visigoths

In 410 the Visigoths under Alaric captured Rome and took a hostage—Galla Placidia, sister of Emperor Honorius. When Alaric died, Galla Placidia was inherited by his brother-in-law Ataulf, who carried the young maiden off on his conquests in southwest France. Ataulf pre-ferred Toulouse to Bordeaux, the Roman capital of Aquitaine, and made it the Visigothic capital. When his wife died, he married Galla Placidia. It was the love match of the Dark Ages, and her genteel Roman manners helped to tame the Visigothic temperment. Ataulf was later killed in a palace conspiracy and Galla Placidia returned to her brother in Ravenna, where she built a beautiful tomb of golden mosaics that can be seen to this day (she later remarried, gave birth to Emperor Valentinian III, and reigned for years as Empress herself). Toulouse remained the elegant capital of the Visigoths until 507 when Clovis, the recently baptised king of the Franks, took it upon himself to wipe out the Arian heresy—the sect of the Visigoths. After Clovis defeated Alaric II in hand-to-hand combat, the Visigoths upped sticks over the Pyrenees for Toledo, which they made their capital until ousted by the Arabs in 716.

Five years later these same Arab armies appeared at the gates of Toulouse. Clovis's succes-sors, the Merovingian 'do-nothing kings' (*rois fainéants*) hadn't failed to neglect Toulouse, but by chance the city had an able duke on hand named Eudes, who organized a brilliant resistance, killed the emir and gave the Moors their very first taste of defeat on 9 June 721. The Arabs' later defeat at Poitiers has always been the more famous one, however, because the victor was Charles Martel, founding father of the Carolingian dynasty that replaced Duke Eudes and the Merovingians in the person of his son, Pepin the Short.

Pepin, recognizing the danger of a renewed Arab attack from over the Pyrenees, spent years hunting down Waiofar, the last Merovingian duke of Aquitaine, in order to establish his authority and guarantee the frontiers of the Franks' growing empire. Pepin's son Charlemagne continued this policy by petting and pampering Toulouse. The most able and loyal counsellors of his sons and grandsons, who inherited these southwest marches, became in 849 the counts of Toulouse, responsible for Languedoc—a vast territory extending from the Rhône to the Garonne and from the Pyrenees to the Dordogne.

The Counts of Toulouse

The counts of Toulouse are often called the Raymondine dynasty—because Raymond was their favourite name. The first to emerge from obscurity was Raymond Saint-Gilles, born in 1041, the younger brother of Count Guilhem. A mighty warrior, Raymond spent his youth battling the Moors in Spain with such audacity that the king of Castile married him to his daughter and put him under the wing of the Cid. In 1090, Count Guilhem died without a male heir, and Raymond was summoned back to Toulouse, where despite his great popularity, his reign as Count Raymond IV was brief; in 1095 Urban II asked him to lead the First Crusade. Before leaving, he oversaw the consecration of the great basilica of Saint-Sernin, and declaring he would never return, installed his son Bertrand as count. For his arms Raymond designed the twelve-pointed red cross that to this day is the symbol of Toulouse and its region. In the Holy Land Raymond was offered the crown of Jerusalem; to everyone's surprise he refused and let the honour go to Godfrey of Bouillon. Before he died in 1105 he saw the birth of his fourth son, baptised in the river Jordan and henceforth known as Alphonse-Jourdain.

Little Alphonse-Jourdain was shipped home to Toulouse to take Bertrand's place as count when the latter succumbed to the crusading itch. Alphonse-Jordain remained on the job long enough to found, in 1152, one of Toulouse's most enduring and original institutions, the *domini de capitulo* (lords of the chapter), a name shortened over the years to *capitouls*. At first they administered justice; by the time of the Revolution they ran the city. Each parish in Toulouse had its own *capitoul* (by 1438 the number was fixed at eight); they were appointed each November by the count (and later by the king's judge, or *viguier*) from a list of names provided by the outgoing *capitouls*, and had to wait three years before they were eligible again.

The next Count Raymond, the fifth, took over at age 14, when his father Alphonse-Jourdain could no longer resist the siren song of the Crusades. Raymond V was a troubadour who presided over a golden age of poetry for Toulouse; more concretely, he continued his father's administrative reforms by granting Toulouse municipal autonomy. Another charter, in 1192, established the very first concern managed by shareholders, the *Moulins du Bazacle*, for centuries one of the largest such installations in Europe; Rabelais wrote 'that they filled the ears with the infernal racket of their wheels that rotated ten heavy millstones.' Although Raymond V is known among non-Toulousain historians as 'the weathervane', inconsistent and ambiguous in his diplomacy, his manoeuvrings were all for the sake of his beloved Languedoc—a small but rich prize greedily coveted by the most powerful rulers of Europe: France, England, Aquitaine and Barcelona all had tenuous claims and were ready to pounce. In 1190, Richard the Lion-Heart did, capturing Cahors and 18 castles on the pretext of avenging alleged attacks on pilgrims passing through the lands of Toulouse. Raymond V quietly got his revenge by having his Mediterranean allies refuse a safe harbour for Richard's ship on his return from the crusades, leading directly to his capture by Leopold of Austria.

To Lose Toulouse, Through Love

When the count died in 1195, his son Raymond VI had already been through three wives (the first died, the second and third were repudiated) and was ready to patch things up with the troublesome Plantagenets by wedding a fourth, Joanna, sister of Richard the Lion-Heart, who bore him an heir before she died. But reproaches on his private life were nothing compared to the reproaches heaped on him for his ambiguous attitude towards the Cathars. In 1208, when one of his Provençal vassals murdered the papal legate Pierre de Castelnau, Pope Innocent III demanded that the count, who knew nothing of the matter, do penance and let himself be stripped to the waist and beaten with rods. Even this humiliation, and the fact that he had undertaken the expense of constructing a new cathedral in Toulouse, failed to convince Innocent that he hated the heretics sufficiently. And he probably didn't. Raymond VI seems to have had quite a modern, tolerant attitude towards the Cathars; they lived honestly without harming anyone, and as count it was his job to defend them. Such an attitude was so threatening to the Church that Innocent began recruiting in the north for what has come down in history as the Albigensian crusade. Raymond and his barons soon enough recognized what it really was—an excuse for the northerners to grab the south of France.

With the pope, the king of France and the crusaders' cruel fanatic of a leader, Simon de Montfort lined up against him, Raymond summoned his brother-in-law, Pere (Pedro) of Aragon, count of Barcelona, offering to unite the counties of Barcelona and Toulouse into a kingdom of the south to defeat the northerners. Pere was fresh from the great victory over the Moors at Las Navas de Tolosa, but he had no qualms about fighting against the pope's team—especially if he could combine war with a visit to his old flame, a certain Azalaïs de Boissezon. Simon de Montfort was near Toulouse at Muret when he intercepted the letter from Pedro, setting up a rendez-vous with Azalaïs. 'How should I respect a king who, for a woman, marches against his God!' declared Montfort. Aragon and Toulouse had 3000 knights against Montfort's 1500 at Muret, and what should have been an easy victory began ominously when King Pedro turned up for battle exhausted, barely able to sit in the saddle. One of his knights traded arms with him, hoping to conceal his identity, but from the beginning the Occitans were outmanoeuvred by Montfort. In the subsequent hand-to-hand combat, the king of Aragon, fearing to be labelled a coward, revealed himself and was quickly slain. The battle of Muret (12 September 1213) turned into a rout and marked the beginning of the end of the south's independence.

In 1215, with the king of France at his side, Simon de Montfort entered Toulouse, where he became count by the will of the pope. He ruled with Bishop Folquet de Marseille, a former troubadour patronized by Raymond V who in 1195 got religion and became the most rabid hellfire bigot of them all (a contemporary wrote: 'And when he was elected Bishop of Toulouse he spread such fire throughout the land that no amount of water will ever suffice to extinguish it; he snuffed out, in body and in soul, the lives of more than fifteen hundred people . . . he is more an Antichrist than a messenger of Rome'). In 1217 when young Raymond, son of the count, orchestrated an uprising in Provence to draw Montfort out of Toulouse, the population welcomed back the exiled Raymond VI 'as if he were the Holy Spirit', and diligently prepared against the furious Montfort's return. The next June, while he besieged Toulouse, a woman, operating a kind of homemade mini-catapult, saw him coming, took aim and lobbed a large rock on his skull, dashing out his brains.

Raymond VI died soon afterwards (his body, while awaiting burial in a monastery corridor, was stolen and never found); he was succeeded by the last Raymond, edition VII. After 17 years of useless fighting to gain back the city, Simon de Montfort's heir ceded his claim to Toulouse to Louis VIII, who embarked on another 'crusade', a fancy name for a scorched-earth campaign to crush the south. In 1229 Raymond VII, seeing the distress of his subjects, sued for terms from the not-so-saintly Louis IX. As put down in the subsequent Treaty of Paris they were: first, the public submission of Raymond in front of Notre-Dame in Paris. Then, the division of booty: eastern Languedoc for the king of France and the Comtat-Vénaissin for the pope (which later allowed the popes to install themselves in Avignon, and helped in the canonization of Louis IX). Jeanne, Raymond's only child, was wed to Alphonse de Poitiers, the king's brother. They too went crusading in the east, and died childless in 1271; Toulouse reverted to France as the chief city of the province of Languedoc.

One side effect of the Albigensian crusade was the founding of the Dominicans (see Les Jacobins, below). A second was the invention of the Inquisition. Raymond VII, in spite of his submission, had little heart for persecuting the Cathars, so Gregory IX in 1233 came up with the idea of a spiritual police force and put the Dominicans in charge of it. This went down like a lead balloon; the *capitouls* themselves ordered an assault on the Jacobins (Dominican friars), forcing the Grand Inquisitors to flee. The count was ordered to take them back, and one night a band of Cathars from Montségur descended from their mountain fastness and slit their throats—an act that tragically sealed the fate of Montségur. A third side effect was the founding of the University of Toulouse: the 1229 Treaty of Paris ordered Raymond to support 14 masters of theology and canon law for a decade. They stuck around to form the second oldest university in France, one controlled for years by Parisians and papal appointees to enforce orthodoxy on the wayward southerners.

A fourth side effect was the boom in the slave trade; the northern French were not only buying up recalcitrant southerners, but they now found the path to Spain clear to capture Muslims to sell in the north. The *capitouls* found it revolting, and in 1226 struck a precocious blow for human rights by granting the right of asylum to any slave, whatever his country of origin. Despite considerable outside pressure, the law remained on the books in Toulouse until the Revolution.

A Second Golden Age, in Pastel

Although the city got through the Hundred Years' War fairly intact, a fire that started in a bakery oven in 1463 destroyed 7000 buildings in the medieval centre. Toulouse sprang back almost immediately thanks to a new cash crop—dyers' woad, locally called *pastel*. Cultivated in the hills of the Lauragais just southeast of Toulouse, pastel leaves were pulverized and squeezed into balls called *coques*. These were left to dry, then crushed into paste, fermented and mixed with urine to produce the deep blue dye so fashionable in the

Renaissance; mixed with other ingredients it became bright green or violet. For a century so much money poured into Toulouse that the Lauragais, the land of the *coques* became the *païs de Cocanha* or Cocaigne, the carefree land of abundance and pleasure. Merchants from across Europe speculated and dealt in *pastel* credits and futures (the whole process from harvest to dye took over a year). These activities were centralized in 1552, with the founding of Toulouse's stock exchange—just before the *pastel* market collapsed in the 1560s with the import of a much cheaper substitute, indigo from South Carolina.

The 17th century brought Toulouse both deep economic depression and spiritual malaise. The clergy were openly corrupt, and many Toulousains, the Cathars of old, were receptive to the preachings of John Calvin. Although the *capitouls* tolerated the new religion (many of them were converts themselves), the parlementarians and intendants—representing royal power in Toulouse—stayed strictly in the Catholic camp, and conflicts were inevitable: a bloody riot broke out in 1562 when Catholic priests stole the body of a dead Protestant woman laid out in a temple, saying she had reconverted on her deathbed; by May it was open warfare in the streets. But the Catholics prevailed in the end, and Toulouse was one of the last cities to recognize Henri IV as king.

In 1632, with the dramatic fall of the governor of Languedoc, the duke of Montmorency (*see* below), Toulouse saw its remaining independence and privileges slowly gobbled up by the absolute monarchy. One bright spot was the digging of the Canal du Midi, linking the Mediterranean and the Atlantic, a project according to legend first envisioned by Charlemagne and brilliantly planned, financed and achieved by Pierre-Paul Riquet, scion of a prominent Italian family in the region. Louis XVI was pleased to take credit for uniting two seas and two worlds in record time (1666–81), but the cost—3,600,000 livres—was borne by Languedoc and the dedicated Riquet, who died ruined.

The new prosperity and agricultural trade (mostly in wheat) brought about by Riquet's ditch may have improved local morale if not local morals. The most popular entertainments in Toulouse were public executions, to the tune of three or four a month, which may be why the population only grew 10 per cent (to around 60,000) while the rest of France shot up 40 per cent in the 1700s. The execution with the most repercussions was the 1761 *affaire Calas*: the son of a fervent Protestant cloth merchant was found strangled. The family claimed they had tried to keep his suicide quiet, to prevent the dishonour of having the body put on trial (as suicide was a crime) but the neighbours had often overheard father and son quarrelling over religion, and were convinced from the beginning that Calas *père* had killed the young man rather than see him convert to Catholicism. Found guilty by the *parlement* of Toulouse, Calas was brutally tortured, then had all his limbs broken with iron bars, and survived another two hours, the whole time stalwartly maintaining his innocence. Voltaire wrote of the case, and soon enough the king of Prussia and Catherine the Great were expressing their great indignation. Funds were raised on the streets of Holland and England for a retrial; the parlement of Paris demanded the dossier, and three years later Calas was found innocent, his family rehabilitated. Encouraged by the result, Voltaire continued his sarcastic attacks, until all the *parlements* in France were universally hated —adding another pile of kindling to the smouldering misery that ignited the Revolution.

Toulouse in the Sky with Diamonds

The mid-19th century found Toulouse a mere departmental capital, a sleepy provincial backwater where the elite invested in property and farms instead of joining the Industrial Revolution. In 1833 journalist Léon Faucher wrote: 'Life is too easy in Toulouse for the people there to feel pushed to be or do anything.' The arrival of the railroad in 1856 shook things up a bit, or at least shook down branches of Paris's banks and department stores.

What proved to be the turning point for modern Toulouse literally fell from the sky. Clément Ader of Muret, born in 1841, gave a preview of coming events when one of his bat-winged, steam-powered *avions*, as he called them, hopped off the ground in 1873; in 1890 he flew 300 yards in the *Eole*, 13 years before Orville Wright's first flight at Kitty Hawk. In 1917, Latécoère founded the first aircraft factory in Toulouse—it was far from the front lines of the First World War, and at its peak produced six combat aeroplanes a day. After the Armistice, Latécoère continued production, for peaceful purposes, and on 12 March 1919 launched a Toulouse–Casablanca airmail route that soon extended to Dakar and

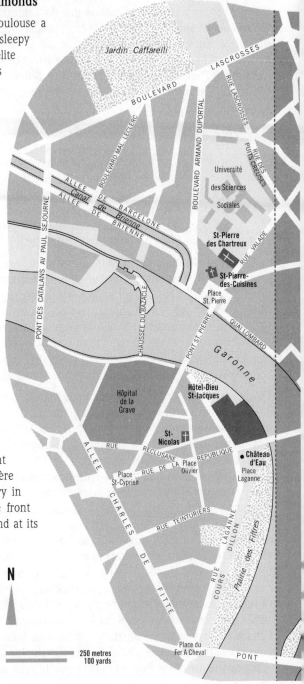

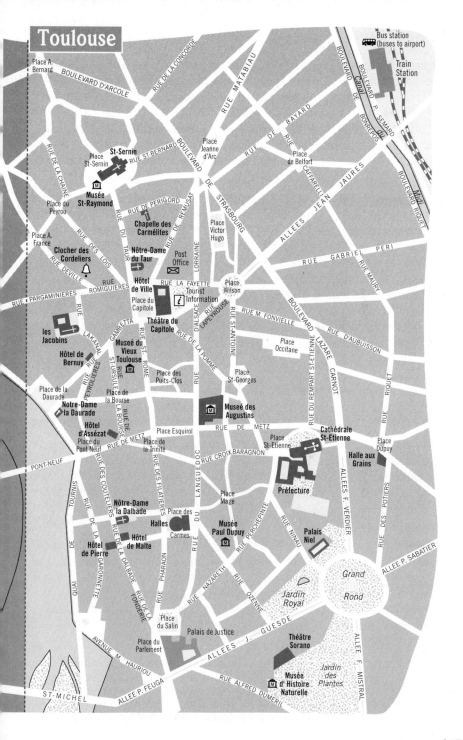

Toulouse

Place A.
Bernard

BOULEVARD D'ARCOLE

RUE DE LA CONCORDE

RUE MATABIAU

Bus station
(buses to airport)

Train
Station

BOULEVARD Canal DU SÉMARD

BOULEVARD DE RUE DE BAYARD

BOULEVARD P. SÉMARD

BOULEVARD RIQUET

Midi

RUE DE LA CHAINE

Place
St-Sernin

St-Sernin

RUE ST-BERNARD

BOULEVARD DE STRASBOURG

Place
Jeanne
d'Arc

Place
de Belfort

CAFFARELLI

ALLEES JEAN JAURES

Place du
Peyrou

**Musée
St-Raymond**

RUE DE PERIGORD

RUE DU TAUR

Place A.
France

**Clocher des
Cordeliers**

RUE DEVILLE

RUE DES LOIS

**Chapelle des
Carmélites**

Place
Victor
Hugo

RUE GABRIEL PERI

RUE MAURY

RUE PARGAMINIERES

RUE
ROMIGUIERES

**Nôtre-Dame
du Taur**

Post
Office
✉

**Hôtel
de Ville**

RUE LA FAYETTE

Place du
Capitole

Place
Wilson

Tourist
Information
ℹ

RUE D'ALSACE LORRAINE

RUE M. FONVIELLE

BOULEVARD LAZARE CARNOT

RUE D'AUBUISSON

RUE RIQUET

les
Jacobins

GAMBETTA

LAKANAL

**Théâtre du
Capitole**

RUE DE LA POMME

RUE CAPEYROUSE

RUE ST-ANTOINE

Place
Occitane

RUE DU REMPART ST-ETIENNE

**Hôtel de
Bernuy**

RUE PEYROLIERES

RUE ST-ROME

RUE STURSULE

**Musée du
Vieux
Toulouse**
Ⓜ

Place des
Puits-Clos

Place
St-Georges

Place de la
Daurade

**Notre-Dame
la Daurade**

RUE DE LA BOURSE

Place de
la Bourse

**Hôtel
d'Assézat**

Place du
Pont Neuf

RUE DE METZ

Place Esquirol

Ⓜ **Museé des
Augustins**

RUE DE METZ

**Cathédrale
St-Etienne** ✝

Place
Dupuy

PONT-NEUF

RUE DES COUTELIERS

Place de
la Trinité

RUE DES FILATIERES

RUE CROIX BARAGNON

Place
St-Etienne

**Halle aux
Grains**

ALLEES F. VERDIER

RUE DES POTIERS

TOURNIS

RUE DE LA GARONNETTE

**Nôtre-Dame
la Dalbade** ✝

Place des
Carmes

Place
Mage

Préfecture

RUE DE LA DALBADE

RUE DU LANGUEDOC

Halles

**Hôtel
de Malte**

RUE DE LA FONDERIE

**Hôtel
de Pierre**

RUE PHARAON

**Musée
Paul Dupuy**
Ⓜ

RUE PERCHEPINTE

RUE NINAU

**Palais
Niel**

ALLEE P. SABATIER

QUAI DE LA DAURADE

RUE NAZARETH

RUE OZENNE

RUE J. GUESDE

Grand
Rond

*Jardin
Royal*

Place
du Salin

AVENUE M. HAURIOU

Place du
Parlement

Palais de Justice

ALLEES J. GUESDE

**Théâtre
Sorano**

ALLEE F. MISTRAL

ST-MICHEL

ALLEE P. FEUGA

RUE ALFRED DUMERIL

Ⓜ **Musée
d'Histoire
Naturelle**

*Jardin
des
Plantes*

347

eventually to South America. For this new airline, the *Compagnie Générale Aéropostale*, he recruited ace pilots—'Archangel' Jean Mermoz, Daurat, Guillaumet and Antoine de Saint-Exupéry, the 'Lord of the Sands' who immortalized them in his books. A second aircraft company, founded in 1920 by Toulousain Emile Dewoitine, was nationalized in 1937 and later became Aérospatiale, the birthplace of Ariane rockets and Hermès, the European space shuttle, as well as Caravelle, Concorde and Airbus jets. CNES, the French space agency, was transferred here in 1968 along with the French national weather service; Matra-Marconi Space makes Europe's satellites. The industry has attracted a bevy of research centres, 600 related high-tech firms and elite schools of engineering and aviation.

The population of Toulouse has grown apace. It was the principal refugee centre during and after the Spanish Civil War, and of the 360,000 or so civilians and Republican soldiers who passed through the city, a quarter stayed and became French citizens (in the 1970s, when Franco executed the anti-fascist Puig Antich, 3000 protestors set fire to the Spanish consulate in Toulouse). Thousands came to work in the new postwar industries; 25,000 *pieds-noirs* from Algeria settled here in the 1960s. Then in 1964, when France decided to ever so slowly reverse the centralizing work of Richelieu, Toulouse was made capital of the largest of France's new regions, the Midi-Pyrénées, the western half of its old province of Languedoc. By then Toulouse, after its slow start, had become the fourth city of France. Although pink in its politics as well as its bricks for most of the 20th century, Toulouse since 1971 has been mayored by the right-wing Baudises, first the father, and now his son, Dominique Baudis—a bundle of itchy ambition who has been trying to make a national name for himself by attacking what right-wingers think is a major cause of France's unemployment and race problems: 'white marriages' of immigrants to French nationals.

Getting Around

By air: Toulouse's international airport at Blagnac, 10km from the centre, has 19 connections daily with Paris (Air Inter, © 61 30 68 68), and at least two a day with London (Air France, reservations © 62 10 01 01, airport © 62 12 87 66; British Airways, © 61 71 96 71; Brit Air, © 61 71 10 00), and once a week in the summer with Montreal (Nouvelles Frontières, © 61 21 03 53). The airport shuttle departs from the bus station (next to the train station) every 20mins, less often after 9pm.

By train: Trains run from Paris–Austerlitz through Gourdon, Souillac, Cahors and Montauban to Toulouse in 6½ hours; TGVs from Paris-Montparnasse do the same in around 5hrs—by way of Bordeaux. The slow trains to Bordeaux take 2½ hours and stop in Montauban, Castelsarrasin, Moissac, Agen and Aiguillon. Other connections include Albi (1hr) and Castres (1½hrs), Auch, Carcassonne and Marseille. For info © 61 62 50 50, reservations © 61 62 85 44.

By bus: The bus station is next to the railway station at 4 Rue Marengo, © 61 48 71 84; there are buses to Foix, Albi, Gaillac, Auch, Nogaro and Montauban, and also to London, Madrid and Barcelona.

By métro and city bus: In 1993 Toulouse proudly opened its first métro line, running northeast to southwest from Joliment, the railway station and the Capitole to the Mirail. City buses are run by SEMVAT, which has an information office at 7 Place Esquirol, ℂ 61 41 70 70. Almost all the sites are in the compact centre, though, and you'll hardly ever need either of these.

By taxi: If you can't find one cruising the streets or at a taxi stand, ℂ 61 42 38 38, 61 21 00 72 or 61 80 36 36 (all night).

By car: Toulouse's rapid growth has led to some major traffic tie-ups; at the time of writing there are over 450 road projects in the city, even as more pedestrian streets are set aside in the city centre. The most convenient pay car parks are at Place du Capitole, Place Wilson and Place St-Etienne; closest free parking is at Place St-Sernin and Place de la Daurade.

By boat: One of the nicest ways to see Toulouse is by canal; 1½hr tours depart from the Port de l'Embouchure (Ponts Jumeaux, bus 16 or 70), ℂ 61 71 45 95, and take you down the Brienne and around the Garonne.

Tourist Information

Donjon du Capitole, Rue Lafayette, behind the Capitole, ℂ 61 11 02 22. For information on the whole of the Midi-Pyrénées region, stop by the Comité Régional du Tourisme Midi-Pyrénées, 54 Bd de l'Embouchure, ℂ 61 13 55 55. If you plan to visit at least three museums in Toulouse, you can save money by purchasing a pass at the first one (20F for 3, 30F for 6), valid for a month.

Place du Capitole

This diginified front parlour of Toulouse dates only from 1850, when the 200-year-long tidying away of excess buildings was completed and the edges rimmed with neoclassical brick façades. In the centre of the pavement is the **Cross of Languedoc**, the same designed by Raymond IV before embarking on the First Crusade. This same golden cross on a red background hangs proudly from Toulouse's city hall, the **Capitole**, or CAPITOLIUM as it reads, bowing to an flagrant bit of local patriotism, a 16th-century story claiming ancient Rome got its Capitol idea from Toulouse's temple of Capitoline Jupiter.

This Capitole, however, is named after the *capitouls*. In 1750, flush with new money brought in by the Canal du Midi, they decided to transform their higgledy-piggledy medieval buildings into a proper Hôtel de Ville. Parts of the original 12th–17th-century complex were saved, at least as much as could be masked by the neoclassical façade designed by municipal artist Guillaume Cammas, who imported stone and marble to alternate with the good home-made brick of Toulouse. Cammas's careful polychromatic effects were only briefly admired when the *capitouls* decided to pass a law ordering every building to be whitewashed or covered with white stucco, the better to reflect the moonlight and make up for the lack of street lighting. The first building to get the treatment was the Capitole itself; the entire Place du Capitole remained under this dull white make-up until 1946, when Toulouse decided to become the *Ville Rose* once more. Other critics have had trouble with its height. '*C'est beau mais c'est bas*' was the only comment of Napoleon, an expert on the subject.

The portal on the right belongs to the **Théâtre du Capitole**, while over the central door eight pink marble columns represent the eight *capitouls*; on weekdays from 8.30 to 5 you may visit the rather pompous historical rooms upstairs, decorated in the 1800s with busts of famous Toulousains.

You may also visit the **Cour Henri IV** with a statue of the king, who in 1602 gave his permission for the construction of the courtyard. He might not have, had he known what was going to go on here 30 years later, thanks to the jealous rivalries and schemes of his two neurotic sons, Louis XIII and Gaston d'Orléans ('Monsieur' for short), and the prime minister and arch-puppeteer, Cardinal Richelieu.

A Conspiracy's Martyr

Henri IV's companion in arms, Henri Duke of Montmorency, First Peer of the Realm and Governor of Languedoc, was succeeded in these titles by his son, Duke Henri II, a brave fighter and governor dedicated to the welfare of Languedoc. Richelieu, whose plans for creating an absolute monarchy included tripping up the kingdom's mightiest barons, made it hot for Montmorency by choking Languedoc with taxes until it was at the point of insurrection. Montmorency hated Richelieu, and attracted the attention of 'Monsieur' who, in cahoots with his scheming mother, Marie de' Medici, was always ready to befriend an enemy of the cardinal. Monsieur offered to send down troops to liberate Languedoc and France from the high-handed cardinal's policies. After much soul-searching, Montmorency cast his lot with Monsieur.

Richelieu must have rubbed his hands with glee. With the king in tow he led an army south to snuff out the revolt. The promised military aid from Monsieur failed to turn up, and Montmorency, realizing he had made a terrible mistake, tried unsuccessfully to surrender, hoping to avoid battle. Richelieu refused. His troops, however, surprised the hapless duke while he was reconnoitring the lines. Montmorency, fighting singlehandedly, was wounded 17 times; he might have escaped, it was said, had he had his proper warhorse. Richelieu was careful to keep Montmorency alive, knowing he could make a more memorable example out of the affair by persuading the king to sentence him to death.

Montmorency's fate quickly became a *cause célèbre* across Europe—Charles I of England, the Pope, the Republic of Venice and most of the nobles of France pleaded for mercy. Louis XIII turned a deaf ear, but on the appointed day of execution, 30 October 1632, popular feeling ran so high that the authorities decided to hold the execution privately in this courtyard rather than in public. In spite of his wounds, Montmorency walked alone to the chopping block (a slab in the pavement marks the spot), his eyes falling on the statue of Henri IV. 'He was a great and generous prince, and I had the honour to be his godson,' were Montmorency's last words. His blood splattered over the statue; the guard dipped their swords in the red pool; a throng of grieving Toulousains were let in to touch and even kiss the sticky pavement as if he had been a martyr. He was buried in St-Sernin, the basilica's first non-saint.

Through the Cour Henri IV, the Square Charles de Gaulle is occupied by the **Donjon** of 1525, where the *capitouls* kept the city archives. The building was restored by Viollet-le-Duc and now houses the city tourist office.

Saint-Sernin

Running north from Place du Capitole, narrow **Rue de Taur** was the road to Cahors in Roman times. The Taur in its name means 'bull', which features in the life of the city's first saint, Sernin, who died here in the 240s.

Sernin (a corruption of Saturnin) was a missionary from Rome who preached in Pamplona and then in Toulouse. One day, runs the legend, he happened by the temple of Capitoline Jupiter, where preparations were under way for the sacrifice of a bull to Mithras. The priests ordered him to kneel before the pagan idol, and when Sernin refused, a sudden gust of wind blew over the statue of Mithras, breaking it to bits. In fury the crowd demanded the sacrifice of Sernin instead, and he was tied under the bull, which, maddened by the extra weight, dragged his body through the city streets. (By coincidence, an identical martyrdom awaited Sernin's disciple Fermin in Pamplona, where he became the patron saint of matadors and is honoured each year by the famous running of the bulls. The official hagiography, however, has Fermin dying in bed as the bishop of Amiens).

After turning the unfortunate Sernin into pulp, the bull left his body where the 14th-century **Notre Dame du Taur** now stands, replacing an oratory built over Sernin's tomb in 360. Its 135ft *clocher mur* looks like a false front in a Wild West town; the nave is surprisingly wide, and has a faded fresco of the Tree of Jesse along the right wall.

Sernin's tomb attracted so many pilgrims and Christians who desired to be buried near him that a *martyrium* was built 300 yards to the north in 403. An imperial decree permitted the removal of the saint's relics to this spot, and over the centuries tombs lined the length of Rue de Taur, as in the Alyschamps in Arles. In 1075, just as the pilgrimage to Compostela was getting under way, Count Guilhem decided Sernin deserved something more grand. The construction, continued by his famous brother Raymond IV, was of such import that in 1096 Pope Urban II came to consecrate its marble altar (the pope was touring that year, preaching the First Crusade).

In the 12th century the **Basilique du Saint Sernin** was finished—at 380ft the largest surviving Romanesque church in the world (only the great abbey church of Cluny, destroyed in the Revolution, was bigger). Its plan is identical to the basilica of St James at Compostela, begun at the same time: it has the form of a cross, ending in a semi-circular apse with five radiating chapels. In the 19th century the abbey buildings and cloister were demolished, and in 1860 Viollet-le-Duc was summoned to restore the basilica. He spent 20 years on the project—and botched the roof so badly that rainwater seeped directly into the stone and brick. A century later the church was found to be in danger of collapse—hence the scaffolding you may well see draped around it, part of a 20 million franc 'de-restoration' project to undo Viollet-le-Duc's mischief.

The Exterior

The apse of Saint-Sernin (seen from Rue Saint-Bernard) is a fascinating play of white stone and red brick, a crescendo culminating in the octagonal bell tower that is Toulouse's most striking landmark; the original three storeys of arcades were increased to five in the 13th century to upstage the tower of the Jacobins. The most elaborately decorated of the portals is an odd, asymmetrical one on the south side, the **Porte Miège-ville**. It faces Rue du Taur; apparently this street, called Miège-ville or 'mid-city' in medieval times, ran right through the spot before the basilica was built. Devotees of medieval Toulousain arcana—a bottomless subject—say that this portal is the real cornerstone of the state the 11th-century counts were trying to create; books have been written about its proportions and the symbolism of its decoration, even claiming that it is the centre of a geomantic construction, with twelve lines radiating from here across the counts' territories, connecting various chapels and villages—forming a Cross of Languedoc, Raymond IV's symbol and the symbol of the Midi-Pyrénées region today.

The tympanum was carved by the 11th-century master Bernard Gilduin, showing the *Ascension of Christ*, a rare scene in medieval art, and one of the most choreographic: Christ surrounded by dancing angels, watched by the Apostles on the lintel. On the brackets are figures of David and others riding on lions; the magnificent capitals tell the story of the Redemption (*Original sin, Massacre of the Innocents, Annunciation*) from the expressive chisel of Gilduin. The north transept door, now walled up, was the royal door; the south transept door, the **Porte des Comtes**, is named after the several 11th-century counts of Toulouse who are buried in paleochristian sarcophagi in the deep *enfeu* near by. The eight capitals here, also by Gilduin (c. 1080), are the oldest Romanesque works to show the torments of hell, most alarmingly a man having his testicles crushed and a woman whose breasts are being devoured by serpents.

The Interior

Begun in 1969, the 'de-restoration' of the barrel-vaulted interior has recently been completed, stripping the majestic brick and stone of all Viollet-le-Duc's ham-handed murals and neo-gothic furnishings. In the process, some 12th-century frescoes have been found, especially the serene angel of the Resurrection in the third bay of the north transept, which also has some of the best capitals.

From here you can pay to enter the **ambulatory** and make what the Middle Agers called 'the circuit of Holy bodies', for the wide selection of saintly anatomies stashed in the five radiating chapels. In the 17th century, bas-reliefs and wood panels on the lives of the saints were added to bring the relics to life, and although these were removed in the 1800s they were restored and replaced in 1980. Opposite the central chapel are seven magnificent marble bas-reliefs of 1096, carved and signed by Bernard Gilduin. The Christ in Majesty set in a mandorla is as serene, pot-bellied and beardless as a Buddah, surrounded by the four Evangelists; the others show a seraph, a cherub, two apostles and a pair of hierarchic, well-coiffed angels; scholars guess these were perhaps modelled after a Roman statue of Orpheus.

The Holy Bodies circuit continues down into the upper crypt, with the silver shrine of St Honoratus (1517) and the 13th-century reliquaries of the Holy Cross and of St Sernin, the latter showing the saint under the hooves of the bull. The lower crypt contains even more bits of bodies, two Holy Thorns, 13th-century gloves and mitres, and a set of six 16th-century painted wooden statues of apostles. In the choir an 18th-century baldachin shelters St-Sernin's tomb, remade in 1746 and supported by a pair of bronze bulls. In the south transept, note the big feet sticking out of a pillar, all that remains of a shallow relief of St Christopher effaced by the hands of centuries of pilgrims.

Around Place Saint-Sernin and the Quartier Arnaud-Bernard

At no. 3, the Lycée Saint-Sernin occupies the Hôtel du Barry, built in 1777 by Louis XV's pimp, the Roué du Barry, who made his fortune by marrying his lover, Jeanne de Bécu, to his brother and making her the king's mistress. (The word *roué*, incidentally, was first used in the 1720s, to describe the bawdy companions of the Regent, the Duke of Orléans; it was invented by some disapproving soul who thought they should have been broken on the wheel.) On the south side of the square stood a pilgrims' hostel, founded in the 1070s by a chanter of St Sernin named Raymond Gayard, who was canonized for his charity to poor. His hostel was succeeded by the collège of St Raymond (1505) for poor university students, and now by the rich archaeological collections of the **Musée Saint-Raymond** *(open daily 10–5, till 6 in the summer; adm)*. Exhibits include examples of the legendary wealth of the Tectosages (especially in solid gold torques, twisted necklaces and bracelets); a superb set of busts of Roman emperors and fine marbles depicting the *Labours of Hercules* from the Gallo-Roman villas of Martres-Toulouse; small bronze statues and keys decorated with figures of animals; and mosaics. The paleochristian, Visigothic and Dark Age artefacts (including a vast coin collection) are frequently rearranged for lack of space. Just south of St-Sernin in Rue de Périgord, the **Chapelle des Carmélites** (1643) has been restored to bring out its lavishly painted ceiling, an unusual allegory on the glory of Carmel by Jean-Baptiste Despax (d. 1773).

This northernmost neighbourhood of medieval Toulouse, the **Quartier Arnaud-Bernard** has been the equivalent of Paris's Latin Quarter ever since 1229 when the **University of Toulouse** was founded in Rue des Lois (part of it now occupies the old seminary of St-Pierre des Chartreaux to the west). Although forced down Toulouse's throat, the university enjoyed a certain prestige in the Middle Ages; among its alumni were three popes and Michel de Montaigne. Rabelais started to study here, where he 'well learned to dance and to play at swords with two hands' but he quickly got out because its regents had a certain problem when it came to freethinkers; several were burned alive at the stake. 'It didn't please God that I linger,' Rabelais continued; 'me with my nature already rather parched, and not in need of any more heat.' The three principal squares of the quarter—Place du Peyrou, Place des Tiercerettes and Place Arnaud-Bernard—became the centre of immigrant life in this century; today they are quickly being gentrified. North of the boulevard, the neighbourhood's 'lung', the **Jardin Compans-Caffarelli**, was laid out in 1982 with exotic plants, a Japanese garden and tea room.

Les Jacobins

Open 10–12 and 2.30–6, July–15 Sept 10–6.30, closed Sun mornings; adm for the cloister.

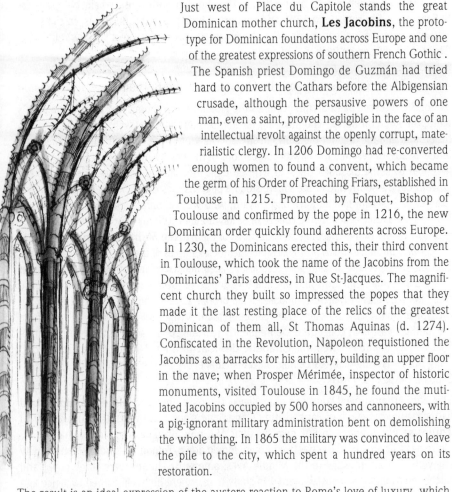

Just west of Place du Capitole stands the great Dominican mother church, **Les Jacobins**, the prototype for Dominican foundations across Europe and one of the greatest expressions of southern French Gothic . The Spanish priest Domingo de Guzmán had tried hard to convert the Cathars before the Albigensian crusade, although the persausive powers of one man, even a saint, proved negligible in the face of an intellectual revolt against the openly corrupt, materialistic clergy. In 1206 Domingo had re-converted enough women to found a convent, which became the germ of his Order of Preaching Friars, established in Toulouse in 1215. Promoted by Folquet, Bishop of Toulouse and confirmed by the pope in 1216, the new Dominican order quickly found adherents across Europe. In 1230, the Dominicans erected this, their third convent in Toulouse, which took the name of the Jacobins from the Dominicans' Paris address, in Rue St-Jacques. The magnificent church they built so impressed the popes that they made it the last resting place of the relics of the greatest Dominican of them all, St Thomas Aquinas (d. 1274). Confiscated in the Revolution, Napoleon requistioned the Jacobins as a barracks for his artillery, building an upper floor in the nave; when Prosper Mérimée, inspector of historic monuments, visited Toulouse in 1845, he found the mutilated Jacobins occupied by 500 horses and cannoneers, with a pig-ignorant military administration bent on demolishing the whole thing. In 1865 the military was convinced to leave the pile to the city, which spent a hundred years on its restoration.

The result is an ideal expression of the austere reaction to Rome's love of luxury, which made both the preaching orders, the Dominicans and Franciscans, so popular in the 13th century. Gargoyles are the only exterior sculpture in this immense but harmonious brick pile of buttresses, alternating with flamboyant windows; its octagonal bell tower of brick and stone crowned with tiny towers is one of the landmarks of the city skyline. The interior is breathtakingly light and spacious, consisting of twin naves divided by seven huge columns, crisscrossed by a fantastic interweaving of ribs in the vault, reaching an epiphany in the massive flamboyant *palmier* in the apse. The painted decoration dates from the 13th to the 16th century, but only the glass of the rose windows on the west side is original. The 19th-century gilded reliquary shrine of St Thomas Aquinas was returned to the high altar in 1974.

A small door leads out into the lovely garden **cloister** (1309), with brick arcades and twinned columns in grey marble, used in the summer for the concert series, *Piano aux Jacobins*. The east gallery gives onto the large **chapter house**, supported by a pair of slender marble columns, and the adjacent **Chapelle Saint-Antonin**, the funerary chapel, painted in the early 1300s with scenes from the life of St Antonin and on the ceiling, southwest France's favourite vision from the Apocalypse: the 24 Elders and angels glorifying Christ. In Rue Pargaminieres, the **Refectory**, nearly 200ft long, contains the **Musée d'Art Moderne** *(open 10–5, closed Tues; adm)* and temporary exhibitions of contemporary art.

Northwest of Les Jacobins, near the Garonne's new hog-backed **Pont St-Pierre** are Toulouse's two churches dedicated to St Peter. **St-Pierre-des-Cuisines**, a little Romanesque priory associated with Moissac, is named after its kitchens where bread could be baked at cheaper rates than at the counts' ovens; used as a warehouse from the Revolution until 1965, the church is slated for a major restoration. **St-Pierre des Chartreaux**, to the north in Rue Valade, was founded in the 17th century by monks fleeing the Huguenots of Castres and, if open, has some fine works from the 17th and 18th century—the grand organ (1686; originally in Les Jacobins), elaborate sculpted wood panels, stuccoes and murals from the 1680s. The leafy banks of the **Canal de Brienne**, linking the Garonne to the Canal du Midi, is one of Toulouse's favourite promenades.

Pastel Palaces and Violets of Gold

Just south of Les Jacobins, at the end of Rue Gambetta, is one of the city's most splendid residences, the **Hôtel de Bernuy**, built in 1504 by a *pastel* merchant from Burgos, Don Juan de Bernuy, a Spanish Jew who fled Ferdinand and Isabella's Inquisition and became a citizen—and *capitoul*—of Toulouse. Although Gothic on the outside, inside his master mason Loys Privat designed an eclectic fantasy courtyard, a mix of Gothic, Plateresque and Loire château, with a lofty tower rivalling those of all the other pastel nabobs. De Bernuy had a chance to repay France for the fortune he made when King François I was captured at the battle of Pavia by Emperor Charles V and imprisoned in Madrid; the king fell gravely ill, but no one could afford the ransom of 1,200,000 gold ecus demanded by the emperor—until de Bernuy bailed him out. In his distress the king had promised an *ex voto* to St Sernin if he survived, and in the ambulatory you can still see the black marble statue he donated when he came in 1533 to thank de Bernuy for his generosity.

Not long after de Bernuy's time the Jesuits converted his hôtel into a college, now the prestigious Lycée Pierre de Fermat, named after its star pupil, the great mathematician (1595–1665) who invented integral calculus six years before Newton and left behind Fermat's Last Theorem, which has teased mathematicians for the last 300 plus years. (It was discovered in a margin of a book after Fermat's death; 'I have just found the most marvellous proof,' he wrote 'But there's not enough room to fit it in this margin.' No one knows if Fermat was just kidding, but 1990s masterminds claim they're closing in on it.)

Just to the east, another 16th-century *hôtel particulier* from the same period houses the **Musée du Vieux Toulouse**, 7 Rue Dumay *(open June–Sept, Mon–Sat 3–6; other times Thurs 2.30–5.30, closed Nov–Feb)* with a fascinating collection of bits and bobs from the city's fragrant history, its former porcelain industry, 19th-century paintings and etchings of the city. Rue Dumay gives onto Rue St-Rome, a street of many names that was the *cardo* of Roman Tolosa and the city's principal north–south axis in the Middle Ages. Now pedestrian-only, it has many 16th-century mansions built by the *capitouls* and wealthy merchants. Don't miss what was the very centre of Roman Toulouse, the triangular **Place de la Trinité**, with a 19th-century fountain supported by bronze mermaids. Near here, you can examine the popular artistic pulse of Toulouse on the ever-changing murals along narrow Rue Coq-d'Inde.

One of the finest private residences built in Toulouse, the **Hôtel d'Assezat** is just west, off Rue de Metz, a wide street rammed through the middle of medieval Toulouse in the 19th century. The *hôtel* was begun in 1555 by *pastel* magnate Pierre d'Assezat, who had a near monopoly on the dye in northern Europe. Designed by Nicolas Bachelier, Toulouse's master architect-sculptor-engineer, it consists of two buildings around a large square court, and a curious tower crowned with an octagonal lantern and dome that served the merchant as an observation post over the Garonne. The decoration, a rhythmic composition of Ionic, Doric and Corinthian columns, is so much like the old Louvre that Bachelier was long thought to have copied the idea, although the records prove that both buildings went up at the same time. Facing the street, an Italianate loggia has seven brackets decorated with *pastel* pods. Since the 19th century, the hôtel has been the **Palais des Académies**, seat of the Académie des Jeux Floraux. Over the portico is a statue of Dame Clemence Isaure, the legendary patroness of the Floral Games.

The Eisteddfod of France

In November 1323, seven burghers of Toulouse met together in a monastery garden. Although not poets, these 'Seven Troubadours' were connoisseurs who regretted that good poetry had vanished along with the counts of Toulouse. To inspire some new verse, the seven decided to invite all the bards of Languedoc to gather in the monastery garden to recite on the 3rd of May, and the poem the seven judged best would receive a violet made of gold. A big crowd showed up, and ever since then the 3rd of May in Toulouse has hosted what has become known as the *Jeux Floraux*. The Seven Troubadours were soon succeeded by the 'Maintainers' of the *College du Gay Scavoir*, the world's oldest literary society, renamed the *Académie des Jeux Floraux* by Louis XIV.

Early on the Seven Troubadours added two other prizes, an eglantine and marigold in silver. To cope with the bewildering disorder of entries in the competition, they commissioned a code from one of Toulouse's top jurists and humanists, Guilhem

Molinier; the resulting *Las Leys d'Amors* in 1356 was widely read, and soon copied in Barcelona, which in 1388 started its own *Jocs Florals*. There the first prize was not a gold rose but a real rose, because like the greatest poetry, a rose can never be imitated. Although the Toulousains will punch anyone in the eye for saying so, Barcelona produced the better poetry; so great was the fear of heresy or challenging accepted moral norms in the home town of the Inquisition that nearly all the poems are safe, bloodless praises of the Virgin Mary that hold little interest today (and as their contemporary, Chaucer, would have told them, the 3rd of May is the Invention of the Cross, the unluckiest day in the year).

Along the Garonne

Rue de Metz continues to Toulouse's oldest bridge, which, as in Paris, is rather confusingly known as the new, or **Pont Neuf**. This Pont Neuf, with its seven unequal arches of brick and stone and curious holes (*oculi*), took from 1544 to 1632 to build, and links Gascony—the Left Bank—with the medieval province of Languedoc. Just down the quay stands the **Ecole des Beaux Arts**, its façade larded with allegorical figures (1895). Hidden under the icing is a 17th-century U-shaped monastery connected to **Notre Dame-la-Daurade**. Only the name recalls what was for centuries one of the wonders of Toulouse, the 10-sided, domed, 5th-century palatine chapel of the Visigothic kings, known as the Daurade ('the golden') after its mosaics. Similar to the churches of Ravenna, it was destroyed in 1761, when the monks who owned it fancied replacing it with a reproduction of the Vatican. Plans for the current church collided with the Revolution and the building was only completed in the mid 19th century. The paintings in the choir are by Ingres's master, Roques. Don't miss the pretty Place de la Daurade just north of the church; it overlooked the Garonne until the rebuilding of the quays in the 19th century.

One of the finest views of the Pont Neuf and riverfront is to the south along the **Quai de Tounis**. Rue du Pont de Tounis, built in 1515 as a bridge over the Garonnette (a now-covered tributary of the Garonne), leads back to the original river bank and **Notre Dame-la-Dalbade** (Our Lady the Whitened, after its medieval whitewash). This church has taken some hard knocks. It was rebuilt in the Renaissance with a 280ft spire; the spire was chopped down in the Revolution, and rebuilt in the 1880s, using such cheap materials that it fell through the roof in 1926. It has a rich Renaissance door, under the tympanum's ceramic reproduction of Fra Angelico's *Coronation of the Virgin* (1874).

Rue de la Dalbade was the favourite address for the nobility, and among its many *hôtels particuliers*, the standout is the sooty **Hôtel de Pierre** (No. 25), which, extravagantly for the *ville rose* is made of stone. In 1538 Nicolas Bachelier designed the façades around the courtyard, the doorway framed by two bearded old men and the monumental chimney. In the early 17th century when the next owner, a president of the parlement, married a *pastel* heiress he added the grandiose Baroque façade to the front in imitation of one he saw in Italy. Just opposite is the grand **Hôtel de Malte** (1680), the headquarters of the Knights of St John in Toulouse since 1115; after 1315, they took over the wealth and duties of the Templars (who before their suppression were at No. 13).

The Quartier du Jardin

At the south end of Rue de la Dalbade/Rue de la Fonderie in Place du Salin stood the fortified residence of the counts of Toulouse, the celebrated Château Narbonnais; it was also
the site of the *parlement*, established in Toulouse in 1443. All was demolished in the 19th
century for the Palais de Justice, with only the square brick tower, the 14th-century royal
treasury (converted into a Protestant church) as a memory. In the adjacent Place du
Parlement is an old house built on the Roman wall, donated to Domingo Guzmán for his
new preaching order, and later converted to the use inscribed over the door: 'Maison de
l'Inquisition'. In Roman times the south gate of the city stood here, at the end of the *cardo*
(here Rue Pharaon).

South of the Place du Parlement, Allées Jules-Guesde replaces the walls torn down in
1752. Here, by the Théâtre Sorano, a plaque marks the exact spot where the hated Simon
de Montfort was brained; near by at No. 35 is Toulouse's fascinating, fusty old **Musée
d'Histoire Naturelle** *(open 2–6, winter till 5, closed Tues and holidays; adm)*. Some
grand architecture was planned here in the mid-17th century but never got built—the
Grand Rond at the end of Allée Jules-Guesde was supposed to be the central garden in the
midst of six wide radiating promenades, or *allées*, of which only four were laid out. The
Jardin Royal was planted outside the walls, and in the 19th century, the **Jardin des
Plantes** was added. The garden's grand 16th–17th-century portal on Allée Frédéric-
Mistral was salvaged from the original Capitole; just south of this is the **Monument to the
Resistance**, with a crypt aligned to be illuminated by the sun on 19 August, the anniver-
sary of the Liberation of Toulouse.

There is one last museum in this quarter, and one not to be missed if you're fond of
Egyptian and Eastern Art. This is the **Musée Georges Labit**, in a neo-Moorish villa at 43
Rue des Martyrs-de-la-Libération, off Allée Frédéric-Mistral *(open 10–6, till 5 in the winter,
closed Tues and holidays; adm)*. Labit was a 19th-century traveller with plenty of money
and a good eye who accumulated an oriental collection considered the best in France after
the Guimet Museum in Paris.

Place du Salin to the Cathedral of St-Etienne

The parlementarians liked to build themselves distingished houses in the homogenous
quarter between the old *parlement* and the cathedral; all uniform pink brick, with light
grey shutters and black wrought-iron balconies. In this mesh of quiet lanes, there are a few
to pick out during a stroll, such as the sumptuously ornate **Hôtel du Vieux Raisin**
(1515), 36 Rue du Languedoc, built by another *capitoul* in love with Italy. A *hôtel* at 13
Rue de la Pleau houses the **Musée Paul-Dupuy** *(open 10–12 and 2–6, closed Tues, Sun
morning and holidays; adm)*, named after the obsessed collector who left to Toulouse his
horde of watches, automata, guns, coins, fans, faïence, pharmaceutical jars and gems like
the 11th-century 'horn of Roland' and other exquisite medieval works in ivory, and a silver
marigold from the Jeux Floraux of 1762. In Rue Ninau the 16th-century **Hôtel de Ulmo**
with a marble baldachin in the courtyard was built by Jean de Ulmo, president of the

Toulouse parlement whose motto *Durum patientia frango* (my constancy breaks adversity) hid a scoundrel to the core; caught selling every favour his office had to dispense, he was flogged, stripped of his possessions and sent off to prison, where he was given the task of keeping the accounts of the prison governor—which he falsified to his own advantage before he was hanged.

Rue Perchepinte and Rue Fermat, lined with antique shops, lead up to Place Saint-Etienne, with Toulouse's oldest fountain (1546) and the massive archbishop's palace (1713), now used as the Préfecture. All are overpowered by the **cathedral of Saint-Etienne**, begun in the 11th century by Raymond IV and, after various fits and starts, completed only in the 17th century. In the three major building campaigns fashions and finances rose and fell, resulting in a church that seems a bit drunk. Have a good look at the façade: in the centre rises a massive brick bell tower with a clock, over the Romanesque base. To the right is a worn, assymmetrical stone Gothic façade, where the portal and rose window are off-centre; to the left extends the bulge of the chapel of Notre-Dame, a small church in itself stuck on the north end.

It's even tipsier inside. In 1215, Bishop Folquet rebuilt most of Raymond IV's church, in the form of a single nave 62ft high and 62ft wide, with ogival crossings that became the model for southern Gothic. In 1275, Bishop Bertrand de L'Isle-Jourdaine decided it was hardly grandiose enough and came up with a plan based on northern French Gothic that involved realigning the axis of the church. The choir was built, but the lack of money after his death put paid to his plan, leaving a doglegged nave (the first was meant to be destroyed, but never was). Where the two meet stands the massive Pilier d'Orléans, one of four intended to support the transept; it bears a plaque marking the tomb of Pierre-Paul Riquet, father of the Canal du Midi. The vaults of Bishop Bertrand's church were designed to be 132ft high, but lack of money limited them to 90ft. Nevertheless what did get built is a fine example of flamboyant Gothic, with beautiful 14th-century glass on the west side; the tapestries, faded into negatives of themselves, date from the 15th and 16th centuries, and the choir is decorated with grotesques. Behind it hovers the organ, a remarkable instrument from the early 1600s that was at the point of collapsing in the 1970s when it was restored and firmly bolted high on its wall bracket like an elephant in a flower vase.

Musée des Augustins

Open 10–6, till 5 in winter, closed Tues and holidays; Wed night until 9pm, adm.

Rue Croix Baragnon, opposite the cathedral, has two beautiful Gothic houses, especially No. 15, decorated with a band of stone carvings. But the greatest medieval art in this part of town is in the **Musée des Augustins**, a block north at the corner of Rue de Metz and Rue d'Alsace. The museum, one of the oldest in France, is housed in a 14th-century Augustinian convent, beautifully restored in 1950.

During the Revolution, the Ville Rose went about gaily smashing up its fabulous architectural heritage as ordered in 1790 by the Convention, 'to leave standing no monument that hinted of slavery'. Enter onto the scene Alexandre Dumège, the self-taught son of a Dutch actor who had such a passion for antiquities that he singlehandedly rescued most of the contents of this museum, opening its doors in 1794. Gothic sculptures occupy the Augustinians' flamboyant chapterhouse: the beautiful 14th-century *Virgin and Child* from Avignon, *Notre Dame de Grasse* from the Jacobins, scenes from a 14th-century retable, the 'Group of three Persons one of which is strangled by a monster', and effigies from tomb-stones. A crooning choir of gargoyles from Toulouse's demolished Franciscan convent keep company with the sarcophaguses around the cloister; one is said to belong to the Visigothic Queen Ranachilde—*la reine Pédauque*, the goose-foot (*see* 'Topics', p.51) perhaps, because of the web-footed bird carved in the side.

The nave of the convent church is devoted to religious paintings (Van Dyck's *Christ aux anges* and *Miracle de la mule*, Rubens's *Christ entre deux Larrons* and *San Diego in extase* by Murillo) and reliefs by Nicolas Bachelier. Best of all are the Romanesque works, most of them rescued from demolished cloisters: from Saint-Sernin, a capital sculpted with the *War of Angels* and an enigmatic bas-relief from the Porte des Comtes showing two women looking at one another, one holding a lion in her arms, the other a ram, a myste-rious image that also appears on the main portal at Compostela. Other capitals, stylistically closely related to those of Moissac, come from the Romanesque cloister of the Daurade; the most beautiful of all are from Raymond IV's 11th-century cloister of St-Etienne—note espe-cially the delicate, almost fluid scene of the Dance of Salome and the beheading of John the Baptist. From the Romanesque portal of St-Etienne's chapterhouse are statue-columns of the Apostles that look ahead to Chartres.

The first floor of the convent is devoted to paintings. There are a pair of paintings of *capi-touls*; one of their oldest prerogatives was the *droit d'image*—the right to have their portraits painted. In the Middle Ages this was quite exceptional; the doge of Venice and the pope were among the few who enjoyed a similar privilege. Among other paintings are a 15th-century Florentine hunt scene, an extremely unpleasant Guido Reni, of *Apollo flaying Marsyas*, works by Simon Vouet, Philippe de Champaigne, a froufrou portrait by Hyacinthe Rigaud, two Guardis, Delacroix, Ingres, Manet, Morisot, Vuillard, Maurice Denis and a pair of Toulouse-Lautrecs.

From the museum, Rue des Arts leads up to **Place Saint-Georges**, once the favourite venue for executions—including that of Jean Calas—as it could hold the most spectators (this is before Place du Capitole was enlarged). Today the many spectators dawdling in the cafés mainly look at one another. The square lent its name to an inner-city development completed in 1982 called the Nouveau Saint-Georges, which stretches off to Place Occitane. Here, in Rue Lapeyrouse, the Nouvelles Galeries department store has a splendid view over Toulouse from its rooftop tearoom.

Rue St-Antoine-de-T (named after the tau symbol on the robes of the monks of St Anthony) leads from Place Saint-Georges to an early, cosier experiment in urban renewal, the ellip-tical **Place Président Wilson**, laid out by municipal architect Jean-Paul Virebent in the early 19th century, with a centrepiece monument to one of the last troubadours, Pierre Godolin (1580–1649).

Toulouse's Left Bank

Although the Left, or Gascon, bank of the Garonne has been settled since the early Middle Ages, the periodic rampages of the river dampened property values until the end of the 19th century, when flood control projects were completed. The main reason for visiting is just over the Pont Neuf: the round, brick, lighthouse-shaped tower of a pumping and filtering station, built in 1817 to provide pure drinking water to the city. In 1974 this found a new use as the **Galerie Municipale du Château-d'Eau** *(open 1–7, closed Tues and holidays)*. The hydraulic machinery is still intact on the bottom level, while upstairs you can visit one of Europe's top photographic galleries—over and over again; exhibits change every month. An annexe has been installed in a dry arch of the Pont Neuf.

Opposite the water tower is the **Hôtel-Dieu St-Jacques**, a medieval pilgrimage hostel rebuilt in the 17th century; ask to visit the grand Salle St-Jacques and Salle St-Lazare for their magnificent ceilings (there are plans to open a museum of medicine here after 1994). Behind the Hôtel-Dieu stands the parish church of the Left Bank, originally dedicated to St Cyprien. When the church was rebuilt in 1300, Cyprien had proved to have such little celestial influence over the Garonne that the church was rededicated to **Saint Nicolas**, patron of sailors and protector of the flooded. It is a small southern Gothic version of the Jacobins and boasts a grand 18th-century altar painted by Despax.

More visual arts, this time graphics, posters, ads and postcards from the 17th century to the present are the subject of the changing exhibits at the **Centre Municipal de l'Affiche, de la Carte Postale and de l'Art Graphique** at 58 Allées Charles-de-Fitte *(Mon–Fri 9–12 and 2–6)*; there's an extensive book, film and record library, and, most popular of all, French commercials—those that used to be shown before films—from 1904 to 1968, on video cassettes.

Le Mirail, Toulouse's Shadow Utopia

In 1993, when Toulouse's new métro was inaugurated, it was with dire warnings of invasions from Le Mirail, now brought within a 10-minute ride from the Capitole. Le Mirail is the home to the last-off-the-boat in Toulouse, including over 80 different nationalities, who live together in an experiment in creative integration in the face of a 30 per cent unemployment rate. This is a far cry from the experiment planned for Le Mirail, but in the end it may well prove more interesting.

Le Mirail ZUP *(zone à urbaniser en priorité)* was envisioned in 1960 as a *bis Toulouse* near the university, a futurist self-contained white-collar utopia for 100,000 people. These were the days when city planners fondly believed that architecture could modify behaviour, and

Toulouse's Socialist government chose as its master builder George Chandalis, who had worked with Le Corbusier on the Cité Radieuse project in Marseille. Chandalis planned a star-shaped city of five separate neighbourhoods of 20,000 inhabitants, each with its own commerce, social and cultural services, with a regional centre in the middle. Cars and pedestrians were to be kept strictly apart, so children could play without danger: vehicles were banished to vast underground car parks under the large central squares of each neighbourhood. Each apartment would have a view over the square, the ideal centre of urban life, and a view over the gardens at the back. Chandalis meant his 13-storey blocks or 'tripods' to be residential cooperatives, linked one to the other by long concourses (the *coursives*) or suspended streets with shops and other services that people would stroll past daily on route to the centralized lifts.

Two of Le Mirail's five neighbourhoods, Bellefontaine and La Reynerie, were built by 1971, when Pierre Baudis became mayor and radically changed the next stage of building to fit into a more traditional idea of a French *faubourg*. No one complained too vehemently; Le Mirail was already going awry. Toulouse's white-collar workers didn't care to be convivial and live in cooperatives, but instead bought bungalows in suburban dreamland, with their own little gardens and gates. Le Mirail's idealistic vision was altered: walls went up in the *coursives* to keep people in their own buildings; new entrances and elevators have gone up to lower the amount of forced public interaction. The empty underground car parks are to be converted into activity centres. One of the liveliest institutions in La Reynerie is the Maison des Racines du Monde, founded by local parents. Artists are beginning to move to Le Mirail by choice, and now there are concerns that the métro will bring too many middle-class people, force up the price of housing and destroy Le Mirail's diversity.

On the Periphery of Toulouse

You can watch Aérospatiale build aircraft at the **Usine Clément Ader** in Colomiers by appointment (contact Taxiway, © 61 15 44 00) or learn about the history of aviation in Toulouse at Aérospatiale's **Aérothèque** on Rue Montmorency, Wed and Fri 2–6 (© 61 93 93 57).

Blagnac (buses 66 or 70) has the tomb-oratory of the 5th-century bishop St Exupère, who on one occassion dispersed a besieging army of Vandals by sprinkling them with holy water, and on another, sold all the goods of his church to buy food for the poor during a famine. When the Toulousains proved to be total ingrates, Exupère stomped off to his father's farm in the Pyrenees. A delegation was sent from Toulouse to bring him back, but he angrily refused, saying he'd return only if the ox goad in his hand burst into bloom. It immediately did, of course, and back he went. Hence the story behind the naive 16th-century frescoes on the walls with their inscriptions in Occitan.

Lastly, **Le Centre Régional d'Art Contemporain** is to the southeast, in the industrial zone of La Bège-Innopole (bus 79), © 61 80 18 21, and specializes in exhibits of lesser-known new artists (*open Wed–Sun 12.30–8*).

Markets and Shopping

There are regular markets Tuesday through Sunday at Place des Carmes and at Les Halles in Bd Victor-Hugo. On Wednesday mornings, Place du Capitole has a lively food and flea market and an organic farm market on Tuesday and Saturday mornings. Sunday morning sees a huge flea market around St-Sernin and along the length of the boulevards, the 'relics' of modern Toulouse that draw thousands of 'pilgrims'. With all the major French department stores—and a Marks & Spencer, just behind the Capitole—the Pink City is the shopping mecca of the southwest, although specifically local products, besides Airbuses, are mostly violet—violet-scented soaps, eau de cologne, and candied-violet *confits*, the last-named made since 1730 (along with superb chocolates) at Olivier, 27 Rue Lafayette; Maison Pillon, at 23 Rue du Languedoc and 2 Rue Ozenne also produces delicious handmade chocolates and other treats. Or pick the ultimate Toulousain taste treat: rubbery anis- or mint-flavoured Cachou pellets, invented by a pharmacist named Lajaunie at 64 Avenue de Larrrieu and sold all over France in the same little metal tins for the past 100 years or so. Two bookshops have titles in English: Librairie Etrangère, 16 Rue des Lois, © 61 21 67 21, and The Bookshop, 17 Rue Lakanal, © 61 22 99 92. For posters and reprints, try the shop in the Centre Municipal de l'Affiche (*see* above).

Sports and Activities

The Toulouse Football Club (T.F.C., pronounced 'tayfessay') plays in France's first division, but the city's heart lies with its rugby team, the Stade, over a hundred years old and ten times champion of France (latest in '85, '86 and '89). They play on Sunday afternoons at the stadium; local teams are divided into Rugby à XV and Rugby à XIII (heretical 'Cathar rugby'). From May to September you can splash around in the various pools and slippery slides at **Aqualand de Toulouse**, part of the sports complex in Parc de Sesquières, north of Toulouse in Allée des Foulques (bus 7 from Place du Capitole), © 61 37 10 00; from October to March you can swish out a figure eight at the **Patinoire Olympique de Blagnac**, an ice rink at 10 Av. du Général de Gaulle, © 61 30 09 79 (buses 66 or 70).

Toulouse ✉ *31000*   **Where to Stay**

Toulouse has chain hotels galore for its numerous business visitors and a short list of reliable independent establishments in the historic centre. Try to avoid the cheep fleabags near the station.

expensive

The most beautiful hotel in Toulouse ★★★★**Grand Hôtel de l'Opéra**, 1 Place du Capitole, © 61 21 82 66, is housed in a former convent, with sumptuous Italianate rooms, indoor pool and a magnificent restaurant (*see* below). ★★★**Capoul**, 13 Place Wilson, © 61 10 70 70, has large, luminous air-conditioned rooms, a jacuzzi and a good *bistrot*.

★★★**Des Beaux Arts**, 1 Place Pont-Neuf, ✆ 61 23 40 50, has pleasant, sound-proofed rooms overlooking the Garonne. Ultra-modern ★★★**Brienne**, 20 Bd du Maréchal Leclerc, ✆ 61 23 60 60, has well-equipped rooms, many with balconies. ★★★**Mermoz**, 50 Rue Matabiau, ✆ 61 63 04 04, stands out as the exception to the hotels near the station, with delightful air-conditioned rooms overlooking inner courtyards and perhaps the best breakfast in Toulouse. If you're driving, you can sleep where the Tectosages once roamed in Vieille-Toulouse (31320), 8km south on the D 4: ★★★**La Flânerie**, Rte de Lacroix-Falgarde, ✆ 61 73 39 12, is a pretty country house with grand views over the Garonne; pool, tennis, and in the environs, a golf course are added bonuses.

inexpensive

★★**Arnaud-Bernard**, Place des Tiercerettes, ✆ 61 21 37 64, in the centre of Toulouse's lively popular quarter near St-Sernin, has recently renovated rooms. In the same area for a bit more, the ★★**Saint-Sernin**, 2 Rue St-Bernard, ✆ 61 21 73 08, has good rooms with full bath, mini bars, TVs, etc. ★★**Park Hotel**, 2 Rue Porte-Sardane, ✆ 61 21 90 58, within easy walking distance the Capitole, has modern rooms with most creature comforts, including a sauna and jacuzzi; equally central, ★★**Albert 1er**, 8 Rue Rivals, ✆ 61 21 17 91, has convenient parking. ★★**Hôtel du Grand Balcon**, at the corner of Place du Capitole, 8 Rue Romiquières, ✆ 61 21 48 08, is one of Toulouse's best loved institutions. The phrase *grand balcon* is what early French pilots used to describe the view from the cockpit, and this is where Saint-Exupéry and friends stayed when on the ground. Three sisters ran it for 50 years, and the current owners have had it for the past 37, carefully preserving the rooms as they were, along with a fascinating collection of photos and memorabilia from France's early days of aviation. The author of *Le Petit Prince* always stayed in no. 32; bring your own soap (closed for Christmas and 3 weeks in Aug).

cheap

Near the Capitole, ★**Anatole France**, 46 Place Anatole France, ✆ 61 23 19 96, has some of the nicest cheap rooms in Toulouse, all with showers and phones. Near Place St-Georges, friendly ★**Des Arts**, 1bis Rue Cantegril, ✆ 61 23 36 21, has good rooms with showers in a lively part of town. Near St-Etienne, ★**Croix-Baragnon**, 17 Rue Croix-Baragnon, ✆ 61 52 60 10, is a good bet: all rooms have bath and shower. The **Auberge de Jeunesse** (youth hostel) is out on the east side of town, at 125 Av. Jean-Rieux, ✆ 61 80 49 93 (from the station, bus 14 to Place Dupuy, then bus 22 to Rue Leygues); in summer ring ahead to make sure there's room.

Eating Out

Toulouse occupies a key place in the southwest bean belt, and claims to make a *cassoulet* that walks all over the *cassoulets* of rivals Caracasonne and

Castelnaudary. To the base recipe of white beans, garlic, herbs, goose fat, salt bacon, fat pork, and *confits* of goose or duck, the Toulousains like to chuck a foot or two of their renowned sausage (*saucisse de Toulouse*), shoulder of mutton, and perhaps some ham. The final touch: sprinkle with breadcrumbs and bake in the oven. To aid in the long and tormented *cassoulet* digestion, the locals recommend a game of rugby, or a tipple of *eau de noix Benoit Serres*, the local walnut *digestif* (or *Get Frères*, if you like peppermint).

expensive

Toulouse's finest gastronomic experience, **Les Jardins de l'Opéra**, 1 Place du Capitole, © 61 23 07 76, is also one of the most beautiful restaurants in the whole southwest. It manages to stay light years from the hubbub just outside the door, a cool and refreshing glass-covered oasis overlooking a garden pool. The food matches the setting, orchestrated by the excellent Dominique Toulousy, who prepares aromatic mushroom dishes (morels stuffed with foie gras, when available), seafood cooked to perfection, a classic *cassoulet* and flavourful regional specialities, topped off by delicate desserts (closed Sun, holidays and most of Aug, 200F lunch menu with wine, other menus at 290 and 480F). Out in Blagnac, in an elegant 19th-century villa with a veranda overlooking 100-year-old trees, **Pujol**, 21 Av. Général Compans, © 61 71 13 58 is named after one the area's finest chefs, Michel Pujol, who bases his perfect *cuisine de terroir* on market availability and the day's catch, all accompanied with an extensive listing of Bordeaux wines; there's a delicious 190F menu, otherwise 350F à la carte.

moderate

North of the station, set in a little park with a pool, **Le Grand Clément**, 233 Route d'Albi, © 61 48 60 60, is a favourite in Toulouse for its well-prepared seafood and exquisite desserts, especially the *chaud-froid feuilleté au chocolat chaud* (menus from 150 to 350F, weekday lunch menu 95F). For something out of the ordinary, **Le Barreau de Toulouse**, 10 Rue Moulins (near Place du Salin), © 61 25 25 52, occupies three floors of an old bakery and serves original dishes that sound bizarre but taste delicious, as well as more tame offerings for shy diners. Good wine list, too (closed Sun and Aug, menus from 145 to 350F). A boat on the Canal de Brienne, **La Belle Chaurienne**, © 61 21 23 95 specializes in *cassoulet* with all the Toulouse trimmings; full meal 200F. Art Deco **Orsi**, 13 Rue Industrie (off Rue de la Colombette), © 61 62 97 43, also has *cassoulet* on the menu, as well as dishes from Provence and Lyon, all deliciously prepared (good-value menus from 135 to 175F; closed Sun). In warm weather, there are worse things to do than sit out on the terrace of **Chez Emile**, 13 Place St-Georges, © 61 21 05 56, and linger over some of the finest seafood in Toulouse or a *confit de canard*; if it's cold try the garden dining room on the first floor (menus from 115 to 210F, closed Sun and Mon).

La Tatina de Burgos, 27 Rue Garonnette, ℂ 61 55 59 29, is a wonderfully zesty tapas bar and restaurant with lots of sherry and Spanish wines, a tasty *zarzuela* (Catalan fish soup) and 30 other Spanish dishes; 50F lunch menu, but could go over 100F for a dinner (closed Sun, Mon and the first half of Aug). Arrive early for the popular 65F buffet lunch at **Les Caves de la Maréchale**, 3 Rue Jules-Chalande, ℂ 61 23 89 88, set in the immense cellar of a 17th-century library; in the evening the menu goes up to 135F (closed Sun and Mon lunch). One of the most beautiful brasseries in Toulouse, **Le Bibent**, is strategically located at 5 Place du Capitole, ℂ 61 23 89 03, with a grand dining room and terrace (around 120F); another, the **Brasserie des Beaux-Arts**, 1 Quai Daurade, ℂ 61 21 12 12 offers traditional seafood platters at 155F, salmon and sorrel, curried lamb, good desserts (menus at 90 and 140F; after 11pm, a special late-night munchie menu at 90F with wine). A 17th-century *jeu de paume* court is now the dining room at **Les Jardins de Li**, 9 Rue Croix-Baragon, ℂ 61 53 00 14, offering light, well prepared lunches at 55F and dinners from 100F (closed Sat lunch, Sun, and Mon night). **Le Ver Luisant**, 41 Rue de la Colombette, ℂ 61 63 06 73, is often packed to the gills, a favourite of local artists and scholars, attracted by the good food and atmosphere—meals around 100F (closed Sat lunch and Sun). At **Benjamin**, 7 Rue des Gestes (off Rue St-Rome), ℂ 61 22 92 66, dine among frescoes and Greek columns on the likes of fennel and courgette terrine and steak with *cèpes* for some of the friendliest prices in town—lunch menus at 60 and 80F, dinner at 90 and 125F (closed Sun).

The first floor of the **Marché Victor-Hugo** is chock-a-block with cheap little beaneries that daily attract Toulousains of every ilk for lunch (exc Mon), including the excellent **Attila** with its succulent *gambas flambées* (menus at 55 and 80F). François Villon would probably feel at home at **Le Picotin**, 5 Impasse Trésorerie, ℂ 61 52 44 54, where the 90F menu is roast meat and plonk—no forks or knives allowed. The same family for three generations has been dishing out southwestern home-cooking at **A la Truffe du Quercy**, 17 Rue Croix-Baragnon, ℂ 61 53 34 24, with a *formule* menu at 50F and a delicious regular menu for 20F more (closed Sun and holidays). Traditional and unusual Algerian dishes are on the board at **La Casbah**, 30 Rue de la Chaîne, ℂ 61 25 55 06; try the lamb with olives (*zitoun maamer*); around 80F (closed Wed). Pasta lovers have a wide choice at **Mille et Une Pâtes**, 1bis Rue Mirapoix, ℂ 61 21 97 83, some fairly orthodox and others more heretical, like chocolate and trifle lasagne; full meals with *vin de pays* and salad under 100F (closed Sat eve and Sun).

Cafés, Bars and Wine Bars

The most resolutely traditional bar in Toulouse is **Le Père Louis**, 45 Place des Tourneurs, between Rue Peyras and Rue de Metz, which has drawn Toulouse's *quinquina* drinkers for over a century; open 10.30–1 and 5–10pm, closed Sun and Mon afternoon. Tequila lubricates the trendy clientele at the **Texas Café**, 26 Rue Castellane; for a wide selection of wines and snacks, try **Le Nabuchodonosor**, 15bis Rue Coq-d'Inde, ✆ 61 53 65 00 (closed Sat and Sun, open til 8pm). **Le Mangevin**, 46 Rue Pharaon, ✆ 61 52 79 16, has a wide variety of wines accompanied by fancy snacks or light meals (open till 11.30pm); and for hardcore oenophiles, the **Bistrot des Vins**, 5 Rue Riguepels, ✆ 61 25 20 41, offers over 400 wines, including two score or so by the glass, and cheese, foie gras, charcuterie or simple meals in the 100F range (till 11.30pm). **Le Griot**, 21 Rue des Blanchers offers African music and snacks; **Dubliners**, 46 Av. Marcel-Langer, is Toulouse's chief Irish pub. Gay bars are clustered around Rue de la Colombette, east of Place Wilson. The feminist, women-only **Bagdam Café**, 4 Rue Delacroix, opens at 7pm Tues–Sat.

Entertainment and Nightlife

The weekly *Flash*, available at any newsstand, will tell you what's on in Toulouse. And thanks to its students, its Spanish blood and the do-re-mi provided by the city's high tech jobs, there's plenty. Since the Second World War, Toulouse has discovered classical music in a big way. In July and August, the city puts on a commendable music festival, including performances by the fine Orchestre Nationale de Chambre de Toulouse; in September the cloister of the Jacobins is the site of the *Festival International Piano aux Jacobins*; book early, ✆ 61 23 32 00. From October to June, the prestigious **Théâtre du Capitole**, Place du Capitole, ✆ 61 23 21 35 presents a series of opera and dance. Toulouse's 40-year-old Orchestre Nationale du Capitole, under the baton of Michel Plasson, is one of the top symphony orchestras in France and may be heard in the acoustically excellent **La Halle aux Grains**, Place Dupuy (just east of Cathédrale St-Etienne), ✆ 61 62 02 70, bookings ✆ 61 63 18 65. **Théâtre Sorano**, 35 Allées Jules-Guesde, ✆ 61 25 66 87 is small but puts on some of the finest plays in Toulouse.

The **Cinémathèque**, 3 Rue Roquelaine, ✆ 61 48 90 75, is the second most important in France, and often shows films in V.O. (*version originale*) as does **Le Cratère**, 95 Grand Rue St-Michel, ✆ 61 53 50 53; **Rex**, 15 Av. Honoré Serres, ✆ 61 23 93 04 and **ABC**, 13 Rue St-Bernard, ✆ 61 29 81 99.

Toulouse stays up later than any other city in this book, but places open and close like flowers in the night—check posters or listings in the aforementioned *Flash*. At the time of writing, **Cav' Rag Time**, 14 Place Arnaud-Bernard, ✆ 61 22 73 01, serves up jazz and latino music as well as drinks until 2am, 5am on Saturdays; for more jazz or blues try **Didjeridoo**, a bar at 6 Rue Joutx Aïgues, ✆ 61 14 10 61 (open till 2am), or **Chantaco**, 4 rue Gabriel Péri, ✆ 61 62 56 31. For a listen to the current state of French poetry, *chanson* and theatre, try **La Cave Poésie**, 71 Rue du Taur, ✆ 61 23 62 00 (every evening exc Sun and holidays). **Eriche Coffie**, 9/11 Rue Joseph Vié, ✆ 61 42 04 27 (near St-Cyprien) is a bar/German brasserie that puts on excellent concerts and lots of R and B. **Au Mandala**, 23 Rue des Amidonniers, ✆ 61 21 19 95, mixes Latin and jazz; salsa livens things up at **El Barrio Latino**, 2 Rue de la Digue, ✆ 61 59 00 58. **Aux Trois Petits Cochons**, 7 Place Marengo, ✆ 61 48 79 45, is a jumping tapas bar with frequent rock concerts; **Swing & Occupation**, 44 Bd de la Gare, ✆ 61 26 05 12, attempts to evoke the music and food of the years 1939–45.

For decades, Toulouse's snobs have got down (or whatever they do) at the **Ubu Club**, 16 Rue St-Rome, ✆ 61 23 97 80, guarded by a stern doorman who can tell how much your clothes cost. Most of the smaller rock or blues bands who pass through Toulouse play at the young and convivial **Bikini**, Route de Lacroix-Flagarde, ✆ 61 55 00 29, with concerts almost every night. Everything from techno to reggae and 1960s nostalgia plays at the futuristic **Le Clap**, with a terrace over the Garonne at 146 Chemin des Etroits (towards Lacroix-Falgarde), ✆ 61 52 87 47 (Wed–Sat); rock and reggae keep them boogeying.

Abbaye: abbey

Arrondissement: a city district

Auberge: inn

Aven: natural well.

Bastide: a fortified new town founded in the Middle Ages; usually rectangular, with a grid of streets and an arcaded central square; sometimes circular in plan.

Caryatid: column or pillar carved in the figure of a woman

Castelnau: a village, often planned, that grew up around a seigneur's castle (often the parish church will be on the edge of a castelnau instead of at its centre)

Castrum: A rectangular Roman army camp, which often grew into a permanent settlement (like Bordeaux and many others); in Quercy, the word was often used in the same sense as *castelnau.*

Cardo: a north-southstreet in a Roman castrum; a street running east-west was called a decumanus

Cave: cellar

Château: mansion, manor house or castle

Château des Anglais: a cave fortress along the cliffs of the Lot or Dordogne, first built by the English in the Hundred Years' War

Chemin: path

Chevet: eastern end of a church, including the apse

Cingles: oxbow bends in a meandering river, such as the Dordogne and Lot

Clocher-mur: the west front of a church that rises high above the roofline for its entire width to make a bell tower; a common feature in medieval architecture in many parts of southwest France

Cloître: cloister

Commandery: local headquarters of a knightly order (like the Templars or Knights Hospitallers), usually to look after the order's lands and properties in an area

Commune: in the Middle Ages, the government of a free town or city; today, the smallest unit of local government, encompassing a town or village.

Cornière: arched portico surrounding the main square of a bastide

Cour d'honneur: the principal courtyard of a palace or large *hôtel*

Glossary

Couvent: convent or monastery

Croquant: peasant guerrilla in the anti-French revolts of the 17th and 18th centuries

Ecluse: canal lock

Eglise: church

Enfeu: niche in a church's exterior or interior wall for a tomb

Gare: railway station (SNCF)

Gariotte: small dry-stone building with a corbelled dome or vault for a roof; many were built as shepherds' huts, others as refuges for villagers in plague times; also called *bories*, *caselles*, or *cabannes* in different parts of the Midi

Gentilhommière: a small country château, especially popular in Périgord in the 18th century

Gisant: a sculpted prone effigy on a tomb

Halle: covered market

Hôtel: originally the town residence of the nobility; by the 18th century the word became more generally used for any large, private residence

Lauze: heavy grey stones used for making steep roofs in the Dordogne, now mostly replaced by machine-made tiles; the rare lauze roofer these days manages to do about a square metre a day

Lavoir: communal fountain, usually covered, for the washing of clothes.

Mairie: town hall

Marché: market

Mas: (from Latin *mansio*) a large farmhouse, or manor, or hamlet

Mascaron: an ornamental mask, usually one carved on the keystone of an arch

Modillon: a stone projecting from the cornice of a church, carved with a face or animal figure

Mozarabic: refers to elements in art and architecure derived from Muslim Spain in the Middle Ages

Parlement: a French juridical body, with members appointed by the king; by the late *ancien régime* parlements exercized a great deal of influence over political affairs

Pays: a region, or a village

Pech: hill

Plan d'eau: artificial lake.

Puy: hill

Retable: a carved or painted altarpiece, often consisting of a number of scenes or sculptural ensembles

Rez-de-chausée (RC): ground floor

Routiers: English mercenaries in the Hundred Years War.

Sauveterre: a village or town founded under a guarantee against violence in wartime, agreed to by the Church and local barons; sauveterres' boundaries are often marked by crosses on all the roads leading in to them

Soleiho: top story of a Quercy town house with an open loggia, especially in Figeac and Cahors

Tour: tower

Transi: in a tomb, a relief of the decomposing cadaver

Tree of Jesse: a pictorial representation of the genealogy of Christ

Trumeau: the column between twin doors of a church portal, often carved with reliefs

Tympanum: semicircular panel over a church door; often the occasion for the most ambitious ensembles of medieval sculpture

Language

Even if your French is brilliant, the soupy southern twang may throw you. Any word with a nasal *in* or *en* becomes something like *aing* (*vaing* for *vin*). The last vowel on many words that are silent in the north get to express themselves in the south as well (*encore* becomes something like *engcora*). What stays the same is the level of politeness: use *monsieur*, *madame* or *mademoiselle* when speaking to everyone, from your first *bonjour* (and never *garçon* in restaurants!) to your last *au revoir*.

Deciphering French Menus

Many of the restaurants in this book don't translate their menus, so we've included the decoder below; try the section on regional specialities (*see* p.13) if an item isn't listed below.

Hors d'oeuvre et Soupes	Starters and soups
Assiette assortie	Mix cold hors d'oeuvres
Bisque	Shellfish soup
Bouchées	Mini vol-au-vents
Bouillon	Broth
Consommé	Clear soup
Crudités	Raw vegetable platter
Potage	Thick vegetable soup
Velouté	Thick smooth soup, often fish or chicken
Vol-au-vent	Puff pastry case with savoury filling

Poissons et Coquillages (Crustacés)	Fish and Shellfish
Aiglefin	Little haddock
Anchois	Anchovies
Anguille	Eel
Bar	Bass, sea-dace
Barbue	Brill
Baudroie	Anglerfish
Belons	Shelled oysters
Bigourneau	Winkle
Blanchailles	Whitebait
Brème	Bream
Brochet	Pike
Bulot	Whelk

Cabillaud	Fresh cod
Calmar	Squid
Carrelet	Plaice
Colin	Hake
Congre	Conger eel
Coques	Cockles
Coquilles St-Jacques	Scallops
Crabe	Crab
Crevettes grises	Shrimp
Crevettes roses	Prawns
Cuisses de grenouilles	Frogs' legs
Darne	Thin slice of fish
Daurade	Sea bream
Ecrevisse	Freshwater crayfish
Eperlans	Smelt
Escabèche	Fish fried, marinated and served cold
Escargot	Snails
Espadon	Swordfish
Flétan	Halibut
Friture	Deep-fried fish
Fruits de mer	Seafood
Gambas	Giant prawns
Gigot de mer	A large fish cooked whole
Grondin	Red gurnard
Hareng	Herring
Homard	Atlantic (Norway) lobster
Huîtres	Oysters
Langouste	Spiny Mediterranean lobster
Langoustines	Norway lobster (often called Dublin Bay Prawns or Scampi)
Limande	Lemon sole
Lotte	Monkfish
Loup (de mer)	Sea bass
Louvine	Sea bass (in Aquitaine)
Maquereau	Mackerel

Merlan	Whiting
Morue	Salt cod
Moules	Mussels
Oursin	Sea urchin
Pagel	Sea bream
Palourdes	Clams
Poulpe	Octopus
Praires	Small clams
Raie	Skate
Rascasse	Scorpion fish
Rouget	Red mullet
Saumon	Salmon
Saint-Pierre	John Dory
Sole (meunière)	Sole (with butter, lemon and parsley)
Stockfisch	Stockfish (wind-dried cod)
Telline	Tiny clam
Thon	Tuna
Truite	Trout
Truite saumonée	Salmon trout

Viandes et Volaille	**Meat and Poultry**
Agneau (de pré salé)	Lamb (grazed in fields by the sea)
Ailerons	Chicken wings
Andouillette	Chitterling (tripe) sausage
Biftek	Beefsteak
Blanc	Breast or white meat
Blanquette	Stew of white meat, thickened with egg yolk
Boeuf	Beef
Boudin blanc	Sausage of white meat
Boudin noir	Black pudding
Brochette	Meat (or fish) on a skewer
Caille	Quail
Canard, caneton	Duck, duckling
Carré	The best end of a cutlet or chop
Cervelles	Brains

Châteaubriand	Porterhouse steak
Cheval	Horsemeat
Chevreau	Kid
Civet	Stew of rabbit (usually), marinated in wine
Confit	Meat cooked and preserved in its own fat
Contre-filet	Sirloin steak
Côte, côtelette	Chop, cutlet
Cuisse	Thigh or leg
Dinde, dindon	Turkey
Entrecôte	Ribsteak
Epaule	Shoulder
Estouffade	A meat stew marinated, fried, and then braised
Faisan	Pheasant
Faux-filet	Sirloin
Foie	Liver
Foie gras	Goose liver
Frais de veau	Veal testicles
Fricadelle	Meatball
Gésier	Gizzard
Gibier	Game
Gigot	Leg of lamb
Graisse	Fat
Grillade	Grilled meat
Grive	Thrush
Jambon	Ham
Jarret	Knuckle
Langue	Tongue
Lapereau	Young rabbit
Lapin	Rabbit
Lard (lardons)	Bacon (diced bacon)
Lièvre	Hare
Maigret, or Magret (de canard)	Breast (of duck)
Marcassin	Young wild boar
Merguez	Spicy red sausage
Museau	Muzzle

Navarin	Lamb stew with root vegetables
Noix de veau	Topside of veal
Oie	Goose
Os	Bone
Perdreau (perdrix)	Partridge
Petit salé	Salt pork
Pieds	Trotters
Pintade	Guinea fowl
Porc	Pork
Poularde	Capon
Poulet	Chicken
Poussin	Baby chicken
Queue de boeuf	Oxtail
Ris (de veau)	Sweetbreads (veal)
Rognons	Kidneys
Rôti	Roast
Sanglier	Wild boar
Saucisses	Sausages
Saucisson	Dry sausage, like salami
Selle (d'agneau)	Saddle (of lamb)
Steak tartare	Raw minced beef, often topped with a raw egg yolk
Suprême de volaille	Fillet of chicken breast and wing
Tête (de veau)	Head (calf's)
Taureau	Bull's meat
Tortue	Turtle
Tournedos	Thick round slices of beef fillet
Travers de porc	Spare ribs
Tripes	Tripe
Veau	Veal
Venaison	Venison

Légumes, herbes, etc.	**Vegetables, herbs, etc.**
Ail	Garlic
Algue	Seaweed
Aneth	Dill

Artichaut	Artichoke
Asperges	Asparagus
Aubergine	Aubergine (eggplant)
Avocat	Avocado
Basilic	Basil
Betterave	Beetroot
Cannelle	Cinnamon
Céleri (-rave)	Celery (celeriac)
Cèpes	Wild dark-brown mushrooms
Champignons	Mushrooms
Chanterelles	Wild yellow mushrooms
Chicorée	Curly endive
Chou	Cabbage
Choufleur	Cauliflower
Choucroute	Sauerkraut
Ciboulettes	Chives
Citrouille	Pumpkin
Coeur de palmier	Heart of palm
Concombre	Cucumber
Cornichons	Gherkins
Courgettes	Courgettes (zucchini)
Cresson	Watercress
Echalote	Shallot
Endive	Chicory
Epinards	Spinach
Estragon	Tarragon
Fenouil	Fennel
Fèves	Broad beans
Flageolets	White beans
Fleurs de courgette	Courgette blossoms
Frites	Chips (French fries)
Genièvre	Juniper
Gingembre	Ginger
Girofle	Clove
Haricots (rouges, blancs)	Beans (kidney, white)

Haricot verts	Green (French) beans
Jardinière	With diced garden vegetables
Laitue	Lettuce
Laurier	Bay leaf
Lentilles	Lentils
Maïs (épis de)	Sweet corn (on the cob)
Marjolaine	Marjoram
Menthe	Mint
Mesclum	Salad of various leaves
Morilles	Morel mushrooms
Moutarde	Mustard
Navet	Turnip
Oignons	Onions
Oseille	Sorrel
Panais	Parsnip
Persil	Parsley
Petits pois	Peas
Piment	Pimento
Pissenlits	Dandelion greens
Poireaux	Leeks
Pois chiches	Chickpeas
Pois mange-tout	Sugar peas/mangetout
Poivron	Sweet pepper; capsicum
Pomme de terre	Potato
Primeurs	Young vegetables
Radis	Radishes
Raifort	Horseradish
Riz	Rice
Romarin	Rosemary
Safran	Saffron
Salade verte	Green salad
Salsafi	Salsify
Sarriette	Savory
Sarrasin	Buckwheat
Sauge	Sage

Seigle	Rye
Serpolet	Wild thyme
Thym	Thyme
Truffes	Truffles

Fruits, Desserts, Noix	**Fruits, Desserts, Nuts**
Abricot	Apricot
Acajous	Cashews
Amandes	Almonds
Ananas	Pineapple
Banane	Banana
Bavarois	Mousse or custard in a mould
Biscuit	Biscuit, cracker, cake
Bombe	Ice-cream dessert in round mould
Bonbons	Sweets, candy
Brebis	Sheep cheese
Brioche	Light sweet yeast bread
Brugnon	Nectarine
Cacahouètes	Peanuts
Cassis	Blackcurrant
Cerise	Cherry
Charlotte	Custard and fruit in almond biscuits
Chausson	Turnover
Chèvre	Goat cheese
Citron	Lemon
Citron vert	Lime
Clafoutis	Berry tart
Coing	Quince
Compôt	Stewed fruit
Corbeille de fruits	Basket of fruit
Coupe	Ice cream
Crème anglaise	Trifle
Crème Chantilly	Sweet whipped cream
Crème fraîche	Sour cream
Crème pâtissière	Thick pastry cream filling made with eggs

Dattes	Dates
Figues (de Barbarie)	Figs (prickly pear)
Fraises (des bois)	Strawberries (wild)
Framboises	Raspberries
Fromage (plateau de)	Cheese (board)
Fromage blanc	Yogurty cream cheese
Fromage frais	Similar to sour cream
Fruit de la passion	Passion fruit
Gâteau	Cake
Génoise	Rich sponge cake
Glace	Ice cream
Grenade	Pomegranate
Groseilles	Redcurrants
Lavande	Lavender
Macarons	Macaroons
Madeleine	Small sponge cake
Mandarine	Tangerine
Mangue	Mango
Marrons	Chestnuts
Merise	Black cherry
Miel	Honey
Mirabelles	Mirabelle plums, Greengage (plums)
Mûres	Mulberries, blackberries
Myrtilles	Bilberries
Noisette	Hazelnut
Noix	Walnuts
Oeufs à la neige	Meringue
Pamplemousse	Grapefruit
Parfait	Frozen mousse
Pastèque	Watermelon
Pêche (blanche)	Peach (white)
Petits fours	Tiny cakes and pastries
Pignons	Pinenuts
Pistache	Pistachio
Poire	Pear

Pomme	Apple
Prune	Plum
Pruneau	Prune
Raisins (secs)	Grapes (raisins)
Sablé	Shortbread
Savarin	A filled cake, shaped like a ring
Tarte, tartelette	Tart, little tart
Tarte tropézienne	Sponge cake filled with custard and topped with nuts
Truffes	Chocolate truffles

Cooking terms, miscellaneous, snacks

Addition	Bill
Aigre-doux	Sweet and sour
Aiguillette	Thin slice
A l'anglaise	Boiled
A l'arlésienne	With aubergines, potatoes, tomatoes, onions and rice
A la châtelaine	With chestnut purée and artichoke hearts
A la grecque	Cooked in olive oil and lemon
A la périgordine	In a truffle and foie gras sauce
A la provençale	Cooked with tomatoes, garlic and olive oil
Allumettes	Strips of puff pastry
A point	Medium steak
Au feu de bois	Cooked over a wood fire
Au four	Baked
Auvergnat	With sausage, bacon and cabbage
Baguette	Long loaf of bread
Barquette	Pastry boat
Beignets	Fritters
Béarnaise	Sauce of egg yolks, shallots and white wine
Beurre	Butter
Bien cuit	Well done steak
Bleu	Very rare steak
Bordelaise	Red wine, bone marrow and shallot sauce

Broche	Roast on a spit
Chasseur	Mushrooms and shallots in white wine
Chaud	Hot
Chou	Puff pastry
Confiture	Jam
Coulis	Strong clear broth
Couteau	Knife
Crème	Cream
Crêpe	Thin pancake
Croque-monsieur	Toasted ham and cheese sandwich
Croustade	Small savoury pastry
Cru	Raw
Cuillère	Spoon
Cuit	Cooked
Diable	Spicy mustard or green pepper sauce
Emincé	Thinly sliced
En croûte	Cooked in a pastry crust
En papillote	Baked in buttered paper
Epices	Spices
Farci	Stuffed
Feuilleté	Flaky pastry
Flambé	Set aflame with alcohol
Forestière	With bacon and mushrooms
Fourchette	Fork
Fourré	Stuffed
Frais, fraîche	Fresh
Frappé	With crushed ice
Frit	Fried
Froid	Cold
Fumé	Smoked
Galantine	Cooked food served in cold jelly
Galette	Flaky pastry case or pancake
Garni	With vegetables
(au) Gratin	Topped with crisp browned cheese and bread crumbs

Grillé	Grilled
Fromage	Cheese
Hachis	Minced
Hollandaise	A sauce of butter and vinegar
Huile (d'olive)	Oil (olive)
Marmite	Casserole
Médaillon	Round piece
Mijoté	Simmered
Mornay	Cheese sauce
Nouille	Noodles
Oeufs	Eggs
Pain	Bread
Pané	Breaded
Pâte	Pastry, pasta
Paupiette	Rolled and filled thin slices of fish or meat
Parmentier	With potatoes
Pavé	Slab
Piquante	Vinegar sauce with shallots and capers
Pissaladière	A kind of pizza with onions, anchovies, etc.
Poché	Poached
Poivre	Pepper
Quenelles	Dumplings of fish or poultry
Raclette	Toasted cheese with potatoes, onions and pickles
Sanglant	Rare steak
Salé	Salted, spicy
Sel	Salt
Sucré	Sweet
Timbale	Pie cooked in a dome-shaped mould
Tranche	Slice
Vapeur	Steamed
Véronique	Green grapes, wine and cream sauce
Vinaigre	Vinegar
Vinaigrette	Oil and vinegar dressing

Boissons	Drinking
Bière (pression)	Beer (draught)
Bouteille (demi)	Bottle (half)
Chocolat (chaud)	Chocolate (hot)
Café	Coffee
Demi	A third of a litre
Doux	Sweet (wine)
Eau (minérale)	Water (mineral, spring)
Eau-de-vie	Aquavitae
Gazeuse	Sparkling
Glaçons	Ice cubes
Infusion (or tisane)	Herbal tea
Lait	Milk
Moelleux	Semi-dry
Pichet	Pitcher
Citron pressé/orange pressée	Fresh lemon/orange juice
Pression	Draught
Sec	Dry
Sirop d'orange/de citron	Orange/lemon squash
Thé	Tea
Verre	Glass
Vin blanc/rosé/rouge	White/rosé/red wine

Page numbers in **bold** refer to main entries; page numbers in *italics* refer to maps. Castles are indexed under *châteaux*; wine *appellations* are listed under wine.

Index